A Commentary on the New Testament from the Talmud and Hebraica
Matthew — I Corinthians

Volume 2
Matthew — Mark

John Lightfoot

BAKER BOOK HOUSE
Grand Rapids, Michigan

HIS DEAR FRIENDS,

THE

STUDENTS OF CATHARINE-HALL,

HEALTH.

THOSE very arguments which, first and chiefly, moved me to turn over the Talmudical writings, moved me also to this present work: so that, from the same reasons whence that reading first proceeded, from them proceed also this fruit and benefit of it.

For, first, when all the books of the New Testament were written by Jews, and among Jews, and unto them; and when all the discourses made there, were made in like manner by Jews, and to Jews, and among them ; I was always fully persuaded, as of a thing past all doubting, that that Testament could not but everywhere taste of and retain the Jews' style, idiom, form, and rule of speaking.

And hence, in the second place, I concluded as assuredly that, in the obscurer places of that Testament (which are very many), the best and most natural method of searching out the sense is, to inquire how, and in what sense, those phrases and manners of speech were understood, according to the vulgar and common dialect and opinion of that nation; and how they took them, by whom they were spoken, and by whom they were heard. For it is no matter what we can beat out concerning those manners of speech on the anvil of our own conceit, but what they signified among them, in their ordinary sense and speech. And since this could be found out no other way than by consulting Talmudic authors, who both speak in the vulgar dialect of the Jews, and also handle

[a] *English folio edit.*, vol. ii. p. 93.—*Leusden's edition*, vol. ii. p. 245.

and reveal all Jewish matters; being induced by these reasons, I applied myself chiefly to the reading these books. I knew, indeed, well enough, that I must certainly wrestle with infinite difficulties, and such as were hardly to be overcome; yet I undervalued them all, and armed myself with a firm purpose, that, if it were possible, I might arrive to a fuller and more deep knowledge and understanding of the style and dialect of the New Testament.

The ill report of those authors, whom all do so very much speak against, may, at first, discourage him that sets upon the reading of their books. The Jews themselves stink in Marcellinus[b], and their writings stink as much amongst all; and they labour under this I know not what singular misfortune, that, being not read, they displease; and that they are sufficiently reproached by those that have read them, but undergo much more infamy by those that have not.

The almost unconquerable difficulty of the style, the frightful roughness of the language, and the amazing emptiness and sophistry of the matters handled, do torture, vex, and tire him that reads them. They do everywhere abound with trifles in that manner, as though they had no mind to be read; with obscurities and difficulties, as though they had no mind to be understood: so that the reader hath need of patience all along, to enable him to bear both trifling in sense and roughness in expression.

I, indeed, propounded three things to myself while I turned them over, that I might, as much as I could, either undervalue those vexations of reading, or soften them, or recreate myself with them, and that I might reap and enjoy fruit from them, if I could, and as much as I could.

I. I resolved with myself to observe those things which seemed to yield some light to the holy Scriptures, but especially either to the phrases, or sentences, or history of the New Testament.

II. To set down such things in my note-books, which carried some mention of[c] certain places in the land of Israel, or afforded[d] some light into the chorography of that land.

---

[b] Lib. xxii. [c. 5. Fœtentium Judæorum et tumultuantium tædio percitus. See Browne's Vulgar Errors, chap. x.]

[c] *English folio edit.*, vol. ii. p. 94.

[d] *Leusden's edit.*, vol. ii. p. 246.

III. To note those things which referred to the history of the Jews, whether ecclesiastical, or scholastic, or civil; or which referred to the Christian history, or the history of the rest of the world.

And now, after having viewed and observed the nature, art, matter, and marrow of these authors with as much intention as we could, I cannot paint out, in little, a true and lively character of them better than in these paradoxes and riddles: There are no authors do more affright and vex the reader; and yet there are none who do more entice and delight him. In no writers is greater or equal trifling; and yet in none is greater or so great benefit. The doctrine of the gospel hath no more bitter enemies than they; and yet the text of the gospel hath no more plain interpreters. To say all in a word, to the Jews, their countrymen, they recommend nothing but toys, and destruction, and poison; but Christians, by their skill and industry, may render them most usefully serviceable to their studies, and most eminently tending to the interpretation of the New Testament.

We here offer some specimen of this our reading and our choice, for the reader's sake, if so it may find acceptance with the reader. We know how exposed to suspicion it is to produce new things; how exposed to hatred the Talmudic writings are; how exposed to both, and to sharp censure also, to produce them in holy things. Therefore, this our more unusual manner of explaining Scripture cannot, upon that very account, but look for a more unusual censure, and become subject to a severer examination. But when the lot is cast, it is too late at this time to desire to avoid the sequel of it; and too much in vain in this place to attempt a defence. If the work and book itself does not carry something with it which may plead its cause, and obtain the reader's pardon and favour; our oration, or begging Epistle, will little avail to do it. The present work, therefore, is to be exposed and delivered over to its fate and fortune, whatsoever it be. Some there are, we hope, who will give it a milder and more gentle reception; for this very thing, dealing favourably and kindly with us, that we have been intent upon our studies; that we have been intent upon the gospel; and that we have endeavoured after truth: they will show us favour that we followed after it, and, if we have not attained it, they will pity us. But as for the wrinkled forehead, and the stern brow, we are pre-pared to bear them with all patience, being armed and satis-fied with this inward patronage, that " we have endeavoured to profit."

But this work, whatever it be, and whatever fortune it is like to meet with, we would dedicate to you, my very dear Catharine-Hall men, both as a debt, and as a desire. For by this most close bond and tie wherewith we are united, to you is due all that we study, all that we can do ; if so be that *all* is any thing at all. And when we desire to profit all (if we could) which becomes both a student and a Christian to do ; by that bond and your own merits, you are the very centre and rest of those desires and wishes. We are suffi-ciently conscious to ourselves how little or nothing we can do either for the public benefit, or for yours; yet we would make a public profession, before all the world, of our desire and study ; and, before you, of our inward and cordial affection.

Let this pledge, therefore, of our love and endearment be laid up by you ; and, while we endeavour to give others an account of our hours, let this give you an assurance of our affections. And may it last in Catharine-Hall, even to future ages, as a testimony of service, a monument of love, and a memorial both of me and you !

From my Study,
The Calends of June, 1658.

HEBREW AND TALMUDICAL

EXERCITATIONS

UPON

THE GOSPEL OF ST. MATTHEW.

CHAP. I.ᵃ

VER. I : Βίβλος γενέσεως Ἰησοῦ Χριστοῦ *The book of the ge-neration of Jesus Christ.*] עשרה יוחסין עלו מבבל וגר״ : *Ten* ᵇ *stocks came out of Babylon :* 1. כהני *Priests.* 2. לוי *Levites.* 3. ישראל *Israelites.* 4. חלילי *Common per-sons,* as to the priesthood : such whose fathers, indeed, were sprung from priests, but their mothers unfit to be admitted to the priests' marriage-bed. 5. גירי *Proselytes.* 6. חרורי *Liberti,* or *servants set free.* 7. ממזורי *Nothi :* such as were born in wedlock ; but that which was unlawful. 8. נתיני *Nethinims.* 9. שתוקי *bastards :* such as came of a certain mother, but of an uncertain father. 10. אסופי *Such as were gathered up* out of the streets, whose fathers and mothers were uncertain.

A defiled generation indeed ! and, therefore, brought up out of Babylon in this common sink, according to the opinion of the Hebrews, that the whole Jewish seed still remaining there might not be polluted by it. כי לא עלה עזרא מבבל עד שעשא כסולת נקייה: *For Ezra went not up out of Ba-bylon, until he had rendered it pure as flour.* They are the words of the Babylonian Gemara, which the Gloss explains thus ; " He left not any there that were illegitimate in any respect, but the priests and Levites only, and Israelites of a

---

ᵃ *Leusden's edition,* vol. ii. p. 247.—*English folio edit.,* vol. ii. p. 95.
ᵇ Talm. in Kiddush. cap. 4. art. 1.

pure and undefiled stock.   Therefore, he brought up with
him these ten kinds of pedigrees, that these might not be
mingled with those, when there remained now no more a Sanhedrim there, which might take care of that matter.   Therefore he brought them to Jerusalem, where care might [c] be
taken by the Sanhedrim fixed there, that the legitimate might
not marry with the illegitimate."

Let us think of these things a little while we are upon our
entrance into the Gospel-history:

I. How great a cloud of obscurity could not but arise to
the people concerning the original of Christ, even from the
very return out of Babylon, when they either certainly saw,
or certainly believed that they saw, a purer spring of Jewish
blood there than in the land of Israel itself!

II. How great a care ought there to be in the families of
pure blood, to preserve themselves untouched and clean from
this impure sink ; and to lay up among themselves genealogical scrolls from generation to generation as faithful witnesses and lasting monuments of their legitimate stock and
free blood!

Hear a complaint and a story in this case: " R. Jochanan[d]
said, By the Temple, it is in our hand to discover who are
not of pure blood in the land of Israel : but what shall I do,
when the chief men of this generation lie hid?" (that is, when
they are not of pure blood, and yet we must not declare so
much openly concerning them.)   " He was of the same
opinion with R. Isaac, who said, משפחת שנטמעה נטמעה
A family (of the polluted blood) *that lies hid, let it lie hid.*
Abai also saith, We have learned this also by tradition, That
there was a certain family called the family of Beth-zeripha,
beyond Jordan, and a son of Zion removed it away."   (The
Gloss is, Some eminent man, by a public proclamation, declared
it impure.)   " But he caused another which was such" [that
is, impure] " to come near.   And there was another which
the wise men would not manifest."

III. When it especially lay upon the Sanhedrim, settled at Jerusalem to preserve pure families, as much as in them lay, pure
still; and when they prescribed canons of preserving the legiti-

c *English folio edition*, vol. ii. p. 96.
d Hieros. Kiddush. fol. 65. 3.   Bab. ibid. fol. 71.

mation of the people (which you may see in those things that follow at the place alleged), there was some necessity to lay up public records of pedigrees with them : whence it might be known what family was pure, and what defiled. Hence [e] that of Simon Ben Azzai deserves our notice : " I saw (saith he [f]) a genealogical scroll in Jerusalem, in which it was thus written ; ' *N.*, a bastard of a strange wife.' " Observe, that even a bastard was written in their public books of genealogy, that he might be known to be a bastard, and that the purer families might take heed of the defilement of his seed. Let that also be noted [g] : " They found a book of genealogy at Jerusalem, in which it was thus written ; ' Hillel was sprung from David. Ben Jatsaph from Asaph. Ben Tsitsith Hacceseth from Abner. Ben Cobisin from Achab,' " &c. And the records of the genealogies smell of those things which are mentioned in the text of the Misna concerning ' wood-carrying :' " The [h] priests' and people's times of wood-carrying were nine : on the first day of the month Nisan, for the sons of Erach, the sons of Judah : the twentieth day of Tammuz, for the sons of David, the son of Judah : the fifth day of Ab, for the sons of Parosh, the son of Judah : the seventh of the same month for the sons of Jonadab the son of Rechab : the tenth of the same for the sons of Senaah, the son of Benjamin," &c.

It is, therefore, easy to guess whence Matthew took the last fourteen generations of this genealogy, and Luke the first forty names of his ; namely, from the genealogical scrolls at that time well enough known, and laid up in the public κειμήλια, *repositories,* and in the private also. And it was necessary, indeed, in so noble and sublime a subject, and a thing that would be so much inquired into by the Jewish people as the lineage of the Messiah would be, that the evangelists should deliver a truth, not only that could not be gainsaid, but also that might be proved and established from certain and undoubted rolls of ancestors.

Ἰησοῦ Χριστοῦ· *Of Jesus Christ.*] That the name of *Jesus* is so often added to the name of *Christ* in the New Testament, is not only that thereby Christ might be pointed out

---

[e] *Leusden's edition*, vol. ii. p. 248.   [g] Hieros. Taanith, fol. 68. 1.
[f] Bab. Jevamoth, fol. 49. 2.   [h] Taanith, cap. 4. hal. 5.

for the *Saviour*, which the name *Jesus* signifies ; but also, that Jesus might be pointed out for true *Christ :* against the unbelief of the Jews, who though they acknowledged a certain *Messiah*, or *Christ*, yet they stiffly denied that *Jesus* of Nazareth was he. This observation takes place in numberless places of the New Testament ; Acts ii. 36, viii. 35 ; 1 Cor. xvi. 22 ; 1 John ii. 22, iv. 15, &c.

Υἱοῦ Δαβίδ· *The Son of David.*] That is, " the true Messias." For by no more ordinary and more proper name did the Jewish nation point out the Messiah than by דוד בן *The Son of David.* See Matt. xii. 23, xxi. 9, xxii. 42 ; Luke xviii. 38 ; and everywhere in the Talmudic writings, but i especially in Bab. Sanhedrim [k] : where it is also discussed, What kind of times those should be when *the Son of David* should come.

The things which are devised by the Jews concerning Messiah Ben Joseph (which the Targum upon Cant. iv. 5 calls ' Messiah Ben Ephraim') are therefore devised, to comply with their giddiness and loss of judgment in their opinion of the Messiah. For, since they despised the true Messiah, who came in the time fore-allotted by the prophets, and crucified him ; they still expect I know not what chimerical one, concerning whom they have no certain opinion : whether he shall be one, or two ; whether he shall arise from among the living, or from the dead ; whether he shall come in the clouds of heaven, or sitting upon an ass, &c.: they expect a *Son of David ;* but they know not whom, they know not when.

Ver. 2 : 'Ιούδαν· *Judas.*] In Hebrew, יהודה *Jehudah.* Which word not only the Greeks, for want of the letter *h* in the middle of a word, but the Jews themselves, do contract into יודה *Judah :* which occurs infinite times in the Jerusalem Talmud. The [l] same person who is called ר' יוסי בי ר' הודה *R. Jose Bi R. Jehudah*, in the next line is called ר' יוסי בי ר' יודה *R. Jose Bi R. Judah.* So also Schabb [m]. And this is done elsewhere [n] in the very same line.

Ver. 5 : Βοὸζ ἐκ τῆς 'Ραχάβ· *Booz of Rachab.*] So far the

---

[i] *English folio edition*, vol. ii. p. 97.

[k] Fol. 97. 1.

[l] Demai, fol. 22. 3.

[m] Fol. 4. 4.

[n] Jom tobh, fol. 62. 3.

Jewish writers agree with Matthew, that they confess Rachab was married to some prince of Israel, but mistaking concerning the person : whether they do this out of ignorance, or wilfully, let themselves look to that. Concerning this matter, the Babylonian Gemara⁰ hath these words : " Eight prophets and those priests sprung from Rachab, and they are these, Neriah, Baruch, Seraiah, Maaseiah, Jeremiah, Hilkiah, Hanameel, and Shallum. R. Judah saith, Huldah also was of the posterity of Rachab." And a little after, " There is a tradition, that she, being made a proselytess, was married to Joshua :" which Kimchi also produceth in Josh. vi. Here the Gloss casts in a scruple : " It sounds somewhat harshly (saith it), that Joshua married one that was made a proselyte, when it was not lawful to contract marriage with the Canaanites, though they became proselytes. Therefore we must say that she was not of the seven nations of the Canaanites, but of some other nation, and sojourned there. But others say that that prohibition took not place before the entrance into the promised land," &c.

Ver. 8 : Ἰωρὰμ δὲ ἐγέννησε τὸν Ὀζίαν· *And Joram begat Ozias.*] The names of Ahazias, Joash, and Amazias, are struck out. See the history in the books of the Kings, and 1 Chron. iii. 11, 12.

I. The promise that "the throne of David should not be empty," passed over, after a manner, for some time into the family of Jehu, the overthrower of Joram's family. For when he had razed the house of Ahab, and had slain Ahaziahᴾ, sprung, on the mother's side, of the family of Ahab, the Lord promiseth him that his sons should reign unto the fourth generation, 2 Kings x. 30. Therefore however the mean time the throne of David was not empty, and that Joash and Amazias sat during the space between, yet their names are not unfitly omitted by our evangelist, both because they were sometimes not very unlike Joram in their manners ; and because their kingdom was very much eclipsed by the kingdom of Israel, when Ahazias was slain by Jehu, and his cousin Amazias taken and basely subdued by his cousin Joash, 2 Chron. xxv. 23.

II. זֶרַע רְשָׁעִים נִכְרָת *The seed of the wicked shall be cut off*, Psalm xxxvii. 28. Let the studious reader observe that, in the original, in this very place, the letter ע (Ain), which is the last letter of רָשָׁע *wicked*; and of זֶרַע *seed*, is cut off, and is not expressed ; when, by the rule of acrostic verse (according to which this Psalm is composed), that letter ought to begin the next following verse.

III. "Thou shalt not make to thyself any graven image, &c. For I the Lord thy God am a jealous God ; visiting the iniquity of the fathers upon the children, unto the third and fourth generation," Exod. xx. 5.

Joram[q] walked in the idolatrous ways of the kings of Israel, according to the manner of the family of Ahab, 2 Kings viii. 18. Which horrid violation of the second command God visits upon his posterity, according to the threatening of that command; and therefore the names of his sons are dashed out unto the fourth generation.

IV. The Old Testament also stigmatizeth that idolatry of Joram in a way not unlike this of the New ; and shows that family unworthy to be numbered among David's progeny, 2 Chron. xxii. 2 : בֶּן־אַרְבָּעִים וּשְׁתַּיִם שָׁנָה אֲחַזְיָהוּ *Ahazias, the son of two and-forty years :* that is, not of his age (for he was not above two-and-twenty, 2 Kings viii. 26), but of the duration of the family of Omri, of which stock Ahazias was, on the mother's side ; as will sufficiently appear to him that computes the years. A fatal thing surely ! that the years of a king of Judah should be reckoned by the account of the house of Omri.

V. Let a genealogical style not much different be observed, 1 Chron iv. 1 ; where Shobal, born in the fifth or sixth generation from Judah, is reckoned as if he were an immediate son of Judah. Compare chap. ii. 50.

In the like manner, Ezra vii, in the genealogy of Ezra, five or six generations are erased.

Ver. 11 : Ἰωσίας δὲ ἐγέννησε τὸν Ἰεχονίαν· *And Josias begat Jechonias.*] The sons of Josias were these : the first-born, Jochanan ; the second, Joachim ; the third, Zedekiah ; the fourth, Shallum, 1 Chron. iii. 15. Who this Shallum was, the Jerusalem Talmudists[r] do dispute : "R. Jochanan saith, Jochanan and Jehoachaz were the same. And when it is

---

written, *Jochanan the first-born*, it means this; that he was
the first-born to the kingdom : that is, he first reigned. And
R. Jochanan saith, Shallum and Zedekias are the same.
And when it is written, Zedekias the third Shallum the
fourth ; he was the third in birth, but he reigned fourth."
The same things are produced in the tract Sotah[s]. But
R. Kimchi[t] much more correctly : " Shallum (saith he) is
Jechonias, who had two names, and was reckoned for the son
of Josias, when he was his grandchild" (or the son of his
son) ; "for the sons of sons are reputed for sons." Compare
Jer. xxii. ver. 11 with 24 ; and the thing itself speaks it.
And that which the Gemarists now quoted say, Zedekiah
was also called *Shallum*, שבימיו שלמה מלכות בית דוד
*because in his days ' Shalmah,' ' an end was put to' the kingdom
of the family of David :* this also agrees very fitly to Jechonias, Jer. xxii. 28—30.

Ver. 12 : Ἰεχονίας ἐγέννησε τὸν Σαλαθιήλ· *Jechonias begat
Salathiel.*] That is, " a son of the kingdom," or successor in
that dignity of the house of David, whatsoever it was, which
was altogether withered in the rest of the sons of Josiah, but
did somewhat flourish again in him, 2 Kings xxv. 27. And
hence it is, that of all the posterity of Josiah, Jechonias only
is named by St. Matthew.

Jechonias, in truth, was ἄτεκνος, *without children*, Jer.
xxii. 30 ; and Salathiel, properly speaking, was the son of
Neri, Luke iii. 27 : but yet Jechonias is said to beget him ;
not that he was truly his father, but that the other was his
successor ; not, indeed, in his kingly dignity, for that was
now perished, but in that which now was the chief dignity
among the Jews. So 1 Chron. iii. 16, Zedekias is called the
son, either of Jehoiakim, whose brother indeed he was, or of
Jechonias, whose uncle he was ; because he succeeded him in
the kingly dignity.

The Lord had declared, and that not without an oath,
that Jechonias should be עֲרִירִי *without children*. The Talmudists do so interpret עֲרִירִי : " R. Judah saith[u], All they
of whom it is said, עֲרִירִים יִהְיוּ, *These shall be ἄτεκνοι, with-*

---

[s] Fol. 22. 3.   [t] In Jer. xxiv. and 1 Chron. iii.
[u] Hieros. in Schabb. fol. 9. 3.

out children; they shall have no children. And those of whom it is said, עֲרִירִים יָמוּתוּ *They shall die without children;* they bury their children." [Lev. xx. 20, 21.]

So Kimchi also upon the place; "The word עֲרִירִי (saith he) means this; That his sons shall die in his life, if he shall now have sons: but if he shall not now have sons, he never shall. But our Rabbins of blessed memory say, That he repented in prison. And they say moreover, Oh! how much doth repentance avail, which evacuates a penal edict! for it is said, 'Write ye this man childless:' but, he repenting[x], this edict turned to his good," &c. " R. Jochanan saith, His carrying away expiated. For when it is said, 'Write this man childless,' after the carrying away it is said, 'The sons of Coniah, Assir his son, Shealtiel his son.'" These things are in Babyl. Sanhedrim[y], where these words are added, אסיר בנו שעברתו אמו [z] בבית האסורין " Assir his son, because his mother conceived him in prison."

But the words in the original [1 Chron. iii. 17.] are these, וּבְנֵי יְכָנְיָה אַסִּר שְׁאַלְתִּיאֵל בְּנוֹ which are thus to be rendered; *Now the sons of Jechonias bound* [or *imprisoned*] *were Shealtiel his son.* Which version both the accents and the order of the words confirm: for Zakeph hung over אַסִּר, to which Munach beneath יְכָנְיָה serves, persuades that it is a conjunct construction; to wit, that יְכָנְיָה *Jechoniah,* and אַסִּר *bound,* should be joined together, that is, a substantive and an adjective. And the word בְּנוֹ *his son,* placed after שְׁאַלְתִּיאֵל *Shealtiel,* not after אַסִּר *bound,* fixeth the genealogy in *Salathiel,* not in אַסִּר *Assir* at all.

Ver. 16: Ἰακὼβ δὲ ἐγέννησε τὸν Ἰωσὴφ ἄνδρα Μαρίας· *And Jacob begat Joseph the husband of Mary.*] משפחת אם אין קרויה משפחה: *The* [a] *mother's family is not to be called a family.* Hence the reason may very easily be given, why Matthew brings down the generation to Joseph, Mary's husband; but Luke to Eli, Mary's father. These two frame the genealogy two ways, according to the double notion of the promise of Christ. For he is promised, as the ' seed of the

woman,' and as the 'Son of David;' that, as a man, this, as a
king.   It was therefore needful, in setting down his genealogy, that satisfaction should be given concerning both.
Therefore Luke declareth him the promised seed of the
woman, deducing his mother's stock, from whence man was
born, from Adam ; Matthew exhibits his royal original, deriving his pedigree along through the royal family of David to
Joseph, his (reputed) father.

Ver. 17 : Γενεαὶ δεκατέσσαρες· *Fourteen generations.* Although all things do not square exactly in this threefold
number of *fourteen generations,* yet there is no reason why
this should be charged as a fault upon Matthew, when in the
Jewish schools themselves it obtained for a custom, yea,
almost for an axiom, to reduce things and numbers to the
very same, when they were near alike.   The thing will be
plain by an example or two, when a hundred almost might be
produced.

Five calamitous things are ascribed to the same day, that
is, to the ninth day of the month Ab.   " For that day (say
they b) it was decreed, That the people should not go into the
promised land : the same day, the first Temple was laid
waste, and the second also : the city Bitter was destroyed,
and the city Jerusalem ploughed up."   Not that they believed
all these things fell out precisely the same day of the month ;
but, as the Babylonian Gemara notes upon it, מגלגלין זכות
ליום זכאי וחובה ליום חייב *That they might reduce a for-
tunate thing to a holy day, and an unfortunate to an unlucky
day.*

The Jerusalem Gemara c, in the same tract, examines the
reason why the daily prayers consist of the number of eighteen,
and among other things hath these words ; " The daily
prayers are eighteen, according to the number of the eighteen
Psalms, from the beginning of the Book of Psalms to that
Psalm whose beginning is, ' The Lord hear thee in the day of
trouble,'" [which Psalm, indeed, is the twentieth Psalm.]
" But if any object, that nineteen Psalms reach thither, you
may answer, The Psalm which begins, ' Why did the heathen
rage,' is not of them," a distinct Psalm.   Behold, with what
liberty they fit numbers to their own case.

b Taanith, cap. 4. art. 6.   Taanith, fol. 65. 3.

Inquiry is made, whence the number of the thirty-nine more principal servile works, to be avoided on the sabbath-day, may be proved.   Among other, we meet with these words ; אלה הדברים דבר דברי דברים " R. Chaninah[d] of Zippor saith, in the name of R Abhu, אלף *Aleph* denotes one, למד *Lamed* thirty, הא *He* five, דבר *Dabar* one, דברים *Debarim* two.   Hence are the forty works, save one, concerning which it is written in the law.   The Rabbins of Cæsarea say, Not any thing is wanting out of his place: אלח *Aleph* one, למד *Lamed* thirty, ח *Cheth* eight : לא מתמנעין רבנן דרשין בין הא לחית *our profound doctors do not distinguish between He and Cheth :*" that they may fit numbers to their case ; for אלה *these*, they write אלח, and change ה (He) and ח (Cheth) at their pleasure.

" R. Joshua Ben Levi saith[e], In all my whole life I have not looked into the [*mystical*] book of Agada but once; and then I looked into it, and found it thus written, A hundred and seventy-five sections of the law ; where it is written, דבר אמר צוה *He spake, he said, he commanded*, they are for the number of the years of our father Abraham."   And a little after ; " A hundred and forty and seven Psalms, which are written in the Book of the Psalms [*note this number*], are for the number of the years of our father Jacob.   Whence this is hinted[f], that all the praises wherewith the Israelites praise God are according to the years of Jacob.   Those hundred and twenty and three times, wherein the Israelites answer Hallelujah, are according to the number of the years of Aaron," &c.

They do so very much delight in such kind of concents, that they oftentimes screw up the strings beyond the due measure, and stretch them till they crack.   So that if a Jew carps at thee, O divine Matthew, for the unevenness of thy fourteens, out of their own schools and writings thou hast that, not only whereby thou mayest defend thyself, but retort upon them.

Ver. 18[g]: Μνηστευθείσης τῆς μητρὸς αὐτοῦ· *When as his mother was espoused.*]   No woman of Israel was married, unless she had been first espoused.   " Before the giving of the

---

[d] Hieros. Schabb. fol. 9. 2.
[e] Id. ibid. fol. 15. 3.

[f] *English folio edit.*, vol. ii. p. 100.
[g] *Leusden's edition*, vol. ii. p. 251.

law (saith Maimonides[h]), if the man and the woman had
agreed about marriage, he brought her into his house, and
privately married her.   But after the giving of the law, the
Israelites were commanded, that, if any were minded to take
a woman for his wife, he should receive her, first, before
witnesses; and thenceforth let her be to him a wife, as it is
written, אִשָּׁה אִישׁ יִקַּח כִּי *If any one take a wife.* This
taking is one of the affirmative precepts of the law, and is
called *espousing.*"   Of the manner and form of espousing, you
may read till you are weary, in that tractate, and in the
Talmudic tract, Kiddushin.

Πρὶν ἢ συνελθεῖν αὐτούς· *Before they came together.*]   "In
many places the man espouseth the woman; but doth not
bring her home to him, but after some space of time." So
the Gloss[i] upon Maimonides.

Distinction is made by the Jewish canons, and that justly
and openly, between יִחוּד *private society* or *discourse,* between
the espouser and the espoused, and הכנסה *the bringing* of
the espoused into the husband's house.   Of either of the two
may those words be understood, πρὶν ἢ συνελθεῖν αὐτοὺς, *before
they came together,* or, rather, of them both.   He had not
only not brought her home to him, but he had no manner of
society with her alone, beyond the canonical limits of discourse, that were allowed to unmarried persons; and yet she
was found with child.

Εὑρέθη ἐν γαστρὶ ἔχουσα· *She was found with child.*]   Namely,
after the space of three months from her conception, when
she was now returned home from her cousin Elizabeth. See
Luke i. 56, and compare Gen. xxxviii. 24.

The masters of the traditions[k] assign this space to discover a thing of that nature.   "A woman (say they) who is
either put away from her husband, or become a widow,
neither marrieth, nor is espoused, but after ninety days:
namely, that it may be known, whether she be big with
child or no; and that distinction may be made between the
offspring of the first husband and of the second.   In like
manner, a husband and wife, being made proselytes, are

---

[h] In אישות cap. 1.

[i] Ad אישות cap. 3.

[k] Maim. in Gerushin, cap. 11.

Talm. in Jevammoth, cap. 4. Chetuboth, cap. 5, largely.

parted from one another for ninety days, that judgment may
be made between children begotten in holiness," (that is,
within the true religion ; see 1 Cor. vii. 14,) " and children
begotten out of holiness."

Ver. 19 : Ἰωσὴφ δὲ δίκαιος ὤν, &c.   *But Joseph, being a just
man*, &c.] There is no need to rack the word δίκαιος, *just*, to
fetch out thence the sense of *gentleness* or *mercy*, which many
do ; for, construing the clauses of the verse separately, the
sense will appear clear and soft enough, *Joseph, being a just
man*, could not, would not, endure an adulteress : *but yet not
willing* παραδειγματίσαι, *to make her a public example*, being a
merciful man, and loving his wife, *was minded to put her away
privily*.

Παραδειγματίσαι· *To make her a public example*.] This doth
not imply death, but rather public disgrace, לפרסמה *to make
her public*. For it may, not without reason, be inquired,
whether she would have been brought to capital punishment,
if it had been true that she had conceived by adultery.   For
although there was a law promulged of punishing adultery
with death, Lev. xx. 10, Deut.[1] xxii. 22, and, in this case, she
that was espoused, would be dealt withal after the same
manner as it was with her who was become a wife ; yet
so far was that law modified, that I say not weakened, by the
law of giving a bill of divorce, Deut. xxiv. 1, &c., that the
husband might not only pardon his adulterous wife, and not
compel her to appear before the Sanhedrim, but scarcely
could, if he would, put her to death.   For why otherwise was
the bill of divorce indulged ?

Joseph, therefore, endeavours to do nothing here, but what
he might, with the full consent both of the law and nation.
The adulteress might be put away ; she that was espoused
could not be put away without a bill of divorce ; concerning
which thus the Jewish laws [m] : " A woman is espoused three
ways ; by money, or by a writing, or by being lain with.
And being thus espoused, though she were not yet married,
nor conducted into the man's house, yet she is his wife.
And if any shall lie with her beside him, he is to be punished
with death by the Sanhedrim.   And if he himself will put her
away, he must have a bill of divorce."

[1] *English folio edition*, vol. ii. p. 101.   [m] Maimon. in אישות cap. 1.

Λάθρα ἀπολῦσαι αὐτήν· *Put her away privily.*] Let the
Talmudic tract ' Gittin ' be looked upon, where they are
treating of the manner of delivering a bill of divorce to a
wife to be put away : among other things, it might be given
privately, if the husband so pleased, either into the woman's
hand or bosom, two witnesses only present.

Ver. 23 : 'Ιδοὺ, ἡ παρθένος ἐν γαστρὶ ἕξει· *Behold, a virgin
shall be with child.*] That the word עַלְמָה, in the prophet,
denotes an *untouched virgin,* sufficiently appears from the
sense of the place, Isa. vii. 14. King Ahaz there was afraid,
lest the enemies that were now upon him might destroy Jerusalem, and utterly consume the house of David[n]. The Lord
meets this fear by a signal and most remarkable promise,
namely, ' that sooner should a pure virgin bring forth a child,
than the family of David perish.' And the promise yields a
double comfort : namely, of Christ hereafter to be born of a
virgin ; and of their security from the imminent danger of
the city and house of David. So that, although that prophecy, of a *virgin's* bringing forth a son, should not be fulfilled till many hundreds of years after, yet, at that present
time, when the prophecy was made, Ahaz had a certain and
notable sign, that the house of David should be safe and
secure from the danger that hung over it. As much as if
the prophet had said, " Be not so troubled, O Ahaz ; does it
not seem an impossible thing to thee, and that never will
happen, that *a pure virgin* should become a mother? But I
tell thee, *a pure virgin* shall bring forth a son, before the
house of David perish."

Hear this, O unbelieving Jew! and shew us now some
remainders of the house of David : or confess this prophecy
fulfilled in *the Virgin's* bringing forth : or deny that a sign
was given, when a sign is given.

§ *In what language Matthew wrote his Gospel.*

"Ο ἐστι μεθερμηνευόμενον· *Which is, being interpreted.*]
I. All confess that the Syriac language was the mother-
tongue to the Jewish nation dwelling in Judea ; and that the
Hebrew was not at all understood by the common people
may especially appear from two things :

[n] *Leusden's edition,* vol. ii. p. 252.

1. That, in the synagogues, when the law and the prophets were read in the original Hebrew, an interpreter was always present to the reader, who rendered into the mother-tongue that which was read, that it might be understood by the common people. Hence [o] those rules of the office of an nterpreter, and of some places which were not to be rendered into the mother-tongue.

2. That Jonathan the son of Uzziel, a scholar of Hillel, about the time of Christ's birth, rendered all the prophets (that is, as the Jews number them, Joshua, Judges, Samuel, the Books of the Kings, Isaiah, Jeremiah, Ezekiel, and the twelve lesser prophets) into the Chaldee language; that is, into a language much more known to the people than the Hebrew, and more acceptable than the mother-tongue. For if it be asked why he translated them at all, and why he translated not rather into the mother-tongue, which was known to all? and if it be objected concerning St. Matthew and St. Paul, that, writing to the Jews, one his Gospel, the other his Epistle (to the Hebrews[p]), they must have written in the Syriac tongue (if so be they wrote not in Hebrew), that they might be understood by all :—we answer,

First, It was not without reason that the paraphrast Jonathan translated out of the Hebrew original into the Chaldee tongue, because this tongue was much more known and familiar to all the people than the Hebrew. The holy text had need of an interpreter into a more known tongue, because it was now in a tongue not known at all to the vulgar. For none knew the Hebrew but such as learned it by study. However, therefore, all the Jews inhabiting the land of Canaan, did not so readily understand the Chaldee language as the Syriac, which was their mother-language, yet they much more readily understood that than the Hebrew, which, to the unlearned, was not known at all. Hence it was not without necessity that the prophets were turned into the Chaldee language by Jonathan, and the law, not much after, by Onkelos, that they might a little be understood by the common people, by whom the Hebrew original was not understood at all. We[q] read also that the Book

---

[o] Bab. Megill. fol. 25, &c. Massech. Sopherim, cap. 11, 12, &c.

[p] *English folio edit.*, vol. ii. p. 102.
[q] Hieros. Schabb. fol. 15. col. 3.

of Job had its Targum in the time of Gamaliel the Elder ;
that is, Paul's master.

Secondly, it is no impertinent question, Why Jonathan
and Onkelos did not rather translate into the Syriac language, which was the mother-language to all the people,
when both they themselves were in Judea, while they were
employed about this work, and laboured in it for the use of
the Jews that dwelt there? To which we give this double
answer ; 1. That, by turning it into the Chaldee language,
they did a thing that might be of use to both them that
dwelt in Judea, and in Babylon also. 2. The Syriac language was not so grateful unto the Jews, who used it for
their mother-tongue, as the Chaldee was ; as being a language more neat and polite, and the mother-tongue to the
brethren in Babylon, and which they that came up out of
Babylon, carried thence with them into Judea. You may
wonder, reader, when you hear that canon which permits a
single man " to say his prayers in any language, when he
asks those things that are needful for him, except only the
Syriac: יחיד שואל צרכיו אומר בכל לשון חוץ מלשון ארמי׃
While [r] *he asketh necessaries for himself, let him use any language but the Syriac.*" But you will laugh when you hear the
reason : " Therefore, by all means, because the angels do not
understand the Syriac language."

Whether they distinguish the Syriac language here from
the pure Chaldee, is not of great moment solicitously to inquire : we shall only produce these things of the Glosser
upon Beracoth [s], which make to our purpose :—" There are
some (saith he) who say, that that prayer which begins קדיש,
is therefore to be made in the Syriac language, because it is
a noble prayer, and that deserves the highest praise ; and
therefore it is framed in the Targumistical language, that
the angels may not understand it, and envy it to us," &c.
And a little after ; " It was the custom to recite that prayer
קריש, אחר הדרשה *after sermon :* and the common people
were there present, who understood not the Hebrew language
at all ; and therefore they appointed it to be framed in the

[r] פסקי הר' אש' i. e. R. Oshaiæ   Beracoth, cap. 2. Bab. Schab. fol.
Rabbæ. See Juchas. fol. 84. 1. in   12. 2. Sotah, fol. 33. 1.   [s] Fol. 3. 1.

Targumistical language, that it might be understood [t] by all; for this is their tongue."

Mark, the Hebrew was altogether unknown to the common people : no wonder, therefore, if the evangelists and apostles wrote not in Hebrew when there were none who understood things so written, but learned men only.

That also must not be passed over, which, at first sight, seems to hint that the Syriac language was not understood even by learned men. " Samuel the Little [u], at the point of death, said, שמעון וישמעאל לחרבא *Simeon and Ismael to the sword;* ושאר כל עמא לביזה *and all the other people to the spoil:* ועקין סגיאין הויין *and there shall be very great calamities.* ובלשון ארמית אמרן ולא ידעו מה אמר *And because he spoke these things in the Syriac language, they understood not what he had said.* This story you have repeated in the Babylonian Gemara, where the words of the dying man are thus related; שמעון וישמעאל לחרבא וחברוהי לקטלא ושאר עמא לביזא ועקן סגיאן עתירין למיתי על עלמא: Let the Glosser [x] upon the place be the interpreter : " *Simeon and Ismael to the sword* [that is, Rabban Simeon the prince, and R. Ismael Ben Elisha the high-priest, were slain with the sword], *and his fellows to slaughter* [that is, R. Akibah and R. Chananiah Ben Teradion were slain by other deaths ; namely R. Akibah by iron teeth, and R. Chananiah by burning alive before idols]; *and the other people for a prey: and very many calamities shall fall upon the world.*"

Now where it is said that, " They understood not what he said, because he spake in the Syrian tongue," we also do not easily understand. What ! for the Jerusalem doctors not to understand the Chaldee language! For Samuel the Little died before the destruction of the city ; and he spake of the death of Rabban Simeon, who perished in the siege of the city ; and he spake these things when some of the learnedest Rabbins were by : and yet that they understood not these words, which even a smatterer in the oriental tongues would very easily understand !

Therefore, perhaps, you may beat out the sense of the

matter from the words of the author of Juchasin[y], who saith,
He prophesied in the Syriac language, התנבא בלשון ארמי
But now, when prophecies were spoken only in the Hebrew
language, however they understood[z] the sense of the words,
yet they reputed it not for a prophecy, because it was not
uttered in the language that was proper for prophetical pre-
dictions. But we tarry not here. That which we would
have is this, that Matthew wrote not in Hebrew (which is
proved sufficiently by what is spoken before), if so be we
suppose him to have written in a language vulgarly known
and understood ; which, certainly, we ought to suppose :
not that he, or the other writers of the New Testament,
wrote in the Syriac language, unless we suppose them to have
written in the ungrateful language of an ungrateful nation,
which, certainly, we ought not to suppose. For when the
Jewish people were now to be cast off, and to be doomed to
eternal cursing, it was very improper, certainly, to extol
their language, whether it were the Syriac mother-tongue,
or the Chaldee, its cousin language, unto that degree of
honour; that it should be the original language of the New
Testament. Improper, certainly, it was, to write the Gospel
in their tongue, who, above all the inhabitants of the world,
most despised and opposed it.

II. Since, therefore, the Gentiles were to be called to the
faith, and to embrace the Gospel by the preaching of it, the
New Testament was written very congruously in the Gentile
language, and in that which, among the Gentile languages,
was the most noble ; viz. the Greek. Let us see what the
Jews say of this language, envious enough against all languages besides their own.

" Rabban Simeon[a] Ben Gamaliel saith, Even concerning
the holy books, the wise men permitted not that they should
be written in any other language than Greek. R. Abhu saith
that R. Jochanan said, The tradition is according to Rabban
Simeon ; that R. Jochanan said, moreover, Whence is that of
Rabban Simeon proved ? From thence, that the Scripture
saith, ' The Lord shall persuade Japhet, and he shall dwell
in the tents of Sem :' the words of Japhet shall be in the

[y] Juchas. fol. 21. 1.   [z] Megillah, fol. 9. 2.
                [a] *English folio edit.,* vol. ii. p. 103.

tents of Sem :" and a little after, יֶפְתְּ אֱלֹהִים לְיֶפֶת *God shall persuade Japhet* ; i. e. יפיותו של יפת יהא באהלי שם *The grace of Japhet shall be in the tents of Sem.* Where the Gloss speaks thus ; " ' The grace of Japhet' is the Greek language ; the fairest of those tongues which belonged to the sons of Japhet."

" Rabban Simeon[b] Ben Gamaliel saith, Even concerning the sacred books, they permitted not that they should be written in any other language than Greek. They searched seriously, and found, שאין התורה יכולה להתרגם כל צורכה אלא יוונית *that the law could not be translated according to what was needful for it, but in Greek.*" You have this latter clause cut off in Massecheth Sopherim[c], where this story also is added : " The five elders wrote the law in Greek for Ptolemy the king : and that day was bitter to Israel, as the day wherein the golden calf was made, because the law could not be translated according to what was needful for it." This story of the ' five interpreters' of the law is worthy of consideration, which you find seldom mentioned, or scarce anywhere else. The tradition next following after this, in the place cited, recites the story of the Seventy. Look at it.

When, therefore, the common use of the Hebrew language had perished, and when the mother Syriac or Chaldee tongue of a cursed nation could not be blessed, our very enemies being judges, no other language could be found, which might be fit to write the (new) divine law, besides the Greek tongue. That this language was scattered, and in use[d] among all the eastern nations almost, and was in a manner the mother tongue, and that it was planted every where by the conquests of Alexander, and the empire of the Greeks, we need not many words to prove ; since it is every where to be seen in the historians. The Jews do well near acknowledge it for their mother-tongue even in Judea.

" R. Jochanan[e] of Beth Gubrin said, There are four noble languages which the world useth ; the mother-tongue, for singing ; the Roman, for war ; the Syriac, for mourning ; and the Hebrew, for elocution : and there are some who say,

---

[b] Hieros. Megill. fol. 71. 3.
[c] Cap. 1. artic. 7.
[d] *Leusden's edit.*, vol. ii. p. 254.
[e] Hieros. Megill. in the place above, col. 2.

the Assyrian for writing." What is that which he calls the
mother-tongue? It is very easily answered, the Greek, from
those encomiums added to it, mentioned before : and that
may more confidently be affirmed from the words of Midras
Tillin[f], respecting this saying of R. Jochanan, and mentioning
the Greek language by name. " R. Jochanan said, There are
three languages; the Roman, for war; the Greek, for speech;
the Assyrian, for prayer." To this also belongs that, that
occurs once and again in Bab. Megillah[g], בלעז יווני *In the
Greek mother tongue.* You have an instance of the thing[h] :
" R. Levi, coming to Cæsarea, heard some קריין שמע
אלוניסתין *reciting the phylacteries in the Hellenistical language.*"
This is worthy to be marked. At Cæsarea flourished the
famous schools of the Rabbins. רבנין דקיסרין *The Rabbins
of Cæsarea* are mentioned in both Talmuds most frequently,
and with great praise, but especially in that of Jerusalem.
But yet among these, the Greek is used as the mother-tongue,
and that in reciting the phylacteries, which, you may well
think, above all other things, in Judea were to be said in
Hebrew.

In that very Cæsarea, Jerome mentions the Hebrew Gospel
of St. Matthew, to be laid up in the library of Pamphilus, in
these words : " Matthew, who was also called Levi, from a
publican made an apostle, first of all in Judea composed the
Gospel of Christ in Hebrew letters and[i] words, for their sakes,
who were of the circumcision and believed. Which Gospel,
who he was that afterward translated it into Greek, it is
not sufficiently known. Moreover, that very Hebrew Gospel
is reserved to this day in the library at Cæsarea, which Pamphilus the martyr, with much care, collected. I also had
leave given me by the Nazarenes, who use this book in Berea,
a city of Syria, to write it out."

It is not at all to be doubted, that this Gospel was found
in Hebrew; but that which deceived the good man was not
the very hand-writing of Matthew, nor, indeed, did Matthew
write the Gospel in that language : but it was turned by
somebody out of the original Greek into Hebrew, that so, if

[f] Midr. Till. fol. 25. 4.   [h] Hieros. Sotah, fol. 21. 2.
[g] Fol. 18. 1.   [i] *English folio edit.*, vol. ii. p. 104.

possible, the learned Jews might read it. For since they had little kindness for foreign books, that is, heathen books, or such as were written in a language different from their own, which might be illustrated from various canons, concerning this matter; some person converted to the gospel, excited with a good zeal, seems to have translated this Gospel of St. Matthew out of the Greek original into the Hebrew language, that learned men among the Jews, who as yet believed not, might perhaps read it, being now published in their language : which was rejected by them while it remained in a foreign speech. Thus, I suppose, this Gospel was written in Greek by St. Matthew, for the sake of those that believed in Judea, and turned into Hebrew by somebody else, for the sake of those that did not believe.

The same is to be resolved concerning the original language of the Epistle to the Hebrews. That Epistle was written to the Jews inhabiting Judea, to whom the Syriac was the mother-tongue ; but yet it was writ in Greek, for the reasons above named. For the same reasons, also, the same apostle writ in Greek to the Romans, although in that church there were Romans, to whom it might seem more agreeable to have written in Latin ; and there were Jews, to whom it might seem more proper to have written in Syriac.

CHAP. II.

A calculation of the times when Christ was born.

VER. 1 : Τοῦ δὲ ᾽Ιησοῦ γεννηθέντος· *Now when Jesus was born.*] We thus lay down a scheme of the times when Christ was born :

I. He was born in the year of the world 3928.

For from the creation of the world to the deluge are commonly reckoned 1656 years.

From the deluge to Abraham's promise are 427 years. This being supposed, that Abraham was born the 130th year of Terah : which must be supposed.

From the promise given, to the going out of Egypt, 430 years, Exod. xii. 40, Gal. iii. 17.

From the going out of Egypt to the laying the foundations of the Temple are 480 years, 1 Kings vi. 1.

The Temple was building 7 years, 1 Kings vi. 38.   Casting up, therefore, all these together, viz.

$$
\begin{array}{r}
1656 \\
427 \\
430 \\
480 \\
7 \\
\hline
\end{array}
$$

The sum of years amounts to 3000

And it is clear, the building of the Temple was finished and completed in the year of the world 3000.

The Temple was finished in the eleventh year of Solomon, 1 Kings vi. 38 : and thence to the revolting of the ten tribes, in the first year of Rehoboam, were 30 years.   Therefore, that revolt was in the year of the world 3030.

From[k] the revolt of the ten tribes to the destruction of Jerusalem under Zedekiah were three hundred and ninety years: which appears sufficiently from the chronical computation of the parallel times of the kings of Judah and Israel: and which is implied by Ezekiel, iv. 4–6 : " Thou[l] shalt sleep upon thy left side, and shalt put the iniquities of the house of Israel upon it, &c. according to the number of the days, three hundred and ninety days.   And when thou shalt have accomplished them, thou shalt sleep upon thy right side the second time, and shalt take upon thee the iniquity of the house of Judah forty days.   Concerning the computation of these years, it is doubted, whether those forty years are to be numbered together within the three hundred and ninety years, or by themselves, as following after those three hundred and ninety years.   We, not without cause, embrace the former opinion, and suppose those forty years to be included within the sum of three hundred and ninety ; but mentioned by themselves particularly, for a particular reason.   For by the space of forty years before the destruction of the city by the Chaldeans, did Jeremiah prophesy daily, namely, from the third year of Josias to the sacking of the city : whom the people not hearkening to, they are marked for that peculiar iniquity with this note.

[k] *English folio edit.*, vol. ii. p. 105.   [l] *Leusden's edit.*, vol. ii. p. 255.

Therefore, these three hundred and ninety years being added to the year of the world, 3030, when the ten tribes fell off from the house of David, the age of the world when Jerusalem perished, arose to the year 3420.

At that time there remained fifty years of the Babylonian captivity to be completed. For those remarkable seventy years took their beginning from the third year of Jehoiakim, Dan. i. 1, whose fourth year begins the Babylonian monarchy, Jer. xxv. 1. And, in the nineteenth year of Nebuchadnezzar, the Temple was destroyed, 2 Kings xxv. 8, when now the twentieth year of the captivity passed; and other fifty remained: which fifty being added to the year of the world 3420, a year fatal to the Temple, the years of the world amount, in the first year of Cyrus, unto 3470.

From the first of Cyrus to the death of Christ are seventy weeks of years, or four hundred and ninety years, Dan. ix. 24. Add these to the three thousand four hundred and seventy, and you observe Christ crucified in the year of the world 3960. When, therefore, you have subtracted thirty-two years and a half, wherein Christ lived upon the earth, you will find him born in the year of the world 3928.

II. He was born in the one-and-thirtieth year of Augustus Cæsar, the computation of his monarchy beginning from the victory at Actium. Of which matter thus Dion Cassius writes: Τοιαύτη τις ἡ ναυμαχία αὐτῶν τῇ δευτέρᾳ τοῦ Σεπτεμβρίου ἐγένετο· Τοῦτο δὲ οὐκ ἄλλως εἶπον, &c. " This [m] their sea-fight was on the second of September: and this I speak upon no other account (for I am not wont to do it), but because then Cæsar first obtained the whole power: so that the computation of the years of his monarchy must be precisely reckoned from that very day." We confirm this our computation, by drawing down a chronological table from this year of Augustus to the fifteenth year of Tiberias, when Christ, having now completed the nine-and-twentieth year of his age, and entering just upon his thirtieth, was baptized. Now this table, adding the consuls of every year, we thus frame:

[m] Dion. Cass. lib. li. in the beginning.

A.M.	A.U.C.	Augus-tus.	A.D.	CONSULS.
3928	754	31	1	Cæs. Aug. XIV. and L. Æmil. Paulus.
3929	755	32	2	Publius Vinicius and Pub. Alfenus Varus.
3930	756	33	3	L. Ælius Lamia, and M. Servilius.
3931	757	34	4	Sext. Æmilius Carus, and C. Sentius Saturninus.
3932	758	35	5	L. Valerius Messala, and Cn. Corn. Cinna Magn.
3933	759	36	6	M. Æmil. Lepidus, and L. Aruntius.
3934	760	37	7	A. Licin. Nerv. Silanus, and Q. Cæcil. Metell. Cret.
3935	761	38	8	Furius Camillus, and Sext. Nonius Quintilianus.
3936	762	39	9	Q. Sulpit. Camarin. and C. Poppæus Sabinus.
3937	763	40	10	Pub. Corn. Dolabella, and C. Junius Silanus.
3938	764	41	11	M. Æmil. Lepid. and T. Statilius Taurus.
3939	765	42	12	Germanicus Cæs. and C. Fonteius Capito.
3940	766	43	13	L. Munatius Plancus, and C. Silius Cæcina.
3941	767	44	14	Sext. Pomp. Sexti F. and Sext. Apuleius Sexti F.

Augustus Cæsar died the 19th day of August : on which day he had formerly entered upon the first consulship. He [n] lived seventy-five years, ten months, and twenty-six days. He bore the empire alone, from the victory at Actium, forty-four years, wanting only thirteen days.

" Tiberius [o] held the empire in great slothfulness, with grievous cruelty, wicked covetousness, and filthy lust [p]."

A.M.	A.U.C.	Tiber.	A.D.	CONSULS.
3942	768	1	15	Drusus Cæs. and C. Norbanus Flaccus.
3943	769	2	16	C. Statil. Sisenna Taurus, and Scribonius Libo.
3944	770	3	17	C. Cæcil. Rufus, and L. Pomponianus Flaccus.
3945	771	4	18	Tiber. Cæs. Aug. III. and Germanicus Cæs. II.
3946	772	5	19	M. Julius Silanus, and L. Norban Flac. vel Balbus.
3947	773	6	20	M. Valerius Messala, and M. Aurel. Cotta.
3948	774	7	21	Tiber. Cæs. Aug. IV. and Drusus Cæs. II.
3949	775	8	22	D. Haterius Agrippa, and C. Sulpitius Galba.
3950	776	9	23	C. Asinius Pollio, and C. Antistius Veter.

[n] Dion. Cass. lib. lvi.   —*Leusden's edit.*, vol. ii. p. 256.
[o] *English folio edit.*, vol. ii. p. 106.   [p] Eutrop. lib. vii.

A.M.	A.U.C. Tiber.		A.D.	CONSULS.
3951	777	10	24	Sext. Cornel. Cethegus, and Visellius Varro.
3952	778	11	25	M. Asinius Agrippa, and Cossus Cornel Lentulus.
3953	779	12	26	Cn. Lentulus Getulicus, and C. Calvisius Sabinus.
3954	780	13	27	M. Licinius Crassus, and P. L. Calphurnius Piso.
3955	781	14	28	Appius Jul. Silanus, and P. Silvius Nerva.
3956	782	15	29	C. Rubellius Geminus, and C. Fusius Geminus.

In the early spring of this year came John baptizing. In the month Tisri Christ is baptized, when he had now accomplished the nine-and-twentieth year of his age, and had now newly entered upon his thirtieth. The thirtieth of Christ is to be reckoned with the sixteenth of Tiberius.

Of Augustus, now entering upon his one-and-thirtieth year, wherein Christ was born, Dion Cassius hath moreover these words: Πληρωθείσης δὲ καὶ τῆς τρίτης δεκαετίας, τὴν ἡγημονίαν καὶ τὸ τέταρτον ἐκβιασθεὶς δῆθεν ὑπεδέξατο, πρᾳότερός τε καὶ ὀκνηρότερος ὑπὸ τοῦ γήρως· "Having now completed thrice ten years, being compelled, indeed, to it, he continued his government, and entered upon a fourth ten of years : being now more easy and slothful by reason of age." In this very year was the taxation under Cyrenius, of which Luke speaks, chap. ii. So that if it be asked when the fifth monarchy of the Romans arose, after the dissolution of those four mentioned by Daniel, an easy answer may be fetched from St. Luke, who relates that in that very year wherein Christ was born, Augustus laid a tax upon the whole world.

III. Christ was born in the thirty-fifth year of the reign of Herod : which we gather from the observation of these things : 1. Herod q reigned, from that time he was first declared king by the Romans, seven-and-thirty years. 2. Between the death of Herod and the death of Augustus there was this space of time :

1. The r ten years current of the reign of Archelaus.

2. Coponius s succeeds him, banished to Vienna in the presidentship of Judea.

---

q Joseph. Antiq. lib. xvii. cap. 10. [xvii. 8. 1.]   r Id. Ibid. c. 15. [xvii. 13. 2.]
s Id. ibid. and lib. xviii. c. 1. [xviii. 1. 1.]

3. Marcus Ambibuchus [Ambivius] succeeds Coponius.

4. Annius Rufus[t] succeeds Ambibuchus [Ambivius], during whose presidentship Augustus dies.

Since, therefore, only fourteen years passed from the nativity of Christ to the death of Augustus, out of which sum when you shall have reckoned the ten years current of Archelaus, and the times of the three presidents, we must reckon that Christ was not born but in the last years of Herod. Thus we conjecture:

In his thirty-fifth Christ was born.

In his thirty-seventh, now newly begun, the wise men came : presently after this was the slaying of the infants; and, after a few months, the death of Herod.

IV. Christ was born about the twenty-seventh year of the presidentship of Hillel in the Sanhedrim.

The rise of the family of Hillel took its beginning at the decease of the Asmonean family (Herod, indeed, succeeded in the kingly government) ; a family sprung from Babylon, and, as was believed, of the stock of David. For[u] " a book of genealogy was found at Jerusalem" (which we mentioned before), " in which it was written, that Hillel was sprung from the stock of David, by his wife Abital." Now Hillel went up out of Babylon to Jerusalem, to inquire of the wise men concerning some things, when now, after the death of Shemaia and Abtalion, the two sons of Betira held the chief seats. And when he who had resorted thither to learn something, had taught them some things of the Passover rites, which they had forgot, they put him into the chair. You have the full story of it in the Jerusalem Talmud[x]. We mention it chap. xxvi. 1.

Now Hillel went up to Jerusalem and took the chair a hundred years before the destruction of the city: הילל ושמעון ‏ " Hillel[y] גמליאל ושמעון נהגו נשיאותן לפני הבית ק׳ שנה and[z] his son Simeon, and his son Gamaliel, and his son Simeon, bare the government for a hundred years before the laying waste of the Temple." Of those hundred years if you take away two-and-thirty and a half of the life of Christ, and

t Joseph. Antiq. lib. xviii. c. 3. [xviii. 2. 2.]

u Hieros. Taanith, fol. 68. 1.

x Pesachin, fol. 33. 1.

y Bab. Schabb. fol. 15. 1.

z *English folio edit.*, vol. ii. p. 107.

forty years (as it is commonly deputed) coming between the
death of Christ and the destruction of the city, there remain[a]
the twenty-seven years of Hillel before the birth of our Saviour.

Hillel held the government forty years: so that his death
happened about the twelfth or thirteenth year of Christ. His
son also held it after him, and his grandsons, in a long suc-
cession, even to R. Judah the Holy. The splendour and pomp
of this family of Hillel had so obscured the rest of the families
of David's stock, that perhaps they believed or expected the
less, that the Messias should spring from any of them. Yea,
one in the Babylonian Gemara was almost persuaded, that
" Rabbi Judah the Holy, of the Hillelian family, was the
Messias. Rabh[b] said, אי מן חייא כגון רבינו הקדוש *If
Messiah be among the living, our Holy Rabbi is such:* if among
the dead, Daniel was he."

V. Christ was born in the month of Tisri; somewhat answering to our September. This we conclude, omitting other
things, by computing backwards from his death. For if he
died in his two-and-thirtieth year and a half, at the feast of
the Passover, in the month Nisan, you must necessarily lay
the time of his birth in the month Tisri. But that he died at
that age, not to make any delay by mentioning more things,
appears hence, that he was baptized now beginning his thirtieth year, and that he lived after his baptism three years
and a half; as the space of his public ministry is determined
by the angel Gabriel, Dan. ix. [27]; " In the half of a
week" (that is, three years and a half), " he shall make the
sacrifice to cease," &c. But of this hereafter.

This month was ennobled in former times, 1. For the creation of the world. Weigh well Exod. xxiii. 15, Joel ii. 23.
2. For the nativity of the first fathers; which the Jews[c] assert
not without reason. 3. For the repairing the tables of the
law. For Moses, after the third fast of forty days, comes
down from the mountain, a messenger of good things, the
tenth day of this month, which was from hence appointed
for the feast of Expiation to following ages. 4. For the
dedication of the Temple, 1 Kings viii. 2. And, 5. For three

---

[a] *Leusden's edition,* vol. ii. p. 257.   [b] Sanhedr. fol. 98. 2.
          [c] Hieros. Rosh Hashanah, fol. 56. 4.

solemn feasts, namely, that of the Beginning of the Year, that of Expiation, and that of Tabernacles. From this month also was the beginning of the Jubilee.

VI. It is probable Christ was born at the feast of Tabernacles.

1. So it ariseth exactly to three-and-thirty years and a half, when he died at the feast of the Passover.

2. He fulfilled the typical equity of the Passover and Pentecost, when, at the Passover, he offered himself for a passover, at Pentecost he bestowed the Holy Ghost from heaven, as at that time the law had been given from heaven. At that time the first-fruits of the Spirit were given by him (Rom. viii. 23), when the first-fruits of corn had been wont to be given, Levit. xxiii. 17. It had been a wonder if he had honoured the third solemnity, namely, the feast of Tabernacles, with no antitype.

3. The institution of the feast of Tabernacles agrees excellently with the time of Christ's birth. For when Moses went down from the mount on the tenth day of the month Tisri, declaring that God was appeased, that the people was pardoned, and that the building of the holy tabernacle was forthwith to be gone in hand with (hitherto hindered by and because of the golden calf), seeing that God now would dwell among them, and forsake them no more; the Israelites immediately pitch their tents, knowing they were not to depart from that place before the divine tabernacle was finished, and they set upon this work with all their strength. Whence the tenth day of that month, wherein Moses came down and brought this good news with him, was appointed for the feast of Expiation; and the fifteenth day, and seven days after, for the feast of Tabernacles, in memory of their dwelling in tents in the wilderness, when God dwelt in the midst of them: which things with how aptly typical an aspect they respect the incarnation, when God dwelt among men in human flesh, is plain enough.

4. Weigh Zech. xiv. 16, 17: "And it shall come to pass, that every one that is left of all the nations which came against Jerusalem shall even go up, from year to year, to worship the King, the Lord of hosts, and to keep the feast of Tabernacles. And it shall be, that whoso will not come up

of all the families of the earth unto Jerusalem, to worship
the King, the Lord of hosts, even upon them shall be no
more rain."

Ἐν Βηθλεέμ· *In Beth-lehem.*   It will not be improper here
to produce the Gemarists themselves, openly confessing that
the Messias was born now a good while ago before their times.
For so they write: " After[d] this the children of Israel shall
be converted, and shall inquire after the Lord their God, and
David their king, Hos. iii. 5.   Our Rabbins say, That is king
Messias : if he[e] be among the living, his name is David ;
or if dead, David is his name.   R. Tanchum said, Thus I
prove it : ' He showeth mercy to David his Messiah' (Psalm
xviii. 50).   R. Joshua Ben Levi saith, His name is צֶמַח *A
branch* (Zech. iii. 8).   R. Judan Bar Aibu saith, His name
is *Menahem* [מְנַחֵם] [that is, παράκλητος, *the comforter*].
And that which happened to a certain Jew, as he was
ploughing, agreeth with this business :—A certain Arabian
travelling, and hearing the ox bellow, said to the Jew at
plough, ' O Jew, loose thy oxen, and loose thy ploughs : for
behold ! the Temple is laid waste.'   The ox bellowed the
second time ; the Arabian said to him, *O Jew, Jew, yoke thy
oxen and fit thy ploughs, for behold ! King Messiah is born.*
יודאי יודאי קטור תוריך וקטור קנקניך דהא יליד מלכא
משיחא :.   But, saith the Jew, ' What is his name ?'   ' Menahem,' saith he.   ' And what is the name of his father ?'
' Hezekiah,' saith the Arabian.   To whom the Jew, ' But
whence is he ?'   The other answered, ' From the palace of
the king of Beth-lehem Judah.'   Away he went, and sold his
oxen and his ploughs, and became a seller of infants' swad-
dling-clothes, going about from town to town.   When he
came to that city [*Beth-lehem*], all the women bought of him,
but the mother of Menahem bought nothing.   He heard the
voice of the women saying, ' O thou mother of Menahem, thou
mother of Menahem, carry thy son the things that are here[f]
sold.'   But she replied, ' May the enemies of Israel be strangled, because on the day that he was born the Temple was
laid waste !'   To whom he said, ' But we hoped, that as it
was laid waste at his feet, so at his feet it would be built

---

d Hieros. Beracoth, fol. 5. 1.   e *English folio edit.*, vol. ii. p. 108.
f *Leusden's edition*, vol. ii. p. 258.

again.' She saith, ' I have no money.' To whom he replied,
' But why should this be prejudicial to him? Carry him what
you buy here; and if you have no money to-day, after some
days I will come back and receive it.' After some days he
returns to that city, and saith to her, ' How does the little
infant?' And she said, ' From the time you saw me last,
spirits and tempests came, and snatched him away out of my
hands.' R. Bon saith, What need have we to learn from an
Arabian? Is it not plainly written, ' And Lebanon shall fall
before the powerful One?' (Isa. x. 34.) And what follows
after? ' A branch shall come out of the root of Jesse'" (Isa.
xi. 1).

The Babylonian doctors yield us a confession not very
unlike the former: " R. Chaninah [g] saith, After four hundred
years are past from the destruction of the Temple, if any one
shall say to you, 'Take to thyself for one penny a field worth
a thousand pence,' do not take it." And again; " After four
thousand two hundred thirty-and-one years from the creation
of the world, if any shall say to you, ' Take for a penny a
field worth a thousand pence,' take it not." The Gloss is,
" For that is the time of redemption; and you shall be
brought back to the holy mountain, to the inheritance of your
fathers: why, therefore, should you mispend your penny?"

You may fetch the reason of this calculation, if you are at
leisure, out of the tract Sanhedrim [h]: " The tradition of the
school of Elias, The world is to last six thousand years," &c.
And a little after; " Elias said to Rabh Judah, ' The world
shall last not less than eighty-five jubilees; and in the last
jubilee shall the Son of David come.' He saith to him,
'Whether in the beginning of it, or in the end?' He answered
him, ' I know not.' ' Whether is this whole time to be
finished first, or not?' He answered him, ' I know not.'
But Rabh Asher asserts that he answered thus, ' Until then
expect him not, but from thence expect him.'" Hear your
own countrymen, O Jew, how many centuries of years are
past by and gone from the eighty-fifth jubilee of the world,
that is, the year 4250, and yet the Messias of your expectation is not yet come.

Daniel's weeks had so clearly defined the time of the true

[g] Avodah Zarah, fol. 9. 2.   [h] Fol. 97.

Messias's coming, that the minds of the whole nation were raised into the expectation of him. Hence it was doubted of the Baptist whether he were not the Messias, Luke iii. 15. Hence it was that the Jews are gathered together from all countries unto Jerusalem [Acts ii.], expecting, and coming to see, because at that time the term of revealing the Messias, that had been prefixed by Daniel, was come. Hence it was that there was so great a number of false Christs, Matt. xxiv. 5, &c., taking the occasion of their impostures hence, that now the time of that great expectation was at hand, and fulfilled : and in one word, " They thought the kingdom of God should presently appear ;" Luke xix. 11.

But when those times of expectation were past, nor did such a Messias appear as they expected (for when they saw the true Messias, they would not see him), they first broke out into various and those wild conjectures of the time ; and at length all those conjectures coming to nothing, all ended in this curse (the just cause of their eternal blindness), תפח רוחן של מחשבי קצין *May their soul be confounded who compute the times!*

Μάγοι ἀπ' ἀνατολῶν· *Wise men from the east.*] Μάγοι, *Magi,* that is, *wizards,* or such as practised ill arts : for in this sense alone this word occurs in holy writ.

From the east. This more generally denotes as much as, ' Out of the land of the heathen,' in the same sense as ' the queen of the south' is taken, Matt. xii. 42 ; that is, ' a heathen queen.' Consider this passage in the Talmud, מרקם למזרח ורקם כמזרח מאשקלון לדרום ואשקלון כדרום מעכו לצפון ועכו כצפון " From Rekam to the east, and Rekam is as the east : from Ascalon to the south, and Ascalon is as the[i] south : from Acon to the north, and Acon is as the north." These words R. Nissim[k] quotes from R. Judah, and illustrates it with this Gloss, " From Rekam to the furthest bounds of the land eastward is heathen land ; and Rekam itself is reckoned for the east of the world, and not for the land of Israel. So also from Ascalon onwards to the south is the heathen country, and Ascalon itself is reckoned for the south :" that is, for heathen land.

Those countries where the sons of Abraham by his wife

[i] *English folio edition,* vol. ii. p. 109.   [k] In Gittin, cap. 1. art. 1.

Keturah were dispersed, are more particularly called the
' eastern' countries, Gen. xxv. 6, Judg. vi. 3, and elsewhere
often.   And hence came these first-fruits of the Gentiles :
whence it is not unlikely that Jethro also came, the first proselyte to the law.   And that which is spoken by the Gemara
concerning the Arabian, the first pointer-out of the Messias
born, is perhaps some shadow of this story of the magicians'
coming out of Arabia, and who first publicly declared him to
be born.

Ver. 2 : Εἴδομεν γὰρ αὐτοῦ τὸν ἀστέρα ἐν τῇ ἀνατολῇ· *For
we have seen his star in the east.*]   We, being in the east,
have seen his star :—that heavenly light, which in that very
night wherein the Saviour was born shone round about the
shepherds of Beth-lehem, perhaps was seen by these magicians, being then a great distance off, resembling a star
hanging over Judea ; whence they might the more easily
guess that the happy sign belonged to the Jews.

Ver. 4[1] : Καὶ συναγαγὼν πάντας τοὺς 'Αρχιερεῖς καὶ Γραμματεῖς τοῦ λαοῦ· *And when he had gathered all the chief priests
and scribes of the people together.*]   That is, he assembled the
Sanhedrim.   Herod is said by very many authors to have
slain the Sanhedrim, but this is neither to be understood
of the whole Sanhedrim, nor, if it were to be understood of
the whole, would it denote the total subversion of the Sanhedrim.   The Babylonian Gemarists do thus relate the story :
" Herod [m] was a servant of the Asmonean family.   He cast
his eyes upon a young maid [*of that family*].   On a certain
day he heard the *Bath Kol* [*a voice from heaven*] saying,
Whatsoever servant shall now rebel shall prosper.   He arose
up against his masters, and slew them all."   And a little
after ; " Herod said, Who is there that interprets these
words, ' Thou shalt set a king over thee out of the midst of
thy brethren?' (Deut. xvii. 15.) The Rabbins [interpreted the
words].   He rose up and slew all the Rabbins, leaving only
Bava Ben Buta, with whom he consulted."

Herod was to overcome two difficulties, that he might,
with the peace and favour of the Jews, become their king.
For, although he had been raised unto the kingdom by the
Romans, nevertheless, that he might establish his throne,

---

[1] *Leusden's edition*, vol. ii. p. 259.   [m] Bava Bathra, fol. 3. 2.

the people remaining quiet and accepting him, first it seemed
necessary to him that the Asmonean family should be removed out of the way, which, formerly governing the people,
they had some affection and love for, and which still remaining, he suspected he could scarce be secure.   Secondly, that
law of setting no king over them but of their brethren de-
barred him, since he himself was of the stock of Edom.
Therefore he took away all those Rabbins, who, adhering
stiffly to this law, opposed, what they could, his coming to
the kingdom.   " But all the Rabbins indeed he slew not
(saith the Gloss upon the place alleged) ; for the sons of
Betira were left alive, who held the chair when Hillel came
out of Babylon."

Therefore he slew not all the elders of the Sanhedrim,
but those only who, taking occasion from that law, opposed
his access to the kingdom.   Out of that slaughter the two
sons of Betira escaped, who held the first places in the Sanhedrim after the death of Shemaiah and Abtalion.   Shammai
also escaped, who, according as Josephus relates, foretold
this slaughter.   Hillel escaped likewise, if he were then present; and Menahem, who certainly was there, and who
thenceforth sat second in the chair.   Bava Ben Buta escaped also, as the Gemara relates, who afterward persuaded
Herod that he should repair the Temple to expiate this
bloody impiety.   And others escaped.

'Αρχιερεῖς· *The chief priests.*]   When the Sanhedrim consisted of priests, Levites, and Israelites (as Maimonides [n]
teacheth), under the word ἀρχιερεῖς, *chief priests*, are comprehended the two former ; namely, whosoever of the clergy
were members of the Sanhedrim ; and under the *scribes of the
people* are comprehended all those of the Sanhedrim who were
not of the clergy.

Among [o] the priests were divers differences :

I. Of the priests some were called כהני עם הארץ, as if
you would say *the plebeian priests ;* namely, such who indeed
were not of the common people, but wanted school education,
and were not reckoned among the learned, nor among such
as were devoted to religion.   For seeing the whole seed of
Aaron was sacerdotal, and priests were not so much made as

---

[n] In Sanhedr. cap. 2.   [o] *English folio edition,* vol. ii. p. 110.

born, no wonder if some ignorant and poor were found among them. Hence is that distinction, עניי ישראל ועניי כהנים מלקטין *The* P *poor Israelites and the poor priests are gatherers.* כהן חבר וכהן עם הארץ *A Votary priest, and a Plebeian priest.* And caution is given, שאין תרומה לכהן עם הארץ *That* q *the oblation be not given to a Plebeian priest.* And the reason of it is added, "Because whosoever giveth an oblation to a Plebeian priest doth all one as if he should give it to a lion; of which it may be doubted whether he will tread it under his feet and eat it or not. So it may be doubted of a Plebeian priest, whether he will eat it in cleanness or in uncleanness." However ignorant and illiterate these were, yet they had their courses at the altar according to their lot, being instructed at that time by certain rules for the performing their office, appointed them by lot. You would stand amazed to read those things r which are supposed concerning the ignorance and rudeness even of the high-priest himself.

II. There were others who were called כהנים הדיוטות *Idiot,* or *private, priests ;* who although they both were learned, and performed the public office at the altar, yet were called *private,* because they were priests of a lower, and not of a worthier, order.

III. The worthier degree of priests was fourfold, besides the degree of the high-priest, and of the sagan his substitute. For, 1. There were ראש משמר *the heads of the Ephemeries,* or courses ; in number twenty-four. 2. There were ראש בית אב *the heads of the families* in every course. Of s both, see the Jerusalem Talmud. 3. ממונים שהיו במקדיש *The presidents over the various offices in the Temple.* Of them, see Shekalim t. 4. Any priests or Levites, indeed, (although not of these orders,) that were chosen into the chief Sanhedrim. Ἀρχιερεῖς, *chief priests,* therefore, here and elsewhere, where the discourse is of the Sanhedrim, were they who, being of the priestly or Levitical stock, were chosen into that chief senate.

Γραμματοῖς τοῦ λαοῦ· *The scribes of the people.*] סופר *A scribe,* denotes more generally any man learned u, and

p Hieros. Trumoth, fol. 44. 1.& 2 .
q Bab. Sanhedr. fol. 90. 2.
r Joma, cap. 1.
s Taanith, fol. 68. 1.
t Cap. 5.
u *Leusden's edition,* vol. ii. p. 260.

is opposed to the word בור *rude*, or *clownish*. " Two [x], who
ate together, are bound to give thanks each by themselves,
אבל אחד כששניהם סופרים *when both of them are scribes*:
סופר ואחד בור סופר מברך ובור יוצא: *But if one be a
scribe, and the other ignorant* [or a *clown*], *let the scribe give
thanks, and thence satisfaction is made for the duty of the ignorant*, or unlearned person." So we read of סופרי כותיים
The[y] scribes of the Samaritans; that is, the learned among the
Samaritans: for among them there were no traditionarians.

More particularly, סופרים *scribes*, denote such, who,
being learned, and of scholastic education, addicted themselves especially to handling the pen, and to writing. Such
were the public notaries in the Sanhedrim, registrars in
the synagogues, amanuenses who employed themselves in
transcribing the law, phylacteries, short sentences to be
fixed upon the door-posts, bills of contracts, or divorce, &c.
And in this sense ספרא *a scribe*, and תנא *a Talmudic
doctor*, are sometimes opposed; although he was not תנא
Tanna, a Talmudic doctor, who was not ספרא *Sophra*, a
scribe, in the sense above mentioned. In [z] the Babylonian
Talmud it is disputed (a passage not unworthy our reading),
what disagreement in calculation may be borne with between
תנא *an expounder* out of the chair, or the pulpits, and ספרא
a writer of contracts, or bills of divorce, or a register, &c.,
in reckoning up the year of the Temple, of the Greek empire,
&c. Concerning which matter, this, among other things,
is concluded on, ספרא בצירא תנא תוספאה that *a scribe
computes more briefly, a doctor more largely*. It will not repent
one to read the place; nor that whole tract called מסכת
סופרים *The tract of the scribes*; which dictates to the *scribes*
of that sort of which we are now speaking, concerning writing
out the law, the phylacteries, &c.

But, above all others, the fathers of the traditions are
called *scribes* (who were, indeed, the elders of the Sanhedrim): which is clear enough in these and such-like expressions: דברי סופרים חביבים מדברי תורה *The words of
the scribes are more lovely than the words of the law*; that is,
traditions are better than the written law: זה מדברי סופרים

---

[x] Bab. Berac. fol. 45. 2.　　　　　[y] Bab. Sotah, fol. 33. 2.
[z] Avodah Zarah, fol. 9, 1, &c.

This is of the words of the scribes : that is, 'this is from the traditionary decrees.'

These, therefore, whom Matthew calls *the scribes of the people,* were those elders of the Sanhedrim, who were not sprung from the sacerdotal or Levitical stock, but of other tribes : the elders of the Sanhedrim, sprung of the blood of the priests, were the *scribes of the clergy,* the rest were *the scribes of the people.*

We[a] may therefore guess, and that no improbable conjecture, that, in this assembly, called together by Herod, these were present, among others :— 1. Hillel, the president. 2. Shammai, vice-president. 3. The sons of Betira, Judah, and Joshua. 4. Bava Ben Buta. 5. Jonathan the son of Uzziel, the Chaldee paraphrast. 6. Simeon, the son of Hillel.

Ver. 6 : Οὐδαμῶς ἐλαχίστη εἶ· *Art not the least.*] These words do not at all disagree with the words of the prophet whence they are taken, Micah v. 2, צָעִיר לִהְיוֹת בְּאַלְפֵי יְהוּדָה which I thus render, " But thou, Beth-lehem Ephrata, it is a small thing that thou art" [or, art reckoned] " among the thousands of Israel ;" for thou art to be crowned with higher dignity ; " for from thee shall go forth a ruler," &c. And in effect to this sense, unless I mistake, does the Chaldee paraphrast plainly render it, whom I suspect to be present at this very council, זְעִיר הֲוֵיתָא לְאִתְמְנָאָה׃ " Thou art within a little to become chief." See the same sense of the word זְעִיר in the Targum upon Psalm lxxiii. 2, Hos. i. 4, &c.

Ver. 9 : Ἀστήρ, ὃν εἶδον ἐν τῇ ἀνατολῇ, προῆγεν αὐτούς· *The star, which they saw in the east, went before them.*] It is probable the star had shone in the very birthnight : and thenceforward to this very time it had disappeared. The wise men had no need of the star to be their guide when they were going to Jerusalem, a city well known ; but going forward thence to Beth-lehem, and that, as it seems, by night, it was their guide.

Ver. 14 : Ἀνεχώρησεν εἰς Αἴγυπτον· *Departed into Egypt.*] Egypt was now replenished with Jews above measure, and that, partly by reason of them that travelled thither under Jochanan, the son of Kareah, Jer. xliii ; partly with them that flocked thither, more latewardly, to the temple of Onias,

of which Josephus writes [b], and both Talmuds [c] : " When
Simeon the Just said, ' I shall die this year,' they said to him,
' Whom, therefore, shall we put in thy place?' He answered,
: הנה בני נחוניון ' *Behold! my son Onias is before you.*' They
made Onias therefore high-priest.   But his brother Simeon
envied him.   Onias, therefore, fled, first into the Royal Mountain, and then into Egypt, and built there an altar, repeating
that of the prophet, ' In that day there shall be an altar to
the Lord in the midst of Egypt.'"

" He [d] that hath not seen the cathedral church of Alexandria hath never seen the glory of Israel.   It was after the
manner of a court-walk, double cloistered.   There were sometimes there so many as doubly exceeded the number of those
that went out of Egypt.   There were seventy golden chairs
set with gems, according to the number of the seventy elders.
A wooden pulpit also placed in the middle, in which the
bishop of the synagogue stood.   And when the law was read,
after every benediction, a sign being given by a private person
waving a handkerchief, they all answered ' Amen.'   But they
sat not confusedly and mixedly together; but every artificer [e]
with the professors of the same art : so that if a stranger
came, he might mingle himself with the workmen of the same
trade, &c.   These did wicked Trajan destroy," &c.

The Babylonian Gemara [f] repeats almost the same things,
alleging these last matters after this manner : " They sat not
confusedly, but the artificers by themselves, the silversmiths
by themselves, the braziers by themselves, the weavers by
themselves, &c; so that if a poor stranger came in, he might
know his own fellow-workmen, and betake himself to them,
and thence receive sustenance for himself and family.

So provision was made for the poverty of Joseph and Mary,
while they sojourned in Egypt (at Alexandria, probably),
partly by selling the presents of the wise men for food and
provision by the way; and partly by a supply of victuals from
their country-folks in Egypt when they had need.

There are some footsteps in the Talmudists of this journey of our Saviour into Egypt, but so corrupted with venom-

[b] Antiq. l. xiii. c. 6. [xiii. 3. 1.]   [d] Id. Succah, fol. 55. 1, 2.
[c] Menachoth, c. 13. Succah, c.   [e] *Leusden's edit.*, vol. ii. p. 261.
5. Hieros. Joma, fol. 43. 4.   [f] Succah, fol. 51. 2.

ous malice and blasphemy (as all their writings are), that
they seem only to have confessed the truth, that they might
have matter the more liberally to reproach him; for so they
speak: " When Jannai g the king slew the Rabbins, R. Josua
Ben Perachiah, and Jesus, went away unto Alexandria in
Egypt. Simeon Ben Shetah sent thither, speaking thus,
' From me Jerusalem the holy city, to thee, O Alexandria in
Egypt, my sister, health. My husband dwells with thee,
while I, in the mean time, sit alone. Therefore h he rose up,
and went." And a little after; " He brought forth four
hundred trumpets, and anathematized" [Jesus]. And a little
before that; " Elisæus turned away Gehazi with both his
hands, and R. Josua Ben Perachiah thrust away Jesus with
both his hands."

" Did i not Ben Satda bring enchantments out of Egypt
in the cutting which was in his flesh?" Under the name of
Ben Satda they wound our *Jesus* with their reproaches,
although the Glosser upon the place, from the authority of
R. Tam, denies it: for thus he; R. Tam saith, This was not
Jesus of Nazareth, because they say here, *Ben Satda* was in
the days of Paphus, the son of Judah, who was in the days of
R. Akiba: but Jesus was in the days of R. Josua, the son of
Perachiah," &c.

Ver. 16: ᾿Απὸ διετοῦς καὶ κατωτέρω· *From two years old, and
under.*] It was now two years ago, or thereabouts, since the
star had shone, and Christ was born. The reason of the
tarrying of Joseph and Mary in Beth-lehem was this; that
they believed that the Messias, who, according to the prophet was born there, should have been brought up nowhere
but there also; nor dared they to carry him elsewhere, before
they had leave to do so by an angel from heaven.

The Jewish nation are very purblind, how and whence the
Messias shall arise; and "Nemo novit, no man knows whence
the Son of man is," John vii. 27; that is, from what original.
It was doubted : אין מי חייא הוא אין מי דמכייא הוא
whether k *he should come from the living or from the dead.*
Only it was confessed by all without controversy, that he
should first make some show of himself from Beth-lehem,
which the priests and scribes of the people assert, ver. 4.

g Bab. Sanhedr. fol. 107. 2.   i Schabb. fol. 104. 2.
h *English folio edit.*, vol. ii. p. 112.   k Hieros. Berac. fol. 5. 1.

Hence you have Christ now in his second year at Beth-lehem, whither Joseph and Mary had again betaken themselves with him, when they had now presented him in the Temple, according to the law, being forty days old, Luke ii. 22. And they had taken care for his education in this place, and not elsewhere, until he himself, going forth from hence, might show himself openly the Messias, if they had not been sent away somewhere else by permission from heaven.

Ver. 23 : Ὅτι Ναζωραῖος κληθήσεται· *He shall be called a Nazarene.*] Those things which are brought from Isa. xi. 1 concerning נֵצֶר *Netzer, the Branch*; and those things also produced concerning Samson the Nazarite, a most noble type of Christ, have their weight, by no means to be despised. We add, that Matthew may be understood concerning the outward, humble, and mean condition of our Saviour. And that by the word Ναζωραῖος, *Nazarene*, he hints his *separation* and *estrangement* from other men, as a despicable person, and unworthy of the society of men.

I. Let it be observed, that the evangelist does not cite some one of the prophets, but all : τὸ ῥηθὲν διὰ τῶν προφητῶν, "spoken by the prophets." But now all the prophets, in a manner, do preach the vile and abject condition of Christ; none, that his original should be out of Nazareth.

II. David, in his person, speaks thus ; מוּזָר הָיִיתִי לְאֶחָי: *I was a stranger to my brethren*, Psalm lxix. 9.

III. If you derive the word Ναζωραῖος, *Nazarene*, which not a few do, from נָזִיר *Nazir*, a *Nazirean*, that word denotes not only a *separation*, dedicated to God, such as that of the *Nazarenes* was; but it signifies also the *separation* of a man from others, as being unworthy of their society; Gen. xlix. 26, "They shall be on the head of Joseph, and on the crown of the head of him that was *separate* from his brethren."

Therefore, let us digest the sense of the evangelist by this paraphrase: Joseph was to depart with Christ to Beth-lehem, the city of David, or to Jerusalem, the royal city, had not the fear of Archelaus hindered him. Therefore, by the signification of an angel, he is sent away into Galilee, a very contemptible country, and into the city Nazareth, a place of no account : whence, from this very place, and the name of it, you may observe that fulfilled to a tittle which is so often declared by the prophets, that the Messias should be

Nazor, [נָזוֹר] a *stranger,* or *separate* from men, as if he were
a very vile person, and not worthy of their company.

CHAP. III.[k]

VER. 1[1]: 'Ιωάννης ὁ Βαπτιστὴς κηρύσσων ἐν τῇ ἐρήμῳ τῆς
'Ιουδαίας· *John the Baptist preaching in the wilderness of Judea.*]
That John was born in Hebron, one may not unfitly conjecture by comparing Luke i. 39 with Josh. xxi. 11 ; and that
he was born about the feast of the Passover, namely, half a
year before the nativity of our Saviour, Luke i. 36. So the
conceptions and births of the Baptist and our Saviour ennobled the four famous *tekuphas* [*revolutions*] of the year :
one being conceived at the summer solstice, the other at
the winter ; one born at the vernal equinox, the other at the
autumnal.

" John lived in the deserts, until he made himself known
unto Israel," Luke i. 80. That is, if the pope's school may
be interpreter, he led the life of a hermit. But,

I. Be ashamed, O papist, to be so ignorant of the sense
of the word ἔρημος, *wilderness,* or *desert ;* which in the
common dialect sounds all one as if it had been said, " He
lived in the country, not in the city ; his education was more
coarse and plain in the country, without the breeding of the
university, or court at Jerusalem." תורה היתה ה״ סאין
ירושלמיות שהן שש מדבריות: *An*[m] *oblation for thanksgiving*
consists of five Jerusalem seahs, which were in value six seahs of
the wilderness ; that is, six country seahs.

" A Jerusalem[n] seah exceeds a seah of the wilderness by
a sixth part."

אילנות מדבריות " *The*[o] *trees of the wilderness* are those
which are common, and not appropriate to one master :" that
is, trees in groves and common meadows.

So 2 Cor. xi. 26 : Κινδύνοις ἐν πόλει, κινδύνοις ἐν ἐρημίᾳ·
that is, " in perils in the city, and in perils in *the country.*"

II. The wildernesses of the land of Canaan were not without towns and cities ; nor was he presently to be called an
Eremite who dwelt in the wilderness. The hill-country of

---

[k] *English folio edit.,* vol. ii. p. 113.   [n] Bab. Erubh. fol. 83. 1.
[l] *Leusden's edition,* vol. ii. p. 262.   [o] Rambam in Demai, cap. 1.
[m] Menachoth, cap. 7. hal. 1.

Judea, John's native soil, is called by the Talmudists, הֵר הַמֶלֶךְ *The royal mountain*, or *hill*; and by the Psalmist, מִדְבַּר הָרִים *The desert hill-country*, Psalm lxxv. 6 ; and yet "in the royal mountain were a myriad of cities P."

III. David passed much of his youth in the wilderness, 1 Sam. xvii. 28 : but yet, who will call him an eremite? In the like sense I conceive John living in the deserts, not only spending his time in leisure and contemplation, but employing himself in some work, or studies. For when I read, that the youth of our Saviour was taken up in the carpenter's trade, I scarcely believe his forerunner employed his youth in no calling at all.

Beginning now the thirtieth year of his age, when, according to the custom of the priests, he ought to have come to the chief Sanhedrim to undergo their examination, and to be entered into the priesthood by them, " the word of God coming unto him," Luke iii. 2, as it had done before to the prophets, he is diverted to another ministry.

Ver. 2 : Μετανοεῖτε· *Repent ye.*] A doctrine most fit for the gospel, and most suitable to the time, and the word or the phrase as agreeable to the doctrine.

I. A nation leavened with the error of the Pharisees, concerning justification by the works of the law, was necessarily to be called off to the contrary doctrine of repentance. No receiving of the gospel was otherwise to be expected.

II. However the schools of the Pharisees had illy defined repentance, which we observe presently, yet they asserted that repentance itself was necessary to the reception of the Messias. Concerning q this matter the Babylonian Gemarists do dispute : whom Kimchi also upon Isa. lix. 19 cites, and determines the question : " From the words of our Rabbins (saith he) it is plain there arose a doubt among them concerning this matter, namely, whether Israel were to be redeemed with repentance or without repentance. And it sprang from this occasion, that some texts of Scripture seemed to go against them : such as those ; ' He saw, and there was no man, and he wondered, that there was none to intercede ; therefore r, his own arm brought salvation.' And

---

p Hieros Taanith, fol. 69. 1.   q Sanhedr. fol. 98, &c.
          r *English folio edit*. vol. ii. p. 114.

also, ' Not for your sake, O Israel, do I this.'   And again,
' I will remember for them my old covenant,' &c.   And these
places, on the other hand, make for repentance : ' Thou shalt
return to the Lord thy God, and shalt hearken to his voice.'
And again ; ' And thence thou shalt seek the Lord thy God,
and shalt find him, if thou seekest him with all thy heart,'
&c.   But these may be reconciled after this manner; namely,
that many of Israel shall repent, when they shall see the
signs of redemption.   And hence is that which is said, ' And
he saw that there was no man,' because they will not repent
until they see the beginning of redemption."

"If Israel[s] shall repent but one day, forthwith the Redeemer
cometh."

Therefore, it is very fitly argued by the Baptist, and by
our Saviour after him, Matt. iv. 17, from the approach of the
kingdom of heaven to repentance, since they themselves to
whom this is preached do acknowledge that thus the kingdom of heaven, or the manifestation of the Messias, is to be
brought in.   For however the Gemarists who dispute of this
were of a later age, yet for the most part they do but speak
the sense of their fathers.

III. The word μετάνοια, *repentance,* as it does very well
express the sense of true repentance, so among the Jews it
was necessary[t] that it should be so expressed, among whom
repentance, for the most part, was thought to consist in the
confession of the mouth only.

" Whosoever[u], out of error or presumption, shall transgress
the precepts of the law, whether they be those that command
or those that forbid, when he repents and returns from his
sins, he is bound to make confession.   Whosoever brings an
offering for a sin, committed either out of ignorance or presumption, his sin is not expiated by the offering, until he
makes an oral confession.   Or whosoever is guilty of death,
or of scourging by the Sanhedrim, his sin is not taken away
by his death, or by his scourging, if he do not repent and
make confession.   And because the scape-goat is the expiation
for all Israel, therefore the high priest makes confession over
him for all Israel."

s Hieros. Taanith, fol. 64. 1.   t *Leusden's edition,* vol. ii. p. 263.
u Maimon. in Teshubah, cap. 1.

It is worthy observing, that, when John urgeth those that came to his baptism to repent, it is said, that they were baptized, "confessing their sins :" which was a sign of repentance highly requisite among the Jews, and necessary for those that were then brought in to the profession of the Gospel; that hereby they might openly profess that they renounced the doctrine of justification by the works of the law.

It is worthy of observing also, that John said not, "Repent, and believe the gospel," which our Saviour did, Matt. iv. 17, (and yet John preached the gospel, Mark i. 1, 2, John i. 7); for his office, chiefly, was to make Christ known, who when he should come was to be the great preacher of the gospel.

Therefore the Baptist doth very properly urge repentance upon those that looked for the Messias; and the text of the Gospel used a very proper word to express true and lively repentance.

Ἥγγικε γὰρ ἡ βασιλεία τῶν οὐρανῶν· *For the kingdom of heaven is at hand.*]   I. *The kingdom of heaven,* in Matthew, is *the kingdom of God,* for the most part, in the other evangelists.   Compare these places :

" *The kingdom of heaven* is at hand," Matt. iv. 17.

"The poor in spirit, theirs is *the kingdom of heaven,*" Matt. v. 3.

"The least in *the kingdom of heaven,*" Matt. xi. 11.

"The mysteries of *the kingdom of heaven,*" Matt. xiii. 11.

"Little children, of such is *the kingdom of heaven,*" Matt. xix. 14.

" *The kingdom of God* is at hand," Mark i. 15.

" Blessed are the poor, for yours is *the kingdom of God,*" Luke vi. 20.

"The least in *the kingdom of God,*" Luke vii. 28.

" The mysteries of *the kingdom of God,*" Luke viii. 10.

Little children, of such is *the kingdom of God,*" Mark x. 14.

And so we have it elsewhere very often. For שָׁמַיִם *Heaven* is very usually, in the Jewish dialect, taken for *God,* Dan. iv. 23, Matt. xxi. 25, Luke xv. 21, John iii. 27. And, in these and such-like speeches, scattered in the Talmudists ; מיתה ביד שמים *Death by the hand of heaven :* נתחלל שם שמים *The name of heaven is profaned :* פולחנא דשמיא *The worship, of heaven :* בסייעתא דשמיא *by the help of heaven,* &c. " For [x] they called God by the name of *Heaven,* because his habitation is in heaven."

The story of the Jews is related, groaning out under their persecution these words, אי שמים *O Heavens!* that is, as the Gloss renders it, ‏אהה ה״‏ *Ah! Jehovah!*

II. This [y] manner of speech, *the kingdom of heaven,* is taken from Daniel, chap. vii. 13, 14 ; where, after the description of the four earthly and tyrannical monarchies, that is, the Babylonian, Mede-Persian, Grecian, and Syro-Grecian, and the destruction of them at last ; the entrance and nature of the reign of Christ is described, as it is universal over the whole world, and eternal throughout all ages : " under whom the rule, and dominion, and authority of kingdoms under the whole heaven is given to the people of the saints of the Most High," ver. 27 : that is, " Whereas, before, the rule had been in the hands of heathen kings, under the reign of Christ there should be Christian kings." Unto which that of the apostle hath respect, 1 Cor. vi. 2 ; " Know ye not that the saints shall judge the world ?"

Truly I admire that the fulfilling of that vision and prophecy in Daniel should be lengthened out still into I know not what long and late expectation, not to receive its completion before Rome and antichrist shall fall ; since the books of the Gospel afford us a commentary clearer than the sun, that that *kingdom of heaven* took its beginning immediately upon the preaching of the Gospel. When both the Baptist and Christ published the approach of *the kingdom of heaven* from their very first preaching ; certainly, for any to think that the fulfilling of those things in Daniel did not then begin, for my part, I think it is to grope in the dark, either through wilfulness or ignorance.

III. *The kingdom of heaven* implies, 1. The exhibition and manifestation of the Messias, Matt. xii. 28 ; " But if I, by the finger of God, cast out devils, the kingdom of God is come upon you :" that is, ' Hence is the manifestation of the Messias.' See John iii. 3, xii. 13, &c. 2. The resurrection of Christ ; death, hell, Satan, being conquered : whence is a

---

[x] Elias Levit. in Tishbi.   [y] *English folio edit.,* vol. ii. p. 115.

most evident manifestation that he is that ' eternal King,' &c.:
see Matt. xxvi. 29, Rom. i. 4.　　3. His vengeance upon the
Jewish [z] nation, his most implacable enemies: this is another,
and most eminent manifestation of him: see Matt. xvi. 28,
xix. 28.　　4. His dominion by the sceptre of the gospel among
the Gentiles, Matt. xxi. 43.　　In this place which is before us
it points out the exhibition and revelation of the Messias.

IV. The phrase מלכות שמים *the kingdom of heaven* very
frequently occurs in the Jewish writers. We will produce
some places; let the reader gather the sense of them:

"R. Joshua [a] Ben Korcha saith, In reciting the phylacteries, why is שְׁמַע *Hear, O Israel*, [Deut. vi. 4, &c.] recited
before that passage וְהָיָה אִם שָׁמֹעַ *And it shall come to pass,
if you shall hearken* [Deut. xi. 13], &c.　To wit, that a man
first take upon himself *the kingdom of heaven*, and then the
yoke of the precept." So the Jerusalem Misna hath it; but
the Babylonian thus: "That a man first take upon himself
the yoke of *the kingdom of heaven*, and then the yoke of the
precept."

"Rabh [b] said to Rabbi Chaijah, לא חזינא ליה לרבי דמקבל
עליה מלכות שמים: *We never saw Rabbi* [Judah] *taking upon
himself the kingdom of heaven*.　Bar Pahti answered, At that
time when he put his hands to his face, he took upon himself *the kingdom of heaven*." Where the Gloss speaks thus;
" We saw not that he took upon himself *the kingdom of
heaven;* for until the time came of reciting the phylacteries,
he instructed his scholars; and when that time was come, I
saw him not interposing any space."

" Doth [c] any ease nature? Let him wash his hands, put on
his phylacteries, repeat them, and pray, וזו היא מלכות שמים
שלמה: *and this is the kingdom of heaven fulfilled*." אם תפרש
שדי ותבדיל תיבות של מלכות שמים *" If* [d] *thou shalt have
explained Shaddai, and divided the letters of the kingdom of
heaven*, thou shalt make the shadow of death to be cool to
thee;" that is, " If, in the repeating of that passage of the
phylacteries [Deut. vi. 4], 'Hear, O Israel, the Lord our God
is one Lord,' &c., you shall pronounce the letters distinctly

[z] *Leusden's edition*, vol. ii. p. 264.

[a] Beracoth, cap. 2. hal. 2.

[b] Gemara Bab. ibid. fol. 13. 2.

[c] Ibid. fol. 15. 1.

[d] Ibid. col. 2. in the Gloss.

and deliberately, so that you shall have sounded out the names of God rightly, 'thou shalt make cool the shades of death.'" For the same Gloss had said, קריאה שמע שהוא קבלת מלכות שמים *The repeating of that passage,* 'Hear, O Israel, &c., *is the taking of the kingdom of heaven upon thee.* But the repeating of that place, 'And it shall be, if thou shalt hearken,' &c. [Deut. xix. 13] והיא אם שמוע שהוא קבלת עול מצוה: *is the taking of the yoke of the precept upon thee.*"

" Rabban[f] Gamaliel recited his phylacterical prayers on the very night of his nuptials. And when his scholars said unto him, ' Hast thou not taught us, O our master, that a bridegroom is freed from the reciting of his phylacteries the first night?' he answered, ' I will not hearken to you, nor will I lay aside *the kingdom of heaven* from me, no, not for an hour.' "

" What[g] is the yoke of *the kingdom of heaven ?* In like manner as they lay the yoke upon an ox, that he may be serviceable ; and if he bear not the yoke, he becomes unprofitable : so it becomes a man first to take the yoke upon himself, and to serve in all things with it : but if he casts it off, he is unprofitable : as it is said, ' Serve the Lord in fear.' What means, ' in fear?' The same that is written, ' The fear of the Lord is the beginning of wisdom.' And this is *the kingdom of heaven.*"

" The[h] scholars of Jochanan Ben Zaccai asked[i], Why a servant was to be bored through the ear, rather than through some other part of the body ? He answered, When he heard with the ear those words from mount Sinai, ' Thou shalt have no other Lord before my face,' he broke the yoke of *the kingdom of heaven* from him, and took upon himself the yoke of flesh and blood."

If by *the kingdom of heaven*, in these and other suchlike places, which it would be too much to heap together, they mean the inward love and fear of God, which indeed they seem to do; so far they agree with our gospel sense, which asserts the inward and spiritual kingdom of Christ especially. And if the words of our Saviour, " Behold, the

---

[f] In eodem, cap. 2. tract. Berac. hal. 5.

[g] Zohar. in Levit, fol. 53.

[h] *English folio edition,* vol. ii. p. 116.

[i] Hieros. Kiddushin, fol. 59. 4.

kingdom of God is within you," Luke xvii. 21, be suited to
this sense of the nation concerning *the kingdom of heaven,*
there is nothing sounds hard or rough in them : for it is as
much as if he had said " Do you think *the kingdom of heaven*
shall come with some remarkable observation, or μετὰ πολλῆς
φαντασίας, *with much show ?* Your very schools teach that the
kingdom of God is within a man."

But, however they most ordinarily applied this manner
of speech hither, yet they used it also for the exhibition and
revelation of the Messiah in the like manner as the evangelical history doth. Hence are these expressions, and the
like to them, in sacred writers ; " The Pharisees asked Jesus
when the kingdom of God should come [k]." " They thought
that the kingdom of God should presently be manifested [l]."
" Josephus of Arimathea waited for the kingdom of God [m]."

And these words in the Chaldee paraphrast, " Say ye to
the cities of Judah, The kingdom of your God is revealed,"
Isa. xl. 9 : " They shall see the kingdom of their Messiah,"
Isa. liii. 11.

The Baptist, therefore, by his preaching, stirs up the minds
of his hearers to meet the coming of the Messiah, now presently to be manifested, with that repentance and preparation as is meet.

Ver. 4 : ʿΗ δὲ τροφὴ αὐτοῦ ἦν ἀκρίδες· *His food was locusts.*]
הנודר מן הבשר יהא אסור בבשר דגים וחגבים : *He [n] that by
vow tieth himself from flesh, is forbidden the flesh of fish and of
locusts.* See the Babylonian Talmud [o] concerning locusts fit
for food.

Ver. 5 [p] : ʿΗ περίχωρος τοῦ Ἰορδάνου· *The region round about
Jordan.*] The word περίχωρος, *the region round about,* is used
by the Jerusalem Gemara : מבית חורון ועד חים מדינה אחת
פרי כורין " From [q] Beth-horon to the sea is one region περίχωρος, *round about,*" or, *one circumjacent region.* Περίχωρος,
perhaps, both in the Talmudist and in the evangelist, is one
and the same thing with a *coast,* or a *country along a coast,*
in Pliny : " The country (saith he [r]) along the coast is Samaria :" that is, the sea-coast, and the country further, lying

[k] Luke xvii. 20.
[l] Luke xix. 11.
[m] Luke xxiii. 52, &c.
[n] Hieros. Nedarim, fol. 40. 2.

[o] Cholin, fol. 65. 1.
[p] *Leusden's edition,* vol. ii. p. 265.
[q] Sheviith, fol. 38. 4.
[r] Lib. v. cap. 13.

along by that coast : which may be said also concerning *the region round about Jordan.* Strabo [r], concerning the plain bordering on Jordan, hath these words ; " It is a place of a hundred furlongs, all well watered and full of dwellings."

§. *A few things concerning Baptism.*

Ver. 6 : Καὶ ἐβαπτίζοντο· *And were baptized.*] It is no unfit or unprofitable question, Whence it came to pass that there was so great a conflux of men to the Baptist, and so ready a reception of his baptism ?

I. The first reason is, Because the manifestation of the Messias was then expected, the weeks of Daniel being now spent to the last four years. Let us consult a little his text :—

Dan. ix. 24. " Seventy weeks [*of years*] are decreed concerning thy people," &c. That is, four hundred and ninety years, from the first of Cyrus to the death of Christ. These years are divided into three parts, and they very unequal.

1. Into seven weeks, or forty-nine years, from the giving of Cyrus's patent for the rebuilding Jerusalem, to the finishing the rebuilding of it by Nehemiah.

2. Into sixty-two weeks, or four hundred thirty-four years, —namely, from the finishing the building of the city to the beginning of the last week of the seventy. In which space [s] of time, the times of the Persian empire (which remained after Nehemiah, if indeed there was any time now remaining), and the times of the Grecian empire, and of the Syro-Grecian, were all run out, and those times also, wherein the Romans ruled over the Jews.

3. The holy text divides the last week, or the last seven years, into two equal parts, ver. 27 ; which I thus render ; " And he shall strengthen, or *confirm*, the covenant with many in that one week : and the half of that week shall make the sacrifice and oblation to cease : *or*, in the half of that week he shall make to cease," &c. Not in the middle of that week, but in the latter half, that is, the latter three years and a half of the seven.

---

[r] [He seems to refer to a passage in book xvi. (Syria), p. 1073 of Falconer's edition. If so, the quotation is not exact.]

[s] *English folio edition,* vol. ii. p. 117.

First, seven weeks having been reckoned up before, and then sixty-two weeks, ver. 25,—now there remained one only of the seventy; and in reference to that, in the middle of it the Messias shall begin his ministry; which being finished in three years and a half (the latter halved part of that week), "he shall make the sacrifice and oblation to cease," &c.

The nation could not but know, could not but take great notice of, the times so exactly set out by the angel Gabriel. Since, therefore, the coming of the Messias was the great wish and desire of all,—and since the time of his appearing was so clearly decreed by the angel that nothing could be more,—and when the latter half of the last seven years, chiefly to be observed, was now, within a very little, come;—it is no wonder if the people, hearing from this venerable preacher that the kingdom of heaven was now come, should be stirred up beyond measure to meet him, and should flock to him. For, as we observed before, "They thought that the kingdom of God would immediately be manifested," Luke xix. 11.

II. Another reason of it was this,—the institution of baptism, for an evangelical sacrament, was first in the hand of the Baptist, who, "the word of the Lord coming to him," (Luke iii. 2,) went forth, backed with the same authority as the chiefest prophets had in times past. But yet the first use of baptism was not exhibited at that time. For baptism, very many centuries of years backwards, had been both known and received in most frequent use among the Jews,—and for the very same end as it now obtains among Christians,—namely, that by it proselytes might be admitted into the church; and hence it was called טבילת גרות *Baptism for proselytism:* and was distinct from טבילת נדה *Baptism* [or *washing*] *from uncleanness.* See the Babylonian Talmud in Jevamoth[s].

I. I ascribe the first use of it, for this end, to the patriarch Jacob, when he chose into his family and church the young women of Sychem, and other heathens who then lived with him. "Jacob said to his family, and to all who were with him, Put away from you the strange gods, and be ye

---

[s] Fol. 45. 2. in the Gloss.

clean, and change your garments," &c. Gen. xxxv. 2. What
that word means, וְהִטַּהֲרוּ *and be ye clean,* Aben Ezra does
very well interpret to be שירחצו הגוף *the washing of the
body,* or *baptism ;* which reason itself also persuades us to
believe.

II. All the nation of Israel do assert, as it were with one
mouth, that all the nation of Israel were brought into the
covenant, among other things, by baptism. " Israel (saith
Maimonides[t], the great interpreter of the Jewish law) was
admitted into the covenant by three things,—namely, by circumcision, baptism, and sacrifice. Circumcision was in Egypt ;
as it is said, ' None uncircumcised shall eat of the passover.'
Baptism was in the wilderness before the giving of the law ;
as it is said, ' Thou shalt sanctify them to-day and to-morrow,
and let them wash their garments.' "

III. They assert, that that infinite number of proselytes in
the day of David and Solomon were admitted[u] by baptism :
" The[x] Sanhedrims received not proselytes in the days of
David and Solomon : not in the days of David, lest they
should betake themselves to proselytism out of a fear of the
kingdom of Israel : not in the days of Solomon, lest they
might do the same by reason of the glory of the kingdom.
And yet abundance of proselytes were made in the days of
David and Solomon before private men; and the great Sanhedrim was full of care about this business : for they would
not cast them out of the church, because they were baptized," &c.

IV. " Whensoever[y] any heathen will betake himself, and
be joined to the covenant of Israel, and place himself under
the wings of the divine Majesty, and take the yoke of the
law upon him, voluntary circumcision, baptism, and oblation, are required : but if it be a woman, baptism and oblation."

That was a common axiom אין גר עד שימול ויטבול
No man is a proselyte until he be circumcised and baptized.
It is disputed by the Babylonian Gemara[z], "A proselyte, that
is circumcised and not baptized, what of him? R. Eliezer

[t] Issure Biah, cap. 13.
[u] *Leusden's edition,* vol. ii. p.
266.
[x] Maimonid. Issure Biah, cap. 13.
[y] Id. ibid.
[z] Jevamoth, fol. 46. 2.

saith, Behold, he is a proselyte : for so we find concerning our
fathers, that they were circumcised, but not baptized. One is
baptized, but not circumcised; what of him? R. Joshua saith,
Behold, he is a proselyte : for so we find concerning the maid-
servants, who were baptized, but not circumcised. But[a] the
wise men say, Is he baptized, and not circumcised? Or, Is he
circumcised, and not baptized? He is not a proselyte, until
he be circumcised and baptized."

But baptism was sufficient for women so far forth as this
held good, אטבלה לההיא נכרית לשם אנתתא יכילנא
לאכשורי " *One*[b] *baptizeth a heathen woman in the name of
a woman, we can assert that for a deed rightly done.*" Where
the Gloss is thus; " To be baptized in the name of a woman,
was to be baptized טבילת נדה *with the washing of a woman
polluted*, and not with the baptism to proselytism. But we
may, nevertheless, assert her, who is so baptized, for a complete proselytess; because that baptism of washing for uncleanness serves for proselytism to her; for a heathen woman
is not baptized [or washed] for uncleanness."

V. They baptized also young children (for the most part
with their parents). גר קטן מטבילין אותו על דעת בד"
They[c] *baptize a little proselyte according to the judgment of the
Sanhedrim :* that is, as the Gloss renders it, " If he be deprived of his father, and his mother brings him to be made
a proselyte, they baptize him [because none becomes a proselyte without circumcision and baptism] according to the
judgment [or right] of the Sanhedrim; that is, that three
men be present at the baptism, who are now instead of a
father to him."

And the Gemara a little after; גר שנתגיירו בניו ובנתיו
עמו דניחא להו במאי דעביד אבוהון *If with a proselyte
his sons and his daughters are made proselytes also, that which
is done by their father redounds to their good.* א"רב יוסף
הגדילו יכולים למחות *R. Joseph saith, When they grow into
years, they may retract.* Where the Gloss writes thus; " This
is to be understood of little children, who are made proselytes
together with their father."

" A[d] heathen woman, if she is made a proselytess, when

a *English folio edit.*, vol. ii. p. 118.   c Bab. Erubhin, fol. 11. 1.
b Jevam. fol. 45. 2.   d Jevam. fol. 78. 1.

she is now big with child,—the child needs not baptism: דסלקא ליה טבילה דאימיה *for the baptism of his mother serves him for baptism."* Otherwise, he were to be baptized.

ישראל שתקף בגוי קטן: *" If*[e] *an Israelite take a Gentile child,* או מצא תינוק גוי *or find a Gentile infant,* and baptizeth him in the name of a proselyte,—behold, he is a proselyte."

We cannot also pass over that, which indeed is worthy to be remembered : " Any[f] one's servant is to be circumcised, though he be unwilling; but any one's son is not to be circumcised, if he be unwilling. R. Jochanan inquired, Behold a little son; do you circumcise him by force? Yea, although he be as the son of Urcan. R. Hezekiah saith, Behold, a man finds an infant cast out, and he baptizeth him in the name of a servant: in the name of a freeman, do you also circumcise him in the name of a freeman."

We have therefore alleged these things the more largely, not only that you may receive satisfaction concerning the thing propounded, namely, how it came to pass that the people flocked, in so universal a concourse, to John's baptism (because baptism was no strange thing to the Jews); but that some other things may be observed hence, which afford some light to certain places of Scripture, and will help to clear some knotty questions about baptism.

First, You see baptism inseparably joined to the circumcision of proselytes. There was, indeed, some little distance of time; for " they[g] were not baptized till the pain of circumcision was healed, because water might be injurious to the wound." But certainly baptism ever followed. We acknowledge, indeed, that circumcision was plainly of divine institution; but by whom baptism, that was inseparable from it, was instituted, is doubtful. And yet it is worthy of observation, our Saviour rejected circumcision, and retained the appendix to it: and when all the Gentiles were now to be introduced into the true religion, he preferred this ' proselytical introductory' (pardon the expression) unto the sacrament of entrance into the gospel.

One might observe the same almost in the eucharist. The

---

[e] Maimon. in Avadim, cap. 8.   [f] Hieros. Jevamoth, fol. 8. 4.
[g] Jevam. fol. 45. 2.

lamb in the Passover was of divine institution, and so indeed
was the bread. But whence was the wine? But yet, rejecting
the lamb, Christ instituted the sacrament in the bread and
wine.

Secondly[h], Observing from these things which have been
spoken, how very known and frequent the use of baptism was
among the Jews, the reason appears very easy why the Sanhedrim, by their messengers, inquired not of John concerning
the reason of baptism, but concerning the authority of the
baptizer; not what baptism meant, but whence he had a
license so to baptize, John i. 25.

Thirdly, Hence also the reason appears why the New Testament doth not prescribe, by some more accurate rule, who
the persons are to be baptized. The Anabaptists object, ' It
is not commanded to baptize infants,—therefore they are not
to be baptized.' To whom I answer, ' It is not forbidden to
baptize infants,—therefore they are to be baptized.' And
the reason is plain. For when Pædobaptism in the Jewish
church was so known, usual, and frequent, in the admission
of proselytes, that nothing almost was more known, usual,
and frequent,—

1. There was no need to strengthen it with any precept,
when baptism was now passed into an evangelical sacrament.
For Christ took baptism into his hands, and into evangelical
use, as he found it; this only added, that he might promote
it to a worthier end and a larger use. The whole nation
knew well enough that little children used to be baptized[i]:
there was no need of a precept for that which had ever, by
common use, prevailed. If a royal proclamation should now
issue forth in these words, " Let every one resort, on the
Lord's day, to the public assembly in the church;" certainly
he would be mad, who, in times to come, should argue hence
that prayers, sermons, singing of psalms, were not to be celebrated on the Lord's day in the public assemblies, because
there is no mention of them in the proclamation. For the
proclamation provided for the celebration of the Lord's day
in the public assemblies in general: but there was no need to
make mention of the particular kinds of the divine worship

[h] *Leusden's edit.*, vol. ii. p. 267.   [i] *English folio edit.*, vol. ii. p. 119.

to be celebrated there, when they were always, and every where, well known and in daily use before the publishing of the proclamation, and when it was published. The case is the very same in baptism. Christ instituted it for an evangelical sacrament, whereby all should be admitted into the possession of the gospel, as heretofore it was used for admission into proselytism to the Jewish religion. The particulars belonging to it,—as, the manner of baptizing, the age, the sex to be baptized, &c.—had no need of a rule and definition; because these were, by the common use of them, sufficiently known even to mechanics and the most ignorant men.

2. On the other hand, therefore, there was need of a plain and open prohibition that infants and little children should not be baptized, if our Saviour would not have had them baptized. For, since it was most common, in all ages foregoing, that little children should be baptized, if Christ had been minded to have that custom abolished, he would have openly forbidden it. Therefore his silence, and the silence of the Scripture in this matter, confirms Pædobaptism, and continueth it unto all ages.

Fourthly, It is clear enough, by what hath been already said, in what sense that is to be taken in the New Testament which we sometimes meet with,—namely, that the master of the family was baptized with his whole family, Acts xvi. 15, 33, &c. Nor is it of any strength which the Anti-pædobaptists contend for, that it cannot be proved there were infants in those families; for the inquiry is not so proper, whether there were infants in those families, as it is concluded truly and deservedly,—if there were, they had all been to be baptized. Nor do I believe this people, that flocked to John's baptism, were so forgetful of the manner and custom of the nation, that they brought not their little children also with them to be baptized.

Some things are now to be spoken of the manner and form which John used.

First, In some things he seems to have followed the *manner* whereby proselytes were baptized; in other things, not to have followed them. Concerning it the Talmudic Canons have these sayings:—

I. בלילה גר מטבילין אין *They[k] do not baptize a prose-lyte by night.* Nor, indeed, " were[l] the unclean to be washed but in the day-time." Maimonides adds, " They[m] baptized not a proselyte on the sabbath, nor on a holy-day, nor by night."

II. שלושה צריך גר *A[n] proselyte hath need of three :* that is, it is required, that three men, who are scholars of the wise men, be present at the baptism of a proselyte; who may take care that the business be rightly performed, and may briefly instruct the catechumen [the person to be baptized], and may judge of the matter itself. For the admission of a prose-lyte was reckoned no light matter; לישראל גרים קשים כספחת: *Proselytes[o] are dangerous to Israel, like the itch,* was an axiom. For they, either tenacious of their former customs, or ignorant of the law of Israel, have corrupted others with their example; or, being mingled with Israel, were the cause that the divine glory did rest the less upon them; because it resteth not on any but upon families of a nobler pedigree. These reasons the Glossers give. When, therefore, the admis-sion of proselytes was of so great moment, they were not to be admitted but by the judicial consistory of *three.*

III. הגרים את מטבילין שם נדה לטבילת הכשר במקוה *They[p] baptize a proselyte in such a confluence of waters as was fit for the washing of a menstruous woman.* Of such a conflu-ence of waters the lawyers have these words : " A[q] man that hath the gonorrhœa is cleansed nowhere but in a fountain : but a menstruous woman, as also all other unclean persons, were washed in some confluence of waters; in which so much water ought to be as may serve to wash the whole body at one dipping. Our wise men have esteemed this proportion to be a cubit square, and three cubits depth : and this measure contains forty seahs of water."

When[r] it is said, that " he that hath the gonorrhœa is to wash in a spring [or a stream]; but a menstruous woman, and all other unclean persons, in some confluence of waters,"—it

---

[k] Jevamoth, fol. 46. 2.
[l] Megillah, fol. 20. 1.
[m] Issure Biah, cap. 13.
[n] Jevam. in the above place.
[o] Jevam. fol. 47. 2.

[p] Maimonid. Issur. Biah, in the above place.
[q] Maim. in Mikvaoth, c. 1. 4. Talmud. in Mikvaoth, c. 2, 3.
[r] *Leusden's edit.,* vol. ii. p. 120.

forbids not a menstruous woman, and other unclean persons, to wash in streams, where they might : but it permits, where they might not, to wash in some confluence of waters; which was not lawful for a man that had the gonorrhœa to do. The same is to be understood concerning the baptism of a proselyte, who was allowed to wash himself in streams : and was allowed also, where there were no streams, to wash in a confluence of waters.

IV. When[s] a proselyte was to be circumcised, they first asked him concerning the sincerity of his conversion to Judaism : whether he offered not himself to proselytism for the obtaining riches, for fear, or for love to some Israelite woman, &c. And when they saw that he came out of love of the law, they instructed him concerning the various articles of the law, of one God, of the evil of idolatry, of the reward of obedience, of the world to come, of the privileges of Israel, &c. All which, if he professed that he embraced them he is forthwith circumcised.

"As[t] soon as he grows whole of the wound of circumcision, they bring him to baptism; and being placed in the water, they again instruct him in some weightier and in some lighter commands of the law. Which being heard, טבל ועלה הרי הוא כישראל לכל דברין: *he plunges himself, and comes up, and behold, he is as an Israelite in all things.* The women place a woman in the waters up to the neck; and two disciples of the wise men, standing without, instruct her about some lighter precepts of the law and some weightier, while she, in the meantime, stands in the waters. ואחר כך טובלת בפניהם: *And then she plungeth herself;* and they, turning away their faces, go out, while she comes up out of the water."

In the baptizing of a proselyte, this is not to be passed over, but let it be observed, namely, that מטבילין אותו *others baptized him,* and that והוא טובל *he baptized himself,* or dipped, or plunged himself in the waters. Now, what that plunging was, you may understand from those things which Maimonides speaks in Mikvaoth in the place before cited. כל טובל "*Every person baptized*" [or *dipped,*

s *English folio edition,* vol. ii. p. 120.
t Jevam. Maimon. in the places above.

whether he were washed from pollution, or baptized into pros-
elytism], "must dip his whole body, now stripped and made
naked, at one dipping. And wheresoever in the law washing
of the body or garments is mentioned, it means nothing else
than the washing of the whole body. For if any wash himself all over, except the very top of his little finger, he is still
in his uncleanness. And if any hath much hair, he must
wash all the hair of his head, for that also was reckoned for
the body. But if any should enter into the water with their
clothes on, yet their washing holds good ; because the water
would pass through their clothes, and their garments would
not hinder it."

And now, a little to compare the baptism of John with
that proselytical baptism, and ours with both, these things
are to be considered :—

I. If you compare the washing of polluted persons, prescribed by the law, with the baptism of proselytes,—both that
and this imply uncleanness, however something different;
that implies legal uncleanness,—this, heathen,—but both pol-
luting. But a proselyte was baptized not only into the wash-
ing-off of that Gentile pollution, nor only thereby to be transplanted into the religion of the Jews ; but that, by the most
accurate rite of translation that could possibly be, he might
so pass into an Israelite, that, being married to an Israelite
woman, he might produce a free and legitimate seed, and an
undefiled offspring. Hence, servants that were taken into a
family were baptized,—and servants also that were to be
made free : not so much because they were defiled with
heathen uncleanness, as that, by that rite כישראל לכל דבר
becoming Israelites in all respects, they might be more fit
to match with Israelites, and their children be accounted as
Israelites. And hence the sons of proselytes, in following
generations, were circumcised indeed, but not baptized. They
were circumcised, that they might take upon themselves the
obligation of the law ; but they needed not baptism, because
they were already Israelites. From these things it is plain
that there was some difference as to the end, between the
Mosaical washings of unclean persons, and the baptism of
proselytes ; and some between the baptism of proselytes and
John's baptism : not as though they concurred not in some

parallel end; but because other ends were added over and above to this or that, or some ends were withdrawn.

II. The baptism of proselytes was the bringing over of Gentiles into the Jewish religion; the baptism of John was the bringing over of Jews into another religion. And hence it is the more to be wondered at, that the people so readily flocked to him, when he introduced a baptism so different from the known proselytical baptism. The reason of which is to be fetched from hence,—that at the coming of the Messias they thought, not without cause, that the state of things was plainly to be changed; and that, from the oracles of the prophets, who, with one mouth, described the times of the Messias for a new world. Hence was that received opinion, אלף שנים שעתיד הק״ בה ״לחדש עולמו: *That God, at that time, would renew the world for a thousand years.* See the Aruch, in the word צדק, and after in chap. xxiv. 3. And that also, that they used עולם הבא *the world to come,* by a form of speech very common among them, for the times of the Messias; which we observe more largely elsewhere.

III. The baptism of proselytes was an obligation to perform the law; that of John was an obligation to repentance. For although proselytical baptism admitted of some ends,—and circumcision [u] of others,—yet a traditional and erroneous doctrine at that time had joined this to both, that the proselyte covenanted in both, and obliged himself to perform the law; to which that of the apostle relates, Gal. v. 3, " I testify [x] again to every man that is circumcised, that he is a debtor to do the whole law."

But the baptism of John was a 'baptism of repentance;' Mark i. 4: which being undertaken, they who were baptized professed to renounce their own legal righteousness; and, on the contrary, acknowledged themselves to be obliged to repentance and faith in the Messias to come. How much the Pharisaical doctrine of justification differed from the evangelical, so much the obligation undertaken in the baptism of proselytes differed from the obligation undertaken in the baptism of John: which obligation also holds amongst Christians to the end of the world.

[u] *Leusden's edit.*, vol. ii. p. 269.   [x] *English folio edit.*, vol. ii. p. 121.

IV. That the baptism of John was by plunging the body (after the same manner as the washing of unclean persons, and the baptism of proselytes was), seems to appear from those things which are related of him; namely, that he "baptized in Jordan;" that he baptized "in Ænon, because there was much water there;" and that Christ, being baptized, "came up out of the water:" to which that seems to be parallel, Acts viii. 38, "Philip and the eunuch went down into the water," &c. Some complain, that this rite is not retained in the Christian church, as though it something derogated from the truth of baptism; or as though it were to be called an innovation, when the sprinkling of water is used instead of plunging. This is no place to dispute of these things. Let us return these three things only for a present answer:—

1. That the notion of washing in John's baptism differs from ours, in that he baptized none who were not brought over from one religion, and that an irreligious one too,—into another, and that a true one. But there is no place for this among us who are born Christians: the condition, therefore, being varied, the rite is not only lawfully, but deservedly, varied also. Our baptism argues defilement, indeed, and uncleanness; and demonstrates this doctrinally,—that we, being polluted, have need of washing: but this is to be understood of our natural and sinful stain, to be washed away by the blood of Christ and the grace of God: with which stain, indeed, they were defiled who were baptized by John. But to denote this washing by a sacramental sign, the sprinkling of water is as sufficient as the dipping into water,—when, in truth, this argues washing and purification as well as that. But those who were baptized by John were blemished with another stain, and that an outward one, and after a manner visible; that is, a polluted religion,—namely, Judaism, or heathenism; from which, if, according to the custom of the nation, they passed by a deeper and severer washing,—they neither underwent it without reason; nor with any reason may it be laid upon us, whose condition is different from theirs.

2. Since dipping was a rite used only in the Jewish nation and proper to it, it were something hard, if all nations should

be subjected under it; but especially, when it is neither
necessarily to be esteemed of the essence of baptism, and is
moreover so harsh and dangerous, that, in regard of these
things, it scarcely gave place to circumcision.   We read that
some, leavened with Judaism to the highest degree, yet wished
that dipping in purification might be taken away, because it
was accompanied with so much severity.   " In[y] the days of
R. Joshua Ben Levi, some endeavoured to abolish this dipping,
for the sake of the women of Galilee ; because, by reason of
the cold, they became barren.   R. Joshua Ben Levi said
unto them, Do ye go about to take away that which hedges
in Israel from transgression ?"   Surely it is hard to lay this
yoke upon the neck of all nations, which seemed too rough
to the Jews themselves, and not to be borne by them, men
too much given to such kind of severer rites.   And if it be
demanded of them who went about to take away that dipping, Would you have no purification at all by water? it is
probable that they would have allowed of the sprinkling of
water, which is less harsh, and not less agreeable to the thing
itself.

3. The following ages, with good reason, and by divine
prescript, administered a baptism differing in a greater matter
from the baptism of John ; and therefore it was less to differ
in a less matter.   The application of water was necessarily
of the essence of baptism ; but the application of it in this or
that manner speaks but a circumstance : the adding also of
the word was of the nature of a sacrament ; but the changing of the word into this or that form, would you not call this
a circumstance also?   And yet we read the form of baptism
so changed, that you may observe it to have been threefold in
the history of the New Testament.

Secondly, In reference to the form of John's baptism
[which thing we have propounded to consider in the second
place], it is not at all to be doubted but he baptized " in the
name of the Messias now ready to come:" and it may be
gathered from his words, and from his story.   As yet he
knew not that Jesus of Nazareth was the Messias; which he
confesseth himself, John i. 31 : yet he knew well enough,
that the Messias was coming ; therefore, he baptized those

y Hieros. Beracoth, fol. 6. 3.

that came to him in his name, instructing them in the doctrine of the gospel, concerning faith in the Messias, and repentance; that they might be the readier to receive the Messias when he should manifest himself.   Consider well Mal. iii. 1, Luke[z] i. 17, John i. 7, 31, &c.   The apostles, baptizing the Jews, baptized them "in the name of Jesus;" because Jesus of Nazareth had now been revealed for the Messias; and that they did, when it had been before commanded them by Christ, "Baptize all nations in the name of the Father, and of the Son, and of the Holy Ghost."   So you must understand that which is spoken, John iii. 23, iv. 2, concerning the disciples of Christ baptizing; namely, that[a] they baptized in 'the name of Jesus,' that thence it might be known that Jesus of Nazareth was the Messias, in the name of whom, suddenly to come, John had baptized.   That of St. Peter is plain, Acts ii. 38; " Be baptized, every one of you, in the name of Jesus Christ:" and that, Acts viii. 16, " They were baptized in the name of Jesus."

But the apostles baptized the Gentiles, according to the precept of our Lord, " In the name of the Father, and of the Son, and of the Holy Ghost," Matt. xxviii. 19.   For since it was very much controverted among the Jews about the true Messias, and that unbelieving nation denied, stiffly and without ceasing, that Jesus of Nazareth was he (under which virulent spirit they labour even to this day), it was not without cause, yea, nor without necessity, that they baptized in the name of Jesus; that by that seal might be confirmed this most principal truth in the gospel, and that those that were baptized might profess it; that Jesus of Nazareth was the true Messias.   But among the Gentiles, the controversy was not concerning the true Messias, but concerning the true God: among them, therefore, it was needful that baptism should be conferred in the name of the true God, " Father, Son, and Holy Spirit."

We suppose, therefore, that men, women, and children came to John's baptism, according to the manner of the nation in the reception of proselytes; namely, that they standing in Jordan were taught by John that they were

---

[z] *English folio edit.*, vol. ii. p. 122.   [a] *Leusden's edit.*, vol. ii. p. 270.

baptized into the name of the Messias, that was now immediately to come ; and into the profession of the doctrine of
the gospel concerning faith and repentance; that they plunged
themselves into the river, and so came out. And that which
is said of them, that they were baptized by him " confessing
their sins," is to be understood according to the tenour of the
Baptist's preaching; not that they did this man by man, or
by some auricular confession made to John, or by openly
declaring some particular sins ; but when the doctrine of
John exhorted them to repentance and to faith in the Messias, they renounced and disowned the doctrine and opinion
of justification by their works, wherewith they had been
beforetime leavened, and acknowledged and confessed themselves sinners.

'Εν τῷ 'Ιορδάνῃ· *In Jordan.*]   John could not baptize in
any part of Jordan, so it were within the bounds of Judea
(which the evangelists assert), which had not been dried up,
and had afforded a passage to the Israelites when they came
out of Egypt, and were now entering into the promised land.

§ *Some few remarks concerning the Pharisees and Sadducees.*

Ver. 7 : 'Ιδὼν δὲ πολλοὺς τῶν Φαρισαίων καὶ Σαδδουκαίων·
And seeing many of the Pharisees and Sadducees.]   To attempt a history of the *Pharisees* and *Sadducees*, after so
many very learned men, who have treated of their original,
manners, and institutions, would be next to madness : we
will briefly touch at a few things, and those, perhaps, less
obvious.

1. That the *Pharisees* do not derive their name (as some
would have it) from the word פרש which signifies to *expound*,
is sufficiently evinced by this, that there were *women-Pharisees*, as well as men. R. Joshua[b] saith, A religious man
foolish, a wicked man crafty, a *woman-Pharisee*, and the
dashing of the *Pharisees* [against the stones], destroy the
world."   Those things are worth observing, which are spoke
by the Babylonian Gemarists on that clause, אִישָׁה פְּרוּשָׁה
A woman-Pharisee.   ת"ר בתולה צלויינית ואלמנה
שובבית וקטן שלא כלו לו חדשיו הרי אלו מבלי עולם:

b Sotah, cap. 3. hal. 4.

" *The Rabbins teach. A praying* [*procax*] *maid, a gadding widow, and a boy whose months are not fulfilled, these corrupt the world.* But R. Jochanan saith, We learn the shunning of sin from a maid, and the receiving of a reward from a widow. ' The shunning of sin from a maid ;' for R. Jochanan heard a certain maid prostrate on her face thus praying ; Eternal Lord, thou hast created Paradise, thou hast created hell also, thou hast created the righteous, and thou hast created the wicked : let it be thy good pleasure that I be not a scandal to men. ' The receiving of a reward from a widow ;' for there was a certain widow, who, when there were synagogues nearer everywhere, she always resorted[c] to the school of R. Jochanan to pray : to whom R. Jochanan said, O my daughter, are there not synagogues at hand round about you ? But she answered, ולא שכר פסיעות יש לי *Will there not be a reward for my steps* [or, for my journey hither] ? for [the tradition] saith, These destroy the world, as Joanna, the daughter of Retib."

בתולה צליינית: , by one Gloss, is rendered בעלת תפילה, that is, *a maid given to prayer,* or *a maid of many prayers.* By another it is rendered, בתולתא צמיינית *a maid given to fasting :* מציימה אובדת בתוליה: *losing her virginity by fasting.*

A gadding widow they call her, " who always goes about from place to place to visit her neighbours ;" they are the words of the Gloss. " And these corrupt the world, because they are no other but bawds and sorceresses, and yet they pretend sanctity."

" Joanna the daughter of Retib [the Gloss also being witness] was a certain sorceress widow, who, when the time of any child's birth drew near, shut up the womb of the child-bearing woman with magic arts, that she could not be delivered. And when the poor woman had endured long and great torments, she would say, ' I will go and pray for you ; perhaps my prayers will be heard :' when she was gone, she would dissolve the enchantments, and presently the infant would be born. On a certain day as a hired man wrought in her house, she being gone to a woman's labour, he heard the

---

[c] *English folio edition,* vol. ii. p. 123.

charms tinkling in a pan; and, taking[d] off the cover, the charms presently came out, and strait the infant is born; and hence it was known that she was a witch."

I have therefore cited these passages, not only that it may be shown that there were *women-Pharisees*, and so that the name is not taken from *interpreting* or *expounding*, but that it may be observed also what kind of women, for the most part, embrace Pharisaism; namely, widows and maids, under the veil of sanctity and devotion, hiding and practising all manner of wickedness. And so much we gain of the history of the *Pharisees*, while we are tracing the etymology of the word.

II. That the *Pharisees* therefore were so called from the word פרש, signifying *separation*, is more commonly asserted, and more truly; and the thing itself, as well as the word, speaks it. So that by a word more known to us, you might rightly call the *Pharisees, Separatists;* but in what sense, has need of more narrow inquiry. The differences of the Jewish people are to be disposed here into divers ranks : and, first, we will begin with the women.

ı. It were an infinite task to search particularly, how their canons *indulged* (shall I say?) or *prescribed* the woman a freedom from very many rites, in which a great part of the Jewish religion was placed. How numberless are the times that that occurs in the Talmudic pandect, נשים ועבדין וקטנים פטורין "Women[e], *servants, and children, are not bound to these things.* Women[f], *servants, and children, are not bound to recite their phylacteries, nor to wear them.* פסחן של נשים רשות *The Passovers of women are at their own will.*" And, not to dwell upon things that are obvious, let this one serve instead of many : "As[g] certain matron asked R. Eleazar, Why, when Aaron sinned in making the golden calf, the people are punished with a threefold death? He answered, Let not a woman be learned beyond her distaff. Hircanus his son said unto him, Because no answer is given her in one word out of the law, she will withdraw from us three hundred tenth cori yearly. To whom he replied, Let them rather go and be burnt, than the words of the law be delivered to women."

---

[d] *Leusden's edition*, vol. ii. p. 271.
[e] Berac. cap. 3. hal. 3.
[f] Hieros. Kiddush. fol. 61. 3.
[g] Bab. Sotah, fol. 21. 2.

From hence it appears that the women that embraced Pharisaism did it of their own free will and vow, not by command : which the men-Pharisees also did.

2. Pass we from the women to the men ; and, first, to the lowest degrees of men in the distinction relating to religion ; namely, to them whom they ordinarily called בור *illiterate,* and עם הארץ *the people of the earth,* or *the plebeians.* Of them, thus the Gemara in Sotah[h] newly cited : " One reads the Scriptures, and recites the Misna, and yet he waits not upon the scholars of the wise men ; what of him ? R. Eleazar said, זה עם הארץ *This is one of the people of the earth.* R. Samuel Bar Nachmani saith, הרי זה בור *Behold, this is an illiterate man.* R. Jannai saith, ' Behold, this is a Cuthean.' R. Achabar saith, ' Behold, this is a magician.' " And a little after, " Who is עם הארץ *the people of the earth ?* R. Meith saith ' He that recites not his phylacteries morning and evening with his prayers. But the wise men say, ' He, whosoever he be, that lays not up his phylacteries.' Ben Azzai saith, ' He who hath not a fringe on his garment.' R. Jochanan Ben Joseph saith, ' He that instructs not his sons in the doctrine of the law.' Others say, ' He who, although he read the Scriptures, and repeats the traditions, yet attends not on the scholars of the wise men, this is, ע״ה *the people of the earth* [or *the plebeians*]. Does he read the Scriptures, and not repeat the tradition ? Behold, this man is בור *illiterate.*' The Gloss upon the place speaks thus, " *The people of the earth* are they of whom there is suspicion of tenths and cleanness :" that is, lest they tithe not rightly, nor take care aright concerning cleansings. And בור *the illiterate* person is גרוע מע״ה *more vile than, or inferior to, the people of the earth.*" Compare that, John vii. 49, " this people that knoweth not the law is cursed."

The[i] תלמידי חכמים and חבירים *colleagues* or *associates,* and *scholars of the wise men,* were opposed to these vulgar persons. Under the title of תלמידי חכמים *scholars of the wise men,* are comprehended all that were learned and studious : under the title of חברים *religious,* as well learned as unlearned. There were some of the learned whom they commonly called חבריהון דרבנין or חברייא דרבנין *colleagues*

[h] Fol. 22. 1.　　　　　　　[i] *English folio edit.,* vol. ii. p. 124.

of the Rabbins; who as yet were candidates, and not pre-ferred to the public office of teaching or judging. The thing may be illustrated by one example: " חבירים מהו ליכנס לקידוש החדש *Do* [k] *the* חבירים, *the colleagues enter in to ap-point the new moon ?* R. Hoshaia said, When I was חבר *a colleague,* R. Samuel Ben R. Isaac led me in to the appoint-ment of the new moon, but I knew not whether I were of the number or no." And a little after; " Do the *colleagues* [or *fellows*] go in to intercalate the year? Let us learn this from the example of Rabban Gamaliel, who said, Let the seven seniors meet me in the chamber. But eight entered, ' Who came in hither,' saith he, ' without leave?' ' I,' an-swered Samuel the Little."

In this sense the word חבר *a colleague,* differs nothing from תלמיד חכם *a scholar of a wise man,* in that both signify a student and a learned man. But the word חבר *a colleague,* hath a wider sense, denoting all such who have more pro-fessedly devoted themselves to religion, and have professed a more devout life and rule than the common people, whether they were learned or unlearned, whether of the sect of the *Pharisees,* or of the *Sadducees,* or some other. Hence you have mention of חבר כות *a* [l] *religious Samaritan,* and of נחתום הבר *a* [m] *religious baker.* And the phrase seems to be drawn from Psalm cxix. 63 ; חָבֵר אָנִי לְכָל־אֲשֶׁר יְרֵאוּךָ " I am [n] *a companion* of all those that fear thee:" קבלו עליהן דברי חברות *They take upon them the habit of religion.* See the Babylonian Talmud in Avodah Zarah [o] in the Gloss. That distinction also is worthy of consideration, of חברייא רברבייא and חברייא זעייריייא *The* [p] *greater and the less re-ligious.*

Yet the word seems sometimes to be appropriated to the *Pharisees,* as being men who, above all others, put on a splendidly cloaked religion, which appears enough from the history of the Gospel. So, perhaps, is that to be understood, חבריא מדכן בגלילא *The* [q] *religious Galileans purify :* that is, as the Gloss explains it, " They cleanse their wine and their oil for a drink-offering, if perhaps the Temple may be built

[k] Hieros. Sanhedr. fol. 18. 3.
[l] Bab. Berac. fol. 44. 2.
[m] Joma, fol. 8. 2.
[n] *Leusden's edition,* vol. ii. p. 272.
[o] Fol. 7. 1.
[p] Hieros. Bava Bathra, fol. 17. 1.
[q] Niddah, fol. 6. 2.

in their days." Which, nevertheless, the Aruch citing, thus explains them חברים אוכלין חוליהן בטהרה: *The religious eat their common food in cleanness.* By which very thing the Gloss defines *Pharisees*; לפרושין לאוכלי חוליהן בטהרה *To*[r] *the Pharisees; that is, to them that eat their common food in cleanness.* Behold, how the word חברים *religious*, and פרושין *Pharisees*, are convertible terms; and how this was the proper notion whereby a *Pharisee* was defined, "That he ate his common food in cleanness:" that is, that he washed his hands when he ate.

III. We must not think that Pharisaism arose altogether and at once, but it was long a-conceiving, and of no fixed form when it was brought forth. The same may, in a manner, be said of this, which is of the traditions: both these and that were the issue of many years. The[s] traditionarians do refer the first conception of the Traditions to the times of Ezra. But how many centuries of years passed before the birth of this whole monster was full ripe? In like manner, the first seeds of Pharisaism were cast long before its birth; and being now brought forth, was a long time growing, before it came to maturity; if so be any can define what its maturity was.

We observe presently, that the foundations of Sadduceeism were laid in the days of Ezra, before there were any Sadducees: in his days also, I suspect, the foundations of Pharisaism were laid long before there were any *Pharisees.* For, since the *Pharisees* were marked with that title because they *separated* themselves from other men, as more profane; and since, in the days of Ezra and Nehemiah, it was the great care, and that a holy care too, to *separate* the seed of Israel from the heathen inhabitants of the land, to wit, the Samaritans, the Ashdodites, the Moabites, &c., not much after; some men, arrogating too much for themselves, took occasion hence of *separating* themselves from the men of the Israelitic seed, as too profane, and very unfit (alas!) for their communion. Which very thing we experience in our present Separatists. For when the Scripture commands Christians that they communicate not " with unbelievers,

r In Chagigah, fol. 18. 2.
s Hieros. Megill. fol. 75. 1. Bab. Bava Kama, fol. 82. 1.

with those who are without," &c., that is, with heathens;
some do hence make a pretence of withdrawing themselves
from the assemblies of Christians : by what right, by what
foundation, let themselves look to it.

We shall not trace the time wherein the name of *Pharisee* first arose; this is done by learneder men : and therefore let it be enough to have observed that only. After
once this pretence of religion was received, " that it was a
pious matter to separate a man's self from the common people," superstition increased every day, which served for a
stay and patronage to this sect and separation. For when
they had espoused a religion so supercilious, that they commonly said, " Stand off, I am holier than thou" (which was
also foretold by the prophet with an execration, Isa. lxv. 5.),
and that they placed the highest sanctimony[t] in this, to
withdraw themselves from the common people, as profane ;
it was certainly necessary to circumscribe, and to put themselves under a more austere rule and discipline, that they
might retain the name and fame of religious persons in other
things besides that separation, that argued so much pride
and arrogancy. Hence the troubles about tithings and
washings arose, and increased age after age : hence sprang
the frequent fastings and prayers, the cares of the phylacteries, fringes, and other matters without number : so that (a
thing fatal to *Separatists*) this sect, at last, was crumbled
into sects, and a *Pharisee* was, in a manner, the same to a
Pharisee, that *the people of the earth* was to *a Pharisee.*

Both[u] Talmuds reckon seven sects of *Pharisees*, and so
does the Aruch[x] : which it will not be irksome to describe
with their pencil, that the reader may see to what a degree
of madness this sect was come, as well as to what a degree of
hypocrisy. שבעה פרושין הן *The Pharisees are seven :*

1. פרוש שכמי *A Shechemite Pharisee.* זה עשה מעשה שכם
This [y] [*Pharisee*] *does as Shechem.* Where the Gloss is,
" Who is circumcised, but not for the honour of God."
טעין מצוותיה על כתפיה *He*[z] *carrieth his precepts upon his
shoulders :* that is, as the Aruch explains it, " wood to

[t] *English folio edition*, vol. ii. p.   tah, fol. 20. 3. Bab. Sotah, fol.
125.   22. 2.
[u] Hieros. in Berac. fol. 13. 2. So-   [x] In פרוש.   [y] Bab.   [z] Hieros.

make a booth [in the feast of Tabernacles], or something of that nature."

2. פרוש ניקפי *A Pharisee struck,* or *dashing.* המנקיף את רגליו *Who* [a] *dasheth his feet.* The Gloss is, " He who walketh in humility, the heel of one foot touching the great toe of the other : nor did he lift up his feet from the earth, so that his toes were dashed against the stones." The Aruch writes, " Who withdrew himself a great way off, that he might not press upon men in the ways, and dashed his feet against the stones." אקיף לי ואנא עבד מצוה : *Strike* [b] *me* (or surround me), *and yet I will perform the command.*

3. פרוש קזאי *A* [c] *Pharisee that lets out his blood.* " He [d] strikes out his blood against the walls." The Gloss is ; " He shows himself such a one as if his eyes were hoodwinked, that he might not look upon a woman ; and hereupon dashed his head against the walls, and let out his blood." The Aruch writes, " He so pressed up himself against the walls, that he might not touch those that passed by, that by the dashing he fetched blood of himself."—" He [e] performed one precept, and one duty, and struck out blood at each."

4. פרוש מדוכיא *A Pharisee of the mortar.* The Aruch thus describes him ; " He went in a loose coat, resembling a mortar with the mouth turned downwards. So he, with his loose garment, was straiter above and broader below." In the Jerusalem Talmud he is called פרוש מנכייה, " who saith, I withdraw whatsoever is mine, and fulfil the command."

5. פרוש מה חובתי ואעשנה " *The Pharisee* which saith, Let me know *what my duty is, and I will do it.*" " I have [f] done my duty, that the command may be performed according to it." The Aruch thus ; " As though he should say, There is no man can show me wherein I have transgressed."

6. פרוש יראה *A Pharisee of fear :* such was Job.

7. פרוש אהבה *A Pharisee of love :* אין לך חביב מכולן אלא פרוש אהבה כאברהם *Among* [g] *all these, none is worthy to be loved but the Pharisee of love : as Abraham.*

Whether Pharisaism ran out into any of these sects in the days of the Baptist, we dispute not. Let it be granted,

---

[a] Bab.   [b] Hieros.   [d] Bab.   [e] Hieros.
[c] *Leusden's edit.,* vol. ii. p. 273.   [f] Hieros.   [g] Hieros.

that the best and the most modest of that order came to his baptism : the best of the *Pharisees* certainly were the worst of men.   And it is so much the more to be wondered at that these men should receive his baptism after that manner as they did ; when it was highly contrary to the rule of the *Pharisees* to converse among the common people, of whom there was so great a concourse to John ; and highly contrary to the doctrine of the *Pharisees,* so much as to dream of any righteousness, besides that which was of the works of the law, which the doctrine of John diametrically contradicted.

The original of the *Sadducees,* learned men as well Jews as Christians, do, for the most part, refer to one *Zadoc,* a scholar of Antigonus Socheus ; which Antigonus took the chief seat in the Sanhedrim after the death of Simeon the Just.   Of him thus speaks the tract Avoth[h] : " Antigonus of Socho received traditions of Simeon the Just.   He said, Be not as servants, who wait upon their master for the sake of the reward ; but be ye like servants who wait upon their master not for the sake of the reward : but let the fear of the Lord rule you."

" This wise man (saith Rambam[i] upon the place) had two scholars, Zadoc and Baithus ; who, when they heard this from their master, said among themselves, when they were gone away, Our master in his exposition teacheth us that there is neither reward nor punishment, nor any expectation at all [for the future] : for they understood not what he meant : therefore, they mutually strengthened one another, and departed from the rule, and forsook the law : and some company adhered to both.   The wise men, therefore, called them *Sadducees* and Baithusees."   And a little after ; " But in these countries, namely in Egypt, they call them *Karaites,* קראים ; but *Sadducees* and Baithusees are their names among the wise men."   See also the Avoth of R. Nathan[k].

Yet[l] that raiseth a scruple here : " At[m] the conclusion of all prayers in the Temple they said, עד עולם *for ever.*   But when the heretics brake in and said, There was no age but

h Cap. 1.

i [A name formed from the initials of the full name, *Rabbi Moses ben Maimon.*, better known among Christians as *Maimonides.*]

k Cap. 5.

l *English folio edit.*, vol. ii. p. 126.

m Bab. Berac. fol. 54.

one, it was appointed to be said, מִן הָעוֹלָם וְעַד הָעוֹלָם *for ever and ever*, or *from age to age*." Upon these words thus the Gloss ; "In the first Temple they said only, 'Blessed be the Lord God of Israel for ever.' But when the heretics brake in and said there was no age but this, Ezra and his consistory appointed that it should be said, מִן הָעוֹלָם וְעַד הָעוֹלָם *for ever and ever*, or *from age to age*, to imply there is a double world [this, and one to come], to root out of the heart the opinion of those that deny the resurrection of the dead."

Take notice, reader, that "there were some who denied the resurrection of the dead in the days of Ezra," when as yet Zadoc, the father of the *Sadducees*, was not born. After Ezra, and his great synagogue (which endured many a year after Ezra was dead), sat Simeon the Just, performing the office of the high-priest, for the space of forty years : and Antigonus Socheus, the master of Zadoc, succeeded him in the chair of the Sanhedrim. So that although the Sadducees, with good reason, do bear an ill report for denying the resurrection, and that was their principal heresy ; yet that heresy was, when as yet there were no heretics, called by the name of *Sadducees*. To which, perhaps, those words do agree (which sufficiently taste of such a heresy), "Ye have said, It is in vain to serve God," &c., Mal. iii. 14.

It is not, therefore, to be denied that the *Sadducee-heretics* were so named from Zadoc ; but that the heresy of the *Sadducees*, concerning the resurrection, was older than that name, one may suppose not without reason ; nor that that cursed doctrine first arose from the words of Antigonus, illy understood by Zadoc and Baithus, but was of an ancienter original, when as yet the prophets Zecharias, Malachi, and Ezra himself, were alive, if that Ezra were not the same with Malachi, as the Jews suppose. Therefore I do rather think that heresy sprang from the misunderstanding of the words of Ezekiel, chap. xxxvii ; which some understanding according to the letter, and, together with it, seeing no resurrection, dreamt that there would be none afterward. And this doctrine increased, and exalted itself into a sect ; when, at length, Zadoc and Baithus asserted that it was so determined out of the chair by their master Antigonus [n], the president of the Sanhedrim.

[n] *Leusden's edition*, vol. ii. p. 274.

When I fetch the rise of the *Sadducees* not much after
the death of Simeon the Just, that does not unseasonably
come into my mind, which is mentioned by the Talmudists,
that the state of things became worse after his death. " All[o]
the days of Simeon the Just, the scape-goat had scarce come
to the middle of the precipice of the mountain [whence he
was cast down], but he was broken into pieces : but, when
Simeon the Just was dead, he fled away [alive] into the
desert, and was eaten by Saracens.   While Simeon the Just
lived, the lot of God [in the day of expiation] went forth
always to the right hand : Simeon the Just being dead, it
went forth sometimes to the right hand and sometimes to
the left.   All the days of Simeon the Just, the little scarlet
tongue looked always white ; but when Simeon the Just was
dead, it sometimes looked white and sometimes red.   All
the days of Simeon the Just, the west light always burnt ;
but when he was dead, it sometimes burnt and sometimes
went out.   All the days of Simeon the Just, the fire upon
the altar burnt clear and bright ; and, after two pieces of
wood laid on in the morning, they laid on nothing else the
whole day : but when he was dead, the force of the fire
languished in that manner that they were compelled to supply it all the day.   All the days of Simeon the Just, a blessing was sent upon the two loaves and the show-bread, so
that a portion came to every priest, to the quantity of an
olive at least ; and there were some who ate till they were
satisfied, and there were others to whom something remained after they had eaten their fill : but when Simeon the
Just was dead, that blessing was withdrawn, and so little
remained to each, that those that were modest withdrew
their-hands, and those that were greedy still stretched them
out."

Γεννήματα ἐχιδνῶν· *Generation of vipers.*]   I. Ὄφεις,
serpents, chap. xxiii. 33.   Not so much " the seed of Abraham," which ye boast of, as " the seed of the serpent," Ὁ
Ἀντίχριστος, ὁ Ἀντικείμενος, *the Antichrist, the Opposer,* 2 Thess.
ii. 4.   A nation and offspring diametrically opposite, and an
enemy to that seed of the woman, and which was to bruise
his heel."

[o] Hieros., Joma, fol. 43. 3.

II. Hence, not without ground, it is concluded that that nation was rejected and given over to a reprobate sense, even before the coming of Christ. They were not only γενεὰ, *a generation*, but γεννήματα, *an offspring* of vipers, serpents sprung from serpents. Nor is it wonder that they were rejected by God, when they had long since rejected God, and God's word, by their traditions. See that Matt. xiii. 13—15, 1 Pet. ii. 10, " Ye were not a people."

There was, indeed, a certain *remnant* among them to be gathered by Christ: and when that was gathered, the rest of the nation was delivered over to everlasting perdition. This P is that λεῖμμα, that *remnant* of the apostle, Rom. xi. 5, which then was, when he writ those things; which then was to be gathered, before the destruction of that nation.

Φυγεῖν ἀπὸ τῆς μελλούσης ὀργῆς· *To fly from the wrath to come.*] These words respect the very last words of the Old Testament, "lest I smite the earth with a curse," Mal. iv. [6]; and denote the most miserable destruction of the nation, and now almost ready to fall upon them.

The receiving of John's baptism signed and fenced those that received it from the ruin that was just coming. To this belongs that of St. Peter, Epist. i. ch. iii. 20, 21 : in that manner as Noah and his sons were by water delivered from the flood, "so also baptism now, the antitype of that type, saveth us" from the deluge of divine indignation, which in a short time is to overflow the Jewish nation. Think here, if those that came to baptism brought not their little ones with them to baptism : when, by the plain words of the Baptist, those that are baptized are said to " fly from the wrath to come ?" that is, ' the wrath of God,' that was not long hence to destroy the nation by a most sad overthrow.

Ver. 9: Μὴ δόξητε λέγειν· *Think not to say.*] A Jerusalem phrase, to be met with everywhere in the Talmud : סבר מימר *To think a word*, or *to be of that opinion.*

Ver. 10: Ἡ ἀξίνη πρὸς τὴν ῥίζαν· *The axe is laid to the root.*] These words seem to be taken from Isa. x. 33, 34. The destruction of the nation was to proceed from the Romans, who

had now a great while held them under the yoke. That axe,
now laid to the root of the tree, shall certainly cut it down,
if from this last dressing by the gospel it bears not fruit.
In the Talmud[q], those words of Isaiah are applied to the
destruction of the city; and thence it is argued, that the
Messias should be born not much after the time of that
destruction, because presently after the threatening of that
ruin follows, " A Branch shall arise out of the stock of Jesse,"
Isa. xi. 1.

Ver. 11 : Οὗ οὐκ εἰμὶ ἱκανὸς τὰ ὑποδήματα βαστάσαι· *Whose
shoes I am not worthy to bear.*] In Luke it is, λῦσαι τὸν ἱμάντα
τῶν ὑποδημάτων, *to unloose the latchet of his shoes:* which comes
to the same thing : both sound to the same import, as if he
had said, ' Whose servant I am not worthy to be.'

" A Canaanite[r] servant is like a farm, in respect of buying:
for he is bought with money, or with a writing, אוֹ בחזקה
or by some service done, as a pledge or pawn. And what is
such a pawning in the buying of servants? Namely, that he
looseth the shoe ·of him [who buys], or binds on his shoe, or
carries to the bath such things as be necessary for him," &c.
These things Maimonides produceth out of the Talmud,
where these words are, " How[s] is a servant[t] bought בחזקה
by service? He looseneth the buyer's shoe; he carrieth such
things after him as are necessary for the bath ; he un-
clothes him ; washes, anoints, rubs, dresses him ; puts on his
shoes, and lifts him up from the earth," &c. See also the
Tosaphta[u].

This, by the way, is to be noted, which the Gloss intimates,
that all servants, of what heathen nation soever, bought by
the Jews, were called ' Canaanite servants,' because it is said
of Canaan, " Canaan a servant of servants."

Ver. 15[x]: Οὕτω πρέπον ἐστὶν ἡμῖν πληρῶσαι πᾶσαν δικαιοσύ-
νην· *Thus it becomes us to fulfil all righteousness.*] That is, ' that
we fulfil every thing that is just.' Now in the baptism of
Christ there were these two just things especially :—I. That
this great priest, being initiated into his ministerial office,
should answer the type of the admission of the Levitical

---

q Hieros. Beracoth, fol. 5. 1.
r Maimon. in מכירה cap. 2.
s Bab. Kiddushin, fol. 22. 2.

t *Leusden's edition,* vol. ii. p. 275.
u Ad Kiddush. cap. 1.
x *English folio edit.,* vol. ii. p. 128.

priests, who were initiated by washing and anointing; so was
he by baptism, and the Holy Ghost.   II. When, by the institution of Christ, those that entered into the profession of
the gospel were to be introduced by baptism, it was just,
yea, necessary, that Christ, being to enter into the same
profession, and to preach it too, should be admitted by
baptism.

Ver. 16: Καὶ βαπτισθεὶς ὁ Ἰησοῦς· *And Jesus being baptized.*]
I. That Christ conversed upon earth two-and-thirty years and
a half (as many years as David lived at Jerusalem ; compare
2 Sam. v. 5), is proved hence :—1. That he was baptized when
he had now completed his twenty-ninth year, and had newly
begun his thirtieth.   That the words of Luke imply, ὡσεὶ ἐτῶν
τριάκοντα ἀρχόμενος ὤν· *He began to be about thirty years old.*
Which words, although they are applied by some Christians
to I know not what large latitude,—yet in the Jewish schools,
and among that nation, they would not admit, certainly, of
another sense than we produce.   For there[y] this axiom holds,
יום אחד בשנה חשוב שנה : *The first day of the year is
reckoned for that year.*   And, questionless, Luke speaks with
the vulgar.   For let it be supposed that the evangelist uttered
these words in some Jewish school, " N. was baptized ἀρχόμενος ὤν ὡσεὶ τριάκοντα ἐτῶν, *beginning to be about thirty years
old:*" how could it be understood by them of the thirtieth
complete (much less of the thirty-first, or thirty-second, as
some wrest it)?   when the words ἀρχόμενος ὡσεὶ, *beginning to
be about*, do so harmoniously agree with the said axiom, as
scarcely any thing can do more clearly.   2. That, from his
baptism to his cross, he lived three years and a half.   This is
intimated by the angel Gabriel, Dan. ix. 27 ; " In the half of
a week" (that is, in three years and a half) " he shall make
the sacrifice and oblation to cease ;" and it is confirmed from
the computation in the evangelists, but especially in John,
who clearly mentioneth four Passovers (chap. ii. 13, v. 1, vi. 4,
and xiii.1) after his forty days' fast, and not a little time spent
in Galilee.

II. Therefore, we suppose Christ was baptized about the
feast of Tabernacles, in the month Tisri, at which time we

[y] Rosh Hashanah, fol. 2. 2.

suppose him born; and that John was born about the feast
of the Passover, and at that time began to baptize. For
when Christ lived two-and-thirty years and a half, and died
at the feast of the Passover, you must necessarily reduce
his birth to the month Tisri, and about the time of the feast
of Tabernacles: and when John the Baptist was elder than he
by half a year, you must necessarily suppose him born about
the feast of the Passover. But of these things we have said
something already.

Ver. 17: Καὶ ἰδοὺ, φωνὴ ἐκ τῶν οὐρανῶν· *And behold, a voice
from heaven.*] Christ was honoured with a threefold testimony,
pronounced by a voice from heaven, according to his threefold
office. See what we say at chap. xvii. 2.

You find not a voice sent from heaven between the giving
of the law and the baptism of Christ. What things the Jews
relate of *Bath Kol*[z], they must pardon me if I esteem them,
partly, for Jewish fables,—partly, for devilish witchcrafts.
They hold it for a tradition: "After[a] the death of the last
prophets, Haggai, Zechariah, Malachi, נסתלקה רוח הקדש
מישראל: *the Holy Spirit departed from Israel* [which was
most true] : ואעפ" כן משתמשין בבת קול *but they used
thenceforth the Bath Kol.*" "The *Bath Kol* was this;
כשקול יוצא מן השמים יוצא מתוכו קול אחר *When*[b] *a
voice* (or *thunder*) *came out of heaven, another voice came out
from it.*"

But why, I pray, was prophecy withdrawn, if heavenly
oracles were to be continued? Why, also, was Urim and
Thummim taken away? Or rather, why was it not restored
after the Babylonian captivity? For "Five things (say they[c])
were wanting under the second Temple[d], which were under
the first; namely, the fire from heaven, the ark, Urim and
Thummim, the oil of anointing, and the Holy Spirit." It
would certainly be a wonder, if God, taking away from his
people his ordinary oracles, should bestow upon them a
nobler oracle, or as noble; and that when the nation had
degenerated, and were sunk into all kind of impiety, supersti-

---

[z] [בַּת קוֹל Hebr. *Filia vocis.* See
Buxtorf Lex. Rabb. col. 320.]
[a] Bab. Sanhed. fol. 11. 1.
[b] Piske Tosaph. in Sanhed. cap. 1.

art. 29.
[c] Hieros. Taanith, fol. 65. 1.
[d] *English folio edition,* vol. ii. p.
129.

tion, heresy.   When the last prophets, Haggai and the rest,
were dead, the Sadducean heresy, concerning the resurrection crept in, and the Pharisaical heresy also, weakening all
Scripture, and making it of none effect by vain traditions.
And shall I believe that God should so indulge his people,
when they were guilty of so grievous apostasy, as to vouchsafe to talk familiarly with them from heaven, and[e] to afford
them oracles so sublime, so frequent, as the prophets themselves had not the like? If I may speak plainly what I
think, I should reduce those numberless stories of the *Bath
Kol* which occur everywhere under these two heads ;
namely, that very many are mere fables, invented for this
purpose, that hence the worth of this or that Rabbin or
story may be illustrated : the rest are mere magical and diabolical delusions.

When I read these and such-like passages, that[f] the *Bath
Kol* in Jericho gave witness to Hillel, that he was worthy to
have the Holy Ghost abide upon him ; that the *Bath Kol* in
Jabneh yielded the same testimony to Samuel the Little ;
that the[g] *Bath Kol* again in Jabneh determined the controversies between the schools of Shammai and Hillel, for those
of Hillel ;" and innumerable other stories of that kind, I
cannot but either suspect these to be tales, or that these
voices were framed by art magic for the honour of the
Rabbins.

It is remarkable what is related in the Jerusalem Talmud[h];
אר״ אלעזר הולכין אחר שמיעת בת קול : *R. Eliezer saith,
They follow the hearing of Bath Kol.* And a little after;
" R. Jochanan, and R. Simeon Ben Lachish, desired to see
the face of Samuel [*the Babylonian Doctor*]; Let us follow,
say they, the hearing of *Bath Kol.* Travelling therefore, near
a school, they heard a boy's voice reading [in 1 Sam. xxv. 1.]
ושמואל מת *And Samuel died.* They observed this, and so
it came to pass, for Samuel of Babylon was dead."

" R. Jonah and R. Josah went to visit R. Acha lying sick :
Let us follow, say they, the hearing of *Bath Kol.* They heard
the voice of a certain woman speaking to her neighbour, ' The

e *Leusden's edit.,* vol. ii. p. 246.
f Bab. Sanhed. in the above
place.

g Hieros. Berac. fol. 3. 2.
h Schab. fol. 8. 3.

light is put out.' To whom she said, ' Let it not be put out, nor let the light of Israel be quenched.' "

Behold! reader, a people very well contented to be deceived with a new kind of *Bath Kol.* Compare these things with *Virgil's lots*[i], of which the Roman historians speak frequently. Not to be more tedious therefore in this matter, let two things only be observed: 1. That the nation, under the second Temple was given to magical arts beyond measure. And, 2. That it was given to an easiness of believing all manner of delusions beyond measure. And one may safely suspect, that those voices which they thought to be from heaven, and noted with the name of *Bath Kol,* were either formed by the devil in the air to deceive the people, or by magicians by devilish art to promote their own affairs. Hence the apostle Peter saith with good reason, that "the word of prophecy was surer than a *voice* from heaven;" 2 Pet. i. 19.

The very same which I judge of the *Bath Kol,* is my opinion also of the frequent appearances of Elias, with which the leaves of the Talmud do every where abound; namely, that in very many places the stories are false, and, in the rest, the apparitions of him were diabolical. See the notes upon the tenth verse of the seventeenth chapter.

CHAP. IV.

VER. 1 : Ἀνήχθη εἰς τὴν ἔρημον ὑπὸ τοῦ Πνεύματος πειρασθῆναι, &c. *He was led up by the Spirit into the wilderness to be tempted, &c.*] The war, proclaimed of old in Eden between the serpent, and the seed of the serpent, and the seed of the woman, Gen. iii. 15, now takes place; when that promised seed of the woman comes forth into the field (being initiated by baptism, and anointed by the Holy Ghost, unto the public office of his ministry) to fight with that old serpent, and at last to bruise his head. And, since the devil was always a most impudent spirit, now he takes upon him a more hardened boldness than ever, even of waging war with him whom he knew to be the Son of God, because from that[k] ancient proclamation of this war he knew well enough that he should bruise his heel.

[i] [See Smith's Dict. G. and R. Antiquities, art. *Sortes.*]
[k] *English folio edition,* vol. ii. p. 133.

The first scene or field of the combat was the 'desert of Judea,' which Luke intimates, when he saith, that "Jesus returned from Jordan, and that he was led by the Spirit into the wilderness;" that is, from the same coast or region of Jordan in which he had been baptized.

The *time* of his temptations was from the middle of the month Tisri to the end of forty days; that is, from the beginning of our month of October to the middle of November, or thereabouts: so that he conflicted with cold, as well as want and Satan.

The *manner* of his temptations was twofold. First, invisibly, as the devil is wont to tempt sinners; and this for forty days: while the tempter endeavoured with all his industry to throw in his suggestions, if possible, into the mind of Christ, as he does to mortal men. Which when he could not compass, because he found 'nothing in him' in which such a temptation might fix itself, John xiv. 30, he attempted another way, namely, by appearing to him in a visible shape, and conversing with him, and that in the form of an angel of light. Let the evangelists be compared. Mark [i. 13.] saith, "he was tempted forty days:" so also doth Luke [iv. 2.]: but Matthew, that "the tempter came to him after forty days;" that is, in a visible form.

The *matter* of his temptations was very like the temptations of Eve. She fell by the "lust of the flesh, the lust of the eye, and the pride of life:" which are the heads of all sins, 1 John ii. 16.

By "the lust of the eyes:" for "she saw the fruit, that it was pleasant to the sight."

By "the lust of the flesh;" she lusted for it, because "it was desirable to be eaten."

By "the pride of life;" not contented with the state of perfection wherein she was created, she affected a higher; and she "took[1] of the fruit, and did eat," that she might become wiser by it.

The same tempter set upon our Saviour with the same stratagems.

I. As Eve was deceived by mistaking his person, supposing a good angel discoursed with her when it was a bad, so the

---

[1] *Leusden's edition*, vol. ii. p. 277.

devil in like manner puts on the good angel here, clothed with light and feigned glory.

II. He endeavours to ensnare Christ by "the lust of the flesh;" "Command that these stones be made bread:" by "the lust of the eye;" "All these things will I give thee, and the glory of them:" by "the pride of life;" "'Throw thyself down,' and fly in the air, and be held up by angels."

Ver. 5 : 'Επὶ τὸ πτερύγιον τοῦ ἱεροῦ· *Upon the pinnacle of the Temple.*] Whether he placed him upon the Temple itself, or upon some building within the holy circuit, it is in vain to seek, because it cannot be found. If it were upon the Temple itself, I should reflect upon the top of the אולם *porch of the Temple:* if upon some other building, I should reflect upon the Στοὰν βασιλικὴν, *the royal gallery.* The priests were wont sometimes to go up to the top of the Temple, stairs being made for this purpose, and described in the Talmudic book entitled Middoth[m]; and they are said to have ascended hither, "when[n] fire was first put to the Temple, and to have thrown up the keys of the chambers of the Temple towards heaven, with these words; 'O thou eternal Lord, because we are not worthy to keep these keys, to thee they are delivered.' And there came, as it were, the form of a hand out of heaven, and took them from them: and they leaped down, and fell into the fire."

Above all other parts of the Temple the אולם *porch of the Temple,* yea, the whole πρόναον, *space before it,* may not unfitly be called τὸ πτερύγιον τοῦ ἱεροῦ, *the wing of the Temple,* because, like *wings,* it extended itself in breadth on each side, far beyond the breadth of the Temple: which we take notice of elsewhere.

If, therefore, the devil had placed Christ in the very precipice of this part of the Temple, he may well be said to have placed him upon *the wing of the Temple,* both because this part was like a wing to the Temple itself, and that that precipice was *the wing* of this part.

But if you suppose him placed ἐπὶ στοὰν βασιλικὴν, *upon the royal gallery,* look upon it thus painted out by Josephus: "On[o] the south part [of the court of the Gentiles] was the

---

m Cap. 4. hal. 5.   n Bab. Taanith, fol. 29. 1.
     o Antiq. lib. xv. cap. 14. [Hudson, p. 703.] [xv. 11. 5.]

στοὰ βασιλικὴ, *the king's gallery*, that deserves to be mentioned
among the most magnificent things under the sun : for upon
a huge depth of a valley, scarcely to be fathomed by the eye
of him that stands above, Herod erected a gallery of a vast
height ; from the top of which if any looked down, σκοτο-
δινιᾷν οὐκ ἐξικουμένης τῆς ὄψεως εἰς ἀμέτρητον τὸν βυθόν· *he
would grow dizzy, his eyes not being able to reach to so vast
a depth."*

Ver. 8[p] : Δείκνυσιν αὐτῷ πάσας τὰς βασιλείας τοῦ κόσμου, &c.
Showed him all the kingdoms of the world, &c.] That is,
Rome with her empire and state. For, 1. That empire is
called πᾶσα οἰκουμένη, *all the world*, (which word Luke [iv. 5.]
useth in this story,) both in sacred and profane writers.
2. At this time all cities were of little account in comparison of Rome, nor did any part of the earth bear any vogue
without that empire. 3. Rome was 'the seat of Satan,'
Rev. xiii. 2 ; and he granted to the beast of that city both
it and the dominion. 4. This therefore seems to be that
whereby he attempts to ensnare our Saviour in this object,
namely, that he promiseth to give him the pomp and power
of Cæsar, and to deliver into his hand the highest empire of
the world, that is, the Roman. This, antichrist afterward
obtained.

Ver. 13 : Καὶ καταλιπὼν τὴν Ναζαρὲθ, ἐλθὼν κατῴκησεν εἰς
Καπερναούμ· *And, leaving Nazareth, he came and dwelt at
Capernaum.*] Why he left Nazareth after he had passed six
or seven-and-twenty years there, the reason appears, Luke
iv. 28, &c. We do not read that he returned thither again ;
and so, unhappy Nazareth, thou perishest by thine own folly
and perverseness. Whether his father Joseph had any inheritance at Capernaum, which he possessed as his heir, or
rather dwelt there in some hired house, we dispute not. This
is certainly called his city, Matt. ix. 1, &c. ; and here, as a
citizen, he paid the half-shekel, Matt. xvii. 24. Where it is
worthy marking what is said by the Jews : כמה יהא בעיר
: ויהא כאנשי העיר יב" חדש *How[q] long does a man dwell in
some city before he be as one of the citizens ? Twelve months.*
The same is recited again[r] elsewhere. The Jerusalem Ge-

mara thus explains it; "If he tarry in the city thirty days,
he becomes as one of the citizens in respect of the alms-chest;
if six months, he becomes a citizen in respect of clothing ; if
twelve months, in respect of tributes and taxes." The Babylonian adds, " if nine months, in respect of burial." That is,
if any abide in a city thirty days, they require of him alms for
the poor ; if six months, he is bound, with the other citizens,
to clothe the poor ; if nine months, to bury the dead poor ; if
twelve months, he is bound to undergo all other taxes with
the rest of the citizens. See the Gloss.

Ver. 15: Γῆ Ζαβουλὼν, καὶ γῆ Νεφθαλείμ· *The land of Zabulon, and the land of Nephthali.*] It is needful that the
words of Isaiah be considered, whence these words are taken.
He had been discoursing, in the eighth chapter towards the
end, concerning the straits and miseries that compassed [s]
the transgressors of the law and the testimony. " To the
law and to the testimony," &c., ver. 20. וְעָבַר בָּהּ נִקְשֶׁה וְרָעֵב
" But if a man transgress against it [that is, תּוֹרָה and תְּעוּדָה
the law and *the testimony*], it will redound to his hardship, and
he shall suffer hunger," &c., ver. 21. " And he shall look to
the earth, and behold trouble and darkness, dimness of an-
guish, and he shall be driven to darkness," ver. 22. And
then it follows, chap. ix. 1, כִּי לֹא מוּעָף לַאֲשֶׁר מוּצָק לָהּ
" For the dimness shall not be like to that wherein it was ill
with him, at what time the former [afflicter] lightly touched
the land of Zabulon, and the land of Nephthali, and the latter
grievously afflicted," &c. " That people who sat in darkness,
saw a great light," &c.

That which the prophet means here is this : 1. That
the contemners of Emanuel and his testimony, that is, the
gospel, should undergo far greater calamities than those
places had undergone, either under their first conqueror
Ben-hadad[t], or under the second, the king of Assyria[u]. For
those places saw light at last restored to them, when the
Messias preached the gospel there : but the contemners of
the gospel are driven into eternal darkness. 2. He foretells
the morning of liberty, and of evangelical light, to arise
there, where the first darkness and the calamities of their

[s] *Leusden's edition*, vol. ii. p.
278.
[t] 1 Kings xv. 20.
[u] 2 Kings xv. 29.

captivity had arisen. St. Matthew citing these words, that
he might show the prophecy to be fulfilled, of that light
that should arise there, omits those words which speak of
their former misery, that is, the first clause of the verse;
and produceth those words only, and that very fitly too,
which make to his purpose, and which aim directly thither
by the prophet's intention. The prophet Hosea affords us
an instance of curtailing[x] a sentence after that manner, chap.
i. 11, ii. 1; when he proclaims Israel and Judah miserable,
he calls them ' Lo-Ammi,' and ' Lo-Ruchamah;' when happy,
' Ammi,' and ' Ruchamah.'

Πέραν τοῦ Ἰορδάνου· *Beyond Jordan.*] Not *by* Jordan, but
beyond Jordan. For the latter afflicter, the king of Assyria,
had carried away that country also into banishment and
bonds, 1 Chron. v. 26. Here is an ellipsis of the conjunction *and*.

Ver. 18: Βάλλοντας ἀμφίβληστρον εἰς τὴν θάλασσαν· *Casting
a net into the sea.*] : טבריה של בימה מחכין *Fishing*[y] *in the
sea of Tiberias*, in Talmudic speech. There the fathers of
the traditions dream that Joshua the son of Nun gave ten
laws to the Israelites, concerning having some things in common, as lawful, and to be allowed of: התנה תנאין י"ר "ת
יהושע *Our Rabbins have a tradition that Joshua ordained
ten conditions:* בחורשין מרעין שיהו *That cattle graze in
common in woody places.* : בשדותיהם עצים ומלקטין *And
that a man gather wood in common in his neighbour's field*, &c.
Among others, טבריה של בימה ומחכין *And that any, in
common, spread his nets for fishing in the sea of Tiberias.* But
yet under this caution, הספינה את ויעמיד קלע יפרוס שלא
That none set up a wall, which may be any stop to ships. The
Gloss is, " It is the manner of fishermen to fasten stakes in
the water, and to make fences of canes or reeds, in which
the fish may be taken: but this is not permitted, because it
is an impediment to the ships." However therefore the sea
of Tiberias belonged to the tribe of Nephthali, yet it was
free for any Israelite to fish in it, so it were under the condition mentioned.

Ver. 19: Ἁλιεῖς ἀνθρώπων· *Fishers of men.*] This phrase

is something agreeable with that of Maimonides [z] upon the Talmud, שׁלֹא ישׁכח דבר מדברי דייגי תורה; *A fisher of the law.*

Ver. 21 : Ἰάκωβον τὸν τοῦ Ζεβεδαίου· *James the son of Zebedee.*] We meet [a] with a certain Rabbin of this very same name, ר' יעקב בר זבדי *R. Jacob the son of Zabdi.*

Ver. 23 : Διδάσκων ἐν ταῖς συναγωγαῖς αὐτῶν· *Teaching in their synagogues.*] Since we meet with very frequent mention of synagogues every where in the books of the Gospel, it may be needful to know something more clearly what the customs and institutions of the synagogues were, for the better understanding very many things which have some reference thereunto in the New Testament : let us here despatch the history of them ἐν ἐπιτομῇ, as briefly as we may, now when the mention of synagogues first occurs.

§ *Of the Synagogues.*

I. A synagogue was not formed anywhere but where there were ten learned men professedly students of the law. 1. Let that of the Talmud [b] be observed. איזה עיר גדולה "*What is a great city ?* כל שיש בה ""י בטלנין : *That in which were ten men of leisure.* פחות מכאן הרי זה כפר : *If there be less than this number, behold, it is a village.*" 2. Observe that of Maimonides [c] ; " Wheresoever there be ten of Israel, there a house must needs be built, to which they may resort to prayers in the time of prayer, and this house is called a synagogue." Not that any ten of Israel made a synagogue ; but wheresoever were ten learned men, and studious of the law, these were called בטלנין *Batlanin, men of leisure ;* " who were not to be esteemed for lazy and idle persons, but בטלנין ממלאכתן ועוסקין בצרכי ציבור such who [d]," not being encumbered with worldly things, " *were at leisure only to take care of the affairs of the synagogues,* and to give themselves to the study of the law."

The [e] reason of the number of ten, though lean and empty enough, is given in the Talmud [f] : and it is this ; עדה היא

---

[z] Torah, cap. 1.
[a] Hieros. Maasar Sheni, fol. 55. 2.
[b] Megill. cap. 1. hal. 3.
[c] Tephillah, cap. 11.

[d] *English folio edition,* vol. ii. p. 133.
[e] *Leusden's edit.,* vol. ii. p. 279.
[f] Sanhedr. cap. 4. hal. 6.

עשרה *A congregation consists of ten :* which they prove hence, because it is said, עַד מָתַי לָעֵדָה הָרָעָה הַזֹּאת "*How long shall I bear with this evil congregation, &c.* (Numb. xiv. 27.) Take away Joshua and Caleb, and there remain only ten ;" namely, of the spies of the land.

II. Of these ten men :

1. Three bear the magistracy, and were called בד "של שלשה *The bench of three:* whose office it was to decide the differences arising between the members of the synagogue, and to take care about other matters of the synagogue. These judged concerning money-matters, thefts, losses, restitutions, ravishing a virgin, of a man enticing a virgin, of the admission of proselytes, χειροθεσία, *laying on of hands*, and divers other things, of which see the tract Sanhedrim g. These were properly, and with good reason, called ἀρχισυνά-γωγοι, *rulers of the synagogue*, because on them laid the chief care of things, and the chief power.

2. Besides these there was ' the public minister of the synagogue,' who prayed publicly, and took care about the reading of the law, and sometimes preached, if there were not some other to discharge this office. This person was called שליח ציבור *the angel of the church,* and חזן הכנסת *the Chazan* or *bishop of the congregation.* The Aruch gives the reason of the name : " The *Chazan* (saith he) is שליח צבור *the angel of the church* (or *the public minister*), and the Targum renders the word רואה by the word חוזה, *one that over-sees* ; שהוא צריך לראות *for it is incumbent on him to over-see* how the reader reads, and whom he may call out to read in the law." The public minister of the synagogue himself read not the law publicly ; but, every sabbath, he called out seven of the synagogue (on other days, fewer) whom he judged fit to read. He stood by him that read, with great care observing that he read nothing either falsely or improperly ; and calling him back and correcting him if he had failed in any thing. And hence he was called חזן, that is, ἐπίσκοπος, or *overseer.* Certainly the signification of the word *bishop*, and *angel of the church*, had been determined with less noise, if recourse had been made to the proper fountains, and men

g Cap. 4. hal. 1.

had not vainly disputed about the signification of words, taken I know not whence. The service and worship of the Temple being abolished, as being ceremonial, God transplanted the worship and public adoration of God used in the synagogues, which was moral, into the Christian church; to wit, the public ministry, public prayers, reading God's word, and preaching, &c. Hence the names of the ministers of the Gospel were the very same, *the angel of the church*, and *the bishop;* which belonged to the ministers in the synagogues.

3. There were also three deacons, or almoners, on whom was the care of the poor; and these were called *Parnasin*[h], [פרכסין] or *Pastors.* And these seven perhaps were reputed שבעה טובי העיר *the seven good men of the city;* of whom there is frequent remembrance in the Talmudists.

Of these *Parnasin* we shall only produce these things. There were two, who demanded alms of the townsmen; and they were called, שני גבאי צדקה *the two*[i] *collectors of alms.* ועוד אחד כדי שיהיו ג׳ לחלק צדקה *To whom was added a third to distribute it.*

"R. Chelbo[k] in the name of R. Ba Bar Zabda saith, They do not make fewer than three *Parnasin.* For I see the judgments about many matters to be managed by three: therefore much more these which concern life. R. Josi in the name of R. Jochanan saith, They do not make two brethren *Parnasin.* R. Josi went to Cephar, intending there to set *Parnasin* over them, but they received him not. He went away, after he had said these words before them, Ben Bebai was only set over the threaded [linen of the lamps], and yet he was reckoned worthy to be numbered with the eminent men of that age. [See Shekalim, cap. 5.] Ye who are set over the lives of men, how much more are ye so ! R. Chaggai, when he appointed the *Parnasin,* argued to them out of the law, all dominion that is given is given from the law. By me kings reign. R. Chaiia Bar Ba מקים ארכונין *set* ἄρχοντας, *rulers,* over them, that is, he *appointed Parnasin.* R. Lazar was a *Parnas.*"

This perhaps holds out a light to those words of the

---

[h] [See Buxtorf Lex. T. & R. sub v. col. 1822.]

[i] Maimon. in Sanhedr. cap. 1.

[k] Hieros. Peah, fol. 21. 1.

apostle, 1 Tim. iii. 13, "They that have performed the office of a deacon well have obtained to themselves a good degree:" that is, being faithful in their care and provision for the poor, as to their corporal life, they may well be probationers for the care of souls. For when those *Parnasin*, as also all the ten, were learned and studious, they might with good reason be preferred from the care of bodies to that of souls. The apostles' deacons are to be reckoned also of the same learned and studious rank. And now let us turn our eyes a little from the synagogues to Christian churches, in the history of the New Testament. When the Romans permitted the Jewish synagogues to use their own laws and proper government, why, I pray, should there not be the same toleration allowed to the apostolical churches? The Roman[1] censure had as yet made no difference between the Judaizing synagogues of the Jews, and the Christian synagogues or churches of Jews; nor did it permit them to live after their own laws, and forbid these. I am not, therefore, afraid to assert, that the churches of that first age were wanting to themselves, if they took not up the same liberty of government as the Romans allowed the Jewish synagogues to use. And I do not think that was said by the apostle, 1 Cor. vi. 2, 3, &c. without this foundation. Therefore, this power of their own government being allowed them, if so be they were minded to enjoy what they might, how easily may those words of the apostle be understood, which have so racked learned men (shall I say?), or which have been so racked by them, 1 Tim. v. 17[m]: Οἱ καλῶς προεστῶτες πρεσβύτεροι, &c. "Let the elders that rule well," &c.

4. We may reckon the eighth man of these ten to be the תורגמן, that is, *the interpreter* in the synagogue; who, being skilled in the tongues, and standing by him that read in the law, rendered in the mother-tongue, verse by verse, those things that were read out of the Hebrew text. The duty of this interpreter, and the rules of his duty, you may read at large in the Talmud[n].

[1] *English folio edition*, vol. ii. p. 134.
[m] *Leusden's edition*, vol. ii. p. 280.

[n] Megill. cap. 4. Maimon. in Tephillah, cap. 12, &c. Massecheth Sopherim, cap. 10, &c. and elsewhere.

The use of such an interpreter, they think, was drawn down to them from the times of Ezra, and not without good reason. וַיִּקְרְאוּ בַסֵּפֶר תּוֹרָה זה המקרא וגו״ " And[o] they *read in the book of the law: that was the text.* מְפוֹרָשׁ זה תרגום *Explaining: that was the Targum.* וְשׂוֹם שֶׂכֶל אִילוּ טעמים *And added the meaning:* they are the accents: וַיָּבִינוּ בַּמִּקְרָא זה המסורת *and they understood the text: that was the Masoreth.*" See Nehem. viii. 8; see also Buxtorf's Tiberias, chap. viii.

5. We do not readily know whom to name for the ninth and tenth of this last three. Let us suppose them to be the *master of the divinity-school,* and his *interpreter:* of whom we shall have a fuller occasion of inquiry. And thus much concerning the head of the synagogue, that learned Decemvirate, which was also the representative body of the synagogue.

III. The days wherein they met together in the synagogue were the sabbath, and the second day and the fifth of every week. Of the sabbath there is no question. They refer the appointment of the second and fifth days to Ezra. " Ezra (say they[p]) decreed ten decrees. He appointed the public reading of the law in the second and fifth days of the week. Also on the sabbath at the time of the sacrifice. He appointed washing to those that had the gonorrhœa. He appointed the session of the judges in cities on the second and fifth days of the week," &c. Hence, perhaps, it will appear in what sense that is to be understood, Acts xiii. 42, Παρεκάλουν τὰ ἔθνη εἰς τὸ μεταξὺ σάββατον λαληθῆναι αὐτοῖς τὸ ῥήματα ταῦτα. " The Gentiles besought that these words might be preached to them the *next sabbath,* or the *sabbath between;*" that is, on the days of that intervening week, wherein they met together in the synagogue.

IV. Synagogues were anciently builded in fields. "To[q] the evening recital of the phylacteries are to be added two prayers going before, and two following after." Where the Gloss thus; "The Rabbins instituted that prayer [יראו עינינו], that they might retain their colleagues in the synagogue. And this certainly respected their synagogues at that time;

---

[o] Hieros. Megill. fol. 74. 4.   Kama, fol. 82. 1.
[p] Ibid. fol. 75. 1.   Bab. Bava   [q] Bab. Beracoth, fol. 2. 1.

because they were situated in the fields, where they might be
in danger." And so Rabbenu Asher[r] upon the same tract;
" Anciently their synagogues were in fields : therefore they
were afraid to tarry there, until the evening prayers were
ended. It was therefore appointed that they should recite
some verses, in which a short sum of all the eighteen prayers
had been compacted ; after which that prayer יראו עינינו was
to be recited."

But the following times brought back their synagogues for
the most part into the cities; and provision was made by
sharp canons, that a synagogue should be built in the highest
place of the city, and that no house should be built higher
than it.

V. The like provision was made, that every one at the
stated times of prayer should frequent the synagogue. " God[s]
does not refuse the prayers, although sinners are mingled
there. Therefore it is necessary that a man associate himself
with the congregation, and that he pray not alone when an
opportunity is given of praying with the congregation. Let
every one therefore come morning and evening to the synagogue." And " It[t] is forbidden to pass by the synagogue in
the time of prayer, unless a man carry some burden upon his
back : or unless there be more synagogues in the same city ;
for then it may be judged that he goes to another; or unless
there be two doors in the synagogue ; for it may be judged
that he passed by one to go in at another. But if he carry
his phylacteries upon his head, then it is allowed him to pass
by, because they bear him witness that he is not unmindful
of the law." These things are taken out of the Babylonian
Talmud[u] : where these are also added : " The holy blessed
one saith, Whosoever employeth himself in the study of the
law, and in the returning of mercy, and whosoever prays with
the synagogue, I account concerning him, as if he redeemed
me and my sons from the nations of the world. And whosoever prays not with the synagogue is called an ' ill neighbour,'
as it is said, ' Thus saith the Lord of all my evil neighbours,' "
&c. Jer. xii. 14.

r Fol. 69. 3.
s Maim. in Tephill. cap. 8.
t Chap. 6.
u Beracoth, fol. 8. 1.

VI.[x] When they were met together in the synagogue on
the sabbath-day (for this being observed, there is no need to
speak any thing of the other days), the service being begun,
the minister of the church calls out seven, whomsoever he
pleases to call out, to read the law in their order.   First, a
priest, then a Levite, if they were present ; and after these
five Israelites.   Hence it is, O young student in Hebrew
learning, that in some editions of the Hebrew Bible you see
marked in the margin of the Pentateuch, 1. כהן *The priest.*
2. לוי *The Levite.*   3. שלישי *The third.*   4. רביעי *The fourth.*
5. חמישי *The fifth.*   6. ששי *The sixth.*   7. שביעי *The seventh :*
—denoting by these words the order of the readers, and mea-
suring out hereby the portion read by each one.   Thus, I suppose, Christ was called out by *the angel of the church* of Nazareth, Luke iv. 16, and reading according to the custom as a
member of that synagogue.

There is no need to mention that prayers were made publicly by *the angel of the church* for the whole congregation,
and that the congregation answered *Amen* to every prayer :
and it would be too much particularly to enumerate what
those prayers were, and to recite them.   It is known enough
to all that prayers, and reading of the law and the prophets,
was the chief [y] business in the synagogue, and that both were
under the care of *the angel of the synagogue.*

I. There seemed to have been catechizing of boys in
the synagogue.   Consider what that means, נשים במאי זכיין
" *What*[z] *is the privilege of women ?* באקרויי בנייהו לבי כנשתא :
This, that their sons read in the synagogue. באתנויי גברייהו
בי רבנן : *That their husbands recite in the school of the doctors.*
Where the Gloss thus, " The boys that were scholars were
wont to be instructed [or to learn] before their master in the
synagogue."

II. The *Targumist*, or *Interpreter*, who stood by him that
read in the law, and rendered what was read out of the Hebrew original into the mother-tongue,—sometimes used a
liberty of enlarging himself in paraphrase.   Examples of this
we meet with in the Talmud [a], and also in the Chaldee paraphrast himself.

[x] *English folio edit.*, vol. ii. p. 135.
[y] *Leusden's edit.*, vol. ii. p. 281.
[z] Bab. Berac. fol. 17. 1.

[a] Hieros. Biccurim, fol. 65. 4.
Sanhedr. fol. 20. 3. Bab. Berac. fol.
28. 1. and elsewhere.

III. Observe that of the Glosser, היו באים לשמוע הדרשה
נשים ועמי הארץ: Women[b] *and the common people were wont
to meet together to hear the exposition or the sermon.* But of
what place is this better to be understood than of the synagogue ? That especially being well weighed which immediately followeth; והיו צריכין דרשנין למשוך את לבבם *And
they had need of expounders* [or preachers] *to affect their hearts :*
which is not much unlike that which is said Acts xiii. 13, Εἰ
ἔστι λόγος ἐν ὑμῖν παρακλήσεως πρὸς τὸν λαόν· *If ye have any
word of exhortation for the people, say on.*

IV. Service being done in the synagogue, they went to
dinner. And after dinner to בית מדרש *the school,* or *the
church,* or *a lecture of divinity ;* call it by what name you
will. It is called also not seldom by the Talmudists ציבור
and כנסת *The synagogue.* In this sense, it may be, is
כנישתא עילייתא *the upper synagogue* to be taken, mentioned
in the Talmud [c] ; if it be not to be taken of the Sanhedrim.
In this place a doctor read to his auditors some traditional
matter, and expounded it. בית המדרש ששם שונין משנה
וגמרא In[d] *the Beth Midrash they taught traditions, and their
exposition.*

There are three things to be taken notice of concerning
the rites used in this place.

I. He that read to the auditors spake not out with an
audible voice, but muttered it with a small whisper in somebody's ear ; and he pronounced it aloud to all the people.
So that here the doctor had his interpreter in this sense, as
well as the reader of the law his in the synagogue. " Rabh[e]
went to the place of R. Shilla, ולא הוה אמורא למיקם עליה
and there was no interpreter to stand by R. Shilla ; Rabh therefore stood by him." Where the Gloss hath these words,
לא הוה אמורא " *He had no speaker,* that is, מתורגמן
he had no *interpreter* present, who stood before the doctor when
he was reading the lecture. והחכם לוחש לו לשון עברית :
*And the doctor whispered him in the ear in Hebrew, and he ren-
dered it in the mother-tongue to the people.*" Hither that of
our Saviour hath respect, Matt. x. 27 ; " What ye hear in

---

[b] In Bab. Schab. fol. 30. 2.
[c] Hieros. Schab. fol. 3. 1.
[d] Gloss. in Bab. Berac. fol. 17. 1.
[e] Bab. Joma, fol. 20. 2.

the ear, that preach ye upon the house-tops." Consult the same place.

2. It was customary in this place, and in these exercises, to propound questions. In that remarkable story of removing Rabban Gamaliel of Jafne from his presidentship, which we meet with in divers[f] places of both Talmuds : when they met together in the Beth Midrash, עמד השואל ושאל "*The questioner stood forth and asked,* The evening prayer, is it observed by way of duty, or of free will?" And after a few lines, the mention of an interpreter occurs : "The whole multitude murmured against it, and said to Hotspith the interpreter, 'Hold your peace;' and he held his peace, &c.

3. While the interpreter preached from the mouth of the doctor, the people sat upon the earth. " Let[g] not a judge go upon the heads of the holy people." The Gloss is, " While the interpreter preached ציבור the *synagogue* [or *the whole congregation*] sat on the ground : and whosoever walked through the middle of them to take his place, seemed as if he walked upon their heads."

One[h] may safely be of opinion that the word συναγωγή, *synagogue*, was used sometimes in the New Testament in this sense ; and that Christ sometimes preached in these divinity-schools, as well as in the synagogues.

But by what right was Christ permitted by the rulers of the synagogue to preach, being the son of a carpenter, and of no learned education? Was it allowed any illiterate person, or mechanic, to preach in the synagogues, if he had the confidence himself to it? By no means. For it was permitted to none to teach there but those that were learned. But there were two things especially that gave Christ admission to preach in every synagogue ; namely, the fame of his miracles, and that he gave out himself the head of a religious sect. For however the religion of Christ and his disciples was both scorned and hated by the scribes and Pharisees, yet they accounted them among the *religious* in the same sense as they did the Sadducees; that is, distinguished from עם הארץ *the common people,* or *the seculars,* who took little care of

---

[f] Hieros. Berac. fol. 7. 4. Taanith, fol. 67. 4. Bab. Berac. fol. 27. 2.

[g] Bab. Sanhedr. fol. 7. 2.

[h] *English folio edition,* vol. ii. p. 136.

religion. When, therefore, Christ was reckoned among the religious, and grew so famous by the rumour of his miracles, and the shining rays of his doctrine, no wonder if he raised among the people an earnest desire of hearing him, and obtained among the governors of the synagogues a liberty of preaching.

CHAP. V.[i]

VERS. 3, 4, 5, &c. : Μακάριοι, μακάριοι, &c. *Blessed, blessed*, &c.] It is commanded, Deut. xxvii, that, upon the entrance of the people into the promised land, blessings and curses should be denounced from the mounts Gerizim and Ebal : the curses being particularly reckoned up, but the blessings not so. Which seems not to be without a mystery, since the law brought the curse with it; but Christ, who should bring the blessing, was yet to come a great while hence. Now he is present pronouncing the blessings, and that on a mountain. The Jewish writers do thus relate that matter :

" Six [k] tribes went up to the top of mount Gerizim, and six to the top of mount Ebal. But the priests and the Levites stood below with the ark of the covenant. The priests compassed the ark ; the Levites compassed the priests; and the whole people of Israel stood on one side and on the other : as it is said, ' All Israel and the elders,' &c. (Josh. viii. 33.) Turning their faces to mount Gerizim, they began with the blessing, ' Blessed is the man that shall make no idol, or molten image,' &c. And both the one and the other answered, Amen. Turning their faces to mount Ebal, they pronounced the curse, ' Cursed is the man who shall make an idol, or molten image :' and both the one and the other answered, Amen. And so of the rest. And at last, turning their faces to Gerizim, they began with the blessing, ' Blessed is the man who shall continue in all the words of the law ;' and the answer on both sides is, Amen. Turning their faces to Ebal, they pronounce the curse, ' Cursed is every one that shall not continue in all the words of the law :' and the answer from both sides is, Amen," &c.

In like manner Christ here, having begun with blessings,

---

[i] *Leusden's edition*, vol. ii. p. 282.
[k] Talm. in Sotah, cap. 7. Tosaph. in Sotah, cap. 8.

" Blessed, blessed," thundereth out curses, " Woe, woe,"
Luke vi. 24—26.

That which many do comment concerning the octonary
number of beatitudes hath too much curiosity, and little
benefit. It hath that which is like it among the Jews : for
thus they write [1] ; " There is a tradition from the school of
R. Esaiah Ben Korcha, that twenty blessings are pronounced
in the Book of the Psalms, and in like manner twenty woes
in the Book of Isaiah. ' But I say,' saith Rabbi, ' that there
are two-and-twenty blessings, according to the number of the
two-and-twenty letters."

" Abraham [m] was blessed with seven blessings."

" These[n] six are blessed, every one with six blessings,
David, Daniel, and his three companions, and king Messias."

Ver. 8[o] : Μακάριοι οἱ καθαροὶ τῇ καρδίᾳ· *Blessed are the pure
in heart.*] Hearken, O Pharisee, all whose praise lies in
outward cleanness. How foolish is this boasting of a Jew !
" Come[p] and see, saith R. Simeon Ben Eleazar, how far the
purity of Israel extends itself : when it is not only appointed,
that a clean man eat not with an unclean woman; but [that
an unclean man eat not with an unclean man] that a Pharisee that hath the gonorrhœa eat not with a common person
that hath the gonorrhœa."

Ver. 9: Μακάριοι οἱ εἰρηνοποιοί· *Blessed are the peacemakers.*]
הבאת שלום בין איש לרעהו [אדם לחבירו:] *Making*[q]
peace between neighbours is numbered among those things
which bring forth good fruit in this life, and benefit in the
life to come.

Ver. 17 : Μὴ νομίσητε ὅτι ἦλθον καταλῦσαι τὸν νόμον, &c.
Think not that I am come to destroy the law, &c.] I. It was
the opinion of the nation concerning the Messias, that he
would bring in a new law, but not at all to the prejudice or
damage of Moses and the prophets : but that he would ad-
vance the Mosaic law to the very highest pitch, and would
fulfil those things that were foretold by the prophets, and
that according to the letter, even to the greatest pomp.

---

[1] Midr. Tillin upon Psal. i. R.
Sol. upon Isa. v.
[m] Baal Turim upon Gen. xii.
[n] Targ. upon Ruth iii.

[o] *English folio edition*, vol. ii. p. 137.
[p] Bab. Schab. fol. 13. 1.
[q] Peah, cap. 1. hal. 1.

II. The scribes and Pharisees, therefore, snatch an occasion of cavilling against Christ ; and readily objected that he was not the true Messias, because he abolished the doctrines of the traditions which they obtruded upon the people for Moses and the prophets.

III. He meets with this prejudice here and so onwards by many arguments, as namely, 1. That he abolished not the law when he abolished traditions ; for therefore he came that he might fulfil the law. 2. That he asserts, that " not one iota shall perish from the law." 3. That he brought in an observation of the law much more pure and excellent than the Pharisaical observation of it was: which he confirms even to the end of the chapter, explaining the law according to its genuine and spiritual sense.

Ver. 18 : 'Αμὴν γὰρ λέγω ὑμῖν· *Verily, I say unto you.*] I. Such an asseveration was usual to the nation, though the syllables were something changed. " A[r] certain matron said to R. Judah Bar Allai, Thy face is like to a swineherd or a usurer. To whom he answered, הימנותא לדידי תרוייהו אסירן *In truth, both are forbidden me.* The Gloss there, הימנותא " *In truth* is a manner of speech used in swearing."

II. But our Saviour useth this phrase by the highest divine right. 1. Because he is " Amen, the faithful witness," Rev. iii. 14, 2 Cor. i. 20 : see also Isa. lxv. 16[s] ; and Kimchi there. 2. Because he published the gospel, the highest truth, John xviii. 37, &c. 3. By this asseveration he doth well oppose his divine oracles against the insolent madness of the traditional doctors, who did often vent their blasphemous and frivolous tales under this seal, באמת אמרו *They speak in truth :* and " wheresoever this is said (say they), it is הלך למשה מסיני *a tradition of Moses from Sinai.*"

'Ιῶτα ἕν· *One jot.*] The Jerusalem Gemarists[t] speak almost to the same sense : " The Book of Deuteronomy came and prostrated itself before God, and said, ' O Lord of the universe, thou hast written in me thy law, but now a testament defective in some part is defective in all. Behold, Solomon endeavours to root the letter Jod out of me' [to wit, in this

---

[r] Bab. Berac. fol. 55. 1.   [s] *Leusden's edition,* vol. ii. p. 283.
[t] Sanhedr. fol. 20. 3.

text, לֹא יַרְבֶּה נָשִׁים, *He shall not multiply wives,* Deut.
xvii. 17]. The holy blessed God answered, ' Solomon and a
thousand such as he shall perish, but the least word shall not
perish out of thee.' R. Honna said in the name of R. Acha,
The letter Jod which God took out of the name of Sarai our
mother, was[u] given half to Sara and half to Abraham.   A
tradition of R. Hoshaia : The letter Jod came and prostrated
itself before God, and said, 'O eternal Lord, thou hast rooted
me out of the name of that holy woman.'   The blessed God
answered, ' Hitherto thou hast been in the name of a woman,
and that in the end [viz. in Sarai]; but henceforward thou
shalt be in the name of a man, and that in the beginning.'
Hence is that which is written, ' And Moses called the name
of Hoshea, Jehoshua.' "   The Babylonians also do relate this
translation of the letter Jod out of the name of Sarai to the
name of Joshua, after this manner: "The[x] letter Jod, saith
God, which I took out of the name of Sarai, stood and cried
to me for very many years, How long will it be ere Joshua
arise? to whose name I have added it."

You have an example of the eternal duration of this very
little letter Jod, in Deut. xxxii. 18, where, in the word תֶּשִׁי,
it is written even less than itself, and yet it stands immortal
in that its diminutive state unto this very day, and so shall
for ever.

There[y] is a certain little city mentioned by name דרוקרת
Derokreth, which, by reason of the smallness of it, was called
Jod in the Gloss.   And[z] there was a rabbin named Rabh
Jod.   Of the letter Jod, see Midrash Tillin upon the hundred
and fourteenth Psalm.

Μία κεραία· *One tittle.*]   It seems to denote the little heads
or dashes of letters, whereby the difference is made between
letters of a form almost alike.   The matter may be illustrated
by these examples, היה דלת ועשאו ריש ריש ועשאו
דלת חייב *If[a] it were Daleth, and a man should have formed
it into Resh* [on the sabbath], *or should have formed Resh into
Daleth, he is guilty.*

---

u *English folio edition,* vol. ii. p.   y Bab. Taanith, fol. 21. 2.
138.   z Fol. 22. 2.
    x Sanhedr. fol. 107. 1.   a Hieros. Schab. fol. 10. 4.

" It[b] is written [Lev. xxii. 32.] לֹא תְחַלְּלוּ אֶת־שֵׁם קָדְשִׁי
Ye shall not profane my holy name: whosoever shall change
ח [Cheth] into ה [He], destroys the world [for then לֹא
תְהַלְלוּ, written with ה [He], makes this sense, *Ye shall not
'praise' my holy name*]. It is written [Ps. cl. 6], כֹּל הַנְּשָׁמָה
תְּהַלֵּל יָהּ *Let every spirit praise the Lord:* whosoever
changeth ה [He] into ח [Cheth], destroys the world. It is
written [Jer. v. 12], כִּחֲשׁוּ בַּיהוָה *They lied against the Lord:*
whosoever changeth בּ [Beth] into כּ [Caph], destroys the
world. It is written [1 Sam. ii. 2], אֵין קָדוֹשׁ כַּיהוָה *There
is none holy as the Lord:* whosoever changeth כּ [Caph] into
בּ [Beth], destroys the world. It is written [Deut. vi. 4],
יְהוָה אֱלֹהֵינוּ יְהוָה אֶחָד *The Lord our God is one Lord:*
he that changeth ד [Daleth] into ר [Resh], destroys the
world."

But that our Saviour, by ἰῶτα καὶ κεραία, *jot and tittle,* did
not only understand the bare letters, or the little marks that
distinguished them, appears sufficiently from verse 19, where
he renders it, one of " these least commands :" in which
sense is that also in the Jerusalem Gemara of Solomon's
rooting out Jod, that is, evacuating that precept לֹא יַרְבֶּה
נָשִׁים *He shall not multiply wives.* And yet it appears enough
hence, that our Saviour also so far asserts the uncorrupt immortality and purity of the holy text, that no particle of the
sacred sense should perish, from the beginning of the law to
the end of it.

To him that diligently considers these words of our Saviour,
their opinion offers itself, who suppose that the whole alphabet
of the law, or rather the original character of it is perished ;
namely, the Samaritan, in which they think the law was first
given and written; and that that Hebrew wherein we now
read the Bible was substituted in its stead. We shall not
expatiate in the question; but let me, with the reader's good
leave, produce and consider some passages of the Talmud,
whence, if I be not mistaken, Christians seem first to have
taken up this opinion.

---

[b] Tanchum, fol. 1. 1.

The Jerusalem Talmud treats of this matter in these
words : " R. Jochanan de Beth Gubrin saith[c], There are
four noble tongues which the world useth : the mother-
tongue, for singing ; the Roman, for war ; the Syriac, for
mourning ; the Hebrew, for elocution : and there are some
which add the Assyrian, for writing. The Assyrian hath
writing [that is, letters or characters], but a language it hath
not. The Hebrew hath a language, but writing it hath not.
They chose to themselves the Hebrew language in the Assyrian character. But why is it called אשורי *the Assyrian ?*
שהוא מאושר בכתבו *Because it is blessed* (or *direct*) *in its
writing.* R. Levi saith, Because it came up into their hands
out of Assyria."

" A tradition. R. Josi saith, Ezra was fit, by whose hands
the law might have been given, but that the age of Moses
prevented. But although the law was not given by his hand,
yet writing [that is, the forms of the letters] and the language
were given by his hand. ' And the writing of the epistle was
writ in Syriac, and rendered in Syriac,' Ezra iv. 7. ' And
they could not read the writing,' Dan. v. 8. From whence is
shown that the writing [that is, the form of the characters
and letters] was given that very same day. R. Nathan saith :
The law was given in breaking[d] [that is, in letters more rude
and more disjoined] : and the matter is as R. Josi saith.
Rabbi [Judah Haccodesh] saith, The law was given in the
Assyrian language ; and when they sinned it was turned into
breaking. And when they were worthy in the days of Ezra,
it was turned for them again into the Assyrian. I show
to-day, that I will render to you משנה *Mishneh, the doubled,*
or, as if he should say *the seconded*[e] (Zech. ix. 12). And he
shall write for himself the *Mishneh* (*the doubled*) of this law
in a book (Deut. xvii. 18), namely, in a writing that was to
be changed. R. Simeon Ben Eleazar saith, in the name
of R. Eleazar Ben Parta, and he in the name of R. Lazar
the Hammodean, The law was given in Assyrian writing.
Whence is that proved ? from those words, וָוֵי הָעַמּוּדִים
(Exod. xxvii. 10). שיהו ווים של תורה דומים לעמודים

---

[c] In Megill. fol. 71. 2, 3.   [d] *Leusden's edition*, vol. ii. p. 284.
[e] *English folio edition*, vol. ii. p. 139.

that the letter ו [*Vau*] *in the law is like a pillar.*" So the Jerusalem Talmudists.

Discourse is had of the same business in the Babylonian
Talmud[f], and almost in the same words, these being added
over : " The law was given to Israel in Hebrew writing, and
in the holy language.   And it was given to them again in the
days of Ezra, in Assyrian writing, and the Syriac language.
The Israelites chose to themselves the Assyrian writing, and
the holy language ; והניחו להדיוטות כתב עברית ולשון
ארמית *and left the Hebrew writing and the Syriac language
to ignorant persons.* מאן הדיוטות But *who are those idiots*
(or *ignorant persons*)? R. Chasda saith, כותאי *The Samaritans.*   And what is the Hebrew writing? R. Chasda saith,
כתב ליבונאה :" that is, according to the Gloss, " Great letters, such as those are which are writ in charms and upon
doorposts."

That we may a little apprehend the meaning of the Rabbins, let it be observed,

I. That by ' the mother-tongue' (the Hebrew, Syriac, Roman, being named particularly) no other certainly can be
understood than the Greek, we have shown at the three-and-
twentieth verse of the first chapter.

II. That that writing which the Gemarists call כתב עברי
and which we have interpreted by a very known word, *Hebrew
writing,*—is not therefore called עברי, because this was proper
to the Israelites, or because it was the ancient writing, but
(as the Gloss very aptly) כתב עברי של בני עבר הנהר
because *the writing* or *character was in use among them that
dwelt beyond Euphrates.*   In the same sense as some would
have Abraham called עִבְרִי *Hebrew,* signifying *on the other side,*
that is, *beyond* or *on the other side of* Amana.

Many nations were united into one language, that is, the
old Syriac,—namely, the Chaldeans, the Mesopotamians, the
Assyrians, the Syrians.   Of these some were the sons of Sem
and some of Ham.   Though all had the same language, it is
no wonder if all had not the same letters.   The Assyrians and
Israelites refer their original to Sem ; these had the Assyrian
writing : the sons of Ham that inhabited beyond Euphrates

[f] Sanhedr. fol. 21. 2. et 22. 1.

had another; perhaps that which is now called by us the Samaritan, which it may be the sons of Ham the Canaanites used.

III. That the law was given by Moses in Assyrian letters, is the opinion (as you see) of some Talmudists; and that, indeed, the sounder by much. For to think that the divine law was writ in characters proper to the cursed seed of Ham, is agreeable neither to the dignity of the law, nor indeed to reason itself. They that assert the mother-writing was Assyrian, do indeed confess that the characters of the law were changed; but this was done by reason of the sin of the people, and through negligence. For when under the first Temple the Israelites degenerated into Canaanitish manners, perhaps they used the letters of the Canaanites, which were the same with those of the inhabitants beyond Euphrates. These words of theirs put the matter out of doubt: "The law was given to Israel in the Assyrian writing in the days of Moses: but when they sinned under the first Temple and contemned the law, it was changed into breaking to them."

Therefore, according to these men's opinion, the Assyrian writing was the original of the law, and endured and obtained unto the degenerate age under the first Temple. Then they think it was changed into the writing used beyond Euphrates or the Samaritan; or, if you will, the Canaanitish (if so be these were not one and the same); but by Ezra it was at last restored into the original Assyrian.

Truly, I wonder that learned men should attribute so much to this tradition (for whence else they have received their opinion, I do not understand), that they should think that the primitive writing of the law was in Samaritan: seeing that which the Gemarists assert concerning the changing of the characters rests upon so brittle and tottering a foundation, that it is much more probable that there was no change at all (but that the law was first writ in Assyrian by Moses, and in the Assyrian also by Ezra), because the change cannot be built and established upon stronger arguments.

A second question might follow concerning Keri and Kethib: and a suspicion might also arise, that the text of the law was not preserved perfect to *one jot and one tittle*, when so many various readings do so frequently occur. Concerning this business we will offer these few things only, that so we may return to our task :—

I. These things are delivered by tradition ; ספרים מצאו ג"‏ בעזרה " *They[g] found three books in the court,* ספר מעוני *the book* מעוני *Meoni, the book* זעטוטי *Zaatuti, and the book* היא *Hi*. In one they found written, באחד מעאו כתוב מעון אלהי קדם ' The eternal God is thy refuge:' but in the two other they found it written, מעונה אלהי קדם (Deut. xxxiii. 27) ; קיימו שנים וביטלו אחד : *They approved* [or *confirmed*] *those two, but rejected that one.* In one they found[h] written, וישלח את זעטוטי בני ישראל but in two it was written[i], וישלח את נערי בני ישראל : ' And he sent young men of the children of Israel' (Exod. xxiv. 5). Those two they confirmed, but that one they rejected. In one they found written, תשע היא *She was nine;* but in the two was written, אחת עשרה היא *She was eleven:* those two they confirmed, and that one they rejected."

I do much suspect that these three books laid up in the court answered to the threefold congregation of the Jews, namely, in Judea, Babylon, and Egypt, whence these copies might be particularly taken. For, however that nation was scattered abroad almost throughout the whole world, yet, by number and companies scarcely to be numbered, it more plentifully increased in these three countries than any where else : in Judea, by those that returned from Babylon ; in Babylon, by those that returned not ; and in Egypt, by the temple of Onias. The two copies that agreed, I judge to be out of Judea and Babylon ; that that differed to be out of Egypt : and this last I suspect by this, that the word זעטוטי *Zaatuti* smells of the Seventy interpreters, whom the Jews of Egypt might be judged, for the very sake of the place, to favour more than any elsewhere. For[k] it is asserted by the Jewish writers, that זעטוטי was one of those changes which the Septuagint brought into the sacred text.

II. It is therefore very probable, that the Keri and Kethib

[g] Hieros. Taanith, fol. 68. 1.
[h] *English folio edition*, vol. ii. p. 140.
[i] *Leusden's edit.*, vol. ii. p. 284.
[k] Massecheth Sopherim, cap. 1. art. 8.

were compacted from the comparing of the two copies of the greatest authority, that is, the Jewish and the Babylonian : which when they differed from one another in so many places in certain little dashes of writing, but little or nothing at all as to the sense, by very sound counsel they provided that both should be reserved, so that both copies might have their worth preserved, and the sacred text its purity and fulness, whilst not *one jot* nor *one tittle* of it perished.

Ver. 21 : ʼΗκούσατε· *Ye have heard.*] That is, ye have received it by tradition. אם שמעו אמרו להם *If*[1] *they have heard* [that is, *learned by tradition*], *they speak to them.* מפי השמועה למדו *They learnèd by hearing,* that is, by tradition ; a saying very frequent in Maimonides.

Ὅτι ἐρρέθη τοῖς ἀρχαίοις· *That it was said by them of old time.*] That is, "it is an old tradition." For the particular passages of the law which are here cited by our Saviour are not produced as the bare words of Moses, but as clothed in the Glosses of the Scribes ; which most plainly appears above the rest, ver. 43, and sufficiently in this first allegation, where those words, " Whosoever shall kill shall be guilty of the judgment," do hold out the false paint of tradition, and, as we observe in the following verses, such as misrepresents the law, and makes it of none effect. If it be asked, why Christ makes mention of " those of old time ?" it may be answered, that the memory of the ancienter Fathers of the Traditions was venerable among the people. Reverend was the name חסידים ראשונים of *the first good men,* and חכמים ראשונים the *first wise men.* Therefore Christ chose to confute their doctrines and Glosses, that he might more clearly prove the vanity of traditions, when he reproved their most famous men. But the sense which we have produced is plain, and without any difficulty ; as if he should say, " It is an old tradition which hath obtained for many ages."

Ver. 22 : Ἐγὼ δὲ λέγω ὑμῖν· *But I say unto you.*] ואני אומר׃ *But I say,* the words of one that refutes or determines a question, very frequently to be met with in the Hebrew writers. To this you may lay that of Isaiah, chap. ii. 3, " And he will teach us of his ways," &c. Where Kimchi writes thus,

---

[1] Sanhedr. cap. 11. hal. 1.

המורה הוא מלך המשיח *This teacher is king Messias.* And
that of Zechariah, chap. xi. 8 ; where this great Shepherd destroys "three evil shepherds," namely, the Pharisee, and the
Sadducee, and the Essene.

῞Οτι [m] πᾶς ὁ ὀργιζόμενος τῷ ἀδελφῷ αὐτοῦ εἰκῆ, &c. *That
whosoever is angry with his brother without a cause, &c.*] First
let us treat of the words, and then of the sentences.

With his brother :] The Jewish schools do thus distinguish
between a brother and a neighbour; that *a brother* signifies
an Israelite by nation and blood : *a neighbour*, an Israelite in
religion and worship, that is, a proselyte. The author of
Aruch, in the word בן ברית *A son of the covenant*, writes
thus ; " The sons of the covenant, these are Israel. And
when the Scripture saith, ' If any one's ox gore the ox of his
neighbour,' it excludes all the heathen, in that it saith, ' of
his neighbour.' " Maimonides writes thus ; " It [n] is all one
to kill an Israelite and a Canaanite servant : for both, the
punishment is death ; but an Israelite who shall kill גר תושב
a stranger-inhabitant shall not be punished with death, because it is said, ' Whosoever shall proudly rise up against his
neighbour to kill him,' Exod. xxi. 14 : and it is needless to
say he shall not be punished with death for killing a heathen."
Where this is to be noted, that heathens and stranger-in-
habitants, who were not admitted to perfect and complete
proselytism, were not qualified with the title of *neighbour*,
nor with any privileges.

But under the Gospel, where there is no distinction of nations or tribes, *brother* is taken in the same latitude as among
the Jews both *brother* and *neighbour* were ; that is, for all pro-
fessing the gospel : and is contradistinguished to the *heathen*,
1 Cor. v. 11, " If any one who is called a *brother :*" and Matt.
xviii. 15, " If thy *brother* sin against thee," &c., ver. 17, " If
he hear not the church, let him be a *heathen*."

But [o] *neighbour* is extended to all, even such as are strangers
to our religion : Luke x. 29, 30, &c.

He shall be guilty :] חייב or מחויב words signifying *guilt*
or *debt*, to be met with a thousand times in the Talmudists.
Isa. xxiv. 23 ; " They shall be gathered together, as captives

[m] *English folio edition*, vol. ii. p. 141.   [n] In רוצח c. 2.
[o] *Leusden's edition*, vol. ii. p. 286.

are gathered into prison." Where R. Solomon speaks thus, מחוייבי גהינום לגהינום, ῎Ενοχοι γέεννῃ εἰς γέενναν, *Guilty of hell unto hell:* which agrees with the last clause of this verse.

Of the council:] Τῷ συνεδρίῳ, *of the Sanhedrim:* that is, of the judgment, or tribunal of the magistrate. For that κρίσει, *judgment,* in the clause before, is to be referred to the *judgment of God,* will appear by what follows.

Ῥακὰ, *Raca.*] A word used by one that despiseth another in the highest scorn: very usual in the Hebrew writers, and very common in the mouth of the nation.

" One [p] returned to repentance: his wife said to him, ריקה *Raca,* if it be appointed you to repent, the very girdle wherewith you gird yourself shall not be your own."

" A [q] heathen said to an Israelite, Very suitable food is made ready for you at my house. What is it? saith the other. To whom he replied, Swine's flesh. *Raca* (saith the Jew), I must not eat of clean beasts with you."

" A [r] king's daughter was married to a certain dirty fellow. He commands her to stand by him as a mean servant, and to be his butler. To whom she said, *Raca,* I am a king's daughter."

" One [s] of the scholars of R. Jochanan made sport with the teaching of his master: but returning at last to a sober mind, Teach thou, O master, saith he, for thou art worthy to teach: for I have found and seen that which thou hast taught. To whom he replied, ריקה, *Raca,* thou hadst not believed, unless thou hadst seen."

" A [t] certain captain saluted a religious man praying in the way, but he saluted him not again: he waited till he had done his prayer, and saith to him, ריקה, *Raca,* it is written in your law," &c.

Εἰς τὴν γέενναν τοῦ πυρός· *Into hell-fire.*] The Jews do very usually express *hell,* or *the place of the damned,* by the word גהינום *Gehinnom,* which might be shown in infinite examples; the manner of speech being taken from the *valley of Hinnom,* a place infamous for foul idolatry committed there; for the howlings of infants roasted to Moloch; filth carried out

[p] Tanchum, fol. 5. col. 2.
[q] Id. fol. 18. col. 4.
[r] Midrash Tillin upon Psal. cxxxvii.
[s] Id. fol. 38. col. 4.
[t] Bab. Berac. fol. 32. 2.

thither ; and for a fire that always was burning, and so most
fit to represent the horror of hell.

" There [u] are three doors of Gehenna ; one in the wilderness, as it is written, ' They went down, and all that belonged
to them, alive into hell ' (Num. xvi. 33.) Another in the sea,
as it is written, ' Out of the belly of hell have I called ; thou
hast heard my voice' (Jonah ii. 2).   The third in Jerusalem,
as it is written, Thus saith the Lord, whose fire is in Sion,
and his furnace in Jerusalem,' Isa. xxxi. 9.   The tradition
of the school of R. Ismael ; 'Whose fire is in Sion,' this is the
gate of Gehenna."

The Chaldee paraphrast upon Isaiah, chap. xxxiii. 14,
גהינום יקידות עלם *Gehenna, eternal fire*, &c.   Γέεννα πυρὸς
αἰωνίου, *the Gehenna of eternal fire.*

We come now to the sentences and sense of the verse.
A threefold punishment is adjudged to a threefold wickedness. *Judgment* to him that is angry חנם, that is, *without
cause* [x]. *Judgment* also, and that by the Sanhedrim, to him
that calls *Raca*. *Judgment of hell* to him that calleth Μωρὲ,
Fool.

That which is here produced of the threefold Sanhedrim
among the Jews pleases me not, because, passing over other
reasons, mention of the Sanhedrim is made only in the middle
clause.

How the judgment in the first clause is to be distinguished
from the judgment of the Sanhedrim in the second, will very
easily appear from this Gloss and commentary of the Talmudists, ' Of not killing :" " He [y] is a manslayer, whosoever shall
strike his neighbour with a stone or iron, or thrust him into
the water, or fire, whence he cannot come out, so that he die,
he is guilty.   But if he shall thrust another into the water or
fire, whence he might come out, if he die, he is guiltless.   A
man sets a dog or serpent on another, he is guiltless." See
also the Babylonian Gemara there; "Whosoever [z] shall slay his
neighbour with his own hand, striking him with his sword, or
with a stone, so that he kills him ; or shall strangle or burn
him so that he die, in any manner whatsoever killing him in
his own person ; behold, such a one is to be put to death by

the Sanhedrim. But he that hires another by a reward to kill his neighbour, or who sends his servants, and they kill him; or he that thrusts him violently upon a lion, or upon some other beast, and the beast kill him; or he that kills himself, כל אחד מאילו שופך דמים *every one of these is a shedder of blood,* and the iniquity of manslaughter is in his hand, and he is liable to death לשמים, *by the hand of God;* but he is not to be punished with death by the Sanhedrim."

Behold a double manslayer! Behold a double judgment! Now let the words of our Saviour be applied to this Gloss of the ancients upon the law of murder : " Do ye hear," saith he, " what is said by the ancients, Whosoever shall kill, after what manner soever a man shall kill him, whether by the hand of one that he hath hired, or by his servants, or by setting a beast on him; he is guilty of the judgment of God, though not of the judgment of the Sanhedrim : and whosoever shall kill his neighbour by himself, none other interposing, this man is liable to the judgment of the Sanhedrim : but I say unto you, That whosoever is rashly angry with his brother, this man is liable to the judgment of God; and whosoever shall say to his brother, *Raca,* he is liable to the Sanhedrim."

These words of our Saviour, perhaps, we shall more truly understand [a] by comparing some more phrases and doctrines, very usual in the Jewish schools. Such as these, פטור מדיני אדם וחייב בדיני שמים *Absolved* [b] *from the judgment of men, but guilty in the judgment of Heaven,* that is, *of God.* מיתה ב״ד ומיתה בידי שמים *Death by the Sanhedrim, and death by the hand of Heaven.*

And in a word, כרת *cutting off,* speaks vengeance by the hand of God. They are very much deceived who understand כרת and כריתות *cutting off,* of which there is very frequent mention in the Holy Bible, concerning the *cutting-off* from the public assembly *by ecclesiastical censure,* when as it means nothing else than *cutting off by divine vengeance.* There is nothing more usual and common among the Hebrew canonists, than to adjudge very many transgressions to *cutting off,* in that worn phrase, אם or חייב על זדונו כרת

[a] *Leusden's edit.,* vol. ii. p. 287.   [b] Hieros. Bava Kama, fol. 5. 2.

מזיד חייב כרת " *If he shall do this out of presumption, he is guilty of cutting off;* but if he shall do it out of ignorance, he is bound for a sacrifice for sin." When they adjudge a thing or a guilty person to cutting off, they deliver and leave him to the judgment of God; nevertheless, a censure and punishment from the Sanhedrim sometimes is added, and sometimes not. Which might be illustrated by infinite examples, but we are afraid of being tedious. Let these two be enough on both sides.

I. Of mere delivering over to the judgment of God, without any punishment inflicted by the Sanhedrim, those words speak, which were lately cited, " He is absolved from the judgment of men, but liable to the judgment of Heaven."

II. Of the judgment of God and of the Sanhedrim joined together, these words in the same place speak: " If he that is made guilty by the Sanhedrim be bound to make restitution, Heaven [or God] doth not pardon him until he pay it." But he that bears a punishment laid on him by the Sanhedrim is absolved from cutting off. " All[c] persons guilty of cutting off, when they are beaten are absolved from their cutting off: as it is said, ' And thy brother become vile in thy sight.' When he shall be beaten, behold, he is thy brother."

Ἔνοχος εἰς γέενναν τοῦ πυρὸς, *Liable or guilty even to the hell-fire.* He had said κρίσει, guilty of *judgment,* and συνεδρίῳ, of *the council,* before; but now he saith εἰς γέενναν, *unto hell,* and that in a higher emphasis; as if he should have said, " Whosoever shall say to his brother, Μωρὲ, *Fool,* shall be guilty of judgment, even unto *the judgment of hell.*"

But what was there more grievous in the word *fool,* than in the word *Raca?* Let king Solomon be the interpreter, who everywhere by a *fool* understands a *wicked and reprobate* person; foolishness being opposed to spiritual wisdom. *Raca* denotes indeed *morosity,* and *lightness of manners and life:* but *fool* judgeth bitterly of the spiritual and eternal state, and decreeth a man to certain destruction. Let the judgings and censures of the scribes and Pharisees concerning the common people serve us instead of a lexicon. They did not only[d] suffer themselves to be styled חכמים *wise men,* but also arro-

[c] Bab. Megill. fol. 7. 2.   [d] *English folio edition,* vol. ii. p. 143.

gated it to themselves, as their merit and due. But what do
they say of the common people? "This people, that knoweth
not the law, is cursed," John vii. 49.

You have a form of speaking, not much unlike this which
is now under our hands : הקורא לחבירו עבד יהא בנדוי
*He[e] that calls his neighbour Servant, let him be in excom-
munication.* The Gloss is, "They therefore excommunicate him, because he vilified an Israelite: him, therefore, they
vilify in like manner."—ממזר סופג את הארבעים "If he
call him *bastard*, let him be punished with forty stripes.
רשע יורד עמו לחיו If *wicked man*, let it descend with him
into his life:" that is, according to the Gloss, "into misery
and penury."

After this manner, therefore, our Saviour suits a different
punishment to different sins by a most just parity, and a very
equal compensation: to unjust anger, the just anger and
judgment of God; to public reproach, a public trial; and
hell-fire to the censure that adjudgeth another thither.

Ver. 23 : Ὅτι ὁ ἀδελφός σου ἔχει τι κατὰ σοῦ, &c. *That thy
brother hath ought against thee, &c.*] The emphasis is chiefly
in the particle τι. For that which the Jews restrained only
to pecuniary damages, Christ extends to all offences against
our brother.

"He[f] that offers an oblation, not restoring that which he
had unjustly taken away, does not do that which is his duty."
And again; "He[g] that steals any thing from his neighbour,
yea, though it be but a farthing, and swears falsely, is bound
to restitution, meeting the wronged party half way." See
also Baal Turim upon Lev. vi.

אין מקריבין את האשם עד שיחזיר הגזלן את הקרן "An[h]
oblation is not offered for a sin, unless that which is [wrong-
fully] taken away, be first restored either to the owner or the
priest." In like manner, "He[i] that swears falsely, either of
the *Pruta* [*small money*], or what the *Pruta* is worth, is
bound to inquire after the owner, even as far as the islands
in the sea, and to make restitution."

Observe, how provision is here made for pecuniary damages

[e] Bab. Kiddushin, fol. 28. 1.   [g] Hal. 5.
Chetubh. fol. 50. 1. and elsewhere.   [h] Maimon. in Gezelah, cap. 8.
[f] Bava Kama, cap. 9. hal. 12.   [i] Cap. 7.

only and bare restitution, which might be done without a charitable mind and a brotherly heart. But Christ urgeth charity, reconciliation of mind, and a pure desire of reunion with our offended brother; and that not only in money matters, but in any other, and for whatever cause, wherein our neighbour complains that he is grieved.

Ver. 24 : Ἄφες ἐκεῖ τὸ δῶρόν σου ἔμπροσθεν τοῦ θυσιαστηρίου· *Leave[k] there thy gift before the altar.*] This business was altogether unusual in gifts offered at the altar, in such a cause. We read, indeed, of the drink-offering, delayed after the sacrifice was offered: " For[l] the wise men say, That a man is not held in his sin, when the drink-offering is put off by some delay; because one may offer his sacrifice to-day, but his drink-offering twenty days hence." We read also that the oblation of a sacrifice presented even at the altar, in some cases hath not only been delayed, but the sacrifice itself hath been rejected; that is, if, in that instant, discovery was made, in sacrificing the beast, either of a blemish, or of somewhat else, whereby it became an illegal sacrifice; or if some uncleanness or other cause appeared in the offerer, whereby he was rendered unfit for the present to offer a gift. Of which things, causing the oblation of the sacrifice already presented at the altar to be deferred, the Hebrew lawyers speak much. But among those things we do not meet at all with this whereof our Saviour is here speaking: so that he seems to enjoin some new matter,—and not new alone, but seemingly impossible. For the offended brother might perhaps be absent in the furthest parts of the land of Israel, so that he could not be spoke with, and his pardon asked in very many days after: and what shall become of the beast in the mean time, which is left at the altar? It is a wonder indeed that our Saviour, treating of the worship at the altar, should prescribe such a duty, which was both unusual (in such a case) and next to impossible. But it is answered:—

I. It was a custom and a law among the Jews, that the sacrifices of particular men should not presently, as soon as they were due, be brought to the altar, but that they should be reserved to the feast next following, whatsoever that were, whether the Passover, or Pentecost, or Tabernacles, to be

[k] *Leusden's edit.*, vol. ii. p. 288. [l] Tosaphta ad Corbanoth, cap. 5.

then offered. "Teeming[m] women, women that have the gonorrhœa, and men that have the gonorrhœa, reserve their pigeons until they go up to the feast."—"The oblations[n] which were devoted before the feast shall be offered at the feast: for it is said, These things shall ye do in their solemnities," &c. But now all the Israelites were present at the feasts; and any brother, against whom one had sinned, was not then far off from the altar. Unto which time and custom of the nation it is equal to think Christ alluded.

II. He[o] does silently chastise the curiosity used in deferring of a sacrifice brought about lesser matters, when this that was greater was unregarded. And he teacheth, that God is worshipped in vain without true charity to our brother. The same also, in effect, do the Gemarists[p] confess.

Ver. 25: Ἕως ὅτου εἶ ἐν τῇ ὁδῷ μετ᾿ αὐτοῦ· *Whilst thou art in the way with him.*] That is, "while thou goest with him *to the magistrate,*" ἐπ᾿ ἄρχοντα, Luke xii. 58; where there is a clear distinction between ἄρχοντα, *the magistrate,* and κριτὴν, *the judge:* so that by ἄρχοντα, *magistrate,* or *ruler,* one may understand the judges in the lower Sanhedrims; by κριτὴν, *judge,* the judges in the highest. That allusion is here made to contentions about money matters, sufficiently appears from the following words, ver. 26; "Thou shalt by no means come out of prison till thou hast paid the uttermost farthing." Now[q] it was the business of the bench, that consisted of three men, to judge of such matters.

The words, therefore, of the verse have this sense : ' Does your neighbour accuse you of some damage, or of money that is due to him? and are ye now going in the way to the bench of three to commence the suit? compound with your adversary, lest he compel you to some higher tribunal, where your danger will be greater.' "For[r] if the lender say to the debtor, ' Let us go, that judgment may be had of our case from the chief Sanhedrim,' they force the debtor to go up thence with him. In like manner, if any accuse another of something taken away from him, or of some damage done

---

[m] Bab. Sanhedr. fol. 11. 1.
[n] Hieros. Rosh. Hashanah, fol. 56. 2.
[o] *English folio edit.*, vol. ii. p. 144.
[p] Bab. Joma, fol. 87. 1.
[q] Sanhedr. cap. 1. hal. 1.
[r] Maimon. in Sanhedr. cap. 6.

him, and he that is the accuser will have the higher Sanhe‐
drim to judge of the suit; they force the debtor to go up
thence with him.   And so it is done with all other things of
that nature.

Before, Christ had argued from *piety*, that men should seek
to be reconciled; now he argues from *prudence*, and an honest
care of a man's self.

Καὶ ὁ κριτής σε παραδῷ τῷ ὑπηρέτῃ· *And the judge deliver*
thee to the officer.] A word answering to שׁוֹטֵר or סרדיוט
or מנגדנא *an executioner, a whipper*, among the Rabbins.
שׁוֹפְטִים וְשׁוֹטְרִים תִּתֶּן־לְךָ בְּכָל־שְׁעָרֶיךָ *Judges and officers*
shalt thou make thee in all thy gates, Deut. xvi. 18.   שׁוֹטְרִים
" are[s] vergers and scourge-bearers [*executioners*] who stand
before the judges.   These go through the lanes and streets
and inns, and take care about weights and measures; and
scourge those that do amiss.   But all their business is by the
order of the judges.   Whomsoever they see doing evil, they
bring before the judges," &c.   And אדם יוצא לשוק יהי דומה
בעיניו כמו שנמסר לסרדיוט *Whosoever[t] goes out into the street,*
let him reckon concerning himself, as if he were already delivered
over to the officer; that is, as the Gloss hath it, " Contentions
and contentious men will there be met with Gentiles and
Israelites: so that let him reckon concerning himself, as
though he were already delivered over to the officer, ready
to lead him away before the judges."   The Gloss upon Babyl.
Joma[u] writes thus; מנגדנא " is the executioner of the San‐
hedrim, whose office is to whip."

Ver. 26: Κοδράντην· *Farthing*.] According to the Jerusa‐
lem Talmud, it is קרדיונטס *Kordiontes;* according to the Ba‐
bylonian, קונטריק *Kontrik*.   For thus they write:

שני איסרין פונדיון : " Two[x] *assars* make a *pondion*[y].
שני מסומסין איסר : Two *semisses* make an *assar*.
שני קרדיונטס מסומס : Two *farthings* a *semissis*.
ב״ פרוטות קרדיונטס : Two *prutahs* a *farthing*.
פונדיונין שני איסרין : A[z] *pondion* is in value two *assars*.
איסר שני מסומסין : An *assar* is two *semisses*.

---

[s] Maimon. in Sanhedr. cap. i.   [y] *Leusden's edition*, vol. ii. p. 289.
[t] Bab. Schabb. fol. 32. 1.   [z] Bab. Kiddush. cap. i. Alphesius,
[u] Fol. 15. 1.   ibid. fol. 625. 2.
[x] Hieros. Kiddushin, fol. 58. 4.

מסמס שני קונטריקין : A *semissis* is two *farthings*.

קונטריק שני פרוטות: A *kontric*, or a *farthing*, is two *prutahs*."

That which is here said by the Jerusalem Talmud, שני פרוטות קרדיונטס *Two prutahs make a farthing*, is the very same thing that is said, Mark xii. 42, Λεπτὰ δύο, ὅ ἐστι κοδράντης, *Two mites, which make a farthing*. A *prutah* was the very least piece among coins. So Maimonides[a], אין פחות משוה פרוטה ממון *That which is not worth a prutah, is*[b] *not to be reckoned among riches*. Hence are those numberless passages in the Talmudic Pandects relating to the prutah: "He[c] that steals less than a *prutah* is not bound to pay five-fold." "No[d] land is bought for a price less than a *prutah*," that is, given as an earnest.

You have the value of these coins in the same Maimonides: "Selaa (saith he[e]) is in value four-pence: a penny, six meahs. Now a meah, in the days of Moses our master, was called a gerah; it contains two pondions; a pondion, two assars; and a prutah is the eighth part of an assar. The weight of a meah, which is also called a gerah, is sixteen barleycorns. And the weight of an assar is four barleycorns. And the weight of a prutah is half a barleycorn."

Luke hath ἔσχατον λεπτὸν, *the last mite*, chap. xii. 59; that is, *the last prutah*, which "משמנה באיסר האטלקי א' *was*[f] *the eighth part of the Italian assarius*. Therefore, κοδρὰνς, *a farthing*, was so called, not that it was the fourth part of a *penny*, but the fourth part of an *assar*; which how very small a part of a penny it was, we may observe by those things that are said by both Gemaras in the place before cited.

שש מעה כסף דינר : "Six silver *meahs* make a *penny*.

מעה שני פונדיונין: A *meah* is worth two *pondions*.

פונדיון שני איסרין: A *pondion* is worth two *assars*."

Let this be noted by the way; מעה a *meah*, which, as Maimonides before testifies, was anciently called a *gerah*, was also commonly called זוז *zuz*, in the Talmudists. For as it is said here, שש מעה כסף דינר *six meahs of silver make a penny*, so in Rambam, דינר ו' זוזים" *a*[g] *penny contains six zuzim*.

[a] Gezelah, c. 7.
[b] *English folio edit.*, vol. ii. p.145.
[c] Gezelah, c. 7.
[d] Id. in Mecherah, cap. 1, &c.

[e] In Tract. Shekalim, cap. 1.
[f] Kiddush. cap. 1. hal. 1.
[g] In Peah, cap. ult. hal. 7.

The *prutah*, as it was the least piece of money among the
Jews, so it seems to have been a coin merely Jewish, not
Roman. For although the Jews, being subjects to the Romans, used Roman money, and thence, as our Saviour argues,
confessed their subjection to the Romans; yet they were permitted to use their own money, which appears by the common use of the shekels and half-shekels among them : with
good reason, therefore, one may hold the κοδράντης, *the farthing*, was the least Roman coin, and the λεπτὸν, *the prutah*,
the least Jewish. Whilst our Saviour mentions both, he is
not inconstant to his own speech, but speaks more to the
capacity of all.

Ver. 27: Ἠκούσατε, ὅτι ἐρρέθη τοῖς ἀρχαίοις, Οὐ μοιχεύσεις· *Ye
have heard, that it hath been said by them of old time, Thou shalt
not commit adultery.*] He citeth not the command or text of
Moses, as barely delivered by Moses, but as deformed by
those of old time with such a gloss as almost evacuated all
the force of the command; for they interpreted it of the act
of adultery only, and that with a married woman. So the
enumeration of the six hundred and thirteen precepts of the
law, and that, Exod. xx. 14, 'Thou shalt not commit adultery,'
hath these words, "This is the thirty-fifth precept of the law,
namely, That no man lie with another man's wife."

Ver. 28: Πᾶς ὁ βλέπων γυναῖκα πρὸς τὸ ἐπιθυμῆσαι, &c.
Whosoever looketh upon a woman to lust after her, &c.] " He[h]
that looketh upon a woman's heel, is as if he looked upon
her belly : and he that looks upon her belly, is as if he lay
with her." And yet, זו דרכי של ר' "ג' "להסתכל בנשים
It[i] was Rabban Gamaliel's custom to look upon women. And
in the other Talmud; " He[j] that looks upon the little finger
of a woman, is as if he looked upon her privy parts." And
yet " Rabh Gidal[k] and R. Jochanan were wont to sit at the
place of dipping, where the women were washed ; and when
they were admonished by some of the danger of lascivi-
ness, R. Jochanan answered, 'I am of the seed of Joseph, over
whom an evil affection could not rule.' "

Ver. 30: Εἰ ἡ δεξιά σου χεὶρ σκανδαλίζει σε, ἔκκοψον αὐτήν·
If thy right hand offend thee, cut it off.] See here Babyl.

---

[h] Hieros. Challah, fol. 58. 3.   [j] Bab. Berac. fol. 24. 8.
[i] Id. Berac. fol. 12. 3.   [k] Ibid. fol. 20. 1.

Niddah, fol. 13, quite through. Among other things, R.
Tarphon saith, "Whosoever brings his hand to his modest
parts, let his hand be cut off unto his navel." And a little
after; "It is better that his belly should be cleft in two, than
that he should descend into the well of corruption." The
discourse is of moving the hand to the privy member, that [1],
by the handling it, it might be known whether the party had
the gonorrhœa, or no : and [m] yet they adjudge never so little
handling it to cutting off the hand. Read the place, if you
have leisure.

Ver. 31 : ῞Ος ἀν ἀπολύσῃ τὴν γυναῖκα, δότω αὐτῇ ἀποστά-
σιον· *Whosoever putteth away his wife, let him give her a bill
of divorcement.*] Notice is to be taken how our Saviour passeth
into these words, namely, by using the particle δὲ, *but.* Ἐρρέθη δὲ, "*But* it hath been said." This particle hath this
emphasis in this place, that it whispers a silent objection,
which is answered in the following verse. Christ had said,
"Whosoever looks upon a woman to lust after her hath
committed adultery already:" but the Jewish lawyers said,
"If any one sees a woman which he is delighted withal above
his wife, let him dismiss his wife and marry her."

Among the chapters of Talmudical doctrine, we meet with
none concerning which it is treated more largely, and more
to a punctilio, than of divorces : and yet there the chief care
is not so much of a just cause of it as of the manner and form
of doing it. To him that turns over the book *Gittin* (as also,
indeed, the whole *Seder Nashim*, that part of the Talmud
that treats of women), the diligence of the Masters about
this matter will appear such that they seem to have dwelt,
not without some complacency, upon this article above all
others.

God, indeed, granted to that nation a law concerning divorces, Deut. xxiv. 1, permitted only "for the hardness of
their hearts," Matt. xix. 8 : in which permission, nevertheless, they boast, as though it were indulged them by mere
privilege. When God had established that fatal law of punishing adultery by death (Deut. xxii.), for the terror of
the people, and for their avoiding of that sin ; the same merciful God foreseeing also how hard (occasion being taken

[1] *Leusden's edition*, vol. ii. p. 290.   [m] *English folio edit.*, vol. ii. p. 146.

from this law) the issue of this might be to the women, by
reason of the roughness of the men ; lusting, perhaps, after
other women, and loathing their own wives ; he more gra-
ciously provided against such kind of wife-killing by a law,
mitigating the former, and allowed the putting away a wife
in the same case, concerning which that fatal law was given ;
namely, in the case of adultery.   So that that law of divorce,
in the exhibition of it, implied their hearts to be hard ; and,
in the use of it, they shewed them to be carnal.   And yet hear
them thus boasting of that law : " The [n] Lord of Israel saith,
כִּי שָׂנֵא שַׁלַּח *That he hateth putting away,* Mal. ii. 16.   Through
the whole chapter, saith R. Chananiah in the name of R. Phineas, he is called the Lord of *Hosts :* but here, of *Israel,* that
it might appear that God subscribed not his name to divorces,
but only among the Israelites.   As if he should say, ' To the
Israelites I have granted the putting away of wives ; to the
Gentiles I have not granted it.'   R. Chaijah Rabbah saith,
Divorces are not granted to the nations of the world."

Some of them interpreted this law of Moses (as by right
they ought to interpret it), of the case of adultery only.   " The[o]
school of Shammai said, A wife is not to be divorced, unless
for filthiness [that is, adultery] only, because it is said, כִּי
מָצָא בָהּ עֶרְוַת דָּבָר *Because he hath found filthy nakedness in
her,"* that is, adultery.

" Rabh Papa said[p], If he find not adultery in her, what
then ?   Rabba answered, When the merciful God revealed concerning him that corrupted a maid, that it was not lawful for
him to put her away in his whole life (Deut. xxii. 29), you are
thence taught concerning the matter propounded, that it is
not lawful to put her away, if he shall not find filthiness in his
wife."

With the like honesty have some commented upon those
words cited out of the prophet, כִּי שָׂנֵא שַׁלַּח *For he hateth
putting away.*   " R. Jochanan saith[q], The putting away of a
wife is odious."   Which others also have granted, indeed, of
the first wife, but not of those that a man took to himself
over and above.   For this is approved among them for a canon,

[n] Hieros. in Kiddushin, fol. 58. 3.   [p] Gemara, ib.
[o] Gittin, cap. 9. hal. ult.   [q] Ibid.

"Let[r] no man put away his first wife unless for adultery."
And " R. Eliezer saith[s], For the divorcing of the first wife,
even the altar itself sheds tears." Which Gloss they fetch
from thence, where it is said, " Let no man deal treacherously
towards the wife of his youth;" Mal. ii. 15.

The Jews used polygamy, and the divorcing of their wives,
with one and the same license : and this, that they might
have change, and all for the sake of lust. " It is lawful (say
they[t]) to have many wives together, even as many as you will :
but our wise men have decreed, That no man have above four
wives." But they restrained this, not so much out of some
principles of chastity, as that lest a man, being burdened with
many wives, might not be able to afford them food and clothing,
and due benevolence : for thus they comment concerning this
bridle of polygamy.

For what causes they put away their wives there is no
need to inquire; for this they did for any cause of their own
free will.

I. " It is commanded to divorce a wife that is not of good
behaviour, and who is not modest as becomes a daughter of
Israel." So they speak in Maimonides and Gittin in the place
above[u] specified : where this also is added in the Gemarists :
" R. Meir saith, As men have their pleasures concerning their
meat and their drink, so also concerning their wives. This
man takes out a fly found in his cup, and yet will not drink :
after such a manner did Papus Ben Judah carry himself :
who, as often as he went forth, bolted the doors and shut in
his wife. Another takes out a fly found in his cup, and drinks
up his cup ; that he doth, who sees his wife talking freely with
her neighbours and kinsfolk, and yet allows of it. And there
is another, who, if he find a fly in his basket, eats it : and
this is the part of an evil man, who sees his wife going out,
without a veil upon her head, and with a bare neck, and sees
her washing[v] in the baths, where men are wont to wash, and
yet cares not for it ; whereas by the law he is bound to put
her away."

---

[r] Maimon. in Gerushin, cap. 10.

[s] Gittin, in the place above.

[t] Maimon. in אישות cap. 10. 14.

[u] *English folio edition*, vol. ii. p.
147.

[v] *Leusden's edition*, vol. ii. p. 291.

II. " If[x] any man hate his wife, let him put her away :"
excepting only that wife that he first married. In like manner, R. Judah thus interprets that of the prophet, כִּי שָׂנֵא
שַׁלַּח *If he hate her, let him put her away.* Which sense some
versions, dangerously enough, have followed. R. Solomon ex-
presses the sense of that place thus: " It is commanded to
put away one's wife, if she obtain not favour in the eyes of
her husband."

III. " The[y] school of Hillel saith, If the wife cook her husband's food illy, by over-salting or over-roasting it, she is to
be put away."

IV. Yea, " If, by any stroke from the hand of God, she become dumb or sottish," &c.

V. But not to relate all the things for which they pronounce a wife to be divorced (among which they produce
some things that modesty allows not to be repeated), let it
be enough to mention that of R. Akibah instead of all : " R.
Akibah said[z], If any man sees a woman handsomer than his
own wife, he may put her away; because it is said, ' If she
find not favour in his eyes.' "

Ἀποστάσιον· *Bill of divorce.*] And βιβλίον ἀποστασίου, *A bill
of divorce*, Matt. xix. 7 ; and in the Septuagint, Deut. xxiv. 1.
Of which Beza thus; " This bill may seem to be called ἀπο-
στάσιον [as much as, *departing away*], not in respect of the
wife put away, as of the husband departing away from his
wife." Something hard, and diametrically contrary to the
canonical doctrine of the Jews : for thus they write, " It[a] is
written in the bill, Behold, thou art put away; Behold, thou
art thrust away, &c. But if he writes, I am not thy husband, or, I am not thy spouse, &c.; it is not a just bill: for
it is said, He shall put *her* away, not, He shall put *himself*
away."

This bill is called by the Jews ספר כריתות *a bill of cutting
off,* and ספר תירוכין *a bill of expulsion,* and גט *an instrument,*
and גט פוטורין *an instrument of dismission,* and איגרת שבוקין
letters of forsaking, &c.

---

[x] Maimonides in the place above.
[y] Gittin, in the place above; and
R. Sol. and R. Nissin there.

[z] Misna, ult. in Gittin, cap. 9.
[a] Maimon. in Gerushin, cap. 1.

I. A wife might not be put away, unless a bill of divorce were given. "Therefore it is called (saith Baal Turim) ספר כריתות *A bill of cutting off*, because there is nothing else that cuts her off from the husband. For although a wife were obtained three ways" [of which see the Talmud[b]], "yet there was no other way of dismissing her, besides a bill of divorce[c]."

II. "A wife was not put away, unless the husband were freely willing; for if he were unwilling, it was not a divorce: but whether the wife were willing or unwilling, she was to be divorced, if her husband would[d]."

III. "A[e] *bill of divorce* was written in twelve lines, neither more nor less." R. Mordecai gives the reason of this number, in these words; "Let[f] him that writes a *bill of divorce* comprise it in twelve lines, according to the value of the number of the letters in the word גט *Get*. But Rabh Saadias interprets, that the *bill of divorce* should be written with the same number of lines wherein the books of the law are separated. For four lines come between the Book of Genesis and the Book of Exodus; four between the Book of Exodus and the Book of Leviticus; four between the Book of Leviticus and the Book of Numbers. But the four between the Book of Numbers and Deuteronomy are not reckoned, because that book is only a repetition of the law," &c.

IV. You have the copy of a bill of divorce in Alphesius upon *Gittin*, in this form:

ספר כריתות

בכך בשבת בכך וכך לירח פלוני בשנת כך וכך לבריאת
עולם במניינא דרגילנא למימני ביה בדוכתא פלוני איך אני
פלוני בר פלוני וכל שום דאית ליה דממתא פלוני צביתי
ברעות נפשי בדלא אניסנא ופטרית ושבקית ותריכית יתיכי
ליכי אנת פלונית בת פלוני וכל שום דאית ליכי דממתא
פלונית דהוית אינתתי מן קדמא דנא וכדו תדוכית יתיכי ליכי
אנת פלניתא בת פלוני וכל שום דאית ליכי דממתא פלוני
דיתהוויין רשאה ושלטאה בנפשיכי למהך להתנסבא לכל גבר

---

[b] Kiddush. cap. 1. hal. 1.
[c] Baal Turim, upon Deut. xxiv.
[d] Maimon. in Gerushin, cap. 1.

[e] Rashba in Tikkun Get, at the end of Gittin, in Alphes.
[f] Ch. 1. upon Tract. Gittin.

דתצתבייין ואינש לא ימחה בידיכי מן יומא דנן ולעלם והרי
את מותרת לכל אדם ודן די יהוי ליכי מינאי ספר תירוכין
ונט פיטורין ואגרת שבוקין כדת משה וישראל :

ראובן בן יעקב עד :
אלעזר בן גלעד עד :

A Bill of Divorce.

" On the day of the week *N.*, of the month of *N.*, of the year of
the world's creation *N.*, according to the computation by which we
are wont to reckon in the province *N.* ; I, *N.*, the son of *N.*, and
by what name soever I am called, of the city *N.*, with the greatest
consent of my mind, and without any compulsion urging me, have
put away, dismissed, and expelled thee ; thee, I [g] say, *N.*, the
daughter of *N.*, by what name soever thou art called, of the city
N., who heretofore wert my wife.   But now I have dismissed thee,
—thee, I say, *N.*, the daughter of *N.*, by what name soever thou
art called, of the city *N.*   So that thou art free, and in thine own
power, to marry whosoever shall please thee ; and let no man hinder
thee, from this day forward even for ever.   Thou art free, therefore,
for any man.   And let this be to thee a bill of rejection from me,
letters of divorce, and a schedule of expulsion [h], according to the law
of Moses and Israel.

REUBEN the son of Jacob witness.

ELIEZER the son of Gilead witness."

See also this form varied in some few words in Maimonides [i].

V. This bill, being confirmed with the husband's seal, and
the subscription of witnesses, was to be delivered into the hand
of the wife, either by the husband himself, or by some other
deputed by him for this office : or the wife might depute somebody to receive it in her stead.

VI. It was not to be delivered to the wife, but in the presence of two, who might read the bill both before it was given
into the hand of the wife and after : and when it was given,
the husband, if present, said thus, " Behold, this is a bill of
divorce to you."

[g] *English folio edition*, vol. ii. p. 148.

[h] *Leusden's edition*, vol. ii. p. 292.

[i] In Gerushin, fol. 273. 2.

VII. The wife, thus dismissed, might, if she pleased, bring this bill to the Sanhedrim, where it was enrolled among the records, if she desired it, in memory of the thing. The dismissed person likewise might marry whom she would : if the husband had not put some stop in the bill, by some clause forbidding it.

Ver. 32 : ʽΟς ἂν ἀπολύσῃ τὴν γυναῖκα αὐτοῦ, &c. *Whosoever shall put away his wife, &c.*] 1. Our Saviour does not abrogate Moses's permission of divorces, but tolerates it, yet keeping it within the Mosaic bounds, that is, in the case of adultery, condemning that liberty in the Jewish canons, which allowed it for any cause.

II. Divorce was not commanded in the case of adultery, but permitted. Israelites were compelled, sometimes even by whipping, to put away their wives, as appears in Maimonides[k]. But our Saviour, even in the case of adultery, does not impose a compulsion to divorce, but indulgeth a license to do it.

III. " He that puts away his wife without the cause of fornication makes her commit adultery :" that is, if she commits adultery : or although she commit not adultery in act, yet he is guilty of all the lustful motions of her that is put away; for he that lustfully desires, is said " to commit adultery," ver. 28.

Ver. 33 : Ἐρρέθη τοῖς ἀρχαίοις, Οὐκ ἐπιορκήσεις, &c. *It hath been said by them of old time, Thou shalt not forswear thyself, &c.*] The law forbids perjury, Levit. xix. 12, &c. To which the Fathers of the Traditions reduced the whole sin of swearing, little caring for a rash oath. In this chapter of oaths they doubly sinned :

I. That they were nothing at all solicitous about an oath, so that what was sworn were not false. They do but little trouble themselves, what, how, how often, how rashly, you swear, so that what you swear be true.

In the Talmudic tract שבועות *Shevuoth*, and in like manner in Maimonides, oaths are distributed into these four ranks :

First, שבועת ביטוי *A promissory oath :* when a man swore

[k] In Gerushin, cap. 2.

that he would do, or not do, this or that, &c. And this was one of the שבועות שתים שהן ארבע *twofold oaths, which were also fourfold;* that is, a negative or affirmative oath; and again, a negative or affirmative oath concerning something past, or a negative or affirmative oath concerning something to come: namely, when any one swears that he hath done this or that, or not done it; or that he will do this or that, or that he will not do it. "Whosoever, therefore, swears any of these four ways, and the thing is not as he swears, (for example, that he hath not cast a stone into the sea, when he hath cast it; that he hath cast it, when he hath not; that he will not eat, and yet eats; that he will eat, and yet eateth not,) behold, this is a false oath, or perjury[1]."

"Whosoever[m] swears that he will not eat, and yet eats some things which are not sufficiently fit to be eaten, this man is not guilty."

Secondly[n], שבועת שוא *A vain* or *a rash oath.* This also is fourfold, but not in the same manner as the former: 1. When they asserted that with an oath which was contrary to most known truth; as, "If he should swear a man were a woman, a stone-pillar to be a pillar of gold," &c.; or when any swore that was or was not, which was altogether impossible; as, "that he saw a camel flying in the air." 2. When one asserted that by an oath, concerning which there was no reason that any should doubt. For example, that "Heaven is heaven, a stone is a stone," &c. 3. When a man swore that he would do that which was altogether impossible; namely, "that he would not sleep for three days and three nights; that he would taste nothing for a full week," &c. 4. When any swore that he would abstain from that which was commanded; as, "that he would not wear phylacteries," &c. These very examples are brought in the places alleged.

Thirdly, שבועת פקדון *An oath concerning something left in trust:* namely, when any swore concerning something left in trust with him, that it was stolen or broke or lost, and not embezzled by him, &c.

---

[1] Maimon. in Shevuoth, c. 1. [m] Talmud in Shevuoth, c. 3.
[n] *English folio edition*, vol. ii. p. 149.

Fourthly, שבועת עדות *A testimonial oath,* before a judge or magistrate.

In three of these kinds of swearing, care is taken only concerning the truth of the thing sworn, not of the vanity of swearing.

They seemed, indeed, to make some provision against a vain and rash oath : namely, 1. That he be beaten, who so[o] swears, and become cursed : which Maimonides hints in the twelfth chapter of the tract alleged : with whom the Jerusalem Gemarists do agree ; " He[p] that swears two is two, let him be beaten for his vain oath." 2. They also added terror to it from fearful examples, such as that is in the very same place. בד בוליות היו בדרום : " *There were twenty-four assemblies in the south,* and they were all destroyed for a vain oath." And in the same tract[q], a woman buried her son for an oath, &c. Yet they concluded vain oaths in so narrow a circle, that a man might swear a hundred thousand times, and yet not come within the limits of the caution concerning vain swearing.

II. It was customary and usual among them to swear by the creatures ; " If[r] any swear by heaven, by earth, by the sun, &c. although the mind of the swearer be under these words to swear by Him who created them, yet this is not an oath. Or if any swear by some of the prophets, or by some of the books of the Scripture, although the sense of the swearer be to swear by Him that sent that prophet, or that gave that book, nevertheless this is not an oath."

" If[s] any adjure another by heaven or earth, he is not guilty."

They[t] swore by Heaven. השמים כן הוא *By Heaven so it is.*

They swore by the Temple. " When[u] turtles and young pigeons were sometime sold at Jerusalem for a penny of gold, Rabban Simeon Ben Gamaliel said, המעון הזה *By this habitation* [that is, *by this Temple*] I will not rest this night, unless they be sold for a penny of silver."

---

[o] *Leusden's edition,* vol. ii. p. 293.
[p] Shevuoth, fol. 34. 4.
[q] Fol. 37. 1.
[r] Maimonid. in the place above, cap. 12.

[s] Talmud in the place above, cap. 4.
[t] Bab. Berac. fol. 55.
[u] Cherithuth, cap. 1. hal. 7.

"R. Zechariah[x] Ben Ketsab said, הזה המעון *By this
Temple*, the hand of the woman departed not out of my
hand." "R. Jochanan[y] said, היכלא *By the Temple*, it is in
our hand," &c.

"Bava Ben Buta[z] swore by the Temple in the end of the
tract Cherithuth, and Rabban Simeon Ben Gamaliel in the
beginning; וזה מנהג בישראל *And so was the custom in
Israel*." Note this, "so was the custom."

They swore by the city Jerusalem. "R. Judah saith[a],
He that saith, ' By Jerusalem,' saith nothing, unless with an
intent purpose he shall vow towards Jerusalem." Where,
also, after two lines coming between those forms of swearing
and vowing are added, ירושלם לירושלם בירושלם היכל
להיכל בהיכל: *Jerusalem, for Jerusalem, by Jerusalem.
The Temple, for the Temple, by the Temple*. The altar, for
the altar, by the altar. The lamb, for the lamb, by the
lamb. The chambers of the Temple, for the chambers of
the Temple, by the chambers of the Temple. The wood,
for the wood, by the wood. The sacrifices on fire, for the
sacrifices on fire, by the sacrifices on fire. The dishes, for
the dishes, by the dishes. By all these things, that I will do
this to you."

They swore by their own heads. "One[b] is bound to swear
to his neighbour, and he saith, דור לי בחיי ראשך *Vow* (or
swear) *to me by the life of thy head*," &c.

Ver. 34: Μὴ ὀμόσαι ὅλως· *Swear not at all*.] In the tract
Demai[c] are some rules prescribed to a religious man: among
others, *That he be not too much in swearing and laughing*,
שלא יהא פרוץ בנדרים ובשחוק. Where the Gloss of R.
Solomon is this; פרוץ בנדרים "means this, Be not *much in
oaths*, although one should swear concerning things that are
true: for in much swearing it is impossible not to profane."
Our Saviour, with good reason, binds his followers with a
straiter bond, permitting no place at all for a voluntary and
arbitrary oath. The sense of these words goes in the middle
way, between the Jew, who allowed some place for an arbi-

---

[x] Chetubboth, cap. 3. et Tosapht.
ibid.
[y] Bab. Kiddushin, fol. 71. 1.
[z] Juchas. fol. 56. col. 1.

[a] Tosapht. ad Nedarim, cap. 1.
[b] Sanhedr. cap. 3. hal. 2.
[c] Cap. 2. halac. 3.

trary oath; and the Anabaptist, who allows none for a necessary one.

Ver. 36[d]: Οὐ δύνασαι μίαν τρίχα λευκὴν ἢ μέλαιναν ποιῆσαι·
Thou canst not make one hair white or black.] That is, Thou
canst not put on gray hairs, or lay them aside.

Ver. 37 : Ἔστω ὁ λόγος ὑμῶν, Ναὶ, ναί· Οὐ, οὔ· *Let your
communication be, Yea, yea ; nay, nay.*] In Hebrew, הֵן הֵן
לֹא לֹא מַשָּׂאָן וּמַתָּנָן שֶׁל תַּלְמִידֵי חֲכָמִים *Giving*[e] *and receiving* [that is, *business*] *among the disciples of the wise men,*
בֶּאֱמֶת וּבֶאֱמוּנָה אָמַר עַל לֹא לֹא וְעַל הֵן הֵן *Let it be in
truth and faith, by saying, Yes, yes ; No, no :* or, according
to the very words, *concerning Yes, yes ; concerning No, no.*

"If[f] it be said to a lunatic, Shall we write a bill of divorce for your wife? and he nod with his head, they try
thrice; and if he answer עַל לֹא לֹא וְעַל הֵן הֵן *to No, no ;
and to Yes, yes ;* they write it, and give it to his wife."

Ver. 38 : Ἠκούσατε ὅτι ἐρρέθη, Ὀφθαλμὸν ἀντὶ ὀφθαλμοῦ, &c.
Ye have heard that it hath been said, An eye for an eye, &c.]
This law he also cites, as clothed in the Gloss of the scribes,
and now received in the Jewish schools. But they resolved
the law[g] not into a just retaliation, but into a pecuniary compensation.

"Does[h] any cut off the hand or foot of his neighbour?
They value this according to the example of selling a servant; computing at what price he would be sold before he
was maimed, and for how much less now he is maimed. And
how much of the price is diminished, so much is to be paid
to the maimed person, as it is said, 'An eye for an eye,' &c.
We have received by tradition, that this is to be understood
of pecuniary satisfaction. But whereas it is said in the law,
'If a man cause a blemish in his neighbour, the same shall be
done to him' [Lev. xxiv. 19]; it means not that he should
be maimed, as he hath maimed another; but when he deserveth maiming, he deserveth to pay the damage to the
person maimed." They seemed, out of very great charity,
to soften that severe law to themselves, when, nevertheless,

---

[d] *English folio edition*, vol. ii. p.
150.
[e] Maimon. in Peah, cap. 5.
[f] Gittin, cap. 7. hal. 1.

[g] *Leusden's edit.*, vol. ii. p. 294.
[h] Bava Kama, cap. 8. et Maimon.
in חוֹבֵל וּמַזִּיק cap. 1.

in the mean time, little care was taken of lively charity,
and of the forgiving an offence,—an open door being still
left them to exaction and revenge, which will appear in what
follows.

Ver. 39 : Ὅστις σε ῥαπίσει ἐπὶ τὴν δεξιάν σου σιαγόνα· *Whosoever shall smite thee on thy right cheek.*] That the doctrine of
Christ may here more clearly shine out, let the Jewish doctrine be set against it; to which he opposeth his.

" Does [i] any one give his neighbour a box on the ear? let
him give him a shilling. R. Judah in the name of R. Josi of
Galilee saith, Let him give him a pound."

סטרו נותן לו מאתים זוז " *Does he give him a blow upon
the cheek? Let him give him two hundred zuzees :* if with the
other hand, let him give four hundred." Compare with this
passage ver. 39 : ' If any shall strike thee on the right cheek,
turn to him the other also.'

צרם באזנו וגו׳ " *Does he twitch him by the ear ;* or does he
pull off his hair; or does he spit, so that his spittle falls upon
him; or does he take away his coat" [note this also, and compare ver. 40 with it, ' He that will take away thy coat,' &c.];
" or does he uncover a woman's head in public? Let him give
four hundred zuzees."

They fetch the reason of so severe a mulct chiefly from the
shame done him that is thus injured, and from the disgrace
of the thing itself: and, moreover, from the dignity of an
Israelite : which is declared at large by the Gemarists upon
the words cited, and by Maimonides [k].

הכל לפי כבודו " Those mulcts [say they] are established
and inflicted *according to the dignity* of the person injured.
But R. Akibah said, ' Even the poorest Israelites are to be
esteemed as though they were persons of quality divested of
their estates, because they are the sons of Abraham, Isaac,
and Jacob.' "

Hence the entrance to our Saviour's doctrine lies easy :
1. He cites the law of retaliation, that, by laying one against
the other, Christian charity and forgiveness might shine the[l]
clearer. 2. He mentions these particulars which seemed to
be the most unworthy, and not to be borne by the high quality

---

[i] Bava Kama, cap. 8. hal. 6.   [l] *English folio edition,* vol. ii. p.
[k] In חובל ומזיק cap. 1.—3, &c.   151.

of a Jew, that he might the more preach up evangelical humility, and patience, and self-denial.   But why was the law of retaliation given, if at last it is melted down into this? On the same reason as the law of death was given concerning adultery, namely, for terror, and to demonstrate what the sin was.   Both were to be softened by charity; this by forgiveness, that by a bill of divorce: or, if the husband so pleased, by forgiveness also.

Ver. 40: Καὶ τῷ θέλοντί σοι κριθῆναι, καὶ τὸν χιτῶνά σου λαβεῖν, &c.   *And if any will sue thee at the law, and take away thy coat,* &c.] Χιτῶνα, *coat,* that is, טַלִּית *Talith.* So in the words of the Talmud alleged, העביר טליתו *he takes his coat.*   Of this garment, thus the Aruch; טלית הוא רדיד *Talith is a cloak:* and why is it called טַלִּית, *Talith?* שהוא למעלה מכל בגדים *Because it is above all the garments;* that is, because it is the outermost garment.

In this upper garment were woven in those fringes that were to put them in mind of the law, of which there is mention Num. xv. 38.   Hence is that, הזהיר בציצית זוכה לטלית נאה *He* [m] *that takes care of his skirts deserves a good coat.* Hereupon the disgrace was increased together with the wrong, when that was taken away, concerning which they did not a little boast, nay, and in which they placed no small religion: Matt. xxiii. 5, χιτὼν καὶ ἱμάτιον, *an upper and an inward garment;* to which טלית וחלוק answer. " If [n] any give a poor man a penny to buy חלוק ἱμάτιον, [an inward garment], let him not buy טַלִּית χιτῶνα [*a coat,* nor an upper garment].''   משאיל לו חלוק וטלית *He* [o] *lends him ἱμάτιον καὶ χιτῶνα, an inner garment and a coat* [p].

Ver. 41: Καὶ ὅστις σε ἀγγαρεύσει μίλιον ἕν, &c.   *And whosoever shall compel thee to go a mile,* &c.]   To him that had some corporeal wrong done him were these five mulcts to be paid, according to the reason and quality of the wrong: בנזק בצער בריפוי בבושת בשבת A [q] mulct for *maiming,* if so be the party were maimed: a mulct for *pain,* caused by the

[m] Bab. Schabb. fol. 23. 2.
[n] Bab. Bava Mezia, fol. 78. 2.
[o] Nedarim. fol. 33. 1.
[p] [Lightfoot has here inverted the

ordinary meaning of the Greek terms. —See Smith's Dict. G. and R. Antiq. art. *Pallium.*]
[q] Bava Kama in the place above.

blow or wound given: a mulct for the *cure* of the wound or
blow; a mulct for the *reproach* brought upon him: and a
mulct for *ceasing*, when, being wounded or beaten, he kept his
bed, and could not follow his business.

To the first, the first words of our Saviour, Μὴ ἀντιστῆναι
τῷ πονηρῷ, *That ye resist not evil*, seem to relate: Do not so
resist or rise up against an injurious person, as to require the
law of retaliation against him. The second and fourth, the
words following seem to respect, viz. Ὅστις σε ῥαπίσει, ' *Whosoever smiteth thee*, so that it cause pain and shame :' and
those words also, Θέλοντι χιτῶνά σου λαβεῖν, *Him that will take
away thy coat.*' To the last do these words under our hand
refer, and to the second certainly, if " some intolerable kind
of service be propounded," which the famous Beza asserts.

The word הלוות, very usual among the Talmudists, whereby [r] they denote accompanying him that goes elsewhere,
out of honour and respect, reaches not the sense of the
word ἀγγαρεύειν, but is too soft and low for it. It is reckoned for a duty to accompany a dead corpse to the grave,
and a Rabbin departing somewhere. Hence is that story,
" Germani [s], the servant of R. Judah Nasi, willing προπέμψαι
(מילווייה) *to conduct* R. Illa going away, met a mad dog," &c.
The footsteps of this civility we meet with among the Christians, Tit. iii. 13 ; John, Ep. iii. ver. 6; they were marks of
respect, love, and reverence : but that which was required by
the Jewish masters, out of arrogance and a supercilious authority, was to be done to a Rabbin, as a Rabbin.

But ἀγαρρεύειν, *to compel* to go a mile, sounds harsher,
and speaks not so much an impulse of duty, as a compulsion
of violence : and the Talmudists retain that very word אנגריא
Angaria, and do show, by examples not a few, what it means.
" It [t] is reported of R. Eliazar Ben Harsum, that his father
bequeathed him a thousand cities on the dry land, and a
thousand ships on the sea : but yet he, every day carrying
along with him a bottle of meal on his shoulder, travelled
from city to city, and from country to country, to learn the
law. On a certain day his servants met him, ועשו בו אנגריא
and *angariate, compel him*. He saith to them, ' I beseech you,

[r] *Leusden's edition*, vol. ii. p. 295.   [s] Hieros. Schabb. 8. 3.
[t] Bab. Joma, fol. 35. 2.

dismiss me, that I may go and learn the law.' They say to
him, ' By the life of R. Eliazar Ben Harsum, we will not dismiss you,' " &c.   Where the Gloss is, אנגריאה " *Angariah* is
עבוד" שר העיר *the service of the governor of the city ;* and he
was here to serve himself [for he was lord of the city].   But
they knew him not, but thought him to belong to one of those
his cities : for it was incumbent on them to attend on their
master."

Again[u] ; " R. Eliezer saith[x], ' Why was Abraham our father
punished, and why were his sons afflicted in Egypt two hundred and ten years ?' מפני שעשה אנגריא בתלמידי חכמים
Because he ' angariavit,' ' compelled' the disciples of the wise men
to go with him : as it is said וַיָּרֶק אֶת־חֲנִיכָיו *he armed his*
catechumens, or *his trained,* or *instructed,* Gen. xiv. 14.

The same almost is said of king Asa : " Rabbaʸ asked,
Why was Asa punished [*with the gout*] ? שעשה אנגריא
בתלמידי חכמים *Because he compelled the disciples of the*
wise men to go along with him : as it is said, ' And Asa
gathered together all Judah, none excepted,' " &c., 1 Kings
xv. 22.

We meet with mention also of *angariating* cattle ; " Anᶻ ass
is hired for a hilly journey ; but he that hireth him travels in
the valley : although both be of the like distance, that is, ten
miles, if an ass dies, he who hired him is guilty, &c.   But
(או שנעשית אנגריא אומר לו הרי שלך לפניך) *if the ass*
were angariated, the hirer saith to the owner, *Behold, take your*
beast to yourself," &c.   The Gloss is, או שנעשית אנגריא " *If*
he were angariated, that is, if they take him for some work of
the king," &c.

You see, then, whither the exhortation of our Saviour tends :
1. To patience under an open injury, and for which there is no
pretence, ver. 39.   2. Under an injury, for which some right
and equity in law is pretended, ver. 40.   3. Under an injury,
compulsion, or violence, patronized by the authority of a king,
or of those that are above us.

Ver. 43 : Μισήσεις τὸν ἐχθρόν σου· *Thou shalt hate thine*
enemy.] Here those poisonous canons might be produced,

---

whereby they are trained up in eternal hatred against the
Gentiles, and against Israelites themselves, who do not, in
every respect, walk with them in the same traditions and
rites.   Let this one example be instead of very many, which
are to be met with everywhere : " The[a] heretical Israelites,
that is, they of Israel that worship idols, or who transgress,
to provoke God : also Epicurean Israelites, that is, Israelites
who deny the law and the prophets, are, by precept to be
slain, if any can slay them, and that openly ; but if not
openly, you may compass their death secretly, and by subtilty." And a little after (O ! the extreme charity of the Jews
towards the Gentiles) ; " But as to the Gentiles, with whom
we have no war, and likewise to the shepherds of smaller
cattle, and others of that sort, they do not so plot their
death ; but it is forbidden them to deliver them from death
if they are in danger of it." For instance ; " A Jew sees one
of them fallen into the sea ; let him by no means lift him out
thence : for it is written, ' Thou shalt not rise up against the
blood of thy neighbour :' but this is not thy neighbour." And
further ; " An[b] Israelite, who alone sees another Israelite
transgressing, and admonisheth him, if he repents not, is
bound to hate him."

Ver. 46 : Οὐχὶ καὶ οἱ τελῶναι τὸ αὐτὸ ποιοῦσι ; *Do not even the
publicans the same ?*] How odious the publicans were to the
Jewish nation, especially those that were sprung of that nation,
and how they reckoned them the very worst of all mankind,
appears many ways in the evangelists ; and the very same is
their character in their own writers.

" It[c] is not lawful to use the riches of such men, of whom
it is presumed that they were thieves ; and of whom it is
presumed that all their wealth was gotten by rapine ; and
that all their business was the business of extortioners, such
as publicans and robbers are ; nor is their money to be mingled with thine, because it is presumed to have been gotten
by rapine."

Among[d] those who were neither fit to judge, nor to give a
testimony in judgment, are numbered הגבאין והמוכסין *the
collectors of taxes, and the publicans.*

---

[a] Maimon. in רוצח cap. 4.   [c] Maimon. in גזלה cap. 5.
[b] Ibid. cap. 13.   [d] Bab. Sanhedr. fol. 25. 2.

Publicans [e] are [f] joined with cut-throats and robbers. נודרין להרגין ולחרמין ולמוכסין " *They swear to cut-throats, to robbers and to publicans [invading their goods],* This is an offering, &c. He is known by his companion."

They were marked with such reproach, and that not without good reason; partly by reason of their rapine, partly, that to the burden laid upon the nation they themselves added another burden.

" When [g] are publicans to be reckoned for thieves? when he is a Gentile; or when of himself he takes that office upon him; or when, being deputed by the king, he doth not exact the set sum, but exacts according to his own will." Therefore the father of R. Zeira is to be reputed for a rare person [h], who, being a publican for thirteen years, did not make the burdens of the taxes heavier, but rather eased them.

" When [i] the king laid a tax [k], to be exacted of the Jews, of each according to his estate, these publicans, being deputed to proportion the thing, became respecters of persons, burdening some and indulging others, and so became plunderers."

By how much the more grievous the heathen yoke was to the Jewish people, boasting themselves a free nation, so much the more hateful to them was this kind of men; who, though sprung of Jewish blood, yet rendered their yoke much more heavy by these rapines.

CHAP. VI.

VER. 1 : Προσέχετε τὴν ἐλεημοσύνην ὑμῶν μὴ ποιεῖν, &c. *Take heed, that ye do not your alms, &c.*] It is questioned, whether Matthew writ ἐλεημοσύνην, *alms,* or δικαιοσύνην, *righteousness.* I answer;

I. That our Saviour certainly said צדקה, *righteousness* (or in Syriac זדקתא), I make no doubt at all; but that that word could not be otherwise understood by the common people than of *alms,* there is as little doubt to be made. For although the word צדקה, according to the idiom of the

---

[e] Nedarim, cap. 3. hal. 4.
[f] *Leusden's edition,* vol. ii. p. 296.
[g] Maimon. in the place above.
[h] Bab. Sanhedr. fol. 25. 2.

[i] *English folio edition,* vol. ii. p. 153.
[k] Gaon in Aruch in מכס.

Old Testament, signifies nothing else than *righteousness*; yet now, when our Saviour spoke those words, it signified nothing so much as *alms*.

·II. Christ used also the same word צדקתא *righteousness* in the three verses next following, and Matthew used the word ἐλεημοσύνη, *alms*: but by what right, I beseech you, should he call it δικαιοσύνην, *righteousness*, in the first verse, and ἐλεημοσύνην, *alms*, in the following,—when Christ every where used one and the same word? Matthew might not change in Greek, where our Saviour had not changed in Syriac.

Therefore we must say, that the Lord Jesus used the word צדקה, or צדקתא, in these four first verses: but that, speaking in the dialect of common people, he was understood by the common people to speak of *alms*.

Now they called *alms* by the name of צדקה *righteousness*, in that the Fathers of the Traditions taught, and the common people believed, that *alms* conferred very much to *justification*. Hear the Jewish chair in this matter:

" For[1] one farthing, given to a poor man in alms, a man is made partaker of the beatifical vision." Where it renders these words אֲנִי בְּצֶדֶק אֶחֱזֶה פָנֶיךָ [Ps. xvii. 15] ' I shall behold thy face in *righteousness*,' after this manner; ' I shall behold thy face *because of alms*.'

One saith, " This[m] money goes for *alms*, that my sons may live, and that I may obtain the world to come."

" A[n] man's table now expiates by *alms*, as heretofore the altar did by sacrifice."

" If[o] you afford *alms* out of your purse, God will keep you from all damage and harm."

" Monobazes[p] the king bestowed his goods liberally upon the poor, and had these words spoke to him by his kinsmen and friends, ' Your ancestors increased both their own riches and those that were left them by their fathers; but you waste both your own and those of your ancestors.' To whom he answered, ' My fathers laid up their wealth on earth; I lay up mine in heaven; as it is written, *Truth shall flourish out of*

---

[1] Bab. Bava Bathra, fol. 10. 1. et Midr. Tillin, upon Psal. xvii. 15.

[m] Bab. Rosh hashanah, fol. 4. 1.

[n] Id. Beracoth, fol. 55. 1.

[o] Hieros. Peah, fol. 15. 2.

[p] Ibid.

the earth, but righteousness shall *look down from heaven.* My
fathers laid up treasure that bears no fruit; but I lay up such
as bear fruit; as it is said, *It shall be well with the just, for
they shall eat the fruit of their works.* My fathers treasured
up where power was in their hands; but I where it is not; as
it is said, *Justice and judgment is the habitation of his throne.*
My fathers heaped up for others; I for myself; as it is said,
And this shall be to thee for righteousness. They scraped
together for this world; I for the world to come; as it is said,
Righteousness shall deliver from death." These things are also
recited in the Babylonian Talmud[q].

You see plainly in what sense he understands *righteousness*,
namely, in the sense of *alms:* and that sense not so much
framed in his own imagination, as in that of the whole nation,
and which the royal catechumen had imbibed from the Pharisees his teachers.

Behold the justifying and saving virtue of *alms* from the
very work done, according to the doctrine of the Pharisaical
chair.   And hence the opinion of this efficacy of *alms* so far[r]
prevailed with the deceived people, that they pointed out alms
by no other name (confined within one single word) than
צדקה *righteousness.*   Perhaps those words of our Saviour are
spoken in derision of this doctrine; "Yea, give those things
which ye have in alms, and behold all things shall be clean to
you," Luke xi. 41. With good reason, indeed, exhorting them
to give *alms*, but yet withal striking at the covetousness[s] of
the Pharisees, and confuting their vain opinion of being clean
by the washing of their hands, from their own opinion of the
efficacy of alms. As if he had said, "Ye assert that *alms*
justifies and saves; and therefore ye call it by the name of
righteousness: why, therefore, do ye affect cleanness by the
washing of hands, and not rather by the performance of
charity?" See the praises of *alms*, somewhat too high for it,
in the Talmud[t].

"R. Jannai[u] saw one giving money openly to a poor man;
to whom he said, It is better you had not given at all, than
so to have given."

[q] Bava Bathra, fol. 11. 1.

[r] *English folio edit.*, vol. ii. p.154.

[s] *Leusden's edition*, vol. ii. p. 297.

[t] Bab. Bava Bathra, fol. 8, 9, 10, 11.

[u] Bab. Chagig. fol. 5. 1.

Εἰ δὲ μήγε, μισθὸν οὐκ ἔχετε· *Otherwise ye have no reward.*]
He therefore seems the rather to speak of a reward, because
they expected a reward for their alms-doing without all doubt;
and that, as we said, for the mere work done.

" R. Lazar [x] was the almoner of the synagogue. One
day going into his house, he said, 'What news?' They answered, ' Some came hither, and ate and drank, and made
prayers for thee.' 'Then,' saith he, ' there is no good reward.'
Another time going into his house, he said, ' What news?'
It was answered, ' Some others came, and ate and drank, and
railed upon you.' ' Now.' saith he, ' there will be a good
reward.' "

Ver. 2 : Μὴ σαλπίσῃς ἔμπροσθέν σου, ὥσπερ οἱ ὑποκριταὶ
ποιοῦσιν ἐν ταῖς συναγωγαῖς, καὶ ἐν ταῖς ῥύμαις· *Do not sound a
trumpet before thee, as the hypocrites do in the synagogues, and
in the streets.*] It is a just scruple, whether this sounding a
trumpet be to be understood according to the letter, or in a
borrowed sense. I have not found, although I have sought
for it much and seriously, even the least mention of a trumpet
in almsgiving. I would most willingly be taught this from
the more learned.

You may divide the ordinary alms of the Jews into three
parts :

I. תמחוי *the alms'-dish.* They gave alms to the public dish or basket : תמחוי *Tamchui* (according to the definition of the author of Aruch, and that out of Bava Bathra
in the place lately cited) was a certain vessel, in which bread
and food was gathered לעניי עולם *for the poor of the world.*
You may not improperly call it *the alms'-basket;* he calls it
קערה *a dish.* By *the poor of the world* are to be understood any *beggars,* begging from door to door; yea, even
heathen beggars. Hence the Jerusalem Talmud in the place
above quoted, תמחוי לכל אדם *The alms'-dish was for every
man.* And the Aruch moreover, "נגבית בכל יום בג
ומתחלקת בג' *This alms was gathered daily by three men,
and distributed by three.* It was gathered of the townsmen by
collectors within their doors; which appears by that caution[y];
גבאי צדקה אין רשאין לפרוש זה מזה אבל פורש זה לשער

---

[x] Hieros. Peah, fol. 21. 1.   [y] Bava Bathra, fol. 8. 2.

וזה לחנות וזה The collec ‏‎ of alms may not separate themselves one from another, unless that one may go by himself to the gate, and another to the shop. That is, as the Gloss explains it, they might not gather this alms separately and by themselves ; that no suspicion might arise, that they privily converted what was given to their own use and benefit. This only was allowed them ; when they went to the gate, one might betake himself to the gate, and another to a shop near it, to ask of the dwellers in both places : yet with this proviso, that withal both were within sight of one another. So that at each door it might be seen that this alms was received by the collectors. And here was no probability at all of a trumpet, when this alms was of the lowest degree, being to be bestowed upon vagabond strangers, and they very often heathen.

II. קופה *The poor's-chest.* They gave alms also in the public poor's-box : which was to be distributed to the poor only of that city. תמחוי לעניי העולם *The alms'-dish is for the poor of the world,* קופה לעניי אותה העיר *but the alms'-chest for the poor only of that city.* This was collected of the townsmen by two *Parnasin,* of whom before, to whom also a third was added, for the distributing it. The Babylonian Gemarists give a reason of the number, not unworthy to be marked : " A tradition of the Rabbins. *The alms'-chest* is gathered by two, and distributed by three. It is gathered by two, שאין עושים שררות פחות משנים על ציבור *because they do not constitute a superior office in the synagogue less than of two,* ומתחלקת בג' כדיני ממונות *and it is distributed by three, as pecuniary judgments are transacted by three.*

This [z] alms was collected in the synagogue, on the sabbath (compare 1 Cor. xvi. 2.), and it was distributed to the poor on the sabbath-eve. Hence is that, קופה מערב שבת לערב שבת " *The alms'-chest is from the sabbath-eve to the sabbath-eve ; the alms'-dish, every day.*"

Whether, therefore, the trumpet sounded in the synagogue when alms were done, it again remains obscure, since the Jewish canonists do not openly mention it, while yet they treat of these alms very largely. Indeed, every synagogue had its trumpet. For,

[z] *English folio edition,* vol. ii. p. 155.

ɪ. They sounded with the trumpet in every city in which was a judiciary bench, at the coming in of the new year. But this was not used but after the destruction of the Temple [a].

2. They sounded with the trumpet when any was excommunicated. Hence among the utensils of a judge is numbered a [b] trumpet. For כלי הדיינין *the instruments of judges*, as appears there, were מקל רצועה שופרא וסנדלא *a rod, a whip, a trumpet, and a sandal* [c]. שופרא לשמתא ונידוי "*A trumpet* (saith the Gloss) *for excommunication and anathematizing: and a sandal for the taking off of the shoe of the husband's brother.*" And in the same place [d] mention is made of the excommunicating of Jesus, four hundred trumpets being brought for that business.

3. The trumpet sounded six times at the coming in of every sabbath : that from thence, by that sign given, all people should cease from servile works. Of this matter discourse is had in the Babylonian Talmud, in the tract of the Sabbath [e].

Thus, there was a trumpet in every synagogue; but whether it were used while alms were done, I still inquire. That comes into my mind, גבאי צדקה ביט לא יהו מכריזין בדרך שמכריזין בחול " *The* [f] *collectors of alms do not proclaim on a feast-day, as they proclaim on a common day :* but collect it privately, and put it up in their bosom." But whether this proclamation did publish what was giving by every one, or did admonish of not giving any thing, but what might rightly be given ; let the more learned judge by looking upon the place.

III. They gave alms also out of the field, and that was especially fourfold : 1. The corner of the field not reaped. 2. Sheaves left in the field, either by forgetfulness, or voluntarily. 3. The gleaning of the vintage; of which see Levit. xix. 9, 10, Deut. xxiv. 19. And, 4. מעשר עני *The poor's tenth ;* of which the Talmudists largely in the tracts, Peah, Demai, and Maaseroth. To the gathering of these, the poor

---

[a] See Rosh. hashanah, cap. 4. hal. 1.
[b] Bab. Sanhedr. fol. 7. 2.
[c] *Leusden's edit.*, vol. ii. p. 298.
[d] Fol. 107. 2.
[e] Fol. 35. 2.
[f] Hieros. Demai, fol. 23. 2.

were called, בג'' אבעיות ביום בשחר ובחצות ובמנחה " *By* [g] *three manifestations in the day ;* namely, *in the morning, and at noon, and at Minchah,*" or ' *the evening.*' That is, the owner of the field openly shewed himself three times in the day, for this end, that then the poor should come and gather : in the morning, for the sake of nurses ; because, in the mean time, while their young children slept, they might the more freely go forth for this purpose : at noon, for the sake of children, who also at that time were prepared to gather : at *Minchah*, for the sake of old men. So the Jerusalem Gemarists, and the Glossers upon the Babylonian Talmud.

There were the ordinary alms of the Jewish people : in the doing which, seeing as yet I cannot find so much as the least sound of a trumpet in their writers, I guess that either our Savour here spoke metaphorically ; or, if there were any trumpet used, that it was used in peculiar and extraordinary alms.

The Jews did very highly approve of alms done secretly ; hence לשכת חשאי *the treasury of the silent* was of famed memory in the Temple ; whither " some [h] very religious men brought their alms in silence and privacy, when the poor children of good men were maintained." And hence is that proverb, גדול העושה צדקה בסתר יותר ממשה רבינו 'O ποιῶν ἐλεημοσύνην ἐν κρυπτῷ. *He* [i] *that doth alms in secret is greater than our master Moses himself.* And yet they laboured under such an itch to make their alms public, lest they should not be seen by men, that they did them not without a trumpet ; or, which was as good as a trumpet, with a proud desire of making them known : that they might the more be pointed at with the finger, and that it might be said of them, ' These are the men.'

Ver. 3 : Μὴ γνώτω ἡ ἀριστερά σου, τί ποιεῖ ἡ δεξιά σου· *Let not thy left hand know what thy right hand doth.*] He seems to speak according to the custom used in some other things ; for in some actions, which pertained to religion, they admitted not the left hand to meet with the right. " The [k] cup of wine which was used to sanctify the coming in of the sabbath, was to be taken with the right hand, without the assistance of the

---

[g] Peah, cap. 4. hal. 5.
[h] Aruch in חש.

[i] Bab. Bava Bathra, fol. 9. 2.
[k] Maimon. in Schabb. cap. 29, &c.

left." " Let no man receive into a vessel the blood of the sacrifice, bring it to the altar, or sprinkle it with his left[1] hand[m]." And in the same tract, it is related of Shammai, that he would feed himself only with one hand[n].

Ver. 5 : Φιλοῦσιν ἐν ταῖς συναγωγαῖς καὶ ἐν ταῖς γωνίαις τῶν πλατειῶν ἑστῶτες προσεύχεσθαι· *They love to pray standing in the synagogues, and in the corner of the streets.*] 1. They prayed standing, Luke xviii. 11, 13, Mark xi. 25. " It[o] is written, ' And Abraham rose early in the morning at the place where he had stood before the Lord.' ואין עמידה אלא תפלה, *But to stand was nothing else than to pray :* as it is said, וַיַּעֲמֹד פִּנְחָס וַיְפַלֵּל *And Phineas stood and judged."*

" One[p] entereth into the synagogue, ומצאן עומדין בתפלה *and found them standing in prayer."* " Let[q] a scholar of the wise men look downwards, כשהוא עומד בתפלה *when he stands praying."* And to name no more, the same Maimonides asserts[r] these things are required in prayer; that he that prayeth, *stand ;* that he turn his face towards Jerusalem ; that he cover his head ; and that he fix his eyes downwards.

II. They loved to *pray in the synagogues.* " He[s] goes to the synagogue to pray."

" Why do they recite their phylacteries in the synagogue, when they are not bound to do it ? R. Josi saith, They do not recite them in the synagogue for that end, that so the whole office of the phylacteries may be performed, but to persevere in prayer. For this recitation was to be said over again, when they came home[t]."

Rabbenu[u] Asher hath these words : " When[x] any returns home in the evening from the field, let him not say, ' I will go into my house ;' but first let him betake himself to the synagogue : and if he can read, let him read something ; if he can recite the traditions, let him recite them. And then let him say over the phylacteries, and pray."

[1] *English folio edition*, vol. ii. p. 156.
[m] Bab. Joma, f. 49. 1.
[n] Fol. 77. 2.
[o] Bab. Berac. fol. 26. 2.
[p] Hieros. f. 20. 1.
[q] Maimon. in Peah, cap. 5.
[r] In Tephillah, cap. 5.
[s] Tanchum, fol. 35. 1.
[t] Piske in Berac. cap. 1. art. 6.
[u] *Leusden's edition*, vol. ii. p. 299.
[x] In Berac. fol. 69. 3.

But that we be not too tedious, even from this very opinion, they were wont to betake themselves to the synagogues, because they were persuaded that the prayers of the synagogue were certainly heard.

III. They prayed in the streets. So Maimonides; "They[y] prayed in the streets on the feasts and public fasts." "What[z] are the rites of the fasts? They brought out the ark into the streets of the city, and sprinkled ashes upon the ark, and upon the head of the president of the Sanhedrim, and the vice-president; and every one put ashes upon his own head. One of the elders makes this exhortation; ' It is not said, O brethren, of the Ninevites, that God saw their sackcloth, or their fastings; but, that he saw their works,' &c. They stand praying, and they set some fit elder before the ark, and he prays four-and-twenty prayers before them."

But doth our Saviour condemn all prayers in the synagogue? By no means. For he himself prayed in and with the synagogue. Nor did he barely reprove those public prayers in the streets, made by the whole multitude in those great solemnities, but prayers everywhere, both in the synagogues and the streets, that were made privately, but yet publicly also, and in the sight of all, that thereby he that prayed might get some name and reputation from those that saw him.

I. While public prayers were uttered in the synagogue, it was customary also for those that hunted after vainglory, to mutter private prayers, and such as were different from those of the synagogue, whereby the eyes of all might be the more fixed upon him that prayed.

" Hath[a] not a man prayed his morning prayers? When he goes into the synagogue, does he find them praying the additionary prayer? If he is sure he shall begin and end, so that he may answer ' Amen' after the angel of the church, let him say his prayers."

II. They prayed also by themselves in the streets. " R. Jochanan said[b], I saw R. Jannai standing and praying in the

---

[y] In Tephillah, cap. 11.
[z] Taanith, cap. 2. hal. 1 & 2.

[a] Hieros. Berac. fol. 83.
[b] Hieros. in the place above.

streets of Tsippor, and going four cubits, and then praying
the additionary prayer."

Two things especially shew their hypocrisy here:

1. That so much provision is made concerning reciting the
phylacteries, and the prayers added (that it might be done
within the just time), that wheresoever a man had been, when
the set time was come, he presently betakes himself to prayers:
" A workman, or he that is upon the top of a tree, he that
rides on an ass, must immediately come down, and say his
prayers," &c. These are the very instances that the canonists
give, which, with more of them, you may find in the tract
Beracoth[c]. Hence, therefore, those vainglorious hypocrites
got an occasion of boasting themselves. For the hour of the
phylacterical prayers being come, their care and endeavour
was, to be taken in the streets: whereby the canonical hour
compelling them to their prayers in that place, they might be
the more seen by all persons, and that the ordinary people
might admire and applaud both their zeal and religion. To
which hypocritical pride they often added this also, that they
used very long pauses, both before they began their prayers,
and after they had done[d] them: so that very usually, for
three hours together, they were seen in a praying habit and
posture. See the Babylonian Talmud[e]. So that the Canonists played the madmen with some reason, when they allowed
the space, from the rising of the morning to the third hour of
the day, for the phylacterical prayers; because those three-
hour praying men scarcely despatched them within less space,
pausing one hour before they began prayer, and as much after
they were ended.

2. They addicted themselves to ejaculations, prayers, and
blessings, upon the sight almost of any thing meeting them
either in the streets or in the way. " When[f] one saw a place,
wherein some miracle was done for Israel; a place, from
whence idolatry was rooted out; or a place, where an idol
now was, a short prayer was to be used. When any saw a
blackamoor, a dwarf, a crooked, a maimed person, &c. they
were to bless. Let him that sees a fair tree, or a beautiful

---

[c] Cap. 1-4.   [e] Berac. fol. 30. 2. et 32. 2.
[d] *English folio edit.*, vol. ii. p. 157.   [f] Berac. cap. 9.

face, bless thus, Blessed be He, who created the beauty of the creature," &c.

Ver. 7: Μὴ βαττολογήσητε, ὥσπερ οἱ ἐθνικοί· *Use not vain repetitions, as the heathen do.*] See the civil *battology* [*vain repetitions*] of the heathen in their supplications : " Let[g] the parricide be dragged : we beseech thee, Augustus, let the parricide be dragged. This is the thing we ask, let the parricide be dragged. Hear us, Cæsar. Let the false accusers be condemned to the lion. Hear us, Cæsar. Let the false accusers be condemned to the lion. Hear us, Cæsar," &c. See also the same author in[g] Severus.

" Antoninus[h] the pious, the gods keep thee. Antoninus the merciful, the gods keep thee. Antoninus the merciful, the gods keep thee." See also Capitolinus, in the Maximini.

Those words savour of vain repetition in prayer, 1 Kings xviii. 26 ; " The priests of Baal called upon the name of Baal from morning to noon, saying, O Baal, hear us."

After the same manner almost as the heathen mixed βαττολογίας, *vain repetitions*, in their prayers, did the Jews in their[i] συνωνυμίαι, *using divers words importing the same thing :* not repeating, indeed, the same things as they in the same words, but speaking the same thing in varied phrases ; which appears sufficiently to him that reads their liturgies through, as well the more ancient as those of a later date. And certainly, the sin is equally the same in using different words of the same thing, as in a vain repetition of the same words ; if so be there were the same deceit and hypocrisy in both ; in words only multiplied, but the heart absent.

And in this matter the Jew sinned little less than the heathen. For this was an axiom with them, כל המרבה תפלה נענה *Every* [k] *one that multiplies prayer is heard.* Christ, therefore, does not so much condemn the bare saying over again the same petitions, either in the same words, or in words of the same import (for he himself spake the same things thrice, when he prayed in the garden), as a false opinion, as if there were some power, or zeal, or piety, in such kind of repetitions ; and that they would be sooner heard, and more prevail with God. While he strikes the

---

[g] Lamprid. in Commodo.
[h] Gallican. in Avidio Cassio.
[i] *Leusden's edition,* vol. ii. p. 300.
[k] Hieros. Taanith, fol. 67. 3.

heathen, he strikes the Jews also, who laboured under the
same phrensy: but there is mention only of the heathen, partly
because this savoured rather of heathen blindness than of the
profession of true religion, which the Jews boasted of; partly,
and especially, that he might not condemn the public prayers
of the Jews without cause, in which they sinned not at all by
using synonymous expressions, if it were done out of a pious
and sincere heart.

Ver. 9: Οὕτως οὖν προσεύχεσθε ὑμεῖς· Πάτερ ἡμῶν, &c.
After this manner therefore pray ye: Our Father, &c.] Some
things, which seem more difficult about this divine form of
prayer, will perhaps pass into a softer sense, if certain things,
very usual in the Jewish church and nation, be observed, to
which the apostles could not but have regard when they
clearly acknowledged here the highest conformity with them.
For that it was customary with our Saviour, for the most
part, to conform himself to the church and nation, both in
religious and civil matters, so they were lawful, most evidently appears also in this form of prayer. Let these things,
therefore, be observed:

I. That the stated prayers of the Jews, daily to be said at
that time when Christ prescribed this form to his disciples,
were eighteen in number, or in a quantity equalling it. Of
this number of their prayers, the Gemarists of both Talmuds
treat at large[1]. Whom consult.

Whether they were reduced to the precise number of
eighteen, in the order that they afterward appeared in while
Christ was upon earth, some scruple ariseth from some
things [m] which are said by the Babylonian Talmudists in the
place alleged: but it might be plainly proved, if there were
need, that little, or indeed nothing at all, wanted of the quantity and bulk of such a number. תנו רבנן שמעון הפקולי
הסדיר יח″ ברכות לפני רג″ וגו׳ " The Rabbins have a tradition (say they), that Simeon Pekoli reduced into order the
eighteen prayers according to their course, before Rabban
Gamaliel in Jafne. Rabban Gamaliel said to the wise men,
‘ Is there any that knows to compose a prayer against the
Sadducees?’ Samuel the Little stood forth and constituted

[1] Hieros. Taanith, fol. 65. 3. Bab. Beracoth, fol. 28. 2.
[m] *English folio edition*, vol. ii. p. 158.

one," &c. That Rabban Gamaliel, which is here spoke of,
was Paul's master. For, although Rabban Gamaliel (who
was commonly styled ' Jafnensis,' *of Jafne*) was the nephew
of Paul's master, Gamaliel, and this thing is mentioned to be
done in Jafne; yet Paul's master also lived in Jafne: and
that this was he of whom is the story before us, sufficiently
appears hence, because his business is with Samuel the Little,
who certainly died before the destruction of the city.

Under Gamaliel the elder, therefore, were those daily
prayers reduced first into that order wherein they were received by the following ages. Which, however it was done
after the death of our Saviour, in regard of their reducing
into order, yet so many there were in daily use at that time
when he conversed on earth. Now he condemned not those
prayers altogether, nor esteemed them of no account; yea,
on the contrary, he joined himself to the public liturgy in
the synagogues, and in the Temple: and when he delivereth this form to his disciples, he extinguisheth not other
forms.

II. When all could not readily repeat by heart those
numerous prayers, they were reduced into a brief summary,
in which the marrow of them all was comprised; and that
provision was made for the memory, that they should have
a short epitome of those prayers, whom the weakness of their
memory, or sometime the unavoidable necessity of business,
permitted not to repeat a longer prayer, or to be at leisure
to do it. This summary they called מעין *a fountain.* "Rabban Gamaliel saith, ' Let every one pray the eighteen prayers
every day.' R. Joshua saith, 'יח מעין יתפלל, *Let him pray
the* מעין, *the summary of those eighteen.* But R. Akibah saith,
אם שגורה תפלתו בפיו מתפלל יח' ואם לוא מעין יח'"
*If prayer be free in his mouth, let him pray the eighteen; but if
not, let him pray the summary of those eighteen* [n]." That our
Saviour comprised the sum of all prayers in this form, is
known to all Christians; and it is confessed that such is the
perfection of this form, that it is the epitome of all things to
be prayed for, as the Decalogue is the epitome of all things
to be practised.

III. It was very usual with the doctors of the Jews,

[n] Bab. Beracoth, in the place above.

1. To compose forms of short prayers, and to deliver them to their scholars (which is asserted also of John, Luke xi. 1); whereof you will find some examples[o], and they not a few, in the Babylonian Gemara, in the tract Beracoth, and elsewhere. Not that by those forms they banished or destroyed the set and accustomed prayers of the nation; but they superadded their own to them, and suited them to proper and special occasions.

2. To the stated prayers, and others framed by themselves, it was very usual to add some short prayer over and above, which one may not amiss call ' the concluding prayer.' Take these examples of these prayers: ר' א' בתר דמסיים צלותיה אמר הכי " *R. Eliezer, when he had finished his prayers, was wont to say thus*, ' Let it be thy good pleasure, O Lord, that love and brotherhood dwell in our portion,' &c. R. Jochanan, when he had finished his prayers, was wont to say thus, ' Let it be thy good pleasure, O Lord, to take notice of our reproach, and to look upon our miseries,' " &c. In like manner,

1. Our Saviour, while he delivers this form to his disciples, does not weaken the set forms of the church; nor does he forbid his disciples not to use private prayers: but he delivers this most exact summary of all prayers, to be added, over and above, to our prayers; his most perfect to our most imperfect.

2. The apostles, sufficiently accustomed to the manners of the nation, could not judge otherwise of this form. In interpreting very many phrases and histories of the New Testament, it is not so much worth, what we think of them from notions of our own, feigned upon I know not what grounds, as in what sense these things were understood by the hearers and lookers on, according to the usual custom and vulgar dialect of the nation. Some inquire by what authority we do subjoin or superadd the Lord's Prayer to ours; and feign arguments to the contrary out of their own brain. But I ask, whether it was possible that the apostles and disciples, who from their very cradles had known and seen such forms instituted for common use, and added more-

---

o *Leusden's edition*, vol. ii. p. 301.

over to the set prayers and others, should judge otherwise
of this form given by our Lord; which bore so great conformity with those, and with the most received rite and custom of the nation?

IV. That church held it for a just canon, and that indeed
no discommendable one neither, לעולם לישתף איניש נפשיה
בהדי ציבורא *He* p *that prays ought always, when he prays, to
join with the church.* Which is not strictly to be understood
only of his presence in the synagogue (that is elsewhere and
otherwise commanded many times over), but wheresoever in
the world he be placed, yea, when he is most alone, that he
say his prayers in the plural number q: for thus the Gloss
explains it, אל יתפלל תק" בלשון יחיד אלא בלשון רבים
Let none pray the short prayer (that is, one different from the
set prayers) *in the singular number, but in the plural.* In
which number our Saviour teacheth us also to pray in this
form; and that upon very good reason, when, in whatsoever
solitude or distance we are, yet we ought to acknowledge
ourselves joined with the church, and to pray for her happiness as well as for our own.

Πάτερ ἡμῶν ὁ ἐν τοῖς οὐρανοῖς· *Our Father which art in
heaven.*] I. This epithet of God was very well known among
the Jews, and very usual with them:

אבינו שבשמים: " *Our* r *Father which art in heaven,* deal so
with us as thou hast promised by the prophets." And in another place this is thrice recited; "Whom s have we whereon
to rely, על אבינו שבשמים *besides our Father which is in
heaven?*" "Blessed t are ye, O Israelites; who cleanseth you?
Your *Father, who is in heaven.*" "Ye u gave not to your
Father, who is in heaven, but to me the priest."

II. But in what sense did the Jews call God *their Father
in heaven,* when they were altogether ignorant of the doctrine and mystery of adoption, besides that adoption whereby
God had adopted them for a peculiar people? I answer,
For that very cause they were taught by God himself so
to call him, Exod. iv. 22, Deut. xxxii. 6, &c. Nor was there
any among them who not only might not do this, but also

---

p Bab. Beracoth, fol. 30. 1.
q *English folio edit.,* vol. ii. p. 159.
r Maimon. in Tephilloth.

s Sotah, cap. 9. hal. 15.
t Joma, cap. 8. hal. 9.
u Hieros. Maaseroth, fol. 50. 3.

who ought not to do it.   While the heathen said to his idol,
‘ Thou art my father,’ Jer. ii. 27, the Israelite was bound to
say, *Our Father which art in heaven*, Isa. lxiii. 16, lxiv. 8.

III. When Christ useth this manner of speech so very
well known to the nation, does he not use it in a sense that
was known to the nation also ?   Let them answer who would
have the Lord's Prayer to be prayed and said by none but
by those who are indeed believers, and who have partook of
true adoption.   In what sense was our Saviour, when he spake
these words, understood of the hearers ?   They were thoroughly
instructed, from their cradles, to call God *the Father in heaven :* they neither hear Christ changing the phrase, nor curtailing any thing from the latitude of the known and used
sense.   Therefore let them tell me, Did not Peter, John, and
the rest of the apostles, think that it was as lawful for all
Christians to say to God, *Our Father which art in heaven*, as
it was lawful for all Jews ?   They called God *Father*, because
he had called them into the profession of him, because he
took care of them, and instructed them, &c.   And what, I
beseech you, hinders, but all Christians, obtaining the same
privileges, may honour God with the same compellation ?
There is nothing in the words of Christ that hinders, and
there is somewhat in the very phrase that permits it.

Ver. 9, 10[x]: Ἁγιασθήτω τὸ ὄνομά σου. Ἐλθέτω ἡ βασιλεία σου·
Hallowed be thy name.   Thy kingdom come.] This obtained for
an axiom in the Jewish schools; כל ברכה שאין בה מלכות
אינה ברכה : *That[y] prayer, wherein there is not mention of the
kingdom of God, is not a prayer.*   Where these words are also
added : " Abai saith, Like to this is that of Rabh to be
reckoned, that it is a tradition לא עָבַרְתִּי מִמִּצְוֹתֶיךָ וְלֹא
שָׁכַחְתִּי *I have not transgressed thy precepts, nor have I forgotten
them*" (they are the words of him that offereth the first-fruits,
Deut. xxvi. 13).   " ‘ I have not transgressed,’ that is, by not
giving thanks : ‘ And I have not forgotten them ;’ that is, I
have not forgot to commemorate thy *name*, and thy *kingdom.*"

Γενηθήτω τὸ θέλημά σου, ὡς ἐν οὐρανῷ, &c. *Thy will be done,
as in heaven, &c.*] " What[z] is the short prayer ?   R. Eliezer

---

saith, עשה רצונך בשמים Do thy will in heaven, and give
quietness of spirit to them that fear thee beneath," or in
earth.

Ver. 11: Τὸν ἄρτον ἡμῶν τὸν ἐπιούσιον, &c. *Our daily bread.*]
That is, provide *to-morrow's bread*, and give it us to-day, that
we be not solicitous for to-morrow; as ver. 34, Ἐπιούσιος from
ἐπιὼν, ἐπιοῦσα, &c. *that which next follows*; not ἐπούσιος, *super-
substantial*, from ἔπειμι.

" The necessities of thy people Israel are many, and their
knowledge small, so that they know not how to disclose their
necessities; let it be thy good pleasure to give to every man
כדי פרנסתו *what sufficeth for food*," &c.

Ver. 13[a]: Ῥῦσαι ἡμᾶς ἀπὸ τοῦ πονηροῦ· *Deliver us from evil.*]
" Rabbi[b] [*Judah*] was wont thus to pray: ' Let it be thy good
pleasure to *deliver* us from impudent men, and impudence;
from an evil man, and from an evil chance; from an evil affection, from an evil companion, from an evil neighbour, from
Satan the destroyer, from a hard judgment, and from a hard
adversary,'" &c.

Ὅτι σοῦ ἐστιν ἡ βασιλεία, &c. *For thine is the kingdom, &c.*]
I. In the public service in the Temple, the commemoration of
the *kingdom of God* was the respond; instead of which the
people answered *Amen*, when the priests ended their prayers.
" For תני לא היו עונין אמן בבית המקדש *the tradition is,
that they answered not ' Amen' in the house of the sanctuary.*
What said they then? ברוך שם כבוד מלכותו לעולם ועד
Blessed be the name of the glory of his kingdom for ever[c]."
Hence in the tract Joma (where the rubric of the day of
Expiation is), after various prayers recited, which, on that
day, the high priest makes, is added, " And the people answered, Blessed be the name of the glory of his kingdom for
ever and ever." See the places[d] of that tract noted in the
margin. There a short prayer of the high priest is mentioned,
in which he thus concludes; " Be ye clean before Jehovah;"
and these words are added, " But the priests and people
standing in the court, when they heard שם המפורש *the
name Jehovah* pronounced out in its syllables, adoring, and

a *English folio edition*, vol. ii. p.
160.
b Berac. fol. 16. 2.

c Hieros. Berac. fol. 13. 2.
d Bab. Joma, fol. 39. 1. 41. 2. but
chiefly fol. 66. 1.

falling prostrate upon their face, they said, "ב"ש"כ ברוך וכו
*Blessed be the name of the glory of his kingdom for ever and
ever.*" See also the tract Taanith[e], where a reason is given
of this doxology in the Gloss there.

II. This also they pronounced softly, and in a gentle
whisper, while they were reciting the phylacteries. It[f] is
said of the men of Jericho, that כורכין את שמע *they folded
up the Schemah*. It is disputed what this means; " And
R. Judah saith, That they made some small pause after the
reciting of this period, ' Hear, O Israel, the Lord our God is
one Lord :' but they said not, ' Blessed be the name of the
glory of his kingdom for ever and ever.' But by what reason
do we say so? R. Simeon Ben Levi explains the mystery, who
saith, Our father Jacob called his sons, and said, ' Gather
yourselves together, and I will declare unto you.' It was in
his mind to reveal to them the end of days, and the Holy
Spirit departed from him : he said, therefore, ' Perhaps there
is something profane in my bed, (which God forbid!) as it
was to Abraham, from whom proceeded Ishmael ; and to
Isaac, from whom proceeded Esau.' His sons said unto him,
' Hear, Israel, the Lord our God is one Lord ;' as, in thy
heart, there is but one ; so, in our hearts, there is but one.
At that time our father Jacob began, and said, "ב"ש"כ
מ"ל"ר. *Blessed be the name of the glory of his kingdom for ever
and ever.* The Rabbins said, What shall we do? Shall we
say this doxology? Our master Moses. said it not. Shall we
not say it? Our father Jacob said it. Therefore it was appointed to say it softly," &c.

You see how very public the use of this doxology was, and
how very private too. Being a response, it was pronounced
in the Temple by all with a loud voice ; being an ejaculation,
it was spoken in the phylacterical prayers, by every single
man, in a very low voice. And you see how great an agreement it hath with the conclusion of the Lord's prayer, " For
thine is the kingdom," &c.

III. As they answered *Amen*, not at all in the public
prayers in the Temple, so they seldom joined it to the end
of their private prayers. In the synagogue, indeed, the people

answered *Amen* to the prayers made by the minister : and also at home, when the master of the family blessed or prayed; but seldom, or indeed never, any one praying privately joined this to the end of his prayers.

And[g] now, to apply those things which have been said to the matter under our hands, consider the following things :

1. That this prayer was twice delivered by our Saviour : first, in this sermon in the mount, when he was not asked ; and afterward, when he was asked, almost half a year after, Luke xi.

2. That this conclusion is added in St. Matthew, " For thine is the kingdom," &c.; but in St. Luke it is not.   In St. Matthew is added moreover the word *Amen ;* but in St. Luke it is wanting.   Upon the whole matter, therefore, we infer,

I. That Christ, in exhibiting this form of prayer, followed a very usual rite and custom of the nation.

II. That the disciples also, receiving this form delivered to them, could not but receive it according to the manner and sense of the nation, used in such cases : since he introduced no exception at all from that general rule and custom.

III. That[h] he scarcely could signify his mind, that this prayer should be universally and constantly used, by any marks or signs more clear than those which he made use of.   For,

First, He commanded all, without any exception or distinction, " After this manner pray ye ;" and, " When ye pray, say, Our Father," &c.

Secondly, As, according to the ordinary custom of the nation, forms of prayer, delivered by the masters to the scholars, were to be used, and were used by them all indifferently, and without distinction of persons ; so also he neither suggested any thing concerning this his prayer, either besides the common custom, or contrary to it.

Thirdly, The form itself carries along with it certain characters, both of its public and private and constant use.   It may certainly with good reason be asked, Why, since Christ

had delivered this prayer in such plain words in his sermon
upon the mount, this command moreover being added, "After
this manner pray ye," it was desired again, that he would
teach them to pray? What! had they forgotten that prayer
that was given them there? Were they ignorant that it was
given them for a form of prayer, and so to be used? But this
seems rather the cause why they desired a second time a form
of prayer, namely, because they might reckon that first for a
public form of prayer; since this might easily be evinced,
both by the addition of the conclusion so like the public
response in the Temple, and especially by the addition of
Amen used only in public assemblies : therefore, they beseech him again, that he would teach them to pray privately ;
and he repeats the same form, but omits the conclusion, and
Amen, which savoured of public use. Therefore you have
in the conclusion a sign of the *public* use, by the agreement
of it to the response in the Temple; and of the *private*, by
the agreement of it to the ejaculation in the phylacterical
prayers. A sign of the public use was in the addition of
Amen ; a sign of the private use was in the absence of it: a
sign of both in the conformity of the whole to the custom
of the nation. Christ taught his disciples to pray, as John
had taught his, Luke xi. 1 : John taught his, as the masters
among the Jews had theirs, by yielding them a form to be
used by all theirs daily, verbatim, and in terms.

Ver. 16 : 'Αφανίζουσι τὰ πρόσωπα αὐτῶν· *They disfigure their
faces*.] That is, they disguised their faces with ashes; as he
heretofore upon another cause, 1 Kings xx. 38 : "In[i] the public fasts every one took ashes, and put upon his head. They[k]
say of R. Joshua Ben Ananiah, that, all the days of his life,
הושחרו פניו מפני תעניות *his face was black by reason of his
fastings.* Why[l] is his name called Ashur? (1 Chron. iv. 5.)
שהושחרו פניו *Because his face was black by fastings.*"

Here let that of Seneca[m] come in ; "This is against nature,
to hate easy cleanliness, and to affect nastiness."

Ver. 17 : Σὺ δὲ νηστεύων ἄλειψαί σου τὴν κεφαλήν, &c.
But thou, when thou fastest, anoint thine head, &c.] For those
that fasted neither anointed themselves nor washed. " On[n]

---

[i] Taanith, c. 2.   [k] Juchasin, f. 59.   [l] Bab. Sotah, fol. 12. 1.
    [m] Epist. 5.   [n] Joma, cap. 8. hal. 1.

the day of Expiation it was forbidden to eat, to drink, to wash, to anoint themselves, to put on their sandals, to lie with their wives. But the king and the bride may wash their faces, and a midwife may put on her sandals." See the Babylonian Gemara [o] here. See also the Babylonian Talmud in the tract Taanith[p], concerning other fasts, and the fasts of private men.

They were wont to anoint their bodies and heads upon a threefold reason :

I. לְתַעֲנוּג *For finer dress.* " Anointing [q] is permitted to be used on the sabbath, whether it be for ornament, or not for ornament. On the day of Expiation both are forbidden. On the ninth day of the month Ab, and in the public fasts, anointing for dress is forbid ; anointing not for dress is allowed."

II. סיכה שלא לתענוג They *anointed* themselves often, *not for excess,* or *bravery,* or *delight,* but for the healing of some disease, or for the health of the body. חושש את ראשו או שעלו בו חטטין סך שמן: *He[r] that is troubled with the head-ache, or on whom scabs arise, let him anoint himself with oil.*

" A [s] tradition of the Rabbins. It is forbidden [*in fasts*] to wash a part of the body, as well as the whole body. But if it be defiled with dirt or dung, let him wash according to the custom, and let him not be troubled. It is also forbidden to anoint a part of the body, as well as the whole body : but if[t] a man be sick, or if a scab arise on his head, let him anoint himself according to the custom."

Hence [u], when the apostles are said " to anoint the sick with oil, and to heal them," Mark vi. 13, they used an ordinary medicine, and obtained an extraordinary and infallible effect.

Hence that of St. James, chap. v. 14 : " Let the sick man call for the elders of the church, and let them pray over him, anointing him with oil in the name of the Lord :" that is, to that ordinary medicine, namely, anointing for recovery of

[o] Fol. 77. 2.
[p] Fol. 12. 2. and 13. 2.
[q] Hieros. in Maasar Sheni, fol. 53. 2. and Schabb. fol. 12. 1.

[r] Hieros. in the place above.
[s] Bab. Joma, fol. 77. 2.
[t] *Leusden's edition,* vol. ii. p.304.
[u] *English folio edit.,* vol. ii. p. 162.

health, let the prayers of the ministers of the church be used.

III. They used sometimes a superstitious anointing of the head, and nothing differing from magical anointing : זה שהוא לוחש נותן שמן על גבי ראשו ולוחש *He*[x] *that mutters, let him put oil upon his head, and mutter.* This *muttering* is to be understood concerning the manner of saying a charm upon the wound, or some place of the body that feels pain ; לוחש על המכה *muttering over the wound ;* of which mention is made in the tract *Sanhedrim*[y]. Mention also is made in the tract *Schabbath*[z] now alleged, that some used this enchanting muttering in the name of Jesus : " One being sick, a certain person came to him, and muttered upon him in the name of Jesus of Pandira, and he was healed." And a little after ; "R. Eliezer Ben Damah was bitten by a serpent. James of Capharsam came to heal him in the name of Jesus : but R. Ismael permitted him not," &c. See Acts xix. 13.

If the words of James before alleged be compared with this cursed custom, they may well sound to this sense ; ' It is customary for the unbelieving Jews to use anointing of the sick joined with a magical and enchanting muttering ; but how infinitely better is it to join the pious prayers of the elders of the church to the anointing of the sick !'

Ver. 22 : 'Eὰν ὁ ὀφθαλμός σου ἁπλοῦς ᾖ· *If thine eye be single.* Ver. 23 : 'Eὰν ὁ ὀφθαλμός σου πονηρὸς ᾖ· *If thine eye be evil.*] That the business here is about a covetous, or a not covetous mind, may be gathered,

I. From the context on either hand : for, ver. 20, 21, the discourse is concerning treasures either earthly or heavenly, and, ver. 24, concerning serving either God or Mammon.

II. From a very usual manner of speech of the nation. For *a good eye,* to the Jews, is the same with *a bountiful mind ;* and an *evil eye* is the same with a *covetous mind.* " This[a] is the measure of the Truma" (or, of the oblation yielded to the priests), עין יפה א׳ מארבעים *A good eye yieldeth one out of forty ;* that is, the fortieth part. " The school of Shammai saith, One out of thirty. A middling eye, one out of fifty. והרעה א׳ מששים *And an evil eye, one out of sixty.* הנותן

---

[x] Hieros. in Maasar Sheni, in the place above, and in Schab. f. 14. 3.

[y] Cap. 10. hal. 1.

[z] Col. 4.

[a] Trumoth, cap. 4. hal. 3.

מתנה להיות נותן בעין יפה *He*[b] *that gives a gift, let him give with a good eye:* and he that dedicates any thing, let him dedicate it with a good eye." See Matt. xx. 15. Hence covetousness is called ἐπιθυμία τῶν ὀφθαλμῶν, *the lust of the eyes,* 1 John ii. 16. Therefore our Saviour shows here with how great darkness the mind is clouded and dimmed by covetousness, and too much care of worldly things.

Ver. 26 : Πετεινὰ τοῦ οὐρανοῦ οὐ σπείρουσιν, &c.: *The fowls of the air, they sow not, &c.*] " Have[c] you ever seen beasts or fowls that had a workshop ? And yet they are fed without trouble of mind," &c. See also Midras Tillin[d].

Ver. 30 : Ὀλιγόπιστοι· *O ye of little faith.*] קטני אמונה *Small of faith,* a phrase very frequent in the Talmudists.

המשמיע קולו בתפלתו הרי זה מקטני אמונה *He*[e] *that prayed with a loud voice, is to be numbered among those that are little of faith,* ὀλιγοπίστους. The[f] Israelites in the wilderness were קטני אמונה ὀλιγόπιστοι, *of little faith.* R. Abuhabh in the preface to *Menorath hammaor;* " R. Eliezer saith, ʻWhosoever hath but a small morsel in his basket, and saith, What have I to eat to-morrow, behold, he is to be reckoned among קטני אמונה *those of little faith.*ʼ "

Ver. 34[g] : Ἀρκετὸν τῇ ἡμέρᾳ ἡ κακία αὐτῆς· *Sufficient to the day is the evil thereof.*] דיה לצרה בשעתה : *There*[h] *is enough of trouble in the very moment.*

CHAP. VII.

Ver. 2 : Ἐν ᾧ μέτρῳ μετρεῖτε· *With what measure ye mete.*] This is a very common proverb among the Jews : במדה שאדם מודד מודדין לו: *In*[i] *the measure that a man measureth, others measure to him.* See also the tract Sotah[k], where it is illustrated by various examples.

Ver. 4 : Ἐκβάλω τὸ κάρφος ἀπὸ τοῦ ὀφθαλμοῦ σου, &c. *Let me pull out the mote out of thine eye, &c.*] And this also was a known proverb among them : " It[l] is written in the days when they judged the judges, that is, in the generation which

---

b Hieros. Bava Bathra, fol. 14. 4.
c Kiddushin, cap. ult. hal. ult.
d Fol. 15. 1.
e Bab. Berac. fol. 24. 2.
f Id. Erachin, fol. 15. 1.
g *English folio edit.*, vol. ii. p.163.

h Bab. Berac. fol. 9. 2.
i Bab. Sanhedr. fol. 100. 1. near the end.
k Cap. 1. hal. 7, 8. 9.
l Bab. Bava Bathra, fol. 15. 2.

judged their judges, When [m] any [*judge*] אומר לו טול קיסם
מבין עיניך said to another, *Cast out the mote out of thine eye* ;
אומד לו טול קורה מבין עיניך : he answered, *Cast you out the
beam out of your own eye,"* &c.

" R. Tarphon [n] said, ' I wonder whether there be any in
this age that will receive reproof : but if one saith to another, Cast out the mote out of thine eye, he will be ready
to answer, Cast out the beam out of thine own eye.' " Where
the Gloss writes thus ; קיסם " Cast out *the mote*, that is, the
small sin that is in thine hand; he may answer, But cast
you out the great sin that is in yours. So that they could
not reprove, because all were sinners." See also the Aruch
in the word קסם.

Ver. 9 : Μὴ λίθον ἐπιδώσει αὐτῷ ; *Will he give him a stone ?*
Here that of Seneca [o] comes into my mind ; " Verrucosus
called a benefit roughly given from a hard man, *panem lapi-
dosum, ' stony bread.' "*

Ver. 12 : Πάντα ὅσα ἂν θέλητε, ἵνα ποιῶσιν ὑμῖν οἱ ἄνθρωποι,
&c. *Whatsoever ye would that men should do unto you,* &c.]
A [p] certain Gentile came to Shammai, and said, ' Make me a
proselyte, that I may learn the whole law, standing upon one
foot :' Shammai beat him with the staff that was in his hand.
He went to Hillel, and he made him a proselyte, and said,
דעלך סני לחברך לא תעביד *That which is odious to thyself,
do it not to thy neighbour :* for this is the whole law.

Ver. 13 : Εὐρύχωρος ἡ ὁδός· *Broad is the way.*] In these
words, concerning the broad and narrow way, our Saviour
seems to allude to the rules of the Jews among their lawyers
concerning the public and private ways. With whom, " a
private way was four cubits in breadth ; a public way was
sixteen cubits." See the Gloss in *Peah* [q].

Ver. 14 [r]: Πύλη· *Gate.*] Under this phrase are very many
things in religion expressed in the Holy Scripture, Gen. xxviii.
17, Psal. cxviii. 19, 20, Matt. xvi. 18, &c. ; and also in the
Jewish writers. ' The gate of repentance' is mentioned by
the Chaldee paraphrast upon Jer. xxxiii. 6 ; and ' the gate of

---

[m] *Leusden's edit.*, vol. ii. p. 305.
[n] Bab. Erachin. fol. 16. 2.
[o] De Benefic. lib. ii. cap. 7.

[p] Bab. Schab. fol. 31. 1.
[q] Cap. 2. hal. 1.
[r] *English folio edit.*, vol. ii. p. 164.

prayers,' and 'the gate of tears.' " Since[s] the Temple was laid waste, the gates of prayer were shut, but the gates of tears were not shut."

Στενὴ πύλη, *Strait gate*, seems to be the Greek rendering of פשפש *Pishpesh*, a word very usual among the Talmudists: פתח את הפשפש "With[t] a key he *opened the little door*, and out of Beth-mokad" (*the place of the fire-hearth*) " he entereth into the court." פשפש, saith the Aruch, *is a little door in the midst of a great door.*

Ver. 15 : Ἐν ἐνδύμασι προβάτων· *In sheep's clothing.*] Not so much in woollen garments as in the very *skins of sheep :* so that outwardly they might seem sheep, but " inwardly they were ravening wolves." Of the ravenousness of wolves among the Jews, take these two examples besides others. " The[u] elders proclaimed a fast in their cities upon this occasion, because the wolves had devoured two little children beyond Jordan. More[x] than three hundred sheep of the sons of Judah Ben Shamoe were torn by wolves."

Ver. 16 : Ἀπὸ τῶν καρπῶν αὐτῶν ἐπιγνώσεσθε αὐτούς· *By their fruits ye shall know them.*] That is a proverb not unlike it. בוצין בוצין מקטפיה ידוע A[y] *gourd, a gourd, is known by its branch.*

Ver. 29 : Ὡς ἐξουσίαν ἔχων, καὶ οὐχ ὡς οἱ γραμματεῖς· *As one having authority, and not as the scribes.*] It is said with good reason, in the verse going before, that " the multitude were astonished at Christ's doctrine :" for, besides his divine truth, depth, and convincing power, they had not before heard any discoursing with that αὐθεντία, *authority*, that he did. The scribes borrowed credit to their doctrine from traditions, and the fathers of them : and no sermon of any scribe had any authority or value, without תנו רבנין *The Rabbins have a tradition*, or חכמים אומרים *The wise men say ;* or some traditional oracle of that nature. Hillel the Great taught truly, and as the tradition was concerning a certain thing ; " But[z], although he discoursed of that matter all day long, לא קבלו ממנו *they received not his doctrine*, until he said at last, So I heard from Shemaia and Abtalion."

---

[s] Bab. Berac. fol. 32. 2.

[t] Tamid, cap. 1. hal. 3.

[u] Taanith, cap. 3. hal. 7.

[x] Hieros. Jom. tobh, fol. 60. 1.

[y] Bab. Berac. fol. 48. 1.

[z] Hieros. Pesachin, fol. 33. 1.

CHAP. VIII.

Ver. 2 : Δύνασαί με καθαρίσαι· *Thou canst make me clean.*]
The doctrine in the law concerning leprosy paints out very
well the doctrine of sin.

I. It teacheth, that no creature is so unclean by a touch
as man. Yea, it may with good reason be asked, whether
any creature, while it lived, was unclean to the touch, beside man? That is often repeated in the Talmudists, that
" he that takes a worm in his hand[a], all the waters of Jordan
cannot wash him from his uncleanness ;" that is, while the
worm is as yet in his hand; or the worm being cast away,
not until the time appointed for[b] such purification be expired. But whether it is to be understood of a living or
dead worm, it is doubted, not without cause, since the law,
treating of this matter, speaketh only of those things that
died of themselves. See Lev. xi. 31 : " Whosoever shall touch
them when they be dead," &c. : and ver. 32, " Upon whatsoever any of them, when they are dead, shall fall," &c. But
whether he speaks of a living worm, or a dead, uncleanness
followed by the touch of it for that day only : for " he shall
be unclean (saith the law) until the evening :" but the carcase
of a man being touched, a week's uncleanness followed. See
Num. xix.

II. Among all the uncleannesses of men, leprosy was the
greatest, inasmuch as other uncleannesses separated the unclean person, or rendered him unclean, for a day, or a week,
or a month; but the leprosy, perhaps, for ever.

III. When the leper was purified, the leprosy was not
healed : but the poison of the disease being evaporated, and
the danger of the contagion gone, the leper was restored to
the public congregation. Gehazi, the servant of Elisha, was
adjudged to perpetual leprosy ; and yet he was cleansed, and
conversed with the king (2 Kings viii. 5); cleansed, not healed.
Thus under justification and sanctification there remain still
the seeds and filth of sin.

IV. He that was full of the leprosy was pronounced

---

[a] *Leusden's edit.*, vol. ii. p. 306.   [b] *English folio edit.*, vol. ii. p. 165.

clean ; he that was otherwise, was not.   Levit. xiii. 12 ; " If
the leprosy shall cover the whole body from head to foot,
thou shalt pronounce him clean," &c.   A law certainly to be
wondered at !   Is he not clean, till the whole body be in-
fected and covered with the leprosy ?   Nor shalt thou, O sin-
ner, be made clean without the like condition.   Either acknowledge thyself all over leprous, or thou shalt not be
cleansed.

Ver. 3 : Ἥψατο αὐτοῦ ὁ Ἰησοῦς· *Jesus touched him.*]   It was
indeed a wonder, that when the leprosy was a creeping infection, the priest, when he judged of it, was not hurt with the
infection.   It cannot be passed over without observation, that
Aaron, being bound under the same guilt with Miriam, bore
not the same punishment : for she was touched with leprosy,
he not, Num. xii.   And also that Uzziah should be confuted
concerning his encroaching upon the priesthood no other way
than by the plague of leprosy.   In him God would magnify
the priesthood, that was to judge of the leprosy ; and he
would shew the other was no priest, by his being touched
with the leprosy.   It can scarcely be denied, indeed, that
the priests sometimes might be touched with that plague ;
but certainly they catched not the contagion while they
were doing their office in judging of it.   This is a noble
doctrine of our High Priest, the Judge and Physician of our
leprosy, while he remains wholly untouched by it.   How much
does he surpass that miracle of the Levitical priesthood !
They were not touched by the contagion when they touched
the leprous person ; he, by his touch, heals him that hath
the infection.

Ver. 4 : Ὕπαγε, σεαυτὸν δεῖξον τῷ ἱερεῖ, &c. *Go, shew thyself
to the priest, &c.*]   I. Our Saviour would not have the extraordinary manner whereby he was healed discovered to the
priest, that he might pay the ordinary duty of his cleansing.
And surely it deserves no slight consideration, that he sends
him to the priest.   However now the priesthood was too degenerate both from its institution and its office, yet he would
reserve to it its privileges, while he would reserve the priesthood itself.   Corruption, indeed, defiles a divine institution,
but extinguishes it not.

II. Those things which at that time were to be done in

cleansing of the leprosy, according to the Rubric, were these :
" Let him bring three beasts: that is, *a sacrifice for sin*
[חַטָּאת], *a sacrifice for transgression* [אָשָׁם], and a burnt-
offering. But a poor man brought a sacrifice for sin of birds,
and a burnt-offering of birds. He stands by the sacrifice for
transgression, and lays both his hands upon it, and slays it :
and two priests receive the blood ; the one in a vessel, the
other in his hand. He who receives the blood in his hand
goes to the leper in the chamber of the lepers :" this was in
the corner of the Court of the Women, looking north-west.
" He placeth him in the gate of Nicanor," the east gate of
the Court of Israel ; " he stretcheth forth his head within
the court, and puts blood upon the lowest part of his ear :
he stretcheth out his hand also within the court, and he
puts blood upon his thumb and his foot, and he puts blood
also upon his great toe, &c. And the other adds oil to the
same members in the same place," &c. The reason why,
with his[c] neck held out, he so thrust forth his head and ears
into the court, you may learn from the Glosser : " The gate
of Nicanor (saith he) was between the Court of the Women
and the Court of Israel : but now it was not lawful for any
to enter into the Court of Israel for whom there was not a
perfect expiation : and, on the contrary, it was not lawful to
carry the blood of the sacrifice for transgression out of the
court." Hence was that invention, that the leper that was
to be cleansed should stand without the court ; and yet his
ears, his thumbs, and his toes, to which the blood was to be
applied, were within the court. We omit saying more ; it is
enough to have produced these things, whence it may be observed what things they were that our Saviour sent back this
healed person to do.

The cure was done in Galilee, and thence he is sent away
to Jerusalem ; silence and sacrifice are enjoined him : Ὅρα
μηδενὶ εἴπῃς, &c. *See thou tell no man*, &c.: καὶ προσένεγκε τὸ
δῶρον, &c.: *and offer the gift*, &c. And why all these things?

First, Christ makes trial of the obedience[d] and gratitude of
him that was cured, laying upon him the charge of a sacrifice
and the labour of a journey.

[c] *English folio edit.*, vol. ii. p. 166.   [d] *Leusden's edit.*, vol. ii. p. 307.

Secondly, He would have him restored to the communion of the church (from which his leprosy had separated him), after the wonted and instituted manner. He provides that he himself give no scandal, and the person healed make no schism: and however both his words and gestures sufficiently argue that he believed in Christ, yet Christ will by no means draw him from the communion of the church, but restore him to it. Hence is that command of his to him; " See thou tell no man, but offer a gift for a testimony to them :" that is, ' Do not boast the extraordinary manner of thy healing; think not thyself freed from the bond of the law, in case of a leper, because of it; thrust not thyself into the communion of the church before the rites of admission be duly performed : but, however you have no business with the priest in reference to the purification and cleansing, go to the priest nevertheless, and offer the gift that is due, for a testimony that you are again restored into communion with them.' This caution of our Saviour hath the same tendency with that, Matt. xvii. 27, " That we be not an offence to them," &c.

Ver. 6: Βέβληται· *Lieth.*] מוטל : *Laid forth.* Thus, מת מוטל *A dead man laid forth*, in order to his being carried out. The power and dominion of the disease is so expressed. The weak person lieth so, that he is moved only by others; he cannot move himself, but is, as it were, next door to carrying out. So, ver. 14, of Peter's mother-in-law, ἦν βεβλημένη καὶ πυρέσσουσα, *was laid, and sick of a fever.*

Ver. 12 : Ἐκβληθήσονται εἰς τὸ σκότος τὸ ἐξώτερον· *Shall be cast out into outer darkness.*] Hear, O Jew, thy most sad but certainly most just judgment, concerning thy eternal blindness and perdition. For whatsoever τὸ σκότος τὸ ἐξώτερον, *outer darkness*, signifies, whether *the darkness of the heathen* (for to the Jews the heathen were οἱ ἔξω, *those that are without*), or that *darkness* beyond that, Isaiah ix. 1, or both ; our Saviour clearly intimates the Jews were thither to be banished ; but that they were to be recalled again, he intimates not anywhere: if so be by υἱοὺς βασιλείας, *children of the kingdom, they* be to be understood : which who is there that denies ?

Ver. 16 : 'Οψίας δὲ γενομένης· *When the even was come.*]
Mark adds, ὅτε ἔδυ ὁ ἥλιος, *when the sun was now set*, and
the sabbath was now gone.

I. The sabbath was ended by the Jews at the supper, or
the feast.   In which they used a candle (as they did upon
the entrance of the sabbath), and wine, and spices ; and the
form of a blessing over a cup of wine, and then over the
candle, and then over the spices: " Does the sabbath end
when he is now in the middle of his feast? He puts an end
to his eating ; washes his hands ; and over a cup of wine
he gives thanks for his food ; and afterward over that cup
he useth the form of prayer in the separation of the sabbath
from[e] a common day : if he be now drinking when the sabbath goes out, he ceaseth from drinking, and recites the form
of separation, and then returns to his drinking[f]."

II. The proper limits of the sabbath were from sun-set to
sun-set.   This is sufficiently intimated by St. Mark, when
he saith, that ὅτε ἔδυ ὁ ἥλιος, *when the sun was now set*, they
brought the sick to be healed : which they held unlawful to
do while the sun was yet going down, and the sabbath yet
present.

The Talmudic canons give a caution of some works, that
they be not begun on the day before the sabbath, if they
may not be ended and finished, מבעוד יום *while it is yet
day :* that is (as they explain it), עם השמש *while the sun is
not yet set[g].* המדליק צריך להדליק מבעוד יום קודם שקיעת
החמה *He that lights a [sabbath] candle, let him light it while
it is yet day, before sun-set[h].* "On the sabbath-eve it is permitted to work until sun-set[i]." The entrance of the sabbath
was at sun-set, and so was the end of it.

III. After the setting of sun, a certain space was called
בין השמשות *Bin Hashmashuth :* concerning which these
things are disputed[k] ; "What is בין השמשות ? R. Tanchuma
saith, It is like a drop of blood put upon the very edge of a
sword, which divides itself every where.   What is בין
השמשות ? It is from that time when the sun sets, whilst one
may walk half a mile.   R. Josi saith, בין השמשות is like a

e *English folio edit.*, vol. ii. p. 167.   h Maimon. in Schab. cap. 5, &c.
f Maimon. Schab. cap. 29.   i Hieros. Sheviith, fol. 33. 1.
g Schab. cap. 1.   k Hieros. Berac. fol. 2. 2.

wink of the eye," &c. בֵּין הַשְּׁמָשׁוֹת properly signifies, *between the suns :* and the manner of speech seems to be drawn thence, that there are said to be two שְׁקִיעוֹת *sun-sets.* Concerning which, read the Glosser upon Maimonides[1]. Where thus also Maimonides himself : " From the time that the sun sets till the three middle stars appear, it is called בֵּין שְׁמָשׁוֹת *between the suns :* and it is a doubt whether that time be part of the day or of the night. However, they every where judge of it לְהַחְמִיר *to render the office heavy.* Therefore, between that time they do not light the sabbatical candle : and whosoever shall do any servile work on the sabbath-eve, and in the going out of the sabbath, is bound to offer a sacrifice for sin." So also the Jerusalem Talmudists in the place last cited : " Does one star appear? Certainly, as yet it is day. Do two? It is doubted whether it be day. Do three? It is night without doubt." And a line after ; " On the sabbath-eve, if any work after one star seen, he is clear : if after[m] two, he is bound to a sacrifice for a transgression ; if after three, he is bound to a sacrifice for sin. Likewise, in the going out of the sabbath, if he do any work after one star is seen, he is bound to a sacrifice for sin ; if after two, to a sacrifice for transgression : if after three, he is clear."

Hence you may see at what time they brought persons here to Christ to be healed, namely, in the going out of the sabbath ; if so be they took care of the canonical hour of the nation, which is not to be doubted of.

Ver. 17 : Αὐτὸς τὰς ἀσθενείας ἡμῶν ἔλαβε· *Himself took our infirmities.*] Divers names of the Messias are produced by the Talmudists[n], among others חִיוְורְתָא דְבִי רַבִּי שְׁמוֹ : " The Rabbins say, *His name is, ' The leper of the house of Rabbi :'* as it is said, Certainly he bare our infirmities," &c. And a little after, " Rabh saith, If Messias be among the living, Rabbenu Haccodesh is he." The Gloss is, " If Messias be of them that are now alive, certainly our holy Rabbi is he, as being one that carries infirmities," &c. R. Judah, whom they called ' the Holy,' underwent very many sicknesses (of whom, and of his sicknesses, you have the story in the Tal-

---

[1] In Schab. cap. 5.   [m] *Leusden's edition,* vol. ii. p. 308.
[n] Bab. Sanhedr. fol. 98. 2.

mud, "Thirteen[o] years Rabbi laboured under the pain of the teeth," &c.); because of which there were some who were pleased to account him for the Messias; because, according to the prophets, Messias should be 'a man of sorrows:' and yet they look for him coming in pomp.

This allegation of Matthew may seem somewhat unsuitable and different from the sense of the prophet: for Isaiah speaks of the Messias carrying our infirmities in himself; but Matthew speaks concerning him healing them in others: Isaiah of the diseases of the soul (see 1 Pet. ii. 24); Matthew of the diseases of the body. But in this sense both agree very well, that Christ's business was with our infirmities and sorrows, and he was able to manage that business: his part was to carry and bear them, and in him was strength and power to carry and bear them. In this sense, therefore, is Matthew to be understood; he healed the demoniacs and all diseased persons with his word, that that of Isaiah might be fulfilled, He it is who is able to bear and carry our sorrows and sicknesses. And so, whether you apply the words to the diseases of the mind or the body, a plain sense by an equal easiness does arise. The sense of Isaiah reacheth indeed further; namely, That Messias himself shall be a man of sorrows, &c., but not excluding that which we have mentioned, which Matthew very fitly retains, as excellently well suiting with his case.

Ver. 28[P]: Εἰς τὴν χώραν τῶν Γεργεσηνῶν· *Into the country of the Gergesenes.*] In Mark and Luke it is, τῶν Γαδαρηνῶν, *of the Gadarenes,* both very properly: for it was the city Gadara, whence the country had its name: there was also Gergasa, a city or a town within that country; which whether it bare its name from the ancient Canaanite stock of the Gergashites, or from the word גרגשתא *Gargushta,* which signifies *clay* or *dirt,* we leave to the more learned to discuss. *Lutetia,* [Paris], a word of such a nature, may be brought for an example.

Δύο δαιμονιζόμενοι ἐκ τῶν μνημείων ἐξερχόμενοι, &c. *Two possessed with devils coming out of the tombs, &c.*] "These[q] are the signs of a שוטה *madman.* He goes out in the night,

---

[o] Hieros. Kilaim, fol. 32. 1.   [P] *English folio edit.,* vol. ii. p. 168.
[q] Hieros. Trumoth, fol. 40. 2.

and lodges among the sepulchres, and teareth his garments, and tramples upon whatsoever is given him. R. Houna saith, But is he only mad in whom all these signs are? I say, Not. He that goes out in the night קניטריכוס is *chondriacus, hypochondriacal.* He that lodgeth a night among the tombs מקטר לשדים *burns incense to devils.* He that tears his garments כוליקוס *is melancholic.* And he that tramples under his feet whatsoever is given him is קורדייקוס *cardiacus, troubled in mind.*" And a little after, פעמים שוטה פעמים חלום " *one while he is mad, another while he is well:* while he is mad, he is to be esteemed for a madman in respect of all his actions: while he is well, he is to be esteemed for one that is his own man in all respects." See what we say at chap. xvii. 15.

Ver. 30: Ἀγέλη χοίρων πολλῶν βοσκομένη· *A herd of many swine feeding.*] Were these Gadarenes Jews, or heathens?

I. It was a matter of infamy for a Jew to keep swine: "R. Jonah[r] had a very red face, which a certain woman seeing said thus, סבא סבא *Seignior, Seignior,* either you are a winebibber, or a usurer, or a keeper of hogs."

II. It was forbidden by the canon: "The[s] wise men forbade to keep hogs anywhere, and a dog, unless he were chained." Hogs upon a twofold account: 1. By reason of the hurt and damage that they would bring to other men's fields. Generally, "the[t] keeping smaller cattle was forbid in the land of Israel;" among which you may very well reckon hogs even in the first place: and the reason is given by the Gemarists, "That they break not into other men's grounds." 2. The feeding of hogs is more particularly forbidden for their uncleanness. For אסור לעשות סחורה בכל דברים טמאים *It is forbidden to trade in any thing that is unclean[u].*

III. Yea, it was forbid under a curse: "The[x] wise men say, Cursed is he that keeps dogs and swine; because from them ariseth much harm."

" Let[y] no man keep hogs anywhere. The Rabbins deliver: When the Asmonean family were in hostility among

[r] Hieros. Shekalim, fol. 47. 3.
[s] Maimon. in Nizke Mammon. cap. 5.
[t] Bava Kama, cap. 7. hal. 7.

[u] Gloss. in Kama, in the place above.
[x] Maimon. in the place before.
[y] Bab. Kama, fol. 82. 2.

themselves, Hyrcanus was besieged within Jerusalem, and Aristobulus was without. The besieged sent money in a box let down[z] by a rope; and they which were without bought with it the daily sacrifices, which were drawn up by those that were within. Among the besiegers there was one skilled in the Greek learning, who said, 'As long as they thus perform the service of the Temple, they will not be delivered into your hands.' The next day, therefore, they let down their money, and these sent them back a hog. When the hog was drawing up, and came to the middle of the wall, he fixed his hoofs to the wall, and the land of Israel was shaken, &c. From that time they said, 'Cursed be he who keeps hogs, and cursed be he who teacheth his son the wisdom of the Greeks.'" This story is cited in Menachoth[a].

Therefore you will wonder, and not without cause, at that which is related in their Talmud : " They[b] said sometimes to Rabh Judah, There is a plague among the swine. He therefore appointed a fast." What! is a Jew concerned for a plague among swine? But the reason is added : " For Rabh Judah thought that a stroke laid upon one kind of cattle would invade all."

You may not, therefore, improperly guess, that these hogs belonged not to the Jews, but to the heathen dwelling among the Gadarene Jews; for such a mixture was very usual in the cities and countries of the land of Israel. Which we observe elsewhere of the town Susitha or Hippo, but some small distance from Gadara.

Or[c] if you grant that they were Jews, their manners will make that opinion probable, as being persons whose highest law the purse and profit was wont to be. Since brawn and swine's flesh were of so great account with the Romans and other heathens, there is no reason to believe that a Jew was held so straitly by his canons, as to value them before his own profit, when there was hope of gain.

CHAP. IX.

VER. 9 : Εἶδεν ἄνθρωπον καθήμενον ἐπὶ τὸ τελώνιον, Ματθαῖον λεγόμενον· *He saw a man sitting at the receipt of custom, called*

---

[z] *Leusden's edition*, vol. ii. p. 309.
[a] Fol. 64. 2.
[b] Bab. Taanith, fol. 21. 2.
[c] *English folio edit.*, vol. ii. p. 171.

Matthew.]   Five disciples of Christ are mentioned by the
Talmudists, among whom Matthew seems to be named :
" The[d] Rabbins deliver, There were five disciples of Jesus,
מתאי נקאי נצר ובוני והודה‏ *Mathai, Nakai, Nezer, and
Boni, and Thodah.*" These, they relate, were led out and
killed. See the place. Perhaps *five* are only mentioned by
them, because five of the disciples were chiefly employed
among the Jews in Judea : namely, Matthew who wrote his
Gospel there, Peter, James, John, and Judas.

Matthew seems to have sat in the custom-house of Capernaum near the sea, to gather some certain toll or rate of those
that sailed over. See Mark, chap. ii. 13, 14.

" He[e] that produceth paper [on the Sabbath] in which
a publican's note is writ, and he that produceth a publican's
note, is guilty." The Gloss is, " When any pays tribute to
the lord of the river, or when he excuses him his tribute,
he certifies the publican by a note [or some bill of free com-
merce], that he hath remitted him his duty : and it was customary in it to write two letters greater than ours." See also
the Gemara there.

Ver. 14 : Ἡμεῖς καὶ οἱ Φαρισαῖοι νηστεύομεν πολλά· *We and
the Pharisees fast oft.*]   Monsters, rather than stories, are
related of the Pharisees' fasts :—

I. It is known to all, from Luke xviii. 12, that they were
wont to fast twice every week. The rise of which custom
you may fetch from this tradition : " Ezra[f] decreed ten
decrees. He appointed the public reading of the law the
second and fifth days of the week : and again on the sabbath
at the *Mincha* [or *evening service*]. He instituted the session
of the judges in cities on the second and fifth days of the
week," &c. Of this matter discourse is had elsewhere : " If[g]
you ask the reason why the decree was made concerning the
second and fifth days, &c., we must answer, saith the Gloss,
from that which is said in Midras concerning Moses; namely,
that he went up into the mount to receive the second tables
on the fifth day of the week, and came down, God being now
appeased, the second day. When, therefore, that ascent and
descent was a time of grace, they so determined of the second

---

d Bab. Sanhedr, fol. 43. 1.   f Bab. Bava Kama, fol. 82. 1.
e Schabb. cap. 8. hal. 2.   g Hieros. in Megill. fol. 75. 1.

and fifth days.   And therefore they were wont to fast also on
the second and fifth days."

II. It was not seldom that they enjoined themselves fasts,
for this end, to have lucky dreams ; or to attain the interpretation of some dream; or to turn away the ill import of a
dream.   Hence was that expression very usual, תענית חלום
A fast for a dream; and it was a common proverb, יפה
תענית לחלום כאש לנעורת *A fast is as fit for a dream, as
fire is for flax.*   For this cause it was allowed to fast on the
sabbath, which otherwise was forbidden.   See the Babylonian
Talmud, in the tract *Schabbath*[h] : where also we meet with
the story of R. Joshua Bar Rabh Idai, who on the sabbath
was splendidly received by R. Ishai, but would not eat because
he was בתענית חלום *under a fast for a dream.*

III. They fasted often to obtain their desires : " R. Josi[i]
fasted eighty fasts, and R. Simeon Ben Lachish three hundred
for this end, that they might see R. Chaijah Rubbah."   And
often to avert threatening evils ; of which fasts the tract
Taanith does largely treat.   Let one example be enough
instead of many ; and that is, of R. Zadok, who for forty
years, that is, from the time when[k] the gates of the Temple
opened of their own accord (a sign of the destruction coming),
did so mortify himself with fastings, that he was commonly
called חלשא *Chalsha,* that is, *The weak.*   And when the city
was now destroyed, and he saw it was in vain to fast any
longer, he used the physicians of Titus to restore his health,
which, through too much abstinence, had been wasted.

Ver. 15[l] : Οἱ υἱοὶ τοῦ νυμφῶνος· *The children of the bridechamber.*] בני חופה *The sons of the bridechamber,* an ordinary phrase.   There is no need to relate their mirth in the
time of the nuptials : I will relate that only, and it is enough,
which is spoke by the Glosser [m], נהגו לשבר זכוכית בנישואין
They were wont to break glass vessels in weddings.   And that
for this reason, that they might by this action set bounds to
their mirth, lest they should run out into too much excess.
The Gemara produceth one or two stories there : " Mar the
son of Rabbena made wedding feasts for his son, and invited

[h] Fol. 11. 1.
[i] Hieros. Kilaim, fol. 32. 2.
[k] *Leusden's edit.,* vol. ii. p. 310.

[l] *English folio edit.,* vol. ii. p. 172.
[m] In Bab. Berac. fol. 31. 1.

the Rabbins : and when he saw that their mirth exceeded its
bounds, אייתי כסא דמוקרא *he brought forth a glass cup*
worth four hundred zuzees, and brake it before them ; whereupon they became sad." The like story is also related of
Rabh Ishai. And the reason of this action is given ; שאסור
לאדם שימלא שחוק פיו בעהז" *Because it is forbidden a
man to fill his mouth with laughter in this world.* [Tantum
aberant a jejunando filii thalami. *Leusd.*]

חופה, or the days of the bridechamber, to *the sons of the
bridechamber,* that is, to the friends and acquaintance, were
seven : hence there is frequent mention of " the seven days of
the marriage-feast :" but to the bride, the days of the bridechamber were thirty. It is forbidden to eat, drink, wash or
anoint oneself on the day of Expiation : והמלך וכלה
ירחצו פניהם *But[n] it is allowed a king and a bride to wash their
faces.* " For the bride is to be made handsome (saith the
Gloss upon the place), that she may be lovely to her husband.
וכל ל' יום לחופתה היא קרויה כלה *And all the thirty
days of her bridechamber she is called The Bride.*"

It is worth meditation, how the disciples, when Christ was
with them, suffered no persecution at all ; but when he was
absent, all manner of persecution overtook them.

Ver. 18 : Ἰδοὺ, ἄρχων· *Behold, a ruler.*] Distinction[o] is
made between חזן הכנסת *the bishop of the congregation,* and
ראש הכנסת *the head of the congregation.* For while the
discourse is there of the high priest reading a certain portion
of the law on the day of Expiation agreeable to the day, thus
it is said, חזן הכנסת נוטל ספר תורה ונותנו לראש הכנסת
*The bishop of the synagogue takes the book of the law, and gives
it* ἀρχισυναγώγῳ, *to the ruler of the synagogue.* Where the
Gloss thus, בית הכנסת " *The synagogue* was in the mount of
the Temple, near the court [which is worthy to be marked] :
חזן הכנסת שמש *The Chazan* [or *bishop,* or *overseer*] *of the
synagogue is the minister :* and the ruler of the synagogue is
he by whose command the affairs of the synagogue are appointed ; namely, who shall read the prophet, who shall recite
the phylacteries, who shall pass before the ark."

Of this order and function was Jairus, in the synagogue

[n] In Joma, cap. 7. hal. 1.   [o] Ibid.

of Capernaum : so that the word ἄρχων, *ruler*, being understood in this sense, admits of little obscurity, although εἷς, *one*, or τὶς, *a certain*, be not there : "he speaking these words, 'Behold, the ruler of that synagogue,'" &c.

Ver. 20 : Αἱμορροοῦσα· *Diseased with an issue of blood.*] זבה *Zeba*, in Talmudic language. The Talmudic tract זבין may serve for a commentary here.

These things were acted in the streets of Capernaum : for there Matthew lived, and there Jairus also : and in his passage from the house of the one to the house of the other, this diseased woman met him. Weigh the story well, and you will easily judge what is to be thought of that story concerning the statues of this woman and Christ, set up at Paneas, or Cæsarea Philippi : of which Eusebius [p] speaks.

Ver. 23 : Ἰδὼν τοὺς αὐλητάς· *Seeing the minstrels.*] Dion Cassius [q] concerning the funeral of Augustus : Ὁ δὲ δὴ Τιβέριος καὶ ὁ Δροῦσος ὁ υἱὸς αὐτοῦ φαιὰν, τὸν ἀγοραῖον τρόπον πεποιημένην, εἶχον. Καὶ τοῦ μὲν λιβανωτοῦ καὶ αὐτοὶ ἔθυσαν· τῷ δὲ αὐλητῇ οὐκ ἐχρήσαντο· *Tiberius, and Drusus his son,......sacrificed frankincense themselves ; but they used not a minstrel.*

אפילי עני שבישראל׳ לא יפחות לה משני חלילים ומקוננת [r] *Even* [s] *the poorest among the Israelites* [his wife being dead], *will afford her not less than two pipes, and one woman to make lamentation.*

"He [t] that hireth an ass-keeper, or a waggoner, to bring חלילים לכלה או למת *pipes, either for a bride, or for a dead person :*" that is, either for a wedding, or a funeral.

"The [u] husband is bound to bury his dead wife, and to make lamentations and mournings for her, according to the custom of all countries. And also the very poorest among the Israelites will afford her not less than two pipes and one lamenting woman : but if he be rich, let all things be done according to his quality."

"If [x] an idolater bring pipes on the sabbath [y] to the house where any one is dead, "an Israelite shall not lament at those pipes."

p Eccles. Hist. lib. vii. cap. 14.
q Lib. lvi. ed. Reimar, p. 830.
r *English folio edit.*, vol. ii. p.173.
s Chetub. cap. 4. hal. 6.
t Bava Mezia, cap. 6. hal. 1.
u Maimon. in אישות cap. 14.
x Schab. cap. 13. hal. 4.

This multitude was got together on a sudden : neighbours, for civility's sake ; *minstrels*, perhaps for the sake of gain ; both the more officious in this business, as we may guess, by how much the parents of the deceased maid were of more eminent quality. She died, when Christ, together with Jairus, was going forward to the house (Mark v. 35) ; and yet, behold what a solemn meeting and concourse there was to lament her. There were two things which, in such cases, afforded an occasion to much company to assemble themselves to the house [y] of mourning :

First, some, as it is very probable, resorted thither to eat and drink : for at such a time some banqueting was used. " A [z] tradition. They drink ten cups in the house of mourning ; two before meat, five while they are eating, and three after meat." And a little after : " When Rabban Simeon Ben Gamaliel died, they added three more. But when the Sanhedrim saw that hence they became drunk, they made a decree against this."

Secondly, others came to perform their duty of charity and neighbourhood : for they accounted it the highest instance of respect to lament the dead, to prepare things for the burial, to take care of the funeral, to put themselves under the bier, and to contribute other things needful for that solemnity with all diligence. Hence they appropriated גמילות חסדים *The rendering* [or *bestowing*] *of mercies* to this duty, in a peculiar sense, above all other demonstrations of charity ; מית חד מנן ולא אתגמל חסד " *One* [a] of the disciples of the wise men *died, and mercy was not yielded him :*" that is, no care was taken of his funeral. " But a certain publican died, ובטילת כל מדינתא מיגמליניה חסד *and the whole city left off work to yield him mercy.*"

Mourning for the dead is distinguished by the Jewish schools into אנינות *Aninuth,* and אבלות *Ebluth.* אנינות was on the day of the funeral only, or until the corpse was carried out ; and then began אבלות, and lasted for thirty days. Of these mournings take these few passages : " He [b] that hath his dead laid out before him, and it is not in his power to bury him, useth not אנינות *Aninuth* [that kind of

[y] *Leusden's edit.,* vol. ii. p. 311.
[z] Hieros. Beracoth, fol. 6. 1.
[a] Hieros. Sanhedr. fol. 23. 3.
[b] Bab. Beracoth, fol. 18. 1.

mourning]. For example : If any die in prison, and the magistrate [or governor of the place], permits not his burial, he that is near of kin to him is not bound to that mourning which is called אנינות," &c. And the reason is given a little after ; namely, because he who hath his dead laid out before him, or upon whom the care of his burial lies, is forbidden to eat flesh, to drink wine, to eat with others, to eat in the same house (under which prohibition, thou, Jairus, now art), and he was free from reciting his phylacteries, and from prayer, and from all such-like precepts of the law. מיד חל עליו אבלות משיצא מפתח ביתו " *But when the funeral is carried out of the door of the house, then presently begins the mourning called* אבלות." From thence he is free from the foregoing prohibitions, and now is subject to others. Hence,

1. כפיית המטה *The bending down of the beds ;* of which the Talmudists speak very much : " From what time (say they) are the beds bended? from that time the dead body is carried out of the gate of the court of the house ; or, as R. Josua, From such time, as גולל the *grave-stone* is stopped up:" for so it is commonly rendered ; but the Gloss somewhere, the *cover,* or the *uppermost board,* of the bier. What this *bending of the beds* should mean, you may observe from those things which are spoken in the tract Beracoth : " Whence[c] is the bending of the beds? R. Crispa, in the name of R. Jochanan saith, From thence, because it is said, וַיֵּשְׁבוּ אִתּוֹ לָאָרֶץ *And they sat with him to the earth* (Job ii. 13). It is not said, ' *upon* the earth,' but לָאָרֶץ ' *to* the earth:' it denotes a thing not far from the earth. Hence it is that they sat upon beds bended down."

2. אבל כל ל"ים ימים אסור לעשו מלאכה "*He that laments all the thirty days is forbidden to do his work ;* and so his sons, and his daughters, and servants, and maids, and cattle[d]," &c.

These things concerned him to whom the dead person did belong. His friends and neighbours did their parts also, both in mourning, and in care of the funeral, employing themselves in that affair by an officious diligence, both

[c] Hieros. Berac. fol. 6. 1.   [d] Massecheth Semach. cap. 5.

out of duty and friendship. כל הרואה מת ואינו מלוהו
"*Whosoever sees a dead corpse* (say they), *and does not accom-
modate* [or *accompany*] *him to his burial, is guilty of that
which is said, 'He that mocketh the poor reproacheth his
Maker,'* &c. But now (say they) no man is so poor as the
dead man e," &c.

Ver. 24 f: Οὐκ ἀπέθανε τὸ κοράσιον, ἀλλὰ καθεύδει· *The maid
is not dead, but sleepeth.*] It was very ordinary among them
to express the death of any one by•the word דמך, which
properly signifies *to sleep.* כד דמך *When N. slept;* that is,
when he died: a phrase to be met with hundreds of times in
the Talmudists. And this whole company would say, דמכת
בת יאיר *The daughter of Jairus sleeps;* that is, *she is dead.*
Therefore it is worthy considering what form of speech
Christ here used. The Syriac hath לא מיתת אלא דמכא,
She is not dead, but asleep.

Ver. 33 : Οὐδέποτε ἐφάνη οὕτως ἐν τῷ Ἰσραήλ· *It was never
so seen in Israel.*] These words seem to refer, not to that
peculiar miracle only that was then done, but to all his miracles. Consider how many were done in that one day, yea,
in the afternoon. Christ dines at Capernaum with Matthew :
having dined, the importunity of Jairus calls him away : going
with Jairus, the woman with the issue of blood meets him,
and is healed : coming to Jairus's house, he raiseth his dead
daughter : returning to his own house (for he had a dwelling
at Capernaum), two blind men meet him in the streets, cry
out *Messias* after him, follow him home, and they are cured.
As they were going out of the house, a dumb demoniac enters,
and is healed. The multitude, therefore, could not but cry
out, with very good reason, "Never had any such thing appeared in Israel."

Ver. 34 g : Ἐν τῷ ἄρχοντι τῶν δαιμονίων, &c. *Through the
prince of the devils, &c.*] See the notes at chap. xii. 24.

CHAP. X.

Ver. 1 : Καὶ προσκαλεσάμενος τοὺς δώδεκα μαθητάς· *And when
he had called to him the twelve disciples.*] Concerning the

---

e Bab. Berac. in the place above.   f *English folio edit.,* vol. ii. p. 174.
g *Leusden's edition,* vol. ii. p. 312.

number of twelve, corresponding to the tribes of Israel, see
Luke xxii. 30, Rev. xxi. 12, 14. These were called the twelve
apostles, שלוחי or שליחי in Talmudic language, under which
title Moses and Aaron are marked by the Chaldee paraphrast, Jer. ii. 1 : a word that does not barely speak *a messenger*, but *such a messenger as represents the person of him
that sends him.* For שלוחו של אדם כמותו *The*[h] '*apostle' of any one is as he himself* from whom he is deputed."
See the fortieth verse of this chapter. If you read over the
tract of Maimonides here, entitled שלוחין ושותפין *messengers and companions,* perhaps you will not repent your
labour.

For these ends were these twelve chosen, as the evangelists
relate :

I. That they might be with him, eyewitnesses of his
works, and students of his doctrine. For they did not presently betake themselves to preach, from the time they were
first admitted disciples, no, nor from the time they were first
chosen; but they sat a long while at the feet of their Master,
and imbibed from his mouth that doctrine which they were to
preach.

II. That they might be his prophets, both to preach and
to do miracles. Thence it comes to pass, that the gift of
miracles, which of a long time had ceased, is now restored to
them.

The ' seven shepherds, and eight principal men,' Micah v. 5,
are the disciples of the Messias, according to Kimchi.

Ἐξουσίαν[i] πνευμάτων ἀκαθάρτων· *Power of unclean spirits.*]
That is, ' *over*, or *upon* unclean spirits :' which therefore are
called, רוחות טומאה *unclean spirits*, that by a clearer anti-
thesis they might be opposed to רוח הקדש *the Holy Spirit,
the Spirit of purity.*

More particularly רוּחַ הַטֻמְאָה *the unclean spirit*, Zech.
xiii. 2 ; and πνεύματα ἀκάθαρτα, *unclean spirits*, Rev. xvi.
13, 14, are diabolical spirits in false prophets, deceiving
Pythons.

By a more particular name yet, according to the Talmudists concerning this business : " There[k] shall not be with

<hr />

[h] Bab. Berac. fol. 34. 2.   [i] *English folio edition,* vol. ii. p. 175.
[k] Bab. Sanhedr. fol. 65. 2.

thee, דּוֹרֵשׁ אֶל־הַמֵּתִים *a necromancer,* Deut. xviii. 11. He
is דּוֹרֵשׁ אֶל־הַמֵּתִים *a necromancer* who mortifies himself
with hunger, and goes and lodges a-nights among the burying-
places for that end, that רוח טמאה, *the unclean spirit* may
dwell upon him. When R. Akibah read that verse he wept.
Does *the unclean spirit,* saith he, come upon him that fasts
for that very end, that *the unclean spirit* may come upon him?
Much more would the Holy Spirit come upon him that fasts
for that end, that the Holy Spirit might come upon him.
But what shall I do, when our sins have brought that on
us which is said, ' Your sins separate between you and your
God?' " Where the Gloss thus; שתשרה רוח טמאה עליו
" *That the unclean spirit dwell upon him:* that is, that the
demon of the burial-place may love him, and may help him in
his enchantments."

When I consider with myself that numberless number of
demoniacs which the evangelists mention, the like to which
no history affords, and the Old Testament produceth hardly
one or two examples, I cannot but suspect these two things
especially for the cause of it:—

First, That the Jewish people, now arriving to the very top
of impiety, now also arrived to the very top of those curses
which are recited, Levit. xxvi. and Deut. xxviii.

Secondly, That the nation, beyond measure addicted to
magical arts, did even affect devils, and invited them to dwell
with them.

Ver. 2: Σίμων· *Simon.*] סימון *Simon* is a name very usual
among the Talmudists for שִׁמְעוֹן *Simeon.* By whieh name
our apostle is also called, Acts xv. 14.

Let these words be taken notice of, ר' א' בעא מר" סימון
" *R. Eliezer*[1] *inquired of R. Simon concerning a certain thing;*
but he answered him not. He inquired of R. Joshua Ben
Levi, and he answered. R. Eliezer was enraged that ר' שמעון
R. Simeon answered him not."

Πέτρος· *Peter.*] Christ changed the names of three dis-
ciples with whom he held more inward familiarity, Simon,
James, and John. Simon was called by him *Peter,* or
Petrosus, that is, referring to a *rock,* because he should con-

---

[1] Hieros. Schab. fol. 11. 2.

tribute not only very much assistance to the church that was
to be built on a *rock,* but the very first assistance, when, the
keys being committed to him, he opened the door of faith to
Cornelius, and so first let in the gospel among the Gentiles.
Of which matter afterward.

'Ανδρέας· *Andrew.*]   This also was no strange name among
the Talmudists.   אנדריי בר חיננא *Andrew Bar Chinna*[m].

Ver. 3: Βαρθολομαῖος· *Bartholomew.*]   Compare the order
wherein the disciples are called, John i, with the order
wherein they are for the most part reckoned, and you will
find *Bartholomew* falling in at the same place with *Nathanael :*
so[n] that one may think he was the same with him: called
Nathanael by his own name, and *Bartholomew* by his father's ;
בר תלמי that is, *the son of Talmai :* for the Greek interpreters render *Talmai* Θολμὶ, *Tolmi,* 2 Sam. xiii. 37.   And
Θολομαῖος, *Tholomæus,* occurs in Josephus[o].

'Αλφαίου[p]· *Of Alpheus.*]   The name חלפי occurs also in
the Talmudists : a word that may admit a double pronunciation ; namely, either to sound *Alphai,* or *Cleophi.*   Hence
that *Alpheus,* who was the father of four apostles, is also
called *Cleopas,* Luke xxiv ; which sufficiently appears from
hence, that she who is called " Mary, the mother of James
the Less, and Joses," Mark xv. 40, by John is called, " Mary
the wife of Cleopas," John xix. 25.

Λεββαῖος ὁ ἐπικληθεὶς Θαδδαῖος· *Lebbeus, whose surname was
Thaddeus.*]   תדאי *Thaddai* was a name known also to the
Talmudists : ר" יוסי בן תדאי *R. Jose*[q] *the son of Thaddeus.*
אלעזר בן תדאי *Eliezer*[r] *Ben Thaddeus.*   It is a warping of
the name *Judas,* that this apostle might be the better distinguished from *Iscariot.*   He was called *Lebbeus,* I suppose,
from the town *Lebba,* a sea-coast town of Galilee : of which
Pliny[s] speaks ; " The promontory Carmel, and in the mountain a town of the same name, heretofore called Ecbatana :
near by Getta *Lebba,*" &c.

Ver. 4: Σίμων ὁ Κανανίτης· *Simon the Canaanite.*]   In Luke
it is Ζηλωτής.   See who are called Ζηλωταὶ, *Zealots,* in Jose-

m Hieros. Megill. cap. 4.
n *Leusden's edition,* vol. ii. p. 313.
o Antiq. lib. xx. cap. 1. [xx. 1. 1.]
p *English folio edit.,* vol. ii. p. 176.

q Massech. Derech Arets, c. 1.
r Hieros. Kilaim, fol. 27. 2. Schab.
fol. 5. 2. See Juchasin, fol. 105. 2.
s Lib. v. cap. 19.

phus. Of whose sect, if you should say this Simon was before
his conversion, perhaps you would do him no more wrong
than you would do his brother Matthew, when you should say
that he was a *publican.*

'Ἰσκαριώτης· *Iscariot.*] It may be inquired whether this
name was given him while he was alive, or not till after his
death. If while he was alive, one may not improperly derive
it from סקורטיא *Skortja,* which is written also, אסקורטיא
Iskortja[t] : where, while the discourse is of a man vowing that
he would not use this or that garment, we are taught these
things ; " He that ties himself by a vow of not using garments, may use sackcloth, veiling cloth, hair cloth, &c. but he
may not use פונדא ופסקיא ואסקורטיא וגו׳." Of which
words the Gloss writes thus ; " These are garments, some, of
of leather, and some of a certain kind of clothing." The
Gemara asketh, " What is אסקורטיא *Iskortja?* Bar Bar
Channah answered, כיתונא דצלא *A tanner's garment.*"
The Gloss is, " A leathern apron that tanners put on over
their clothes." So that *Judas Iscariot* may perhaps signify
as much as *Judas with the apron.* But now in such *aprons*
they had purses sewn, in which they were wont to carry their
money, as you may see in Aruch, in the words אפונדה and
תרמיל, which we shall also observe presently. And hence,
it may be, Judas had that title of *the purse-bearer,* as he was
called *Judas with the apron.*

Or what if he used the art of a tanner before he was
chose into discipleship? Certainly we read of one Simon a
tanner, Acts ix. 43; and that this Judas was the son of Simon,
John xii. 4.

But if he were not branded with this title till after his
death, I should suppose it derived from אסכרא *Iscara* ;
which word what it signifies, let the Gemarists speak :
" Nine[u] hundred and three kinds of death were created in
the world, as it is said, וְלַמָּוֶת תּוֹצָאוֹת *and the issues of
death,* Psalm lxviii. 21. The word תּוֹצָאוֹת *issues* arithme-
tically ariseth to that number. Among all those kinds,
אסכרא *Iscara* is the roughest death, נשיקה[x] is easiest."

[t] Bab. Nedarim, fol. 55. 2.
[u] Bab. Berac. fol. 8. 1.
[x] [נְשִׁיקָה] *Osculatio.* Est genus   mortis placidissimæ et suavissimæ
See Buxtorf. Lex. T. and R. sub v.
col. 1405.]

Where the Gloss is, אסכרא אסטראנגולמנט בלועז ' *Iscara*'
in the mother-tongue is estrangulament, [étranglement.] By
learned men for the most part it is rendered *angina, the
quinsy.*   The Gemara sets out the roughness of it by this
simile, אסכרא דמיא כחיזרא בגבבא דעמרא דלאחורי נשרא
"They Iscara is like to branches of thorns in a fleece of wool;
which if a man shake violently behind, it is impossible but
the wool will be pulled off by them." It is thus defined in
the Gloss, אסכרא המתחיל במעים וגומר בגרון ' *The Iscara*' *begins in the bowels, and ends in the throat.* See the
Gemara there.

When Judas therefore perished by a most miserable strangling, being strangled by the devil (which we observe in its
place), no wonder if this infamous death be branded upon his
name, to be commonly styled Judas *Iscariot*, or ' that Judas
that perished מאסכרא *by strangling.*'

'O[z] καὶ παραδοὺς αὐτόν· *Who also betrayed him.*] Let that of
Maimonides be observed: " It[a] is forbidden to betray an
Israelite into the hands of the heathen, either as to his person, or as to his goods," &c. "And whosoever shall so betray
an Israelite shall have no part in the world to come." Peter
spake agreeably to the opinion of the nation, when he said concerning Judas, "He went unto his own place," Acts i. 25. And
so doth Baal Turim concerning Balaam; "' Balaam went to
his place,' Num. xxiv. 25; that is (saith he), ויירד לגהנום,
he went down to hell."

Ver. 5[b]: Εἰς πόλιν. Σαμαρειτῶν μὴ εἰσέλθητε· *Into any city of
the Samaritans, enter ye not.*] Our Saviour would have the
Jews' privileges reserved to them, until they alienated and
lost them by their own perverseness and sins. Nor does he
grant the preaching of the gospel to the Gentiles or Samaritans, before it was offered to the Jewish nation. The Samaritans vaunted themselves sons of the patriarch Jacob, John
iv. 12 (which, indeed, was not altogether distant from the
truth); they embraced also the law of Moses; and being
taught thence, expected the Messias as well as the Jews:
nevertheless, Christ acknowledges them for his sheep no more
than the heathen themselves.

---

[y] Schabb. fol. 33. 1.
[z] *English folio edit.*, vol. ii. p. 177.

[a] In חובל ומזיק cap. 1.
[b] *Leusden's edition*, vol. ii. p. 314.

I. Very many among them were sprung, indeed, of the seed of Jacob, though now become renegades and apostates from the Jewish faith and nation, and hating them more than if they were heathens, and more than they would do heathens. Which also, among other things, may perhaps be observed in their very language. For read the Samaritan version of the Pentateuch; and, if I mistake not, you will observe that the Samaritans, when, by reason of the nearness of the places, and the alliance of the nations, they could not but make use of the language of the Jews, yet used such a variation and change of the dialect, as if they scorned to speak the same words that they did, and make the same language not the same.

II. In like manner they received the Mosaic law, but, for the most part, in so different a writing of the words, that they seem plainly to have propounded this to themselves, that retaining indeed the law of Moses, they would hold it under as much difference from the Mosaic text of the Jews as ever they could, so that they kept something to the sense. "R. Eliezer[c] Ben R. Simeon said, 'I said to the scribes of the Samaritans, Ye have falsified your law without any manner of profit accruing to you thereby. For ye have written in your law, אצל אלוני מורה שכם, *near the oaken groves of Moreh, which is Sychem,*'" &c. (the word שכם is added.) Let the Samaritan text at Deut. xi. 30 be looked upon.

III. However they pretended to study the religion of Moses, yet, in truth, there was little or no difference between them and idolaters, when they knew not what they worshipped; which our Saviour objects against them, John iv. 22: and had not only revolted as apostates from the true religion of Moses, but set themselves against it with the greatest hatred. Hence the Jewish nation held them for heathens, or for a people more execrable than the heathens themselves. A certain Rabbin thus reproaches their idolatry: "R. Ismael[d] Ben R. Josi went to Neapolis [that is, Sychem]: the Samaritans came to him, to whom he spake thus; 'I see that you adore not this mountain, but the idols which are under it:

---

[c] Hieros. Sotah, fol. 21. 3.   Bab. Sotah, fol. 33. 2.
[d] Hieros. Avodah Zarâh, fol. 44. 4.

for it is written, Jacob hid the strange gods under the wood,
which is near Sychem.'"

It is disputed[e] whether a Cuthite ought to be reckoned for
a heathen, which is asserted by Rabbi, denied by Simeon;
but the conclusion, indeed, is sufficiently for the affirmative.

IV. The metropolis of the Samaritans laboured under a
second apostasy, being brought to it by the deceit and witch-
craft of Simon Magus, after the receiving of the gospel from
the mouth of our Saviour himself. Compare Acts viii. 9 with
John iv. 41.

From all these particulars, and with good reason for the
thing itself, and to preserve the privileges of the Jews safe,
and that they might not otherwise prove an offence to that
nation, the Samaritans are made parallel to the heathen, and
as distant as they from partaking of the gospel.

Ver. 9[f]: Εἰς τὰς ζώνας ὑμῶν, &c. *In your purses, &c.*] These
things, which are forbidden the disciples by our Saviour, were
the ordinary provision of travellers; to which the more religious
added also the book of the law.

" Some[g] Levites travelled to Zoar, the city of palm-trees :
and when one of them fell sick by the way, they brought him
to an inn. Coming back, they inquired of the hostess concerning their companion. ' He is dead,' said she, ' and I have
buried him.'" And a little after, הוציאה להם מקלו
ותרמילו וספר תורה שהיה בידו: *she brought forth to
them his staff, and his purse, and the book of the law, which
was in his hand.* So the Babylonian Misna : but the Jerusalem adds also *shoes :* and instead of that which in the
Misna is תרמילו, *his purse,* in the Gemara is אפונדתו,
which was an *inner garment,* with pockets to hold money and
necessaries.

That also is worthy mention; לא יכנס להר הבית לא
במקלו ולא במנעלו ולא בפונדתו ולא באבק שעל רגליו
*Let[h] no man enter into the mount of the Temple with his staff,
nor with his shoes, nor with his purse, nor with dust on his
feet.* Which words are thus rendered by the Gemara : " Let
no man enter into the mount of the Temple, neither with

---

[e] Hieros. Shekal. fol. 46. 2.
[f] *English folio edit.*, vol. ii. p. 178.
[g] Jevamoth, cap. 16. hal. ult.
[h] Berac. cap. 9. hal. 5.

his staff in his hand, nor with his shoes upon his feet, nor with money bound up in his linen, *nor with a purse hanging on his back,* לאחריו [i] ובפנדתו מופשלת." Where the Gloss thus: פונדתו אזור חלול שנותנין בו מעות פונדא ' *Ponditho*' *is a hollow girdle* [or *a hollow belt*]*, in which they put up their money.* See the Aruch in אפונדה *Aponda,* and פונדה *Ponda.*

Ver. 10 : Μὴ πήραν εἰς ὁδόν· *Nor scrip for your journey.*] The Syriac version reads, ולא תרמלא *No purse.* The word תרמיל and תורמיל is very frequent in the Talmudists. " תורמיל[j] is[k] *a leather pouch,* which shepherds hang about their necks, in which they put their victuals." R. Solomon[l] saith almost the same thing, but that he appropriates it not to shepherds. The Aruch also in effect the same.

A proselyte is brought in thus speaking[m]; " If an Israelite approaching to the holy things shall die, how much more a stranger, שבא במקלו ובתרמילו *who comes with his staff and his pouch !*"

Μηδὲ δύο χιτῶνας· *Nor two coats.*] A single coat bespake a meaner condition ; a double, a more plentiful. Hence is that counsel of the Baptist, Luke iii. 11, " He that hath two coats, let him impart to him that hath none." It is disputed by the Babylonian Talmudists, how[n] far it is lawful to wash garments בחולו של מועד *on the common days of a festival-week;* and the conclusion is, " It is lawful for him שאין לו אלא חלוק אחד *that hath one coat only,* to wash it."

Μηδὲ ὑποδήματα· *Neither shoes.*] That *shoes* are here to be understood, and not *sandals,* appears from Mark vi. 9 : and that there was a difference between these, sufficiently appears from these very places. The contrary to which I read in Beza, not without wonder : " But then from this place (saith he), as also from Acts xii. 8, it appears that the evangelists put no difference between ὑποδήματα, *shoes,* and σανδάλια, *sandals,* as Erasmus hath rightly observed."

Let the Jewish schools be heard in this matter : [o] " The

[i] Bab. Berac. fol. 62. 2.
[j] Rambam in Kelim, cap. 16. hal. 4.
[k] *Leusden's edition,* vol. ii. p. 315.
[l] Rambam in Kelim, cap. 16. hal. 4.
[m] Bab. Schab. fol. 31. 1.
[n] Taanith, fol. 29. 2. Moed Katon, fol. 18. 1.
[o] Jevamoth, cap. 12. hal. 1.

pulling off of *the shoe* [of the husband's brother, Deut. xxv. 9]
is right : and of *the sandal*, if it hath a heel, is right ; but if
not, it is not right."

" R. Josi P saith, I went to Nisibin, and I saw there a
certain elder, and I said to him, ' Are you well acquainted
with R. Judah Ben Betira ?' And he answered, ' I am a money
changer in my city ; and he came to my table very often.'
I said, ' Did you ever see him putting off *the shoe?* What
did he put off, *shoe* or *sandal?*' He answered, ' O Rabbi, are
there *sandals* among us ?' Whence therefore, say I, did R.
Meir say, אין חולצין במנעל *They do not put off the shoe?*
Rabbi Ba, Rabh Judah say, in the name of Rabh, If Elias
should come, and should say, ' They pull off the *shoe* of the
husband's brother, let them hearken to him :' if he should say,
' They pull off the *sandal*,' let them not hearken to him. And
yet, for the most part, the custom is to pull off the *sandal :*
and custom prevails against tradition." See more there, and
in the Babylonian tract *Jevamoth* q.

Shoes r were of more delicate use ; *sandals* were more ordinary, and more for service. מנעל של עור רך *A shoe was*
of softer leather, סנדל של עור קשה *a sandal of harder* s, &c.
There were *sandals* also, whose sole, or lower part, was of
wood, the upper of leather ; and these were fastened together by nails t. There were some *sandals* also made of rushes,
or of the bark of palm-trees u, &c. Another difference also
between *shoes* and *sandals* is illustrated by a notable story
in the tract *Schabbath*, in the place just now cited : " In a
certain time of persecution, when some were hidden in a cave,
they said among themselves, ' He that will enter, let him
enter ; for he will look about him before he enters, that the
enemies see him not : but let none go out ; for perhaps the
enemies will be near, whom he sees not when he goes out,
and so all will be discovered.' One of them by chance put
on his *sandals* the wrong way : for *sandals* were open both
ways, so that one might put in his foot either before or behind : but he putting on his the wrong way, his footsteps,

P Hieros. ibid. fol. 12. 1.   s Gloss. in Jevam. Bab. fol.101.1.
q Fol. 102. 1.   t See Bab. Schabb. fol. 60. 1. in
r *English folio edition*, vol. ii. p. Gloss.
179.   u Joma, fol. 78. 2.

when he went out, seemed as if he went in, and so their hiding-place was discovered to the enemies," &c.

Money therefore in the girdle, and provision in the scrip, were forbidden the disciples by Christ; first, that they might not be careful for temporal things, but resign themselves wholly to the care of Christ; secondly, they ought to live of the gospel, which he hints in the last clause of this verse, " The workman is worthy of his hire."

That, therefore, which he had said before, " Freely ye have received, freely give," forbade them to preach the gospel for gain : but he forbade not to take food, clothing, and other necessaries for the preaching of the gospel.

Two coats and *shoes* are forbidden them, that they might not at all affect pride or worldly pomp, or to make themselves fine; but rather, that their habit and guise might bespeak the greatest humility.

Ver. 11 : Τίς ἐν αὐτῇ ἄξιος· *Who in it is worthy.*] In the Talmudic language, מי זכה *who deserves.*

Ver. 14 : Ἐκτινάξατε τὸν κονιορτὸν τῶν ποδῶν· *Shake off the dust of your feet.*] The schools of the scribes taught that *the dust* of heathen land defiled by the touch. " The [x] *dust* of Syria defiles, as well as the *dust* of other heathen countries."

" A [y] tradition-writer saith, ' They bring not herbs into the land of Israel out of a heathen land : but our Rabbins have permitted it.' מאי ביניידהו *What difference is there between these?* R. Jeremiah saith, הושׁשׁין לגושׁידהן איכא ביניידהו *The care of their [z] dust is among them.*" The Gloss is, " They take care, lest, together with the herbs, something of *the dust* of the heathen land be brought, which defiles in the tent, and defiles the purity of the land of Israel."

" By [a] reason of six doubts, they burn the *truma* : the doubt of a field, in which heretofore might be a sepulchre; the doubt of *dust* brought from a heathen land," &c.   Where the Gloss is this; " Because it may be doubted of all the *dust* of a heathen land, whether it were not from the sepulchre of the dead."

" Rabbi [b] saw a certain priest standing in a part of the

[x] Tosapht. ad Kelim, cap. 1.   [a] Bab. Schab. fol. 15. 2.
[y] Bab. Sanhedr. fol. 12. 1.   [b] Gloss. in Sanhedr. fol. 5. 2.
[z] *Leusden's edition*, vol. ii. p. 316.

city Aco, which part was without the bounds of the land of
Israel ; he said to him, ' Is not that heathen land concerning
which they have determined that it is as unclean as a bury-
ing-place c ?' "

Therefore that rite of *shaking the dust off the feet*, commanded the disciples, speaks thus much ; " Wheresoever a
city of Israel shall not receive you, when ye depart, shew,
by *shaking off the dust from your feet*, that ye esteem that city,
however a city of Israel, for a heathen, profane, impure city ;
and, as such, abhor it."

Ver. 17 : 'Εν ταῖς συναγωγαῖς αὐτῶν μαστιγώσουσιν ὑμᾶς·
They shall scourge you in their synagogues.] Beza here, as he
does very often when he cannot explain a case, suspects it :
for thus he writes ; " When I neither find synagogues elsewhere to have their names from *houses of judgment*, as the
Hebrews speak, nor that civil punishments were taken in synagogues, I suspect this place." But without any cause, for,

I. In every synagogue there was a civil triumvirate, that is,
three magistrates, who judged of matters in contest arising
within that synagogue ; which we have noted before.

II.d מכות בשלשה *Scourging*e *was by that bench of* three.
So that fivefold scourging of St. Paul (2 Cor. xi. 24) was in
the synagogue ; that is, בבד" של שלשה *By that bench of*
three magistrates, such as was in every synagogue.

It is something obscure that is said, Προσέχετε δὲ ἀπὸ τῶν
ἀνθρώπων, *But beware of men.* Of whom else should they
beware ? But perhaps the word ἄνθρωποι, *men*, may occur in
that sense, as אנשי *men*, in these forms of speech ; אנשי
אנשי בית דין : and כנסת הגדלה that is, *the men of the*
great assembly, and, *the men of the house of judgment*, &c. But
we will not contend about it.

Ver. 23 : Οὐ μὴ τελέσητε τὰς πόλεις τοῦ Ἰσραὴλ, &c. *Ye*
shall not have gone over the cities of Israel, &c.] " Ye shall not
have travelled through the cities of Israel preaching the
gospel, before the Son of man is revealed by his resurrection," Rom. i. 4. Lay to this Acts iii. 19, 20, " Repent ye
therefore, and be converted, that your sins may be blotted
out, ὅπως ἂν ἔλθωσι, *that* the times of refreshment *may come*"

c See Pisk. Tosaph. in Sanhedr.   d *English folio edit.*, vol. ii. p. 180.
cap. 1. artic. 30.   e Sanhedr. cap. 1. hal. 2.

(for ye expect refreshment and consolation under the Messias); and he may send Jesus Christ first preached to you." And ver. 26, " To you first God, raising up his Son, sent him to bless you," &c.   The epoch of the Messias is dated from the resurrection of Christ.

Ver. 25 : Βεελζεβούλ· *Beelzebub.*] See chap. xii. 24.

Ver. 27 : Ὅ εἰς τὸ οὖς ἀκούετε· *What ye hear in the ear.*] We have observed before, that allusion is here made to the manner of the schools, where the doctor whispered, out of the chair, into *the ear* of the interpreter, and he with a loud voice repeated to the whole school that which was *spoken in the ear.*

" They[f] said to Judah Bar Nachmani, מתורגמניה דריש לקיש *the interpreter of Resh Lachish,* קום עליה באמורא *Do you stand for his expositor.*"   The Gloss is, " To tell out the exposition to the synagogue, מה שילחוש לך *which he shall whisper to you.*"   We cannot here but repeat that which we produced before, החכם לוחש לו לשון עברית *The doctor whispered him in the ear in Hebrew.*   And we cannot but suspect that that custom in the church of Corinth which the apostle reproves, of speaking in the synagogue in an unknown tongue, were some footsteps of this custom.

We read of whispering in the ear done in another sense, namely, to a certain woman with child, which longed for the perfumed flesh; " Therefore[g] Rabbi said, זילו לחושו לה *Go whisper her* that it is the day of Expiation. לחושו לה ואילחישא *They whispered to her, and she was whispered :*" that is, she was satisfied and at quiet.

Κηρύξατε ἐπὶ τῶν δωμάτων· *Preach ye upon the housetops.*] Perhaps allusion is made to that custom when[h] the minister of the synagogue on the sabbath-eve sounded with a trumpet six times upon the roof of an exceeding high house, that thence all might have notice of the coming in of the sabbath. The first sound was, that they should cease from their works in the fields ; the second, that they should cease from theirs in the city ; the third, that they should light the sabbath candle, &c.

Ver. 34 : Μὴ νομίσητε ὅτι ἦλθον βαλεῖν εἰρήνην, &c.   *Think*

---

[f] Bab. Sanhedr. fol. 7. 2.   [g] Bab. Joma, fol. 82. 2.
[h] Bab. Schab. fol. 35. 2.

not that I am come to send peace, &c.] Although these words
may be understood truly of the differences [i] between believers
and unbelievers by reason of the gospel, which all interpreters observe ; yet they do properly and primarily point
out, as it were with the finger, those horrid slaughters [k] and
civil wars of the Jews among themselves, such as no other
age ever saw, nor story heard.

" R. Eliezer [l] saith, The days of the Messias are forty years,
as it is said, ' Forty years was I provoked by this generation.'"
And again ; " R. Judah [m] saith, In that generation, when the
Son of David shall come, the schools shall be harlots ; Galilee
shall be laid waste ; Gablan shall be destroyed ; and the inhabitants of the earth [the Gloss is ' the Sanhedrim'] shall
wander from city to city, and shall not obtain pity ; the
wisdom of the scribes shall stink ; and they that fear to sin
shall be despised ; and the faces of that generation shall be
like the faces of dogs ; and truth shall fail, &c. Run over
the history of these forty years, from the death of Christ to
the destruction of Jerusalem (as they are vulgarly computed),
and you will wonder to observe the nation conspiring to its
own destruction, and rejoicing in the slaughters and spoils of
one another beyond all example, and even to a miracle. This
phrensy certainly was sent upon them from heaven. And
first, they are deservedly become mad who trod the wisdom
of God, as much as they could, under their feet. And secondly, the blood of the prophets and of Christ, bringing the
good tidings of peace, could not be expiated by a less vengeance. Tell me, O Jew, whence is that rage of your nation
towards the destruction of one another, and those monsters
of madness beyond all examples? Does the nation rave for
nothing, unto their own ruin? Acknowledge the Divine vengeance in thy madness, more than that which befell thee from
men. He that reckons up the differences, contentions, and
broils of the nation, after the dissension betwixt the Pharisees
and the Sadducees, will meet with no less between the scholars of Shammai and Hillel, which increased to that degree,
that at last it came to slaughter and blood.

---

[i] *Leusden's edition,* vol. ii. p. 317.   [l] Bab. Sanhedr. fol. 99. 1.
[k] *English folio edit.,* vol. ii. p. 181.   [m] Fol. 97. 1.

" The[n] scholars of Shammai and Hillel came to the chamber of Chananiah Ben Ezekiah Ben Garon, to visit him: that was a woful day, like the day wherein the golden calf was made. The scholars of Shammai stood below, and slew some of the scholars of Hillel. The tradition is, That six of them went up, and the rest stood there present with swords and spears."

It passed into a common proverb, that " Elias the Tishbite himself could not decide the controversies between the scholars of Hillel and the scholars of Shammai." They dream they were determined by a voice from heaven; but certainly the quarrels and bitternesses were not at all decided.

" Before[o] the *Bath Kol* [in Jabneh] went forth, it was lawful equally to embrace either the decrees of the school of Hillel, or those of the school of Shammai. At last the *Bath Kol* came forth, and spake thus; ' The words, both of the one party and the other, are the words of the living God; but the certain decision of the matter is according to the decrees of the school of Hillel.' And from thenceforth, whosoever shall transgress the decrees of the school of Hillel is guilty of death."

And thus the controversy was decided; but the hatreds and spites were not so ended. I observe, in the Jerusalem Gemarists[p], the word שמותי *Shamothi*, used for *a scholar of Shammai:* which I almost suspect, from the affinity of the word שמתא *Shammatha*, which signifies *Anathema*, to be a word framed by the scholars of Hillel, in hate, ignominy, and reproach of those of *Shammai*. And when I read more than once of R. Tarphon's being in danger by robbers, because in some things he followed the custom and manner of the school of Shammai; I cannot but suspect snares were daily laid by one another, and hostile treacheries continually watching to do each other mischief.

" R. Tarphon[q] saith, ' As I was travelling on the way, I went aside to recite the phylacteries, according to the rite of the school of Shammai, and I was in danger of thieves.' They said

---

[n] Hieros. in Schabb. fol. 3. 3.
[o] Hieros. Beracoth, fol. 3. 2.
[p] See Trumoth, fol. 43. 3. Succah, 53. 1. Jom. Tobh, fol. 60. 3,
&c.
[q] Bab. Beracoth, cap. 1. hal. 3.

to him, and deservedly too, ' Because thou hast transgressed the words of the school of Hillel.' " This is wanting in the Jerusalem Misna.

" R. Tarphon[r] went down to eat figs of his own, according to the school of Shammai. The enemies saw him, and kicked against him : when he saw himself in danger, ' By your life,' saith he, ' carry word unto the house of Tarphon, that grave-clothes be made ready for him.' "

Thus, as if they were struck with a phrensy from heaven, the doctors of the nation rage one against another ; and from their very schools and chairs flow not so much doctrines, as animosities, jarrings, slaughters, and butcheries. To these may be added those fearful outrages, spoils, murders, devastations of robbers, cut-throats, zealots, and amazing cruelties, beyond all example. And if these things do not savour of the divine wrath and vengeance, what ever did ?

CHAP. XI.[s]

VER. 3 : Σὺ εἶ ὁ ἐρχόμενος, ἢ ἕτερον προσδοκῶμεν; *Art thou he that should come, or do we look for another?*] The reason of the message of John to Christ is something obscure :

First, That it was not because he knew not Christ, is without all controversy, when he had been fully instructed from heaven concerning his person, when he was baptized ; and when *he had* again and again most evidently *borne witness to him*, in those words, " This is the Lamb of God," &c.

Secondly[t], Nor was that message certainly, that the disciples of John might receive satisfaction about the person of Christ : for, indeed, the disciples were most unworthy of such a master, if they should not believe him without further argument, when he taught them concerning him.

Thirdly, John therefore seems in this matter to respect his own imprisonment, and that his question, " Art thou he which should come," &c. tends to that. He had heard that miracles of all sorts were done by him, that the blind received their sight, the dead were raised, devils were cast out, &c. And why, therefore, among all the rest, is not John set at liberty ? This scruple, as it seems, stuck with the good

---

[r] Hieros. Sheviith, fol. 65. 2.   [s] *English folio edition*, vol. ii. p. 182.
[t] *Leusden's edition*, vol. ii. p. 318.

man; ' Why do all receive benefit and comfort from Christ,
but only I?' Perhaps he laboured under that dim-sighted-
ness which the disciples of Christ and the whole nation did
concerning his earthly kingdom, victories, and triumphs:
from which how distant (alas!) was this, that his forerunner
and the chief minister should lie in chains! ' If thou art he,
concerning whose triumphing the prophets declare so much,
why am I so long detained in prison? Art thou he, or is
another to be expected, from whom these things are to be
looked for?'

First, " That I am he that should come, these things which
I do bear witness, ' The blind receive their sight, the lame
walk,' " &c.

Secondly, " As to the present case of John, who expects
somebody to come to deliver him out of bonds, and to free
the people from the yoke of men, Let him (saith he) acquiesce
in my divine dispensation, and, ' Blessed is he, whosoever shall
not be offended in me,' however all things are not according
to his mind, which he hath expected to fall out, for his present
and bodily advantage."

And the words of our Saviour, ver. 11, seem to express
some secret reproof of this error in John, " He that is less in
the kingdom of heaven, is greater than he." The Vulgar
version renders well the word μικρότερος, *less*, not *least*: as if
he should say, " When ye went out into the desert to John,
ye neither looked for trifles nor earthly pomp, neither ' a reed
shaken with the wind,' nor ' a man clothed in soft raiment;'
but ye looked in good earnest for a prophet: and in that ye
did very well; for he was the greatest of prophets, nay, of
men, as to his office; honoured in this above all others, that
he is the forerunner of the Messias. Howbeit, there are
some, which, indeed, in respect of office, are much less than
he in the kingdom of heaven, or in the commonwealth of
Christ, who yet are greater than he in respect of the knowledge of the state and condition of his kingdom." A comparison certainly is not here made, either in respect of office,
or in respect of dignity, or in respect of holiness, or in respect
of eternal salvation; for who, I pray, exceeded the Baptist in
all these, or in any of them? but in respect of clear and dis-

tinct knowledge, in judging of the nature and quality of the kingdom of heaven.

Let the austerity of John's life, and the very frequent fasts which he enjoined his disciples, be well considered, and what our Saviour saith of both, and you will easily believe that John also, according to the universal conceit of the nation, expected temporal redemption by the Messias, not so clearly distinguishing concerning the nature of the kingdom and redemption of Christ. And you will the more easily give credit to this, when you shall have observed how the disciples of Christ themselves, that conversed a long time with him, were dimsighted, likewise, in this very thing.

Ver. 12[u] : ʽH βασιλεία τῶν οὐρανῶν βιάζεται· *The kingdom of heaven suffereth violence.*] And these words also make for the praise of John. That he was a very eminent prophet, and of no ordinary mission or authority, these things evince ; that from his preaching, the kingdom of heaven took its beginning, and it was so crowded into by infinite multitudes, as if they would take and seize upon the kingdom by violence. The divine warmth of the people in betaking themselves thither by such numberless crowds, and with so exceeding a zeal, sufficiently argued the divine worth both of the teacher and of his doctrine.

Ver. 14 : Εἰ θέλετε δέξασθαι, αὐτός ἐστιν ʼHλίας· *If ye will receive it, this is Elias.*] תקבלו אין *If ye will receive it.* The words hint some suspicion, that they would not receive his doctrine ; which the obstinate expectation of that nation unto this very day, that Elias is personally to come, witnesseth also. Upon what ground some Christians are of the same opinion, let themselves look to it. See the notes on chap. xvii. 10.

Ver. 21 : ʼEν Τύρῳ καὶ Σιδῶνι· *In Tyre and Sidon.*] He compares the cities of the Jews with the cities of the Canaanites, who were of a cursed original ; " but yet these cities, of a cursed seed and name, if they had been partakers of the miracles done among you, had not hardened themselves to such a degree of madness and obstinacy as you have

---

[u] *English folio edition*, vol. ii. p. 183.

done: but had turned from their heathenism and Canaanitism unto the knowledge of the gospel; or, at least, had betook themselves to such a repentance as would have prevented vengeance." So the repentance of the Ninevites, however it were not to salvation, yet it was such as preserved them, and freed their city from the wrath and scourge that hung over them. The most horrid stiffness of the Jews is here intimated, of all impious men the most impious, of all cursed wretches the most cursed.

Ver. 22 [x]: Ἡμέρᾳ κρίσεως· *At the day of judgment.*] ביום דינא *In the day of judgment:* and ביום דינא רבא *In the day of the great judgment:* a form of speech very usual among the Jews.

Ver. 29: Τὸν ζυγόν μου· *My yoke.*] So אול תורה *The yoke of the law:* עול מצוה *The yoke of the precept:* עול מלכות שמים *The yoke of the kingdom of heaven.*

CHAP. XII.[y]

Ver. 1: Ἐν ἐκείνῳ τῷ καιρῷ ἐπορεύθη ὁ Ἰησοῦς τοῖς σάββασι διὰ τῶν σπορίμων· *At that time Jesus went on the sabbath day through the corn.*] The time is determined by Luke in these words, ἐν σαββάτῳ δευτεροπρώτῳ· that is, *on the sabbath from the second-first.*

I. Provision was made by the divine law, that the sheaf of firstfruits should be offered on the second day of the Passover-week, Lev. xxiii. 10, 11: מִמָּחֳרַת הַשַּׁבָּת יְנִיפֶנּוּ הַכֹּהֵן *On the morrow after the sabbath the priest shall shake [or wave] it.* Not on the morrow after the ordinary sabbath of the week, but the morrow after the first day of the Passover week, which was a sabbatic day, Exod. xii. 16; Lev. xxiii. 7. Hence the Seventy, ἐπαύριον τῆς πρώτης, *the morrow of the first day;* the Chaldee, מבתר יומא טאב *after the holy-day.* The Rabbins Solomon and Menachem, ממחרת יום טוב הראשון של פסח *on the morrow after the first day of the Passover-feast:* of which mention had been made in the verses foregoing.

II. But now, from that second day of the Passover-solemnity, wherein the sheaf was offered, were numbered seven

weeks to Pentecost.   For the day of the sheaf and the day
of Pentecost did mutually respect each other.   For on this
second day of the Passover, the offering of the sheaf was sup-
plicatory, and by way of prayer, beseeching a blessing upon
the new corn, and leave to eat it, and to put in the sickle
into the standing corn.   Now the offering of the first fruit
loaves on the day of Pentecost (Lev. xxiii. 15—17) did respect the giving of thanks for the finishing and inning of
barley harvest.   Therefore, in regard of this relation, these
two solemnities were linked together, that both might respect the harvest : that, the harvest beginning ; this, the
harvest ended : this depended on that, and was numbered
seven weeks after it.   Therefore, the computation of the time
coming between could not but carry with it the memory of
that second day of the Passover-week; and hence Pentecost
is called the ' Feast of weeks' (Deut. xvi. 10).   The true
calculation of the time between could not otherwise be retained as to sabbaths, but by numbering thus; This is σάββατον δευτερόπρωτον, *the first sabbath after the second day of the
Passover.*   This is δευτεροδεύτερον, *the second sabbath after that
second day.*   And so of the rest.   In the Jerusalem Talmud [z],
the word שבת פרוטוגמייא *the sabbath* πρωτογαμίας, *of the
first marriage,* is a composition not very unlike.

When they numbered by days, and not by weeks, the
calculation began on the day of the sheaf : " A [a] great number of certain scholars died between the Passover and Pentecost, by reason of mutual respect not given to one another.   There is a place where it is said that they died fif-
teen days before Pentecost, that is, thirty-three days after
the sheaf."

At the end of the Midrash of Samuel which I have, it is
thus concluded ; " This work was finished the three-and-
thirtieth day after the sheaf."

III. Therefore by this word δευτεροπρώτῳ, *the second-first,*
added by St. Luke, is shown, first, that this *first sabbath*
was *after the second day of the Passover* ; and so, according
to the order of evangelic history, either that very sabbath
wherein the paralytic man was healed at the pool of Be-

thesda, John v, or the sabbath next after it. Secondly, that these ears of corn plucked by the disciples were of barley: how far, alas! from those dainties wherewith the Jews are wont to junket, not out of custom only, but out of religion also! Hear their Gloss, savouring of the kitchen and the dish, upon that of the prophet Isaiah, chap. lviii. 13 : " ' Thou shalt call the sabbath a delight :'—It is forbidden," say they, " to fast on the sabbath ; but, on the contrary, men are bound to delight themselves with meat and drink. For we must live more delicately on the sabbath than on other days : and he is highly to be commended who provides the most delicious junkets against that day. We must eat thrice on the sabbath, and all men are to be admonished of it. And even the poor themselves who live on alms, let them eat thrice on the sabbath. For he that feasts thrice on the sabbath shall be delivered from the calamities of the Messias, from the judgment of hell, and from the war of Gog and Magog [b]." ' Whose god is their belly,' Phil. iii. 19.

IV. But was the standing corn ripe at the feast of the Passover? I answer,

I. The seed-time of barley was presently after the middle of the month Marchesvan ; that is, about the beginning of our November: " He [c] heard that the seed sown at the first rain [d] was destroyed by hail; he went and sowed at the second rain, &c. : and when the seed of all others perished with the hail, his seed perished not." Upon which words the Gloss writes thus ; " The first rain was the seventeenth day of the month Marchesvan ; the second rain, the three-and-twentieth day of the same month ; and the third was in the beginning of the month Chisleu. When, therefore, the rain came down, that which was sown at the first rain was now become somewhat [e] stiff, and so it was broken by the hail; but that which was sown at the second rain, by reason of its tenderness, was not broken, &c. Therefore the barley was sown at the coming in of the winter, and growing by the mildness of the weather, in winter, when the Passover came in, it became ripe : so that from that time

---

[b] Maimon. Schab. cap. 30. Kimchi, in Isai. cap. lviii.

[c] Bab. Berac. fol. 18. 2.

[d] *English folio edition*, vol. ii. p. 185.

[e] *Leusden's edit.*, vol. ii. p. 320.

(the sheaf being then offered) barley-harvest took its beginning.

2. But if, when the just time of the Passover was come,
the barley were not ripe, the intercalary month was added
to that year, and they waited until it ripened: " For [f], for
three things they intercalated the year; for the equinox, for
the new corn, and for the fruit of the trees. For the elders
of the Sanhedrim do compute and observe if the vernal
equinox will fall out on the sixteenth day of the month Nisan, or beyond that; then they intercalate that year, and
they make that Nisan the second Adar; so that the Passover might happen at the time of new corn. Or if they observe that there is no new corn, and that the trees sprouted
not when they were wont to sprout, then they intercalate the
year," &c.

You have an example of this thing: " Rabban [g] Gamaliel
to the elders of the great Sanhedrim, our brethren in Judea
and Galilee, &c.; health. Be it known unto you, that since
the lambs are too young, and the doves are not fledged, and
there is no young corn, we have thought good to add thirty
days to this year," &c.

Οἱ δὲ μαθηταὶ αὐτοῦ ἐπείνασαν· *And his disciples were an
hungred.*] The custom of the nation, as yet, had held them
fasting; which suffered none, unless he were sick, to taste
any thing on the sabbath before the morning prayers of the
synagogue were done. And on common days also, and that
in the afternoon, provision was made by the canons, " That [h]
none, returning home from his work in the evening, either
eat, or drink, or sleep, before he had said his prayers in the
synagogue."

Of the public or private ways that lay by the corn-fields,
let him that is at leisure read Peah, chap. ii.

Ver. 2: Ποιοῦσιν ὃ οὐκ ἔξεστι ποιεῖν ἐν σαββάτῳ· *They do
that which is not lawful to do on the sabbath day.*] They do
not contend about the thing itself, because it was lawful,
Deut. xxiii. 25; but about the thing done on the sabbath.

---

[f] Maimon. in Kiddush. Hodesh.   fol. 11. 2.
cap. 4.
    [h] Piske Tosaph. in Berac. cap. 1.
  [g] Hieros. Maasar Sheni, fol. 56. 3.   artic. 4. R. Asher ibid.
Sanhedr. fol. 18. 4. Bab. Sanhedr.

Concerning which the Fathers of the Traditions write thus ;
קוצר גרונות חייב ותולש תולדות קוצר " He [i] that reaps on
the sabbath, though never so little, is guilty.   And to pluck
the ears of corn is a kind of reaping ; and whosoever plucks
any thing from the springing of his own fruit is guilty, under
the name of a reaper." But under what guilt were they
held ? He had said this before, at the beginning of chap. vii,
in these words : " The works whereby a man is guilty of
stoning and cutting off, if he do them presumptuously; but
if ignorantly, he is bound to bring a sacrifice for sin, מהן
אבות ומהן תולדות *are either primitive or derivative.*" Of
' primitive,' or of the general kinds of works, are nine-and-
thirty reckoned ; " To plough [k], to sow, to reap, to gather
the sheaves, to thrash, to sift, to grind, to bake, &c.; to shear
sheep, to dye wool," &c.   תולדות The *derivative* works, or
the particulars of those generals, are such as are of the same
rank and likeness with them.   For example, digging is of
the same kind with ploughing ; chopping of herbs is of the
same rank with grinding ; and plucking the ears of corn is
of the same nature with reaping.   Our Saviour, therefore,
pleaded the cause of the disciples so much the more eagerly,
because now their lives were in danger ; for the canons of
the scribes adjudged them to stoning for what they had done,
if so be it could be proved that they had done it presumptuously.   From hence, therefore, he begins their defence, that
this was done by the disciples out of necessity, hunger compelling them, not out of any contempt of the laws.

Ver. 3 : Δαβὶδ, καὶ οἱ μετ' αὐτοῦ· *David, and those that were
with him.*] For those words of Ahimelech are to be understood comparatively, " Wherefore art thou alone, and no
man with thee ?" [1 Sam. xxi. 1.] that is, comparatively to
that noble train wherewith thou wast wont to go attended,
and which becomes the captain-general of Israel.   David
came to Nob, not as one that fled, but as one that came to
inquire at the[l] oracle concerning the event of war, unto which
he pretended to come by the king's command.   Dissembling,
therefore, that he hastened to the war, or to expedite some

---

[i] Maimon. Schabb. cap. 8.   [k] Talm. Schab. cap. 7.
[l] *English folio edition*, vol. ii. p. 186.

warlike design, he dissembles likewise that he sent his army
to a certain place; and that he had turned aside thither
to worship God, and to inquire of the event; that he had
brought but a very few of his most trusty servants along
with him, for whom, being an hungred, he asketh a few
loaves.

῞Οτε ἐπείνασεν· *When he was an hungred.*] Here
hearken to Kimchi, producing the opinion of the ancients
concerning this story in these words: " Our Rabbins, of
blessed memory, say, that he gave him the show-bread, &c.
The interpretation also of the clause, וְאַף כִּי הַיּוֹם יִקְדַּשׁ
בַּכֶּלִי *yea, though it were sanctified this day in the vessel,* [v. 6.]
is this; It is a small thing to say, that it is lawful for us to
eat these loaves taken from before the Lord when we are
hungry; for it would be lawful to eat this very loaf which
is now set on, which is also sanctified in the vessel (for the
table sanctifieth); it would be lawful to eat even this, when
another loaf is not present with you to give us, and we are
so hunger-bitten." And a little after; " There is[m] nothing
which may hinder taking care of life, beside idolatry, adultery,
and murder."

These words do excellently agree with the force of our
Saviour's arguments; but with the genuine sense of that
clause, methinks they do not well agree. I should, under
correction, render it otherwise, only prefacing this before-
hand, that it is no improbable conjecture that David came
to Nob either on the sabbath itself, or when the sabbath
was but newly gone. " For[n] the show-bread was not to be
eaten unless for one day and one night; that is, on the sabbath and the going-out of the sabbath; David, therefore,
came thither in the going-out of the sabbath." And now I
render David's words thus; " Women have been kept from
us these three days," [so that there is no uncleanness with
us from the touch of a menstruous woman], "and the vessels
of the young men were holy, even in the common way," [that
is, while we travelled in the common manner and journey];
" therefore, much more are they holy as to their vessels this
[sabbath] day." And to this sense perhaps does that come:

---

[m] *Leusden's edit.*, vol. ii. p. 321.   [n] R. Esaias in 1 Sam. xxi.

דָּאֵג נֶעְצָר לִפְנֵי יְהוָה "But there was there one of the servants of Saul *detained that day before the Lord*," [v. 8.] The reverence of the sabbath had brought him to worship, and as yet had detained him there.

Ver. 5: Οἱ ἱερεῖς ἐν τῷ ἱερῷ τὸ σάββατον βεβηλοῦσι, καὶ ἀναίτιοί εἰσι· *The priests in the Temple profane the sabbath, and are guiltless.*] עבודה שהיא לשם קדושים אין עבודה "*The*[o] *servile work which is done in the holy things is not servile.* The same works which were done in the Temple on other days were done also on the sabbath.*" And אין שבות במקדש כלל *There is no sabbatism at all in the Temple* [p].

Ver. 8: Κύριος γάρ ἐστι καὶ τοῦ σαββάτου ὁ υἱὸς τοῦ ἀνθρώπου· *For the Son of man is Lord also of the sabbath.*] I. He opposed this very argument against their cavils before the Sanhedrim, John v. When he was summoned into the court concerning his healing the paralytic man on this very sabbath, or on the sabbath next before, he shews his dominion over the sabbath from this very thing, that he, the Son, was invested and honoured with the same authority, power, and dignity, in respect of the administration of the New Testament, as the Father was in regard of the Old.

II. The care of the sabbath lay upon the first Adam under a double law, according to his double condition : 1. Before his fall, under the law of nature written in his heart : under which he had kept the sabbath, if he had remained innocent. And here it is not unworthy to be observed, that although the seventh day was not come before his fall, yet the institution of the sabbath is mentioned before the history of his fall. 2. After his fall, under a positive law. For when he had sinned on the sixth day, and the seventh came, he was not now bound under the bare law of nature to celebrate it ; but according as the condition of Adam was changed, and as the condition of the sabbath was not a little changed also, a new and positive law concerning the keeping the sabbath was superinduced upon him. It will not be unpleasant to produce a few passages from the Jewish masters of that first sabbath :—

"Circumcision[q]," saith R. Judah[r], "and the sabbath, were

---

o Hieros. Schab. fol. 17. 1.   q *English folio edit.,* vol. ii. p. 187.
p Maimon. in Pesach. cap. 1.   r Mid. Tillin, fol. 15. 3.

before the law." But how much backward before the law? Hear Baal Turim[s] : " The Israelites were redeemed (saith he) out of Egypt, because they observed circumcision and the sabbath-day." Yea, and further backward still : " The inheritance[t] of Jacob is promised to those that sanctify the sabbath, because he sanctified the sabbath himself." Yea, and more backwards yet, even to the beginning of the world : " The[u] first psalm in the world was, when Adam's sin was forgiven : and when the sabbath entered, he opened his mouth and uttered the psalm of the sabbath." So also the Targum upon the title of Psalm xcii : " The psalm or song which Adam composed concerning the sabbath-day." Upon which psalm, among other things, thus Midrash Tillin : " What did God create the first day? Heaven and earth. What the second? The firmament, &c. What the seventh? The sabbath. And since God had not created the sabbath for servile works, for which he had created the other days of the week, therefore it is not said of that as of the other days, ' And the evening and the morning was the seventh day.' " And a little after, " Adam was created on the eve of the sabbath : the sabbath entered when he had now sinned, and was his advocate with God," &c.

" Adam[x] was created on the sabbath-eve, that he might immediately be put under the command."

III. Since, therefore, the sabbath was so instituted after the fall, and that by a law and condition which had a regard to Christ now promised, and to the fall of man, the sabbath could not but come under the power and dominion of *the Son of man*, that is, of the promised seed, to be ordered and disposed by him as he thought good, and as he should make provision, for his own honour and the benefit of man.

Ver. 10 : Εἰ ἔξεστι τοῖς σάββασι θεραπεύειν; *Is it lawful to heal on the sabbath days?*] These are not so much the words of inquirers, as deniers. For these were their decisions in that case ; " Let[y] not those that are in health use physic on the sabbath day. Let not him that labours under a pain in

---

[s] In Exod. i.
[t] R. Sol. in Isa. lviii. 14.
[u] Targ. in Cant. i.

[x] Bab. Sanhedr. fol. 38. 1.
[y] Maimon. in Schabb. c. 21.

his loins, anoint the place affected with oil and vinegar ; but with oil he may, so it be not oil of roses, &c. He that hath the toothache, let him not swallow vinegar to spit it out again; but he may swallow it, so he swallow it down[z]. He that hath a sore throat, let him not gargle it with oil: but he may swallow down the oil, whence if he receive a cure it is well. Let no man chew mastich, or rub his teeth with spice for a cure ; but if he do this to make his mouth sweet, it is allowed. They do not put wine into a sore eye. They do not apply fomentations or oils to the place affected," &c. All which things, however they were not applicable to the cure wrought by Christ (with a word only), yet they afforded them an occasion of cavilling : who, indeed, were sworn together thus to quarrel him ; that canon affording them a further pretence, " This[a] certainly obtains, that whatsoever was possible to be done on the sabbath eve driveth not away the sabbath." To which sense he speaks, Luke xiii. 14.

Let[b] the reader see, if he be at leisure, what diseases they judge dangerous, and what physic is to be used on the sabbath.

Ver. 11 : 'Εὰν ἐμπέσῃ πρόβατον τοῖς σάββασιν εἰς βόθυνον, &c. *If a sheep fall into a ditch on the sabbath days, &c.*] It was a canon, חוס על ניכסידן של ישראל *We*[c] *must take a tender care of the goods of an Israelite.* Hence,

" If[d] a beast fall into a ditch, or into a pool of waters, let [*the owner*] bring him food in that place if he can ; but if he cannot, let him bring clothes and litter, and bear up the beast ; whence, if he can come up, let him come up," &c.

" If a beast, or his foal, fall into a ditch on a holy-day, R. Lazar saith[e], ' Let him lift up the former to kill him, and let him kill him : but let him give fodder to the other, lest he die in that place.' R. Joshua saith, ' Let him lift up the former, with the intention of killing him, although he kill him not : let him lift up the other also, although it be not in his mind to kill him.' "

Ver. 16[f] : 'Ίνα μὴ φανερὸν αὐτὸν ποιήσωσι· *That they should*

---

[z] *Leusden's edition*, vol. ii. p. 322.

[a] Talm. Schabb. cap. 19.

[b] In Hieros. Avodah Zarah, fol. 40. 4.

[c] Hieros. Jom Tobh, fol. 62. 1.

[d] Maimon. in Schabb. c. 25.

[e] Hieros. in the place above.

[f] *English folio edit.*, vol. ii. p. 188.

not make him known.] But this, not that he refused to heal
the sick, nor only to shun popular applause; but because he
would keep himself hid from those who would not acknowledge
him.   This prohibition tends the same way as his preaching
by parables did, Matt. xiii. 13; "I speak to them by parables,
because seeing they see not." He would not be known by
them who would not know him.

Ver. 20: Κάλαμον συντετριμμένον οὐ κατεάξει· *A bruised reed
shall he not break.*] These words are to be applied, as appears
by those that went before, to our Saviour's silent transaction
of his own affairs, without hunting after applause, the noise
of boasting, or the loud reports of fame.   He shall not make
so great a noise as is made from the breaking of a reed now
already bruised and half broken, or from the hissing of smoking
flax only when water is thrown upon it.   How far different is
the Messias thus described, from the Messias of the expectation of the Jews! And yet it appears sufficiently that Isaiah,
from whom these words are taken, spake of the Messias, and
the Jews confess it.

῎Εως ἂν ἐκβάλῃ εἰς νῖκος τὴν κρίσιν· *Till he send forth judgment unto victory.*] The Hebrew and LXX in Isaiah read
it thus, " He shall bring forth judgment unto truth." The
words in both places mean thus much, That Christ should
make no sound in the world, or noise of pomp, or applause,
or state, but should manage his affairs in humility, silence,
poverty, and patience, both while he himself was on earth,
and by his apostles, after his ascension, labouring under
contempt, poverty, and persecution; but at last " he should
bring forth judgment to victory;" that is, that he should
break forth and show himself a judge, avenger, and conqueror, against that most wicked nation of the Jews, from
whom both he and his suffered such things: and then, also,
" he sent forth judgment unto truth," and asserted himself
the true Messias, and the Son of God, before the eyes of
all; and confirmed the truth of the gospel, by avenging his
cause upon his enemies, in a manner so conspicuous and so
dreadful.   And hence it is, that that sending forth and execution of judgment against that nation is almost always
called in the New Testament " his coming in glory." When
Christ and his kingdom had so long lain hid under the veil

of humility, and the cloud of persecution, at last he brake forth a revenger, and cut off that persecuting nation, and shewed himself a conqueror before the eyes of all, both Jews and Gentiles. Let it be observed in the text before us, how, after the mention of that judgment and victory (against the Jews), presently follows, " And in his name shall the Gentiles trust."

Ver. 24 : Ἐν τῷ Βεελζεβοὺλ ἄρχοντι τῶν δαιμονίων· *By Beelzebub, the prince of the devils.*] For the searching out the sense of this horrid blasphemy, these things are worthy observing :

I. Among the Jews it was held, in a manner, for a matter of religion, to reproach idols, and to give them odious names.

" R. Akibah [g] saith, Idolatry pollutes, as a menstruous woman pollutes : as it is said, ' Thou shalt cast away the [*idol*] as something that is menstruous, and thou shalt say to it, Get thee hence' (Isa. xxx. 22). R. Lazar saith, Thou shalt say to it, Get thee hence : that which they call the face of *God*[h], let them call[i] the face of a *dog :* that which they call עֵין כּוֹס *the fountain of a cup,* let them call עֵין קֵרֵץ *the fountain of toil* [or *of flails*]: that which they call גְּדֵירָה *fortune,* let them call גְּלֵייָא *a stink,* &c. That town which sometimes was called *Beth-el,* was afterward called *Beth-aven.*" See also the tract *Schabbath*[k], where these same words are[l].

כָּל לִיצָנוּתָא אֲסִירָא חוּץ מִלִּיצָנוּתָא דְּעַ״ז *All*[m] *jeering is forbidden, except the jeering of idolatry.* This also is repeated in the tract *Megillah*[n] : where this is added, " It is lawful for a Jew to say to a Cuthite, שִׁקְלֵיהּ לְעַ״ז וְאַנְחֵיהּ בְּשִׁין תִּיוֹ״ *Take your idol, and put it under your buttocks.*"

II. Among the ignominious names bestowed upon idols, the general and common one was[o] זְבוּל *Zebul, dung,* or *a dunghill.* " Even[p] to them who have stretched out their hands בְּזֶבוּל *in a dunghill* [that is, in an idol-temple, or in

---

[g] Hieros. Avodah Zarah, fol. 43. 3.

[h] See Strabo, lib. 16. p. apud me 874.

[i] *Leusden's edit.,* vol. ii. p. 323.

[k] Fol. 11. 4.

[l] [See more in Buxtorf, Lex. T. & R. sub v. פַּרְיָא col. 1086, 7.]

[m] Bab. Sanhedr. fol. 93. 2.

[n] Fol. 25. 2.

[o] *English folio edition,* vol. ii. p. 189.

[p] Hieros. Beracoth, fol. 12. 2.

idolatry], there is hope. Thou canst not bring them [into the church], because they have stretched forth their hands בזבול *in a dunghill:* but yet you cannot reject them, because they have repented." And a little after, ראה אותם מזבלין וגו' ליעז " *He that sees them 'dunging'* [for מזבחים, that is, *'sacrificing'*] *to an idol,* let him say, Cursed be he that sacrifices to a strange god."

Let them therefore, who dare, form this word in Matthew into *Beelzebub.* I am so far from doubting that the Pharisees pronounced the word *Beelzebul,* and that Matthew so wrote it, that I doubt not but the sense fails if it be writ otherwise.

III. Very many names of evil spirits or devils occur in the Talmudists, which it is needless here to mention. Among all the devils, they esteemed that devil the worst, the foulest, and, as it were, the prince of the rest, who ruled over the idols, and by whom oracles and miracles were given forth among the heathens and idolaters. And they were of this opinion for this reason, because they held idolatry above all other things chiefly wicked and abominable, and to be the prince and head of evil. This demon they called בעל זבול *Baal-zebul,* not so much by a proper name, as by one more general and common; as much as to say, the *lord of idolatry:* the worst devil, and the worst thing: and they called him the " prince of devils," because idolatry is the prince (or chief) of wickedness.

We meet with a story[q], where mention is made of רבהון דרוחיא *the prince of spirits.* Whether it be in this sense, let the reader consult and judge. Also in the Aruch[r] we meet with these words, שידא אשמדון רבהון דרוחתא *the demon Asmodeus, the prince of spirits.*

IV. The Talmudists, being taught by these their fathers, do give out, horribly blaspheming, that Jesus of Nazareth our Lord was a magician, a broacher of strange and wicked worship; and one that did miracles by the power of the devil, to beget his worship the greater belief and honour.

" Ben[s] סטדא *Satda* brought magic out of Egypt, by cut-

----

[q] Hieros. Peah, fol. 21. 2.   [r] Ex Rabboth.
[s] Bab. Schab. fol. 104. 2. [See more in Buxtorf, Lex. T. & R. sub v. סטד coll. 1458 foll.]

tings which he had made in his flesh." By בן סטדא *Ben Satda*, they understand Jesus of Nazareth, as we have said before; whom they dishonour by that name, that they might, by one word and in one breath, reproach him and his mother together. For סטדא *Satda*, or *Stada*, sounds as much as an *adulterous wife*, which the Gemara shews after a few lines, סטת דא מבעלה *She went aside from her husband.* They feign[t] that Jesus travelled with Joshua Ben Perachiah into Egypt, when the said Joshua fled from the anger and sword of Janneus the king, which we have mentioned at the second chapter; and that he brought thence magical witchcrafts with him, but under the cutting of his flesh, that he might not be taken by the Egyptian magicians, who strictly examined all that went out of that land, that none should transport their magic art into another land. And in that place they add these horrid words, ישו כשף והסית יהדיה את ישראל *Jesus practised magic, and deceived, and drove Israel to idolatry.* Those whelps bark, as they were taught by these dogs.

To this, therefore, does this blasphemy of the Pharisees come; as if they should say, " He casts out devils indeed; but he doth this by the help of the devil, the lord of idols, that dwells in him; by him, that is the worst of all devils, who favours him and helps him, because it is his ambition to drive the people from the worship of the true God to strange worship."

Ver. 25 : Εἰδὼς δὲ ὁ Ἰησοῦς τὰς ἐνθυμήσεις αὐτῶν· *But Jesus knowing their thoughts.*] Behold, O Pharisee, a sign of the true Messias, for[u] a sign you would have: he smells out a wicked man.

"It[x] is written of Messias, The Spirit of the Lord shall rest upon him, וַהֲרִיחוֹ בְּיִרְאַת ה *and shall make him smell in the fear of the Lord.* Rabba said, he shall smell and judge; as it is said, he shall not judge by the sight of his eyes, &c. Ben Cozba reigned two years and a half, and said to the Rabbins, I am the Messias: they said to him, It is written of Messias that he shall smell and judge (the Gloss is, he

---

[t] Sanhedr. fol. 107. 2.   [u] Signum veri Messiæ, etiam quod optas: *Leusd.*
[x] Bab. Sanhedr. fol. 93. 2.

shall smell out [y] the man, and shall judge and know whether
he be guilty). Let us see whether thou canst smell and
judge. [z] כיון דחזייה דלא מריח ודאין קטילוה *And when
they saw that he could not smell 'and judge, they slew him."*

Ver. 27 : Οἱ υἱοὶ ὑμῶν ἐν τίνι ἐκβάλλουσι; *By whom do your
children cast them out ?*] By *your children,* Christ seems to
understand some disciples of the Pharisees; that is, some of
the Jews, who using exorcisms seemed to cast out devils
such as they, Acts xix. 13[a]; and yet they said not to them,
" Ye cast out devils by Beelzebul." It is worthy marking,
that Christ presently saith, "If I by the Spirit of God cast
out devils, then the kingdom of God is come among you."
For what else does this speak, than that Christ was the first
who should cast out devils? which was an undoubted sign
to them that the kingdom of heaven was now come. But
that which was performed by them by exorcisms was not so
much a casting out of devils, as a delusion of the people ;
since Satan would not cast out Satan, but by compact with
himself and with his company he seemed to be cast out,
that he might the more deceive.

The sense, therefore, of Christ's words comes to this :
" That your disciples cast out devils, ye attribute not to Beelzebul, no nor to magic ; but ye applaud the work when it is
done by them : they, therefore, may in this matter be your
judges, that you pronounce these words of my actions out of
the rankness and venom of your minds."

In[b] the Gloss mention is made of a devil cast out by a Jew
at Rome.

Ver. 32 : Οὐκ ἀφεθήσεται αὐτῷ, οὔτε ἐν τούτῳ τῷ αἰῶνι, οὔτε
ἐν τῷ μέλλοντι· *It shall not be forgiven him, neither in this world,
nor in that which is to come.*] They that endeavour hence to
prove the remission of some sins after death, seem little to
understand to what Christ had respect when he spake these
words. Weigh well this common and most known doctrine
of the Jewish schools, and judge :

" He[c] that transgresses an affirmative precept, if he presently repent, is not moved until the Lord pardon him. And

[y] Subolebit ei de homine: *Leusd.*
[z] *Leusden's edition,* vol. ii. p. 324.
[a] *English folio edit.,* vol. ii. p. 190.

[b] Bab. Joma, fol. 57. 1.
[c] Hieros. Sanhedr. fol. 37. 3.
Bab. Joma, fol. 86. 1.

of such it is said, ' Be ye converted, O backsliding children,
and I will heal your backslidings.' He that transgresses a
negative precept and repents, his repentance suspends judgment, and the day of expiation expiates him; as it is said,
' This day shall all your uncleannesses be expiated to you.'
He that transgresses to cutting off [*by the stroke of God,*] or
to death by the Sanhedrim, and repents, repentance and the
day of expiation do suspend judgment, and the strokes that
are laid upon him wipe off sin ; as it is said, ' And I will visit
their transgression with a rod, and their iniquity with
scourges.' But he by whom the name of God is profaned
[or blasphemed], repentance is of no avail to him to suspend
judgment, nor the day of expiation to expiate it, nor scourges
[or corrections inflicted] to wipe it off, but all suspend judgment, and death wipes it off." Thus the Babylonian Gemara
writes: but the Jerusalem thus ; " Repentance and the day
of expiation expiate as to the third part, and corrections as
to the third part, and death wipes it off: as it is said, and
your iniquities shall not be expiated to you until ye die.
הא למדנו שמיתא ממרקת *Behold, we learn that death wipes
off.*" Note this, which Christ contradicts, concerning blasphemy against the Holy Ghost ; " It shall not be forgiven,
(saith he,) neither in this world, nor in the world to come ;"
that is, neither before death, nor, as you dream, by death.

'Ἐν τῷ αἰῶνι τῷ μέλλοντι· *In the world to come.*] I. Some
phrases were received into common use, by which in common speech they opposed the heresy of the Sadducees, who
denied immortality. Of that sort were עולם הבא *αἰὼν ὁ
μέλλων, the world to come*: גן עדן *παράδεισος, paradise:*
גהנום *γέεννα, hell,* &c.

" At[d] the end of all the prayers in the Temple" (as we
observed before) " they said עד עולם *for ever.* But when
the heretics brake in and said, 'There was no age but one,' it
was appointed to be said, מן העולם ועד העולם *for ever
and ever.*"

This distinction of עולם הזה *this world,* and of עולם
הבא *the world to come,* you may find almost in every page of
the Rabbins.

" The [e]Lord recompense thee a good reward for this thy

d Bab. Beracoth, fol. 54. 1.   e Targ. in Ruth, chap. ii. 15.

good word בְּעַלְמָא הָדֵין *in this world*, and let thy reward be perfected בְּעַלְמָא דְאָתֵי *in the world to come*."

" It[f] [that is, the history of the creation and of the Bible] begins therefore with the letter ב [Beth] [in the word בְּרֵאשִׁית *Bereshith*], because two worlds were created, this world, and a world to come."

II. עוֹלָם הבא *The world to come*, hints two things especially (of which see Rambam[g]) : 1. The times of the Messias : "Be[h] mindful of the day wherein thou camest out of Egypt, all the days of thy life. The wise men say, By 'the days of thy life,' is intimated 'this world :' by 'all the days of thy life,' the days of the Messias are superinduced." In sense the apostle seems to speak, Hebrews ii. 5, and vi. 5. 2. The state after death, ע״ הב״ לאחר שיצא האדם מע״ה *The[i] world to come is, when a man is departed out of this world.*

Ver. 39[k] : Γενεὰ πονηρὰ καὶ μοιχαλὶς σημεῖον ἐπιζητεῖ, &c. *An evil and adulterous generation seeketh after a sign.*] I. Their schools also confessed, that signs and miracles were not to be expected but by a fit generation.

" The[l] elders being once assembled at Jericho, the Bath Kol went forth and said, There is one among you who is fit to have the Holy Ghost dwell upon him, אלא שאין הדור כדיי *but that [this] generation is not fit.* They fix their eyes upon Hillel the Elder. The elders being assembled again in ὑπερῴῳ, *an upper room* in Jabneh, *Bath Kol* came forth and said, There is one among you who is fit to have the Holy Spirit dwell upon him, אלא שאין הדור כדיי *but that the generation is not fit.* They cast their eyes upon Samuel the Little."

II. That *generation* by which and in which the Lord of life was crucified lay, and that deservedly, under an ill report for their great wickedness above all other, from the beginning of the world until that day. Whence that of the prophet, " Who shall declare his *generation?*" Isaiah liii. 2 ; that is, his *generation* (viz. that *generation* in which he should

---

f Baal Turim, & Tanch. in Gen. i. 1.

g In Sanhedr. cap. Chelek.

h Berac. cap. 1, hal. ult.

i Tanchum, fol. 52.

k *English folio edit.*, vol. ii. p. 191. —*Leusden's edition*, vol. ii. p. 325.

l Hieros. Sotah, fol. 24. 2.

live) should proceed to that degree of impiety and wickedness, that it should surpass all expression and history. We
have observed before, how the Talmudists themselves confess, that that *generation* in which the Messias should come
should exceed all other ages in all kinds of amazing wickedness.

III. That nation and *generation* might be called *adulterous*
literally ; for what else, I beseech you, was their irreligious
polygamy than continual adultery ? And what else was their
ordinary practice of divorcing their wives, no less irreligious,
according to every man's foolish or naughty will ?

Ver. 39 : Εἰ μὴ τὸ σημεῖον Ἰωνᾶ τοῦ προφήτου· *But the sign
of Jonah the prophet.*] Here and elsewhere, while he gives
them the sign of Jonah, he does not barely speak of the
miracle done upon him, which was to be equalled in the Son
of man, but girds them with a silent check[m]; instructing them
thus much, that the Gentiles were to be converted by him,
after his return out of the bowels of the earth, as heathen
Nineveh was converted, after Jonah was restored out of the
belly of the whale. Than which doctrine scarce anything bit
that nation more sharply.

Ver. 40 : Ἔσται ὁ υἱὸς τοῦ ἀνθρώπου ἐν τῇ καρδίᾳ τῆς γῆς
τρεῖς ἡμέρας καὶ τρεῖς νύκτας· *The Son of man shall be three days
and three nights in the heart of the earth.*] 1. The Jewish
writers extend that memorable station of the unmoving sun
at Joshua's prayer to six-and-thirty hours ; for so Kimchi
upon that place : " According to more exact interpretation,
the sun and moon stood still for six-and-thirty hours : for
when the fight was on the eve of the sabbath, Joshua feared
lest the Israelites might break the sabbath : therefore he
spread abroad his hands, that the sun might stand still on
the sixth day, according to the measure of the day of the
sabbath, and the moon, according to the measure of the
night of the sabbath, and of the going-out of the sabbath ;
which amounts to six-and-thirty hours."

II. If you number the hours that passed from our Saviour's giving up the ghost upon the cross to his resurrection, you shall find almost the same number of hours ; and

---

[m] [Sed tacito etiam stimulo eos pungit, Lat.]

yet that space is called by him " three days and three nights,"
when as two nights only came between, and only one complete
day. Nevertheless, while he speaks these words, he is not
without the consent both of the Jewish schools, and their
computation. Weigh well that which is disputed in the tract
Schabbath[o], concerning the uncleanness of a woman for three
days; where many things are discussed by the Gemarists
concerning the computation of this space of three days.
Among other things these words occur; " R. Ismael saith,
עונות ד׳ שהן פעמים *Sometimes*[p] *it contains four* עונות *Onoth*,
sometimes five, sometimes six. But [q] how much is the space
of עונה *an Onah?* R. Jochanan saith either a day or a night."
And so also the Jerusalem Talmud; " R. Akiba[r] fixed a day
for an *Onah*, and a night for an *Onah*: but the tradition is,
that R. Eliezar Ben Azariah said, ומקצת עונה ולילה יום
עונה ככולה *A day and a night make an Onah, and a part of*
an Onah is as the whole." And a little after, עבר ישמעאל ר׳
מקצת עונה ככולה *R. Ismael computeth a part of the Onah*
for the whole.

It [s] is not easy to translate the word עונה *Onah* into good
Latin: for to some it is the same with the half of a natural
day; to some it is all one with νυχθήμερον, *a whole natural*
day. According to the first sense we may observe, from the
words of R. Ismael, that sometimes four עונות *Onoth*, or
halves of a natural day, may be accounted for three days:
and that they also are so numbered that one part or the
other of those halves may be accounted for a whole. Compare the latter sense with the words of our Saviour, which
are now before us: " A day and a night (saith the tradition)
make an *Onah*, and a part of an *Onah* is as the whole."
Therefore Christ may truly be said to have been in his grave
three *Onoth*, or τρὶς νυχθήμερον, *three natural days* (when yet
the greatest part of the first day was wanting, and the night
altogether, and the greatest part by far of the third day also),
the consent of the schools and dialect of the nation agreeing
thereunto. For, " the least part of the *Onah* concluded the
whole." So that according to this idiom, that diminutive

o Cap. 9. hal. 3.
p Bab. fol. 86. 1.
q Bab. Avod. Zar. fol. 75. 1.

r Schabb. fol. 12. 1.
s *English folio edition*, vol. ii. p.
192.

part of the third day upon which Christ arose may be computed for the whole day, and the night following it.

Ver. 45 [t]: Οὕτως ἔσται καὶ τῇ γενεᾷ ταύτῃ τῇ πονηρᾷ· *So
shall it be to this evil generation.*] These words foretell a dreadful apostasy in that nation and generation.

I. It is something difficult so to suit all things in the
parable aforegoing, that they may agree with one another :
1. You can hardly understand it of unclean spirits cast out
of men by Christ ; when through the whole evangelic history there is not the least shadow of probability that any
devil cast out by him did return again into him out of whom
he had been cast.   2. Therefore our Saviour seems to allude
to the casting out of devils by exorcisms : which art, as the
Jews were well instructed in, so in practising it there was
need of dexterous deceits and collusions.   3. For it is
scarcely credible that the devil in truth finds less rest in dry
places than in wet : but it is credible that those diabolical
artists have found out such kind of figments for the honour
and fame of their art.   For, 4. It would be ridiculous to
think that they could by their exorcisms cast a devil out of
a man into whom he had been sent by God.   They might,
indeed, with a compact with the devil, procure some lucid
intervals to the possessed ; so that the inhabiting demon
might deal gently with him for some time, and not disturb
the man : but the demoniacal heats came back again at last,
and the former outrages returned.   Therefore, here there was
need of deceits well put together, that so provision might the
better be made for the honour of the exorcistical art ; as,
that the devil, being sent away into dry and waste places,
could not find any rest ; that he could not, that he would
not always wander about here and there, alone by himself,
without rest ; that he therefore returned into his old man-
sion, which he had formerly found so well fitted and prepared for him, &c.

Therefore these words seem to have been spoken by our
Saviour according to the capacity of the common people, or
rather, according to the deceit put upon them, more than
according to the reality or truth of the thing itself ; taking a

[t] *Leusden's edition*, vol. ii. p. 326.

parable from something commonly believed and entertained, that he might express the thing which he propounded more plainly and familiarly.

II. But however it was, whether those things were true indeed, or only believed and conceived so, by a most apt and open comparison is shown that the devil was first cast out of the Jewish nation by the gospel; and then, seeking for a seat and rest among the Gentiles, and not finding it, the gospel everywhere vexing him, came back into the Jewish nation again, fixed his seat there, and possessed it much more than he had done before. The truth of this thing appears in that fearful apostasy of an infinite multitude of Jews, who received the gospel, and most wickedly revolted from it afterward ; concerning which the New Testament speaks in abundance of places.

CHAP. XIII.[u]

Ver. 2 : "Ωστε αὐτὸν καθῆσθαι, καὶ πᾶς ὁ ὄχλος εἱστήκει· *So·that he sat, and the whole multitude stood.*] So was the manner of the nation, that the masters when they read their lectures *sat*, and the scholars *stood :* which honorary custom continued to the death of Gamaliel the Elder ; and then so far ceased, that the scholars *sat* when their masters *sat.* Hence is that passage : " From[x] that time that old Rabban Gamaliel died, the honour of the law perished, and purity and Pharisaism died." Where the Gloss, from *Megillah,* writes us ; " Before his death health was in the world, and they learned the law *standing ;* but when he was dead sickness came down into the world, and they were compelled to learn the law *sitting.*"

Ver. 3 : Ἐν παραβολαῖς· *In parables.*] I. No figure of Jewish rhetoric was more familiarly used than that of *parables :* which perhaps, creeping in from thence, among the heathen ended in fables. It is said, in the place of the Talmud just now cited, משמת רמ״ ביטלו משלים משלים *From the time that R. Meir died, those that spake in parables ceased :* not that that figure of rhetoric perished in the nation from that time, but because he surpassed all others in these

---

flowers ; as the Gloss there from the tract *Sanhedrim* speaks ; תלתא שמעתא ותלחא אגדתא ותלתא מתלי *A third part* [of his discourses or sermons] *was tradition, a third part allegory, and a third part parable.* The Jewish books abound everywhere with these figures, the nation inclining by a kind of natural genius to this kind of rhetoric. One might not amiss call their religion *Parabolical,* folded up within the coverings of ceremonies ; and their oratory in their sermons was like to it. But it is a wonder indeed, that they who were so given to and delighted in *parables,* and so dextrous in unfolding them, should stick in the outward shell of ceremonies, and should not have fetched out the parabolical and spiritual sense of them ; neither should he be able to fetch them out.

II. Our Saviour (who always and everywhere spake with the vulgar) useth the same kind of speech, and very often the same preface, as they did in their parables. למה הדבר דומה Τίνι ὡμοιώθη, &c., *to what is it likened,* &c. But in him, thus speaking, one may both acknowledge the Divine justice, who speaks darkly to them that despise the light ; and his Divine wisdom likewise, who so speaks to them that see, and yet see not, that they may see the shell and not see the kernel.

Ver. 4 [y] : ᾿Α μὲν ἔπεσε παρὰ τὴν ὁδόν, &c. *Some fell by the way side,* &c.] Concerning the husbandry of the Jews, and their manner of sowing, we meet with various passages in the tracts *Peah, Demai, Kilaim, Sheviith :* we shall only touch upon those things which the words of the text under our hands do readily remind us of.

There were ways and paths as well common as more private along the sown fields ; see chap. xii. 1. Hence in the tract *Peah* [z], where they dispute what those things are which divide a field so that it owes a double corner to the poor ; thus it is determined, "These things divide : a river, an aqueduct, a private way, a common way, a common path, and a private path," &c. See the place and the Gloss.

Ver. 5 [a] : ᾿Αλλα δὲ ἔπεσεν ἐπὶ τὰ πετρώδη· *Some fell among stony places.*] Discourse is had [b] concerning some laws of the

[y] *Leusden's edit.,* vol. ii. p. 327.   [a] *English folio edit.,* vol. ii. p. 194.
[z] Cap. 2.   [b] Hieros. Kilaim, fol. 27. 1.

Kilaim (or, *of the seeds of different kinds*), and of the seventh
year : where, among other things, we meet with these words ;
" R. Simeon Ben Lachish saith that he is freed [*from those
laws*] who sows his seed by the sea, עג″ פטרה עג״ סעלים
עג״ טרשים upon *rocks, shelves, and rocky places.*" These
words are spoken according to the reason and nature of the
land of Israel, which was very rocky ; and yet those places
that were so were not altogether unfit for tillage.

Ver. 7 : Ἄλλα δὲ ἔπεσεν ἐπὶ τὰς ἀκάνθας· *Others fell among
thorns.*] Here the distinction comes into my mind of שדה
לבן *a white field*, that is, which is all sown ; and of שדה אילן
a woody field, that is, in which trees and bushes grow here
and there : concerning which see the tract *Sheviith* [c]. So
there is very frequent mention in the Talmudists of מלבנות
beds, in fields and vineyards, ערוגות [d] which speaks the same
thing. And [e] of קרחה בשדה *baldness in a field*: that is,
when some places are left not sown, and some places lying
between are [f].

Ver. 8 : Ἐδίδου καρπὸν, ὁ μὲν ἑκατὸν, &c. *And brought forth
fruit, some a hundred, &c.*] These words are spoken according
to the fruitfulness of the land of Israel ; concerning which
the Talmudists speak much, and hyperbolically enough :
which nevertheless they confess to be turned long since into
miserable barrenness ; but are dim-sighted as to the true
cause of it.

They [g] treat of this matter, and various stories are produced,
which you may see : we will only mention these two :—

" R. Jochanan said, The worst fruit which we eat in our
youth excelled the best which we now eat in our old age :
for in his days the world was changed.

" R. Chaijah Bar Ba said סאה ארבלית *The Arbelite bushel*
formerly yielded a bushel of flour, a bushel of meal, a bushel
of bran, and a bushel of coarse bran, and a bushel of coarser
bran yet, and a bushel of the coarsest bran also : but now one
bushel scarcely comes from one bushel."

Ver. 13 : Βλέποντες οὐ βλέπουσι, &c. *They seeing see not.*]
Here you may observe this people to have been given up to a
reprobate mind, and a spirit of deep sleep, now a great while

[c] Cap. 2.   [d] Pcah, cap. 2.   [e] Kilaim, c. 3.
[f] Kilaim, c. 4.   [g] Hieros. Peah, fol. 20. 1, 2.

before the death of Christ. Which being observed, the sense
of the apostle will more easily appear, Rom. xi. 8 ; where these
very words are repeated. If you there state aright the rejection of that people, you will understand more clearly the apostle concerning their call, which is there handled. Pharisaism
and the sottishness of traditions had, now a good while ago,
thrown them into blindness, stupidity, and hardness of heart ;
and that for some ages before Christ was born : but when the
gospel came, the Lord had his gleanings among them, and
there were some that believed, and unto whom the participa-
tion of the promises was granted : concerning them the apostle
speaks in that chapter : see ver. 5, Ἐν τῷ νῦν καίρῳ λεῖμμα κατ'
ἐκλογήν, &c.   *At this present time there is a remnant according to election,"* &c., which we have observed before at
chap. iii. ver. 7.

Ver. 25: Ζιζάνια· *Tares.*] זונין *Zunin,* in Talmudic language.
החטים והזונין אינן כלאים זה בזה *Wheat*[h] *and* זונין ' *Zunin'*
are not seeds of different kinds. Where the Gloss is this ; "זונין
is a kind of wheat, which is changed in the earth, both as to
its form, and to its nature." By the best Lexicographers it
is rendered *zizania,* in Latin.

So[i] that that field, in this parable, was sown by the lord
with good wheat ; by the enemy, with bad and degenerate
wheat ; but all of it was sown with wheat, one or the other.
These words do not so barely mean good and bad men, as
good and bad Christians ; both distinguished from other men,
namely, from heathens, as wheat is distinguished from other
seeds : but they are distinguished also among themselves, as
good wheat is distinguished from that which is degenerate.
So chap. xxv, all those ten women, expecting the bridegroom, are virgins ; but are distinguished into wise and
foolish.

Ver. 32: Ὃ μικρότερον μέν ἐστι πάντων τῶν σπερμάτων, &c.
Which, indeed, is the least of all seeds, &c.] Hence it is passed
into a common proverb, כזרע הרדל *According to the quantity
of a grain of mustard:* and כטיפת הרדל *According to the
quantity of a little drop of mustard,* very frequently[k] used by

---

[h] Kilaim, cap. 1. hal. 1.   [i] *English folio edition,* vol. ii. p. 195.
[k] *Leusden's edition,* vol. ii. p. 328.

the Rabbins, when they would express the smallest thing, or the most diminutive quantity.

Μεῖζον τῶν λαχάνων ἐστί· *Is the greatest among herbs.*] " There[1] was a stalk of *mustard* in Sichin, from which sprang out three boughs : of which, one was broke off, and covered the tent of a potter, and produced three cabes of mustard. R. Simeon Ben Chalaphta said, A stalk of *mustard* was in my field, into which I was wont to climb, as men are wont to climb into a fig-tree."

Ver. 33 : Εἰς ἀλεύρου σάτα τρία· *In three (sata) measures of meal.*] That is, *in an ephah of meal.* Exod. xvi. 36; " Now an omer is the tenth part of an *ephah.*" The Chaldee reads, חד מן עסרא כתלת סאין *The tenth part of three sata.* The LXX reads, Δέκατον τῶν τριῶν μέτρων, *The tenth part of three measures.* And Ruth ii. 17, " It was as *an ephah* of barley." Where the Targum reads, כתלת סאין סעורין *As it were three sata of barley.*

" A[m] *seah* contains a double hin, six cabes, twenty-four *login*, a hundred and forty-four *eggs.*"

Ver. 52 : Ἐκβάλλει ἐκ τοῦ θησαυροῦ αὐτοῦ καινὰ καὶ παλαιά· *Bringeth forth out of his treasury things new and old.*] These words are spoken according to the dialect of the schools, where the question was not seldom started, What wine, what corn, or fruits were to be used in the holy things, and in some rites, new or more old ; namely, *of the present year, or the years past* [חדש או ישן]. But now, a thrifty man, provident of his own affairs, was stored both with the one and the other, prepared for either, which should be required. So it becomes a scribe of the gospel to have all things in readiness, to bring forth according to the condition and nature of the thing, of the place, and of the hearers. " Do ye understand all these things (saith Christ), both the things which I have said, and why I have said them ? So a scribe of the gospel ought to bring forth," &c.

---

[1] Hieros. Peah, fol. 20. 2.
[m] Alphes. in Pesach. cap. 5. Kimchi in Miclol.

CHAP. XIV.[n]

Ver. 2 : Οὗτός ἐστιν Ἰωάννης, &c. *This is John, &c.*] Was not Herod of the Sadducean faith? For that which is said by Matthew, " Beware of the leaven of the Pharisees and Sadducees," chap. xvi. 6, is rendered by Mark, " Beware of the leaven of the Pharisees, and of the leaven of Herod," chap. viii. 15 ; that is, ' of their doctrine.'

If, therefore, Herod embraced the doctrine of the Sadducees, his words, " This is John the Baptist, he is risen from the dead," seem to be extorted from his conscience, pricked with the sting of horror and guilt, as though the image and ghost of the Baptist, but newly butchered by him, were before his eyes : so that his mind is under horror ; and forgetting his Sadduceism, groaning and trembling, he acknowledgeth the resurrection of the dead, whether he will or no.

Or let it be supposed, that with the Pharisees he owned the resurrection of the dead ; yet certainly it was unusual for them that confessed it to dream of the resurrection of one that was but newly dead : they expected there should be a resurrection of the dead hereafter : but this, which Herod speaks, believes, and suspects, is a great way distant from that doctrine, and seems, indeed, to have proceeded from a conscience touched from above.

Ver. 4 : Οὐκ ἔξεστί σοι ἔχειν αὐτήν· *It is not lawful for thee to have her.*] " There[o] are thirty-six cuttings off in the law :" that is, sinners who deserve cutting off. And among the rest, הבא על אשה אחיו *he that lies with his brother's wife.* Philip[p] was now alive, and lived to the twentieth year of Tiberius.

Ver. 6 : Γενεσίων δὲ ἀγομένων τοῦ Ἡρώδου· *And when Herod's birthday was kept.*] The Jewish schools esteem the keeping of *birthdays* a part of idolatrous worship : perhaps they would pronounce more favourably and flatteringly of thine, O tetrarch, because thine.

These[q] are the times of idolaters : קלנדא *the Kalends ;*

---

[n] *English folio edition,* vol. ii. p. 196.
[o] Cherithuth, cap. 1. hal. 1.
[p] Joseph. Antiq. lib. 18. cap. 6. [xviii. 4. 6.]
[q] Avodah Zarah, cap. 1. hal. 3.

סטרנורא *the Saturnalia;* קרטסים κρατήσεις [that is, when they first took upon them the empire]; וגנוסיא של מלכים *and the* γενέσια, *the birthday of the kingdom;* ויום הלידה *and the day of a man's birth."* While they distinguish γενέσια *and a birthday,* they understand the beginning of that kingdom : of which distinction the Gemarists have many disputes.

'Ωρχήσατο ἡ θυγάτηρ, &c. *The daughter of Herodias danced.*] Not so much out of lightness, as according to the custom of the nation, namely, to express joy and to celebrate the day. The Jews were wont in their public and more than ordinary rejoicings, and also in some of their holy festivals, to express their cheerfulness by leaping and dancing. Omitting the examples which occur in the holy Bible, it is reported by the Fathers of the Traditions, that the chief part of the mirth in the feast of Tabernacles consisted in such kind of dancing : the chief men, the aged, and the most religious, dancing in the Court of the Women; and by how much the more vehemently they did it, so much the more commendable it was. The[r] gesture, therefore, or motion of the girl that danced took not so much with Herod, as her mind and affection : namely, because hereby she shewed honour towards his birthday[s], and love and respect towards him, and joy for his life and health: from whom, indeed, Herod had little deserved such things, since he had deprived her father Philip of his wife, and defiled her mother with unlawful wedlock and continual incest.

Ver. 7[t]: Μεθ' ὅρκου ὡμολόγησεν αὐτῇ, &c. *He promised her with an oath, &c.*] This kind of oath is called by the Talmudists שבועת בטוי *a rash oath :* concerning which see Maimonides[u], and the Talmudic tract under that title. If the form of the oath were " by his head," which[x] was very usual, the request of the maid very fitly, though very unjustly, answered to the promise of the king; as if she should say, ' You swore by your head that you would give me whatsoever I shall ask ; give me, then, the head of John Baptist.'

Ver. 10 : 'Απεκεφάλισε τὸν 'Ιωάννην· *He beheaded John.*]

---

[r] Sotah, cap. 5.
[s] *Leusden's edition,* vol. ii. p. 329.
[t] *English folio edit.,* vol. ii. p. 197.

[u] In שבועות cap. 1.
[x] Sanhedr. c. 3. hal. 2.

Josephus relates that John was imprisoned by Herod in Machærus: Ὑποψίᾳ τῇ Ἡρώδου δέσμιος εἰς τὸν Μαχαιροῦντα πεμφθείς· *Through the suspicion of Herod he was sent prisoner to Machærus.* Now Machærus was the utmost bounds of Perea[z]: and Perea was within Herod's jurisdiction[a]. But now if John lay prisoner there, when the decree went out against his life, the executioner must have gone a long journey, and which could scarcely be performed in two days from Tiberias, where the tyrant's court was, to execute that bloody command. So that that horrid dish, the head of the venerable prophet, could not be presented to the maid but some days after the celebration of his birthday.

The time of his beheading we find out by those words of the evangelist John[b], " but now the Passover was nigh," by reasoning after this manner: It may be concluded, without all controversy, that the disciples, as soon as they heard of the death of their master, and buried him, betook themselves to Christ, relating his slaughter, and giving him caution by that example to take care of his own safety. He hearing of it passeth over into the desert of Bethsaida, and there he miraculously feeds five thousand men, when the Passover was now at hand, as John relates, mentioning that story with the rest of the evangelists. Therefore we suppose the beheading of the Baptist was a little before the Passover, when he had now been in durance half a year, as he had freely preached by the space of half a year before his imprisonment.

Ver. 13 : Ἀνεχώρησεν ἐκεῖθεν ἐν πλοίῳ εἰς ἔρημον τόπον, &c. *He departed thence by ship into a desert place, &c.*] That is, from Capernaum[c] into the desert of Bethsaida, which is rendered by John[d], Ἀπῆλθεν πέραν τῆς θαλάσσης, *He went over the sea.* Which is to be understood properly, namely, from Galilee into Perea. The chorographical maps have placed Bethsaida in Galilee, on the same coast on which Capernaum is also : so also commentators feign to themselves a bay of the sea only coming between these two cities, which

---

[y] Antiq. lib. xviii. cap. 7. [xviii. 5. 2.]
[z] Id. de Bell. lib. iii. cap. 4. [iii. 3. 3.]
[a] Id. de Bell. lib. ii. cap. 9. [ii. 6. 3.]
[b] Chap. vi. 4.   [c] Luke ix. 10.
[d] John vi. 1.

was our opinion once also with them : but at last we learned
of Josephus, that Bethsaida was ἐν τῇ ἄνω Γαυλανιτικῇ, *in the
upper Gaulanitis,* (which we observe elsewhere,) on the east
coast of the sea of Gennesaret in Perea.

Ἠκολούθησαν αὐτῷ πεζῇ· *They followed him on foot.*] From
hence interpreters argue that Capernaum and Bethsaida lay
not on different shores of the sea, but on the same : for how
else, say they, could the multitude follow him afoot? Very
well, say I, passing Jordan near Tiberias, whose situation I
have elsewhere shewn to be at the efflux of Jordan out of the
sea of Galilee.   They followed him afoot ἀπὸ τῶν πόλεων,
from the cities, saith our evangelist : now there were cities of
some note very near Capernaum, Tarichea on one side, Tiberias on the other.   Let it be granted that the multitude
travelled out of these cities after Christ ; the way by which
they went afoot was at the bridge of Jordan in Chammath :
that place was distant a mile or something less from Tiberias,
and from Capernaum three miles or thereabouts.   Passing
Jordan, they went along by the coast of Magdala ; and, after
that, through the country of Hippo : now Magdala was distant one mile from Jordan, Hippo two ; and after Hippo
was Bethsaida, at the east shore of the sea ; and after Bethsaida was a bay of the sea, thrusting out itself somewhat into
the land ; and from thence was the desert of Bethsaida.
When, therefore[e], they returned back from thence, he commands his disciples to get into a ship, and to go to Bethsaida,
while he sent the multitude away, whence he would afterward
follow them on foot, and would sail with them thence to
Capernaum.

Ver. 17 : Δύο ἰχθύας· *Two fishes.*]   What kind of *fish* they
were we do not determine.   That they were brought hither
by a boy to be sold, together with the five loaves, we may
gather from John, chap. vi. 9.   The Talmudists discourse
very much of מליח *salt fish.*   I render the word *salt fish,*
upon the credit of the Aruch : he citing this tradition out of
Beracoth[f], הביאו לפניו מליח " *Do they set before him first
something salt,* and with it a morsel? He blesseth[g] over the
salt meat, and omits [*the blessing*] over the morsel, because

the morsel is, as it were, an appendix to it. מליח *The salt meat*, saith he, is to be understood of fish, as the tradition teacheth, that he that vows abstinence from salt things is restrained from nothing but from salt fish." Whether these were *salt fish*, it were a ridiculous matter to attempt to determine ; but if they were, the manner of blessing which Christ used is worthy to be compared with that which the tradition now alleged commands.

Ver. 20 : Καὶ ἔφαγον πάντες, καὶ ἐχορτάσθησαν· *And they did all eat, and were filled.*] So סעודה *eating*, or *a repast after food*, is defined by the Talmudists ; namely, " When they eat their fill. Rabh[h] saith, כל סעודה שאין בה מלח אינה סעודה *All eating, where salt is not, is not eating.*" The Aruch citing these words, for מלח *salt*, reads מליח *something seasoned*, and adds, " It is no eating, because they are not filled."

Ver. 22 : Καὶ εὐθέως ἠνάγκασε τοὺς μαθητὰς, &c. *And immediately he compelled his disciples, &c.*] The reason of this compulson is given by St. John[i], namely, because the people seeing the miracle were ambitious to make him a king : perhaps that the disciples might not conspire to do the same, who as yet dreamed too much of the temporal and earthly kingdom of the Messias.

Ver. 23 : Ὀψίας δὲ γενομένης· *When the evening was come.*] So ver. 15, but in another sense : for that denotes the lateness of the day ; this, the lateness of the night. So ערב *evening*, in the Talmudists, signifies not only the declining part of the day, but the night also : " from[k] what time do they recite the phylacteries בערבית *in the evening?* From the time when the priests go in to eat their *T'ruma,* even to the end of the first watch, as R. Eliezer saith ; but, as the wise men say, unto midnight ; yea, as Rabban Gamaliel saith, even to the rising of the pillar of the morning." Where the Gloss is, בערבית בלילה *in the evening, that is, in the night.*

Ver. 25 : Τετάρτῃ δὲ φυλακῇ τῆς νυκτός· *In the fourth watch of the night.*] That is, after cock crowing : the Jews acknowledge only three watches of the night, for this with them was the third ; אשמורת שליש הא של של לילה *The watch is the*

---

[h] In Bab. Berac. fol. 44. 1.   [i] Chap. vi. 15.
[k] Berac. cap. 1. hal. 1.

third part of the night. Thus the Gloss upon the place now
cited. See also the Hebrew commentators upon Judg. vii. 19.
Not that they divided not the night into four parts, but that
they esteemed the fourth part, or the watch, not so much for
the night as for the morning. So Mark xiii. 35, that space
after cockcrowing is called πρωΐ, *the morning.* See also
Exod. xiv. 24. There were, therefore, in truth, four watches
of the night, but only three of deep night. When, therefore,
it is said that Gideon set upon the Midianites in the "middle
watch of the night," Judg. vii. 19, it is to be understood of
that watch which was indeed the second of the whole night,
but the middle watch of the deep night: namely, from the
ending of the first watch to midnight.

CHAP. XV.[1]

VER. 2 : Παραβαίνουσι τὴν παράδοσιν τῶν πρεσβυτέρων; *Why
do they transgress the tradition of the elders?*] How great a
value they set upon their traditions, even above the word of
God, appears sufficiently from this very place, ver. 6. Out of
infinite examples which we meet with in their writings, we
will produce one place only; חביבים דברי סופרים מדברי
תורה *The*[m] *words of the scribes are lovely above the words of
the law :* for the words of the law are weighty and light ; but
the words of the scribes are all weighty."

" He that shall say, 'There are no phylacteries, transgressing the words of the law,' is not guilty ; but he that shall
say, 'There are five *Totaphoth,* adding to the words of the
scribes,' he is guilty."

חמורים דברי זקנים מדברי נביאים : " *The words* πρεσβυτέρων *of the elders are weightier than the words of the prophets.*"

" A prophet and πρεσβύτερος *an elder,* to what are they
likened? To a king sending two of his servants into a province. Of one he writes thus, 'Unless he shew you my seal,
believe him not :' of the other thus, 'Although he shews you
not my seal, yet believe him.' Thus it is written of the prophet, 'He shall shew thee a sign or a miracle ;' but of the
elders thus, 'According to the law which they shall teach
thee,'" &c. But enough of blasphemies.

---

[1] *English folio edit.,* vol. ii. p. 199.   [m] Hieros. Berac. fol. 3. 2.

Οὐ γὰρ νίπτονται τὰς χεῖρας αὐτῶν, &c. *For they wash not their hands, &c.*] The [n] undervaluing of the washing of hands is said to be among those things for which the Sanhedrim excommunicates: and therefore that R. Eleazar Ben Hazar was excommunicated by it, שפקפק בנטילת ידים *because he undervalued the washing of hands;* and that when he was dead, by the command of the Sanhedrim, a great stone was laid upon his bier. " Whence you may learn (say they) that the Sanhedrim stones the very coffin of every excommunicate [o] person that dies in his excommunication."

It would require a just volume, and not a short commentary, or a running pen, to lay open this mystery of Pharisaism concerning washing of hands, and to discover it in all its niceties: let us gather these few passages out of infinite numbers:

I. נטילת ידים וטבילתן מדברי סופרים *The* [p] *washing of hands and the plunging of them is appointed by the words of the scribes:* but by whom, and when, it is doubted. Some ascribe the institution of this rite to Hillel and Shammai, others carry it back to ages before them: " Hillel [q] and Shammai decreed concerning the washing of hands. R. Josi Ben Rabbi Bon, in the name of R. Levi, saith, ' That tradition was given before, but they had forgotten it :' these second stand forth, and appoint according to the mind of the former."

II. " Although [r] it was permitted to eat unclean meats, and to drink unclean drinks, yet the ancient religious eat their common food in cleanness, and took care to avoid uncleanness all their days; and they were called Pharisees. And this is a matter of the highest sanctity, and the way of the highest religion; namely, that a man separate himself, and go aside from the vulgar, and that he neither touch them, nor eat nor drink with them: for such separation conduceth to the purity of the body from evil works," &c. Hence that definition of a Pharisee which we have produced before, פרושין אוכלין חולין בטהרה *The Pharisees eat their common food in cleanness:* and the Pharisaical ladder of heaven, " Whosoever [s] hath his seat in the land of Israel,

---

[n] In Bab. Berac. fol. 46. 2.
[o] *Leusden's edition*, vol. ii. p. 331.
[p] Maimon. in Mikvaoth, cap. 11.
[q] Hieros. Schab. fol. 3. 4.
[r] Maimon. in אוכלין טומאת.
[s] Hieros. in the place above.

and eateth his common food in cleanness, and speaks the
holy language, and recites his phylacteries morning and
evening, let him be confident that he shall obtain the life of
the world to come."

III. Here that distinction is to be observed between
מאכלות אסורות *forbidden meats,* and אוכלין טמאין *unclean
meats.* Of both Maimonides wrote a proper tract. *Forbidden meats,* such as fat, blood, creatures unlawful to be
eaten (Levit. ii.), were by no means to be eaten : but *meats,
unclean* in themselves, were lawful indeed to be eaten, but
contracted some uncleanness elsewhere : it was lawful to eat
them, and it was not lawful ; or, to speak as the thing indeed
is, they might eat them by the law of God, but by the canons
of Pharisaism they might not.

IV. The distinction also between טמא *unclean,* and פסול
profane or *polluted,* is to be observed. Rambam, in his preface to *Toharoth,* declares it.

פסול עניינו שלא יטמא זולתו *Profane* or *polluted denotes
this, that it does not pollute another beside itself.* For every
thing which uncleanness invades so that it becomes unclean,
but renders not another thing unclean, is called פסול *profane.* And hence it is said of every one that[t] eats unclean
meats, or drinks unclean drinks, נפסלה גווייתו *that his body
is polluted :* but he pollutes not another. Note that, " the
body of the eater is polluted by unclean meats." To which
you may add that which follows in[u] the same Maimonides, in
the place before alleged : " Separation from the common
people, &c., conduces to the purity of the body from evil
works ; the purity of the body conduceth to the sanctity of
the soul from evil affections ; the sanctity of the soul conduces unto likeness to God, as it is said, ' And ye shall be
sanctified, and ye shall be holy, because I, the Lord that
sanctify you, am holy.' " Hence you may more clearly perceive the force of Christ's confutation, which we have ver.
17—20.

V. They thought that clean food was polluted by unclean
hands, and that the hands were polluted by unclean meats.
You would wonder at this tradition : " Unclean[u] meats and

---

[t] *English folio edit.,* vol. ii. p. 200. [u] Rambam in the place before.

unclean drinks do not defile a man if he touch them not, but if he touch them with his hands, then his hands become unclean ; if he handle them with both hands, both hands are defiled ; if he touch them with one hand only, one hand only is defiled."

VI. This care, therefore, laid upon the Pharisee sect, that meats should be set on free, as much as might be, from all uncleanness : but especially since they could not always be secure of this, that they might be secure that the meats were not rendered unclean by their hands. Hence were the washings of them not only when they knew them to be unclean, but also when they knew it not.

Rambam in the preface to the tract ידים *of hands*, hath these words ; " If the hands are unclean by any uncleanness, which renders them unclean ; or if it be hid from a man, and he knows not that he is polluted ; yet he is bound to wash his hands in order to eating his common food," &c.

VII. To these most rigid canons they added also bugbears and ghosts to affright them.

מילתא דשיבתא הוה : *It*[x] *was the business of Shibta.* Where the Gloss is, " *Shibta* was one of the demons who hurt them that wash not their hands before meat." The Aruch writes thus, " *Shibta* is an evil spirit which sits upon men's hands in the night : and if any touch his food with unwashen hands, that spirit sits upon that food, and there is danger from it."

Let these things suffice as we pass along : it would be infinite to pursue all that is said of this rite and superstition. Of the quantity of water sufficient for this washing ; of the washing of the hands, and of the plunging of them ; of the first and second water ; of the manner of washing ; of the time ; of the order, when the number of those that sat down to meat exceeded five, or did not exceed ; and other such like niceties : read, if you have leisure, and if the toil and nauseousness of it do not offend you, the Talmudic tract ידים *of hands*, Maimonides upon the tract מקוואות *lavers*, and Babyl. *Beracoth*[y] : and this article, indeed, is inserted through the whole volume entitled טהרות *cleanness.* Let this discourse be ended with this canon; "For [z] a cake, and for the washing of hands, let a man walk as far as four miles."

Ver. 5 : Δῶρον, ὃ ἐὰν ἐξ ἐμοῦ ὠφεληθῇς, &c. *It is a gift by whatsoever thou mightest be profited by me, &c.*] I. Beside the law alleged by Christ, "Honour thy father and thy mother," &c., they acknowledge this also for law, בן מאכיל אביו ומשקה מלביש ומכסה מוציא ומכניס ומרחץ פניו ידיו ורגליו *A [a] son is bound to provide his father meat and drink, to clothe him, to cover him, to lead him in and out, to wash his face, hands, and feet.* Yea, that [b] goes higher, "A son is bound to nourish his father, yea, to beg for him." Therefore it is no wonder if these things which are spoken by our Saviour are not found verbatim in the Jewish pandect; for they are not so much alleged by him to shew that it was their direct design to banish away all reverence and love towards parents, as to show how wicked their traditions were, and into what ungodly consequences they oftentimes fell. They denied not directly the nourishment of their parents, nay, they commanded it, they exhorted to it; but consequently by this tradition they made all void. They taught openly, indeed, that a father was to be made no account of in comparison of a Rabbin that taught them the law [c]; but they by no means openly asserted that parents were to be neglected : yet openly enough they did by consequence drawn from this foolish and impious tradition.

II. One might readily comment upon this clause, δῶρον, "it is a *gift*" (or, as Mark, Κορβᾶν, "it is *Corban*") *by whatsoever thou mightest be profited by me,* if we have read the Talmudic tracts *Nedarim* and *Nazir*, where the discourse is of vows and oaths; and the phrase which is before us speaks a vow or a form of swearing.

1. Vows were distinguished into two ranks, נדרי הקדש *vows of consecration,* and נדרי איסור *vows of obligation,* or *of prohibition.* A *vow of consecration* was when any thing was devoted to holy uses, namely, to the use of the altar or the Temple : as when a man, by a vow, would dedicate this or

---

[z] Hieros. Challah, fol. 58. 3.
[a] Tosaphta, in Kiddushin, cap. 1.

[b] Hieros. Kiddushin, fol. 61. 2, 3.
[c] Maimon. in Gezelah, cap. 12.

that for sacrifice, or to buy wood, salt, wine, &c. for [d] the altar: or לברק הבית *for the reparation of the Temple,* &c. נדר איסור *A vow of obligation* or *prohibition* was, when a man bound himself by a vow from this or that thing, which was lawful in itself; as, that he would not eat, that he would not put on, that he would not do this or that, &c.

2. This went for a noted axiom among them, כל כינויי נדרים כנדרים *All[e] epithets of vows are as the vows themselves.* They added certain short forms, by which they signified a vow, and which carried with it the force of a vow, as if the thing were spoken out in a larger periphrasis: as for example, "[f] If one should say to his neighbour, קונם קונה קונם *Konem, Konah, Kones,* behold, these are epithets of a thing devoted unto sacred uses."

The word קונם *Konem,* Rambam thus explains; כהקדש יהא עלי *Let[g] it be upon me as a thing devoted.* So also R. Nissim[h], קונם קונה הרי לשון הקדש הוא *Konem, Koneh, are words of devoting.*

We produced before, at chap. v. 33, some forms of oaths, which were only *Assertive:* these under our hands are *Votive* also. In the place from *Beracoth* just now alleged, one saith, קונם היין שאני טועם שהיין קשה לבני מעים *Let the wine be ' Konem,' which I shall taste, for wine is hard to the bowels:* that is, Let the wine which I taste be as devoted wine: as though he had said, I vow that I will not taste wine. "To which others answered, Is not old wine good for the bowels? Then he held his peace."

III. But above all such like forms of vowing, the word קרבן Κορβᾶν, *Corban,* was plainest of all; which openly speaks a thing devoted and dedicated to sacred use. And the reader of those tracts which we have mentioned shall observe these forms frequently to occur, קרבן שאני נהנה לך, and קונם שאני נהנה לך. *Let it be ' Corban,' whereby I am profitable to thee;* and, *Let it be ' Konem,' whereby I am profitable to thee.* Which words sound the very same thing, unless I am very much mistaken, with the words before us, "Let it be Κορβᾶν,

---

[d] *English folio edition,* vol. ii. p. 201.

[e] Nedarim, cap. 1. hal. 1.

[f] Ibid. hal. 2.

[g] In Bab. Berac. fol. 51. 1.

[h] In Nedarim, cap. 1.

Corban, or δῶρον, *a gift*, by whatsoever thou mayest be profited by me."

Which words that they may be more clearly understood,
and that the plain and full sense of the place may be discovered, let these things be considered :

First, That the word δῶρον is rather to be rendered, *Let it
be a gift*, than *It is a gift*. For *Konem* and *Corban*, as we have
noted, signified not היה כהקדש '*It is*' *as something devoted*, but
יהא כהקדש '*Let it be*' *as something devoted*. And he, of whom
we had mention before, who said, קונם היין שאני טועם
meant not, *The wine which I shall taste is as something devoted*, but *Let whatsoever wine I shall taste be as something
devoted*: that is, *To me let all wine be devoted, and not to be
tasted*.

Secondly, This form of speech קרבן שאני נהנה לך Δῶρον,
ὃ ἐὰν ἐξ ἐμοῦ ὠφεληθῆς *A gift, by whatsoever thou mightest be profited by me*, does neither argue, that he who thus spake devoted his goods to sacred uses, nor obliged him (according to
the doctrine[i] of the scribes) to devote them ; but only restrained him by an obligation from that thing, for the denying
of which he used such a form; that is, from helping him by
his goods, to whom he thus spake. He might help others
with his wealth, but him he might not.

Thirdly, The words are brought in as though they were
pronounced with indignation; as if, when the needy father
required food from his son, he should answer in anger and
with contempt, *Let it be as a thing devoted, whatsoever of mine
may profit thee*. But now, things that were devoted were not
to be laid out upon common uses.

Fourthly, Christ not only cites the law, ' Honour thy father
and mother,' but adds this also, Ὁ κακολογῶν πατέρα ἢ μητέρα,
He that curseth father or mother. But now there was no κακο-
λογία, *cursing*, here at all; if the son spoke truly and modestly,
and as the thing was, namely, that all his estate was devoted
before.

Fifthly, Therefore, although these words should have been
spoken by the son irreverently, wrathfully, and inhumanly,
towards his father, yet such was the folly, together with the

---

i *Leusden's edition*, vol. 2. p. 333.

impiety, of the traditional doctrine in this case, which pronounced the son so obliged by these his words, that it was
lawful by no means to succour his needy father.   He was not
at all bound by these words to dedicate his estate to sacred
uses; but not to help his father he was inviolably bound.   O
excellent doctrine and charity !

Sixthly, The words of the verse, therefore, may thus be
rendered, without any addition put between, which many interpreters do : *Whosoever shall say to his father or mother, Let
it be a* [devoted] *gift, in whatsoever thou mayest be helped by me :
then let him not honour his father and mother at all.*

Ver. 11 : Κοινοῖ τὸν ἄνθρωπον· *Defileth the man.*] Or, *maketh
him common*; so the word פָּסוּל seems to be rendered in the
Pharisaic idiotism, as I may so speak ; because they esteemed
defiled men for *common* and *vulgar* men : on the contrary, a
religious man among them is יָחִיד *a singular man.*   In Acts
x. 14[k], κοινὸν ἢ ἀκάθαρτον, *common or unclean,* seem to speak
the same thing with פָּסוּל אוֹ טָמֵא among the Talmudists.

Ver. 20 : Ἀνίπτοις χερσί· *With unwashen hands.*] He saith
not with *unclean* hands, but *unwashen*; because, as we said
before, they were bound to wash, although they were not conscious that their hands were unclean.   In Mark it is κοιναῖς
χερσὶ, *with common or defiled hands,* Mark vii. 2 ; which seem
to be called by the Talmudists *impure* hands, merely because
not washed.   Judge from that which is said in the tract
Challah : " A[l] cake is owing out of that dough which they
knead with the juice of fruits : וְנֶאֱכֶלֶת בְּיָדַיִם מְסוּבָּאוֹת
and it is eaten with unclean hands."

Ver. 22 : Γυνὴ Χαναναία· *A woman of Canaan.*] In Mark it
is, Ἑλληνὶς, Συροφοίνισσα τῷ γένει, *A Greek woman, a Syrophœnician by nation,* chap. vii. 26.

I. Χαναναία, *of Canaan.*   It is worthy observing, that the
Holy Bible, reckoning up ז" אוּמוֹת *the seven nations,* which
were to be destroyed by the Israelites, names the Perizzites,
who were not at all recited among the sons of Canaan, Gen. x.,
and the Canaanites as a particular nation, when all the seven,
indeed, were Canaanites.   See Deut. vii. 1, Josh. ix. 1, xi. 3,
Judg. iii. 5, &c.

---

[k] *English folio edit.*, vol. ii. p. 202.   [l] Cap. 2. hal. 2.

The reason of the latter (with which our business is) is to be fetched thence, that Canaan himself inhabited a peculiar part of that (northern) country, with his first-born sons, Sidon and Heth : and thence the name of Canaanites was put upon that particular progeny, distinguished from all his other sons ; and that country was peculiarly called by the name of ' Canaan,' distinctly from all the rest of the land of Canaan.   Hence Jabin, the king of Hazor, is called the ' king of Canaan,' Judg. iv. 2, and the kings of Tyre and Sidon, if I mistake not, are called ' the kings of the Hittites,' 1 Kings x. 29.

II. Ἑλληνὶς, Συροφοίνισσα· *A Greek woman, a Syrophœnician.*] Although Judea, and almost the whole world, had now a long while stooped under the yoke of the Romans, yet the memory of the Syro-Grecian kingdom, and the name of the nation, was not yet vanished. And that is worthy to be noted, בגולה אין מונין אלא למלכי יונים *In*[m] *the captivity, they compute the years only from the kingdom of the Greeks.*   They said before, "That[n] the Romans, for a hundred and fourscore years, ruled over the Jews before the destruction of the Temple ;" and yet they do not compute the times to that destruction by the years of the Romans, but by the years of the Greeks.   Let the Jews themselves well consider this, and the Christians with them, who reckon the Roman for the fourth monarchy in Daniel.

Therefore that woman that is here spoken of (to reduce all into a short conclusion) was a Syro-Grecian by nation, a Phœnician in respect of her habitation, and from thence called *a woman of Canaan.*

Ver. 26 : Τοῖς κυναρίοις· *To the dogs.*] By this title the Jews, out of spite and contempt, disgraced the Gentiles, whose first care it was to hate, to mock, and to curse, all beside themselves.   אומות עולם נמשלו ככלבים *The*[o] *nations of the world* [that is, *the heathen*] *are likened to dogs.* From the common speech of the nation, rather than from his own sense, our Saviour uses this expression, to whom ' the Gentiles' were not so hateful, and whose custom was to speak with the vulgar.

[m] Bab. Avodah Zarah, fol. 10. 1.　　　[n] Fol. 8. 2.
[o] Midr. Tillin, fol. 6. 3.

This ignominious name, like a stone cast at the heathen, at length fell[p] upon their own heads; and that by the hand and justice of God directing it: for although they out of pride and contempt fixed that disgraceful name upon the Gentiles, according to their very just desert, the Holy Spirit recoiled it upon themselves. See Psal. lix. 6; Phil. iii. 2; Rev. xxii. 15, &c.

Ver. 36[q]: Εὐχαριστήσας ἔκλασε· *He gave thanks and brake.*] See here the tract *Beracoth*[r], where it is discoursed of the manner of giving thanks when many ate together: שלשה שאכלו חייבי לזמן *Three who eat together ought to give thanks together:* that is, one gave thanks for the rest (as the Gloss writes) " in the plural number, saying, Let *us* give thanks." So when there were ten, or a hundred, or a thousand or more, one gave thanks for all, and they answered after him *Amen*, or some words which he had recited[s].

CHAP. XVI.

Ver. 3 : Διακρίνειν τὰ σημεῖα τῶν καιρῶν οὐ δύνασθε; *Can ye not discern the signs of the times?*] The Jews were very curious in observing the seasons of the heavens, and the temper of the air.

" In[t] the going out of the last day of the feast of Tabernacles, all observed the rising of the smoke. If the smoke bended northward, the poor rejoiced, but the rich were troubled; because there would be much rain the following year, and the fruits would be corrupted: if it bended southward, the poor grieved, and the rich rejoiced; for then there would be fewer rains that year, and the fruit would be sound: if eastward, all rejoiced: if westward, all were troubled." The Gloss is, " They observed this the last day of the feast of Tabernacles, because the day before, the decree of their judgment concerning the rains of that year was signed, as the tradition is, In the feast of Tabernacles they judged concerning the rains."

" R. Acha[u] said, If any wise man had been at Zippor when

---

p *Leusden's edition*, vol. ii. p. 334.
q *English folio edit.*, vol. ii. p. 203.
r Cap. vii.
s See halac. 3.
t Bab. Joma, fol. 21. 2.
u Hieros. Taanith, fol. 65. 2.

the first rain fell, he might foretell the moistness of the year
by the very smell of the dust," &c.

But they were dim-sighted at the signs of times; that is,
at those eminent signs, which plainly pointed, as with the
finger and by a visible mark, that now those times that were
so much foretold and expected, even the days of the Messias, were at hand. As if he had said, " Can ye not distinguish that the times of the Messias are come, by those
signs which plainly declare it? Do ye not observe Daniel's
weeks now expiring? Are ye not under a yoke, the shaking
off of which ye have neither any hope at all nor expectation
to do? Do ye not see how the nation is sunk into all manner
of wickedness? Are not miracles done by me, such as were
neither seen nor heard before? Do ye not consider an infinite
multitude flowing in, even to a miracle, to the profession of
the gospel? and that the minds of all men are raised into a
present expectation of the Messias? Strange blindness, voluntary, and yet sent upon you from heaven: your sin and your
punishment too! They see all things which may demonstrate
and declare a Messias, but they will not see."

Ver. 6: Προσέχετε ἀπὸ τῆς ζύμης τῶν Φαρισαίων, &c. *Beware
of the leaven of the Pharisees, &c.*] There were two things,
especially, which seem to have driven the disciples into a mistaken interpretation of these words, so that they understood
them of *leaven* properly so called.

I. That they had more seldom heard *leaven* used for *doctrine.* The metaphorical use of it, indeed, was frequent
among them in an ill sense, namely, for evil affections, and
the naughtiness of the heart; but the use of it was more rare,
if any at all, for evil doctrine.

Thus one prays: " Lord[x] of ages, it is revealed and known
before thy face that we would do thy will; but do thou subdue that which hinders: שאור שבעיסה ושעבוד מלכיות
namely, *the leaven which is in the lump, and the tyranny of*
[*heathen*] *kingdoms.*" Where the Gloss is thus; " The '*leaven
which is in the lump,*' are evil affections, which leaven us in
our hearts."

כורש החמיץ: *Cyrus*[y] *was leavened,* that is, grew worse.

[x] Bab. Berac. fol. 17. 1.   [y] Id. Rosh Hashanah, fol. 3. 2.

Sometimes it is used in a better sense ; " The Rabbins say[z],
Blessed is that judge who leaveneth his judgment." But
this[a] is not to be understood concerning doctrine, but concerning deliberation in judgment.

II. Because very exact care was taken by the Pharisaical
canons, what leaven was to be used and what not ; disputa-
tions occur here and there, whether heathen leaven is to be
used, and whether Cuthite leaven[b], &c. With which caution the disciples thought that Christ armed them, when he
spake concerning the leaven of the Pharisees : but withal
they suspected some silent reproof for not bringing bread
along with them.

Ver. 13 : Τίνα με λέγουσιν οἱ ἄνθρωποι εἶναι, τὸν υἱὸν τοῦ
ἀνθρώπου; *Whom do men say that I the Son of man am ?*]
I. That phrase or title, *the Son of man,* which Christ very
often gives himself, denotes[c] not only his humanity, nor his
humility (for see that passage, John v. 27, "He hath given
him authority of executing judgment, because he is *the Son
of man*") ; but it bespeaks the 'seed promised to Adam, the
second Adam :' and it carried with it a silent confutation of
a double ignorance and error among the Jews: 1. They knew
not what to resolve upon concerning the original of the
Messias ; and how he should rise, whether he should be of
the living, as we noted before, the manner of his rise being
unknown to them ; or whether of the dead. This phrase
unties this knot and teaches openly, that he, being a seed
promised to the first man, should arise and be born from the
seed of the woman. 2. They dreamed of the earthly victories of the Messias, and of nations to be subdued by him ;
but this title, *The Son of man,* recalls their minds to the first
promise, where the victory of the promised seed is the bruising
of the serpent's head, not the subduing of kingdoms by some
warlike and earthly triumph.

II. When, therefore, the opinion of the Jews concerning
the person of the Messias, what he should be, was uncertain
and wavering, Christ asketh, not so much whether they acknowledged him the Messias, as acknowledging the Messias,
what kind of person they conceived him to be. The apostles

---

[z] Kimchi in Isai. chap. i. 17.   [b] See Hieros. Schabb. fol. 3, 3, &c.
[a] *English folio edit.*, vol. ii. p. 204.   [c] *Leusden's edition,* vol. ii. p. 334.

and the other disciples whom he had gathered, and were very many, acknowledged him the Messias : yea, those blind men, chap. ix. 27, had confessed this also : therefore that question had been needless as to them, " Do they think me to be the Messias?" but that was needful, " What do they conceive of me, the Messias?" and to this the answer of Peter has regard, " Thou art Christ, the Son of the living God :" as if he should say, " We knew well enough a good while ago that thou art the Messias ; but as to the question, ' What kind of person thou art,' I say, ' Thou art the Son of the living God.' " See what we note at chap. xvii. 54.

Therefore the word τίνα, *whom*, asks not so much concerning the person, as concerning the quality of the person. In which sense also is the word מִי *who*, in those words, 1 Sam. xvii. 55, בֶּן־מִי־זֶה ; not, " The son of *whom*," but the son " *of what kind of man*," is this youth?

Ver. 14 : Ἕτεροι δὲ Ἰερεμίαν· *But others, Jeremias.*] The reason why they name Jeremiah only of all the prophets, we give at chap. xxvii. 9. You observe that recourse is here made to the memory of the dead, from whom the Messias should spring, rather than from the living : among other things, perhaps, this reason might persuade them so to do, that that piety could not in those days be expected in any one living, as had shined out in those deceased persons. (One of the Babylonian Gemarists suspects that Daniel, raised from the dead, should be the Messias.) And this perhaps persuaded them further, because they thought that the kingdom of the Messias should arise after the resurrection : and they that were of this opinion might be led to think that the Messias himself was some eminent person among the saints departed, and that he rising again should bring others with him.

Ver. 17 : Σὰρξ καὶ αἷμα· *Flesh and blood.*] The Jewish writers use this form of speech infinite times, and by it oppose *men* to God.

" If[d] they were about to lead me לִפְנֵי מֶלֶךְ בָּשָׂר וָדָם *before a king of flesh and blood*, &c. ; but they are leading me before the King of kings."

" A[e] king *of flesh and blood* forms his picture in a table,

d Bab. Berac. fol. 28. 2.   e Tanchum, fol. 12. 4.

&c.; the Holy Blessed One, his, &c." This phrase occurs five times in that one column: "the[f] Holy Blessed God doth not[g], as *flesh and blood* doth, &c. *Flesh and blood* wound with one thing and heal with another: but the Holy Blessed One wounds and heals with one and the same thing. Joseph was sold for his dreams, and he was promoted by dreams."

Ver. 18: Σὺ εἶ Πέτρος, &c. *Thou art Peter*, &c.] I. There is nothing, either in the dialect of the nation, or in reason, forbids us to think that our Saviour used this very same Greek word, since such Græcizings were not unusual in that nation. But be it granted (which is asserted more without controversy) that he used the Syriac word; yet I deny that he used that very word כיפא *Cepha,* which he did presently after: but he pronounced it *Cephas,* after the Greek manner; or he spoke it כיפאי *Cephai,* in the adjective sense, according to the Syriac formation. For how, I pray, could he be understood by the disciples, or by Peter himself, if in both places he had retained the same word אנת כיפא *Thou art a rock,* ועל כיפא *and upon this rock* I will build my church? It is readily answered by the Papists, that "Peter was the rock." But let them tell me why Matthew used not the same word in Greek, if our Saviour used the same word in Syriac. If he had intimated that the church should be built upon Peter, it had been plainer and more agreeable to the vulgar idiom to have said, "Thou art Peter, and upon *thee* I will build my church."

II. The words concerning the *rock* upon which the church was to be built are evidently taken out of Isaiah, chap. xxviii. 16; which, the New Testament being interpreter, in very many places do most plainly speak Christ. When therefore Peter, the first of all the disciples (from the very first beginning of the preaching of the gospel), had pronounced most clearly of the person of Christ, and had declared the mystery of the incarnation, and confessed the deity of Christ, the minds of the disciples are, with good reason, called back[h] to those words of Isaiah, that they might learn to acknowledge who that *stone* was that was set

---

f Id. fol. 18. 3.   g *English folio edition,* vol. ii. p. 205.

h *Leusden's edition,* vol. ii. p. 336.

in Sion for a foundation never to be shaken, and whence it
came to pass that that foundation remained so unshaken ;
namely, thence, that he was not a creature, but God himself,
the Son of God.

III. Thence, therefore, Peter took his surname ; not that
he should be argued to be that *rock*, but because he was so
much to be employed in building a church upon a *rock :*
whether it were that church that was to be gathered out of
the Jews, of which he was the chief minister, or that of the
Gentiles (concerning which the discourse here is principally
of), unto which he made the first entrance by the gospel.

Ver. 19 : Καὶ δώσω σοὶ τὰς κλεῖς τῆς βασιλείας τῶν οὐρανῶν·
And I will give thee the keys of the kingdom of heaven.] That is,
Thou shalt first open the door of faith to the Gentiles.   He
had said that he would build his church to endure for ever,
against which " the gates of hell should not prevail," which
had prevailed against the Jewish church : " and to thee,
O Peter (saith he), I will give the keys of the kingdom of
heaven, that thou mayest open a door for the bringing in the
gospel to that church." Which was performed by Peter in
that remarkable story concerning Cornelius, Acts x. And I
make no doubt that those words of Peter respect these words
of Christ, Acts xv. 7 ; Ἀφ᾽ ἡμερῶν ἀρχαίων ὁ Θεὸς ἐν ἡμῖν ἐξε-
λέξατο διὰ τοῦ στόματός μου ἀκοῦσαι τὰ ἔθνη τὸν λόγον τοῦ εὐαγγελίου, καὶ πιστεῦσαι· *A good while ago God made choice
among us, that the Gentiles should hear the word of the gospel by
my mouth, and believe.*

Καὶ ὃ ἐὰν δήσῃς ἐπὶ τῆς γῆς, &c. *And whatsoever thou shalt
bind on earth*, &c. Καὶ ὃ ἐὰν λύσῃς ἐπὶ τῆς γῆς, &c. *And whatsoever thou shalt loose on earth*, &c.] I. We believe the keys
were committed to Peter alone, but the power of binding and
loosing to the other apostles also, chap. xviii. 18.

II It is necessary to suppose that Christ here spake according to the common people, or he could not be understood without a particular commentary, which is nowhere
to be found.

III. But now *to bind and loose*, a very usual phrase in the
Jewish schools, was spoken of *things*, not of *persons ;* which is
here also to be observed in the articles ὃ and ὅσα, *what* and
whatsoever, chap. xviii.

One [i] might produce thousands of examples out of their writings: we will only offer a double decad ; the first, whence the frequent use of this word may appear ; the second, whence the sense may :

1. " R. Jochanan [k] said [to those of Tiberias], ' Why have ye brought this elder to me? **דאנא שרי והוא אסר ואסר** **והוא שרי** *Whatsoever I loose, he binds ; whatsoever I bind, he looseth.* ' "

2. **לא תאסור ולא תשרי** *Thou* [l] *shalt neither bind nor loose.*

3. " Nachum [m], the brother of R. Illa, asked R. Jochanan concerning a certain matter. To whom he answered, **לא תאסור ולא תשרי** *Thou shalt neither bind nor loose.*"

4. **חד אסר וחד שרי** *This* [n] *man binds, but the other looseth.*

5. " R. Chaija [o] said, **כל מה שאסרתי לך ממקום אחת הותרתי לך כאן** *Whatsoever I have bound to you elsewhere, I will loose to you here.*"

6. **שאל לחכם ואסר** *He* [p] *asked one wise man, and he bound :* **לא ישאל לחכם אחר שמא אחר יתיר** *Do not ask another wise man, lest perhaps he loose.*

7. **פה שאסר הוא פה שהתיר** *The* [q] *mouth that bindeth is the mouth that looseth.*

8. **אף על פי שאלו אוסרין ואלו מתירין** *"Although* [r] of the disciples of Shammai, and those of Hillel, *the one bound, and the other loosed ;* yet they forbade not but that these might make purifications according to the others."

9. **חכם שדן את הדין טמא וטיהר אסר והתיר :** *A* [s] *wise man that judgeth judgment, defileth and cleanseth [that is, he declares defiled or clean] ; he looseth and bindeth.* The same also is in Maimonides [t].

10. Whether it is lawful to go into the necessary-house with the phylacteries only to piss? **רבינא שרי רב אדא אסר** *Rabbena* [u] *looseth, and Rabh Ada bindeth.* **בעל אגדה שאינו**

[i] *English folio edit.*, vol. ii. p. 206.
[k] Hieros. Jom. Tobh, fol. 60. 1.
[l] Ibid.
[m] Id. ibid. fol. 63. 1.
[n] Bab. Megillah, fol. 26. 7.
[o] Hieros. Orlah, fol. 61. 2.
[p] Id. Schabb. fol. 16. 4.   Bab.

Avodah Zarah, fol. 7. 1.
[q] Demai, cap. 6. hal. 11.   Maimon. in Gezelah, cap. 4.
[r] Tosaphta in Jevam. cap. 1.
[s] Id. ib. cap. 4.
[t] In Mamrim, cap. 1.
[u] Bab. Berac. fol. 23. 1.

לא ולאאוסר מתיר *The* [x] *mystical doctor, who neither bindeth nor looseth.*

The other decad shall show the phrase applied to things:

1. "In[y] Judea they did [*servile*] works on the Passover-eve" (that is, on the day going before the Passover), " until noon, but in Galilee not. ב'ש' אוסרין בה" מתירין עד הנץ החמה But that which *the school of Shammai binds* until the night, *the school of Hillel looseth until the rising of the sun.*"

2. " A[z] festival-day may teach us this, שהתירו בו משום מלאכה *in which they loosed by the notion of a* [*servile*] *work*," killing and boiling, &c., as the Gloss notes. ואסרו בו משום שבות *But in which they bound by the notion of a sabbatism:* that is, as the same Gloss speaks, 'The bringing in some food from without the limits of the sabbath.'

3. " They[a] do not send letters by the hand of a heathen on the eve of a sabbath, no, nor on the fifth day of the week. בש" אוסרין אפילו ברביעי ובה" מתירין: *Yea, the school of Shammai binds it, even on the fourth day of the week; but the school of Hillel looseth it.*"

4.[b] " They[c] do not begin a voyage in the great sea on the eve of the sabbath, no, nor on the fifth day of the week. בש" אוסרין אפילו ברביעי ובה' מתירין: *Yea, the school of Shammai binds it, even on the fourth day of the week; but the school of Hillel looses it.*"

5. " To[d] them that bathe in the hot-baths in the sabbath-day, אסרו להן רחיצה והתירו להן זיעה: *they bind washing, and they loose sweating.*"

6. " Women[e] may not look into a looking-glass on the sab-bath-day, if it be fixed to a wall, רבי מתיר וחכמים אוסרין: *Rabbi loosed it, but the wise men bound it.*"

7. " Concerning[f] the moving of empty vessels [on the sabbath-day], of the filling of which there is no intention; בש" אוסרין ובה" מתירין *the school of Shammai binds it, the school of Hillel looseth it.*"

8. " Concerning[g] gathering wood on a feast-day scattered

---

[x] Hieros. Horaioth, fol. 48. 3.
[y] Pesachin, cap. 4. hal. 5.
[z] Ibid. cap. 6. hal. 2.
[a] Hieros. Schab. fol. 4. 1.
[b] Id. ibid.

[c] *Leusden's edit.,* vol. ii. p. 337.
[d] Hieros. Schab. fol. 6. 1.
[e] Id. ibid. fol. 7. 4.
[f] Id. ibid. fol. 16. 2.
[g] Id. Jom Tob, fol. 61. 1.

about a field, the school of Shammai *binds* it, the school of Hillel *looseth* it."

9. מעולם לא שרו לן עורבא ולא אסרו לן יונה *They* [h] *never loosed to us a crow, nor bound to us a pigeon.*

10. "Doth [i] a *seah* of unclean *Truma* fall into a hundred *seahs* of clean *Truma?* The school of Shammai *binds* it, the school of Hillel *looseth* it." There are infinite examples of this nature.

Let a third decad also be added (that nothing may be left unsaid in this matter), giving examples of the parts of the phrase distinctly and by themselves:

1. דברים שלא אסרו אותן כדי לעשות סייג "*The* [k] *things which they bound not, that they might have a hedge* to the law."

2. סופרים אסרוהו "*The* [l] *scribes bound the leaven.*"

3. לא קנסו ואסרו אלא בחמץ עצמו *They* [m] *neither punished nor bound, unless concerning the leaven itself.*

4. אסרו חכמים לאכל חמץ "*The* [n] *wise men bound the eating of leaven* from the beginning of the sixth hour," of the day of the Passover.

5. "R. Abhu [o] saith, R. Gamaliel Ben Rabbi asked me. What if I should go into the market? ואסרתי לו *and I bound it him.*"

1. בד" שהתיר שני דבדים אל ימהר להתיר דבר שלישי *The* [p] *Sanhedrim, which looseth two things, let it not hasten to loose three.*

2. [q] "R. Jochanan [r] saith, מדוחק התירו שאלת שלום בשבת *They necessarily loose saluting on the sabbath.*"

3. חכמים מתירין הכל השמנים *The* [s] *wise men loose all oils,* or *all fat things.*

4. "The [t] school of Shammai saith, They do not steep ink, colours, and vetches" on the eve of the sabbath, "unless they be steeped before the day be ended: ובית הלל מתירין *but*

---

h Bab. Sanhedr. fol. 100. 1.

i Truma, cap. 5. hal. 4.

k Maimon. Mamrim, cap. 2.

l Id. in Hamets et Matsah, cap. 1.

m Id. ibid. cap. 5.

n Id. ibid. cap. 9.

o Hieros. Avod. Zarah, fol. 39. 2.

p Maimon. Mamrim, cap. 2.

q *English folio edition,* vol. ii. p. 207.

r Tanchum, fol. 1. 3.

s Id. fol. 74. 3.

t Schabb. cap. 1. hal. 5.

the school of Hillel looseth it." Many more such like instances occur there.

5. מאיר התיר לטרוף ר' " *R. Meir* [u] *loosed the mixing* of wine and oil, to anoint a sick man on the sabbath."

To these may be added, if need were, the *frequent* (shall I say?) or *infinite* use of the phrases, אסור ומותר *bound and loosed*, which we meet with thousands of times over. But from these allegations, the reader sees abundantly enough both the frequency and the common use of this phrase, and the sense of it also; namely, first, that it is used in doctrine, and in judgments, concerning things allowed or not allowed in the law. Secondly, That to *bind* is the same with to *forbid*, or to *declare forbidden*. To think that Christ, when he used the common phrase, was not understood by his hearers in the common and vulgar sense, shall I call it a matter of laughter or of madness?

To this, therefore, do these words amount : When the time was come, wherein the Mosaic law, as to some part of it, was to be abolished and left off; and as to another part of it, was to be continued, and to last for ever : he granted Peter here, and to the rest of the apostles, chap. xviii. 18, a power to abolish or confirm what they thought good, and as they thought good, being taught this and led by the Holy Spirit : as if he should say, " Whatsoever ye shall *bind* in the law of Moses, that is, *forbid*, it shall be *forbidden*, the Divine authority confirming it; and whatsoever ye shall *loose*, that is, *permit*, or shall *teach*, that it is *permitted* and *lawful*, shall be *lawful* and *permitted*."

Hence they *bound*, that is, *forbade*, circumcision to the believers; eating of things offered to idols, of things strangled, and of blood for a time to the Gentiles; and that which they *bound* on earth was confirmed in heaven. They *loosed*, that is, *allowed* purification to Paul, and to four other brethren, for the shunning of scandal, Acts xxi. 24 : and in a word, by these words of Christ it was committed to them, the Holy Spirit directing that they should make decrees concerning religion, as to the use or rejection of Mosaic rites and judgments, and that either for a time or for ever.

---

[u] Hieros. Schabb. fol. 3. 1.

Let the words be applied, by way of paraphrase, to the matter that was transacted at present with Peter : " I am about to build a Gentile church (saith Christ) ; and to thee, O Peter, do I give the keys of the kingdom of heaven, that thou mayest first open the door of faith to them ; but if thou askest, by what rule that church is to be governed, when the Mosaic rule may seem so improper for it, thou shalt be so guided by the Holy Spirit[x], that whatsoever of the law of Moses thou shalt *forbid* them shall be *forbidden ;* whatsoever thou *grantest* them shall be *granted*, and that under a sanction made in heaven."

Hence in that instant, when he should use his keys, that is, when he was now ready to open the gate of the gospel to the Gentiles, Acts x. 28, he was taught from heaven, that the consorting of the Jew with the Gentile, which before had been *bound,* was now *loosed ;* and the eating of any creature convenient for food was now *loosed*, which before had been *bound ;* and he, in like manner, *looses* both these.

Those words of our Saviour, John xx. 23, " Whose sins ye remit, they are remitted to them," for the most part are forced to the same sense with these before us ; when they carry quite another sense. Here the business is of *doctrine* only, not of *persons ;* there of *persons*, not of *doctrine :* here of things lawful or unlawful in religion to be determined by the apostles ; there of persons obstinate or not obstinate, to be punished by them, or not to be punished.

As to doctrine, the apostles were doubly instructed : 1. So long sitting at the feet of their Master, they had imbibed the evangelical doctrine. 2. The Holy Spirit directing them, they were to determine concerning the legal doctrine and practice ; being completely instructed and enabled in both by the Holy Spirit descending upon them. As to their persons, they were endowed with a peculiar gift, so that the same Spirit directing them, if they would retain and punish the sins of any, a power was delivered into their hands of delivering to Satan, of punishing with diseases, plagues, yea, death itself ; which Peter did to Ananias and Sapphira ; Paul to Elymas, Hymeneus, and Philetus, &c.

---

[x] *Leusden's edition*, vol. ii. p. 338.

CHAP. XVII.[y]

VER. 2 : Καὶ μετεμορφώθη· *And was transfigured.*] When
Christ was baptized, being now ready to enter upon his evangelical priesthood, he is sealed by a heavenly voice for the
High Priest, and is anointed with the Holy Spirit, as the high
priests were wont to be with holy oil.

In this transfiguration, he is sealed for the high priest:
for mark, 1. How two of the greatest prophets, Moses and
Elias, resort to him. 2. How to those words, " This is my
beloved Son, in whom I am well pleased," which also were
heard from heaven at his baptism, is added that clause,
" hear ye him :" which compare with the words of Moses,
concerning a prophet to be raised up by God, Deut. xviii.
19, " Whosoever shall not hearken to my words, which I
shall put into his mouth," &c. 3. How the heavenly voice
went out of the cloud that overshadowed them, when at his
baptism no such cloud appeared. Here that is worthy observing, which some Jews note, and reason dictates, namely,
That the cloud of glory, the conductor of Israel, departed
at the death of Moses; for while he lived, that cloud was the
people's guide in the wilderness; but when he was dead, the
ark of the covenant led them. Therefore, as that cloud departed at the death of Moses, that great prophet, so such a
cloud was now present at the sealing of the greatest Prophet.
4. Christ here shines with such a brightness, nay, with a
greater than Moses and Elias now glorified; and this both
for the honour of his person and for the honour of his doctrine; both which surpassed by infinite degrees the persons
and the doctrines of both of them. When you recollect the
face of Christ transfigured, shining with so great lustre when
he talked with Moses and Elias, acknowledge the brightness
of the gospel above the cloudy obscurity of the law and of the
prophets.

Ver. 4 : Ποιήσωμεν ὧδε τρεῖς σκηνὰς, &c. *Let us make here
three tabernacles, &c.*] The transfiguration of Christ was by
night. Compare Luke ix. 37. The form of his face and
garments is changed while he prays; and Moses and Elias

come and discourse with him concerning his death (it is uncertain how long), while as yet the disciples that were present
were overcharged with sleep. When they awaked, O what a
spectacle had they ! being afraid, they observe and contem-
plate, they discover the prophets : whom, now departing,
Peter would detain; and being loath that so noble a scene
should be dispersed, made this proposition, " Let us make
here three tabernacles," &c. Whence he should know them
to be prophets, it is in vain to seek, because it is nowhere to
be found; but being known, he was loath they should depart
thence, being ravished with the sweetness of such society,
however astonished at the terror of the glory; and hence
those words, which when he spake he is said by Luke " not
to know what he said;" and by Mark, " not to know what
he should say;" which are rather to be understood of the
misapplication of his words, than of the sense of the words.
He knew well enough that he said these words, and he
knew as well for what reason he said them; but yet " he
knew not what he said;" that is, he was much mistaken
when he spake these words, while he believed that Christ,
Moses, and Elias, would abide and dwell there together in
earthly tabernacles.

Ver. 5: Ἔτι αὐτοῦ λαλοῦντος, ἰδοὺ, νεφέλη, &c. *While he yet
spake, behold, a cloud, &c.*] Moses and Elias now turning their
backs, and going out of the scene, Peter speaks his words;
and as he speaks them when the prophets were now gone,
" Behold, a cloud," &c. They had foretold Christ of his death
(such is the cry of the Law and of the Prophets, that "Christ
should suffer," Luke xxiv. 44); he preaches his deity to his[z]
disciples, and the heavenly voice seals him for the true Messias. See 2 Pet. i. 16, 17.

Ver. 10[a]: Τί οὖν οἱ γραμματεῖς λέγουσιν, ὅτι Ἠλίαν δεῖ
ἐλθεῖν πρῶτον; *Why therefore say the scribes that Elias must
first come?*] I. It would be an infinite task to produce all
the passages out of the Jewish writings which one might
concerning the expected coming of Elias : we will mention a
few things ἐν παρόδῳ, *in passing*, which sufficiently speak out
that vain expectation, and the ends also of his expected
coming.

I. Let David Kimchi first be heard upon those words of Malachi, "Behold, I send you Elias the prophet:" "God (saith he) shall restore the soul of Elias, which ascended of old into heaven, into a created body, like to his former body: for his first body returned to earth when he went up to heaven, each element to its own element. But when God shall bring him to life in the body, he shall send him to Israel before the day of judgment, which is 'the great and terrible day of the Lord:' and he shall admonish both the fathers and the children together to turn to God; and they that turn shall be delivered from the day of judgment," &c. Consider whither the eye of the disciples looks, in the question under our hands. Christ had commanded in the verse before, "Tell the vision" of the transfiguration "to no man, until the Son of man be risen from the dead." But now, although they understood not what the resurrection from the dead meant, (which Mark intimates,) yet they roundly retort, "Why therefore say the scribes that Elias shall first come?" that is, before there be a resurrection and a day of judgment: for as yet they were altogether ignorant that Christ should rise. They believed, with the whole nation, that there should be a resurrection at the coming of the Messias.

2. Let Aben Ezra be heard in the second place: "We find (saith he) that Elias lived in the days of Ahaziah the son of Ahab: we find also, that Joram the son of Ahab and Jehoshaphat, inquired of Elisha the prophet; and there it is written [2 Kings iii. 11], 'This is Elisha the son of Shaphat, אֲשֶׁר יָצַק *who poured water* upon the hands of Elijah.' And this is a sign that Elias was first gone up into heaven in a whirlwind: because it is not said יוֹצֵק 'who *poureth* water,' but 'who *poured*.' Moreover, Elisha departed not from Elijah from the time that he first waited upon him until Elias went up. And yet we find that, after the death of Jehoshaphat, in the days of Ahaziah his son it was written, 'And a letter came to him from Elijah the prophet.' And this proves that he then writ and sent it: for if it had been written before his ascension, it would be said, a letter was found or brought to him, which Elias had left behind him. And it is without controversy, that he was seen in the days of

our holy wise men. God of his mercy hasten his prophecy, and the times of his coming." So he upon Mal. iv.

3. The Talmudists do suppose Elias keeping the sabbath in mount Carmel: " Let not the *Trumah* (saith one[b]), of which it is doubted whether it be clean or unclean, be burnt; lest Elias, keeping the sabbath in mount Carmel, come and testify of it on the sabbath that it is clean."

4. The Talmudical books abound with these and the like trifles: " If[c] a man finds any thing that is lost, he is bound to declare it by a public outcry; but if the owners come not to ask for it, let him lay it up by him until Elias shall come." And, "If[d] any find a bill of contract between his countrymen, and knows not what it means, let him lay it up until Elias shall come."

5. That we be not tedious, it shall be enough to produce a few passages out of Babyl. *Erubhin*[e]: where, upon this subject, " If any say, Behold, I am a Nazarite, on the day wherein the Son of David comes, it is permitted to drink wine on the sabbaths and feast-days," it is disputed what day of the week Messias shall come, and on what day, Elias: where, among other things, these words occur, לא אתא אליהו מאתמול *Elias came not yesterday:* that is, the same day wherein he comes he shall appear in public; and shall not lie hid to day, coming yesterday. The Gloss thus: " If thou sayest, perhaps he shall come on the eve of the sabbath, and *shall preach the gospel* (יבשר) on the sabbath; you may answer with that text, ' Behold, I send you Elias the prophet, before the day of the Lord come:' you may argue, that he shall preach on that very day in which he shall come."

מובטח להן לישראל וגו' " *The Israelites are certain* that Elias shall come, neither on the sabbath eves, nor on the eves of the feast days, מפני טורח *by reason of labour.*" And again, לא אתי אליהו בשבת *Elias cometh not on the sabbath day.* Thus speak the scholars of Hillel[f]: " We are sure Elias will not come on the sabbath, nor on a feast day." The Glossers give the reason, " Not on the sabbath eves, or the eves of the feast days, by reason of labour;" that is, by

---

b Hieros. Pesach. fol. 30. 2.
c Maimon. in Gezelah, c. 13.
d Bava Mezia, cap. 1. hal. ult. &c.

e Fol. 43. 2.
f Hieros. Pesach. fol. 30. 2.

reason of the preparation for the sabbath ; namely, lest they
should leave the necessaries for the sabbath unfinished, to go
to meet him : " Nor on the sabbaths, by reason of labour" in
the banquets : that they omit not those feastings and eat-
ings g which were esteemed so necessary to the sabbath,
whilst they went out to meet Elias.

Let these three observations out of the Glossers upon the
page cited serve for a conclusion :—

1. לפני ביאת בן דוד יבא אליהו לבשר *Before the coming
of the Son of David, Elias shall come to preach of him.*

2. לא אתי משיח בחד בשבת " *Messias cometh* h *not on
the first day of the sabbath,* because Elias shall not come on
the sabbath." Whence it appears that Elias is expected the
day before the Messias's appearing.

3. הלא משיח בן יוסף יש לו לבא תחילה. *Is not Messias Ben Joseph to come first ?*

II. We meet with numberless stories in the Talmudists
concerning the apparitions of Elias : according to that which
was said before by Aben Ezra, " It is without controversy
that Elias was seen in the days of our wise men." There is
no need of examples, when it may not be so much doubted
who of these wise men saw Elias, as who saw him not. For
my part I cannot esteem all those stories for mere fables ;
but in very many of them I cannot but suspect witchcrafts,
and the appearances of ghosts, which we also said before
concerning the *Bath Kol.* For thus the devil craftily deluded this nation, willing to be deceived ; and even the capacity of observing that the coming of the Messias was now
past was obliterated, when here and there, in this age and
in the other, his forerunner Elias appeared, as if he intended
hence to let them know that he was yet to come.

Ver. 11 : Καὶ ἀποκαταστήσει πάντα· *And he shall restore all
things.*] The Jews feign many things which Elias shall restore : יטהר הממזרים " *He* i *shall purify the bastards,* and
restore them to the congregation. He shall render to Israel
the pot of manna, the vial of holy oil, the vial of water ; and
there are some who say, the rod of Aaron k." Which things,

g *English folio edition,* vol. ii. p.
210.

h *Leusden's edition,* vol. ii. p. 340.

i Bab. Kiddushin, fol. 71. 1. Kimchi, in Zech. chap. ix.

k Tanchum, in Exod. i. &c.

alas! how far distant are they from those which are spoken concerning the office of Elias!

'Αποκαταστήσει, *he shall restore*, or *make up*, not into the former state, but into a better.   There were χρόνοι ἀποκατα- στάσεως πάντων, *times of restitution of all things*, determined by God, Acts iii. 21; wherein all things were to be framed into a gospel-state, and a state worthy of the Messias : a church was to be founded, and the doctrine of the gospel dispersed, the hearts of the fathers, the Jews, to be united to the sons, the Gentiles; and the hearts of the sons, the Gentiles, to the fathers the Jews : which work was begun by the Baptist, and finished by Christ and the apostles.   Which term of the restitution of all these expiring, the commonwealth of the Jews expired also; and the gifts of revelation and miracles granted for this purpose, and so necessary to it, failed. "However, therefore, ye have crucified Christ," saith Peter in that place of the Acts now cited, " yet God shall still send you Jesus Christ in the preaching of the gospel to fulfil these things.   Him, indeed, as to his person the heavens do contain, and shall contain, until all these things be perfected; expect not, therefore, with the erring nation, his personal presence always on earth : but he shall make up and consti- tute all things by us his ministers, until the times deter- mined and prefixed for the perfecting of this restitution shall come."

Ver. 15 : Σεληνιάζεται· *He is lunatic.*]   Luke ix. 39, πνεῦμα λαμβάνει αὐτὸν, *a spirit taketh him*; Mark ix. 17, ἔχει πνεῦμα ἄλαλον, *hath a dumb spirit.*

I. He that is skilled in the Talmudic writings will here remember what things are said concerning חרש ושוטה *a deaf and mad man*, concerning whom there is so much mention in their writings.

" There[1] are five who do not pay the *Trumah*; but if they do, their *Trumah* is no *Trumah* : חרש ושוטה *the deaf and dumb, the lunatic*," &c.   " Any[m] one is fit to sacrifice a beast, except חרש ושוטה וקטן *a dumb and deaf, a lunatic, and a child:*" and very many passages of this nature, &c.   I have rendered חרש *deaf and dumb*, according to the sense of the

---

[1] Trumah, cap. i. hal. i.   [m] Cholin, cap. i. hal. i.

masters, who, in the first place cited, do thus interpret the
word; חרש " concerning which the wise men speak, is *he
who neither heareth nor speaketh.*" See there the Jerusalem
Gemara, where, among other things, this occurs not unworthy
our noting; " That all the sons of R. Jochanan Ben Gudgoda
were חרשׁין *deaf and dumb.*"

II. It[n] was very usual to the Jews to attribute some of the
more grievous diseases to evil spirits, specially those wherein
either the body was distorted, or the mind disturbed and
tossed with a phrensy.

מי שהיה רוח רעה מבעתת אותו ואמר כשהתחיל בו
החולי: " *If*[o] *any one, vexed with an evil spirit, shall say,
when the disease did first invade him,* Write a bill of divorce
for my wife," &c.

מי שאחזו קורדייקוס: " *If*[p] *any, whom Kordicus vexeth,*
say, Write a bill of divorce for my wife," &c. " *Kordicus,*
say the Glossers, is a demon, which rules over those that
drink too much new wine. מאי קורדייקוס *What is 'Kordicus?'* Samuel saith, When new wine out of the press hath
caught any one." Rambam[q], upon the place, hath these
words; " *Kordicus* is a disease, generated from the repletion
of the vessels of the brain, whereby the understanding is confounded; and it is a kind of falling-sickness." Behold the
same a demon and a disease! to which the Gemarists applied
exorcisms and a diet[r].

" Shibta[s] is an evil spirit, who, taking hold on the necks of
infants, dries up and contracts their nerves."

" He[t] that drinks up double cups, עי" שדים *is punished by the devils.*"

From this vulgar opinion of the nation, namely, that devils
are the authors of such kind of diseases, one evangelist brings
in the father of this child, saying[u] of him, σεληνιάζεται, *he is
lunatic,* another, ἔχει πνεῦμα, *he hath a spirit.* He had been
dumb and deaf from his birth; to that misery was added a
phrensy, or a lycanthropy, which kind of disease it was not un-

---

[n] *English folio edition,* vol. ii. p.
211.
[o] Maimon. in *Gerushin,* cap. 2.
[p] Gittin, cap. 7. hal. 1.
[q] Gemar. Bab. which see.

[r] Babyl. Gittin, fol. 67. 2.
[s] Aruch, in *Shibta.* [שבתא]
[t] Bab. Berac. fol. 51. 2.
[u] *Leusden's edition,* vol. ii. p. 341.

usual with the nation to attribute to the devil; and here, in truth, a devil was present.

Ver. 17: Ὦ γενεὰ ἄπιστος καὶ διεστραμμένη, &c. *O faithless and perverse generation, &c.*] The edge of these words is levelled especially against the scribes (see Mark ix. 14); and yet the disciples escaped not altogether untouched.

Christ and his three prime disciples being absent, this child is brought to the rest to be healed: they cannot heal him, partly, because the devil was really in him; partly, because this evil had adhered to him from his very birth. Upon this the scribes insult and scoff at them and their master. *A faithless and perverse generation*, which is neither overcome by miracles, when they are done, and vilify, when they are not done! The faith of the disciples (ver. 20) wavered by the plain difficulty of the thing, which seemed impossible to be overcome, when so many evils were digested into one, deafness, dumbness, phrensy, and possession of the devil; and all these from the cradle.

Ver. 20: Πίστιν ὡς κόκκον σινάπεως, &c. *Faith as a grain of mustard seed, &c.*] : כורע חרדל or כזרע פת חרדל *As a seed of mustard, or as a drop of mustard*, in Talmudic language. See chap. xiii. 23.

Ἐρεῖτε τῷ ὄρει τούτῳ, &c. *Ye shall say to this mountain, &c.*] See what we note at chap. xxi. 21.

Ver. 21: Τοῦτο τὸ γένος οὐκ ἐκπορεύεται, εἰ μὴ ἐν προσευχῇ καὶ νηστείᾳ· *This kind goeth not out but by prayer and fasting.*] It is not much unlike this, which is said[x], מפני רוח רעה יחיד רשאי לסגף את עצמו: *By reason of an evil spirit a singular* or *religious man may afflict himself* with fastings.

Ver. 24: Οἱ τὰ δίδραχμα λαμβάνοντες· *They that receive the (didrachma) tribute-money.*] Two things persuade me that this is to be understood of the half-shekel, to be yearly paid into the treasury of the Temple:

1. The[y] word itself whereby this tribute is called, δίδραχμα. Concerning this, thus Josephus writes: Φόρον δὲ τοῖς ὅπου δή-ποτ᾽ οὖσιν Ἰουδαίοις ἐπέβαλε, δύο δραχμὰς ἕκαστον κελεύσας ἀνὰ πᾶν ἔτος εἰς τὸ Καπετώλιον φέρειν, ὥσπερ πρότερον εἰς τὸν ἐν

Ἱεροσολύμοις νεὼν συνετέλουν· "He[z] laid a tax upon all the Jews wheresoever they were, namely, *two drachms;* commanding every one, of whatever age, to bring it into the Capitol, as before they had paid it into the Temple at Jerusalem." And Dion Cassius of the same thus, Καὶ ἀπ' ἐκείνου δίδραχμον ἐτάχθη, &c. "He[a] commanded all to bring *the didrachm* yearly to Jupiter Capitolinus."

The Seventy Interpreters, indeed, upon Exod. xxx. 13, render it ἥμισυ τοῦ διδράχμου, *half a didrachm;* but adding this moreover, ὅ ἐστιν κατὰ τὸ δίδραχμον τὸ ἅγιον, *which is according to the holy didrachm.* Be it so; the whole shekel was δίδραχμον ἅγιον, *the holy didrachm:* then let the half shekel be, δίδραχμον δημόσιον, *the common didrachm.* However, the thing is, he that paid the half-shekel, in the vulgar dialect, was called, *he that paid the shekels;* and that which is here said by Matthew, δίδραχμα λαμβάνοντες, *they that receive the didrachm,* the Talmudists express, תובעין שקלים or גובין *they that demand* or *collect the shekels.* The Targumists render that place, Exod. xxx. [13], פלגות סלעא *the half of the shekel;* the reason of which see, if you please, in Maimonides[b]. "The shekel (saith he) concerning which the Law speaks, did weigh three hundred and twenty grains of barley; but the wise men sometime added to that weight, and made it to be of the same value with the money סלע *Sela,* under the second Temple, that is, three hundred eighty-four middling grains of barley." See the place and the Gloss.

2. The answer of Christ sufficiently argues that the discourse is concerning this tax, when he saith, He is son of that king for whose use that tribute was demanded: for, "from thence were bought the daily and additional sacrifices, and their drink offerings, the sheaf, the two loaves (Lev. xxiii. 17), the shewbread, all the sacrifices of the congregation, the red cow, the scapegoat, and the crimson tongue, which was between his horns[c]," &c.

But here this objection occurs, which is not so easy to answer. The[d] time of the payment of the half shekel was about the feast of the Passover; but now that time was far

[z] De Bell. lib. vii. cap. 27. [Hudson, p. 1311. l. 18.] [vii. 6. 6.]
[a] Lib. lxvi.
[b] Shekal. cap. 1.
[c] Ibid. cap. 4. hal. 1, 2.
[d] Ibid. cap. 1. hal. 3.

gone, and the feast of Tabernacles at hand. It may be answered, 1. That Matthew, who recites this story, observed
not the course and order of time, which was not unusual with
him, as being he among all the evangelists that most dis-
joints the times of the stories. But let it be granted that
the order of the history in him is right and proper here, it is
answered, 2. Either Christ was scarcely present at the Passover last past; or if he were present, by reason of the danger
he was in by the snares of the Jews, he could not perform
this payment in that manner as it ought to have been.
Consider those words which John speaks of the Passover
last past, chap. vi. 4, " The Passover, a feast of the Jews,
was near;" and chap. vii. 1, " After these things Jesus
walked in Galilee; for he would not walk any more in Jewry,
because the Jews sought to kill him." 3. It was not unusual
to defer the payment of the half shekels of this year to the
year following, by reason of some urgent necessity. Hence it
was, when they sat to collect and receive this tribute, the
collectors had before them two chests placed; in one of which
they put the tax of the present year, in the other of the year
past[c].

But[f] it may be objected, Why did the collectors of Capernaum require the payment at that time, when, according
to custom, they began not to demand it before the fifteenth
day of the month Adar? I answer, 1. It is certain there
were, in every city, *moneychangers* (שׁוּלְחָנִין) to collect it,
and, being collected, to carry it to Jerusalem. Hence is
that in the tract cited, " The fifteenth day of the month
Adar, the collectors sit in the cities," to demand the half
shekel; " and the five-and-twentieth they sit in the Temple."
2. The uncertain abode of Christ at Capernaum gave these
collectors no unjust cause of demanding this due, whensoever they had him there present; at this time especially,
when the feast of Tabernacles was near, and they about to
go to Jerusalem, to render an account, perhaps, of their
collection.

But if any list to understand this of the tax paid the Romans, we do not contend. And then the words of those

---

[c] See Shekal. cap. 2. Maimon. ibid.
[f] *Leusden's edition,* vol. ii. p. 342.

that collected the tribute, "Does not your master pay the didrachm?" seem to sound to this effect, "Is your master of the sect of Judas of Galilee?"

CHAP. XVIII.[g]

VER. 1: Τίς ἄρα μείζων ἐστὶν ἐν τῇ βασιλείᾳ τῶν οὐρανῶν; *Who is the greatest in the kingdom of heaven?*] It cannot be passed over without observation, that the ambitious dispute of the disciples concerning primacy, for the most part followed the mention of the death of Christ and his resurrection. See this story in Mark ix. 31—33, and Luke ix. 44—46: "He said to his disciples, Lay up these discourses in your ears: for the time is coming that the Son of man is delivered into the hands of men. But they knew not that saying, &c.; and there arose a contest between them, who among them should be greatest." Also Matt. xx. 18—20: "He said to them, Behold, we go up to Jerusalem; and the Son of man shall be betrayed unto the chief priests, &c. Then came to him the mother of Zebedee's children with her sons, saying, Grant that these my two sons may sit, one on thy right hand," &c. And Luke xxii. 22—24; "The Son of man indeed goeth as it is determined, &c.; and there arose a contention among them, who of them should seem to be the greater."

The dream of the earthly kingdom of the Messias did so possess their minds (for they had sucked in this doctrine with their first milk), that the mention of the most vile death of the Messias, repeated over and over again, did not at all drive it thence. The image of earthly pomp was fixed at the bottom of their hearts, and there it stuck; nor by any words of Christ could it as yet be rooted out, no, not when they saw the death of Christ, when together with that they saw his resurrection: for then they also asked, "Wilt thou at this time restore the kingdom to Israel?" Acts i. 6.

However, after Christ had oftentimes foretold his death and resurrection, it always follows in the evangelists that "they understood not what was spoken;" yet the opinion formed in their minds by their doctors, that the resurrection should go before the kingdom of the Messias, supplied them with such an interpretation of this matter, that they lost not an ace of the opinion of a future earthly kingdom.

See more at chap. xxiv. 3.

Ver. 6: Συμφέρει αὐτῷ, ἵνα κρεμασθῇ μύλος ὀνικὸς, &c. *It were better for him that a millstone were hanged about his neck,* &c.] Συμφέρει αὐτῷ, נוח לו *It is good for him,* in Talmudic language.

Μύλος ὀνικὸς seems to be said in distinction from those very small mills wherewith they were wont to grind the spices that were either to be applied to the wound of circumcision, or to be added to the delights of the sabbath. Hence the Gloss of R. Solomon upon Jer. xxv. 10; " The sound of mills and the light of the candle :" " The sound of mills (saith he), wherewith spices were ground and bruised for the healing of circumcision."

That Christ here speaks of a kind of death, perhaps nowhere, certainly never used among the Jews; he does it either to aggravate the thing, or in allusion to drowning in the Dead sea, in which one cannot be drowned without some weight hung to him: and in which *to drown* any thing, by a common manner of speech, implied to devote to rejection, hatred, and execration; which we have observed elsewhere.

Ver. 10: Ἄγγελοι αὐτῶν ἐν οὐρανοῖς διὰ παντὸς βλέπουσι, &c. *Their angels in heaven do always behold,* &c.] This one may very well expound by laying to it that which is said, Heb. i. 14, "The angels are ministering spirits, sent to minister for them who shall be heirs of the salvation to come:" as if he should say, " See that ye do not despise one of these little ones, who have been received with their believing parents into the gospel-church : for I say unto you, that after that manner as the angels minister to adult believers, they minister to them also."

Ver. 12 [h] : Ἐὰν πλανηθῇ ἓν, ἀφεὶς τὰ ἐννενηκονταεννέα, &c. *If one of them be gone astray, doth he not leave the ninety-and-nine,* &c.] A very common form of speech :—" In [i] distributing some grapes and dates to the poor, although *ninety-nine* say, ' Scatter them ;' and only *one,* 'Divide them :' they hearken

[h] *English folio edit.,* vol. ii. p. 214.   [i] Peah, cap. 4. hal. 2.

to him, because he speaks according to the tradition." "If [k] *ninety-nine* die by an evil eye," that is, by bewitchings; "and but *one* by the hand of Heaven," that is, by the stroke of God, &c. " If *ninety nine* die by reason of cold, but *one* by the hand of God," &c.

Ver. 15 [1]: Ἔλεγξον αὐτὸν μεταξὺ σοῦ καὶ αὐτοῦ μόνου· *Tell him his fault between thee and him alone.*] The reason of the precept is founded in that charitable law, Levit. xix. 17; " Thou shalt not hate thy brother in thy heart; but thou shalt surely reprove him, and shalt not suffer sin in him."

Here the Talmudists speak not amiss: " The [m] Rabbins deliver, 'Thou shalt not hate thy brother in thy heart.' Perhaps he does not beat him, he does not pull off his hair, he does not curse him: the text saith, 'in thy heart,' speaking of hatred in the heart. But whence is it proved that he that sees his brother doing some foul action is bound to reprove him? Because it is said, הוכיח תוכיח *In reproving, thou shalt reprove.* He reproves, ולא קיבל *but he heareth not:* whence is it proved he is bound to a second reproof? The text saith, 'In reproving, thou shalt reprove.' " And a little after, " How long must we reprove? Rabh saith, 'Even to blows;'" that is, until he that is reproved strikes him that reproves him : " Samuel saith, ' Until he is angry.' " See also Maimonides [n].

Ver. 16 : Παράλαβε μετὰ σοῦ ἔτι ἕνα ἢ δύο, &c. *Take with thee one or two more, &c.*] The Hebrew lawyers require the same thing of him that sins against his brother: " Samuel [o] saith, ' Whosoever sins against his brother, he must say to him, I have sinned against thee. If he hear, it is well: if not, let him bring others, and let him appease him before them. If perhaps he die, let him appease him at his sepulchre, and say, I have sinned against thee.' "

But our Saviour here requires a higher charity; namely, from him who is the offended party. In like manner, " The [p] great Sanhedrim admonished a city lapsed to idols, by two disciples of the wise men. If they repented, well : if not,

---

k Hieros. Schab. fol. 14. 3.   1 *Leusden's edit.*, vol. ii. p. 343.
    m Bab. Erachin, fol. 16. 2.   n In Peah, c. 6.
        o Hieros. Joma, fol. 45. 3. et Bab. Joma, fol. 87. 1.
            p Maimon. in Avod. Zarah, cap. 4.

all Israel waged war against it." In like manner also, " The jealous husband warned his wife before two witnesses, ' Do not talk with *N.*' "

Ver, 17 : Εἰπὲ τῇ ἐκκλησίᾳ· *Tell it unto the church.*] That which was incumbent upon him against whom the sin was committed was this, that he should deliver his soul by reproving his brother, and by not suffering sin in him. This was the reason that he had need of witnesses, for what else could they testify? They could not testify that the brother had sinned against him that reproved him ; for this, perhaps, they were altogether ignorant of: but they might testify this, that he against whom the sin was committed used due reproof, and omitted nothing which was commanded by the law in that case, whereby he might admonish his brother, and, if possible, bring him back into the right way. The witnesses also added their friendly admonition : whom if the offender hearkened not unto, " let it be told the church."

We do not here enter upon that long dispute concerning the sense of the word *church* in this place. However you take it, certainly the business here is not so much concerning the censure of the person sinning, as concerning the vindication of the person reproving; that it might be known to all that he discharged his duty, and freed his soul.

It was very customary among the Jews to note those that were obstinate in this or that crime after public admonition given them in the synagogue, and to set a mark of infamy upon them.

כולן צריכין הכרוזה בבית דין [q] *All* [r] *these have need of public admonition in the consistory.* The business there is about some shepherds, collectors, and publicans ; and it is declared how incapable they are of giving evidence in any judiciary matter; but not before public admonition is gone out against them in the consistory.

" If [s] any deny to feed his children, they reprove him, they shame him, they urge him : if he still refuse, they make proclamation against him in the synagogue, saying, ' *N.* is a cruel man, and will not nourish his children : more cruel than the unclean birds themselves, for they feed their young ones,' " &c.

" A [t] provoking wife who saith, ' I will create vexation to my husband, because he hath done thus or thus to me, or because he hath miscalled me, or because he hath chid me,' &c. The consistory by messengers send these words to her, ' Be it known unto you, if you persist in your perverseness, although your dowry be a hundred pounds, you have lost it all.' ואחר כך מכריזין עליה בבתי כנסיות ובבתי מדרשות *And moreover they set forth a public proclamation against her in the synagogues, and in the divinity schools* every day for four sabbaths."

Ἔστω σοὶ ὥσπερ ὁ ἐθνικὸς καὶ ὁ τελώνης· *Let him be to thee as a heathen and a publican.*] He saith, Ἔστω σοι, *Let him be to ' thee ;'* not Ἔστω τῇ ἐκκλησίᾳ, *Let him be to ' the church :'* because the discourse is of peculiar and private scandal against a single man ; who, after three admonitions given, and they to no purpose, is freed from the law of brotherly obligation ; and he who being admonished does not repent, is not to be esteemed so much for a brother to him, as for a heathen, &c.

I. Christ does not here prescribe concerning every of-fender, according to the full latitude of that law, Levit. xix. 17 ; but of him that particularly [u] offends against his brother ; and he does particularly teach what is to be done to that brother.

II. Although he, against whom the offence is committed, had a just cause, why he should be loosed from the obligation of the office of a brother towards him, who neither would make satisfaction for the wrong done, nor be admonished of it ; yet to others in the church there is not the same reason.

III. The words plainly mean this ; " If, after a threefold and just reproof, he that sinned against thee still remains untractable, and neither will give thee satisfaction for the injury, nor, being admonished, doth repent, thou hast deli-vered thine own soul, and art free from brotherly offices to-wards him ;" just as the Jews reckon themselves freed from

[t] Id. ibid. cap. 14. [u] *Leusden's edition,* vol. ii. p. 344.

friendly offices towards *heathens* and *publicans*. That of Maimonides is not much different : " A[x] Jew that apostatizes, or breaks the sabbath presumptuously, is altogether like a *heathen*."

1. They reckoned not *heathens* for brethren or neighbours : " If[y] any one's ox shall gore his neighbour's ox : his neighbour's, not a *heathen's :* when he saith *neighbour's*, he excludes *heathens*." A quotation which we produced before.

2. They reputed *publicans* to be by no means within religious society : A[z] חבד שנעשה גבאי דוחין אותו מחבורתו *religious man, who becomes a publican, is to be driven out of the society of religion.*

3. Hence they ate neither with *heathens* nor with *publicans :* concerning which thing they often quarrel [*with*] our Saviour. Hence that of the apostle, 1 Cor. v. 11 ; " With such an one no not to eat," is the same with what is spoke here, " Let him be to thee as a *heathen*," &c.

" It[a] is forbidden a Jew to be alone with *a heathen*, to travel with *a heathen*," &c.

4. They denied also brotherly offices to *heathens* and *publicans :* " It[b] is forbidden to bring home any thing of a *heathen's* that is lost." " It[c] is lawful for *publicans* to swear that is an oblation which is not ; that you are of the king's retinue when you are not," &c. that is, *publicans* may deceive, and that by oath.

Ver. 18 : Ὅσα ἐὰν δήσητε ἐπὶ τῆς γῆς, &c. *Whatsoever ye shall bind on earth, &c.*] These words depend upon the former. He had been speaking concerning being *loosed* from the office of a brother in a particular case : now he speaks of the authority and power of the apostles of *loosing* and *binding* " any thing" whatsoever seemed them good, being guided in all things by the Holy Ghost. We have explained the sense of this phrase at chap. xvi. ; and he gives the same authority in respect of this, to all the apostles here, as he did to Peter there ; who were all to be partakers of the same Spirit and of the same gifts.

---

[x] In Gerushin, cap. 3.
[y] Aruch in בן ברית.
[z] Hieros. Demai, fol. 23. 1.

[a] Maimon. in רוצח cap. 12.
[b] Maimon. Gezelah, cap. 11.
[c] Nedarim, cap. 3. hal. 4.

This[d] power was built upon that noble and most self-sufficient foundation, John xvi. 13, " The Spirit of truth shall lead you into all truth." There lies an emphasis in those words, " into all truth." I deny that any one, any where, at any time, was led, or to be led, into *all* truth, from the ascension of Christ, unto the world's end, beside the apostles. Every holy man, certainly, is led into all truth necessary to him for salvation : but the apostles were led into all truth necessary both for themselves and the whole church ; because they were to deliver a rule of faith and manners to the whole church throughout all ages. Hence, whatsoever they should confirm in the law was to be confirmed ; whatsoever they should abolish was to be abolished : since they were endowed, as to all things, with a spirit of infallibility, guiding them by the hand into all truth.

Ver. 19 : Ὅτι ἐὰν δύο ὑμῶν συμφωνήσωσιν ἐπὶ τῆς γῆς, &c. *That if two of you shall agree upon earth, &c.*] And these words do closely agree with those that went before : there the speech was concerning the apostles' determination in all things respecting men ; here, concerning their grace and power of obtaining things from God.

I. Δύο ὑμῶν· *Two of you.*] Hence Peter and John act jointly together among the Jews, Acts ii, iii, &c., and they act jointly among the Samaritans, Acts viii. 14 ; and Paul and Barnabas among the Gentiles, Acts xiii. 2. This bond being broke by Barnabas, the Spirit is doubled as it were upon Paul.

II. Συμφωνήσωσι· *Agree together.*] That is, to obtain something from God ; which appears also from the following words, οὗ ἐὰν αἰτήσωνται, *touching any thing that they shall ask :* suppose, concerning conferring the Spirit by the imposition of hands, of doing this or that miracle, &c.

Ver. 20 : Οὗ γάρ εἰσι δύο ἢ τρεῖς συνηγμένοι εἰς τὸ ἐμὸν ὄνομα, ἐκεῖ εἰμὶ ἐν μέσῳ αὐτῶν· *For where two or three are gathered together in my name, there am I in the midst of them.*] The like do the Rabbins speak of two or three sitting in judgment, that שכינה *the divine presence* is in the midst of them.

Ver. 21 : 'Αφήσω αὐτῷ ; ἕως ἑπτάκις ; *Shall 1 forgive him ?*
till seven times ?] This question of Peter respects the words
of our Saviour, ver. 15. " How far shall I forgive my brother
before I proceed to the extremity ? What ! seven times ?"
He thought that he had measured out, by these words, a
large charity, being, in a manner, double to that which was
prescribed by the schools : " He[e] that is wronged (say they)
is forbidden to be difficult to pardon ; for that is not the
manner of the seed of Israel. But when the offender im-
plores him once and again, and it appears he repents of his
deed, let him pardon him : and whosoever is most ready to
pardon is most praiseworthy." It is well[f]; but there lies a
snake under it ; " For (say they[g]) they pardon a man once,
that sins against another ; secondly, they pardon him ;
thirdly, they pardon him ; fourthly, they do not pardon
him," &c.

CHAP. XIX.[h]

VER. 1 : ῏Ηλθεν εἰς τὰ ὅρια τῆς 'Ιουδαίας πέραν τοῦ 'Ιορδάνου·
He came unto the coasts of Judea beyond Jordan.] If it were
barely said, ὅρια τῆς 'Ιουδαίας πέραν τοῦ 'Ιορδάνου, *the coasts*
of Judea beyond Jordan, by *the coasts of Judea* one might understand *the bounds of the Jews beyond Jordan.* Nor does such
a construction want its parallel in Josephus ; for " Hyrcanus
(saith he[i]) built a fortification, the name of which was Tyre,
μεταξὺ τῆς τε 'Αραβίας καὶ τῆς 'Ιουδαίας πέραν τοῦ 'Ιορδάνου, οὐ
πόρρω τῆς 'Εσσεβωνίτιδος, *between Arabia and Judea, beyond*
Jordan, not far from Essebonitis." But see Mark here, chap.
x. 1, relating the same story with this our evangelist: ῎Ερχε-
ται εἰς τὰ ὅρια τῆς 'Ιουδαίας, διὰ τοῦ πέραν τοῦ 'Ιορδάνου· *He came,*
saith he, *into the coasts of Judea,* (taking a journey from Galilee,) *along the country beyond Jordan.*

Ver. 3 : Εἰ ἔξεστιν ἀνθρώπῳ ἀπολῦσαι τὴν γυναῖκα αὐτοῦ κατὰ
πᾶσαν αἰτίαν ; *Is it lawful for a man to put away his wife for*
every cause ?] Of the causes, *ridiculous* (shall I call them ?) or
wicked, for which they put away their wives, we have spoke
at chap. v. 31. We will produce only one example here ;

e Maimon. in חובל cap. 5.
f *Leusden's edition,* vol. ii. p. 345.
g Bab. Joma, fol. 86. 2.

h *English folio edition,* vol. ii. p.
217.
i Antiq. lib. 12. cap. 5. [xii. 4. 11.]

רב כי מקלע לדרשיש מכריז מאן הויא ליומא "*When Rabh
went to Darsis* ('whither,' as the Gloss saith, 'he often went'),
*he made a public proclamation, What woman will have me for
a day?* Rabh Nachman, when he went to Sacnezib, made a
public proclamation, What woman will have me for a day?"
The Gloss is, "Is there any woman who will be my wife while
I tarry in this place [j]?"

The question here propounded by the Pharisees was disputed in the schools, and they divided into parties concerning
it, as we have noted before. For the school of Shammai permitted not divorces, but only in the case of adultery; the
school of Hillel, otherwise[k].

Ver. 8: Ὅτι Μωσῆς πρὸς τὴν σκληροκαρδίαν ὑμῶν ἐπέτρεψεν,
&c. *Because Moses for the hardness of your hearts suffered, &c.*]
Interpreters ordinarily understand this of the unkindness of
men towards their wives; and that not illy: but at first sight
σκληροκαρδία, *hardness of heart*, for the most part in Scripture
denotes rather obduration against God than against men.
Examples occur everywhere. Nor does this sense want its
fitness in this place: not to exclude the other, but to be
joined with it here.

I. That God delivered that rebellious people for the hardness of their hearts to spiritual fornication, that is, to
idolatry, sufficiently appears out of sacred story, and particularly from these words of the first martyr Stephen, Acts
vii. 42: Ἔστρεψε δὲ ὁ Θεός, καὶ παρέδωκεν αὐτοὺς λατρεύειν τῇ
στρατιᾷ τοῦ οὐρανοῦ, &c. *God turned, and gave them up to
worship the host of heaven*, &c. And they seem not less
given up to carnal fornication, if you observe the horrid records of their adulteries in the Holy Scripture, and their not
less horrid allowances of divorces and polygamies in the
books of the Talmudists: so that the particle πρὸς carries
with it a very proper sense, if you interpret it *to*, according to
its most usual signification; "Moses *to* the hardness of your
hearts added this, that he permitted divorces; something
that savours of punishment in itself, however you esteem it
for a privilege."

II. But you may interpret it more clearly and aptly of the

---

[j] Bab. Joma, fol. 18. 2.   [k] See Hieros. Sotah, fol. 16. 2.

inhumanity of husbands towards their wives: but this is to be understood also under restriction: for Moses permitted not divorces, because, simply and generally men were severe and unkind towards their wives; for then, why should he restrain divorces to the cause of adultery? but because, from their fierceness and cruelty towards their wives, they might take hold of and seek occasions from that law which punished adultery with death, to prosecute their wives with all manner of severity, to oppress them, to kill them.

Let[1] us search into the divine laws in case of adultery a little more largely.

1. There was a law made upon the suspicion of adultery, that the wife should undergo a trial by the bitter waters, Num. v: but it is disputed by the Jewish schools, rightly and upon good ground, whether the husband was bound in this case by duty to prosecute his wife to extremity, or whether it were lawful for him to connive at and pardon her, if he would. And there are some who say חובה, that is, he was bound by *duty;* and there are others who say רשות that it was left to his *pleasure*[m].

2. There was a law of death made in case of the discovery of adultery, Deut. xxii. 21—23: "If a man shall be found lying with a married woman, both shall die," &c. Not that this law was not in force unless they were taken in the very act; but the word יִמָּצֵא *shall be found,* is opposed to suspicion, and means the same as if it were said, "When it shall be found that a man hath lain," &c.

3. A law of divorce also was given in case of adultery discovered, Deut. xxiv. 1; for in that case only, and when it is discovered, it plainly appears from our Saviour's gloss, and from the concession of some Rabbins also, that divorces took place: for, say they in the place last cited, "Does a man find something foul in his wife? he cannot put her away, שלא מצא בה ערוה: *because he hath not found foul nakedness in her;*" that is, *adultery.*

But[n] now, how do the law of death and that of divorce consist together? It is answered, They do not so consist

---

[1] *English folio edit.*, vol. ii. p. 218.   [m] See Hieros. Sotah, as before.
[n] *Leusden's edition*, vol. ii. p. 346.

together that both retain their force; but the former was
partly taken off by the latter, and partly not. The Divine
Wisdom knew that inhuman husbands would use that law of
death unto all manner of cruelty towards their wives: for
how ready was it for a wicked and unkind husband to lay
snares even for his innocent wife, if he were weary of her,
to oppress her under that law of death ! And if she were
taken under guilt, how cruelly and insolently would he triumph over her, poor woman, both to the disgrace of wedlock
and to the scandal of religion ! Therefore the most prudent,
and withal merciful lawgiver, made provision that the woman,
if she were guilty, might not go without her punishment;
and if she were not guilty, might go without danger; and
that the wicked husband that was impatient of wedlock
might not satiate his cruelty. That which is said by one
does not please me, " That there was no place for divorce
where matrimony was broke off by capital punishment ;" for
there was place for divorce for that end, that there might not
be place for capital punishment. That law indeed of death
held the adulterer in a snare, and exacted capital punishment
upon him, and so the law made sufficient provision for
terror: but it consulted more gently for the woman, the
weaker vessel, lest the cruelty of her husband might unmer-
cifully triumph over her.

Therefore, in the suspicion of adultery, and the thing not
discovered, the husband might, if he would, try his wife by
the bitter waters ; or if he would, he might connive at her.
In case of the discovery of adultery, the husband might put
away his wife, but he scarce might put her to death ; because
the law of divorce was given for that very end, that provision
might be made for the woman against the hardheartedness
of her husband.

Let this story serve for a conclusion; " Shemaiah[o] and
Abtalion compelled Carchemith, a libertine woman-servant,
to drink the bitter waters." The husband of this woman
could not put her away by the law of Moses, because she was
not found guilty of discovered adultery. He might put her
away by the traditional law, which permitted divorces without

---

[o] Bab. Berac. fol. 19. 1.

the case of adultery; he might not, if he had pleased, have
brought her to trial by the bitter waters; but it argued the
hardness of his heart towards his wife, or burning jealousy,
that he brought her. I do not remember that I have anywhere in the Jewish pandect read any example of a wife
punished with death for adultery. There P is mention of
the daughter of a certain priest committing fornication in
her father's house, that was burnt alive; but she was not
married.

Ver. 12 : Εὐνοῦχοι ἐκ κοιλίας μητρός· *Eunuchs from their
mother's womb.* Εὐνοῦχοι, οἵτινες εὐνουχίσθησαν ὑπὸ τῶν ἀνθρώ-
πων· *Eunuchs, which were made eunuchs of men.*] סריס חמה
and סריס אדם, in the Talmudists q.

Ver. 13 r: Τότε προσηνέχθη αὐτῷ παιδία· *Then were little
children brought unto him.*] Not for the healing of some
disease; for if this had been the end propounded, why did
the disciples keep them back above all others, or chide any
for their access? Nor can we believe that they were the
children of unbelieving Jews, when it is scarcely probable
that they, despising the doctrine and person of Christ, would
desire his blessing. Some therefore of those that believe
brought their infants to Christ, that he might take particular notice of them, and admit them into his discipleship,
and mark them for his by his blessing. Perhaps the disciples thought this an excess of officious religion; or that
they would be too troublesome to their Master; and hence
they opposed them: but Christ countenanceth the same
thing, and favours again that doctrine which he had laid
down, chap. xviii. 3; namely, that the infants of believers
were as much disciples and partakers of the kingdom of
heaven as their parents.

Ver. 18 : Οὐ φονεύσεις, &c. *Thou shalt do no murder, &c.*]
It is worthy marking, how again and again in the New Testament, when mention is made of the whole law, only the
second table is exemplified, as in this place; so also Rom.
xiii. 8, 9, and James ii. 8, 11, &c. Charity towards our neighbour is the top of religion, and a most undoubted sign of love
towards God.

---

p Hieros. Sanhedr. fol. 24. 2.   sub v. סרים, col. 1554.]
q [See Buxtorf Lex. T. & R.   r *English folio edit.,* vol. ii. p. 219.

Ver. 21 : Πώλησόν σου τὰ ὑπάρχοντα, καὶ δὸς πτωχοῖς· *Sell that thou hast, and give to the poor.*] When Christ calls it *perfection* to sell all and give to the poor, he speaks according to the idiom of the nation, which thought so: and he tries this rich man, boasting of his exact performance of the law, whether, when he pretended to aspire to eternal life, he would aspire to that *perfection* which his countrymen so praised. Not that hence he either devoted Christians to voluntary poverty, or that he exhorted this man to rest ultimately in a Pharisaical *perfection* ; but lifting up his mind to the renouncing of worldly things, he provokes him to it by the very doctrine of the Pharisees which he professed.

" For[s] these things the measure is not stated ; for the corner of the field" to be left for the poor; "for the firstfruits for the appearance in the Temple" (according to the law, Exod. xxiii. 15, 17, where, what, or how great an oblation is to be brought, is not appointed), " for the shewing mercy, and for the study of the law." The casuists, discussing that point of ' shewing mercy,' do thus determine concerning it : " A stated measure is not indeed prescribed to the shewing of mercy, as to the[t] affording poor men help with thy body," that is, with thy bodily labour ; " but as to money there is a stated measure, namely, the fifth part of thy wealth; nor is any bound to give the poor above the fifth part of his estate, לבד אם עשה כן במדת הסידות *unless he does it out of extraordinary devotion.* See Rambam upon the place, and the Jerusalem Gemara : where the example of R. Ishbab is produced, distributing all his goods to the poor.

Ver. 24 ; Κάμηλον διὰ τρυπήματος ῥαφίδος διελθεῖν, &c. *A camel to go through the eye of a needle, &c.*] A phrase used in the schools, intimating a thing very unusual and very difficult. There, where the discourse is concerning dreams and their interpretation, these words are added. לא מחוו ליה לאיניש לא דקלה דדהבא ולא פילא דעייל בקופא דמחטא *They[u] do not shew a man a palm tree of gold, nor an elephant going through the eye of a needle.* The Gloss is, " A thing

s Peah, cap. 1. hal. 1.   t *Leusden's edition,* vol. ii. p. 347.
u Babyl. Berac. fol. 55. 2.

which he was not wont to see, nor concerning which he ever thought."

In like manner R. Sheshith answered R. Amram, disputing with him and asserting something that was incongruous, in these words; " Perhaps [x] thou art one of those of Pombeditha, who can make an elephant pass through the eye of a needle :" that is, as the Aruch interprets it, " who speak things that are impossible."

Ver. 28 [y]: Ὑμεῖς οἱ ἀκολουθήσαντές μοι, ἐν τῇ παλιγγενεσίᾳ· *Ye that have followed me, in the regeneration.*] That the world is to be renewed at the coming of the Messias, and the preaching of the gospel, the Scriptures assert, and the Jews believe; but in a grosser sense, which we observe at chap. xxiv. Our Saviour, therefore, by the word παλιγγενεσία, *regeneration,* calls back the mind of the disciples to a right apprehension of the thing ; implying that renovation, concerning which the Scripture speaks, is not of the body or substance of the world ; but that it consists in the renewing of the manners, doctrine, and a dispensation conducing thereunto : *men* are to be renewed, regenerated,—not the *fabric* of the world. This very thing he teaches Nicodemus, treating concerning the nature of the kingdom of heaven, John iii. 3.

Ὅταν καθίσῃ ὁ υἱὸς τοῦ ἀνθρώπου ἐπὶ θρόνου δόξης αὐτοῦ, καθίσεσθε καὶ ὑμεῖς· *When the Son of man shall sit upon the throne of his glory, ye also shall sit.*] These words are fetched out of Daniel, chap. vii. 9, 10, רְמִיו כָּרְסָן ; which words I wonder should be translated by the interpreters, Aben Ezra, R. Saadia, and others, as well Jews as Christians, *thrones were cast down.* R. Solomon the Vulgar, and others, read it righter, *thrones were set up:* where Lyranus thus, " He saith *thrones* in the plural number, because not only Christ shall judge, but the apostles, and perfect men, shall assist him in judgment, sitting upon *thrones.*" The same way very many interpreters bend the words under our hands, namely, that the saints shall at the day of judgment sit with Christ, and approve and applaud his judgment. But, 1, besides that the scene of the last judgment, painted out in the Scripture, does always represent as well the saints as the wicked standing before the tribunal of Christ, Matt. xxv. 32, 2 Cor. v. 10, &c.; we have mention here only of " twelve thrones." And, 2, we have mention only of judging the " twelve tribes of Israel." The sense, therefore, of the place may very well be found out by weighing these things following:

I. That those thrones set up in Daniel are not to be understood of the last judgment of Christ, but of his judgment in his entrance upon his evangelical government, when he was made by his Father chief ruler, king, and judge of all things: Psalm ii. 6, Matt. xxviii. 18, John v. 27. For observe the scope and series of the prophet, that, after the four monarchies, namely, the Babylonian, the Medo-Persian, the Grecian, and the Syro-Grecian, which monarchies had vexed the world and the church by their tyranny, were destroyed, the kingdom of Christ should rise, &c. Those words, " The kingdom of heaven is at hand," that judiciary scene set up Rev. iv. and v., and those thrones Rev. xx. 1, &c. do interpret Daniel to this sense.

II. The throne of glory, concerning which the words before us are, is to be understood of the judgment of Christ to be brought upon the treacherous, rebellious, wicked, Jewish people. We meet with very frequent mention of the coming of Christ in his glory in this sense; which we shall discourse more largely of at chap. xxiv.

III. That the sitting of the apostles upon thrones with Christ is not to be understood of their *persons*, it is sufficiently proved; because Judas was now one of the number: but it is meant of their *doctrine*: as if he had said, " When I shall bring judgment upon this most unjust nation, then your doctrine, which you have preached in my name, shall judge and condemn them." See Rom. ii. 16.

Hence it appears that the gospel was preached to all the twelve tribes of Israel before the destruction of Jerusalem.

CHAP. XX.[z]

Ver. 1 : 'Εξῆλθεν ἅμα πρωὶ μισθώσασθαι ἐργάτας· *Who went out early in the morning to hire labourers.*] You have

such a parable as this, but madly applied, in the Talmud : we
will produce it here for the sake of some phrases : " To a what
was R. Bon Bar Chaija like ? למלך ששכר פועלים *To a king
who hired many labourers ;* among which there was one hired,
who performed his work extraordinary well.   What did b the
king ? He took him aside, and walked with him to and fro.
לעיתותי ערב ὀψίας γενομένης, *When even was come,* those labourers came, ליטול שכרן *ἵνα λήψωνται τὸν μισθὸν αὐτῶν, that
they might receive their hire,* and he gave him a complete hire
with the rest. והיו הפועלים מתרעמין Καὶ ἐγόγγυζον οἱ
ἐργάται λέγοντες, *And the labourers murmured,* saying, אנו
יגענו כל היום ' *We have laboured hard all the day,* and this
man only two hours, yet he hath received as much wages as
we :' the king saith to them, ' He hath laboured more in
those two hours than you in the whole day.' So R. Bon
plied the law more in eight-and-twenty years than another
in a hundred years."

Ἅμα πρωΐ· *Early in the morning.*]   " The c time of working
is from sunrising to the appearing of the stars, and not from
break of day : and this is proved from the chapter אמר להם
הממונה *the president of the priests saith to them* d ; where they
say, ' It is light all in the east, and men go out to hire labourers :' whence it is argued that they do not begin their
work before the sun riseth.   It is also proved from the tract
Pesachin, where it is said that it is prohibited on the day of
the Passover to do any servile work after the sun is up ; intimating this, that that was the time when labourers should
begin their work," &c.

Μισθώσασθαι ἐργάτας· *To hire labourers.*] Read here, if you
please, the tract *Bava Mezia,* cap. vii. ; which begins thus,
שוכר את הפועלים *He that hireth labourers :* and Maimonides,
שכירות, a tract entitled *Hiring* e.

Ver. 2 : Συμφωνήσας ἐκ δηναρίου τὴν ἡμέραν· *Agreed for a
penny a day.*] A *penny* of silver, which one of gold exceeded
twenty-four times ; for דינר זהב הוא כ"ה דנרי כסף *A penny
of gold is worth five-and-twenty of silver* f.   The canons of the

a Hieros. Berac. fol. 5. 3.
b *Leusden's edit.,* vol. ii. p. 348.
c Gloss. in Bab. Bava Mezia, fol.
83. 2.
d Joma, cap. 3. Tamid, cap. 3.
e Cap. 9. 8. 11.
f Gloss. in Cherithuth, cap. 2.

Hebrews concerning hiring of labourers distinguish, as reason requires, between שכיר יום *being hired by the day*, and שכיר שעות *being hired* (only) *for some hours* : which may be observed also in this parable : for in the morning they are hired for all the day, and for a penny, but afterward for certain hours ; and have a part of a penny allotted them, in proportion to the time they wrought.

Ver. 8 : Κάλεσον τοὺς ἐργάτας, &c. : *Call the labourers.*] For " it is one of the affirmative precepts of the law, that a hired labourer should have his wages paid him when they are due, as it is said, ' You shall pay him his wages in his day :' and if they be detained longer, it is a breach of a negative precept ; as it is said, ' The sun shall not go down upon him g,' " &c.

Ver. 13 h : Οὐχὶ δηναρίου συνεφώνησάς μοι ; *Didst not thou agree with me for a penny ?*] In hiring of labourers, the custom of the place most prevailed ; hence came that axiom, לחזי היכי נהיגי בעיר *Observe the custom of the city* i ; speaking of this very thing. There is also an example, " Those k of Tiberias that went up to Bethmeon to be hired for labourers, were hired according to the custom of Bethmeon," &c. By the by also we may observe that which is said by the Babylonians in the place cited, ונחזי מהיכא קא אתו בנקוטאי that is, as the Gloss renders it, " Notice must be taken whether they come from several places ; for at some places they go to work sooner, and at some later."

Hence two things may be cleared in the parable before us : 1. Why they are said to be hired at such different hours ; namely, therefore, because they are supposed to have come together from several places. 2. Why there was no certain agreement made with those that were hired at the third, sixth, and ninth hours, as with those that were hired early in the morning ; but that he should only say, " Whatsoever is right I will give you :" that is, supposing that they would submit to the custom of the place. But, indeed, when their wages were to be paid them, there is, by the favour of the lord of the vineyard, an equality made between those that were hired for some hours, and those that were hired for the

---

g Maimon. שכירות cap. 11.　　　i Bab. Bava Mezia, fol. 83. 2.
h *English folio edit.*, vol. ii. p. 222.　k Hieros. Mezia, fol. 11. 2.

whole day; and when these last murmured, they are answered from their own agreement, Συνεφώνησάς μοι, *You
agreed with me.*   Note here the canon; " The[1] master of
the family saith to his servant, ' Go, hire me labourers for
fourpence :' he goes and hires them for threepence ; although
their labour deserves fourpence, they shall not receive but
three, שקיבלו על עצמן ויש להם תרעומת על שליח *because
they bound themselves by agreement, and their complaint*" (γογ-
γυσμὸς, *murmuring,* in the 11th verse,) " *is against the servant.*"

Ver. 22 : Τὸ βάπτισμα, ὃ ἐγὼ βαπτίζομαι· *The baptism
that I am baptized with.*] The phrase that goes before this,
concerning *the cup,* is taken from divers places of Scripture,
where sad and grievous things are compared to draughts of
a bitter cup.   You may think that כוס פורענות *the cup of
vengeance,* of which there is mention in Bab. *Beracoth*[m],
means the same thing, but it is far otherwise : give me leave
to quote it, though it be somewhat out of our bounds : " Let
them not talk (say they) over their cup of blessing ; and let
them not bless over their *cup of vengeance.* מאי כוס פורענות
What is the cup of vengeance? The second cup, saith R. Nachman Bar Isaac."   Rabbena Asher and Piske are more clear :
" If he shall drink off two cups, let him not bless over the
third."   The Gloss, " He that drinks off double cups is
punished[n] by devils."   But to the matter before us.

So cruel a thing was the baptism of the Jews, being a
plunging of the whole body into water, when it was never so
much chilled with ice and snow, that, not without cause,
partly, by reason of the *burying* as I may call it under water,
and partly by reason of the cold, it used to signify the most
cruel kind of death.   The Jerusalem Talmudists relate, that
" in the days of Joshua Ben Levi, some endeavoured quite to
take away the washings [טבילה *baptisms*] of women, because
the women of Galilee grew barren by reason of the coldness
of the waters ;" which[o] we noted before at the sixth verse of
the third chapter.

[1] Maimon. as before, cap. 9.
[m] Fol. 51. 2.
[n] *Leusden's edit.,* vol. ii. p. 349.
[o] Berac. 6. 3.

CHAP. XXI.

VER. 1 P: Πρὸς τὸ ὄρος τῶν Ἐλαιῶν· *To the mount of Olives.*]
הר הזיתים *Mons Olivarum*, Zech. xiv. 4.   Natæ illic sunt
aliæ arbores præter oleas; ast ab illis nomen, et quod major
harum numerus, et dignior earum fructus.

Ficus produxit hic mons: quod patet per ficum maledictam.
Atque inde forte nomen loci *Bethphage,* id est, *Locus Gros-
sorum.*   Et ficuosus forsan fuit iste tractus *Bethphage* oppo-
situs.   Alibi forte mons magis olivosus: unde nomen loci
Gethsemani ; id est, *Torcular oleaceum.*

Cedros etiam aliquas genuit, easque miras, si Gemaristis
Hierosolymitanis hic fides.   "Duæ cedri (inquiunt) erant in
monte Oliveti.   Sub una quatuor erant tabernæ, vendentes
necessaria ad purificationes.   Ex altera deduxerunt uno-
quoque mense quadraginta *Seas* columbarum[q]."   Nimietate
historiæ historiam perdunt.

Ver. 2: Ὄνον καὶ πῶλον· *An ass and her foal.*]   In the
Talmudists we have the like phrase, חמור וגיידור קטון *an*[r]
ass and a little colt.   In that treatise Mezia, they speak concerning a hired ass, and the terms that the hired is obliged
to.   Among other things there, the Babylon Gemara[s] hath
these words, כל מעביר על דעת של בעל בית נקרא גזלן
*Whosoever transgresses against the will of the owner is called a
robber.*   For[t] instance, if any one hires an ass for a journey
on the plains[u], and turns up to the mountains, &c.   Hence
this of our Saviour appears to be a miracle, not a robbery;
that without any agreement or terms this ass should be led
away; and that the owner and those that stood by should
be satisfied with these bare words, "The Lord hath need of
him."

Ver. 5: Πραΰς, καὶ ἐπιβεβηκὼς ἐπὶ ὄνον· *Meek, and sitting
upon an ass.*]   This triumph of Christ completes a double
prophecy: 1. This prophecy of Zechariah here mentioned.
2. The taking to themselves the Paschal lamb, for this was
the very day on which it was to be taken, according to the

P See " Pauca interserenda in
quædam Horarum Hebraicarum et
Talmudicarum Loca:" in Leusden's
edition, vol. iii. p. 101.
q Taanith, fol. 69. 1.

r Hieros. Bava Mezia, fol. 11. 1.
s Cap. 6. halac. 3.
t Fol. 78. 1.
u *English folio edit.*, vol. ii. p. 223.

command of the law, Exod. xii. 3 ; " In the tenth day of this
month, they shall take to them every man a lamb."

It scarce appears to the Talmudists, how those words of
Daniel concerning the Messias, that " he comes with the
clouds of heaven," are[x] consistent with these words of Zechariah, that " he comes sitting upon an ass." " If (say
they[y]) the Israelites be good, then he shall come with the
clouds of heaven; but if not good, then riding upon an ass."
Thou art much mistaken, O Jew : for he comes " in the
clouds of heaven," as judge and revenger, because you are
evil and very wicked ; but *sitting upon an ass*, not because
you are, but because he is, good. אמר ליה שבור מלכא
לשמואל *King Sapores said to Samuel*, ' You say your Messias
will come upon an ass, I will send him a brave horse.'   He
answers him, ' You have not a horse with a hundred spots as
is his ass[z]." In the greatest humility of the Messias they
dream of grandeur, even in his very ass.

Ver. 8 : Κλάδους ἐστρώννυον ἐν τῇ ὁδῷ· *Strewed branches in
the way*.] Not that they strewed garments and boughs just
in the way under the feet of the ass to be trod on ; this
perhaps might have thrown down the rider ; but by the way-
side they made little tents and tabernacles of clothes and
boughs, according to the custom of the feast of Tabernacles.
John also adds, that taking *branches of palm trees* (לולבין)
in their hands, they went forth to meet him.   That book of
Maimonides entitled סוכה ולולב *Tabernacles and palm-
branches*, will be an excellent comment on this place, and so
will the Talmudic treatise, *Succah*.   We will pick out these
few things, not unsuitable to the present story : " Doth[a] any
one spread his garment on his tabernacle against the heat of
the sun, &c.? it is absurd; but if he spread his garment for
comeliness and ornament, it is approved."   Again, " The[b]
boughs of palm trees, of which the law, Lev. xxiii. 40, speaks,
are the young growing sprouts of palms, before their leaves
shoot out on all sides ; but when they are like small staves,
and these are called לולב."   And a little after, " It is a
notable precept, to gather לולב *young branches of palms*, and

[x] Dan. vii. 13.
[y] See Bab. Sanhedr. fol. 98. 1.
[z] Ibid.
[a] Maimon. Succah, cap. 5. artic. 17.
[b] Cap. 7.

the boughs of myrtle and willow, and to make them up into a small bundle, and to carry them in their hands," &c.

Ver. 9 : Ὡσαννὰ τῷ υἱῷ Δαβίδ· *Hosanna to the Son of David.*] Some are at a loss why it is said τῷ υἱῷ, *to the Son,* and not ὦ υἱὲ, *O Son :* wherefore they fly to Caninius as to an oracle, who tells us, that those very bundles of boughs are called *Hosanna ;* and that these words, *Hosanna to the Son of David,* signify no more than *boughs to the Son of David*[c]." We will not deny that *bundles* are sometimes so called, as seems in these clauses, לא לדוץ איניש ללולבא בהושענא[d] and לא ליגנוז שוניש לולבא בהושענא where it is plain, that a branch of palm is called לולב *Lulab,* and boughs of myrtle and willow bound together are called הושענא *Hosanna*[e] *:* but, indeed, if *Hosanna to the Son of David* signifies *boughs to the Son of David,* what do those words mean, *Hosanna in the highest?* The words therefore here sung import as much as if it were said, *We now sing Hosanna to the Messias*[f].

In the feast of Tabernacles, the *great Hallel,* as they call it, used to be sung, that is, Psalm cxiii, cxiv, cxv, cxvi, cxvii, and cxviii. And while the words of the Psalms were sung or said by one, the whole company used sometimes to answer at certain clauses, *Halleluia.* Sometimes the same clauses that had been sung or said were again repeated by the company : sometimes the bundles of boughs were brandished or shaken. " But when were the bundles shaken?" The rubric of the Talmud saith[g], " At that clause הודו לה" *Give thanks unto the Lord,* in the beginning of Psalm cxviii[h], and at the end. ובאנא ה" הושענא *and at that clause, Save now, I beseech thee, O Lord,* (Psalm cxviii. 25,) as saith the school of Hillel : but the school of Shammai saith also, at that clause, ה" הצליחה נא *O Lord, I beseech thee, send now prosperity.* R. Akibah said, I saw R. Gamaliel and R. Joshuah, when all the company shook their bundles they did not shake theirs, but only at that clause, *Save now, I beseech thee, O Lord*[i]."

[c] See Baronius at the year of Christ 34.

[d] Bab. Succah, fol. 37. 2.

[e] [See Buxtorf Lex. T. & R. sub v. col. 992.]

[f] See the Gloss.

[g] *Leusden's edit.,* vol. ii. p. 350.

[h] *English folio edit.,* vol. ii. p. 224.

[i] Succah, cap. 3. halac. 9.

On every day of the feast, they used once to go round
the altar with bundles in their hands, singing this, ה׳ אנא
הושיעה נא ה׳ הצליחה נא *Save now, I beseech thee, O
Lord; I beseech thee, O Lord, send now prosperity.* But on
the seventh day of the feast they went seven times round
the altar[k], &c. " The tossing or shaking of the bundles
was on the right hand, on the left hand, upwards and
downwards[l]."

" The reason of the bundles was this, because it is written,
' Then let all the trees of the wood sing,' (Psalm xcvi. 12.)
And afterward it is written, ' Give thanks unto the Lord,
because he is good,' (Psalm cvi. 1.) And afterward, ' Save
us, O Lord, O our God,' &c. (Psalm cvi. 47.) And the reason
is mystical. In the beginning of the year, Israel and the
nations of the world go forth to judgment; and being ignorant who are to be cleared and who guilty, the holy and
blessed God commanded Israel that they should rejoice with
these bundles, as a man rejoiceth who goeth out of the presence of his judge acquitted. Behold, therefore, what is
written, ' Let the trees of the wood sing;' as if it were said,
Let them sing with the trees of the wood, when they go out
justified from the presence of the Lord," &c.[m]

These things being premised concerning the rites and customs of that feast, we now return to our story :—

I. It is very much worth our observation, that the company receives Christ coming now to the Passover with the
solemnity of the feast of Tabernacles. For what hath this
to do with the time of the Passover? If one search into the
reason of the thing more accurately, these things occur;
First, The mirth of that feast above all others; concerning
which there needs not much to be said, since the very name
of the feast (for by way of emphasis it was called חג, that
is, *Festivity* or *Mirth*) sufficiently proves it. Secondly, That
prophecy of Zechariah[n], which, however it be not to be understood according to the letter, yet from thence may sufficiently be gathered the singular solemnity and joy of that
feast above all others; and, perhaps, from that same pro-

[k] Maimon. on Succah, cap. 6.
[l] Bab. Succah, fol. 27. 2.
[m] Rabbenu Asher on Succah, fol. 66. 2, 3.
[n] Chap. xiv. 16.

phecy, the occasion of this present action was taken.   For
being willing to receive the Messias with all joyfulness, triumph, and affection of mind (for by calling him the *Son
of David*, it is plain they took him for the *Messias*), they
had no way to express a more ardent zeal and joy at his
coming, than by the solemn procession of that feast.   They
have the Messias before their eyes; they expect great things
from him; and are therefore transported with excess of joy
at his coming.

II. But whereas the *Great Hallel*, according to the custom,
was not now sung, by reason of the suddenness of the present
action, the whole solemnity of that song was, as it were,
swallowed up in the frequent crying out and echoing back of
Hosanna; as they used to do in the Temple, while they went
round the altar.   And one while they sing *Hosanna to the Son
of David;* another while, *Hosanna in the highest;* as if they
had said, " Now we sing *Hosanna to the Son of David; save
us, we beseech thee, O thou* [who dwellest] *in the highest, save us
by the Messias.*"

Ver. 12 : 'Εξέβαλε πάντας τοὺς πωλοῦντας καὶ ἀγοράζοντας ἐν
τῷ ἱερῷ· *He cast out all them that sold and bought in the
Temple.*]   I. There was always a constant market in the
Temple in that place which was called חֲנִיּוֹת *the shops;*
where every day was sold wine, salt, oil, and other requisites
to sacrifices; as also oxen and sheep, in the spacious Court
of the Gentiles.

II. The nearness of the Passover had made the market
greater; for innumerable beasts being requisite to this solemnity, they were brought hither to be sold.   This brings to
mind a story of Bava Ben Buta: " He[o] coming one day into
the court found it quite empty of beasts.   'Let their houses,'
said he, ' be laid waste, who have laid waste the house of our
God.'   He sent for three thousand of the sheep of Kedar;
and having examined whether they were without spot, brought
them into the Mountain of the House;" that is, into the Court
of the Gentiles.

Τὰς τραπέζας τῶν κολλυβιστῶν κατέστρεψε· *Overthrew the tables
of the moneychangers.*]   Who those *moneychangers* were, may

---

[o] Hieros. Jom Tobh, fol. 61. 3.

be learned very well from the Talmud, and Maimonides in the treatise *Shekalim* :—

" It[p] is an affirmative precept of the law[q], that every Israelite should give half a shekel yearly : even the poor, who live by alms, are obliged to this ; and must either beg the money of others, or sell their clothes to pay half a shekel ; as it is said, ' The[r] rich shall give no more, and the poor shall give no less.' "

" In[s] the first day of the month Adar, they made a public proclamation concerning these shekels, that every one should provide his half shekel, and be ready to pay it.   Therefore, on the fifteenth day of the same month, *the exchangers* (השולחנין) sat in every city, civilly requiring this money : they received it of those that gave it, and compelled those that did not.   On the five-and-twentieth day[t] of the same month they sat in the Temple ; and then compelled them to give ; and from him that did not give they forced a pledge, even his very coat."

" They[u] sat in the cities, with two chests before them ; in one of which they laid up the money of the present year, and in the other the money of the year past.   They sat in the Temple with thirteen chests before them ; the first was for the money of the present year ; the second, for the year past ; the third, for the money that was offered to buy pigeons," &c.   They called these chests שופרות *trumpets*, because, like *trumpets*, they had a narrow mouth, and a wide belly.

" It[x] is necessary that every one should have half a shekel to pay for himself.   Therefore, when he comes to the exchanger to change a shekel for two half shekels, he is obliged to allow him some gain, which is called קולבון (κόλλυβος) *kolbon*.   And when two pay one shekel [between them], שניהם חייבין בקולבון *each of them is obliged to allow the same gain* or *fee*."

And not much after, כמה הוא שיעור הקולבון " *How much is that gain?*   At that time when they paid pence for

---

p *English folio edition*, vol. ii. p. 225.

q Maim. Shekal. cap. 1.

r Exod. xxx. 15.

s Id. ibid. Talm. Shekal. cap. 1.

t *Leusden's edit.*, vol. ii. p. 351.

u Talm. Shekal. cap. 2.

x Idem, cap. 3.

the half shekel, *a kolbon* [or the fee that was paid to the money-changer] was half a *mea*, that is, the twelfth part of a penny, and never less. But the *kolbons* were not like the half shekel; but the exchangers laid them by themselves till the holy treasury were paid out of them." You see what these *moneychangers* were, and whence they had their name. You see that Christ did not overturn the chests in which the holy money was laid up, but the tables on which they trafficked for this unholy gain.

Τῶν πωλούντων τὰς περιστεράς· *Of those that sold doves.*] מזבני קינים *sellers of doves.* See the Talmudic treatise of that title. עמדו קינים בירושלם בדינרי זהב : " *Dove*[y] *were at one time sold at Jerusalem for pence of gold.* Whereupon Rabban Simeon Ben Gamaliel said, המעון הזה *By this temple*, I will not lie down this night, unless they be sold for pence of silver, &c. Going into the council-house, he thus decreed, A woman of five undoubted labours, or of five undoubted fluxes, shall be bound only to make one offering; whereby doves were sold that very day for two farthings." The offering for women after childbirth, and fluxes, for their purification, were pigeons[z], &c. But now, when they went up to Jerusalem with their offerings at the feasts only, there was at that time a greater number of beasts, pigeons, and turtles, &c. requisite. See what we have said at the fifth chapter, and the three-and-twentieth verse.

Ver. 15 : Παῖδας κράζοντας ἐν τῷ ἱερῷ, καὶ λέγοντας Ὡσαννά· *The children crying in the temple, and saying, Hosanna.*] *Children*, from their first infancy, were taught to manage the bundles, to shake them, and in shaking, to sing Hosanna. קטון היודע לנענע חייב לולב, *A child*[a], *so soon as he knows how to wave the bundle, is bound to carry a bundle.* Where the Gemara saith thus; " The Rabbins teach, that so soon as a little child can be taught to manage a bundle, he is bound to carry one : so soon as he knows how to veil himself, he must put on the borders : as soon as he knows how to keep his father's phylacteries, he must put on his own : as soon as he can speak, let his father teach him the law, and to say the phylacteries," &c.

---

[y] Cherithuth, cap. 1. halac. 7.　　　　[z] Levit. xii. and xv.
[a] Succah, cap. 3. halac. last.

Ver. 19 : Οὐδὲν εὗρεν ἐν αὐτῇ εἰ μὴ φύλλα μόνον· *Found nothing thereon but leaves only.*] This place is not a little obscure, being compared with Mark xi. 13, who seems to say, that therefore figs were not found on this tree, because *it was not yet the time of figs*, οὐ γὰρ ἦν καιρὸς σύκων. Why then did our Saviour expect figs, when he might certainly know that *it was not yet the time of figs ?* And why, not finding them, did he curse the tree, being innocent and agreeable to its own nature ?

I. We will first consider the situation of this tree. Our evangelist saith, that it was *in the way*, ἐπὶ τῆς ὁδοῦ. This minds me of a distinction used very often by the Talmudists, between[b] מופקר and שמור that is, between the fruits of trees of *common* right, which did not belong to any peculiar master, but grew in woody places, or in *common* fields ; and the fruits of trees which grew in gardens, orchards, or fields, that had a proper owner. How much difference was made between these fruits by the canonists, as to tithing, and as to eating, is in many places to be met with through the whole classes, entitled זרעים *Seeds*. This fig-tree seems to have been of the former kind : תאנה מדברות *a wild fig-tree*, בהפקר growing in a place or field, not belonging to any one in particular, but *common* to all. So that our Saviour did not injure any particular person, when he caused this tree to wither ; but it was such a tree, that it could not be said of it, that it was *mine* or *thine*.

II. *He found nothing thereon but leaves*, because the time of figs was not yet a great while, Mark xi. 13.

1. " At[c] what time in the seventh year do they forbear to lop their trees? The school of Shammai saith, כל האילנות משיוציאו *All trees from that time, they bring forth* [leaves]. The Gloss, " The beginning of leaves is in the days of Nisan."

2. " Rabban[d] Simeon[e] Ben Gamaliel saith, From the putting forth of leaves, till there be green figs, is fifty days ; from the green figs, till the buds fall off, fifty days ; and from that time till the figs be ripe are fifty days." If, therefore, the first putting out of the leaves was in the month Nisan, and that was five months' time before the figs came to be ripe, it is

---

[b] *English folio edit.*, vol. ii. p. 226.
[c] Bab. Pesachin, fol. 52. 2.
[d] Jerus. Sheviith, fol. 35. 4.
[e] *Leusden's edition*, vol. ii. p. 352.

plain enough that the figs of that year coming on were not expected by our Saviour, nor could be expected.

That we may pursue the matter somewhat home, and make it appear that the text of Mark, as it is commonly read, *for the time of figs was not yet,* is uncorrupted,

I. We must first observe what is said about the intercalation of the year: " They intercalate the year upon three accounts ; for the green year, for the fruit of the tree, and for *Tekupha* [f]." Maimonides is more large ; whom see [g]. Now if you ask what means the intercalation for the fruit of the tree, the Gloss answers, " If the fruit be not ripened till Pentecost is past, they intercalate the year ; because Pentecost is the time of bringing the firstfruits : and if at that time one should not bring them along with him when he comes to the feast, he would be obliged to make another journey." But now this is not to be understood of all trees, but of some only, which put forth their fruit about the time of the Passover, and have them ripe at the feast of Pentecost. For thus Maimonides in the place cited : " If the council sees that there is not yet any green ear, and that the fruit of the trees which used to bud at the feast of the Passover is not yet budded [mark that, ' used to bud '], moved by these two causes, they intercalate the year." Among these the fig-tree can by no means be reckoned : for since, our Saviour being witness [h], the putting forth of its leaves is a sign that summer is at hand, you could not expect any ripe figs, nay (according to the Talmudists), not so much as the putting out of leaves, before the Passover. When it is before said that Pentecost was the time of bringing the firstfruits, it must not be so understood as if the firstfruits of all trees were then to be brought, but that before Pentecost it was not lawful to bring any ; for thus it is provided for by a plain canon, " The firstfruits are not to be brought before Pentecost. The inhabitants of mount Zeboim brought theirs before Pentecost, but they did not receive them of them, because it is said in the law [i], ' And

[f] Bab. Sanhedr. fol. 11. 2. [See Buxtorf Lex. T. & R., sub. v. תְּקוּפָה, col. 2003.]

[g] Kiddush Hodesh. cap. 4.

[h] Matt. xxiv. 32.

[i] Exod. xxiii. 16. Biccurim, cap. 1. hal. 13.

the feast of harvest, the firstfruit of thy labours which thou
hast sown in thy field.' "

II. There are several kinds of figs mentioned in the Talmudists besides these common ones; namely, figs of a better
sort, which grew in gardens and paradises : 1. שיתין *shithin.*
Concerning which the tract *Demai* [k], הקלין שבדמאי שיתין
וגו' that is, among those things which were accounted to
deserve lesser care, and among those things which were
doubtful as to tithing, were שיתין *shithin :* which the
Glosser tells us were תאני מדבריות *wild figs.* 2. There is
mention also in the same place of בנות שקמה which, as
some will have it, was *a fig mixed with a plane-tree,* תאנה
מורכבת בערמון : 3. But among all those kinds of figs, they
were memorable which were called פרסאות ; and they yet
more, which were called בנות שוח ; which, unless I mistake,
make to our purpose : not that they were more noble than
the rest, but their manner of bearing fruit was more unusual.
There is mention of these in *Sheviith* [l], in these words, בנות
שוח שביעית שלהם שניה שהן עושות לשלוש שנים ר'
יהודה אומ" הפרסאות שביעית שלהן מוצאי שביעי" שהן
עושות לב" שנים We will render the words in the paraphrase
of the Glossers : " בנות שוח are white figs, and פרסאות
are also a kind of fig : the seventh year" (that is, the year of
release) " is to those the second" (viz. of the seven years
following) ; " to these, the going out of the seventh. בנות
שוח put forth fruit every year, but it is ripe only every third
year : so that on that tree every year one might see three
sorts of fruit, namely, of the present year, of the past, and of
the year before that. Thus the פרסאות bring forth ripe
fruit in two years," &c.

Concerning בנות שוח thus the Jerusalem Gemara : " Do
they bear fruit every year, or once in three years? They
bear fruit every year ; but the fruit is not ripe till the third
year. But how [m] may one know which is the fruit of each
year? R. Jona saith, ' By the threads that hang to them.'
The tradition of Samuel, ' He makes little strings hang to
it,' " &c.

III. The fruit of very many trees hung upon them all

[k] Cap. 1. hal. 1.   [l] Cap. 5. hal. 1.
[m] *English folio edition,* vol. ii. p. 227.

the winter, by the mildness of the weather, if they were not gathered or shaken off by the wind : nay, they ripened in winter. Hence came those cautions about tithing : " The[n] tree which puts forth its fruit before the beginning of the year of the world" [that is, before the beginning of the month Tisri, in which month the world was created], " must be tithed for the year past : but if after the beginning of the world, then it must be tithed for the year coming on. R. Judan Bar Philia answered before R. Jonah, ' Behold the tree Charob puts forth its fruit before the beginning of the world, and yet it is tithed for the year following.' R. Jissa saith, ' If it puts forth a third part before the year of the world, it must be tithed for the year past ; but if after, then for the year following.' R. Zeira answers before R. Jissa ' Sometimes palm-trees do not bring forth part of their fruit till after the beginning of the year of the world ; and yet they must be tithed for the year before.' Samuel Bar Abba saith, ' If it puts[o] forth the third part of its fruit before the fifteenth day of the month Shebat, it is to be tithed for the year past; if after the fifteenth day of the month Shebat, for the year to come.' " Hence that axiom in Rosh Hasha-nah, " The[p] first day of the month Shebat is the beginning of the year for trees, according to the school of Shammai ; but, according to that of Hillel, the fifteenth day."

However, fig-trees were not among those trees that put forth their fruit after the beginning of Tisri ; for you have seen before, out of the Talmudists, that they used to put forth their leaves in the month Nisan : and that their fruit used to be ripe in thrice fifty days after this. Yet, perhaps, it may be objected about them, what we meet with in the Jerusalem Gemara, at the place before cited : " One gathers figs (say they), and knows not at what time they were put forth" (and thereby is at a loss for what year to tithe them). " R. Jonah saith, ' Let him reckon a hundred days back-wards ; and if the fifteenth day of the month Shebat falls within that number, then he may know when they were put forth.' " But this must be understood of figs of a particular sort, which do not grow after the usual manner, which is

---

[n] Jerus. Sheviith, fol. 35. 4.   [o] *Leusden's edition*, vol. ii. p. 353.
[p] Cap. 1. hal. 1.

plain also from that which follows; for, " they say to him,
' With you at Tiberias there are fig-trees that bear fruit
in one year:' to which he answers, ' Behold, with you at
Zippor there are trees that bear fruit in two years.' " Concerning common fig-trees, their ordinary time of putting out
green figs was sufficiently known; as also the year of tithing
them : but concerning those trees of another sort, which had
ripe fruit only in two or three years, it is no wonder if they
were at a loss in both.

IV. Christ, therefore, came to the tree seeking fruit on it,
although the ordinary time of figs was not yet; because it
was very probable that some fruit might be found there. Of
the present year, indeed, he neither expected nor could
expect any fruit, when it was so far from being the *time of
figs*, καιρὸς σύκων, that it was almost five months off: and it
may be doubted whether it had yet so much as any leaves
of the present year. It was now the month Nisan, and that
month was the time of the first putting out of leaves ; so
that if the buds of the leaves had just peeped forth, they
were so tender, small, and scarce worth the name of leaves
(for it was but the eleventh day of the month), that to expect
figs of the same year with those leaves had not been only
in vain, but ridiculous. Those words seem to denote something peculiar, ἔχουσαν φύλλα, *having leaves;* as if the other
trees thereabout had been without leaves, or, at least, had
not such leaves as promised figs. Mark seems to give the
reason why he came rather to that tree than to any other ;
namely, because he saw leaves on it, and thereby hoped to
find figs. " For when he saw (saith he) a fig tree afar off
having leaves, he came, if haply he might find any thing
thereon." From the leaves he had hopes of figs : these,
therefore, certainly were not the leaves of the present spring,
for those were hardly so much as in being yet : but they
were either the leaves of the year past, that had hung upon
the tree all winter ; or else this tree was of that kind which
had figs and leaves together hanging on it for two or three
years before the fruit grew ripe. And I rather approve of
this latter sense, which both renders the matter itself more
clear, and better solves the difficulties that arise from the
words of Mark. This tree, it seems, had leaves which pro-

mised fruit, and others had not so; whereas, had they all
been of the same kind, it is likely they would all have had
leaves after the same manner.   But when others had lost all
their leaves of the former year by winds and the winter, and
those of the present year were not as yet come out, this kept
its leaves, according to its nature and kind, both summer and
winter.   St. Mark, therefore, in that clause, which chiefly
perplexes interpreters, οὐ γὰρ ἦν καιρὸς σύκων, *for the time of
figs was not yet,* doth not strictly and only give the reason
why he found no figs, but gives the reason of the whole
action; namely, why on that mountain which abounded with
fig trees he saw but one that had such leaves; and being
at a great distance when he saw it, he went to it, expecting
figs only from it.   The reason, saith he, was this, " Because
it was not the usual time of figs:" for had it been so, he
might have gathered figs from the trees about him; but
since it was ⁹ not, all his expectation was from this, which
seemed to be the kind of פרסאות or בנות שוח, which never
wanted leaves or figs.   For to take an instance in the tree
בנות שוח: That tree (suppose) bore figs such a summer,
which hung upon the boughs all the following winter; it
bore others also next summer; and those, together with the
former, hung on the boughs all this winter too: the third
summer it bore a third degree, and this summer brought
those of the first bearing to ripeness, and so onwards continually; so that it was no time to be found without fruit of
several years.   It is less, therefore, to be wondered at, if
that which promised so much fruitfulness by its looks, that
one might have expected from it at least the fruit of two
years, did so far deceive the hopes it had raised, as not to
afford one fig; if that, I say, should suffer a just punishment
from our Lord, whom it had so much, in appearance, disap-
pointed: an emblem of the punishment that was to be inflicted upon the Jews for their spiritual barrenness and
hypocrisy.

Ver. 21 : Κἂν τῷ ὄρει τούτῳ εἴπητε, Ἄρθητι καὶ βλήθητι εἰς
τὴν θάλασσαν, γενήσεται· *But if ye shall say unto this mountain,
Be thou removed, and be thou cast into the sea; it shall be done.*]

---

⁹ *English folio edit.,* vol. ii. p. 228.

This is a hyperbolical way of speaking, taken from the common language of the schools of the Jews, and designed[r] after a manner for their refutation.   Such a hyperbole concerning this very mountain you have Zech. xiv. 4.

The Jews used to set out those teachers among them, that were more eminent for the profoundness of their learning, or the splendour of their virtues, by such expressions as this; הוא עוקר הרים *He is a rooter up* (or *a remover*) *of mountains.*   "Rabh[s] Joseph is Sinai, and Rabbah is *a rooter up of mountains.*"   The Gloss; "They called Rabh Joseph *Sinai,* because he was very skilful in clearing of difficulties; and Rabbah Bar Nachmani, *A rooter up of mountains,* because he had a piercing judgment."   "Rabba[t] said, I am like Ben Azzai in the streets of Tiberias."   The Gloss; "Like Ben Azzai, who taught profoundly in the streets of Tiberias; nor was there in his days עוקר הרים כמותו such another *rooter up of mountains as he.*"   "He[u] saw Resh Lachish in the school, as if he were *plucking up mountains* and grinding them one upon another."

The same expression with which they sillily and flatteringly extolled the learning and virtue of their men, Christ deservedly useth to set forth the power of faith, as able to do all things, Mark ix. 23.

Ver. 33: Ἐφύτευσεν ἀμπελῶνα· *Planted a vineyard.*]   Concerning vines and their husbandry see Kilaim[x], where there is a large discourse of the beds of a vineyard, the orders of the vines, of the measure of the winepress, of the hedge, of the trenches, of the void space, of the places within the hedge which were free from vines, whether they were to be sown or not to be sown, &c.

Ver. 35: Ἔδειραν, *beat;* ἀπέκτειναν, *killed;* ἐλιθοβόλησαν, *stoned.*]   There seems to be an allusion to the punishments and manners of death in the council: 1. Ἔδειραν, which properly signifies the *flaying off of the skin,* is not amiss rendered by interpreters *beat;* and the word seems to relate to *whipping,* where forty stripes save one did miserably *flay off the skin* of the poor man.   See what the word סופג properly

r *Leusden's edition,* vol. ii. p. 354.
s Bab. Beracoth, fol. 64. 1.
t Id. Erubhin, fol. 29. 1.
u Id. Sanhedr. fol. 24. 1.
x Cap. 4, 5, 6, and 7.

means in that very usual phrase, expressing this whipping ‎סִיפֵּג אֵת הָאַרְבָּעִים *beaten with forty stripes.* 2. Ἀπέκτειναν, *killed,* signifies a death by the sword, as ‎הרג doth in the Sanhedrim; ‎ד' מיתות נמסרו לבד" סקילה שריפה הרג ‎וחנק *Four kinds of death are delivered to the Sanhedrim, stoning, burning, killing, and strangling*[y].

Ver. 38[z]: Οὗτός ἐστιν ὁ κληρονόμος, &c. *This is the heir, &c.*] Compare this verse with John xi. 48; and it seems to hint, that the rulers of the Jews acknowledged among themselves that Christ was the Messias; but being strangely transported beside their senses, they put him to death; lest, bringing in another worship and another people, he should either destroy or suppress their worship and themselves.

Ver. 44: Καὶ ὁ πεσὼν ἐπὶ τὸν λίθον τοῦτον, συνθλασθήσεται, &c. *And whosoever shall fall on this stone shall be broken, &c.*] Here is a plain allusion to the manner of stoning, concerning which thus *Sanhedrin*[a] : "The place of stoning was twice as high as a man. From the top of this, one of the witnesses striking him on his loins felled him to the ground: if he died of this, well; if not, the other witness threw a stone upon his heart," &c. "R. Simeon[b] Ben Eleazar saith, There was a stone there as much as two could carry: this they threw upon his heart."

CHAP. XXII.

VER. 9: Πορεύεσθε ἐπὶ τὰς διεξόδους τῶν ὁδῶν, &c. *Go ye into the highways, &c*] That is, 'Bring in hither the travellers.' "What[c] is the order of sitting down to meat? The travellers come in and sit down upon benches or chairs, till all are come that were invited." The *Gloss*; "It was a custom among rich men to invite poor travellers to feasts."

Ver. 16: Μετὰ τῶν Ἡρωδιανῶν· *With the Herodians.*] Many things are conjectured concerning the *Herodians.* I make a judgment of them from that history which is produced by the author *Juchasin*[d], speaking of Hillel and Shammai. "Heretofore (saith he) Hillel and Menahem were (heads of the council); but Menahem withdrew into the

---

[y] Sanhedr. cap. 7. hal. 1.
[z] *English folio edit.*, vol. ii. p. 229.
[a] Cap. 6. hal. 4.

[b] Bab. Gemara.
[c] Bab. Beracoth, fol. 43. 1.
[d] Fol. 19. 1.

family of Herod, together with eighty men bravely clad."
These, and such as these, I suppose were called *Herodians,*
who partly got into the court, and partly were of the faction
both of the father and son. With how great opposition of
the generality of the Jewish people Herod ascended and
kept the throne, we have observed before. There were some
that obstinately resisted him; others that as much defended
him: to these was deservedly given the title of *Herodians;*
as endeavouring with all their might to settle the kingdom in
his family: and they, it seems, were of the Sadducean faith
and doctrine; and it is likely had leavened Herod, who was
now tetrarch, with the same principles. For (as we noted
before) 'the leaven of the Sadducees' in Matthew[e], is in
Mark[f] ' the leaven of Herod.' And it was craftily con-
trived on both sides that they might be a mutual establish-
ment to one another, they to his kingdom, and he to their
doctrine. When I read of Manaem or Menahem[g], the
foster-brother of Herod the tetrarch[h], it readily brings to
my mind the name and story before mentioned of Menahem,
who carried over with him so many eminent persons to the
court of Herod.

Ver. 20[i]: Τίνος ἡ εἰκὼν αὕτη καὶ ἡ ἐπιγραφή; *Whose is this
image and superscription?*] They endeavour by a pernicious
subtilty to find out whether Christ were of the same opinion
with Judas of Galilee. Which opinion those lewd disturbers
of all things, whom Josephus brands everywhere under the
name of *zealots,* had taken up; stiffly denying obedience and
tribute to a Roman prince; because they persuaded themselves and their followers that it was a sin to submit to a
heathen government. What great calamities the outrageous
fury of this conceit brought upon the people, both Josephus
and the ruins of Jerusalem at this day testify. They chose
Cæsar before Christ; and yet because they would neither
have Cæsar nor Christ, they remain sad monuments to all
ages of the divine vengeance and their own madness. To
this fury those frequent warnings of the apostles do relate,
"That every one should submit himself to the higher powers[k]."

e Matt. xvi. 6.
f Mark viii. 19.
g *Leusden's edition,* vol. ii. p. 355.
h Acts xiii. 1.
i *English folio edit.,* vol. ii. p. 230.
k Rom. xiii. 1. 1 Pet. ii. 13, &c.

And the characters of these madmen, " they contemn domin-
ions[1]," and " they exalt themselves against every thing that
is called God[m]."

Christ answers the treachery of the question propounded,
out of the very determinations of the schools[n], where this
was taught, " Wheresoever the money of any king is current,
there the inhabitants acknowledge that king for their lord."
Hence is that of the Jerusalem *Sanhedrin*[o] : "Abigail said to
David, ' What evil have I done, or my sons, or my cattle?'
He answered, ' Your husband vilifies my kingdom.' ' Are you
then,' said she, ' a king?' To which he, ' Did not Samuel anoint
me for a king?' She replied, : עדיין מוניטה דמרן שאול
קיים ' *The money of our lord Saul as yet is current:*" that is,
' Is not Saul to be accounted king, while his money is still
received commonly by all?'

Ver. 23 : Σαδδουκαῖοι, οἱ λέγοντες μὴ εἶναι ἀνάστασιν· *The
Sadducees, who say that there is no resurrection.*] "The[p] Sadducees cavil, and say, The cloud faileth and passeth away; so
he that goeth down to the grave doth not return." Just after
the same rate of arguing as they use that deny infant baptism ; because, forsooth, in the law there is no express mention of the resurrection. Above, we suspected that the Sadducees were Herodians, that is to say, courtiers : but these
here mentioned were of a more inferior sort.

Ver. 32 : Οὐκ ἔστιν ὁ Θεὸς Θεὸς νεκρῶν· *God is not the God
of the dead.*] Read, if you please, the beginning of the chapter
Chelek[q], where you will observe with what arguments and
inferences the Talmudists maintain לתחיית המתים מן
התורה *the resurrection of the dead out of the law* ; namely,
by a manner of arguing not unlike this of our Saviour's. We
will produce only this one ; " R. Eliezer Ben R. Josi said, In
this matter I accused the scribes of the Samaritans of false-
hood, while they say, That the resurrection of the dead cannot be proved out of the law. I told them, You corrupt your
law, and it is nothing which you carry about in your hands;
for you say, That the resurrection of the dead is not in the
law, when it saith, ' That soul shall be utterly cut off; his

---

[1] 2 Pet. ii. 10. Jud. ver. 8.
[m] 2 Thess. ii. 4.
[n] Maim. on Gezelah, cap. 5.
[o] Fol. 20. 2.
[p] Tanchum, fol. 3. 1.
[q] In Bab. Sanhedr.

iniquity is upon him[r].' 'Shall be utterly cut off;' namely, in this world. 'His iniquity is upon him:' when? Is it not in the world to come?" I have quoted this, rather than the others which are to be found in the same place; because they seem here to tax the Samaritan text of corruption; when, indeed, both the text and the version, as may easily be observed, agree very well with the Hebrew. When, therefore, the Rabbin saith, that they have *corrupted their law* (וייכתם תורתכם), he doth not so much deny the purity of the text, as reprove the vanity of the interpretation: as if he had said, "You interpret your law falsely, when you do not infer the resurrection from those words which speak it so plainly."

With the present argument of our Saviour compare, first, those things which are said by R. Tanchum[s]: "R. Simeon Ben Jochai saith, God, holy and blessed, doth not join his name to holy men while they live, but only after their death; as it is said, 'To[t] the saints that are in the earth.' When are they saints? When they are laid in the earth; for while they live, God doth not join his name to them; because he is not sure but that some evil affection may lead them astray: but when they are dead, then he joins his name to them. But we find that God joined his name to Isaac while he was living: 'I am the God of Abraham and the[u] God of Isaac[x].' The Rabbins answer, He looked on his dust as if it were gathered upon the altar. R. Berachiah said, Since he became blind, he was in a manner dead." See also R. Menahem on the Law[y].

Compare also those words of the Jerusalem Gemara[z]: "The righteous, even in death, are said to live; and the wicked, even in life, are said to be dead. But how is it proved that the wicked, even in life, are said to be dead? From that place where it is said, לֹא אֶחְפּוֹץ בְּמוֹת הַמֵּת *I have no delight in the death of the dead.* Is he already dead, that is already here called מֵת *dead?* And whence is it proved that the righteous, even in death, are said to live? From that passage, 'And[a] he said to him, This is the land, concerning

r Numb. xv. 31.
s Fol. 13. 3.
t Psal. xvi. 3.
u *English folio edit.*, vol. ii. p. 231.

x Gen. xxviii. 13.
y Fol. 62. 1.
z Berac. fol. 5. 4.

which I sware to Abraham, to Isaac, and to Jacob,' לֵאמֹר. What is the meaning of the word לֵאמֹר? He saith to him, Go and tell the fathers, whatsoever I promised to you, I have performed to your children."

The opinion of the Babylonians[b] is the same; "The living know that they shall die. They are righteous who, in their death, are said to live: as it is said, 'And Benaiah, the son of Jehoiada, the son of אִישׁ חַי *a living man,*' [*The son of a valiant man.* A. V. 2 Sam. xxiii. 20.]" &c. And a little after; "The dead know nothing: They are the wicked who, even in their life, are called *dead*, as it is said, וְאַתָּה חָלָל רָשָׁע נְשִׂיא יִשְׂרָאֵל: *And thou, dead wicked prince of Israel.*" The word חָלָל, which is commonly rendered *profane* in this place, they render it also in a sense very usual, namely, for one *wounded* or *dead*.

There are, further, divers stories alleged[c], by which they prove that the dead so far live, that they understand many things which are done here; and that some have spoke after death, &c.

Ver. 35[d]: Εἷς ἐξ αὐτῶν νομικός.] Si distinguendum sit inter γραμματέα et νομικὸν, ut alius sit hic ab illo, νομικοὶ sunto illi, qui ipsum textum legis explicarunt, et non traditiones. דרשנים, non תנאים. Exempla sumamus ex hac historia.

Rabbi Judah transiit per oppidum Simoniam, et Simonienses prodierunt ei obviam, et dixerunt ei, Rabbi, præbe nobis virum[e] aliquem prælecturum nobis, δευτεροῦντα nobis, et judicaturum nobis judicia nostra. Dedit iis R. Levi Ben Susi. Struxerunt ei suggestum magnum, atque illum in eo collocarunt. Proposuerunt ei quæstiones [ex Deut. xxv. 9. excitatas] גרמת יבמה היאך הולצת *Si truncata manibus sit fratria, quomodo detrahendus per eam est calceus leviri?* רקקה דם מהו *Si consputet sanguinem; quid tum?* [Quæstiones profundæ, et quæ Œdipum aliquem traditionarium, eumque Œdiposissimum, requirerent.] "Quibus cum ille nihil haberet quod responderet, dixerunt, דלמא לית בר אולפן בר אגדה הוא *Forte ille non est doctor traditionum,*

---

[a] *Leusden's edit.*, vol. ii. p. 356.
[b] Berac. fol. 18. 1.
[c] Ibid. col. 2.
[d] See " Pauca interserenda in

quædam Horarum Hebraicarum et Talmudicarum loca." *Leusden's edition*, vol. iii. p. 101.
[e] *Leusden's edit.*, vol. iii. p. 102.

sed doctor explicationis.	Proponunt ergo ei textum [ex Dan. x. 21.] explicandum."

Sub hac classe ordinare licet explicationes istas, quæ vulgo vocantur *Rabboth.* In quibus traditionum quidem parum, ast Glossemata in textum varia, atque ut plurimum vafra satis.

In hisce Commentariis occurrit infinitis vicibus hæc phrasiologia, פתח ר׳ *Rabbi N. aperuit.* Scio vocem פתח reddi posse *incepit.* Cui opponitur חתם *Finiit:* ast reddo *Aperuit*, partim ex ipsa rei memoratæ evidentia, et partim ex verbis hisce Magistrorum : [f] רבנין פותחין פתחא להאי קרא *Rabbini aperiunt apertionem* (vel *ostium*) *huic Scripturæ.* Prævaricati sunt contra Dominum. Nam filios alienos genuerunt; jam devorabit mensis eos et portiones eorum. [Hos. v. 7.] Ad docendum, quod cum mortuus esset Josephus, inane reddiderunt fœdus circumcisionis, et dixerunt, Erimus sicut Ægyptii. Unde discis, quod Moses circumcidit eos, cum egrederentur. Quod cum fecisset, immutavit Deus amorem, quo eos amaverant Ægyptii, in odium . . . . . Ad implendum illud quod dicitur, Devorabit eos mensis cum portionibus suis[g].

Et ubicunque de aliquo dicitur, quod פתח (quod dicitur infinities) Rabbinus iste in manus sumit aliquem textum Scripturæ, et aut verba ejus explicat, aut sensum applicat, aut utrumque. Exempla sunt innumera : præsertim in Bereshith Rabba, atque in introductione ista ad Midras Echa, quam vocant פתחתא דהכימי *Apertiones*, vel *Explicationes Sapientum.*

Illos ergo, qui sese explicandis Scripturis addixerunt hoc modo, νομικοὺς ego dici arbitror, ut distinctos ab iis, qui operam dederunt docendis atque illustrandis traditionibus.

CHAP. XXIII.

VER. 2 : Ἐπὶ τῆς Μωσέως καθέδρας, &c. *In Moses' seat, &c.*] This is to be understood rather of the *legislative seat* (or chair), than of the merely *doctrinal:* and Christ here asserts the authority of the magistrate, and persuadeth to obey him in lawful things.

---

[f] Shemoth Rabba, sect. 1.	[g] Vid. Bemidb. Rab. fol. 257. 3.

Concerning the chairs of the Sanhedrim there is mention made in Bab. *Succah*[h] : " There were at Alexandria seventy-one golden chairs, according to the number of the seventy-one elders of the great council." Concerning the authority of Moses and his vicegerent in the council, there is also mention in *Sanhedrim*[i] : " The great council consisted of seventy-one elders. But whence was this number derived? From that place where it is said, ' Choose me out seventy men of the elders of Israel : and Moses was president over them.' Behold seventy-one ! "

What is here observed by Galatinus from the signification of the aorist ἐκάθισαν, *sat*, is too light and airy : " He saith, They *sat* (saith he), and not, They *sit*, that he might plainly demonstrate, that their power was then ceased[j]." But if we would be so curious to gather any thing from this aorist, we might very well transfer it to this sense rather : " The scribes and Pharisees, the worst of men, have long usurped Moses's seat ; nevertheless, we ought to obey them, because, by the dispensation of the divine providence, they bear the chief magistracy."

Concerning their authority, thus Maimonides[k] : " The great council of Jerusalem was עיקר ועמוד (στύλος καὶ ἑδραίωμα, *the*[l] *pillar and ground*) *the ground* of the traditional law, and *the pillar* of doctrine : whence proceeded statutes and judgments for all Israel. And concerning them the law asserts this very thing, saying, ' According[m] to the sentence of the law which they shall teach thee.' Whosoever, therefore, believes Moses our master and his law, is bound to rely upon them for the things of the law."

Christ teacheth, that they were not to be esteemed as oracles, but as magistrates.

Ver. 4 : Φορτία βαρέα· *Heavy burdens.*] חומרי, in the Talmudic language. Hence[n] איסור חמור *a heavy prohibition ;* הולך אחרי המחמיר *Let*[o] *him follow him that imposeth heavy things.* There are reckoned up four-and-twenty things מחומרי ב״ה מקולי ב״ש *of the weighty things of the school*

[h] Fol. 51. 2.
[i] Cap. 1. hal. 6.
[j] Cap. 6. book 4.
[k] In Mamrim; cap. 1.

[l] See 1 Tim. iii. 15.
[m] Deut. xvii. 11.
[n] Jerus. Rosh hashanah, fol. 56. 4.
[o] Maim. in Mamr. cap. 1.

of Hillel, and the light things of that of Shammai P. " R. Joshua
saith q, A foolish religious man, עָרוּם רָשָׁע r *a crafty wicked
man*, a she-pharisee, and the voluntary dashing of the Pharisees, destroy the world." It is disputed by the Gemarists,
who is that רָשָׁע עָרוּם *crafty wicked man* : and it is answered
by some, " He that prescribes light things to himself, and
heavy to others."

Ver. 5 : Πλατύνουσι δὲ τὰ φυλακτήρια αὐτῶν· *They make broad
their phylacteries.*] These four places of the law,

> Exod. xiii. 3, 4, 5, 6, 7, 8, 9, 10.
> Exod. xiii. 11, 12, 13, 14, 15, 16.
> Deut. vi. 5, 6, 7, 8, 9.
> Deut. xi. 13, 14, 15, 16, 17, 18, 19, 20, 21 ;

being writ upon two parchment labels (which they called
תְּפִלִּין *tephillin* s), were carried about with them constantly
with great devotion, being fastened to their forehead and
their left arm. To the forehead, in that place t שִׂמוּחוּ שֶׁל
תִּינוֹק רוֹפֵף *where the pulse of an infant's brain is.* This of
the forehead was most conspicuous, and *made broad:* hence
came that u, " Let nobody pass by the synagogue while prayers
are saying there.—But if he hath phylacteries upon his head,
he may pass by, because they show that he is studious of
the law."—" It is not lawful to walk through burying-places
with phylacteries on one's head, and the book of the law
hanging at one's arm x."

They are called in Greek *phylacteries*, that is, *observatories* ;
because they were to put them in mind of the law ; and perhaps they were also called *preservatories*, because they were
supposed to have some virtue in them to drive away devils :
" It is necessary that the *phylacteries* should be repeated at
home a-nights, בִּשְׁבִיל לְהַבְרִיחַ אֶת הַמַּזִּיקִין *to drive away
devils* y."

Concerning z the curious writing of the *phylacteries*, see

p Jerus. Jom Tobh, fol. 60. 2. and
Sotah, fol. 19. 2.

q Ibid. cap. 3. hal. 4.

r *English folio edit.*, vol. ii. p. 232.

s [See more in Buxtorf Lex.
T.& R. sub v. תְּפִלָּה col. 1743.]

t Bab. Taanith, fol. 16. 1. in the
Gloss.

u Maimon. on Tephillah, cap. 8.

x Bab. Berac. fol. 18. 1.

y Jerus. Berac. fol. 2. 4. Pisk in
Berac. cap. 1. art. 6. Rabben. Asher.
ibid. cap. 1. col. 1.

z *Leusden's edition*, vol. ii. p.
357.

Maimonides on *Tephillin*[z]. Concerning their strings, marked
with certain small letters, see *Tosaphoth* on *Megillah*[a]. Concerning the repeating of them, see both the Talmuds in
Beracoth[b]. How the Jews did swear touching their *phylacteries*, see Maimonides in *Shevuoth*[c]: and how God is
brought in swearing by the *phylacteries*, see Tanchum[d].

Our Saviour does not so much condemn the bare wearing
of them, as the doing it out of pride and hypocrisy. It is not
unlikely that he wore them himself, according to the custom
of the country: for the children of the Jews were to be
brought up from their infancy in saying *the phylacteries;* that
is, as soon as they were capable of being catechised[e]. The
scribes and Pharisees made theirs very *broad* and visible, that
they might obtain a proportional fame and esteem for their
devotion with the people; these things being looked upon as
arguments of the study of the law, and signs of devotion.

Μεγαλύνουσι τὰ κράσπεδα τῶν ἱματίων αὐτῶν· *Enlarge the
borders of their garments.*] See Numb. xv. 38; Deut. xxii. 12.
—"He[f] that takes care of the candle of the sabbath,* his
children shall be the disciples of wise men. He that takes
care to stick up labels against the posts shall obtain a glorious house; and he that takes care of the צִיצִית, of making
borders to his garment, shall obtain a good coat."

Ver. 7: Καὶ καλεῖσθαι ῾Ραββὶ, ῾Ραββί. *And to be called
Rabbi, Rabbi.*] I. Concerning the original of this title, see
Aruch[g]: "The elder times, which were more worthy, had no
need of the title either of *Rabban,* or *Rabbi,* or *Rabh,* to adorn
either the wise men of Babylon or the wise men of the land
of Israel: for, behold, Hillel comes up out of Babylon, and
the title of *Rabbi* is not added to his name: and thus it was
with those who were noble among the prophets; for he saith,
Haggai the prophet [not *Rabbi* Haggai]. Ezra did not come
up out of Babylon, &c. [not *Rabbi* Ezra]; whom they did not
honour with the titles of *Rabbi* when they spoke their names.
And we have heard that this had its beginning only in the
presidents [of the council] from Rabban Gamaliel the old
man, and Rabban Simeon his son, who perished in the de-

z Cap. 1. 2.   a Fol. 26. 2.   e Berac. fol. 22. 1. in the Gloss.
b Cap. 1. 2, 3.   f Bab. Schabb. fol. 23. 2.
c Cap. 11.   d Fol. 6. 3.   g In the word אבי׳׳.

struction of the second Temple : and from Rabban Jochanan
Ben Zaccai, who were all presidents.   And the title also of
Rabbi began from those that were promoted [to be elders]
from that time, *Rabbi* Zadok, and R. Eliezer Ben Jacob : and
the thing went forth from the disciples of Rabban Jochanan
Ben Zaccai, and onwards.   Now the order, as all men use it,
is this : *Rabbi* is greater than *Rabb*, and *Rabban* is greater
than *Rabbi;* and he is greater who is called by his own
(single) name, than he who is called *Rabban.*"

That[h] this haughty title of *Rabbi* was not in use before
the times of Hillel sufficiently appears from thence, that the
doctors before that were called by their plain names, and
knew nothing of this title.   Antigonus Socheus, Shemaiah
and Abtalion, Gebihah Ben Pesisa, Calba Savua, Admon and
Hanan, Hillel and Shammai, and many others, whose names
we meet with in the Jewish story.   Yet you shall find these,
that were more ancient, sometimes officiously honoured by
the writers of their nation with this title, which they themselves were strangers to.   They feign[i] that king Jehoshaphat
thus called the learned men : "When he saw (say they) a
disciple of the wise men, he rose up out of his throne and
embraced him, and kissed him, and called him אבי אבי
רבי רבי מרי מרי *O Father, Father, Rabbi, Rabbi, Lord,
Lord."*   And Joshua Ben Perachia[k] is called *Rabbi* Joshua.
רבי אבי מורי are here rendered *Rabbi* in the eighth verse;
'*father,*' in the ninth ; and '*master,*' καθηγητὴς, in the tenth.
We do not too nicely examine the precise time when this
title began ; be sure it did not commence before the schism
arose between the schools of Shammai and Hillel : and from
that schism, perhaps, it had its beginning.

II. It was customary, and they loved it, to be saluted with
this honourable title, notwithstanding the dissembled axiom
among them, אחוב את המלאכה ושנא את הרבנות *Love
the work, but hate the title*[l].

1. Disciples were thus taught to salute their masters[m] : " R.
Eliezer saith, המתפלל אחורי רבו *he that prayeth behind the
back of his master,* יהנותן שלום לרבו והמחזיר שלום לרבו

[h] *English folio edition,* vol. ii. p.
233.
[i] Bab. Maccoth, fol. 24. 1.

[k] Sanhedr. fol. 107. 3.
[l] Maim. on Talm. Tor. c. 3.
[m] Bab. Berac. fol. 27. 1.

and he that salutes his master,—or returns a salute to his master,—
and he that makes himself a separatist from the school of
his master,—and he that teaches any thing, which he hath
not heard from his master,—he provokes the Divine Majesty
to depart from Israel." The Glossers on these words, 'He
that salutes, or returns a salute to his master,' thus comment ; "he that salutes his master in the same form of words
that he salutes other men, and doth not say to him, שלום
עליך רבי *God save you, Rabbi*[n]." It is reported also, that[o]
the council excommunicated certain persons four and twenty
times, על כבוד רב *for the honour of master ;* that is, for not
having given due honour to the *Rabbins.*

2. The masters saluted one another so. "R. Akibah[p]
said to R. Eleazar, *Rabbi, Rabbi.*"—"R. Eleazar[q] Ben[r]
Simeon, of Magdal Gedor, came from the house of his master,
sitting upon an ass : he went forward along the bank of the
river rejoicing greatly, and being very much pleased with
himself, because he had learned so much of the law.   There
meets him a very deformed man, and said, שלום עליך רבי
Save you, Rabbi : he did not salute him again, but on the
contrary said thus, ' Raca, how deformed is that man ! perhaps all your townsmen are as deformed as you.'   He answered, ' I know nothing of that, but go you to the workman
that made me, and tell him, how deformed is this vessel which
thou hast made !'" &c.   And a little after, "when that deformed man was come to his own town, his fellow citizens
came out to meet him and said, שלום עליך רבי רבי מורי
מורי *Save you, O Rabbi, Rabbi, master, master.* He [R.
Eleazar] saith to them, ' To whom do you say *Rabbi, Rabbi ?'*
They answer, ' To him that followeth thee.'   He replied,
' If this be a *Rabbi,* let there not be many such in Israel.'"

Ver. 13 : Κατεσθίετε τὰς οἰκίας τῶν χηρῶν· *Ye devour widows'*
houses.] The scribes and Pharisees were ingenious enough
for their own advantage.   Hear one argument among many,
forged upon the anvil of their covetousness, a little rudely
drawn, but gainful enough : "The[s] Lord saith, ' Make me an

---

[n] See also Hieros. Shevuoth, fol.
34. 1.
[o] Id. ibid. fol. 19. 1.
[p] Jerus. Moed Katon, fol. 81. 1.

[q] Bab. Taanith, fol. 2.
[r] *Leusden's edit.*, vol. ii. p. 358.
[s] Bab. Joma, fol. 72. 2.

ark of shittim wood.' מכאן לתח "שבני עירו מצווין לעשות
לו מלאכתו *Hence it is decided* (say they) *in behalf of a disciple of the wise men, that his fellow citizens are bound to perform his servile work for him."*—O money, thou mistress of
art and mother of wit! So he that was preferred to be president of the council, was to be maintained and enriched by
the council! See the Gloss on Babylonian *Taanith*[t].

They angled with a double hook among the people for respect, and by respect for gain.

I. As doctors of the law : where they, first and above all
things, instilled into their disciples and the common people,
that a wise man, or a master, was to be respected above all
mortal men whatsoever. Behold the rank and order of
benches according to these judges ! " A[u] wise man is to
take place of a king ; a king of a high priest ; a high priest
of a prophet ; a prophet of one anointed for war ; one
anointed for war of a president of the courses ; a president
of the courses of the head of a family ; the head of a family
of a counsellor ; a counsellor of a treasurer ; a treasurer of
a private priest ; a private priest of a Levite ; a Levite of
an Israelite ; an Israelite of a bastard ; a bastard of a Nethinim ; a Nethinim of a proselyte ; a proselyte of a freed
slave. But when is this to be? namely, when they are alike
as to other things : but, indeed, if a bastard be a disciple, or
a wise man, and the high priest be unlearned, the bastard is
to take place of him. A wise man is to be preferred before[x]
a king : for if a wise man die, he hath not left his equal ; but
if a king die, any Israelite is fit for a kingdom."

This last brings to my mind those words of Ignatius the
martyr, if indeed they are his, in his tenth epistle, Τίμα, φησὶν,
υἱὲ, τὸν Θεὸν, &c. : " *My son, saith he, honour God* and the
king : but I say, ' Honour God as the cause and Lord of all :
the bishop as the chief priest, bearing the image of God ; in
respect of his rule bearing God's image, in respect of his
priestly office, Christ's ; and, after him, we ought to honour
the king also.' "

II. Under a pretence of mighty devotion, but especially
under the goodly show of long prayers, they so drew over

the minds of devout persons to them, especially of women,
and among them of the richer widows, that by subtle at-
tractives they either drew out or wrested away their goods
and estates. Nor did they want nets of counterfeit authority, when from the chair they pronounced, according to
their pleasures, of the dowry and estate befalling a widow,
and assumed to themselves the power of determining concerning those things. Of which matter, as it is perplexed with
infinite difficulties and quirks, you may read, if you have
leisure, the treatises *Jevamoth, Chetuboth,* and *Gittin.*

Concerning the length of their prayers, it may suffice to
produce the words of the Babylon Gemara in *Beracoth* y :
" The religious anciently used to tarry an hour [*meditating
before they began their prayers*] : whence was this ? R. Joshua
Ben Levi saith, ' It was because the Scripture saith, אַשְׁרֵי
יוֹשְׁבֵי בֵיתֶךָ *Blessed are they who sit in thy house.*' R. Joshua
Ben Levi saith also, ' He that prays ought to tarry an hour
after prayers: as it is said, The just shall praise thy name,
יֵשְׁבוּ יְשָׁרִים אֶת־פָּנֶיךָ *the upright shall sit before thy face :*' it
is necessary, therefore, that he should stay [*meditating*] an
hour before prayers, and an hour after ; and the religious
anciently used to stay an hour before prayers, an hour they
prayed, and an hour they stayed after prayers. Since, therefore, they spent nine hours every day about their prayers,
how did they perform the rest of the law ? and how did they
take care of their worldly affairs ? Why herein, in being religious, both the law was performed, and their own business
well provided for." And in the same place z, " Long prayers
make a long life."

Ver. 15 : Ποιῆσαι ἕνα προσήλυτον· *To make one proselyte.*]
The Talmudists truly speak very ill of proselytes : "Our a Rabbins teach, גרים והמשהקים בתינוקות מעכבין את המשיח
that *proselytes and Sodomites hinder the coming of the Messias.*
גרים לישראל כספחת *Proselytes are as a scab to Israel.*
The Gloss ; " For this reason, that they were not skilled
in the commandments, that they brought in revenge, and
moreover, that the Israelites perchance may imitate their
works," &c.

Yet in making of these they used their utmost endeavours for the sake of their own gain, that they might some way or other drain their purses, after they had drawn them in under the show [b] of religion, or make some use or benefit to themselves by them. The same covetousness, therefore, under a veil of hypocrisy, in devouring widows' houses, which our Saviour had condemned in the former clause, he here also condemns in hunting after *proselytes ;* which the scribes and Pharisees were at all kind of pains to bring over to them. Not that they cared for *proselytes,* whom they accounted as " a scab and plague ;" but that the more they could draw over to their religion, the greater draught they should have for gain, and the more purses to fish in. These, therefore, being so proselyted, " they made doubly more the children of hell than themselves." For when they had drawn them into their' net, having got their prey, they were no further concerned what became of them, so they got some benefit by them. They might perish in ignorance, superstition, atheism, and all kind of wickedness : this was no matter of concern to the scribes and Pharisees ; only let them remain in Judaism, that they might lord it over their consciences and purses.

Ver. 16 : ῞Ος δ᾽ ἂν ὀμόσῃ ἐν τῷ χρυσῷ τοῦ ναοῦ, ὀφείλει, &c.: *Whosoever shall swear by the gold of the Temple, he is a debtor.*] These words agree in the same sense with those of the *Corban,* chap. xv. 5. We must not understand the *gold of the Temple* here, of that gold which shined all about in the walls and ceilings ; but the gold here meant is that which was offered up in the *Corban.* It was a common thing with them, and esteemed as nothing, to swear הַמֵּעוֹן הַזֶּה *by the Temple,* and הַמִּזְבֵּחַ *by the altar,* which we have observed at the 31st verse of the fifth chapter : and therefore they thought themselves not much obliged by it; but if they swore קָרְבָּן *Corban,* they supposed they were bound by an indispensable tie. For example : if any one should swear thus, ' By the Temple, or, By the altar, my money, my cattle, my goods [c] shall not profit you ;' it was lawful, nevertheless, for the swearer, if he pleased, to suffer them to be profited by

---

[b] *Leusden's edition,* vol. ii. p. 359.
[c] *English folio edition,* vol. ii. p. 235.

these : but if he should swear thus, ' *Corban*, my gold is for the Temple, *Corban*, my cattle are for the altar,' this could noways be dispensed with.

Ver. 23 : 'Αποδεκατοῦτε τὸ ἡδύοσμον, &c.: *Ye pay tithe of mint*.] I. " This is the general rule about tithes ; whatsoever serves for food, whatsoever is kept [*that is, which is not of common right*], and whatsoever grows out of the earth, shall be tithed [d]."

II. According to the law, cattle, corn, and fruit were to be tithed : the way and measure of which, as the scribes teach, was this : " Of bread-corn that is thrashed and winnowed, 1. A fifth part is taken out for the priest ; this was called תרומה גדולה *the great offering*. 2. A tenth part of the remainder belonged to the Levite ; this was called מעשר ראשון *the first tenth*, or *tithe*. 3. A tenth part again was to be taken out of the remainder, and was to be eaten at Jerusalem, or else redeemed ; this was called מעשר שני *the second tithe*. 4. The Levite gives a tenth part out of his to the priest ; this was called מעשר המעשר *the tithe of the tithe*." These are handled at large in *Peah, Demai, Maaseroth*, &c.

III. מעשר ירק דרבנן *The tithing of herbs is from the Rabbins* [e]. This tithing was added by the scribes, and yet approved of by our Saviour, when he saith, " Ye ought not to have left these undone." Hear this, O thou who opposest tithes. The tithing of herbs was only of ecclesiastical institution, and yet it hath the authority of our Saviour to confirm it, " Ye ought not to have left these things undone :" and that partly on account of the justice of the thing itself, and the agreeableness of it to law and reason, partly that it was commanded by the council sitting in Moses's chair, as it is, ver. 2.

IV. Τὸ ἡδύοσμον, *mint* : this is sometimes called by the Talmudists [f] הדנדנה ; and is reckoned among those things which come under the law of the seventh year. Where Rambam saith, " In the Aruch it is מינטא *minta*." It is called sometimes מינתא *mintha* : where R. Solomon writes, " In the Aruch it is מינטא *minta* in the mother tongue,

---

[d] Maaseroth, cap. 1. hal. 1.
[e] Bab. Joma, fol. 83. 2.

[f] Sheviith, cap. 1. hal. 1.
[g] Oketsim, cap. 1. hal. 2.

and it hath a sweet smell; therefore they strew it in synagogues for the sake of its scent."

Tὸ ἄνηθον, *anise :* in the Talmudists שבת[h], where R. Solomon, " שבת is a kind of herb, and is tithed, both as to the
seed and herb itself." Rambam writes thus : " It is eaten
raw after meat, and is not to be boiled ; while, therefore, it
is not boiled, it comes under the law of tithing." The Gloss[i]
שבת " in the Roman language is *anethum* [anise], and is
tithed, whether it be gathered green or ripe."

Tὸ κύμινον, *cummin ;* with the Talmudists כמון. It is
reckoned among things that are to be tithed[k].

Ver. 27 : Παρομοιάζετε τάφοις κεκονιαμένοις· *Ye are like
whited sepulchres.*] *Sepulchres* are distinguished by the masters of the Jews into קבר תהום *a deep sepulchre*, which
cannot be known to be a sepulchre ; μνημεῖον ἄδηλον, *graves
that appear not*[l]*;* and קבר מצוין *a painted sepulchre*, such as
were all those that were known, and to be seen. Our Saviour
compares the Scribes and Pharisees to both ; to those, in the
place of Luke last mentioned ; to these, in the place before
us, each upon a different reason.

Concerning the *whiting* of *sepulchres*, there are these traditions[m] : " In the fifteenth day of the month Adar they
mend the ways, and the streets, and the common sewers,
and perform those things that concern the public, ומצייינין
את הקברות *and they paint* (or *mark*) *the sepulchres.*" The
manner is described in *Maasar Sheni*[n] ; מצייינין קברו בסיד
ממחה ושופך *They paint the sepulchres with chalk, tempered
and infused in water.* The Jerusalem Gemarists give the
reason[o] of it in abundance of places : " Do they not mark
the sepulchres (say they) before the month Adar ? Yes, but
it is supposed that the colours are wiped off. For what
cause do they paint them so ? That this matter may be like
the case of the leper. The leprous man crieth out, ' Unclean,
unclean ;' and here, in like manner, uncleanness cries out to
you and saith, ' Come not near.' " R. Illa, in the name of

[h] Oketsim, cap. 3. hal. 4.
[i] Bab. Avodah Zarah, fol. 7. 2.
[k] Demai, cap. 2. hal. 1.
[l] Luke xi. 44.
[m] Shekalim, cap. 1. hal. 1.
[n] Cap. 1. hal. 1.
[o] *Leusden's edition*, vol. ii. p. 360.

R. Samuel Bar Nachman, allegeth that of Ezekiel[n]; " If one
passing through the land seeth a man's bone, he shall set up
a burial sign by it[o]."

The Glossers deliver both the reason and the manner of
it thus : " From the fifteenth day of the month Adar they
began their search ; and wheresoever they found a sepulchre
whose whiting was washed off with the rain, they renewed
it, that the unclean place might be discerned, and the priests
who were to eat the *Trumah* might avoid it." Gloss on
Shekalim, and again on *Maasar Sheni :* " They marked the
sepulchres with chalk in the likeness of bones ; and mixing
it with water, they washed the sepulchre all about with it,
that thereby all might know that the place was unclean,
and therefore[p] to be avoided." Concerning this matter also,
the Gloss[q] speaks ; " They made marks like bones on the
sepulchres with white chalk," &c. See the place.

Ver. 28 : Οὕτω καὶ ὑμεῖς ἔξωθεν μὲν φαίνεσθε τοῖς ἀνθρώποις
δίκαιοι, &c. *Even so ye also outwardly appear righteous unto
men.*] Such kind of hypocrites are called צבועין *distained*[r],
or *coloured.* Jannai the king, when he was dying, warned his
wife that she should take heed מן הצבועין שדומין מפרשין
שמעשיהן כמעשה זמרי ומבקשין שכר כפינחס *of painted
men, pretending to be Pharisees, whose works are as the works of
Zimri, and yet they expect the reward of Phineas.* The Gloss
is צבועין " Those *painted* men are those whose outward show
doth not answer to their nature ; they are *coloured* without,
אין תוכן כברם *but their inward part doth not answer to their
outward ;* and their works are evil, like the works of Zimri ;
but they require the reward of Phineas, saying to men, That
they should honour them as much as Phineas." They had
forgotten their own axiom, תח׳ שאין תוכו כברו אין תח׳, *A
disciple of the wise, who is not the same within that he is without,
is not a disciple of the wise*[s].

Ἔσωθεν δὲ μεστοί ἐστε ὑποκρίσεως καὶ ἀνομίας· *But within ye
are full of hypocrisy and iniquity.*] The masters themselves

[n] Ezek. xxxix. 15.
[o] See Jerus. Maasar Sheni, fol.
55. 3. Moed katon, fol. 80. 2, 3.
Sotah, fol. 23, 3.

[p] *English folio edit.*, vol. ii. p. 236.
[q] Bab. Moed katon, fol. 5. 10.
[r] Bab. Sotah, fol. 22. 2.
[s] Bab. Joma, fol. 72. 2.

acknowledge this to their own shame.   They inquire[t], what
were those sins under the first Temple for which it was
destroyed; and it is answered, " Idolatry, fornication, and
bloodshed."   They inquire, what were the sins under the
second; and answer, " Hate without cause, and secret iniquity;" and add these words, " To those that were under the
first Temple their end was revealed, because their iniquity
was revealed: אחרונים שלא נתגלה עונם לא נתגלה קיצם
*but to those that were under the second their end was not re-
vealed, because their iniquity was not revealed.*"   The Gloss,
" They that were under the first Temple did not hide their
iniquity; therefore their end was revealed to them: as it is
said, ' After seventy years I will visit you in Babylon:' but
their iniquity under the second Temple was not revealed:
בני מקדש שני חיו רשעים נסתר: *those under the second
Temple were secretly wicked.*"

    Ver. 29: Κοσμεῖτε τὰ μνημεῖα τῶν δικαίων·   *Ye garnish the
sepulchres of the righteous.*]   בונין לו נפש על קברו[u]   The
Glossers are divided about the rendering of the word נפש.
Some understand it of a kind of building or pillar; some of
the whiting or marking of a sepulchre above spoken of.   The
place referred to speaks concerning the remains of the di-
drachms paid for the redemption of the soul: and the question is, if there be any thing of them due, or remaining from
the man now dead, what shall be done with it; the answer
is, " Let it be laid up till Elias come: but R. Nathan saith,
בונין לו נפש על קברו   *Let them raise some pillar* [or *building*] *upon his sepulchre.*"   Which that it was done for the
sake of adorning the sepulchres is proved from the words
of the Jerusalem Gemara[x] upon the place; אין עושין נפשות
לצדיקים דבריהן הן זכרונן   Οὐ κοσμοῦσι μνημεῖα τῶν δικαίων,
*They do not adorn the sepulchres of the righteous, for their own
sayings are their memorial.*   Whence those buildings or orna-
ments that were set on their sepulchres seem to have been
sacred to their memory, and thence called נפשות, as much
as *souls,* because they preserved the life and soul of their
memory.
    These things being considered, the sense of the words

---

[t] Bab. Joma, fol. 9. 2.   [u] Shekalim, cap. 2. hal. 5.
                    [x] Fol. 47. 1.

before us doth more clearly appear. Doth it deserve so
severe a curse, to adorn the sepulchres of the prophets and
righteous men? Was not this rather an act of piety than a
crime? But according to their own doctrine, O ye scribes and
Pharisees, דבריהן הן זכרונן *their own* acts and sayings are
a sufficient *memorial for them.* Why do ye not respect,
follow, and imitate these? But neglecting and trampling
upon these, you persuade yourselves that you have performed
piety enough to them, if you bestow some cost in adorning
their sepulchres, whose words indeed you despise.

Ver. 33[y]: 'Απὸ τῆς κρίσεως τῆς γεέννης· *The damnation of
hell.*] דינת של גהינום: *The judgment of Gehenna.* See the
Chaldee paraphrast[z] on Ruth ii. 12; Baal Turim on Gen. i. 1;
and Midras Tillin[a].

Ver. 34: Σοφοὺς καὶ γραμματεῖς· *Wise men and scribes.*]
חכמים *wise men,* and סופרים *scribes.* Let them observe
this, who do not allow the ministers of the word to have a
distinct calling. The Jews knew not any that was called
חכם *a wise man,* or סופר *a scribe,* but who was both learned,
and separated from the common people by a distinct order
and office.

Ver. 35: ῞Εως τοῦ αἵματος Ζαχαρίου υἱοῦ Βαραχίου· *Unto
the blood of Zacharias son of Barachias.*] That the discourse
here is concerning Zacharias the son of Jehoiada[b], killed by
king Joash, we make appear by these arguments:

I. Because no other Zacharias is said to have been slain
before these words were spoken by Christ. Those things
that are spoke of Zacharias, the father of the Baptist, are
dreams; and those of Zacharias, one of the twelve prophets,
are not much better. The killing of our Zacharias in the
Temple is related in express words: and why, neglecting
this, should we seek for another, which in truth we shall
nowhere find in any author of good credit?

II. The Jews observe, that the death of this Zacharias,
the son of Jehoiada, was made memorable by a signal character [*nota*] and revenge: of the martyrdom of the other
Zacharias they say nothing at all.

[y] *English folio edit.,* vol. ii. p. 237.   [a] Fol. 41. 2, 3, &c.
[z] *Leusden's edition,* vol. ii. p. 361.   [b] 2 Chron. xxiv.

'Hear both the Talmuds[c] : " R. Jochanan said, Eighty thousand priests were killed for the blood of Zacharias. R. Judah asked R. Acha, ' Whereabouts they killed Zacharias, whether in the Court of the Women, or in the Court of Israel ?' He answered, ' Neither in the Court of Israel nor in the Court of the Women, but in the Court of the Priests.' And that was not done to his blood which useth to be done to the blood of a ram or a kid. Concerning these it is written, ' And he shall pour out his blood, and cover it with dust.' But here it is written, ' Her[d] blood is in the midst of her ; she set it upon the top of a rock, she poured it not upon the ground.' And why this? ' That[e] it might cause fury to come up to take vengeance. I have set her blood upon a rock, that it should not be covered.' They committed seven wickednesses in that day. They killed a priest, a prophet, and a judge : they shed the blood of an innocent man : they polluted the court : and that day was the sabbath day, and the day of Expiation. When therefore Nebuzar-adan went up thither, he saw the blood bubbling : so he said to them, ' What meaneth this ?' ' It is the blood,' say they, ' of calves, lambs, and rams, which we have offered on the altar.' ' Bring then,' said he, ' calves, lambs, and rams, that 1 may try whether this be their blood.' They brought them and slew them, and that blood still bubbled, but their blood did not bubble. ' Discover the matter to me,' said he, ' or I will tear your flesh with iron rakes.' Then they said to him, ' This was a priest, a prophet, and a judge, who foretold to Israel all these evils which we have suffered from you, and we rose up against him, and slew him.' ' But I,' saith he, ' will appease him.' He brought the Rabbins, and slew them upon that blood ; and yet it was not pacified : he brought the children out of the school, and slew them upon it, and yet it was not quiet : he brought the young priests, and slew them upon it, and yet it was not quiet. So that he slew upon it ninety-four thousand, and yet it was not quiet. He drew near to it himself, and said, ' O Zacharias, Zacharias ! thou hast destroyed the best of thy people ' [that is, they have been killed for your

---

[c] Hieros. in Taanith, fol. 69. 1, 2. Bab. in Sanhedr. fol. 96. 2.
[d] Ezek. xxiv. 7.   [e] Ver. 8.

sake]; 'would you have me destroy all?' Then it was quiet, and did not bubble any more," &c.

The truth of this story we leave to the relators: that which makes to our present purpose we observe: that it was very improbable, nay, next to impossible, that those that heard the words of Christ (concerning Zacharias slain before the Temple and the altar) could understand it of any other but of this, concerning whom and whose blood they had such famous and signal memory; and of any other Zacharias slain in the Temple there was a profound silence. In Josephus, indeed, we meet with the mention of one Zacharias, the son of Baruch, (which is the same thing with Barachias,) killed in the Temple, not long[f] before the destruction of it: whom some conjecture to be prophetically marked out here by our Saviour: but this is somewhat hard, when Christ expressly speaks of time past, ἐφονεύσατε, *ye slew;* and when, by no art nor arguments, it can be proved that this Zacharias ought to be reckoned into the number of prophets and martyrs.

There are two things here that stick with interpreters, so that they cannot so freely subscribe to our Zacharias: 1. That he lived and died long before the first Temple was destroyed; when the example would have seemed more home and proper to be taken under the second Temple, and that now near expiring. 2. That *he* was plainly and notoriously the son of *Jehoiada;* but *this* is called by Christ "the son of *Barachias.*"

To which we, after others who have discoursed at large upon this matter, return only thus much:

I. That Christ plainly intended to bring examples out of the Old Testament; and he brought two, which how much the further off they seemed to be from deriving any guilt to this generation, so much heavier the guilt is if they do derive it. For a Jew would argue, "What hath a Jew to do with *the blood of Abel,* killed almost two thousand years before Abraham the father of the Jews was born? And what hath this generation to do with *the blood of Zacharias,* which was expiated by cruel plagues[g] and calamities many ages since?" Nay, saith Christ, *this generation* hath arrived to that degree

---

[f] *English folio edit.,* vol. ii. p. 238.   [g] *Leusden's edit.,* vol. ii. p. 362.

of impiety, wickedness, and guilt, that even these remote examples of guilt relate, and are to be applied to it: and while you think that *the blood of Abel*, and the following martyrs doth nothing concern you, and believe that *the blood of Zacharias* hath been long ago expiated with a signal punishment; I say unto you, that the blood both of the one and the other, and of all the righteous men killed in the interval of time between them, *shall be required of this generation*; 1. Because you kill him who is of more value than they all. 2. Because by your wickedness you so much kindle the anger of God, that he is driven to cut off his old church; namely, the people that hath been of a long time in covenant with him. For when Christ saith, *That on you may come all the righteous blood*, &c.; it is not so much to be understood of their personal guilt as to that blood, as of their guilt for the killing of Christ, in whose death, the guilt of the murder of all those his types and members is in some measure included: and it is to be understood of the horrible destruction of that generation, than which no former ages have ever seen any more woful or amazing, nor shall any future, before the funeral of the world itself. As if all the guilt of the blood of righteous men, that had been shed from the beginning of the world, had flowed together upon that generation.

II. To the second, which has more difficulty, namely, that *Zacharias* is here called the son of *Barachias*, when he was the son of *Jehoiada*, we will observe, by the way, these two things out of the writings of the Jews, before we come to determine the thing itself:

1. That that very *Zacharias* of whom we speak is by the Chaldee paraphrast called the son of *Iddo*. For thus saith he on Lament. iii. 20: " 'Is it fit that the daughters of Israel should eat the fruit of their womb?' &c. The rule of justice answered and said, ' Is it also fit that they should slay a priest and prophet in the Temple of the Lord, as ye slew *Zacharias* the son of *Iddo*, the high priest and faithful prophet, in the house of the Sanctuary, on the day of Expiation?' " &c.

2. In the place of Isaiah[h], concerning Zechariah the son

[h] Chap. viii. 2.

of Jeberechiah, the Jews have these things[i] : " It is written, 'I took unto me faithful witnesses to record, Uriah the priest, and Zechariah the son of Barachiah,' [ברכיהו writ without Jod prefixed,] Isa. viii. 1. But what is the reason that Uriah is joined with Zechariah? for Uriah was under the first Temple; Zechariah under the second: but the Scripture joineth the prophecy of Zechariah to the prophecy of Uriah. By Urias it is written, 'For your sakes Sion shall be ploughed as a field.'   By Zechariah it is written, 'As yet old men and ancient women shall sit in the streets of Jerusalem.'   When the prophecy of Uriah is fulfilled, the prophecy of Zechariah shall also be fulfilled."   To the same sense also speaks the Chaldee paraphrast upon the place : " 'And I took unto me faithful witnesses.'   The curses which I foretold I would bring, in the prophecy of Uriah the priest, behold they are come to pass: likewise all the blessings which I foretold I would bring, in the prophecy of Zechariah the son of Jeberechiah, I will bring to pass."   See also there RR. Jarchi and Kimchi.

From both these we observe two things : 1. If *Iddo* did not signify the same thing with *Jehoiada* to the Jewish nation, why might not our Saviour have the same liberty to call *Barachias* the father of *Zacharias*, as the Chaldee paraphrast had to call him *Iddo?* 2. It is plain that the Jews looked upon those words of Isaiah as the words of God speaking to Isaiah, not of Isaiah relating a matter of fact historically ; which, indeed, they conjecture very truly and exactly according to the printing of the first word וְאָעִידָה for the conjunction *Vau*, being pointed with *Sheva*, it is a certain token that the verb is to be rendered[k] in the future tense, not in the preter ; which also the Interlineary Version hath well observed, rendering it thus, *Et testificari faciam mihi testes fideles, And I will make faithful witnesses testify to me.*

For if it had been to be construed in the preter tense, it should have been pointed by Kamets, וְאָעִידָ *Et testificari feci, And I caused to witness.* Which being well observed, (as I confess it hath not been by me heretofore,) the difficulty under our hand is resolved, as I imagine, very clearly : and I suppose that Zechariah the son of Jeberechiah in Isaiah is the very same with our *Zacharias* the son of Jehoiada ; and that the sense of Isaiah comes to this : in that and the foregoing chapter[1] there is a discourse of the future destruction of Damascus, Samaria, and Judea. For a confirmation of the truth of this prophecy, God makes use of a double testimony : first, he commands the prophet Isaiah to write, over and over again, in a great volume, from the beginning to the end, " Le maher shalal hash baz :" that is, " To hasten the spoil, he hastened the prey :" and this volume should be an undoubted testimony to them, that God would certainly bring on and hasten the forementioned spoiling and destruction. " And moreover (saith God), I will raise up to myself two faithful martyrs," (or witnesses,) who shall testify and seal the same thing with their words and with their blood, namely, Uriah the priest, who shall hereafter be crowned with martyrdom for this very thing, Jer. xxvi. 20, 23, and Zechariah the son of Barachiah, or Jehoiada, who is lately already crowned : *he*, the first martyr under the first Temple ; *this*, the last. Hear, thou Jew, who taxest Matthew in this place : your own authors assert, that Uriah the priest is to be understood by that Uriah who was killed by Jehoiakim ; and that truly. We also assert, that Zechariah the son of Jehoiadah is to be understood by Zechariah the son of Jeberechiah ; and that Matthew and Christ do not at all innovate in this name of Barachias, but did only pronounce the same things concerning the father of the martyr Zacharias, which God himself had pronounced before[m] them by the prophet Isaiah.

Objection. But since our Saviour took examples from the Old Testament, why did he not rather say, " from the blood of Abel to the blood of Uriah the priest ?" that is, from the beginning of the world to the end of the first Temple ? I answer,

1. The killing of Zechariah was more horrible, as he was more high in dignity ; and as the place wherein he was killed was more holy.

---

[1] See chap. vii. 8. 17, 18, &c. viii. 4. 7, 8, &c.
[m] *Leusden's edition*, vol. ii. p. 363.

2. The consent of the whole people was more universal to his death.

3. He was a more proper and apparent type of Christ.

4. The requiring of vengeance is mentioned only concerning Abel and Zechariah : " Behold[n], the voice of thy brother's blood crieth unto me." And, " Let[o] the Lord look upon it, and require it."

5. In this the death of Christ agrees exactly with the death of Zechariah ; that, although the city and nation of the Jews did not perish till about forty years after the death of Christ, yet they gave themselves their death's wound in wounding Christ. So it was also in the case of Zechariah : Jerusalem and the people of the Jews stood indeed many years after the death of Zechariah, but from that time began to sink, and draw towards ruin. Consult the story narrowly, and you will plainly find, that all the affairs of the Jews began to decline and grow worse and worse, from that time when " blood touched blood[p]," (the blood of the sacrificer mingled with the blood of the sacrifice), and when " the people became contentious and rebellious against the priest[q]."

Ver. 37 : Ἰερουσαλήμ, ἡ ἀποκτείνουσα τοὺς προφήτας· *Jerusalem, that killest the prophets.*] R. Solomon on those words, " But[r] now murderers ;" " They have killed (saith he) Uriah, they have killed Zechariah." Also on these words, " Your[s] sword hath devoured your prophets ;" " Ye have slain (saith he) Zechariah and Isaiah." " Simeon[t] Ben Azzai said, ' I have found a book of genealogies at Jerusalem, in which it was written, Manasseh slew Isaiah,' " &c.

CHAP. XXIV.[u]

Ver. 1 : Ἐπιδεῖξαι αὐτῷ τὰς οἰκοδομὰς τοῦ ἱεροῦ· *To shew him the buildings of the Temple.*] " He[x] that never saw the Temple of Herod never saw a fine building. What was it built of ? Rabba saith, Of white and green marble. But some say, Of white, green, and spotted marble. He made the laver to sink

---

[n] Gen. iv. 10.
[o] 2 Chron. xxiv. 22.
[p] Hos. iv. 2.   [q] Id. ver. 4.
[r] Is. i. 21.
[s] Jer. ii. 31.

[t] Bab. Jevam. fol. 49. 2.
[u] *English folio edition,* vol. ii. p. 240.
[x] Bab. Bava Bathra, fol. 4. 1. Succah, fol. 51. 2.

and to rise" (that is, the walls were built winding in and out, or indented after the manner of waves), " being thus fitted to receive the plaster, which he intended to lay on ; but the Rabbins said to him, ' O let it continue, for it is very beautiful to behold : for it is like the waves of the sea :' and Bava Ben Buta made it so," &c. See there the story of Bava Ben Buta and Herod consulting about the rebuilding of the Temple.

Ver. 2 : Οὐ μὴ ἀφεθῇ ὧδε λίθος ἐπὶ λίθον· *There shall not be left one stone upon another.*] The Talmudic Chronicles[y] bear witness also to this saying, " On the ninth day of the month Ab the city of Jerusalem was ploughed up ;" which Maimonides[z] delivereth more at large : " On that ninth day of the month Ab, fatal for vengeance, the wicked Turnus Rufus, of the children of Edom, ploughed up the Temple, and the places about it, that that saying might be fulfilled, ' Sion shall be ploughed as a field.' " This Turnus Rufus, of great fame and infamy among the Jewish writers, without doubt is the same with Terentius Rufus, of whom Josephus speaks[a], Τερέντιος Ῥοῦφος ἄρχων τῆς στρατιᾶς κατελέλειπτο, *Terentius Rufus was left general of the army by Titus ;* with commission, as it is probable, and as the Jews suppose, to destroy the city and Temple. Concerning which matter, thus again Josephus in the place before quoted[b], Κελεύει Καῖσαρ ἤδη τήν τε πόλιν ἅπασαν καὶ τὸν νεὼν κατασκάπτειν· *The emperor commanded them to dig up the whole city and the Temple.* And a little after, Οὕτως ἐξωμάλισαν οἱ κατασκάπτοντες, &c. " *Thus those that digged it up laid all level,* that it should never be inhabited, to be a witness to such as should come thither."

Ver. 3 : Καὶ τί τὸ σημεῖον τῆς σῆς παρουσίας, καὶ τῆς συντελείας τοῦ αἰῶνος; *And what shall be the sign of thy coming, and of the end of the world?*] What the apostles intended by these words is more clearly conceived by considering the opinion of that people concerning the times of the Messias. We will pick out this in a few words from Babylonian *Sanhedrin.*[c]

" The tradition of the school of Elias : The righteous, whom

y Taanith, c. 5.
z Taanith, cap. 4. hal. 6.
a De Bell. lib. vii. cap. 7. [Hud-
son, p. 1298.] [vii. 2. 2.]
b Cap. 1. [vii. 1. 1.]
c Fol. 92.

the Holy Blessed God will raise up from the dead, shall not
return again to their dust; as it is said, ' Whosoever shall be
left in Zion and remain in Jerusalem shall be called holy,
every one being written in the book of life.' As the Holy
(God) liveth for ever, so they also shall live for ever. But if
it be objected, What shall the righteous do in those years in
which the Holy God will renew his world, as it is said, ' The
Lord only shall be exalted in that day ?' the answer is, That
God will give them wings like an eagle, and they shall swim
(or float) upon the face of the waters." Where the Gloss
says thus; " The righteous, whom the Lord shall raise from
the dead in the days of the Messiah, when they are restored
to life, shall not again return to their dust, neither in the
days of the Messiah, nor in the following age : but their flesh
shall remain upon them till they return and live לעתיד לבוא
to eternity. And[d] in those years, when God shall renew his
world (or age), ויהיה עולם זה חרב אלף שנים, *this world
shall be wasted for a thousand years;* where, then, shall those
righteous men be in those years, when they shall not be
buried in the earth?" To this you may also lay that very
common phrase, עולם הבא *the world to come;* whereby is
signified *the days of the Messiah :* of which we spoke a little at
the thirty-second verse of the twelfth chapter : " If[e] he shall
obtain (*the favour*) to see the world to come, that is, the exal-
tation of Israel," namely, in the days of the Messiah. " The[f]
Holy Blessed God saith to Israel, In this world you are afraid
of transgressions ; but in the world to come, when there shall
be no evil affection[g], you shall be concerned only for the good
which is laid up for you; as it is said[h], ' After this the
children of Israel shall return, and seek the Lord their God,
and David their king,' " &c.; which clearly relate to the times
of the Messiah. Again, " Saith[i] the Holy Blessed God to
Israel, ' In this world, because my messengers (*sent to spy out
the land*) were flesh and blood, I decreed that they should not
enter into the land : but in the world to come, I suddenly

---

[d] *Leusden's edition*, vol. ii. p.
364.
[e] Gloss. in Bab. Berac. fol.
9. 2.
[f] Tanchum, fol. 9. 2.

[g] *English folio edition*, vol. ii. p.
241.
[h] Hos. iii. 5.
[i] Tanchum, fol. 77. 3.

send to you my messenger, and he shall prepare the way before my face[k].' "

See here the doctrine of the Jews concerning the coming of the Messiah :

1. That at that time there shall be a resurrection of the just : מָשִׁיחַ עָתִיד לְיוֹנִין יְשֵׁינֵי עָפָר׃ *The Messias shall raise up those that sleep in the dust*[l].

2. Then shall follow the desolation of this world : עוֹלָם זֶה חָרֵב אֶלֶף שָׁנִים *This world shall be wasted a thousand years*. Not that they imagined that a chaos, or confusion of all things, should last the thousand years; but that this world should end and a new one be introduced in that thousand years.

3. After which עָתִיד לָבוֹא *eternity should succeed*.

From hence we easily understand the meaning of this question of the disciples :—

1. They know and own the present Messiah; and yet they ask, what shall be the signs of his coming?

2. But they do not ask the signs of his coming (as we believe of it) at the last day, to judge both the quick and the dead : but,

3. When he will come in the evidence and demonstration of the Messiah, raising up the dead, and ending this world, and introducing a new; as they had been taught in their schools concerning his coming.

Ver. 7 : Ἐγερθήσεται γὰρ ἔθνος ἐπὶ ἔθνος· *Nation shall rise against nation*.] Besides the seditions of the Jews, made horridly bloody with their mutual slaughter, and other storms of war in the Roman empire from strangers, the commotions of Otho and Vitellius are particularly memorable, and those of Vitellius and Vespasian, whereby not only the whole empire was shaken, and " totius orbis mutatione fortuna imperii transiit" (they are the words of Tacitus), *the fortune of the empire changed with the change of the whole world*, but Rome itself being made the scene of battle, and the prey of the soldiers, and the Capitol itself being reduced to ashes. Such throes the empire suffered, now bringing forth Vespasian to the throne, the scourge and vengeance of God upon the Jews.

[k] Mal. iii. 1.   [l] Midr. Tillin, fol. 42. 1.

Ver. 9 : Τότε παραδώσουσιν ὑμᾶς εἰς θλίψιν· *Then shall they*
deliver you up to be afflicted.] To this relate those words of
Peter, 1 Ep. iv. 17, " The time is come that judgment must
begin at the house of God ;" that is, the time foretold by our
Saviour is now at hand, in which we are to be delivered up to
persecution, &c.   These words denote that persecution which
the Jews, now near their ruin, stirred up almost everywhere
against the professors of the gospel.   They had indeed op-
pressed them hitherto on all sides, as far as they could, with
slanders, rapines, whippings, stripes, &c. which these and
such like places testify; 1 Thess. ii. 14, 15; Heb. x. 33, &c.
But there was something that put a rub in their way, that,
as yet, they could not proceed to the utmost cruelty ; " And[m]
now ye know what withholdeth ;" which, I suppose, is to be
understood of Claudius enraged at and curbing in the
Jews[n].   Who being taken out of the way, and Nero, after
his first five years, suffering all things to be turned topsy
turvy, the Jews now breathing their last (and Satan therefore breathing his last effects in them, because their time was
short), they broke out into slaughter beyond measure, and
into a most bloody persecution : which I wonder is not set
in the front of the ten persecutions by ecclesiastical writers.
This is called by Peter[o] (who himself also at last suffered in
it) πύρωσις πρὸς πειρασμὸν, *a fiery trial;* by Christ[p], dic-
tating the epistles to the seven churches, θλίψις ἡμερῶν δέκα,
tribulation for ten days; and ἡ ὥρα τοῦ πειρασμοῦ ἡ μέλλουσα ἔρχε-
σθαι ἐπὶ τῆς οἰκουμένης ὅλης, *the*[q] *hour of temptation, which shall*
come upon all the world of Christians.   And this is " the revelation of that wicked one" St. Paul[r] speaks of, now in lively,
that is, in bloody colours, openly declaring himself Antichrist,
the enemy of Christ.   In that persecution James suffered at
Jerusalem, Peter in Babylon, and Antipas at Pergamus, and
others, as it is probable, in not a few other places.   Hence,
Rev. vi. 11, 12 (where the state of the Jewish nation is delivered under the type of six seals[s]), they are slain, who were
to be slain[t] for the testimony of the gospel under the fifth

[m] 2 Thess. ii. 6.   [r] 2 Thess. ii. 8.
[n] Acts xviii. 2.   [s] *Leusden's edition,* p. 365.
[o] 1 Pet. iv. 12.   [p] Rev. ii. 10.   [t] *English folio edit.,* vol. ii. p. 242.
[q] Rev. iii. 10.

seal; and immediately under the sixth followed the ruin of
the nation.

Ver. 12 : Ψυγήσεται ἡ ἀγάπη τῶν πολλῶν· *The love of many
shall wax cold.*] These words relate to that horrid apostasy
which prevailed everywhere in the Jewish churches that had
received the gospel. See 2 Thess. ii. 3, &c. ; Gal. iii. 1 ;
1 Tim. i. 15, &c.

Ver. 14 : Καὶ κηρυχθήσεται τοῦτο τὸ εὐαγγέλιον τῆς βασιλείας ἐν ὅλῃ τῇ οἰκουμένῃ· *And this gospel of the kingdom shall
be preached in all the world.*] Jerusalem was not to be destroyed before the gospel was spread over all the world :
God so ordering and designing it that the world, being first
a catechumen in the doctrine of Christ, might have at length
an eminent and undeniable testimony of Christ presented to
it ; when all men, as many as ever heard the history of
Christ, should understand that dreadful wrath and severe
vengeance which was poured out upon that city and nation
by which he was crucified.

Ver. 15 : Τὸ βδέλυγμα τῆς ἐρημώσεως· *The abomination of
desolation.*] These words relate to that passage of Daniel
(chap. ix. 27), וְעַל כְּנַף שִׁקּוּצִים מְשׁוֹמֵם which I would render
thus ; " In the middle of that week," namely, the last of the
seventy, " he shall cause the sacrifice and oblation to cease,
even until *the wing* or *army of abomination shall make desolate,*" &c.; or, *even by the wing of abominations making desolate.*
כָּנָף is an *army*, Isa. viii. 8 : and in that sense Luke [u] rendered these words, " when you shall see Jerusalem compassed
about with an army," &c.

Ὁ ἀναγινώσκων νοείτω· *Let him that readeth understand.*]
This is not spoken so much for the obscurity as for the cer-
tainty of the prophecy : as if he should say, " He that reads
those words in Daniel, let him mind well that when the army
of the prince which is to come, that army of abominations,
shall compass round Jerusalem with a siege, then most
certain destruction hangs over it ; for, saith Daniel, ' the
people of the prince that shall come shall destroy the city,
and the sanctuary,' &c., ver. 26. And the army of abominations shall make desolate even until the consummation, and

[u] Chap. xxi. 20.

that which is determined shall be poured out upon the desolate.' Flatter not yourselves, therefore, with vain hopes,
either of future victory, or of the retreating of that army,
but provide for yourselves; and he that is in Judea, let him
fly to the hills and places of most difficult access, not into the
city." See how Luke clearly speaks out this sense in the
twentieth verse of the one-and-twentieth chapter.

Ver. 20: ῞Ινα μὴ γένηται ἡ φυγὴ ὑμῶν χειμῶνος· *That your
flight be not in the winter.*] R. Tanchum observes a favour of
God in the destruction of the first Temple, that it happened
in the summer, not in winter. For thus he [x] : " God vouchsafed a great favour to Israel; for they ought to have gone
out of the land on the tenth day of the month Tebeth, as he
saith, ' Son of man, mark this day; for on this very day,' &c.
What then did the Lord, holy and blessed? ' If they shall now
go out in the winter,' saith he, ' they will all die :' therefore
he prolonged the time to them, and carried them away in
summer."

Ver. 22 [y] : Κολοβωθήσονται αἱ ἡμέραι ἐκεῖναι· *Those days
shall be shortened.*] God lengthened the time for the sake of
the elect, before the destruction of the city; and in the destruction, for their sakes he shortened it. Compare with
these words before us 2 Pet. iii. 9, " The Lord is not slack
concerning his promise," &c. It was certainly very hard
with the elect that were inhabitants of the city, who underwent all kinds of misery with the besieged, where the plague
and sword raged so violently that there were not living
enough to bury the dead; and the famine was so great, that
a mother ate her son (perhaps the wife of Doeg Ben Joseph,
of whom see such a story in Babyl. Joma [z]). And it was
also hard enough with those elect who fled to the mountains,
being driven out of house, living in the open air, and wanting
necessaries for food: their merciful God and Father, therefore, took care of them, shortening the time of their misery,
and cutting off the reprobates with a speedier destruction;
lest, if their stroke had been longer continued, the elect
should too far have partaken of their misery.

---

[x] Fol. 57. 2.   [y] *English folio edition*, vol. ii. p. 243.   [z] Fol. 38. 2.

The Rabbins dream that God shortened the day on which wicked king Ahab died, and that ten hours; lest he should have been honoured with mourning [a].

Ver. 24: Δώσουσι σημεῖα μεγάλα καὶ τέρατα· *Shall shew great signs and wonders.*] It is a disputable case, whether the Jewish nation were more mad with superstition in matters of religion, or with superstition in curious arts.

I. There was not a people upon earth that studied or attributed more to dreams than they. Hence

1. They often imposed fastings upon themselves to this end, that they might obtain happy dreams; or to get the interpretation of a dream; or to divert the ill omen of a dream: which we have observed at the fourteenth verse of the ninth chapter.

2. Hence their nice rules for handling of dreams [b]; such as these, and the like: יצפה אדם לחלום טוב עד כב׳ שנה *Let one observe a good dream two-and-twenty years*, after the example of Joseph [c]: " If you go to bed merry, you shall have good dreams [d]," &c.

3. Hence many took upon them the public profession of interpreting dreams; and this was reckoned among the nobler arts. A certain old man (Babyl. Beracoth [e]) relates this story; " There were four-and-twenty interpreters of dreams in Jerusalem : and I, having dreamed a dream, went to them all: every one gave a different interpretation, and yet they all came to pass," &c. You have [f] R. Joses Ben Chelpatha, R. Ismael Ben R. Joses, R. Lazar, and R. Akiba interpreting divers dreams, and many coming to them for interpretation of their dreams. Nay, you see there the disciples of R. Lazar in his absence practising this art. See there also many stories about this business, which it would be too much here to transcribe.

II. There were hardly any people in the whole world that more used, or were more fond of, amulets, charms, mutterings, exorcisms, and all kinds of enchantments. We might here produce innumerable examples; a handful shall serve us out of the harvest: ולא בקמיע מזמן שאינו מן המומחה

---

[a] See R. Sol. on Isa. xxxviii.

[b] *Leusden's edit.*, vol. ii. p. 366.

[c] Beracoth, fol. 14. 1.

[d] Schab. fol. 30. 2, in the Gloss.

[e] Fol. 55. 2.

[f] Jerusal. Maasar Sheni, fol. 52. 2. 3.

" Let[g] not any one go abroad with his amulet on the sabbath day, unless that amulet be prescribed by an approved physician" (or, " unless it be an approved amulet;" see the Gemara). Now thesé amulets were either little roots hung about the necks of sick persons, or, what was more common, bits of paper with words written on them (כתב של קמיע or קמיע של עקרין) whereby they supposed that diseases were either driven away or cured : which they wore all the week, but were forbid to wear on the sabbath, unless with a caution : " They[h] do not say a charm over a wound on the sabbath, that also which is said over a mandrake is forbid" on the sabbath. " If any one say, Come and say this versicle over my son, or lay the book" of the law " upon him, to make him sleep ; it is forbid :" that is, on the sabbath, but on other days is usual.

אומרים היו שיר פגועין בירושלם : " *They used to say the psalm of meetings* (that is, *against unlucky meetings*) *at Jerusalem.* R. Judah saith, Sometimes after such a meeting, and sometimes when no such meeting had happened. But what is the Psalm of Meetings ? The third psalm, ' Lord, how are my foes increased !' even all the psalm : and the ninety-first psalm, ' He that dwelleth in the secret place of the Most High,' to the ninth verse." There is a discourse[i] of many things, which they used to carry about with them, as remedies against certain ailments ; and of mutterings over wounds : and there you may see, that while they avoid[k] the enchantments of the Amorites, they have and allow their own. You have, *Bab. Joma*, fol. 84. 1, the form of an enchantment against a mad dog. And, *Avodah Zarah*, fol. 12. 2, the form of enchantment against the devil of blindness. You have, *Hieros. Schab.* fol. 13. 4, and *Avod. Zarah*, fol. 40. 4, mutterings and enchantments, even in the name of Jesus. See also the *Babyl. Sanhedr.* fol. 101. 1, concerning these kind of mutterings.

III. So skilful were they in conjurings, enchantments, and sorceries, that they wrought σημεῖα μεγάλα, *great signs*, many villanies, and more wonders. We pass by those things which

---

g Schabb. cap. 6. hal. 6.
h Jerus. ibid. fol. 8. 2.

i Ibid. col. 3.
k *English folio edit.*, vol. ii. p. 244.

the sacred story relates of Simon Magus, Elymas, the sons of Sceva, &c., and Josephus, of others; we will only produce examples out of the Talmud, a few out of many.

You will wonder, in the entrance, at these two things, in order to the speaking of their magical exploits; and thence you will conjecture at the very common practice of these evil arts among that people: 1. That " the senior who is chosen into the council ought to be skilled in the arts of astrologers, jugglers, diviners, sorcerers, &c., that he may be able to judge of those who are guilty of the same[1]. 2. The Masters tell us, that a certain chamber was built by a magician in the Temple itself: " The[m] chamber of Happarva was built by a certain magician, whose name was Parvah, by art-magic." " Four-and-twenty[n] of the school Rabbi, intercalating the year at Lydda, were killed by an evil eye :" that is, with sorceries. R. Joshua[o] outdoes a magician in magic, and drowns him in the sea. In Babyl. Taanith[p], several miracles are related that the Rabbins had wrought. Elsewhere[q], there is a story told of eighty women-sorceresses at Ascalon, who were hanged in one day by Simeon Ben Shetah: " and the women of Israel (saith the Gloss) had generally fallen to the practice of sorceries :" as we have mentioned before. It is related of abundance of Rabbies, that they were מלומדים בנסים *skilful in working miracles:* thus Abba Chelchia, and Chanin[r], and R. Chanina Ben Dusa[s]; of which R. Chanina Ben Dusa there is almost an infinite number of stories concerning the miracles he wrought, which savour enough and too much of magic[t].

And, that we may not be tedious in producing examples, what can we say of the fasting Rabbies causing it to rain in effect when they pleased? of which there are abundance of stories in Taanith. What can we say of the Bath Kol very frequently applauding the Rabbins out of heaven? of which we have spoken before. What can we say of the death or

[1] Maimon. Sanhedr. cap. 2.
[m] Gloss. on Middoth, cap. 5. hal. 3.
[n] Hieros. Sanhedr. fol. 18. 3.
[o] Ibid. fol. 25. 4.
[p] Fol. 24.

[q] Hieros. Sanhedr. fol. 23.3. Bab. Sanhedr. fol. 44. 2.
[r] Juchas. fol. 20. 1.
[s] Id. fol. 56. 2.
[t] See Bab. Berac. fol. 33. et 34.

plagues foretold by the Rabbins to befall this or that man? which came to pass just according as they were foretold. I rather suspect some magic art in most of these, than fiction in all.

IV. False Christs broke out, and appeared in public with their witchcrafts, so much the frequenter and more impudent, as the city and people drew nearer to its ruin; because the people believed the Messias should be manifested before the destruction of the city; and each of them pretended to be the Messias by these signs. From the words of Isaiah[u], "Before her pain came, she was delivered of a man child," the doctors concluded, "that the Messias should be manifested before the destruction of the city." Thus the Chaldee paraphrast upon the place; "She shall be saved before her utmost extremity, and her king shall be revealed before her pains of childbirth." Mark that also; "The[x] Son of David will not come, till the wicked empire [*of the Romans*] shall have spread itself over all the world nine months; as it is said[y], ' Therefore will he give them up, until the time that she which travaileth hath brought forth.' "

Ver. 27 : ῞Ωσπερ γὰρ ἡ ἀστραπὴ, &c. *For as the lightning, &c.*] To discover clearly the sense of this and the following clauses, those two things must be observed which we have formerly given notice of :—

1. That the destruction of Jerusalem is very frequently expressed in Scripture as if it were the destruction of the whole world, Deut. xxxii. 22; "A fire is kindled in mine anger, and shall burn unto the lowest hell" (the discourse there is about the wrath of God consuming that people; see ver. 20, 21), "and shall consume the earth with her increase, and set on fire the foundations of the mountains." Jer. iv. 23; "I beheld the earth, and lo, it was without form and void; and the heavens, and they had no light," &c. The discourse there also is concerning the destruction of that nation, Isa. lxv. 17; "Behold, I create new heavens and a new earth: and the former shall not be remembered," &c. And more passages of this sort among the prophets. According to this sense,

---

[u] Chap. lxvi. 7.   [x] Bab. Joma, fol. 10. 1.   [y] Micah v. 3.

Christ speaks in this place; and Peter speaks in his Second
Epistle, third chapter; and John, in the sixth of the Revelation; and Paul, 2 Cor. v. 17, &c.

2. That Christ's taking vengeance of that exceeding wicked
nation is called Christ's "coming in glory," and his "coming
in the clouds," Dan. vii.   It is also called, "the day of the
Lord."   See Psalm i. 4; Mal. iii. 1, 2, &c.; Joel ii. 31; Matt.
xvi. 28; Rev. i. 7, &c.   See what we have said on chap. xii.
20; xix. 28.

The[z] meaning, therefore, of the words before us is this:
"While they shall falsely say, that Christ is to be seen here
or there: 'Behold, he is in the desert,' one shall say; another,
'Behold, he is in the secret chambers:' he himself shall come,
like lightning, with sudden and altogether unexpected vengeance: they shall meet him whom they could not find; they
shall find him whom they sought, but quite another than what
they looked for.

Ver. 28: Ὅπου γὰρ ἐὰν ᾖ τὸ πτῶμα, &c. *For wheresoever the
carcase is, &c.*]   I wonder any can understand these words of
pious men flying to Christ, when the discourse here is of quite
a different thing: they are thus connected to the foregoing:
Christ shall be revealed with a sudden vengeance; for when
God shall cast off the city and people, grown ripe for destruction, like a carcase thrown out, the Roman soldiers, like
eagles, shall straight fly to it with their eagles (ensigns) to
tear and devour it.   And to this also agrees the answer of
Christ, Luke xvii. 37; when, after the same words that are
spoke here in this chapter, it was inquired, "Where, Lord?"
he answered, "Wheresoever the body is," &c.; silently hinting
thus much, that Jerusalem, and that wicked nation which he
described through the whole chapter, would be the carcase,
to which the greedy and devouring eagles would fly to prey
upon it.

Ver. 29: Ὁ ἥλιος σκοτισθήσεται, &c. *The sun shall be darkened, &c.*]   That is, the Jewish heaven shall perish, and the
sun and moon of its glory and happiness shall be darkened,
and brought to nothing.   The *sun* is the religion of the church;
the *moon* is the government of the state; and the *stars* are the

judges and doctors of both. Compare Isa. xiii. 10, and Ezek. xxxii. 7, 8, &c.

Ver. 30: Καὶ τότε φανήσεται τὸ σημεῖον τοῦ υἱοῦ τοῦ ἀνθρώπου· *And then shall appear the sign of the Son of man.*] Then shall *the Son of man* give a proof of himself, whom they would not before acknowledge : a proof, indeed, not in any visible figure, but in vengeance and judgment so visible, that all the tribes of the earth shall be forced to acknowledge him the avenger. The Jews would not know him : now they shall know him, whether they will or no, Isa. xxvi. 11. Many times they asked of him a *sign :* now a *sign* shall appear, that he is the true Messias, whom they despised, derided, and crucified, namely, his signal vengeance and fury, such as never any nation felt from the first foundations of the world.

Ver. 31: Καὶ[a] ἀποστελεῖ τοὺς ἀγγέλους αὐτοῦ, &c. *And he shall send his angels, &c.*] When Jerusalem shall be reduced to ashes, and that wicked nation cut off and rejected, then shall the Son of man send his ministers with the trumpet of the gospel, and they shall gather together his elect of the several nations from the four corners of heaven : so that God shall not want a church, although that ancient people of his be rejected and cast off : but, that Jewish church being destroyed, a new church shall be called out of the Gentiles.

Ver. 34: Οὐ μὴ παρέλθῃ ἡ γενεὰ αὕτη, &c. *This generation shall not pass, &c.*] Hence it appears plain enough, that the foregoing verses are not to be understood of the last judgment, but, as we said, of the destruction of Jerusalem. There were some among the disciples (particularly John), who lived to see these things come to pass. With Matt. xvi. 28, compare John xxi. 22. And there were some Rabbins alive at the time when Christ spoke these things, that lived till the city was destroyed, viz.[b] Rabban Simeon, who perished with the city, R. Jochanan Ben Zaccai, who outlived it, R. Zadoch, R. Ismael, and others.

Ver. 36: Οὐδεὶς οἶδεν, οὐδὲ οἱ ἄγγελοι· *No man knoweth, no, not the angels.*] This is taken from Deut. xxxii. 34 : " Is not

[a] *Leusden's edition,* vol. ii. p. 368.
[b] *English folio edition,* vol. ii. p. 368.

this laid up in store with me, and sealed up among my
treasures ?"

Ver. 37 : "Ὥσπερ δὲ αἱ ἡμέραι τοῦ Νῶε, &c. *But as the days
of Noe were, &c.*] Thus Peter placeth as parallels, the ruin
of the old world, and the ruin of Jerusalem, 1 Pet. iii. 19—21;
and by such a comparison his words will be best understood.
For, see how he skips from the mention of the death of
Christ to the times before the flood, in the eighteenth and
nineteenth verses, passing over all the time between. Did
not the Spirit of Christ preach all along in the times
under the law ? Why then doth he take an example only
from the times before the flood ? that he might fit the
matter to his case, and shew that the present state of the
Jews was like theirs in the times of Noah, and that their
ruin should be like also. So, also, in his Second Epistle,
chap. iii. ver. 6, 7.

דור המבול אין להם חלק לע״ הבא *The*[c] *age* or *generation of the flood hath no portion in the world to come :* thus Peter
saith, that "they were shut up in prison :" and here our Saviour intimates that "they were buried in security," and so
were surprised by the flood.

CHAP. XXV.

Ver. 1 : Δέκα παρθένοις· *Ten virgins.*] The nation of the
Jews delighted mightily in the number *ten*, both in sacred
and civil matters : אין עירה פחותה מעשרה *A synagogue
consisted not but of ten at the least :* which we have observed
before, when we spoke about synagogues. This also was
current among them, אין שורה פחותה מעשרה *An order
or ring of men consisted not but of ten at the least*[d]. The text
is speaking of a company to comfort mourners : which the
Gloss thus describes, "When the company was returned from
burying a dead body, היו עושין שורות סביב האבל *they set
themselves in order about the mourners,* and comforted them :
but now such an order or ring consisted of ten at the least."
To this commonly received number there seems to be an
alluding in this place : not but that they very frequently ex-

---

c Sanhedr. cap. 10. hal. 2.   d Gloss. in Bab. Berac. fol. 16. 2.

ceeded that number of virgins in weddings of greater note, but rarely came short of it.

Εἰς ἀπάντησιν τοῦ νυμφίου· *To meet the bridegroom.*] To go to a wedding was reckoned among the works of mercy.

גמילות חסדים "The[e] *shewing of mercy* implies two things: 1. That one should assist an Israelite with one's wealth, namely, by alms and redeeming of captives. 2. That one should assist him in one's own person; to wit, by comforting the mourners, by attending the dead to burial, ולבא לחופת חתנים *and by being present at the chambers of bridegrooms.*" The presence of virgins also adorned the pomp and festivity of the thing. Marriages are called by the Rabbins נישואין *receivings*, &c. הכנסת כלה *the introducing of the bride*, namely, into the house of her husband. There were no marriages but of such as had been before betrothed; and, after the betrothing, the bridegroom might not lie with the bride in his father-in-law's house before he had brought her to his own. That 'bringing' of her was the consummation of the marriage. This parable supposeth that the bride was thus fetched to the house of her husband, and that the virgins were ready against her[f] coming; who yet, being either fetched a great way, or some accident happening to delay her, did not come till midnight.

Λαβοῦσαι τὰς λαμπάδας· *Took lamps.*] The form of *lamps* is described by Rambam and R. Solomon[g], whom see. These things are also mentioned by R. Solomon: "It is the fashion in the country of the Ismaelites to carry the bride from the house[h] of her father to the house of the bridegroom before she is put to bed; and to carry before her about ten wooden staves, having each of them on the top a vessel like a dish, in which there is a piece of cloth with oil and pitch: these, being lighted, they carry before her for torches." The same things saith the Aruch in לפד.

Ver. 2: Πέντε φρόνιμοι· *Five wise*; πέντε μωραί· *Five foolish.*] A parable, not unlike this, is produced by Kimchi[i]: "Rabban Jochanan Ben Zaccai saith (as he hath it), This thing is like a king, who invited his servants, but did not

---

[e] Rambam on Peah, fol. 1. 1.
[f] *English folio edition*, vol. ii. p. 247.
[g] In Kelim, cap. 2. hal. 8.
[h] *Leusden's edit.*, vol. ii. p. 369.
[i] On Isa. lxv. 13, 14.

appoint them any set time. פקחים שבהם *Those of them that were wise* adorned themselves, and sat at the gate of the palace; טפשים שבהם *those that were foolish* were about their own business. The king on a sudden called for his servants: those went in adorned; these, undressed. The king was pleased with the wise, and angry at the foolish."

Ver. 5: Ἐνύσταξαν πᾶσαι καὶ ἐκάθευδον· *They all slumbered and slept.*] : נתנמנמו ונרדמו or נתנמנמו וישנו in Talmudic language[k]: "If some sleep" [while they celebrate the paschal supper], "let them eat; if all, let them not eat. R. Josi saith, נתנמנמו יאכלו *Do they slumber? let them eat.* נרדמו לא יאכלו *Do they sleep? let them not eat.*" The Gemarists inquire, היכי דמי מתנמנם "*Whence a man is to be reputed as a slumberer?* R. Ishi saith, He sleeps and doth not sleep, he wakes and is not awake. If you call him, he answers; לא ידע לאהדורי סברא *but he cannot answer to the purpose.*" The Gloss, "If you speak to him, he will answer הין או לא *yes, or no;* but if you ask any thing that hath need of thinking; as, for instance, where such a vessel is laid up? he cannot answer you."

Ver. 15: Καὶ ᾧ μὲν ἔδωκε πέντε τάλαντα, &c. *And unto one he gave five talents, &c.*] You have a like and almost the same parable, Luke xix.; yet, indeed, not the very same; for, besides that there is mention there of *pounds* being given, here of *talents,*—*that* parable was spoken by Christ, going up from Jericho to Jerusalem, before the raising up of Lazarus; *this,* as he was sitting on Mount Olivet, three days before the Passover. *That,* upon this account, "because he was nigh to Jerusalem, and because they thought that the kingdom of God should immediately appear," Luke xix. 11, and that he might shew that it would not be long before Jerusalem should be called to an account for all the privileges and benefits conferred upon it by God (see verses the fourteenth and seventeenth); but *this,* that he might warn all to be watchful, and provide with their utmost care concerning giving up their accounts at the last judgment.

Ver. 27: Ἔδει οὖν σε βαλεῖν τὸ ἀργύριόν μου τοῖς τραπεζίταις, &c. *Thou oughtest therefore to have put my money to the exchangers,*

&c.] The lord did not deliver the talents to his servants with
that intent, that they should receive the increase and profit
of them by usury; but that, by merchandise and some honest
way of trade, they should increase them. He only returns
this answer to the slothful servant, as fitted to what he had
alleged; "You take me for a covetous, griping, and sordid
man: why then did you not make use of a manner of gain
agreeable to these qualities, namely, interest or usury (since
you would not apply yourself to any honest traffic), that you
might have returned me some increase of my money, rather
than nothing at all?" So that our Lord, in these words, doth
not so much approve of usury, as upbraid the folly and sloth
of his servant.

Τραπεζίταις[1], *exchangers,* answering to the word שולחני very
usual among the Talmudists: שולחני הוא מכר מטבעות
" *An exchanger*[m] *(trapezita) sells money;* and because *a table*
is always before him, upon which he buys and sells, therefore
he is called *mensarius,*" *one that stands at a table.*

Of the same employment was חנוני *the shopkeeper,* of
whom is as frequent mention among them. He exercised
the employment of a usurer in buying and changing of fruits,
as the other in money: for in these two especially consisted
usury: of which you may see, if you please, the tract *Bava
Mezia*[n].

CHAP. XXVI.

§ *Of the present Authority of the Council, and
of its Place.*

VER. 3: Συνήχθησαν εἰς τὴν αὐλὴν ἀρχιερέως· *Assembled together unto the palace of the high priest.*] Those ominous pro-
digies are very memorable, which are related by the Talmudists to have happened forty years before the destruction of
the Temple.

" A tradition[o]. Forty years before the Temple was destroyed, the western candle" (that is, the middlemost in the
holy candlestick) " was put out. And the crimson tongue"
(that was fastened to the horns of the scapegoat, or the

---

[1] *English folio edit.,* vol. ii. p. 248.   [m] Aruch.   [n] Cap. 5.
[o] Jerus. Joma, fol. 43. 3.

doors of the Temple) "kept its redness. And the lot of the Lord" (for the goat that was to be offered up on the day of Expiation) "came out on the left hand. And the gates of the Temple, which were shut over night, were found open in the morning. Rabban Jochanan Ben Zaccai said, 'Therefore, O Temple, wherefore dost thou trouble us? we know thy fate; namely, that thou art to be destroyed: for it is said, Open, O Lebanon [p], thy gates, that the flame may consume thy cedars.'" "A tradition [q]. Forty years before the Temple was destroyed, judgment in capital causes was taken away from Israel." "Forty [r] years before the Temple was destroyed, the council removed and sat in the sheds."

With these two last traditions lies our present business. What the Jews said, John xviii. 31, Ἡμῖν οὐκ ἔξεστιν ἀποκτεῖναι οὐδένα· *It is not lawful for us to put any man to death,* signifies the same thing with the tradition before us, "Judgments in capital causes are taken away from Israel." When were they first taken away? "Forty years before the destruction of the Temple," say the Talmudists: no doubt before the death of Christ; the words of the Jews imply so much. But how were they taken away? It is generally received by all that the Romans did so far divest the council of its authority, that it was not allowed by them to punish any with death; and this is gathered from those words of the Jews, "It is not lawful for us to put any man to death."

But if this, indeed, be true, 1. What do then those words of our Saviour mean [s], παραδώσουσιν ὑμᾶς εἰς συνέδρια, *they will deliver you up to the councils?* 2. How did they put Stephen to death? 3. Why was Paul so much afraid to commit himself to the council, that he chose rather to appeal to Cæsar?

The Talmudists excellently well clear the matter: "What signifieth that tradition (say they) of the removal of the council forty years before the ruin of the Temple? Rabh Isaac Bar Abdimi saith, 'It signifieth thus much, that they did not judge of fines.'" And a little after; "But R. Nachman Bar Isaac saith, 'Do not say that it did not judge of

[p] *Leusden's edition*, vol. ii. p. 370.
[q] Idem, Sanhed. fol. 24. 2.
[r] Bab. Avodah Zarah, fol. 8. 2.
[s] Chap. x. 17.

fines, but that it did not judge in capital causes.' And the
reason was this, כיון דחזו דנפישי להו רוצחין ולא יכלי
למידן *because they saw murderers so much increase that they
could not judge them.* They said therefore, ' It is fit that we
should remove from place to place, that so we may avoid the
guilt.'" That is, the number and boldness of thieves and
murderers growing so great that, by reason thereof, the authority of the council grew weak, and neither could nor dared
put them to death. " It is better (say they) for us to remove from hence, out of this chamber Gazith, where, by the
quality of the place, we are obliged to judge them, than that, by
by sitting still here, and not judging them, we should render
ourselves guilty." Hence it is that neither in the highest
nor in the inferior councils any one was punished with death.
(" For they did not judge of capital matters in the inferior
councils in any city, but only when the great council sat in
the chamber Gazith," saith the Gloss.) The authority of
them was not taken away by the Romans, but rather relin-
quished by themselves. The slothfulness of the council destroyed its own authority. Hear it justly [t] upbraided in this
matter [u] : " The council which puts but one to death in seven
years is called Destructive. R. Lazar Ben Azariah said,
' Which puts one to death in seventy years.' R. Tarphon
and R. Akiba said, ' If we had been in the council' (when it
judged of capital matters), ' there had none ever been put to
death by it.' R. Simeon Ben Gamaliel said, ' These men
have increased the number of murderers in Israel.'" Most
certainly true, O Simeon! for by this means the power of
the council came to be weakened in capital matters, because
they, either by mere slothfulness, or by a foolish tenderness,
or, as indeed the truth was, by a most fond estimation of an
Israelite as an Israelite, they so far neglected to punish bloodshed and murder, and other crimes, till wickedness grew so
untractable that the authority of the council trembled for
fear of it, and dared not kill the killers. In this sense their
saying must be understood, *It is not lawful for us to put any
man to death:* their authority of judging not being taken
from them by the Romans, but lost by themselves, and despised by their people.

[t] *English folio edit.*, vol. ii. p. 249.   [u] Maccoth, cap. 1. hal. 17.

Notwithstanding it was not so lost, but that sometimes
they exercised it; namely, when they observed they might
do it safely and without danger. " Dat veniam corvis," &c.
spares crows, but vexeth pigeons. Thieves, murderers, and
wicked men armed with force, they dared not call into their
judgment; they were afraid of so desperate a crew : but to
judge, condemn, torture, and put to death poor men and
Christians, from whom they feared no such danger, they
dreaded it not, they did not avoid it. They had been ready
enough at condemning our Saviour himself to death if they
had not feared the people, and if Providence had not otherwise determined of his death.

We may also, by the way, add that also which follows
after the place above cited, בימי שמעון בן יוחי ניטלו דיני
ממונות מישראל *In*[x] *the day of Simeon Ben Jochai, judgments
of pecuniary matters were taken away from Israel.* In[y] the
same tract this is said to have been in " the days of Simeon
Ben Shetah," long before Christ was born : but this is an
error of the transcribers.

But now, if the Jewish council lost their power of judging
in pecuniary causes by the same means as they lost it in capital, it must needs be that deceits, oppressions, and mutual
injuries were grown so common and daring that they were let
alone, as being above all punishment. The Babylonian Gemarists allege another reason ; but whether it be only in
favour of their nation, this is no fit place to examine[z].

That we may yet further confirm our opinion, that the
authority of that council in capital matters was not taken
away by the Romans, we will produce[a] two stories, as clear
examples of the thing we assert : one is this[b] ; " R. Lazar
son of R. Zadok said, ' When I was a little boy, sitting on
my father's shoulders, I saw a priest's daughter that had
played the harlot compassed round with fagots and burnt.'"
The council no doubt judging and condemning her, and this
after Judea had then groaned many years under the Roman
yoke; for that same R. Lazar saw the destruction of the city.

The other you have in the same tract[c], where they are

---

[x] Hieros. Sanhedr. fol. 24. 1.
[y] Fol. 18. 1.
[z] See Avodah Zarah as before.

[b] Hieros. Sanhedr. fol. 24. 2.
[a] *Leusden's edition*, vol. ii. p. 371.
[c] Fol. 25. 4.

speaking of the manner of pumping out [*expiscandi*] evidence
against a heretic and seducer of the people : " They place
(say they) two witnesses in ambush, in the inner part of the
house, and him in the outward, with a candle burning by him
that they may see and hear him.   Thus they dealt with Ben
Satda in Lydda.   They placed two disciples of the wise in
ambush for him, and they brought him before the council,
and stoned him."   The Jews openly profess that this was
done to him in the days of R. Akiba, long after the destruction of the city ; and yet then, as you see, the council still
retained its authority in judging of capital causes.   They
might do it for all the Romans, if they dared do it to the
criminals.

But so much thus far concerning its authority : let us now
speak of its present seat.   " The[d] council removed from the
chamber Gazith to the sheds, from the sheds into Jerusalem,
from Jerusalem to Jafne, from Jafne to Osha, from Osha to Shepharaama, from Shepharaama to Bethshaarim, from Bethshaarim to Tsippor, from Tsippor to Tiberias," &c.   We conjecture
that the great bench was driven from its seat, the chamber
Gazith, half a year, or thereabout, before the death of Christ ;
but whether they sat then in the sheds [a place in the Court
of the Gentiles] or in the city, when they debated about the
death of Christ, does not clearly appear, since no authors
make mention how long it sat either here or there.   Those
things that are mentioned in chap. xxvii. 4—6, seem to argue
that they sat in the Temple ; these before us, that they sat
in the city.   Perhaps in both places ; for it was not unusual
with them to return thither, as occasion served, from whence
they came ; only to the chamber Gazith they never went
back.   Whence the Gloss upon the place lately cited, " They
sat in Jafne in the days of Rabban Jochanan ; in Osha, in
the days of Rabban Gamaliel ; for they returned from Osha
to Jafne," &c.   Thus the council, which was removed from
Jerusalem to Jafne before the destruction of the city, returned thither at the feast, and sat as before.   Hence Paul
is brought before the council at Jerusalem when Jafne at that
time was its proper seat.   And hence Rabban Simeon, presi-

_d Bab. Rosh hashanah, fol. 31. 1.

dent of the council, was taken and killed in the siege of the city; and Rabban Jochanan his[e] vice-president was very near it, both of them being drawn from Jafne to the city, with the rest of the bench, for observation of the Passover.

Whether the hall of the high priest were the ordinary receptacle for the council, or only in the present occasion, we do not here inquire. It is more material to inquire concerning the bench itself, and who sat president in judging. The president of the council at this time was Rabban Gamaliel, (Paul's master,) and the vice-president, Rabban Simeon his son, or Rabban Jochanan Ben Zaccai (which we do not dispute now). Whence therefore had the chief priest, here and in other places, the precedence and the chief voice in judging? For thus in Stephen's case the high priest is the chief of the inquisition, Acts vii. 1 ; also in Paul's case, Acts xxiii. 2, see also Acts ix. 1. Had the priests a council and judgment seat of their own? or might they in the chief council, when the president was absent, hear causes of life and death? To this long question, and that enough perplexed, we reply these few things:

I. We confess, indeed, that the priests had a bench and council of their own, yet denying that there was a double council, one for ecclesiastical, the other for civil affairs, as some would have it.

We meet often with mention of the *chamber of the counsellors,* לשכת בולווטי, next the court, which is also called לשכת פרהדרין : concerning which thus the Babyl. *Joma*[f]; "The tradition of R. Juda. What, was it the chamber of פרהדרין ? Was it not the chamber בולווטי βουλευτῶν, *of the counsellors ?* At first it was called the chamber of the *counsellors,* βουλευτῶν, לשכת בולווטי : but when the high priesthood came to be bought with money, and changed yearly, כפרהדרין *as the king's presidents,* πρόεδροι, are changed every year, from that time forward it was called the chamber of the *presidents,* προέδρων."

Hear the Glosser on this place : " The high priests were wicked, and did not fulfil their whole year ; and he that succeeded the other changed this building and adorned it, that it might be called by his own name." Hear also the Ge-

mara; " The first Temple stood four hundred and ten years,
and there were not above eighteen priests under it.   The
second stood four hundred and twenty years, and there were
more than three hundred under it.   Take out forty years of
Simeon the Just, eighty of Jochanan, ten of Ismael Ben
Phabi, and eleven of Eleazar Ben Harsum, and there doth
not remain one whole year to each of the rest."

Behold the chamber of the βουλευτῶν, *counsellors*, properly
so called, because the priests did meet and sit there not to
judge, but to consult; and that only of things belonging to
the Temple! Here they consulted, and took care that all
persons and things belonging and necessary to the worship
of God should be in readiness; that the buildings of the
Temple and the courts should be kept in repair; and that
the public Liturgy should be duly performed: but in the
meantime they wanted all power of judging[g] and punishing;
they had no authority to fine, scourge, or put to death, yea,
and in a word, to exercise any judgment; for by their own
examination and authority they could not admit a candi-
date into the priesthood, but he was admitted by the authority of the council: " In[h] the chamber Gazith sat the council
of Israel, and held the examinations of priests: whosoever
was not found fit was sent away in black clothes, and a black
veil; whosoever was found fit was clothed in white, and had
a white veil, and entered and ministered with his brethren the
priests."

2. We meet also with mention of בֵּית דִּין שֶׁל כֹּהֲנִים *the
council house of the priests.*   שֶׁעָשׂוּ הַכֹּהֲנִים גְּדוֹלִים קָבַע
" The[i] *high priests made a decree*, and did not permit an
Israelite to carry the scapegoat into the wilderness." But
in the Gloss, לֹא הָיוּ בד" שֶׁל כֹּהֲנִים מַנִּיחַ *The council of
the priests did not permit this.*   בד" שֶׁל כֹּהֲנִים *"The[k] council
of the priests* exacted for the portion of a virgin four hundred
zuzees, and the wise men did not hinder it."

First, This was that council of which we spoke before in
the chamber of the counsellors.   Secondly, That which was
decreed by them concerning the carrying away of the scape-
goat belonged merely to the service of the Temple, as being

---

g *Leusden's edition*, vol. ii. p. 372.   i Bab. Joma, fol. 66. 1. in Gemara.
h Bab. Joma, fol. 19. 1.   k Chetub. chap. 1. hal. 5.

a caution about the right performance of the office in the day
of atonement. Thirdly, and that about the portion of a virgin
was nothing else but what any Israelite might do: and so the
Gemarists confess ; " If any noble family in Israel (say they)
would do what the priests do, they may." The priests set a
price upon their virgins, and decreed by common consent,
that not less than such a portion should be required for them;
which was lawful for all the Israelites to do for their virgins
if they pleased.

3. There[1] is an example brought of "Tobias a physician,
who saw the new moon at Jerusalem, he and his son, and his
servant whom he had freed. The priests admitted him and
his son for witnesses, his servant they rejected : but when
they came before בד *the bench*, they admitted him and his
servant, and rejected his son." Observe, 1. That בית דין
the council is here opposed to the priests. 2. That it belonged
to the council to determine of the new moon, because on
that depended the set times of the feasts: this is plain enough
in the[m] chapter cited. 3. That what the priests did was
matter of examination only, not decree.

4. זְקְנֵי הָעִיר זֶה בַּד שֶׁל שְׁלֹשָׁה *The*[n] *elders of the city*
(Deut. xxii. 18,) *are the triumvirate bench :* הַשַּׁעְרָה זֶה בַּד
שֶׁל כֹּהֵן גָּדוֹל ' *at the gate*' (ver. 24.) *means the bench of the
chief priest.* The matter there in debate is about a married
woman, who is found by her husband to have lost her virginity, and is therefore to be put to death : Deut. xxii. 13, &c.
In that passage, among other things, you may find these
words, ver. 18 ; " And the elders of that city shall lay hold of
that man and scourge him." The Gemarists take occasion
from thence to define what the phrase there and in other
places means, " The elders of the city:" and what is the
meaning of הַשַּׁעְרָה the word *gate*, when it relates to the
bench : " *That* (say they) signifies the triumvirate bench :
this the bench or council of the high priest :" that is, unless I
be very much mistaken, every council of twenty-three ; which
is clear enough both from the place mentioned and from
reason itself :

1. The words of the place quoted are these : " R. Bon Bar

1 Rosh hashanah, cap. 1. hal. 7.   m *English folio edit.*, vol. ii. p. 251.
n Jerus. Chetub. fol. 28. 3.

Chaija inquired before R. Zeira, What if the father [*of the virgin*] should produce witnesses which invalidate the testimony of the husband's witnesses? if the father's witnesses are proved false, he must be whipped, and pay a hundred selaim in the triumvirate court; but the witnesses are to be stoned by the bench of the twenty-three, &c. R. Zeira thought that this was a double judgment: but R. Jeremias, in the name of R. Abhu, that it was but a single one: but the tradition contradicts R. Abhu; for אֶל זִקְנֵי הָעִיר *To the elders of the city*, ver. 5, זֶה בַּד" שֶׁל שְׁלֹשָׁה is, *To the triumvirate-bench.* הַשַּׁעְרָה זֶה בַּד" כֹּהֵן גָּדוֹל but *at the gate*, means *the bench of the high priest.*" It is plain, that *the bench of the high priest* is put in opposition to *the triumvirate bench ;* and, by consequence, that it is either the chief council, or the council of the twenty-three, or some other council of the priests, distinct from all these. But it cannot be this third, because the place cited in the Talmudists, and the place in the law cited by the Talmudists, plainly speak of such a council, which had power of judging in capital causes. But they that suppose the ecclesiastical council among the Jews to have been distinct from the civil, scarce suppose that that council sat on capital causes, or passed sentence of death; much less is it to be thought that that council sat only on life and death; which certainly ought to be supposed from the place quoted, if בַּד" שֶׁל כֹּהֵן גָּדוֹל *the council of the high priest* did strictly signify such a council of priests. Let us illustrate the Talmudical words with a paraphrase: " R. Zeira thought, that that cause of a husband accusing his wife for the loss of her virginity belonged to the judgment of two benches; namely, of the triumvirate, which inflicted whipping and pecuniary mulcts; and of the ' twenty-three,' which adjudged to death; but Rabbi Abhu thinks it is to be referred to the judgment of one bench only. But you are mistaken, good Rabbi Abhu; and the very phrase made use of in this case refutes you; for the expression which is brought in, " To the elders of the city," signifies the triumviral bench; and the phrase[o], " at the gate," signifies the bench of twenty-three ; for the chief council never sat in the gate.

2. Now the council of *twenty-three* is called by the Tal-

---

[o] *Leusden's edition*, vol. ii. p. 373.

mudists *the bench*, or *the council of the chief priest*, alluding
to the words of the lawgiver, Deut. xvii. 9, where the word
priests denotes the inferior councils, and *judge* the chief
council.

II. In the chief council, the president sat in the highest
seat, (being at this time, when Christ was under examination,
Rabban Gamaliel, as we said); but the high priest excelled
him in dignity everywhere: for the president of the council
was chosen not so much for his quality, as for his learning
and skill in traditions. He was מקבל (a phrase very much
used by the author of *Juchasin*, applied to presidents), that
is, *keeper, father*, and *deliverer of traditions;* and he was chosen
to this office, who was fittest for these things. Memorable
is the story of Hillel's coming to the presidentship, being
preferred to the chair for this only thing, because he solved
some doubts about the Passover, having learned it, as he saith
himself, from Shemaiah and Abtalion. We will not think it
much to transcribe the storyP: " The sons of Betira once
forgot a tradition: for when the fourteenth day [on which
the Passover was to be celebrated] fell out on the sabbath,
they could not tell whether the Passover should take place of
the sabbath or no. But they said, There is here a certain
Babylonian, Hillel by name, who was brought up under
Shemaiah and Abtalion; he can resolve us whether the Passover should take place of the sabbath or no. They sent
therefore for him, and said to him, ' Have you ever heard in
your life, [that is, have you received any tradition,] whether,
when the fourteenth day falls on the sabbath, the Passover
should take place of the sabbath or no?' He answered,
' Have we but one Passover that takes place of the sabbath
yearly? or are there not many Passovers that put by the
sabbath yearly? namely, the continual sacrifice.' He proved
this by arguments *a pari*, from the equality of it, from the
less to the greater, &c. But they did not admit of this from
him, till he said, ' May it thus and thus happen to me, if I
did not hear this of Shemaiah and Abtalion.' When they
heard this they immediately submitted, and promoted him to
the presidentship," &c.

It q belonged to the president chiefly to sum up the votes

P Jerus. Pesach. fol. 33. 1.   q *English folio edit.*, vol. ii. p. 252.

of the elders, to determine of a tradition, to preserve it, and
transmit it to posterity ; and, these things excepted, you will
scarce observe any thing peculiar to him in judging which
was not common to all the rest.   Nothing therefore hindered
but that the high priest and the other priests (while he excelled in quality, and they in number) might promote acts
in the council above the rest, and pursue them with the
greatest vigour ; but especially when the business before
them was about the sum of religion, as it was here, and in
the examples alleged of Paul and Stephen.   It was lawful
for them, to whose office it peculiarly belonged to take care
of sacred things, to show more officious diligence in matters
where these were concerned than other men, that they might
provide for their fame among men, and the good of their
places.   The council, indeed, might consist of Israelites
only, without either Levites or priests, in case such could
not be found fit: " Thus [r] it is commanded that in the great
council there should be Levites and priests ; but if such
are not to be found, and the council consists of other Israelites only, it is lawful."   But such a scarcity of priests and
Levites is only supposed, was never found ; they were always
a great part, if not the greatest, of the council.   Rabban
Jochanan Ben Zacchai, the priest, was either now vice-president of the council, or next to him.   Priests were everywhere in such esteem with the people and with the council,
and the dignity and veneration of· the high priest was so
great, that it is no wonder if you find him and them always the chief actors, and the principal part in that great
assembly.

Ver. 6 : Τοῦ δὲ Ἰησοῦ γενομένου ἐν Βηθανίᾳ, &c. *Now when
Jesus was in Bethany, &c.*] That this supper in Bethany was
the same with that mentioned John xiii, I dare venture to
affirm ; however that be taken by very many for the paschal
supper.   Let us examine the matter a little home :

I. This supper was before the Passover ; so was that :
that this was, none need doubt ; no more may they of the
other, if we consider these things :

1. It is said by John in express words, πρὸ τῆς ἑορτῆς τοῦ
Πάσχα, *before the feast of the Passover*, ver. 1.   Πάσχα,

Passover, indeed, not seldom signifies the lamb itself; some-times the very time of eating the lamb; sometimes the sa-crifice of the day following, as John xviii. 28. But ἑορτὴ τοῦ Πάσχα, *the feast of the Passover*, alway signifies the whole seven days' paschal feast, both in the language of the Scrip-ture and of the Talmudists: a Jew would laugh at one that should interpret it otherways.

2. When Christ said to Judas going out, " What thou doest, do quickly," some thought he meant this, " Buy those things that we have need of against the feast," at the twenty-ninth verse. For what *feast*, I pray? for the paschal supper? That, according to the interpreters which we here oppose, was just past. For the remaining part of the *feast* of that solemnity? Alas, how unseasonable! Where were those things, I pray, then to be bought, if this were the very night on which they had just eaten the lamb? The night of a feast day was festival: where were there any such markets to be found then? It was an unusual thing indeed, and unheard of, to rise from the paschal supper to go to market: a market on a festival-night[s] was unusual and unheard of. It would argue some ne-gligence, and a little good husbandry, if those things that were necessary for the feast were not yet provided; but that they must be to run, now late at night, to buy those things they knew not where, they knew not how. It is certainly very harsh, and contrary to reason, to understand these things thus, when, from the first verse, the sense is very plain, *before the feast of the Passover*. The Passover was not yet come, but was near at hand: the disciples, therefore, thought that our Saviour had given order to Judas to provide all those things that were ne-cessary to the paschal solemnity against it came.

3. Observe that also of Luke, chap. xxii. 3, &c.: " Satan entered into Judas, and he went his way, and communed with the chief priests," &c. And after, in the seventh verse, " Then came the day of unleavened bread." Hence I inquire, Is the method of Luke direct or no? If not, let there be some reason given of the transposition; if it be direct, then it is plain that the devil entered into Judas before the Pass-over: but he entered into him at that supper in John xiii. 27; therefore that supper was before the Passover. For,

<hr>

[s] *Leusden's edition*, vol, ii. p. 374.

4. Let them who take that supper in John xiii. for the paschal supper, tell me how this is possible, that Judas after the paschal supper (at which they do not deny that he was present with the rest of the disciples) could make his agreement with the priests, and get his blades[s] together ready to apprehend our Saviour, and assemble all the council, ver. 57. The evangelists say that he made an agreement with the chief priests, Matt. xxvi. 14, καὶ τοῖς στρατηγοῖς, *and with the captains,* Luke xxii. 4, and " with all the council," Mark xiv. 10, 11. But now, which way was it possible that he could bargain with all these in[t] so small a space as there was between the going out of Judas from supper and the betraying of our Lord in the garden? What! were these all together at supper that night? This is a matter to be laughed at rather than credited. Did he visit all these from door to door? And this is as little to be thought, since he had scarce time to discourse with any one of them. Every one supped this night at home, the master of a family with his family. It would be ridiculous to suppose that these chief priests supped together, while, in the mean time, their families sat down at home without their head. It is required by the law that every master of a family should be with his family that night, instructing them, and performing sacred rites with and for them. These were, therefore, to be sought from house to house by Judas, if that were the first time of his treating with them about this matter : and let reason answer whether that little time he had were sufficient for this? We affirm, therefore, with the authority of the evangelists, that that supper, John xiii, was before the Passover; at which, Satan entering into Judas, he bargained with the priests before the Passover, he appointed the time and place of his betraying our Saviour, and all things were by them made ready for this wicked deed before the Passover came. Observe the method and order of the story in the evangelists, Matt. xxvi. 14—17; Mark xiv. 10—12: " Then went Judas to the priests, and said, ' What will ye give me,' &c. And from that time he sought opportunity to betray him. Now, the first day of the feast of unleavened bread, the disciples came

---

[s] [Turbam sicariorum.]   [t] *English folio edition,* vol. ii. p. 253.

came," &c.   When was it that Judas came to the priests to treat about betraying Christ ?   surely before the first day of unleavened bread.   Luke also, whom we quoted before, proceeds in the very same method : " From that time (say they), he sought for an opportunity to betray him."   If then first he went to and agreed with the priests when he rose up from the paschal supper, as many suppose, he did not then seek for an opportunity, but had found one.   The manner of speaking used by the evangelists most plainly intimates some space of deliberation, not sudden execution.

5. Let those words of John be considered, chap. xiv. 31, Ἐγείρεσθε, ἄγωμεν ἐντεῦθεν, *Arise, let us go hence,* and compared with the words, chap. xviii. 1, " When Jesus had spoken these words, he went forth with his disciples over the brook Cedron."   Do not these speak of two plainly different departures ?   Did not Christ rise up and depart when he said, " Arise, let us go hence ?"   Those words are brought in by the evangelist without any end or design, if we are not to understand by them that Christ immediately changed his place : and certainly this change of place is different from that which followed the paschal supper, John xviii. 1.

6. In that thirteenth chapter of John there is not the least mention nor syllable of the paschal supper.   There is, indeed, plain mention of a supper *before the feast of the Passover*, that is, before the festival day ; but of a paschal supper there is not one syllable.   I profess seriously, I cannot wonder enough how interpreters could apply that chapter to the paschal supper, when there is not only no mention at all in it of the paschal supper, but the evangelist hath also pronounced, in most express words, and than which nothing can be more plain, that that supper of which he speaks was not *on* the feast of the Passover, but *before* the feast.

7. If those things which we meet with, John xiii, of the sop given to Judas, &c. were acted in the paschal supper, then how, I pray, was it possible for the disciples to mistake the meaning of those words, "What thou doest, do quickly ?" In the paschal supper he said, " He that dips with me in the dish is he ;" and the hand of Judas, as some think, was at that very moment in the dish.   To Judas asking, " Is it I ?" he plainly answered, " Thou hast said :" and besides, he gave

him a sop for a token, as they say who maintain that opinion:
then with what reason, or with what ignorance[u], after so clear
a discovery of the thing and person, could the disciples imagine that Christ said, " Buy quickly those things that are
necessary, or give something to the poor?"

8. And to what *poor*, I pray? It was unseasonable, truly,
late at night, to go to seek for poor people here and there,
who were now dispersed all about in several *families* (φρατρίαι),
eating the passover: for the poorest Israelite was obliged to
that duty as well as the richest. They who supposed that
Christ commanded him to give something to the poor, could
not but understand it of a thing that was presently to be
done. For it had been ridiculous to conceive, that Christ
sent him so hastily away from supper to give something to
the poor to-morrow. But, if it be granted that the matter
was transacted at Bethany, and that two days before the
Passover, which we assert, then it is neither necessary you
should suppose that supper to have been so late at night; nor
were poor people, then and there, to be far sought for, since
so great a multitude of men followed Christ everywhere.

II. This supper was at Bethany, two days before the Passover: the same we conclude of that supper, John xiii, both as
to the place and time; and that, partly, by the carrying on of
the story to that time, partly, by observing the sequel of that
supper. Six days before the Passover Christ sups at Bethany, John xii. 1.

The next day (five days before the Passover)[x] he came to
Jerusalem riding on an ass, John xii. 12: and in the evening
he returned to Bethany, Matt. xxi. 17; Mark xi. 11.

The day following (four days before the Passover) he went
to Jerusalem, Mark xi. 11, 15, &c; and at evening he returned the same way to Bethany, Mark xi. 19.

The day after (three days before the Passover), he goes
again to Jerusalem, Mark xi. 27. In the evening, he went
out to the mount of Olives, Matt. xxiv. 1, 3; Mark xiii. 1, 3;
Luke xxi. 37. Now where did he sup this night? at Bethany.
For so Matthew and Mark, " After two days was the Passover," &c. " Now when Jesus was in Bethany." And from

---

[u] *Leusden's edition*, vol. ii. p. 375.　　　[x] *English folio edit.* vol. ii. p. 254.

this time forward there is no account either of his supping or
going to Jerusalem till the evening of the Passover.

From that supper both the evangelists begin their story
of Judas's contriving to betray our Lord; Matt. xxvi. 14;
Mark xiv. 10: and very fitly; for at that supper the devil
had entered into him, and hurried him forward to accom-
plish his villany.

We therefore thus draw up the series of the history out
of the holy writers : *Before the feast of the Passover* (John
xiii. 1), namely, *two days* (Matt. xxvi. 2, 6), as Jesus was
supping in Bethany, a woman anoints his head : and some of
the disciples murmur at it.   Our Saviour himself becomes
both her advocate and encomiast.   Before supper was done
Christ riseth from the table, and washeth his disciples' feet;
and, sitting down again, acquaints them with the betrayer.
John asking privately about him, he privately also gives him
a token by a sop, and gives a sop to Judas.   With this the
devil entered into him, and now he grows ripe for his wickedness : "The devil had before put it into his heart to betray
him," ver. 2 ; now he is impatient till he hath done it.   He
riseth up immediately after he had the sop, and goes out.
As he was going out, Jesus said to him, "What thou doest,
do quickly :" which some understood of buying necessaries for
the feast, that was now two days off.   It was natural and
easy for them to suppose, that he, out of his diligence (having
the purse, and the care of providing things that were necessary), was now gone to Jerusalem, though it were night, there
being a great deal to be done, to get all things ready against
the feast.   He goes away; comes to Jerusalem ; and the
next day treats with the priests about betraying our Lord,
and concludes a bargain with them.   They were afraid for
themselves, lest they should be either hindered by the people,
or suffer some violence from them on the feast day.   He frees
them from this fear, provided they would let him have soldiers
and company ready at the time appointed.   Our Saviour
lodges at Bethany that night, and spends the next day and
the night after there too : and, being now ready to take his
leave of his disciples, he teaches, instructs, and comforts them
at large.   Judas, having craftily laid the design of his
treachery, and set his nets in readiness, returns, as is pro-

bable, to Bethany; and is supposed by the disciples, who
were ignorant of the matter, to have performed his office
exceeding diligently, in providing necessaries for the approaching feast. On the day itself of the Passover, Jesus
removes from Bethany with his disciples : "Arise (saith he),
let us go hence," John xiv. 31, and comes to Jerusalem.

Ver. 7 : Κατέχεεν ἐπὶ τὴν κεφαλὴν αὐτοῦ ἀνακειμένου· *Poured
it upon his head, as he sat at meat.*] Therefore, it was not the
same supper with that in John xii. 1 ; for then our Saviour's
feet were anointed, now his *head*. I admire that any one
should be able to confound these two stories. Oil, perfumed
with spices, was very usual in feasts, especially sacred ; and it
was wont to be poured upon the head of some one present.

"They school of Shammai saith, He holds sweet oil in his
right hand, and a cup of wine in his left. He says grace
first over the oil, and then over the wine. The school of
Hillel saith, Oil in his right hand, and wine in his left. He
blesseth the sweet oil, and anoints the head of him that
serves : but if the waiter be a disciple of the wise, he anoints
the wall ; for it is a shamez for a disciple of the wise to smell
of perfumes." Here the waiter anoints the head of him that
sits down.

Ver. 8 : Εἰς τί ἡ ἀπώλεια αὕτη ; *To what purpose is this
waste ?*] It was not without cause that it was called "precious ointment," ver. 7, and "very costly," John xii. 3 : to
shew that it was not of those common sorts of ointments
used in feasts, which they thought it no waste to pour upon
the waiter's head, or to daub upon the wall. But this ointment was of much more value, and thence arose the cavil.

Ver. 9a : Καὶ δοθῆναι τοῖς πτωχοῖς· *And be given to the poor.*]
That it was Judas especially who cavilled at this, we have
reason to believe from what is said of him in another supper,
John xii. 4. Compare this with those words, John xiii. 29.
When Jesus said to Judas, "What thou doest, do quickly,"
some thought he had meant, "Give something to the poor."
That supper, I presume, was the same with this : and see,
how these things agree! When a complaint arose of that pro-
digal waste of the ointment here, and before in John xii, and

y Hieros. Berac. fol. 11. 2.   z *Leusden's edition*, vol. ii. p. 376.
a *English folio edition*, vol. ii. p. 255.

that it seemed unfit to some that that should be spent so unadvisedly upon our Lord which might have been bestowed much better, and more fitly, upon the poor, how easily might the others think that Christ had spoken to him about giving somewhat to the poor, that he might show his care of the poor, notwithstanding what he had before said concerning them, and the waste of the ointment.

Ver. 12 : Πρὸς τὸ ἐνταφιάσαι με ἐποίησεν· *She did it for my burial.*] She had anointed his feet, John xii. 3, out of love, duty, and honour to him; but this (which is added over and above to them) is upon account of his burial; and that not only in the interpretation of Christ, but in the design of the woman. She, and she first, believes that Christ should die; and, under that notion, she pours the ointment upon his head, as if she were now taking care of his body, and anointing it for burial: and it is as if Christ had said to those that took exceptions and complained, " You account her too officious and diligent for her doing this; and wasteful rather than prudent, in the immoderate profession of her friendship and respect; but a great and weighty reason moves her to it. She knows I shall die, and now takes care of my burial: what you approve of towards the dead, she hath done to one ready to die. Hence her fame shall be celebrated, in all ages, for this her faith, and this expression of it."

Ver. 15 : Τριάκοντα ἀργύρια. *Thirty pieces of silver.*] The price of a slave, Exod. xxi. 32. Maimon.[b] " The price of a slave, whether great or little, he or she, is סלעין ל׳ *thirty selaim* of pure silver : if the slave be worth a hundred pounds, or worth only one penny." Now סלע a *selaa*, in his weight, weighed three hundred and eighty-four barleycorns[c].

Ver. 17 : Ποῦ θέλεις ἑτοιμάσωμεν, &c. *Where wilt thou that we prepare, &c.*] For they might anywhere; since the houses at Jerusalem were not to be hired, as we have noted elsewhere, but during the time of the feast they were of common right[d].

Ver. 19 : Ἡτοίμασαν τὸ Πάσχα· *They made ready the Passover.*] Peter and John were sent for this purpose, Luke xxii. 8 : and perhaps they moved the question ποῦ θέλεις

---

[b] In נזקי ממון cap. 11.   [c] Shekalim, c. 1.
[d] Bab. Joma, fol. 12. 1.

ἐτοιμάσωμεν, *where wilt thou*, &c.   They only knew that Judas
was about another business, while the rest supposed he was
preparing necessaries for the Passover.

This Peter and John were to do, after having spoken with
the landlord, whom our Saviour pointed out to them by a
sign, to prepare and fit the room.

I. A lamb was to be bought, approved, and fit for the
Passover.

II. This lamb was to be brought by them into the court
where the altar was.

" The[e] Passover was to be killed only in the court where
the other sacrifices were slain : and it was to be killed on
the fourteenth day after noon, after the daily sacrifice, after
the offering[f] of the incense," &c.   The manner of bringing
the Passover into the court, and of killing it, you have in
Pesachin[g], in these words : " The Passover is killed in three
companies ; according as it is said, [Exod. xii. 6,] וְשָׁחֲטוּ

אוֹתוֹ כֹּל קְהַל עֲדַת יִשְׂרָאֵל *and all the assembly of the con-*
gregation of Israel shall kill it (*the Passover*) ; *assembly, congre-*
gation, and *Israel.*   The first company enters and fills the
whole court: they lock the doors of the court : the trumpets
sound : the priests stand in order, having golden and silver
vials in their hands : one row silver, and the other gold ; and
they are not intermingled : the vials had no brims, lest the
blood should stay upon them, and be congealed or thickened:
an Israelite kills it, and a priest receives the blood, and gives
it to him that stands next, and he to the next, who, taking
the vial that was full, gives him an empty one.   The priest
who stands next to the altar sprinkles the blood at one
sprinkling against the bottom of the altar[h] : that company
goes out, and the second comes in," &c.   Let them tell me
now, who suppose that Christ ate his Passover one day sooner
than the Jews did theirs, how these things could be performed by him or his disciples in the Temple, since it was
looked upon as a heinous offence among the people not to
kill or eat the Passover in the due time.   They commonly
carried the lambs into the court upon their shoulders : this

---

[c] Maimon. in Korban Pesach, cap. 1.   [f] *English folio edit.*, vol. ii. p. 256.
   [g] Cap. 5. hal. 5, 6.   [h] *Leusden's edition*, vol. ii. p. 377.

is called הרכבתו *its carrying*, in *Pesachin*[i]: where the Gloss,
" The carrying of it upon a man's shoulders, to bring it into
the court, as into a public place."

III. It was to be presented in the court פסח לשם *under
the name of the Paschal lamb*, and to be killed למנויין *for the
company mentioned*.   See what the Gemarists say of this thing
in *Pesachin*[k]: " If they kill it for such as are not to eat, or
as are not numbered, for such as are not circumcised or
unclean, it is profane : if for those that are to eat, and not to
eat, numbered and not numbered, for circumcised and not
circumcised, clean and unclean, it is right:" that is, for
those that are numbered, that atonement may be made for
the not numbered ; for the circumcised, that atonement may
he made for the uncircumcised, &c.   So the Gemarists and
the Glosses.

IV. The blood being sprinkled at the foot of the altar,
the lamb flayed, his belly cut up, the fat taken out and
thrown into the fire upon the altar, the body is carried back
to the place where they sup: the flesh is roasted, and the
skin given to the landlord.

V. Other things were also provided.   Bread according to
God's appointment, wine, some usual meats, and the same
called חרוסת[l] *Charoseth*: of which commentators speak
everywhere.

Ver. 20: Ἀνέκειτο μετὰ τῶν δώδεκα· *He sat down with the
twelve.*]   היסב : is the word among the Talmudists.

I. The schools of the Rabbins distinguish between ישיבה
sitting at the table, and הסיבה *lying* at the table: היו[m]
יושבין לאכול " If *they sit to eat*, every one says grace for
himself; הסיבו if they *lie*, one says grace for all."   But now
" that lying," as the Gloss on the place saith, " was when
they leaned on their left side upon couches, and ate and
drank as they thus leaned."   And the same Gloss in another
place; " They used to eat lying along upon their left side,
their feet being on the ground, every one on a single couch :"
Babyl. Berac.[n]   As also the Gemara[o]; פרקן לא שמיה

---

[i] Pesachin, cap. 6. hal. 1.
[k] Cap. 5. hal. 3.
[l] [See Buxtorf Lex. T. et R. sub v. col. 831.]
[m] Berac. cap. 6. hal. 6.
[n] Bab. Berac. fol. 46. 2.
[o] Pesachin, fol. 108. 1.

הסיבה הסיבת ימין לא שמיה הסיבה *to lie on one's back is not called lying down ; and to lie on one's right side is not called lying down.*

II. The Israelites accounted such lying down in eating a very fit posture requisite in sacred feasts, and highly requisite and most necessary in the Paschal supper : "We[p] do not use lying down but only to a morsel," &c. " And indeed to those that did eat leaning, leaning was necessary. But now our sitting is a kind of leaning along. They were used to lean along every one on his own couch, and to eat his meat on his own table : but we eat all together at one table."

אפילו עני שבישראל לא יאכל עד שיסב: *Even[q] the poorest Israelite must not eat till he lies down.* The canon is speaking about the Paschal supper; on which thus the Baby-lonians : " It is said that the feast of unleavened bread requires leaning or lying down, but the bitter herbs not : concerning wine, it is said in the name of Rabh Nachman that it hath need of lying down : and it is said in the name of Rabh Nachman, that it hath not need of lying down : and yet these do not contradict one another ; for *that* is said of the two first cups, *this* of the two last[r]." They lie down on the left side, not on the right, " because they must necessarily use their right hand in eating." So the Gloss there.

III. They used and were fond of that custom of lying down, even to superstition, because it carried with it a token and signification of liberty : "R. Levi saith[s], It is the manner of slaves to eat standing : but now let them eat lying along, that it may be known that they are gone out of bondage to liberty. R. Simon in the name of R. Joshua Ben Levi[t], Let that which a man eats at the Passover, and does his duty, though it be but as big as an olive, let it be eaten lying along." " They[u] eat the unleavened bread the first night lying down, because it is a commemoration of deliverance. The bitter herbs have no need of lying down, because they are in memory of bondage. Although it be the bread of affliction, yet it is to be eaten after the manner of liberty."

[p] Another Gloss in Berac. cap. 6. in the place above.

[q] Pesach. cap. 10. hal. 1.

[r] Bab. Pesach. fol. 108. 1.

[s] Hieros. Pesach. fol. 37. 2.

[t] *English folio edit.*, vol. ii. p. 257.

[u] Bab. in the place above in the Gloss.

See more there. " We[x] are obliged to lie down when we eat, that we may eat after the manner of kings and nobles."

IV. " When there were two beds, גדול מיסב בראש *the worthiest person lay uppermost;* the second to him, next above him. But when there were three beds, the worthiest person lay in the middle, the second above him, the third below him[y]." On which thus the Gloss: " When there were two, the principal person lay on the first couch, and the next to him lay above him, that is, on a couch placed at the pillow of the more worthy person. If there were three, the worthiest lay in the middle, the next above him, and the third below him[z]; that is, at the coverlids of his feet. If the principal person desires to speak with the second, he must necessarily raise himself so as to sit upright; for as long as he sits bending he cannot speak to him; for the second sat behind the head of the first, and the face of the first was turned another away: and it would be better with the second [*in respect of discourse*] if he sat below him; for then he might hear his words, even as he lay along." This affords some light to that story, John xiii. 23, 24; where Peter, as seems likely, lying behind our Saviour's head in the first place next after him, could not discourse with him, nor ask about the betrayer: therefore looking over Christ's head upon John, he gave him a sign to inquire. He sitting in the second place from Christ with his face towards him, asketh him,

Ver. 22 : Μήτι ἐγώ εἰμι, Κύριε ; *Lord, is it I ?*] The very occasion, namely, eating together and fellowship, partly renews the mention of the betrayer at the Paschal supper; as if he had said, " We are eating here friendly together, and yet there is one in this number who will betray me :" partly, that the disciples might be more fully acquainted with the matter itself : for at the supper in John xiii, he had privately discovered the person to John only; unless perhaps Peter understood it also, who knew of John's question to Christ, having at first put him upon it by his beckoning. The disciples ask, *Is it I ?* partly through ignorance of the thing, partly out of a sincere and assured profession of the contrary.

[x] Maimon. in פירוש משניות.   Bab. Berac. fol. 46. 2.
[y] Hieros. Taanith, fol. 68. 1. et   [z] *Leusden's edition,* vol. ii. p. 378.

Ver. 24. Καλὸν ἦν αὐτῷ, εἰ οὐκ ἐγεννήθη· *It had been good for him if he had not been born.*] : נוח לו שלא נברא *It*[a] *were better for him that he were not created.* A very usual way of speaking in the Talmudists.

Ver. 26. Λαβὼν ὁ Ἰησοῦς τὸν ἄρτον, &c. *Jesus took bread, &c.*] *Bread* at supper, the cup after supper : " After supper he took the cup," saith Luke, chap. xxii. 20 ; and Paul, 1 Cor. xi. 25 ; but not so of the bread.

That we may more clearly perceive the history of this supper in the evangelists, it may not be amiss to transcribe the rubric of the paschal supper, with what brevity we can, out of the Talmudists ; that we may compare the things here related with the custom of the nation.

I. The paschal supper began with a cup of wine : " They[b] mingle the first cup for him. The school of Shammai saith, He gives thanks, first for the day, and then for the wine : but the school of Hillel saith, He first gives thanks for the wine, and then for the day." The Shammeans confirm their opinion, שהיום גורם ליין שיבא *Because the day is the cause of their having wine:*" that is, as the Gloss explains it, שיבא קודם סעודה *that they have it before meat.* " They[c] first mingle a cup for every one, and [*the master of the family*] blesseth it ; ' Blessed be he that created the fruit of the vine :' and then he repeats the consecration of the day, וזמן [that is, he gives thanks in the plural number for all the company, saying, ' Let *us* give thanks,'] and drinks up the cup. " And afterward he blesseth concerning the washing of hands, and washeth." Compare this cup with that, Luke xxii. 17.

II. Then[d] the bitter herbs are set on : " They[e] bring in a table ready covered, upon which there is מרור וירק אחר *sour sauce and other herbs.*" הביאו לפניו מטבל בחזרת עד שמגיע לפרפרת הפת[f] Let the Glossers[g] give the interpretation : " They do not set the table till after the consecration of the day : and upon the table they set lettuce. After he hath blessed over the wine, they set herbs, and he eats lettuce dipped, but not in חרוסת *the sour sauce,* for that

[a] Bab. Berac. fol. 17. 1, &c.
[b] Pesach. cap. 10. hal. 2.
[c] Maimon. in Chamets umatsah, cap. 8.
[d] *English folio edit.*, vol. ii. p.258.
[e] Maimon.
[f] Pesachin, as before.
[g] Bab. fol. 114. 1.

is not yet brought: and this is not meant simply of lettuce, unless when there be other herbs." עד שמגיע לפרפרת הפת His meaning is this, before he comes to those bitter herbs which he eats after the unleavened bread, when he also gives thanks for the eating of the bitter herbs, "as it is written," Ye shall eat (*it*) with unleavened bread and bitter herbs: "First unleavened bread, and then bitter herbs. And this first dipping is used only for that reason, that children may observe and inquire; for it is unusual for men to eat herbs before meat."

III. "Afterward there is set on unleavened bread, and the sauce called חרוסת, and the lamb, and the flesh also of the *Chagigah* of the fourteenth day." Maimonides doth not take notice of any interposition between the setting on the bitter herbs, and the setting on the unleavened bread: but the Talmudic Misna notes it in these words; הביאו לפניו מצה *They set unleavened bread before him.* Where the Gloss, " This is said, because they have moved the table from before him who performed the duty of the Passover: now that removal of the table was for this end, that the son might ask the father, and the father answered him, 'Let them bring the table again, that we may make the second dipping;' then the son would ask, ' Why do we dip twice ?' Therefore they bring back the table with unleavened bread upon it, and bitter herbs," &c.

IV. He begins, and blesseth, " ' Blessed be He that created the fruits of the earth:' and he takes the herbs and dips them in the sauce *Charoseth*, and eats as much as an olive, he, and all that lie down with him; but less than the quantity of an olive he must not eat: then they remove the table[h] from before the master of the family[i]." Whether this removal of the table be the same with the former is not much worth our inquiry.

V. מזגו לו כוס שני " *Now they mingle the second cup for him:* and the son asks the father; or if the son doth not ask him, he tells him himself, how much this night differs from all other nights. ' On other nights (saith he) we dip but once, but this night twice. On other nights we eat either leavened or unleavened bread; on this, only unleavened, &c.

h *Leusden's edition*, vol. 2, p. 379.   i Maimon.

On other nights we eat either sitting or lying; on this, all lying.'"

VI. "The table is set before them again; and then he saith, 'This is the passover, which we therefore eat, because God passed over the houses of our fathers in Egypt.' Then he lifts up the bitter herbs in his hand and saith, ' We therefore eat these bitter herbs, because the Egyptians made the lives of our fathers bitter in Egypt.' He takes up the un-leavened bread in his hand, and saith, ' We eat this unleavened bread, because our fathers had not time to sprinkle their meal to be leavened before God revealed himself and redeemed them. We ought therefore to praise, celebrate, honour, mag-nify, &c. him, who wrought all these wonderful things for our fathers and for us, and brought us out of bondage into liberty, out of sorrow into joy, out of darkness into great light; let us therefore say, Hallelujah: Praise the Lord, praise him, O ye servants of the Lord, &c. *to*, And the flint-stone into fountains of waters' [that is, from the beginning of Psalm cxiii to the end of Psalm cxiv]. And he concludes, ' Blessed be thou, O Lord God, our King eternal, redeeming us, and redeeming our fathers out of Egypt, and bringing us to this night; that we may eat unleavened bread and bitter herbs:' and then he drinks off the second cup."

VII. "Then washing his hands, and taking two loaves, he breaks one, and lays the broken upon the whole one, and blesseth it; 'Blessed be he who causeth bread to grow out of the earth:' and putting some bread and bitter herbs toge-ther, he dips them in the sauce *Charoseth*,—and blessing, 'Blessed be thou, O Lord God, our eternal King, he who hath sanctified us by his precepts, and hath commanded us to eat,' he eats the unleavened bread and bitter herbs toge-ther; but if he eats the unleavened bread and bitter herbs by themselves, he gives thanks severally for each. And after-ward, giving thanks after the same manner over the flesh of the *Chagigah* of the fourteenth day, he eats also of it, and in like manner giving thanks over the lamb, he eats of it."

VIII. "From thenceforward he lengthens out the supper, eating this or that as he hath a mind, and last of all he eats of the flesh of the passover, at least as much as an olive; but after this he tastes not at all of any food." Thus far

Maimonides in the place quoted, as also the Talmudists in several places in the last chapter in the tract *Pesachin.*

And now was the time when Christ, taking bread, instituted the eucharist: but whether was it after the eating of those *farewell morsels,* as I may call them, of the lamb, or instead of them? It seems to be in their stead, because it is said by our evangelist and Mark, 'Εσθιόντων αὐτῶν, &c. *As they were eating, Jesus took bread.* Now, without doubt, they speak according to the known and common custom of that supper, that they might be understood by their own people. But all Jews know well enough, that after the eating of those morsels of the lamb it cannot be said, *As they were eating;* for the eating was ended[k] with those morsels. It seems therefore more likely that Christ, when they were now ready to take those morsels, changed the custom, and gave about morsels of bread in their stead, and instituted the sacrament. Some are of opinion, that it was the custom to taste the unleavened bread last of all, and to close up the supper with it; of which opinion, I confess, I also sometimes was. And it is so much the more easy to fall into this opinion, because there is such a thing mentioned in some of the rubrics about the passover; and with good reason, because they took up this custom after the destruction of the Temple.

Εὐλογήσας, ἔκλασε· *Blessed and brake it.*] First he blessed, then he brake it. Thus it always used to be done, except in the paschal bread. One of the two loaves was first divided into two parts, or, perhaps, into more, before it was blessed. חולק אחד מהן *One of them is divided:* they are the words of Maimonides, who also adds, "But why doth he not bless both the loaves after the same manner as in other feasts? Because this is called לחם עוני *the bread of poverty.* Now poor people deal in morsels, and here likewise are morsels."

אין בוצע רשאי לבצוע עד שיכלה אמן מפי העונים
Let not him that is to break the bread, break it before Amen be pronounced from the mouths of the answerers[l].

Τοῦτό ἐστι τὸ σῶμά μου· *This is my body.*] These words, being applied to the Passover now newly eaten, will be more clear: " *This* now is my body, in that sense, in which the paschal

---

[k] *English folio edition,* vol. ii. p. 259.   [l] Bab. Berac. fol. 47. 1.

lamb hath been my body hitherto." And in the twenty-
eighth verse, " *This* is my blood of the new testament, in the
same sense, as the blood of bulls and goats hath been my
blood under the Old." Exod. xxiv., Heb. ix.

Ver. 27: Τὸ ποτήριον· *The cup*.] Bread was to be here at
this supper by divine institution : but how came the wine to
be here ? and how much ? and of what sort ?

I. " A tradition [m]. It is necessary that a man should cheer
up his wife and his children for the feast. But how doth he
cheer them up ? With wine." The same things are cited [n] in
the Babylonian Talmud [o] : " The Rabbins deliver," say they,
" that a man is obliged to cheer up his wife and his do-
mestics in the feast ; as it is said, ' And thou shalt rejoice in
thy feast.' (Deut. xvi. 14). But how are they cheered up ?
With wine. R. Judah saith, ' Men are cheered up with
something agreeable to them ; women, with that which is
agreeable to them.' That which is agreeable to men to
rejoice them is wine. But what is that which is agreeable
to women to cheer them ? Rabh Joseph saith, ' Dyed garments in Babylon, and linen garments in the land of Israel.' "

II. Four cups of wine were to be drunk up by every one :
הכל חייבין בד' כוסות " *All are obliged to four cups*, men,
women, and children : R. Judah saith, ' But what have
children to do with wine ?' But they give them wheat and
nuts,' " &c.

The Jerusalem Talmudists give the reason of the number,
in the place before quoted, at full. Some, according to the
number of the four words made use of in the history of the
redemption of Israel out of Egypt, וְהוֹצֵאתִי וְהִצַּלְתִּי וְגָאַלְתִּי
וְלָקַחְתִּי *And I will bring forth, and I will deliver, and I will
redeem, and I will take:* some, according to the number of
the repetition of the word כוֹס *cup*, in Gen. xl. 11, 13, which
is four times ; some, according to the number of the four
monarchies ; some, according to the number of the four cups
of vengeance which God shall give to the nations to drink,
Jer. xxv. 15 ; li. 7 ; Psalm xi. 6 ; lxxv. 8. And according to
the number of the four cups which God shall give Israel to

[m] Jerus. Pesachin, fol. 37. 2.   [n] *Leusden's edit.*, vol. ii. p. 380.
[o] Pesach. fol. 109. 1.

drink, Psalm xxiii. 5 ; xvi. 5 ; cxvi. 13. כוס ישועות אשא תריין *the cup of two salvations.*

III. The measure of these cups is thus determined P: ארבעה כוסות שאמרו ישנן רביעית יין באיטלקי " Rabbi Chaia saith, *Four cups contain an Italian quart of wine.*" And more exactly in the same place : " How much is the measure of a cup? אצבעיים על אצבעיי' על רום אצבע ומחצה ושליש אצבע *Two fingers square, and one finger and a half, and a third part of a finger deep* q." The same words you have in the Babylonian Talmud at the place before quoted, only with this difference, that instead of שליש אצבע *the third part of a finger,* there is חומש אצבע *the fifth part of a finger.*

IV. מצוה לצאת ביין אדום *It is commanded, that he should perform this office with red wine.* So the Babylonian r, צריך שיהא בו טעם ומראה " *It is necessary that it should taste, and look* like wine." The Gloss, שיהא אדום *that it should be red.*

V. שתאן חי יצא s *If he drinks wine pure,* and not mingled with water, *he hath performed his duty ;* but commonly they mingled water with it : hence, when there is mention of wine in the rubric of the feasts, they always use the word מזגו *they mingle* him a cup. Concerning that mingling, both Talmudists dispute in the forecited chapter of the Passover: which see. " The t Rabbins have a tradition. Over wine which hath not water mingled with it they do not say that blessing, ' Blessed be He that created the fruit of the vine ;' but, ' Blessed be he that created the fruit of the tree.' " The Gloss, יינם חזק מאד *Their wine was very strong,* and not fit to be drunk without water," &c. The Gemarists a little after : " The wise agree with R. Eleazar, ' That one ought not to bless over the cup of blessing till water be mingled with it.' " The mingling of water with every cup was requisite for health, and the avoiding of drunkenness. We have before taken notice of a story of Rabban Gamaliel, who found and confessed some disorder of mind, and unfitness for serious buisness, by having drunk off an Italian quart of wine.

P Jerus. Schabb. fol. 11. 1.
q Pesach.
r Hieros. as before.

s *English folio edition,* vol. ii. p. 260.
t Bab. Berac. fol. 50. 2.

These things being thus premised, concerning the paschal wine, we now return to observe this cup of our Saviour.

After those things which used to be performed in the paschal supper, as is before related, these are moreover added by Maimonides : " Then he washeth his hands, ומברך ברכת המזון *and blesseth the blessing of the meat*" [that is, gives thanks after meat], " over the third cup of wine, and drinks it up." That cup was commonly called כוס הברכה *the cup of blessing* ; אכסא דברכתא in the Talmudic dialect. כוס של ברכה ברכת המזון *The cup of blessing is when they give thanks after supper*, saith the Gloss on *Babyl. Berac.*[u] Where also in the text many things are mentioned of this cup : " Ten things are spoken of the cup of blessing. הדחה ושטיפה *Washing and cleansing :*" [that is, to wash the inside and outside, namely, that nothing should remain of the wine of the former cups]. חי " Let *pure wine*" be poured into the cup, and water mingled with it there. ומלא " Let it be *full :* עיטור *the crowning ;*" that is, as the Gemara, " by the disciples." While he is doing this, let the disciples stand about him in a crown or ring. עיטוף *The veiling ;* that is, " as Rabh Papa, he veils himself and sits down ; as R. Issai, he spreads a handkerchief on his head. נוטלו בשתי ידיו *He takes up the cup in both hands,* but puts it into his right hand ; he lifts it from the table, fixeth his eyes upon it, &c. Some say he imparts it (as a gift) to his family."

Which of these rites our Saviour made use of, we do not inquire ; the cup certainly was the same with the " cup of blessing :" namely, when, according to the custom, after having eaten the farewell morsel of the lamb, there was now an end of supper, and thanks were to be given over the third cup after meat, he takes that cup, and after having returned thanks, as is probable, for the meat, both according to the custom, and his office, he instituted this for a cup of eucharist or thanksgiving ; Τὸ ποτήριον τῆς εὐλογίας ὃ εὐλογοῦμεν, *The cup of blessing which we bless,* 1 Cor. x. 16. Hence it is that Luke and Paul say that he took the cup " after supper ;" that is, that cup which closed up the supper.

[u] Fol. 51. 1.

It must not be passed by, that when he instituted the eucharistical [x] cup, he said, " This is my blood of the new testament," as Matthew and Mark : nay, as Luke and Paul, " This cup is the new testament in my blood." Not only the seal of the covenant, but the sanction of the new covenant : the end of the Mosaical economy, and the confirming of a new one. The confirmation of the old covenant was by the blood of bulls and goats, Exod. xxiv., Heb. ix., because blood was still to be shed : the confirmation of the new was by a cup of wine ; because, under the new testament, there was no further shedding of blood. As it is here said of the cup, " This cup is the new testament in my blood," so it might be said of the cup of blood (Exod. xxiv. 8), " That cup was the old testament in the blood of Christ." There, all the articles of that covenant being read over, Moses sprinkled all the people with blood, and said, " This is the blood of the covenant which God hath made with you :" and thus that old covenant or testimony was confirmed. In like manner, Christ having published all the articles of the new covenant, he takes the cup of wine, and gives them to drink, and saith, " This is the new testament in my blood :" and thus the new covenant is established.

There was, besides, a fourth cup, of which our author speaks also ; " Then he mingled a fourth cup, and over it he finished the *Hallel ;* and adds, moreover, *the blessing of the hymn,* ברכת השיר which is, ' Let all thy works praise thee, O Lord,' &c. ; and saith, ' Blessed is He that created the fruit of the vine ;' and afterward he tastes of nothing more that night," &c. ' Finisheth the *Hallel ;*' that is, he begins there where he left off before, to wit, at the beginning of Psalm cxv., and goes on to the end of Psalm cxviii.

Whether Christ made use of this cup also, we do not dispute ; it is certain he used the hymn, as the evangelist tells us, ὑμνήσαντες, *when they had sung a hymn,* at the thirtieth verse. We meet with the very same word היּמנון in *Midras Tillim* [y].

And now looking back on this paschal supper, let me ask those who suppose the supper in John xiii. to be the

---

[x] *Leusden's edition,* vol. ii. p. 381.   [y] Fol. 4. 2. & 42. 1.

same with this, What part of this time they do allot to the washing [z] of the disciples' feet? what part to Judas's going out? and what part to his discoursing with the priests, and getting ready his accomplices for their wicked exploit?

I. It seems strange, indeed, that Christ should put off the washing of the disciples' feet to the paschal supper, when, 1. That kind of action was not only unusual and unheard of at that supper, but in nowise necessary or fitting: for, 2. How much more conveniently might that have been performed at a common supper before the Passover, as we suppose, when he was not straitened by the time, than at the paschal supper, when there were many things to be done which required despatch!

II. The office of the paschal supper did not admit of such interruption, nor was it lawful for others so to decline from the fixed rule as to introduce such a foreign matter: and why should Christ so swerve from it, when in other things he conformed himself to the custom of the nation, and when he had before a much more fit occasion for this action than when he was thus pressed and straitened by the time?

III. Judas sat at supper with the rest, and was there when he did eat, Matt. xxvi. 20, 21; Mark xiv. 18: and, alas! how unusual was it for any to depart, in that manner, from that supper before it was done! It is enough doubted by the Jewish canons whether it were lawful; and how far any one, who had joined himself to this or that φρατρία, *family*, might leave it to go to another, and take one part of the supper here, and another part there: but for a person to leave the supper and go about another business, is a thing they never in the least dreamed of; they would not, they could not, suppose it. You see how light a matter Judas's going away to buy necessaries, as the disciples interpreted it, seemed to them, because he went away from a common supper: but if they had seen him thus dismissed, and sent away from the paschal supper, it would have seemed a monstrous and wonderful thing. What! to leave the paschal supper, now begun, to go to market! To go from a common supper at Bethany, to buy necessaries for the Passover, against the time of the Passover, this was nothing strange or unusual: but to go from the paschal supper, before it was done, to a market or fair, was more unusual and strange than that it should be so lightly passsed over by the disciples.

We, therefore, do not at all doubt that Judas was present both at the Passover and the eucharist; which Luke affirms in direct words, chap. xxii. 20, 21 : nor do we doubt much of his being present at the hymn, and that he went not away before all was done: but when they all rose up from the table, and prepared for their journey to mount Olivet (in order to lie at Bethany, as the disciples supposed), the villanous traitor stole away, and went to the company [*cohortes*], that he had appointed the priests two days before to make ready for him at such a time and place. Methinks I hear the words and consultations of this bloody wretch : "To-morrow (saith he) will be the Passover, and I know my Master will come to it: I know he will not lie at Jerusalem, but will go back to Bethany, however late at night, where he is used to lie. Make ready, therefore, for me armed men, and let them come to a place appointed immediately after the paschal supper; and I will steal out privately to them while my Master makes himself ready for his journey; and I will conduct them to seize upon him in the gardens without the city, where, by reason of the solitariness of the place and the silence of the night, we shall be secure enough from the multitude. Do[a] ye make haste to despatch your passovers, that you may meet together at the council after supper, to examine and judge him, when we shall bring him to you; while the silence of the night favours you also, and protects you from the multitude." Thus, all things are provided against the place and time appointed; and the thief, stealing away from the company of the disciples as they were going out towards the mount of Olives and hastening to his armed confederates without delay, brings them prepared along with him, and sets upon his Master now in the garden.

Ver. 34 : Πρὶν ἀλέκτορα φωνῆσαι, τρὶς ἀπαρνήσῃ με· *Before the cock crow, thou shalt deny me thrice.*] The same also he had said, John xiii. 38, "The cock shall not crow till thou hast denied me thrice." Therefore some say, that that was the same supper with this of the Passover. Very right, indeed, if ἀλέκτωρ οὐ φωνήσει ought to be rendered, *the cock shall not crow once,* or *the cock shall not crow at all.* But it is not so; but it amounts to this sense, "Within the time of cockcrowing" thou shalt deny me thrice; for Peter had denied him but once before the first crowing of the cock, and thrice before the second, Mark xiv. 68, 72. From hence, therefore, we may easily observe in what sense those words are to be understood, which were spoken to Peter two days before the Passover, John xiii. 38, "The cock shall not crow," &c: not that the cock should not crow at all between that[b] time and Peter's denying; but as if our Saviour had said, "Are you so secure of yourself, O Peter? Verily, I say unto you, the time shall be, and that shortly, when you shall deny me thrice within the time of cockcrowing." Ἐν ἀλεκτορο-φωνίᾳ, *at cockcrowing,* Mark xiii. 35. At the Paschal supper it is said, " *This night,* before the cock crow," &c. Matt. xxvi. 34; Mark xiv. 30; Luke xxii. 34. But there is nothing of this said in that supper, John xiii.

Concerning the cockcrowing, thus the masters: " R. Shilla[c] saith, Whosoever begins his journey before cockcrowing, his blood be upon his head. R. Josia saith, If before the second crowing: but some say, Before the third. But of what kind of cock is this spoken?" בתרנגול בינוני *Of a middling cock ;* that is, as the Gloss explains it, " a cock that doth not crow too soon nor too late." The Misna on which this Gloss is hath these words; " Every day they remove the ashes from the altar about cockcrowing; but on the day of atonement at midnight," &c.

You may wonder that a dunghill cock should be found at Jerusalem, when it is forbid by the canons that any cocks should be kept there : אין מגדלין תרנגולין בירושלם מפני קדושים " They[d] *do not keep cocks at Jerusalem, upon account of the holy things ;* nor do the priests keep them throughout all the land of Israel." The Gloss gives the reason; " Even Israelites are forbid to keep cocks at Jerusalem, because of the holy things : for Israelites have eaten there peace offerings and thank offerings : but now it is the custom of dunghill cocks to turn over dunghills, where perhaps they might

---

b *English folio edition,* vol. ii. p. 262.   c Bab. Joma, fol. 21. 1.
d Bava Kama, cap. 7. hal. ult.

find creeping things that might pollute those holy things
that are to be eaten." By what means, and under what
pretence, the canon was dispensed with, we do not dispute.
It is certain there were cocks at Jerusalem, as well as at
other places. And memorable is the story of a cock which
was stoned by the sentence of the council for having killed
a little child [e].

Ver. 36 : Γεθσημανῆ· *Gethsemane.*] *The place of the olive-
presses*, at the foot of mount *Olivet*. In John [f], it is "a
garden beyond Cedron." "They [g] do not make gardens or
paradises in Jerusalem, *because of the stink*, משום סירחא·
The Gloss, " Because of the stink that riseth from the weeds
which are thrown out: besides, it is the custom to dung
gardens ; and thence comes a stink." Upon this account
there were no gardens in the city, (some few gardens of roses
excepted, which had been so from the days of the prophets [h],)
but all were without the walls, especially at the foot of Olivet.

Ver. 49 : Κατεφίλησεν αὐτόν· *Kissed him.*] It was not
unusual for a master to *kiss* his disciple; but for a disciple to
kiss his master was more rare. Whether therefore Judas
did this under pretence of respect, or out of open contempt
and derision, let it be inquired.

Ver. 60: Πολλῶν ψευδομαρτύρων προσελθόντων· *Many false
witnesses came.*] Inquire whether these are to be called
עדים זוממים of which the Talmudists speak at large; especially in the treatise *Maccoth* [i]. זוממים are commonly rendered *false witnesses ;* and deservedly : and yet Maimonides
reckons up these as necessary in that city where the council
of twenty-three is placed : " Why (saith he) is such a council
not set up but in a city where there are a hundred and
twenty men ? Namely, that there may be three-and-twenty
for the council, and three ranks consisting of sixty-nine men,
and ten men to attend upon the affairs of the synagogue :
two scribes, two *bishops* [*episcopi*], two to be judged, two
witnesses." שני זוממין ושני זוממי זוממין &c. The reason
of the thing is a little obscure : the characters of the men
you may take in these examples : " The witnesses say, We

---

[e] Jerus. Erubhin, fol. 26. 1.
[f] Chap. xviii. 1.
[g] Bava Kama, in the place above.
[h] Avoth R. Nathan, fol. 9. 1.
[i] Cap. 1.

testify that N. killed N. They say to them, How do you
depose this, when the killer, or he that was killed, was with us
in such a place on that day? These as yet are not זוממין.
But [k] if they should say, How can you testify this when you
were with us on that day l?" &c. On which Misna, thus Maimonides ; " The witnesses depose that Reuben killed Simeon :
and afterward Kohath and Hushim come, והזימו *and disprove* their testimony : there come afterward other witnesses,
and depose the same with the former ; namely, that Reuben
killed Simeon ; and Kohath and Hushim disprove their testimony also : if a second, third, and fourth, nay, if a thousand pair [m] come and depose the same thing, while those two
so disprove them, they must all die by the testimony of these
two," &c.

There was the like testimony in other things : thus in the
first *halacah* of the chapter quoted; כיצד העדים נעשים
זוממין *" How are witnesses made* זוממים? We testify concerning N., that he is the son of a divorced woman, &c. They
do not say, Let this witness [if he prove false] be made the
son of a divorced woman instead of the other, but he is
beaten with forty stripes." The words are obscure enough,
but their meaning is this : Since a false witness was by the
law to suffer the same things which, by his perjury, he had
designed to bring upon another, it is here inquired, in what
cases a witness is so far to be accounted false as to undergo
such a retaliation? And it is answered, Not in all : and this
reason is alleged, If any one, by false witness, should endeavour to deprive another of his legitimacy, and, by consequence of the privileges of being legitimate, by saying that
he is the son of a divorced woman, though he were indeed
עד זומם *a false witness*, yet he must not be punished in the
like kind, to be made as the son of a divorced woman ; but
he must be whipped. But in capital cases the custom was,
that whosoever endeavoured to procure death to another person by false witness, must himself be put to death.

Ver. 65. Τότε ὁ ἀρχιερεὺς διέρρηξε τὰ ἱμάτια αὐτοῦ· *Then the
high priest rent his clothes.*] "When[n] witnesses speak out
the blasphemy which they heard, then all, hearing the blas-

---

[k] *Leusden's edit.*, vol. ii. p. 383.
[l] Maccoth, cap. 1. fol. 6.
[m] *English folio edit.*, vol. ii. p. 263.
[n] Maimon. in Avod. Zarah, cap. 2.

phemy, are bound to rend their clothes." See more there. "They[o] that judge a blasphemer, first ask the witnesses, and bid him speak out plainly what he hath heard; and when he speaks it, the judges standing on their feet rend their garments, and do not sew them up again," &c. See there the Babylonian Gemara discoursing at large why they stand upon their feet, why they rend their garments, and why they may not be sewed up again.

CHAP. XXVII.

Ver. 1: Πρωΐας δὲ γενομένης, &c. *When the morning was come, &c.*] Let us trace a little the proceedings of this council:—

I. They spend the night in judging on a capital cause, which is expressly forbid by their own canon: דיני נפשות דנין. ביום וגומרין ביום *They handle capital causes in the day time, and finish them by day*[p]. Money matters indeed that were begun by day might be ended in the night, which is asserted in that place; but capital causes were only to be handled by day: but here, in sitting upon the life and death of our Saviour, there is need of night and darkness. This judgment is begun in the night, and carried on all the night through in a manner.

II. This night was the evening of a feast day, namely, of the first day of the paschal week, at what time they were also forbid to sit in judgment: "They[q] do not judge on a feast day." How the lawyers are divided on this point, I will not trouble you now with recounting. This very canon is sufficient ground for scruple, which we leave to them to clear, who, through rancour and hatred towards Christ, seem to slight and trample under feet their own canons.

III. Πρωΐας γενομένης· *When it was morning.*] This was the time of saying their phylacteries, namely, from the first day-light to the third hour[r]. But where was these men's religion to-day? Did you say your phylacteries this morning, my good fathers of the council, before you came to sit on the bench? Another business that you had in hand (effectually to destroy

---

[o] Sanhedr. cap. 7. hal. 10.
[p] Sanhedr. cap. 4. hal. 1.
[q] Moed Katon, cap. 5. hal. 2.
[r] Berac. cap. 1. hal. 2.

Jesus), either robbed you of your prayers, or robbed your
prayers of charity.

IV. Now appears יט" ראשון של הפסח, *the first feast day of
the Passover,* when they used to present themselves in the
Temple and offer their gifts, Exod. xxiii. 15. But when and
how was this performed by them to-day? They take heed of
going into the judgment (or Prætor's) hall, lest they should
be defiled, but that they might eat the *Chagigah*[s], or *Passover*[t]:
but you will scarce find what time they allowed to-day for that
purpose; nor indeed was it lawful for them to eat any thing
on that day; it being provided by a canon, "That when the
council shall have adjudged any one to die, let them not taste
any thing that day[u]."

Συμβούλιον ἔλαβον ὥστε θανατῶσαι αὐτόν· *Took counsel to put
him to death.*] Let that be considered; דיני ממונות דנין
ביום וגומרין בלילה " *Cases*[x] *of money are heard*[y] *in the day-
time, and may be determined in the night.* Capital causes are
tried in the day, and finished in the day. Judgment in cases
of money is passed the same day, whether it be for fining or
acquitting. Judgment in capital causes is passed the same
day, if it be for acquitting: but if it be for condemning, it is
passed the day after." The reason of this difference is given
by the Gemarists; whom see. The reason of the latter is thus
expressed: אשרי הדיין שמחמץ את דינו *Blessed is the
judge who leveneth his judgment:* that is, as the Gloss, "who
delays his judgment, and lets it rest all night, that he may
sift out the truth."

The difference between דנין and גומרין is greater than the
reader may perhaps think at first sight. By the word דנין
they signify the whole process of the trial, the examining of
the plaintiff and defendant, and of the witnesses, the taking
the votes of the council, and the entering of them by the
scribes: גומרין signifies only the passing of judgment, or
giving a definitive sentence. You may better perceive the
difference from the Glossary on Babyl. *Sanhedrin*[z]: in the text

---

[s] *English folio edition,* vol. ii. p.
264.
   [t] See John xviii. 28. and Chagig.
cap. 1.
   [u] Bab. Sanhedr. fol. 63. 1.

[x] Sanhedr. in the place quoted,
cap. 4.
   [y] *Leusden's edition,* vol. ii. p.
384.
   [z] Fol. 35. 1.

this is decreed, אין דנין לא בערב שבת ולא בערב יום טוב
*Let them not judge on the eve of the sabbath, nor on the eve of a
feast day;* which is also repeated in other places[a]. The reason of the prohibition is this, namely, that the trials which
were begun on the eve of the sabbath, or a feast day, should
not be finished on the sabbath or feast day. " Which indeed
(saith the Gloss), is observed in pecuniary trials, and care is
taken that there be no writing" (for it is forbid to write so
much as a letter on the sabbath): " but in capital causes it
takes not place upon that account ; for the votes of those that
acquitted or condemned were written the day before."

You see in the history of the gospel, 1. The trial concerning
our Saviour's life, was not despatched at one and the same
sitting. 2. And that too on a feast-day.

Ver. 5: 'Aπήγξατο· *Hanged himself.*] *Strangulatus est, was
strangled:* namely, by the devil, who had now been in him
three days together. The words of Peter, Acts i. 18, do not
suffer me to understand this of hanging himself. Πρηνὴς
γενόμενος ἐλάκησε μέσος· *Falling headlong he burst asunder in
the midst.* Interpreters take a great deal of pains to make
these words agree with his hanging himself; but indeed all
will not do. I know the word ἀπήγξατο is commonly applied
to a man's *hanging himself,* but not to exclude some other
way of *strangling.* And I cannot but take the story (with
good leave of antiquity) in this sense: After Judas had thrown
down the money, the price of his treason, in the Temple, and
was now returning again to his mates, the devil, who dwelt
in him, caught him up on high, strangled him, and threw him
down headlong ; so that dashing upon the ground, he burst
in the midst, and his guts issued out, and the devil went out
in so horrid an exit. This certainly agrees very well with the
words of Peter now mentioned, and also with those that follow, " This was known to all that dwelt at Jerusalem." It
agrees also very well with the deserts of the wicked wretch,
and with the title of Iscariot. The wickedness he had committed was above all example, and the punishment he suffered was beyond all precedent. There had been many instances of persons who had hanged themselves ; this would not

---

[a] Hieros. Chetub. fol. 24. 4. and Moed Katon, fol. 63. 1.

so much have stirred up the people of Jerusalem to take notice
of it, as such a strangling and throwing down headlong, which
we suppose horrible above measure, and singular beyond example. See what we have said at the tenth chapter concerning the word *Iscariot*.

Ver. 9: Τὸ ῥηθὲν διὰ Ἱερεμίου τοῦ προφήτου· *That which
was spoken by Jeremy the prophet.*] How much this place
hath troubled interpreters, let the famous Beza, instead of
many others, declare: " This knot hath hampered all the most
ancient interpreters, in that the testimony here is taken out of
Zechariah, and not from Jeremiah; so that it seems plainly
to have been ἁμάρτημα μνημονικὸν, *a failing of memory*, as
Augustine supposes in his third book, ' De consensu evange-
listarum,' chapter the seventh; as also Eusebius in the
twentieth book[b] Ἀποδείξεως, *of demonstration*. But if any one
had rather impute this error to the transcribers, or (as I
rather suppose) to the unskilfulness of some person, who
put in the name of *Jeremiah*, when the evangelist had writ
only, as he often doth in other places, διὰ τοῦ προφήτου, *by
the prophet*, yet we must confess that this error hath long
since crept into the Holy Scriptures, as Jerome expressly
affirms," &c.

But (with the leave of so great men) I do not only deny
that so much as one letter is spurious, or crept in without
the knowledge of the evangelist, but I do confidently assert
that Matthew wrote *Jeremy*, as we read. it, and that it was
very readily understood and received by his countrymen. We
will transcribe the following monument of antiquity out of the
Talmudists[c], and then let the reader judge: " A tradition of
the Rabbins. This is the order of the prophets. The Book
of Joshua, Judges, Samuel, Kings, Jeremiah, Ezekiel, Isaiah,
and the twelve." And a little after: " But since Isaiah was
before both Jeremiah and Ezekiel, he ought to have been set
before them : כֵּיוָן דמלכים סופיה חורבנא but *since the Book
of Kings ends with destruction,* וירמיה כוליה חורבנא *and
all Jeremiah is about destruction,* and since Ezekiel begins with
destruction and ends with comfort; and all Isaiah is about
comfort, סמכינן חורבנא לחורבנא ונחמתא לנחמתא

*they joined destruction with destruction, and comfort with com-
fort:"* that is, they placed these books together which treat
of destruction, and[d] those together which treat of comfort.

You have this tradition quoted by David Kimchi in his
preface to Jeremiah. Whence it is very plain that Jeremiah
of old had the first place among the prophets: and hereby
he comes to be mentioned above all the rest, Matt. xvi. 14,
because he stood first in the volume of the prophets, therefore he is first named. When, therefore, Matthew produceth
a text of Zechariah under the name. of *Jeremy*, he only
cites the words of the volume of the prophets under his
name who stood first in the volume of the prophets. Of
which sort is that also of our Saviour, Luke xxiv. 44; " All
things must be fulfilled, which are written of me in the Law,
and the Prophets, and the Psalms." " In the Psalms;" that
is, in the Book of Hagiographa, in which the Psalms were
placed first.

Ver. 16: Βαραββᾶν· *Barabbas.*] בר אבא *Bar Abba*, a
very usual name in the Talmudists: " R. Samuel Barabba,
and R. Nathan Barabba[e]." *Abba Bar Abba*[f], אבא בר אבא
In the Jerusalem dialect it is very often uttered בר בא *Bar
Ba:* " Simeon Bar Ba[g]." " R. Chaijah Bar Ba[h]." This
brings to my mind what Josephus[i] relates to have been done
in the besieging of the city, Σκοποὶ ἐπὶ τῶν πύργων καθεζό-
μενοι προεμήνυον, ὁπόταν σχασθείη τὸ ὄργανον, καὶ ἡ πέτρα φέ-
ροιτο, τῇ πατρίῳ γλώσσῃ βοῶντες, ὁ υἱὸς [ἰὸς Huds.] ἔρχεται·
*When huge stones were thrown against the city by the Roman
slings, some persons sitting in the towers gave the citizens warn-
ing by a sign to take heed, crying out in the vulgar dialect, ' The
Son cometh,'* that is, בר בא. The Son of man indeed then
came in the glory of his justice and his vengeance, as he
had often foretold, to destroy that most wicked and profligate
nation.

Ver. 19: Μηδὲν σοὶ καὶ τῷ δικαίῳ ἐκείνῳ· *Have thou nothing
to do with that just man.*] לא ליהוי לך עסק דברים בהדי
צדיק: " When[k] king Sapores went about to afflict Rabbah,

d *Leusden's edition*, vol. ii. p. 385.
e Hieros. Moed Katon, fol. 82. 1.
f Bab. Berac. fol. 18. 2.
g Taanith, fol. 66. 1.

h Chagigah, fol. 76. 6, &c.
i De Bell. lib. v. cap. 18. [Hud-
son, p. 1232. l. 35.] [v. 6. 3.]
k Bab. Taanith, fol. 25. 2.

his mother sent to him, saying, לא ליהוי לך עסק דברים
בהדי יהודאי *Have thou nothing to do with that Jew*," &c.

Ver. 26: Τὸν δὲ Ἰησοῦν φραγελλώσας παρέδωκεν ἵνα σταυ-
ρωθῇ· *When he had scourged Jesus, he delivered him to be crucified.*] Such was the custom of the Romans towards those
that were to be crucified: Οὓς[1] μάστιξι προαικισάμενος ἀνε-
σταύρωσεν· *Whom after he had beaten with whips, he crucified.*
And a little after, Μαστιγῶσαι πρὸ τοῦ βήματος, καὶ σταυρῷ
προσηλῶσαι· *To be whipped before the judgment seat, and to be
nailed to the cross.*

Ver. 29[m]: Κάλαμον ἐπὶ τὴν δεξιάν· *A reed in his right hand.*]
See those fictions in Tanchum[n], concerning an angel that
appeared in the shape of Solomon: וקנה בידו *In whose hand
there was a reed:* ומכין אותו בקנה *and whom they struck
with a reed.*

Ver. 31: Ἀπήγαγον αὐτὸν εἰς τὸ σταυρῶσαι· *Led him away
to crucify him.*] These things are delivered in Sanhedrim[o], of
one that is guilty of stoning: " If there be no defence found
for him, they lead him out to be stoned, and a crier went
before, saying aloud thus, ' N. the son of N. comes out to be
stoned, because he hath done so and so. The witnesses
against him are N. and N.: whosoever can bring any thing
in his defence, let him come forth and produce it.' " On
which thus the Gemara of Babylon: " The tradition is, that
on the evening of the Passover Jesus was hanged, and that a
crier went before him for forty days making this proclamation, ' This man comes forth to be stoned, because he
dealt in sorceries, and persuaded and seduced Israel; whosoever knows of any defence for him, let him come forth and
produce it:' but no defence could be found, therefore they
hanged him on the evening of the Passover. Ulla saith, His
case seemed not to admit of any defence, since he was a
seducer, and of such God hath said, ' Thou shalt not spare
him, neither shalt thou conceal him,' " Deut. xiii. 8.

They led him that was to be stoned out of the city, Acts
vii. 58: so also him that was to be crucified: " The[p] place
of stoning was without the three camps; for at Jerusalem

[1] Joseph. de Bell. lib. ii. cap. 25.   [n] Fol. 59. 4.
Hudson, p. 1080. l. 45. [ii. 14. 9.]   [o] Cap. 6. hal. 4.
    [m] *English folio edit.*, vol. ii. p. 266.   [p] Gloss. in Bab. Sanhed. fol. 42. 2.

there were three camps," (namely, God's, the Levites', and the people's, as it was in the encamping in the wilderness :) "and in every city also where there was a council," (namely, of twenty-three,) "the place of stoning was without the city. For all cities that have walls bear a resemblance to the camp of Israel."

Because Jesus was judged at a heathen tribunal, therefore a death is inflicted on him not usual with the Jewish council, namely, crucifixion. In several things the circumstances and actions belonging to his death differed from the custom of the Jews in putting persons to death.

1. אין דנין שנים ביום אחר *They never judge two on the same day*[q]. But here, besides Christ, are two thieves judged.

2. They never carried one that was to be hanged to hanging till near sunset[r]: משהין אותו עד סמוך לשקיעת החמה וגומרין את דינו וממיתין אותו *They stay till near sunset, and then they pass sentence, and execute him.* And the reason is given by the Glosser; "They do not perfect his judgment, nor hang him in the morning, lest they should neglect his burial, and happen to forget[s] themselves," and the malefactor should hang till after sunset; "but near sunsetting, so that they may bury him out of hand." But Christ was sentenced to death before noon; and at noon was nailed to the cross. For,

3. ממיתין אותו ואחר כך תולין אותו *They first put the condemned person to death, and then hanged him upon a tree:* but the custom of the (*Roman*) empire is first to hang them, and then to put them to death[t]."

4. They did not openly lament for those that were led forth to be put to death; but for Jesus they did, Luke xxiii. 27, 28. The reason of this difference is not to be sought from the kind of the death, but from the persons : לא היו מתאבלין אבל אונני שאין אנינות אלא בלב *They[u] did not bewail for a person led out to execution, but they lamented inwardly in their hearts.* You will wonder at the reason which the Gloss thus gives you : "They did not openly bewail him, upon this account, that his being vilified" [when nobody

q Sanhedr. cap. 6. hal. 4.
r Ibid. in Gemara.
s *Leusden's edition*, vol. ii. p. 386.
t Sanhedr. in Gemara.
u Ibid.

openly lamented him] " might help to atone for him ; but they sorrowed for him in their hearts; for this did not tend to his honour, nor lessen the atonement." Those were better instructed, who lamented for Christ both as to the thing and person.

Ver. 33 : Γολγοθά· *Golgotha.*] Beza pretends that this is written amiss for *Golgoltha*, Γολγολθά, when yet it is found thus written in all copies. But the good man censures amiss; since such a leaving out of letters in many Syriac words is very usual : you have this word thus written without the second λ, by the Samaritan interpreter, in the first chapter of Numbers.

Ver. 34 [x] : Ἔδωκαν αὐτῷ πιεῖν ὄξος μετὰ χολῆς μεμιγμένον· *They gave him vinegar to drink mingled with gall.*] " To those [y] that were to be executed they gave a grain of *myrrh* infused in wine to drink, that their understanding might be disturbed," (that is, that they might lose their senses) ; " as it is said, ' Give strong drink to them that are ready to die, and wine to those that are of a sorrowful heart,' &c. And the tradition is, That some women of quality in Jerusalem allowed this freely of their own cost," &c.

But it makes a scruple that in Matthew it is ὄξος μετὰ χολῆς, *vinegar with gall;* in Mark, ἐσμυρνισμένον οἶνον, *wine mingled with myrrh.* If *wine*, why is it called *vinegar?* If wine mingled with *myrrh*, why *gall?* Ans. The words of Mark seem to relate to the custom of the nation ; those of Matthew, to the thing as it was really acted. I understand Mark thus, They gave him, according to the custom of the nation, that cup which used to be given to those that were led to execution ; but (as Matthew has it) not the usual mixture; namely, wine and frankincense, or myrrh ; but for the greater mockery, and out of more bitter rancour, *vinegar* and *gall.* So that we may suppose this cup not to have been prepared by those honourable women, compassionating those that were to die, but on purpose by the scribes, and the other persecutors of Christ, studying to heap upon him all kind of ignominy and vexation. In this cup they afterward dipped a sponge, as may be supposed : see the 48th verse.

---

[x] *English folio edition*, vol. ii. p. 267. [y] Bab. Sanhedr. fol. 43. 1.

Ver. 35 : Διεμερίσαντο τὰ ἱμάτιά μου· *Parted my garments.*]
Of stoning, we have this account[z] ; "When he is now four
cubits from the place of stoning, they strip him of his clothes ;
and if it be a man, they hang a cloth before him ; if a
woman, both before and behind. These are the words of
R. Juda : but the wise say, A man is stoned naked, a
woman not naked." So that it is plain enough he was crucified naked.

Ver. 38 : Δύο λησταί· *Two thieves.*]   See, in Josephus, who
they were that, at that time, were called λησταὶ, and how
much trouble and pains the governors of Judea were at to
restrain and root out this cursed sort of men : Ἐζεκίας ἀρχι-
ληστὴς χειρωθεὶς ὑφ' Ἡρώδου· *Ezekias*[a]*, the chief robber, was
subdued by Herod.* Σίμων τις περιιὼν μεθ' ὧν ἤθροισε ληστῶν
τὰ ἐν Ἱεριχοῖ βασίλεια καταπίμπρησι[b]· *One Simon, straggling
about with the robbers with whom he associated, burnt the palaces
in Jericho.* [Φήλιξ] ἀρχιληστὴν Ἐλεάζαρον ἔτεσιν εἴκοσι τὴν χώραν δῃωσάμενον, καὶ πολλοὺς τοὺς σὺν αὐτῷ ζωγρήσας, &c. [*Felix*[c]]
*having caught the chief robber Eleazar, who for twenty years had
wasted the country with fire and sword, sent him to Rome, and
many others with him.* Ἕτερον εἶδος ληστῶν ἐν Ἱεροσολύμοις
ὑπεφύετο, οἱ καλούμενοι σικάριοι, &c. *Another*[d] *kind of robbers
sprang up in Jerusalem, called sicarii,* who slew men in the
day time, and in the midst of the city," &c.

There is a rule set down[e], and the art shewed, of dis-
covering and apprehending robbers : " Go to the victualling-
houses at the fourth hour" (the Gloss, " That was the hour
of eating, and they went all to the victualling-houses to eat") ;
" and if you see there a man drinking wine, and holding the
cup in his hand, and sleeping, &c., he is a thief ; lay hold on
him," &c.

Among the monsters of the Jewish routs, preceding the
destruction of the city, the multitude of robbers, and the
horrible slaughters committed by them, deservedly claim the
first consideration ; which, next to the just vengeance of God

z Sanhedr. cap. 4. hal. 3.
a De Bell. lib. ii. cap. 6. [Hud-
son, p. 1053.] [ii. 4. 1.]
b Ibid. [ii. 4. 2.]

c Ibid. cap. 22. [Hudson, p. 1075.
12.] [ii. 13. 2.]
d Ibid. cap. 23. [ii. 13. 3.]
e Bab. Bava Mezia, fol. 83. 2.

against that most wicked nation, you may justly ascribe to divers originals.

1. It is no wonder, if that nation abounded beyond measure with a vagabond, dissolute, and lewd sort of young men; since, by means of polygamy, and the divorces of their wives at pleasure, and the nation's unspeakable addictedness to lasciviousness and whoredoms, there could not but continually spring up bastards, and an offspring born only to beggary or rapine, as wanting both sustenance and ingenuous education.

2. The foolish and sinful indulgence of the council could not but nurse up all kind of broods[f] of wicked men, while they scarce ever put any one to death, though never so wicked, as being an Israelite; who must not by any means be touched.

3. The opposition of the Zealots to the Roman yoke made them study only to mischief the Romans[g], and do all the mischief they could to those Jews that submitted to them.

4. The governors of Judea did often, out of policy, indulge a licentiousness to such kind of rapines, that they might humble that people they so much hated, and which was continually subject to insurrections, by beating them, as it were, with their own clubs; and sometimes getting a share in the booty. Thus Josephus concerning Florus: Δήμους[h] ἀθρόους ἐλυμαίνετο, &c. "He spoiled all the people, and he did in effect proclaim, that all might go out in the country to rob, that he might receive a share in the spoils." And thus a sword, that first came out of their own bowels, was sheathed in them.

Ver. 39: Κινοῦντες τὰς κεφαλάς· *Wagging their heads.*] קלות ראש *To shake the head*, with the Rabbins, signifies irreverence and lightness.

Ver. 46: Ἠλὶ, Ἠλὶ, λαμὰ σαβαχθανί· *Eli, Eli, lama sabachthani.*] I. All the rout indeed and force of hell was let loose at that time against Christ, without either bridle or chain: he calls it himself, ἐξουσίαν τοῦ σκότους, *the power of dark-*

---

f *Leusden's edition*, vol. ii. p. 387.　　h De Bell. lib. ii. cap. 24. [Hud-
g *English folio edit.*, vol. ii. p. 268.　son, p. 1078. 8. [ii. 14. 2.]

ness, Luke xxii. 53. God who had foretold of old, that the
serpent should bruise the heel of the promised seed, and now
that time is come, had slackened the devil's chain, which, in
regard of men, the Divine Providence used to hold in his
hand; so that all the power and all the rancour of hell might,
freely and without restraint, assault Christ; and that all
that malice that was in the devil against the whole elect of
God, summed up and gathered together into one head, might
at one stroke and onset be brandished against Christ without
measure.

II. Our most blessed Saviour, therefore, feeling such torments as either hell itself, or the instruments of hell, men
conspiring together in villany and cruelty, could pour out
upon him, cries out, under the sharpness of the present providence, " My God ! my God ! why hast thou delivered me
up and left me to such assaults, such bitternesses, and such
merciless hands?" The Talmudists[i] bring in Esther using
such an ejaculation, which is also cited in the Gloss on Joma[k]:
" Esther stood in the inner court of the palace. R. Levi saith,
When she was now just come up to the idol-temple, the divine
glory departed from her: therefore she said, *Eli, Eli, lamma
azabhtani.*"

Ver. 47 : 'Ηλίαν φωνεῖ οὗτος· *This man calleth for Elias.*
Ver. 49: "Ἴδωμεν εἰ ἔρχεται 'Ηλίας σώσων αὐτόν· *Let us see
whether Elias will come to save him.*] That Christ here used
the Syriac dialect, is plain from the word *sabachthani:* but
the word *Eli, Eli,* is not so properly Syriac: and hence
arose the error and misconstruction of the standers by. In
Syriac he should have said, מרי מרי *Mari, Mari:* but *Eli*
was strange to a Syrian ear: this deceived the standers-by,
who, having heard more than enough of the apparitions of
Elias from the Jewish fables, and being deceived by the
double meaning of the word, supposed that Christ was tainted
with the same folly and mistake, and called out to Elias for
help; which it was no strange thing for that deluded people
to expect.

Ver. 51 : Τὸ καταπέτασμα τοῦ ναοῦ ἐσχίσθη εἰς δύο, &c. *The
veil of the Temple was rent in twain, &c.*] Let us hear what

---

[i] Bab. Megill. fol. 15. 2. [k] Fol. 29. 1.

the Fathers of the Traditions say concerning this *catapetasm*
or *veil*[1] : " The wall of the pronaon was five cubits, the pronaon itself eleven. The wall of the Temple was six, the
Temple forty. אמה טרקסין, *the* τάραξις *one cubit*, and the
entrance, twenty." What *taraxis* means, Maimonides[m] will
tell you; " In the first Temple there was a wall one cubit
thick, separating the Holy from the Holy of Holies; but
when they built the second Temple, it was doubted whether
the thickness of that wall should be accounted to belong to
the measure of the Holy, or to the measure of the Holy of
Holies. Wherefore they made the Holy of[n] Holies twenty
cubits complete, and the Holy forty cubits complete; and
they left a void cubit between the Holy and the Holy of
Holies, but they did not build any wall there in the second
Temple : only they made two hangings, one contiguous to
the Holy of Holies, and the other to the Holy; between
which there was a void cubit, according to the thickness of
the wall that was in the first Temple; in which there was but
one *catapetasm* [or *veil*] only."

" The[o] high priest [on the day of atonement] goes forward
in the Temple, till he comes to the two hangings that divide
the Holy from the Holy of Holies, between which there was a
cubit. R. Josi saith, There was but one hanging there; as it
is said, ' And the hanging shall separate [to, or] between the
Holy and the Holy of Holies.' " On which words thus the
Gemara of Babylon[p] : " R. Josi saith rightly to the Rabbins,
and the Rabbins to thee : for he speaks of the tabernacle,
and they, of the second Temple; in which since there was
not a partition-wall, as there was in the first Temple, there
was some doubt made of its holiness, namely, whether it should
belong to the outward part of the Temple or to the inward ;
whereupon they made two hangings."

While, therefore, their minds were *troubled* about this
affair, not knowing whether they should hang the veil at the
Temple, or at the inmost recess of it, and whether the void
space between of a cubit thick should belong to this or that;
they called the place itself by the Greek word τάραξις, that is,

---

[1] Middoth, cap. 4. hal. 7.   [n] *English folio edit.*, vol. ii. p. 269.
[m] In Beth habbechirah, cap. 4.   [o] Joma, cap. 5. hal. 1.   [p] Fol. 51. 2.

trouble, as Aruch plainly affirms, and they hung up two veils, that they might be sure to offend neither against this part nor that.

You will wonder[q], therefore, that Matthew doth not say καταπετάσματα, *veils,* in the plural; or perhaps you will think that only one of these two veils was rent, not both. But it was enough for the evangelists Matthew and Mark, who speak of this miracle, to have shewed that that fence between, which hindered seeing into the Holy of Holies, and going into it, was cleft and broken. This is it they mean, not being solicitous in explaining particulars, but contented to have declared the thing itself. Perhaps the priest, who offered the incense that evening, was in the Temple at the very moment when this miracle happened : and when he went out amazed to the people, and should tell them, *The veil of the Temple is rent,* it would easily be understood of a passage broken into the Holy of Holies by some astonishing and miraculous rending of the hangings. Compare Heb. x. 19, 20.

When the high priest went into the inmost recess of the Temple on the day of atonement, he went in by the south side of the outward hanging, and the north side of the inner[r]. But now both are rent in the very middle, and that from the top to the bottom.

Ver. 52 : Καὶ πολλὰ σώματα τῶν κεκοιμημένων ἁγίων ἠγέρθη· *And many bodies of saints which slept arose.*] You can hardly impute the rending of the hangings to the earthquake, but it must be ascribed rather to another peculiar miracle; since it is more proper for an earthquake to break hard things than soft, and to rend rocks rather than curtains. Rocks were rent by it in those places where sepulchres had been built, so that now the gates of the resurrection were thrown open, the bonds of the grave were unloosed, and the bodies of dead men were made ready, as it were, for their rising again when Christ, the firstfruits, was raised. The Jews had a fancy that the kingdom of the Messias would begin with the resurrection of the dead, as we have noted before; vainly indeed, as to their sense of it; but not without some truth, as to the thing itself : for from the resurrection of Christ the glorious

---

q *Leusden's edition,* vol. ii. p. 383.   r Joma, in the place before.

epoch of the kingdom of God took its beginning, as we said
before (which he himself also signifieth in those words Matt.
xxvi. 29); and when he arose, not a few others arose with
him. What they thought of the resurrection that was to be
in the days of Messias, besides those things which we have
already mentioned, you may see and smile at in this one example: " R. Jeremiah s commanded, ' When you bury me,
put shoes on my feet, and give me a staff in my hand, and
lay me on one side; that when the Messias comes I may be
ready.' "

Ver. 54: Ἀληθῶς Θεοῦ υἱὸς ἦν οὗτος· *Truly this was the
Son of God.*] That is, " This was indeed the Messias."
Howsoever the Jews deny the Son of God in that sense in
which we own it, that is, as the second Person in the Holy
Trinity, yet they acknowledge the Messias for the Son of
God (not indeed by nature, but by adoption and deputation;
see Matt. xvvi. 63), from those places, 1 Chron. xvii. 13;
Psalm t ii. 12; lxxxix. 26, 27, and such-like. The centu-
rion had learned this from the people by conversing among
them, and, seeing the miracles which accompanied the death
of Christ, acknowledged him to be the Messias of whom he
had heard so many and great things spoken by the Jews. In
Luke u we have these words spoken by him, " Certainly this
was a righteous man :" which, I suppose, were not the same
with these words before us; but that both they *and* these
were spoken by him, " Certainly this was a righteous man :
truly this was the Messias, the Son of God." Such are
the words of Nathanael, John i. 49, " Thou art the Son of
God; thou art the King of Israel." Peter, when he declared
that " Christ was the Son of the living God," Matt. xvi. 16,
spoke this in a more sublime sense than the Jews either
owned or knew; as we have said at that place.

Ver. 56: Μαρία ἡ Μαγδαληνή· *Mary Magdalene.*] That
Magdalene was the same with Mary the sister of Lazarus
Baronius x proves at large; whom see. It is confirmed enough
from this very place; for if Mary Magdalene was not the
same with Mary the sister of Lazarus, then either Mary

---

s Jerus. Chetubboth, fol. 35. 1.   u Chap. xxiii. 47.
t *English folio edition*, vol. ii. p.   x Annal. ad An. Christ. 32, p.
270.   147, 148, &c.

the sister of Lazarus was not present at the crucifixion of Christ, and at his burial, or else she is passed over in silence by the evangelists; both which are improbable. Whence she was called *Magdalene*, doth not so plainly appear; whether from *Magdala*, a town on the lake of Gennesaret, or from the word מגדלא which signifies a *plaiting* or *curling of the hair*, a thing usual with harlots. Let us see what is spoken by the Talmudists concerning מרים מגדלא *Mary Magdala*, who, they say, was mother of Ben Satda[y]:

"They stoned the son of Satda in Lydda, and they hanged him up on the evening of the Passover. Now this son of Satda was son of Pandira. Indeed, Rabh Chasda said, 'The husband [*of his mother*] was Satda; her husband was Pandira; her husband was Papus the son of Juda: but yet I say his mother was Satda, מרים מגדלא נשיא namely, *Mary, the plaiter of women's hair;* as they say in Pombeditha, סטת דא מבעלה *she departed from her husband.*'" These words are also repeated in *Schabbath*[z]: "Rabh Bibai, at a time when the angel of death was with him, said to his officer, Go, אייתי לי מרים מגדלא שיער נשייא *bring me Mary the plaiter of women's hair.* He went and brought to him מרים מגדלא דרדקי *Mary, the plaiter of young men's hair,*" &c. The[a] Gloss; "The angel of death reckoned up to him what he had done before: for this story of *Mary, the plaiter of women's hair,* was under the second Temple, for she was the mother of *N.,* as it is said in *Schabbath.*" See the Gloss there at the place before quoted.

"There[b] are some who find a fly in their cup, and take it out and will not drink; such was Papus Ben Judas, who locked the door upon his wife, and went out." Where the Glosser says thus; "Papus Ben Juda was the husband מרים מגדלא נשייא of *Mary, the plaiter of women's hair;* and when he went out of his house into the street, he locked his door upon his wife, that she might not speak with anybody; which, indeed, he ought not to have done: and hence sprang a difference between them, and she broke out into adulteries." See Alphesius on *Gittin*[c].

[y] Bab. Sanhedr. fol. 67. 1.
[z] Fol. 104. 2. Chagigah, fol. 4. 2.
[a] *Leusden's edit.,* vol. ii. p. 389.
[b] Gittin, fol. 90. 1.
[c] Fol. 605.

I pronounce בן סטדא *Ben 'Satda,'* not that I am ignorant
that it is called *'Ben Stada'* by very learned men. The reason
of our thus pronouncing it we fetch from hence, that we
find he was called בן סוטדה *Ben Sutdah* by the Jerusalem
Talmudists [d]; to which the word *Satda* more agrees than
Stada. By the like agreement of sounds they call the same
town both מגדלא *Magdala,* and מוגדלא *Mugdala,* as we
have observed elsewhere.

As they contumeliously reflect upon the Lord Jesus under
the name of *Ben Satda,* so there is a shrewd suspicion that,
under the name of מרים מגדלא *Mary Magdala,* they also
cast reproach upon *Mary Magdalene.* The title which they
gave their Mary is so like this of ours, that you may with
good reason doubt whether she was called *Magdalene* from
the town *Magdala,* or from that word of the Talmudists,
מגדלא *a plaiter of hair.* We leave it to the learned to
decide.

Ver. 56 : Ἰωσῆ· *Joses.*] יוסי *Josi ;* a very usual name in
the Talmudists [e] : " Five were called בי ר' יוסי *Be R. Josi,*
Ismael, Lazar, Menahem, Chelpatha, Abdimus." Also, " R. [f]
Jose Ben R. Chaninah [g]," &c. One may well inquire why
this Mary is called the mother of ' James and Joses,' and
not also of ' Judas and Simon,' as Mark vi. 3.

Ver. 58 [h] : Ἡτήσατο τὸ σῶμα τοῦ Ἰησοῦ· *Begged the body of
Jesus.*] It was not lawful to suffer a man to hang all night
upon a tree, Deut. xxi. 23 : nay, nor to lie all night unburied :
כל המלין את מתו עובר בלא תעש : *Whosoever suffers a
dead body to lie all night unburied violates a negative precept.*
But they that were put to death by the council were not to
be buried in the sepulchres of their fathers ; but two burying-
places were appointed by the council, one for those that were
slain by the sword and strangled, the other for those that
were stoned [*who also were hanged*] and burnt." There, according to the custom, Jesus should have been buried, had
not Joseph, with a pious boldness, begged of Pilate that he
might be more honourably interred : which the fathers of the
council, out of spite to him, would hardly have permitted, if

---

[d] Sanhedr. fol. 25. 4.
[e] Jerus. Jevamoth, fol. 2. 2.
[f] Ibid. fol. 4. 3.

[g] See Juchasin, fol. 61. 62.
[h] *English folio edit.,* vol. ii. p. 271.

they had been asked ; and yet they did not use to deny the
honour of a funeral to those whom they had put to death, if
the meanness of the common burial would have been a disgrace to their family.   As to the dead person himself, they
thought it would be better for him to be treated dishonour-
ably after death, and to be neither lamented nor buried ; for
this vilifying of him they fancied amounted to some atonement for him ; as we have seen before.   And yet, to avoid
the disgrace of his family, they used, at the request of it, to
allow the honour of a funeral [i].

CHAP. XXVIII.

Ver. 1 : 'Οψὲ δὲ σαββάτων· *In the end of the sabbath.*]
In the Jerusalem Talmudists it is בפוקי שובא *in the coming
forth of the sabbath;* vulgarly, במוצאי שבת *in the going out
of the sabbath :* חדא ערובת שובא *On*[k] *a certain eve of the
sabbath,* namely, when the sabbath began, " there was no
wine to be found in all Samaria : בפוקי שובא but *at the end
of the sabbath* there was found abundance, because the Aram-
ites had brought it, and the Cuthites had received it."   'Οψὲ
signifies *all the night.*

Εἰς μίαν σαββάτων· *Towards the first day of the week.*]   The
Jews reckon the days of the week thus ; אחד בשבא *One
day* (or *the first day*) *of the sabbath :* תרי בשבא *two* (or *the
second day*) *of the sabbath :* " Two[l] witnesses come and say,
בחד בשבא *The first of the sabbath* this man stole, &c. ובתרי
בשבא *and, on the second day of the sabbath,* judgment passed
on him."

שלישי בשבת *The third of the sabbath :* " A virgin is married on the fourth day of the week ; for they provide for the
feast אחד בשבת *the first day of the week.*   שני בשבת
The second day of the week : שלישי בשבת and *the third day
of the week*[m]."

ברביעי בשבת " *On the fourth day of the week* they set
apart him who was to burn the red heifer[n]."

בחמישי בשבת *On the fifth of the sabbath.* " Ezra ordained that they should read the law publicly on the second

---

[i] See Bab. Sanhedr. fol. 46. 2 ;
47. 1.
[k] Avodah Zarah, fol. 44. 4.

[l] Bab. Maccoth. fol. 5. 1.
[m] Bab. Chetub. fol. 21.
[n] Gloss. in Parah, cap. 2.

and fifth days of the sabbath, &c. He appointed that judges should sit in the cities on the second and fifth days[o]. Ezra also appointed that they should wash their clothes בה" בשבת on *the fifth day of the sabbath*[p]."

The sixth day they commonly called ערב השבת *the eve of the sabbath:* "To[q] wash[r] their clothes on the fifth day of the sabbath, and eat onions on *the eve of the sabbath.*" חמישי בשבת וערב שבת ושבת, *On the fifth day of the sabbath* [or *week*], *and the eve of the sabbath, and the sabbath*[s].

The first day of the week, which is now changed into the sabbath or Lord's day, the Talmudists call יום נוצרי *the Christians', or the Christian day:* יום נוצרי עולם אסור, *On*[t] *the Christians' day it is always forbidden* for a Jew to traffic with a Christian. Where the Gloss saith thus: נוצרי *A Nazarene* or *Christian* is he who followeth the error of the man who commanded them לעשות להם יום איד בא" בשבת *to make the first day of the week a festival day to him:* and according to the words of Ismael, it is always unlawful to traffic with them[u] three days before that day and three days after; that is, not at all the week through." We cannot here pass by the words of the Glossers on Babyl. *Rosh ha-shanah*[x]; "The Baithusians desire that the first day of the Passover might be on the sabbath, so that the presenting of the sheaf might be on the first day of the week, and the feast of Pentecost on the first day of the week."

With good reason did our blessed Saviour remove the sabbath to this day, the day of his resurrection, *the day which the Lord had made,* Psalm cxviii. 24, when now *the stone which the builders refused was become the head stone of the corner.* For,

I. When Christ was to make a new world, or a new creation, it[y] was necessary for him to make a new sabbath. The sabbath of the old creation was not proper for the new.

II. The kingdom of Christ took its beginning principally from the resurrection of Christ: when he had now overcome death and hell. (The Jews themselves confess that the king-

---

[o] Hieros. Meg. fol. 75. 1.
[p] Bab. Bava Kama, fol. 82.
[q] *Leusden's edit.*, vol. ii. p. 390.
[r] Bab. Bava Kama, fol. 82.
[s] Id. fol. 37. 2.

[t] Bab. Avodah Zarah, fol. 6. 1; 7. 2.
[u] *English folio edit.*, vol. ii. p. 272.
[x] Fol. 22. 2.
[y] Isa. lxv. 17.

dom of the Messiah was to begin with the resurrection of the dead, and the renewing of the world.)   Therefore it was very proper that that day from which Christ's kingdom took its beginning should pass into the sabbath, rather than the old sabbath, the memorial of the creation.

III. That old sabbath was not instituted till after the giving the promise of Christ, Gen. iii. 15; and the rest of God on that seventh day was chiefly in having perfected the new creation in Christ : that also was the sabbatical rest of Adam.   When therefore that was accomplished which was then promised, namely, the bruising of the serpent's head by the resurrection[z] of Christ, and that was fulfilled which was typified and represented in the old sabbath, namely, the finishing of a new creation, the sabbath could not but justly be transferred to that day on which these things were done.

IV. It was necessary that the Christians should have a sabbath given them distinct from the sabbath of the Jews, that a Christian might be thereby distinguished from a Jew. For as the law took great care to provide that a Jew might be distinguished from a heathen; so it was provided by the gospel with the like care, that partly by the forsaking of those rites, partly by the bringing in of different manners and observances, a Christian might be distinguished from a Jew. The law was not more solicitous to mark out and separate a Jew from a heathen by circumcision than the gospel hath been that by the same circumcision a Christian should not Judaize.   And the same care it hath deservedly taken about the sabbath : for since the Jews, among other marks of distinction, were made of a different colour, as it were, from all nations, by their keeping the sabbath, it was necessary, that by the bringing in of another sabbath (since of necessity a sabbath must be kept up), that Christians might be of a different colour from the Jews.

Ver. 9: Χαίρετε· *All hail.*]   In the vulgar dialect of the Jews[a], איישר "The Rabbins saw a certain holy man of Caphar Immi, and said איישר χαῖρε, *All hail*[b]."   מה שואלין בשלומו של ישראל *How do they salute an Israelite ?* יישר *All hail*[c].

[z] Heb. ii. 14.
[a] Hieros. Taanith, fol. 64. 2.

[b] Ib. Sheviith, f. 35. 2; 36. 1.
[c] Id. Gittin, fol. 47. 3.

'Εκράτησαν αὐτοῦ τοὺς πόδας· *They held him by the feet.*]
This seems to have been done to kiss his feet. So 2 Kings iv.
27. For this was not unusual : " As R. Janni and R. Jonathan
were sitting together, a certain man came and kissed the
feet of R. Jonathan[d]." Compare the evangelists here, and
you will find that this was done by Mary Magdalene only,
who formerly had kissed Christ's feet, and who had gone
twice to the sepulchre, however Matthew makes mention but
of once going. The story, in short, is thus to be laid together : At the first dawning of the morning Christ arose, a
great earthquake happening at that time. About the same
time Magdalene and the other women left their houses to go
to the sepulchre : while they met together and made all
things ready, and took their journey to the tomb, the sun
was up. When they were come, they are informed of his resurrection by the angels, and sent back to the disciples. The
matter being told to the disciples, Peter and John run to the
sepulchre ; Magdalene also followed after them. They having
seen the signs of the resurrection return to their company,
but she stays there. Being ready to return back, Christ appears to her, *she supposing him to be the gardener.* As soon as she
knew him, she worships him ; and embracing his feet, kisseth
them. And this is the history before us, which Matthew relates in the plural number, running it over briefly and com-
pendiously, according to his manner.

Ver. 19[e] : Πορευθέντες οὖν μαθητεύσατε πάντα τὰ ἔθνη, βαπτίζοντες αὐτούς, &c. *Go ye therefore and teach all nations,
baptizing them, &c.*] I. The enclosure is now thrown down,
whereby the apostles were kept in from preaching the gospel
to all the Gentiles, Matt. x. 5. For, first, the Jews had now
lost their privilege, nor were they henceforward to be counted
a peculiar people ; nay, they were now become " Lo-ammi."
They had exceeded the heathens in sinning, they had slighted,
trampled upon, and crucified the Creator himself, appearing
visibly before their eyes in human flesh ; while the heathens
had only conceived amiss of the Creator, whom they neither

---

[d] Hieros. Kiddushin, f. 61. 3.
[e] *English folio edition*, vol. ii. p. 273.—*Leusden's edition*, vol. ii. p. 391.

had seen nor could see, and thereby fallen to worship the creature. Secondly, Christ had now by his blood paid a price for the heathens also. Thirdly, he had overcome Satan, who held them captive. Fourthly, he had taken away the wall of partition: and fifthly, had exhibited an infinite righteousness.

II. Μαθητεύσατε, that is, *make disciples.* Bring them in by baptism, that they may be taught. They are very much out, who from these words cry down infant-baptism, and assert that it is necessary for those that are to be baptized to be taught before they are baptized. 1. Observe the words here, μαθητεύσατε, *make disciples;* and then after, διδάσκοντες, *teaching,* in the twentieth verse. 2. Among the Jews, and also with us, and in all nations, those are made disciples that they may be taught. A certain[f] heathen came to the great Hillel, and saith, שתלמדני עמ" גייריני *Make me a proselyte, that thou mayest teach me.* He was first to be proselyted, and then to be taught. Thus first, *make them disciples* (μαθητεύσατε) by baptism; and then, *teach them to observe all things,* &c. διδάσκετε αὐτοὺς τηρεῖν πάντα.

III. Βαπτίζοντες, *baptizing.* There are divers ends of baptism:—1. According to the nature of a sacrament it visibly teacheth invisible things, that is, the washing of us from all our pollutions by the blood of Christ, and by the cleansing of grace, Ezek. xxxvi. 25. 2. According to the nature of a sacrament, it is a seal of divine truth. So circumcision is called, Rom. iv. 11; "And he received the sign of circumcision, the seal of the righteousness of faith," &c. So the Jews, when they circumcised their children, gave this very title to circumcision. The words used when a child was circumcised you have in their Talmud. Among[g] other things, he who is to bless the action saith thus, "Blessed be he who sanctified him that was beloved from the womb, and set a sign in his flesh, וצאצאיו חתם באות ברית קדש *and sealed his children with the sign of the holy covenant,* &c.

But in what sense are sacraments to be called seals? Not that they seal (or confirm) to the receiver his righteousness; but that they seal the divine truth of the covenant and pro-

---

mise. Thus the apostle calls circumcision ' the seal of the righteousness of faith :' that is, it is the seal of this truth and doctrine, that 'justification is by faith,' which righteousness Abraham had when he was yet uncircumcised. And that is the way whereby sacraments confirm faith, namely, because they do doctrinally exhibit the invisible things of the covenant ; and, like seals, do by divine appointment sign the doctrine and truth of the covenant. 3. According to the nature of a sacrament, it obligeth the receivers to the terms of the covenant : for as the covenant itself is of mutual obligation between God and man ; so the sacraments, the seals of the covenant, are of like obligation. 4. According to its nature, it is an introductory into the visible church. And, 5. It is a distinguishing sign between a Christian and no Christian, namely, between those who acknowledge and profess Christ, and Jews, Turks, and Pagans, who do not acknowledge him. Μαθητεύσατε πάντα τὰ ἔθνη βαπτίζοντες· *Disciple all nations, baptizing.* When they are under baptism, they are no longer under heathenism ; and this sacrament puts a difference between those who are under the discipleship of Christ, and those who are not. 6. Baptism also brings its privilege along with it, while it opens the way to a partaking of holy things in the church, and placeth the baptized within the church, over which God exerciseth a more singular providence than over those that are out of the church.

And now, from what hath been said, let us argue a little in behalf of infant-baptism. Omitting that argument which is commonly raised from the words before us, namely, that when Christ had commanded to baptize all nations, infants also are to be taken in as parts of the family, these few things may be observed :

I. Baptism, as a sacrament, is a seal of the covenant. And why, I pray, may not this seal be set on infants ? The seal of divine truth hath sometimes been set upon inanimate things, and that by God's appointment. The bow in the cloud is a seal of the covenant[h] : the law engraven on the altar, Josh. viii, was a seal of the covenant. The blood sprinkled on the twelve pillars that were set up to represent the twelve tribes was a seal and bond of the covenant, Exod. xxiv. And now tell me, why are not infants capable, in like manner, of such a sealing? They were capable heretofore of circumcision; and *our* infants have an equal capacity. The sacrament doth not lose this its end, through the indisposition of the receiver. Peter and Paul, apostles, were baptized: their baptism, according to its nature, sealed to them the truth of God in his promises concerning the washing away of sins, &c. And they, from this doctrinal virtue of the sacrament, received confirmation of their faith. So also Judas and Simon Magus, hypocrites, wicked men, were baptized: did not their baptism, according to the nature of it, seal this doctrine and truth, "that there was a washing away of sins?" It did not, indeed, seal the thing itself to them; nor was it at all a sign to them of the 'washing away' of theirs: but baptism doth in itself seal this doctrine. You will grant that this axiom[i] is most true, "Abraham received the sign of circumcision, the seal of the righteousness of faith." And is not this equally true? Esau, Ahab, Ahaz, received the sign of circumcision, the seal of the righteousness of faith: is not circumcision the same to all? Did not circumcision, to whomsoever it was administered, sign and seal this truth, that there 'was a righteousness of faith?' The sacrament hath a sealing virtue in itself, that doth not depend *on the disposition of the receiver*.

II. Baptism, as a sacrament, is an obligation. But now infants are capable of being obliged. Heirs are sometimes obliged by their parents, though they are not yet born: see also Deut. xxix. 11, 15. For that to which any one is obliged obtains a right to oblige " ex æquitate rei," *from the equity of the thing*, and not " ex captu obligati," *from the apprehension of the person obliged*. The law is imposed upon all under this penalty, " Cursed be every one that doth not continue in all," &c. It is ill arguing from hence, that a man hath power to perform the law; but the equity of the thing itself is very well argued hence. Our duty obligeth us to every thing which the law commands; but we cannot perform the least tittle of it.

---

[i] *Leusden's edition*, vol. ii. p. 392.

III. An infant is capable of privileges, as well as an old man ; and baptism is privilegial. An infant hath been crowned king in his cradle : an infant may be made free who is born a slave. The Gemarists[k] speak very well in this matter ; " Rabh Houna saith, They baptize an infant proselyte by the command of the bench. מאי קמ״ל *Upon what is this grounded ?* דזכות הוא לו On this, that baptism *becomes a privilege to him.* וזכין לאדם שלא בפניו *And they may endow an absent person with a privilege :* or they may bestow a privilege upon one, though he be ignorant of it. Tell me then, why an infant is not capable of being brought into the visible church, and of receiving the distinguishing sign between a Christian and a heathen, as well as a grown person.

IV. One may add, that an infant is part of his parent : upon this account, Gen. xvii. 14, an infant is to be cut off if he be not circumcised, when, indeed, the fault is his parents' ; because thus the parents are punished in a part of themselves, by the cutting off of their child. And hence is that of Exod. xx. 5, " Visiting the sins of the fathers upon the children," because children are a part of their fathers, &c. From hence ariseth also a natural reason of infant-baptism : the infants of baptized parents are to be baptized, because they are part of them, and that the whole parents may be baptized[l]. And upon this account they used of old, with good reason, to baptize the whole family, with the master of it.

Εἰς τὸ ὄνομα τοῦ πατρὸς, &c. *In the name of the Father, &c.*] I. Christ commands them to go and baptize the nations ; but how much time was past before such a journey was taken ! And when the time was now come that this work should be begun, Peter doth not enter upon it without a previous admonition given him from heaven. And this was occasioned hereby, that, according to the command of Christ, the gospel was first to be preached to Judea, Samaria, and Galilee.

II. He commands them to baptize *in the name of the Father, and of the Son, and of the Holy Ghost :* but among the Jews they baptized only *in the name of Jesus ;* which we have observed before, from Acts ii. 38 ; viii. 16 ; xix. 5. For this reason, that thus the baptizers might assert, and the baptized

---

[k] Bab. Chetubboth, fol. 11. 1.　　　　[l] [Ut patres toti baptizentur.]

confess, Jesus to be the true Messias; which was chiefly controverted by the Jews.

Of the same nature is that apostolic blessing, "Grace and peace from God the Father, and from our Lord Jesus Christ." Where then is the Holy Ghost? He is not excluded, however he be not named. The Jews did more easily consent to the Spirit of the Messias, which they very much celebrate, than to the person of the Messias. Above all others, they deny and abjure Jesus of Nazareth. It belonged to the apostles, therefore[m], the more earnestly to assert Jesus (to be the Messias), by how much the more vehemently they opposed him : which being once cleared, the acknowledging of the Spirit of Christ would be introduced without delay or scruple. Moses (in Exod. vi. 14) going about to reckon up all the tribes of Israel, goes no further than the tribe of Levi only; and takes up with that to which his business and story at that present related. In like manner the apostles, for the present, baptize *in the name of Jesus,* bless in the name of the Father and of Jesus, that thereby they might more firmly establish the doctrine of Jesus, which met with such sharp and virulent opposition ; which doctrine being established among them, they would soon agree about the Holy Ghost.

III. Among the Jews, the controversy was about the true Messiah; among the Gentiles, about the true God; it was, therefore, proper among the Jews to baptize *in the name of Jesus,* that he might be vindicated to be the true Messias : among the Gentiles, *In the name of the Father, and of the Son, and of the Holy Ghost,* that they might be hereby instructed in the doctrine of the true God. Hear this, O Arian and Socinian !

IV. The Jews baptized proselytes *into the name of the Father,* that is, into the profession of God, whom they called by the name of *Father.* The apostles baptize the Jews *into the name of Jesus, the Son :* and the Gentiles, *into the name of the Father, and of the Son, and of the Holy Ghost.*

V. *The Father* hath revealed himself in the old covenant,

m *English folio edition,* vol. ii. p. 275.

the Son in the new; in human flesh, by his miracles, doctrine, resurrection, and ascension; *the Holy Ghost*, in his gifts and miracles.   Thus the doctrine of the ever-blessed Trinity grew by degrees to full maturity: for the arriving at the acknowledgment of which it was incumbent upon all who professed the true God to be three in one to be baptized *into his name.*

HORÆ

HEBRAICÆ ET TALMUDICÆ;

OR,

HEBREW AND TALMUDICAL

EXERCITATIONS

UPON THE

GOSPEL OF ST. MARK.

SACRED[a]

TO GOD AND THE KING,

AN ALTAR

IS HERE TO BE ERECTED BEFORE THE PORCH;

AND

THANKSGIVINGS TO BE OFFERED ON IT,

FOR THIS LEISURE GRANTED TO THE STUDIES OF LEARNING;

FOR THE MUSES PRESERVED,

FOR ME AND MINE SNATCHED FROM IMMINENT RUIN,—

TO

JEHOVAH THE DELIVERER,

AND TO

CÆSAR THE PRESERVER:

TO CÆSAR THE THINGS WHICH ARE CÆSAR'S,

AND

TO GOD THE THINGS WHICH ARE GOD'S.

COME hither, stranger, [*viator*], and stand by me, while I am sacrificing; and when you hear me relating my own story, help my prayers with yours; assist me in this holy office, and worship the same deities with me.

I sing the mercy of God, and the clemency of the king, by which I was preserved from suffering shipwreck, when I had been already shipwrecked; and from being driven out of doors, when I had been already driven out.

This rectory of Great Mundon, which I have now enjoyed for almost twenty years, belongs to the royal donation and grant, *pleno jure*, as they use to speak. By which right two rectors were placed

---

[a] *Leusden's edition*, vol. ii. p. 394.

here heretofore by two kings : persons they were of eminent name, of no ordinary worth, and the like to whom their times produced not many. One was the very famous George Downham, S.T.D., presented by king James, who was promoted hence, and sent over to the bishopric of Derry in Ireland. And he leaving it, that excellent person Samuel Ward, S.T.D., master of Sidney Sussex College, in the university of Cambridge, and also the most grave and learned professor of the lady Margaret in the same university, was made his successor by king Charles. Upon his decease I succeeded here ; far unequal (alas !) to so great men : and as unhappy, that I was not admitted by the same right, but by that power that then, while the wars prevailed, possessed all. The brittleness of this my weak title lay not concealed ; but when the king's majesty, in which we now rejoice, by a happy turn of Providence returned to his own rights, it was presently discovered ; and this rectory was granted to one who was a suitor for it, by the royal donation.

Thus I and my fortunes are shipwrecked, and my affairs are come to that last extremity, that nothing now remains for me but to leave my house and these quiet retirements wherein for so many years I followed my studies with the highest satisfaction and the sweetest leisure. But another thing there was that stuck more close, namely, that I seemed to see royal majesty offended with me, and that brow that shined on others with a most sweet serenity, sad, clouded, bended on me ; and certainly to perish under the displeasure of a king is twice to perish.

Under these straits what should I do ? There was no place for hope, when the fatal instrument was now signed against me : but to despair is to subscribe to one's own misfortune, is to derogate from the king's mercy, is to submit to certain ruin under uncertain suspicion. Perhaps the most merciful king is not angry with me at all, for eagles do not use to be angry with flies. Nor, perhaps, is it too late, nor altogether to no purpose, to seek after a remedy for my wound, not yet incurable ; for as yet the fatal decree was not gone out without repeal. Perhaps my case is altogether unknown to the best king, or disguised by some unjust complaint ; and it is a comfort that my business lies before a *king*, not before a *common* man.

To the altar, therefore, of his mercy I humbly fly in a lowly supplication, begging and entreating him to consider my case, to revoke the destructive decree, and to vouchsafe to continue and establish my station in this place. Take now[b], O England, a measure of

---

[b] *Leusden's edition*, vol. ii. p. 395.

thy king ; and, even from this one example, learn what a prince
thou hast to boast of. The royal father of his country received my
supplication cheerfully, complied with my desires, and granted me
his donation,—established it with his great seal, and (which I desire
might be written in letters of gold to last for ever) by a particular,
and, as it were, paternal care, took order that hereafter none, by any
means whatsoever, should proceed to do any thing that tended either
to my danger or ruin.

O ! how would I commemorate thee, thou best of princes, greatest
Charles, how would I commemorate thee ! What praises or what expressions shall I use to celebrate or set forth so great clemency, com-
miseration, and goodness ? Those are light obligations that speak,
these my obligations stand amazed, are speechless, and swallowed
up in admiration. It is for common men to do benefits that may
be expressed in words, it is for Charles to oblige beyond all that
can be spoken.

I will add another thing also, O stranger, which the same mercy
and goodness also added. For when I feared the same fortune in
the university as I had felt in the country, and fled again to the
same altar, the royal bounty heard me, granted my petition, ratified
my desires, and confirmed and strengthened my station there also.

To comprise all in a word, which indeed exceeds all words.
Although I were an obscure person and of no note, altogether
unworthy and of no merit, wholly unknown to the king's majesty,
and lying possibly under some kind of accusations, (for it wanted
not an accusation that I was put into these places by that authority that I was,) yet twice within two weeks by the royal favour
I obtained his grant, confirmed by his hand, and the great seal of
England. And thus rooted out here he replanted me ; and ready
to be rooted out elsewhere he preserved me, rescued me from
danger, freed me of my fear : so that now I, as well as my
worthy predecessors, have this to boast of, that I have a king to
my patron.

But far be it, far be it, from me, most unworthy man, to boast :
all this, most great, most merciful prince, redounds to your praise
alone ; and let it do so : rather let England glory in such a prince,
and let the prince glory in such mercy. Triumph, Cæsar, triumph
in that brave spirit of yours, as you well may. You are Charles,
and you conquer; you subdue all by pitying, delivering, giving, and
forgiving all.

That conquest I shall always acknowledge with all humility and
thankfulness : and thou, little book, and you, trifling sheets, where-

soever ye shall fly, tell this abroad in my name everywhere, and to every man, that although there be nothing else in you worthy to be read, yet that this my sincere profession may be read and heard ; that, next after the divine mercy, I owe to the mercy of the king, that I enjoy this sweet leisure for learning, that I enjoy these quiet retirements, that I enjoy a house, that I enjoy myself.

So, O father of the country, may the Father of mercies reward you sevenfold, and seventy times sevenfold into your bosom ; and may you feel every day the benefit and sweetness of doing good by the recompenses that are made you by Heaven. Thus may your mercy ever triumph, and ever reap as the fruit of it the eternal favour of the Divine mercy. Thus may England be crowned for a long time with her king ; and may the king be crowned for ever with the love of God, with his protection, his blessing, his grace, his glory.

Made these vows,
Jan. 1, 1661.

RIGHT REVEREND FATHER IN CHRIST,

GILBERT,

BY THE DIVINE PROVIDENCE, LORD BISHOP OF LONDON. [a]

THE sacrifice by the law was to be delivered into the hands of the priest, and to be offered by him : and since your hands, reverend prelate, vouchsafed to offer my εὐκτικὰ, *petitions*, to the king's majesty, I now become an humble petitioner that those hands would please to offer also my χαριστήρια, *these testimonials of my thanks.*

I bring the firstfruits of my replantation which the royal favour indulged me by the intercession of your honour, when I had been rooted up. For since by that favour I am restored to these seats, to peace, and my studies, there is nothing I now desire besides, nothing more than that that most excellent prince may perceive, that he hath not been a benefactor to an ungrateful person, however unworthy, however obscure : and that your honour may see that you have not interceded for a forgetful person, howsoever undeserving.

I shall never forget, great sir, with how much kindness and candour your honour received me in my straits, altogether unknown to you, and whose face you had never before seen : with how great concern you pleaded my cause before the king's majesty, before the most honourable the lord chancellor of England, and before the right reverend my diocesan : how your honour consulted for me, wrote letters, laid stops, that my ruin might not proceed beyond a possibility of restoration. All which while I reflect upon, which I ever do, and while, together with that reflection, I consider what obligation lays upon me on one hand, and my own meanness on the

---

[a] *Leusden's edition*, vol. ii. p. 396.

other ; on one hand how unworthy I am of so great favour, and how altogether unable to make any recompense on the other ; what else is left me but to fly again to the same kindness, humbly imploring it, that as it at first so obligingly received me, a person unknown and unworthy ; so it would now entertain me, known and bound by so great obligation, and approaching with all the thanks I can give. Those thanks so due to your honour I have committed to these papers; unlearned indeed they are, and undressed [*impolitis*] ; but such as carry sincerity with them, though not learning, thankfulness, though not eloquence. And I have intrusted this charge with them the rather, because I suppose they may disperse themselves far and near, and perhaps may live to posterity : and that which I desire of them is, that they would declare to all how indebted he is to your honour, and to your great humanity, with how great obligations he is bound to you, and with how grateful a mind and inward affection he professeth all this, and will acknowledge it for ever, who is,

My Lord,

Your Honour's most obliged servant,

JOHN LIGHTFOOT.

EXERCITATIONS

THE GOSPEL OF ST. MARK[a].

CHAP. I.

Ver. 1 : 'Αρχὴ τοῦ εὐαγγελίου· *The beginning of the gospel.*] The preaching and baptism of John were the very gate and entrance into the state and dispensation of the gospel. For,

I. He opened the door of a new church by a new sacrament of admission into the church.

II. Pointing, as it were with the finger, at the Messias that was coming, he shewed the beginning עולם הבא *of the world to come.*

III. In that manner as the Jews by baptism admitted Gentile proselytes into the Jewish church, he admits both Jews and Gentiles into the gospel church.

IV. For the doctrine of justification by works, with which the schools of the scribes had defiled all religion, he brings in a new (and yet not a new) and truly saving doctrine of faith and repentance.

Ver. 2 : 'Ωs γέγραπται ἐν τοῖς προφήταις· *As it is written in the prophets.*] Here a doubt is made of the true meaning : namely, whether it be ἐν τοῖς προφήταις, *in the prophets*, or ἐν 'Hσαΐα τῷ προφήτῃ, *in Esaias the prophet.* These particulars make for the former :

I. When[b] two places are cited out of two prophets, it is

-----

[a] *English folio edit.*, vol. ii. p. 331.—*Leusden's edit.*, vol. ii. p. 435.
[b] *English folio edit.*, vol. ii. p. 332.

far more congruously said, *as it is written in the prophets ;*
than, *as it is written in Esaias :* but especially when the place
first alleged is not in *Esaias,* but in another *prophet.*

II. It was very customary among the Jews (to whose
custom in this matter it is very probable the apostles conformed themselves in their sermons) to hear many testimonies cited out of many prophets under this form of speech,
ככתוב בנביאים *as it is written in the prophets.* If one only
were cited, if two, if more, this was the most common manner of citing them, *as it is written in the prophets.* But
it is without all example, when two testimonies are taken
out of two prophets, to name only the last, which is done
here, if it were to be read, *as it is written in Esaias the
prophet.*

III. It is clear enough, from the scope of the evangelist,
that he propounded to himself to cite those two places,
both out of Malachi and out of Esaias. For he doth two
things most evidently: 1. He mentions the preaching of
the Baptist ; for the illustrating of which he produceth the
same text which both Matthew and Luke do out of Esaias.
2. He saith that that preaching was " the beginning of
the gospel," to prove which he very aptly cites Malachi, of
" sending a messenger," and of " preparing the way of the
Lord."

But what shall we answer to antiquity, and to so many
and so great men reading, *as it is written in Esaias the
prophet ?* " I wonder (saith the very learned Grotius), that
any doubt is made of the truth of this writing, when, beside
the authority of copies, and Irenæus so citing it, there is
a manifest agreement of the ancient interpreters, the Syriac,
the Latin, the Arabic." True [c], indeed ; nor can it be denied that very many of the ancients so read : but the ancients read also, *as it is written in the prophets.* One
Arabic copy hath, *in Isaiah the prophet :* but another
hath, *in the prophets.* Irenæus once reads *in Isaiah :*
but reads twice, *in the prophets* [d]. And " so we find it
written," saith the famous Beza (who yet follows the other
reading), " in all our ancient copies except two, and that

---

[c] *Leusden's edition,* vol. ii. p. 436.   [d] Lib. iii. cap. 11. 18.

my very ancient one, in which we read, ἐν 'Ησαίᾳ τῷ προφήτῃ, *in Esaias the prophet.*"

The whole knot of the question lies in the cause of
changing the reading; why, *as it is written in Esaias the
prophet,* should be changed into, *as it is written in the prophets.* The cause is manifest, saith that very learned man,
namely, because a double testimony is taken out of two
prophets. " But there could be no cause (saith he) of
changing of them." For if Mark, in his own manuscript,
wrote, *as it is written in the prophets,* by what way could this
reading at last creep in, *as it is written in Esaias,* when two
prophets are manifestly cited?

Reader, will you give leave to an innocent and modest
guess? I am apt to suspect that in the copies of the Jewish
Christians it was read, *in Isaiah the prophet;* but in those
of the Gentile Christians, *in the prophets:* and that the
change among the Jews arose from hence, that St. Mark
seems to go contrary to a most received canon and custom
of the Jews[e]: " He that reads the prophets in the synagogues, אין מדלגין מנביא לנביא *let him not skip from one
prophet to another.* But in the lesser prophets he may skip;
with this provision only, that he skip not backward: that is,
not from the latter to the former."

But you see how Mark *skips* here (from whom far be it
to be subject to such foolish canons) from a prophet of one
rank, namely, from a prophet who was one of the twelve, to
a prophet of another rank: and you see also how he *skips*
backward from Malachi to Isaiah. This, perhaps, was not so
pleasing to the Christian Jews, too much Judaizing yet: nor
could they well bear that this allegation should be read in
their churches so differently from the common use. Hence,
in Isaiah the prophet, was inserted for *in the prophets.* And
that they did so much the more boldly, because those words
which are cited out of Malachi are not exactly agreeable
either to the Hebrew original or the Greek version, and
those that are cited from Isaiah are cited also by Matthew
and Luke; and the sense of them which are cited from
Malachi may also be fetched from the place alleged out of
Isaiah.

[e] Megill. fol. 24. 1.

Ver. 6 : Ἐνδεδυμένος τρίχας καμήλου· *Clothed with camel's hair.*] In the Talmudists it would be read צמר גמלים *camel's wool :* "He[f] hath not a garment besides a woollen one ; לרבות צמר גמלים וצמר ארנבים *to add wool* (or *hair*) *of camels, and wool of hares :* צמר רחלים וצמר גמלים שעירבו *wool[g] of sheep, and wool of camels, which they mix*, &c." And a little after, ואפילו עשה בגד מצמר גמלים " *If he make a garment of camel's hair,* and weave in it but one thread of linen, it is forbidden, as things of different kinds."

There[h] is one that thinks that those garments of Adam concerning which it is said [Gen. iii. 21.], that God made for them כתנות עור *coats of skins*, were of *camel's hair :* בתורת ר׳ם׳ מצאו כתוב כתנות אור " In the law of R. Meir they found written כתנות אור *garments of light*. R. Isaac saith[i] that they were like those thin linen garments which come from Bethshan. R. Samuel Bar Nachman saith they were of *the wool* (or *hair*) *of camels,* and the wool of hares."

We cannot pass that by without observation, that it is said, " That in the law of R. Meir they found written כתנות אור *garments of light,* for כתנות עור *garments of skins.*" The like to which is that, " In[k] the law of R. Meir they found it written, instead of והנה טוב מאד *Behold, it was very good,* והנה טוב מות *And behold death is a good thing.* Where by *the law of R. Meir* seems to be understood some volume of the law, in the margin of which, or in some papers put in, that Rabbin had writ his critical toys and his foolish pieces of wit upon the law, or some such trifling commentary of his own upon it.

Ἐσθίων ἀκρίδας· *Eating locusts.*] They who had not nobler provision hunted after *locusts* for food. The Gemarists[l] feign that there are eight hundred kinds of them, namely, of such as are clean. That lexicographer certainly would be very acute who could describe all these kinds particularly by their names.

" The Rabbins deliver : הצד הגבים והגין וגו׳ He[m] that hunts locusts, wasps (*a kind of locusts*), hornets, and flies, on

---

[f] Menacoth, fol. 39. 2.
[g] Orach. Chaijim, lib. ii. 309.
[h] *English folio edition,* vol. ii. p. 333.
[i] Beresh Rab. sect. 20.
[k] Ibid. sect. 9.
[l] Hieros. Taanith, fol. 69. 2.
[m] Bab. Schabb. fol. 106. 2.

the sabbath, is guilty." The Gloss there, " הגזין are a kind of clean locusts, and are eaten." And the Gemara, a little after; " He that hunts locusts in the time of the dew (*on the sabbath*) is not guilty." The Gloss there writes thus; "The locusts in the time of the dew are purblind, so that if you hunt them at that time they stop their pace." The Gemara goes on, " Eliezer Ben Mabbai saith, ' If they go in flocks he is not guilty.'" The Gloss writes, " If they flock together in troops, and be, as it were, ready to be taken, he is not guilty who hunts them even in the time of heat."

Ver. 13[n]: Καὶ ἦν μετὰ τῶν θηρίων· *And was with the wild beasts.*] He was among the wild beasts, but was not touched by them. So Adam first before his fall.

Καὶ οἱ ἄγγελοι διηκόνουν αὐτῷ· *And angels ministered unto him.*] Forty days he was tempted by Satan invisibly, and angels ministered to him visibly. Satan, at last, put on the appearance of an angel of light, and pretending to wait on him, as the rest also did, hid his hook of temptation the more artificially.

Ver. 24: Ἦλθες ἀπολέσαι ἡμᾶς; *Art thou come to destroy us?*] *Us?* Whom? The devils? or those Galileans in the synagogue? See what the masters[o] say: " In that generation, in which the Son of David shall come, saith Rabban Gamaliel, Galilea shall be laid waste, and the Galileans shall wander from city to city, and shall not obtain mercy." If such a report obtained in the nation, the devil thence got a very fit occasion in this possessed man of affrighting the Galileans from receiving Christ, because they were to expect nothing from his coming but devastation.

Ver. 38: Κωμοπόλεις· *Towns.*] What this word means may be excellently well discovered by searching into the distinction between כרכים and כפרים and עיירות, to which πόλεις, *cities,* and κῶμαι, *villages,* and κωμοπόλεις, *towns,* in the evangelists, do answer:—

I. I render כרכים by πόλεις, *cities:* but by what word, you will say, will you render עיירות? By κωμοπόλεις, *towns:* —" A[p] man cannot compel his wife to follow him to dwell, לא מעיר לכרך ולא מכרך לעיר *from town to city, nor*

---

from city to town." The proper English of which take from
what follows : בשלמא מכרך לעיר " *It is plain why he cannot force* her from city to town ; דבכרך שכיחי כל מילי
because in a city any thing · is to be found," or to be had ;
אלא בעיר *but in a town any thing is not to be had.* The
Gloss writes, כרך גדול מעיר ' *Kerac' is greater than ' Ir,'*
(that is, a *city* than a *town*); and there is a place of broad
streets, where all neighbouring inhabitants meet at a market,
and there any thing is to be had." So the same Gloss[r] elsewhere ; " *Kerac* is a place of broad streets, where men meet
together from many places," &c.

The Gemarists go on : " R. Josi Bar Chaninah saith,
Whence is it that dwelling in כרכין *Kerachin* (*cities*) is more
inconvenient ? For it is said, ' And they blessed all the people
who offered themselves willingly to dwell at Jerusalem' "
(Neh. xi). Note, by the way, that Jerusalem was כרך
Kerac. The Gloss there is, " Dwelling in ' *Kerachin*' is worse,
because all dwell there, and the houses are straitened, and
join one to another, so that there is not free air : but בעיר
in a town are gardens, and paradises by the houses, and the
air is more wholesome."

כרכים *Kerachim* therefore were, 1. Cities girt with walls.
Hence is that distinction, כרכין המוקפין חומה מימי יהושוע
*that there were some 'Kerachin' which were girt with walls from
the days of Joshua,* and some walled afterward. 2. Trading
and mart cities, and those that were greater and nobler than
the rest.

II. כפרים therefore were *villages* or *country towns,* in
which no synagogue was. Hence is that פסקי הראש in
Megill. cap. 1: כרך שאין בו י׳ בטלנין נדון ככפר *A Kerac*
(*a city*), *in which are not ten men to make a synagogue, is to be
reckoned for a village.* And Megill. cap. 1, where some of a
village are bound to read the Book of Esther in the feast of
Purim : ומקדימים ליום הכניסה *It is indulged to them to do
it on a synagogue-day :* that is, when they had not a synagogue
among them, but must resort to some neighbour town where
a synagogue was, it was permitted them to go thither on
some weekday, appointed for meeting together in the syna-

gogue, and that they might not take the trouble of a journey on another day, however that day was appointed by law for that lection.

III. עִיר, which word is commonly rendered *urbs*, or *civitas*, *a city*; and denoted generally fortified cities, and towns also not fortified, where synagogues were, and villages, where they were not. Hence is that distinction, עִיר גְדוֹלָה "That was *a great city* where there was a synagogue:" עִיר קְטַנָּה " *a small city* where there was not."

By κωμοπόλεις therefore here are to be understood towns where there were synagogues, which nevertheless were not either fortified or towns of trade; among us English called *church-towns*.

CHAP. II.

VER. 4: Ἀπεστέγασαν τὴν στέγην, &c.   *They uncovered the roof, &c.*] Here I recollect that phrase דֶרֶךְ גַגִין *the way of the roof*: " When[s] Rabh Houna was dead, his bier could not be carried out through the door," the door being too strait; סָבוּר לְשַׁלְשׁוּלֵי דֶרֶךְ גַגִין " therefore *they thought good to draw it out and let it down through the roof*, or *through the way of the roof*. But Rabh Chasda said to them, 'Behold, we have learned from him that it redounds to the honour of a wise man to be carried out by the door.' "

" It[t] is written, 'And they shall eat within thy gates' (Deut. xxvi. 12); that is, when[u] the entrance into the house is by the gate, לְאַפּוֹקֵי דֶרֶךְ גַגוֹת *to except the way through the roof*." " Does[v] he enter into the house, דֶרֶךְ פְתָחִים מִשְׁתַּמֵּשׁ אוֹ דֶרֶךְ גַגִין מִשְׁתַּמֵּשׁ *using the way through the gate, or using the way through the roof?*" The place treats of a house, in the lower part of which the owner dwells; but *the upper part*, that which is called ὑπερῷον, is let out to another. It is asked, what way he must enter who dwells in an upper room, whether by the door and the lower parts, where the owner dwells; or whether he must climb up to the roof דֶרֶךְ גַגִין *by the way to the roof*: that is, as the Gloss hath it, " That he ascend without the house by a ladder set against

s Bab. Moed Katon, fol. 25. 1.   u *Leusden's edition*, vol. ii. p. 438.
t Bava Mezia, fol. 88. 1.   v Ibid. fol. 117. 1.

it for entrance into the ὑπερῷον, *the upper room,* and so go
into the upper room."

By ladders set up, or perhaps fastened there before, they
first draw up the paralytic ἐπὶ δῶμα, *upon the roof,* Luke v. 19.
Then seeing there was a door in every roof through which
they went up from the lower parts of the house into the roof,
and this being too narrow to let down the bed and the sick
man in it, they widen that space by pulling off the tiles that
lay about it.

Well[w], having made a hole through the roof, the paralytic
is let down εἰς τὸ ὑπερῷον, *into the upper chamber.* There
Christ sits, and the Pharisees and the doctors of the law
with him, and not in the lower parts of the house. For it was
customary for them, when they discoursed of the law or religion, to go up into the upper chamber.

" These[x] are the traditions which they taught בעליית *in
the upper chamber* of Hananiah, Ben Hezekiah, Ben Garon."
" They[y] elders went up לעליית *into an upper chamber* in
Jericho. They went up also into an upper chamber in Jabneh."
" Rabh[z] Jochanan and his disciples went up εἰς ὑπερῷον, *to an
upper chamber,* and read and expounded." Compare Mark
xiv. 15; Acts i. 13; xx. 8.

Ver. 7 : Τίς δύναται ἀφιέναι ἁμαρτίας; *Who can forgive sins ?*]
" A certain heretic[a] said to Rabh Idith, It is written, ' And
he said unto Moses, Come up unto the Lord,' Exod. xxiv. 1.
It should rather have been said, ' Come up to me.' He answereth, This is *Mitatron*[b], whose name is like the name of
his Lord, as it is written, ' My name is in him,' Exod. xxiii. 21.
If it be so, then said the other, he is to be worshipped. To
whom Idith replied, It is written אל תמר בו אל תמירני בו
properly, *Do not imbitter* or *provoke him;* but they illy and
perversely read, *Do not change for him, do not exchange me for
him.* If that be the sense, said the other, what is the meaning of that, ' He will not forgive your sins?' He answered,
True indeed, דאפילו כפרוונקא נמי לא קבלניה *for we received him not so much as for a messenger.*" The Gloss is,

---

[w] *English folio edition,* vol. ii.
p. 335.
[x] Schabb. cap. i. hal. 7.
[y] Hieros. Sanhedr. fol. 24. 3.

[z] Juchas. fol. 23. 2.
[a] Sanhedr. fol. 38. 2.
[b] [See Buxtorf Lex. T. et R.
sub v. מְטַטְרוֹן col. 1192.]

" ' He will not forgive your sins ;' that is, He cannot pardon
your sins ; and then, what advantage is there from him? For
he had not the power of pardoning our sins ; we therefore rejected him," &c.   Ye rejected him, indeed, in whom was
the name of Jehovah ; but alas! how much to your own
mischief!

Ver. 9: Τί ἐστιν εὐκοπώτερον εἰπεῖν· *Whether is it easier to say,
&c.*]   He that observes the use of the word נִיחָא *it is easy,*
and קַשְׁיָא *it is hard,* in the Jewish schools (and the school-
men were now with Christ), cannot think it improper that
εὐκοπώτερον should be of the same import with נִיחָא, which
word denotes the thing or the sense plain, smooth, and without scruple ; קַשְׁיָא *it is hard,* denotes the contrary.   As if
our Saviour had said, " Were not the sense plainer, and more
suited to the present business to have said, ' Arise and take
up thy bed,' than to say, ' Thy sins are forgiven thee?'   But I
say thus, that ye may know that the Son of man hath
power," &c.   He does not speak of the easiness of the pronunciation of the words, but of the easiness of the sense.
And I should thus render the words, " It is easier to say to
the paralytic, Thy sins are forgiven thee, than to say," &c.
' Whether to say,' as it is vulgarly rendered, hath a sense not
to be disapproved of ; but, ' than to say,' hath a sense more
emphatical.   Is not the sense easier as to the present business
to say, ' Thy sins are forgiven,' than to say, ' Rise up and
walk ?'

Ver. 12 : Ἐξῆλθεν ἐναντίον πάντων· *He went out before them
all.*]   It is very well rendered, "*before* them all :" and it
might truly be rendered "*against* them all," according to
another signification of the word ἐναντίον.   That is, when
the multitude was so crowded that there was no way of
going out through it, he, being not only made whole, but
strong and lusty, pressed through the press of the multitude,
and stoutly made his way with his bed upon his shoulders.

Ver. 16 : Καὶ ἁμαρτωλῶν· *And sinners.*]   Who were they?
" Dicers[c], usurers, plunderers, publicans, shepherds of lesser
cattle, those that sell the fruit of the seventh year," &c.

Ver. 26[d] : Ἐπὶ Ἀβιάθαρ τοῦ ἀρχιερέως· *In the days of*

---

[c] Sanhedr. fol. 25. 2.   [d] *English folio edition,* vol. ii. p. 336.

Abiathar the high priest.] It is well enough known what is here said in defence of the purity of the text; namely, that Ahimelech the father was called *Abiathar*, and *Abiathar* the son was called also Ahimelech. But I suppose that something more was propounded by our Saviour in these words. For it was[e] common to the Jews under *Abiathar* to understand the Urim and Thummim. Nor without good reason, when it appears, that under the father and the son, both of that name, the mention of inquiring by Urim and Thummim is more frequent than it is ever anywhere else; and, after *Abiathar* the son, there is scarcely mention of it at all. Christ therefore very properly adds, ἐπὶ ᾿Αβιάθαρ ἀρχιερέως, *in the days of Abiathar the high priest,* therein speaking according to a very received opinion in the nation: as though he had said, " David ate the shewbread given him by the high priest, who had the oracle by Urim and Thummim present with him, and who acted by the divine direction."

" Ahitophel[f], that is, a counsellor, Benaiah, the son of Jehoiada, that is, the Sanhedrim; אביתר אילו אורים ותמים, *Abiathar, that is, Urim and Thummim.*"

CHAP. III.

VER. 5 : Οἱ δὲ ἐσιώπων· *But they held their peace.*] This reminds me of the like carriage of the Sanhedrim in judging a servant of king Jannæus, a murderer, when Jannæus himself was present in the Sanhedrim[g]. It was found sufficiently that he was guilty; but, for fear, they dared not to utter their opinion; when Simeon Ben Sheta, president of the Sanhedrim, required it : נפנה לימינו כבשו פניהם בקרקע " *He looked on his right hand, and they fixed their eyes upon the earth; on his left hand, and they fixed their eyes upon the earth,*" &c.

Ver. 17 : Βοανεργές· *Boanerges.*] I. See what Beza saith here. To which our very learned Hugh Broughton, a man very well exercised in these studies, replies : " The Jews to this very day pronounce *Scheva* by *oa,* as *Noabhyim* for *Nebhyim.* So *Boanerges.* When Theodore Beza will have it

---

[e] *Leusden's edit.,* vol. ii. p. 439.   [f] Bab. Sanhedr. fol. 16. 2.
[g] Sanhedr. fol. 19. 1.

written *Benerges,* the very Jews themselves will defend our gospel."

Certainly, it is somewhat hard and bold to accuse the Scripture of St. Mark as corrupt for this manner of pronunciation, when, among the Jews, the pronouncing of some letters, vowels, and words was so different and indifferent, that they pronounced one way in Galilee, another way in Samaria, and another way in Judea. "And I remember (saith the famous Ludovicus de Dieu[h]), that I heard the excellent Erpenius say, that he had it from the mouth of a very learned Maronite, that it could not be taught by any grammatical rules, and hardly by word of mouth, what sound *Scheva* hath among the Syrians."

That castle of noted fame which is called *Masada* in Josephus, Pliny[i], Solinus, and others (in Hebrew מצדה), in Strabo[k] is *Moasada,* very agreeable to this our sound : Πέτρας τινὰς ἐπικεκαυμένας δεικνύουσι τραχείας περὶ Μοασάδα· *They shew some scorched rocks about 'Moasada.'* Where, without all controversy, he speaks of *Masada.*

II. There is a controversy also about the word *erges:* it is obscure, in what manner it is applied to *thunder.* But give me your judgment, courteous reader, what ריגשא is in this story: "The[l] father of Samuel sat in the synagogue of Shaph, and Jathib, in Nehardea : אתיא שכינה *the divine glory came;* שמע קול ריגשא ולא נפק *he heard the voice of* ריגשא '*Rigsha,'* and *went not out:* the angels came, and he was affrighted."

Of the word ריגשא *Rigsha,* the Glossers say nothing. And we do not confidently render it *thunder;* nor yet do we well know how to render it better: if so be it doth not denote[m] ἦχος ὥσπερ φερομένης πνοῆς βιαίας, *the sound as of a mighty rushing wind,* Acts ii. 2 : but let the reader judge.

III. As obscure is the reason of the name imposed upon these two disciples, as the derivation of the word. We have only this certain in this business, that we never find them called by this name elsewhere. Christ called Simon *Peter,* and likewise others called him *Peter,* and he calls himself so.

---

[h] In his Præfat. ad Apoc. Syriac.

[i] [Nat. Hist. v. 17.]

[k] Strab. Geograph. lib. xvi. [c. 2.]

[l] Megill. fol. 29. 1.

[m] *English folio edit.,* vol. ii. p. 337.

But you never find James called *Boanerges*, or John so called, either by themselves or by others. We must trust conjecture for the rest.

IV. It is well enough known what the phrase בת קול *Bath Kol, the daughter of thunder*, means among the Jews. Our Saviour, using another word, seems to respect another etymology of the name. But it is demanded, what that is. He calls Simon *Peter* with respect had to the work he was to ply in building the church of the Gentiles upon a *rock*. For he first opened the door to let in the gospel among the Gentiles. Whether were James and John called *sons of thunder* with respect had to their stout discoursing against the Jews, we neither dare to say, nor can we deny it. James did this, as it seems, to the loss of his life, Acts xii.

But what if allusion be here made to the two registrars, or scribes of the Sanhedrim? whereof one sat on the right hand, and the other on the left; one wrote the votes of those that acquitted, the other the votes of those that condemned[m]. Or to the president himself, and the vice-president? whose definitive sentence, summing up the votes of the whole Sanhedrim, was like thunder and lightning to the condemned persons, and seemed to all like the oracles given from Sinai out of lightning and thunder.

V. But whatsoever that was in the mind of our Saviour, that moved him to imprint this name upon them, when these two brethren, above all the other disciples, would have fire fall[n] from heaven upon that town of the Samaritans which refused to give Christ entertainment, Luke ix. 54, they seem to act according to the sense of this surname. And when the mother of these desired a place for one of them on Christ's right hand, and for the other on his left, she took the confidence of such a request probably from this, that Christ had set so honourable a name upon them above the other disciples. And when John himself calls himself *the elder*, κατ' ἔμφασιν, and he was sufficiently known to those to whom he writ under that bare title, ὁ πρεσβύτερος, *the elder;* I cannot but suspect this distinguishing character arose hence. All the apostles, indeed, were *elders*, which Peter saith of himself,

[m] Sanhedr. fol. 35. 1. and Maimon. in Sanhedr. cap. 1.
[n] *Leusden's edition*, vol. ii. p. 440.

1 Pet. v. 1: but I ask, whether any of the twelve, besides this our apostle (his brother James being now dead), could be known to those that were absent under this title, *the elder*, by a proper, not additional name, as he is in his two latter Epistles.

Ver. 21: Ὅτι ἐξέστη· *He is beside himself.*] In the Talmudists it is נטרפה דעתו *his judgment is gone*, and שף דעתיה *his understanding is ceased.* "If[o] any becomes mute, ונכונה דעתו *and yet is of a sound mind*, and they say to him, Shall we write a bill of divorce for thy wife? and he nods with his head, they try him thrice, &c. And it is necessary that they make trial of him more exactly, שמא נטרפה דעתו *lest, perhaps, he might be deprived of his senses.*" This is to be understood of a dumb person, made so by some paralytical or apoplectical stroke, which sometimes wounds the understanding.

"The[p] Rabbins deliver: If any one is sick, and in the mean time any of his friends die, they do not make it known to him that such a one is dead, שמא תטרף דעתו *lest his understanding be disturbed.*" "One[q] thus lamented R. Simeon Ben Lachish; 'Where art thou, O Bar Lachish? Where art thou, O Bar Lachish?' והוה קא צוח עד דשף דעתיה *And so cried out until his understanding perished.*" For so the Gloss renders it.

How fitly this word ἐξέστη expresseth these phrases is readily observed by him who understandeth both languages. And a Jew, reading these words in Mark, would presently have recourse to the sense of those phrases in his nation; which do not always signify *madness*, or being bereft of one's wits, in the proper sense, but sometimes, and very frequently, some discomposure of the understanding for the present, from some too vehement passion. So say Christ's friends, נטרפה דעתו *His knowledge is snatched away;* he hath forgotten himself, and his own health; he is so vehement and hot in discharging his office, and in preaching, that he is transported beyond himself, and his understanding is disturbed, that he neither takes care of his necessary food nor of his sleep." Those his friends, indeed, have need of an apology, that they

o Maimon. Gerush. cap. 2. p Moed Katon, fol. 26. 2.
q Bava Mezia, fol. 84. 1.

had no sounder, nor holier, nor wiser conceit of him; but it is scarcely credible that they thought him to be fallen into plain and absolute madness, and pure distraction. For he had conversed among the [r] multitudes before, at all times in all places; and yet his friends do not say this of him. But now he was retired to his own house at Capernaum, where he might justly expect rest and repose; yet the multitudes rush upon him there, so that he could not enjoy his table and his bed at his own home. Therefore his friends and kinsfolk of Nazareth (among whom was his mother, ver. 31), hearing this, unanimously run to him to get him away from the multitude; for they said among themselves, Ἐξέστη, *He is too much transported* beyond himself, and is forgetful of himself.

CHAP. IV.

Ver. 1: Ἤρξατο διδάσκειν· *He began to teach.*] That is, *he taught;* by a phrase very usual to these holy writers, because very usual to the nation: שרי רב כהנא מאריך בצלותיה *Rabh [s] Canah began to be tedious in his prayer;* that is, *he was tedious.* שרי ההוא תלמידא בכי *that [t] scholar began to weep;* that is, *he wept.* שרי גֵעֵי " the [u] ox *began to low;*" that is, *he lowed.* " When the tyrant's letter was brought to the Rabbins, שרון בכיין *they began to weep [x];*" that is, *they wept.*

This our evangelist useth also another word, and that numberless times almost: the others also use it, but not so frequently; namely, the word εὐθὺς, and εὐθέως, *presently;* which answereth to the word מיד *out of hand,* most common among the Talmudists. We meet with it in this our evangelist seven or eight times in the first chapter, and elsewhere very frequently: and that not seldom according to the custom of the idiom, more than out of the necessity of the thing signified.

Ver. 4: Ὁ μὲν ἔπεσε· *And some fell.*] כדי נפילה: *According [y] to what falls.* The Gloss there, " According to the measure which one sows." And there the Gemarists speak of

---

[r] *English folio edit.*, vol. ii. p. 338.
[s] Hieros. Sanhed. fol. 18. 3.
[t] Ibid. fol. 23. 3.
[u] Beresh. Rabb. sect. 33.
[x] Ibid. sect. 64.
[y] Bava Mezia, fol. 105.

מפולת יד *seed falling out of the hand :* that is, that is cast out of the hand of the sower: and of מפולת שוורים *seed falling from the oxen :* that is, " that which is scattered and sown" by the sowing oxen. " For (as the Gloss speaks) sometimes they sow with the hand, and sometimes they put the seed into a cart full of holes, and drive the oxen[z] upon the ploughed earth, and the seed falls through the holes."

Ver. 5 : Διὰ τὸ μὴ ἔχειν βάθος γῆς· *Because it had no depth of earth.*] For it was rocky, whose turf nevertheless was thick enough, and very fruitful; but this ground which the parable supposeth wanted that thickness. " You[a] have not a more fruitful land among all lands than the land of Egypt ; nor a more fruitful country in Egypt than Zoan. And yet Hebron, which was rocky, exceeded it sevenfold." Note that ' it was *rocky*, and yet so *fruitful*.'

Ver. 7 : Εἰς τὰς ἀκάνθας· *Among thorns.*] The parable supposeth, שדה לא שנתקוצה *a field not freed from thorns*[b].

Ver. 11[c] : Ἐκείνοις δὲ τοῖς ἔξω· *Unto them that are without.*] Οἱ ἔξω, *those without,* in Jewish speech, were *the Gentiles ;* a phrase taken hence, that they called all lands and countries besides their own, חוצה לארץ *without the land.* Would you have an exact instance of this distinction ? " A tree[d], half of which grows within the land of Israel, and half without the land, the fruits of it which are to be tithed, and the common fruits are confounded : they are the words of Rabba. But Rabban Simeon Ben Gamaliel saith, ' That part which grows within the place, that is bound to tithing" [that is, within the land of Israel], " is to be tithed: that which grows in the place free from tithing" (that is, without the land) " is free." The Gloss is, " For if the roots of the tree are without the land, it is free, although the tree itself extends itself sixteen cubits within the land."

Hence ספרים חיצונים *books* οἱ ἔξω, *that are without,* are heathen books : ספרים החיצונים של חכמת יוונית *extraneous books of Greek wisdom*[e].

This is the common signification of the phrase. And, certainly it foretells dreadful things, when our blessed Sa-

---

[z] *Leusden's edit.,* vol. ii. p. 441.
[a] Setah, fol. 34. 2. Chetub. 112. 1.
[b] See Sheviith, cap. 4. hal. 2.
[c] *English folio edit.,* vol. ii. p. 339.
[d] Bava Bathra, fol. 27. 2.
[e] Aruch in the word מרום.

viour stigmatizeth the Jewish nation with that very name that they were wont to call the heathens by.

The word חיצונים *those without*, occurs also in the Talmudists, when it signifies the Jews themselves ; that is, some of the Jewish nation.   Here [f] קראים *the Karaites*, who rejected traditions, there חיצונים οἱ ἔξω, *those without*, are opposed to חכמים *the wise men :* "He that puts his phylacteries on his forehead, or in the palm of his hand, הרי זו דרך הקראים *behold ! he follows the custom of the Karaites.*   And he that overlays one of them with gold, and puts it upon his garment which is at his hand, הרי זו דרך החיצונים *behold ! he follows the custom of those that are without.*   Where the Gloss, "חיצונים are men who follow their own will, and not the judgment of the wise men."   They are supposed to wear phylacteries, and to be Jews ; but when they do according to their pleasure, and despise the rules of the wise men, they are esteemed as *those that are without*, or *heathens.*   So was the whole Jewish nation according to Christ's censure, which despised the evangelical wisdom.

Ἐν παραβολαῖς τὰ πάντα γίνεται· *All things are done in parables.*]   I. How much is the Jewish nation deceived concerning the times of the Messias !   They think his forerunner Elias will explain all difficulties, resolve scruples, and will render all things plain ; so that when the Messias shall come after him, there shall be nothing obscure or dark in the law and in religion.   Hence these expressions, and the like to them :   "One [g] found a bill of contracts in his keeping, and knew not what it meant, יהא מונח עד שיבא אליהו *Let it be laid up till Elias shall come.*"   And more in the same tract, concerning things found, when it is not known to whom they are to be restored, "Let them be laid up till Elias come."   פרשה זו עתיד אליהו לפרשה *That* [h] *passage*, (Ezek. xiv. 18, 19, where עולה *a burnt offering* is called חטאת *a sacrifice for sin,*) *Elias will unfold.*"   Infinite examples of that sort occur.

But, alas ! thou art deceived, O Jew.   All things are made clear which make to eternal salvation, Elias and Messias,

[f] Megill. fol. 24. 2.   [g] Bav. Mezia, cap. 1. hal. ult.
          [h] Menacoth, fol. 45. 1.

John and Christ preaching the gospel when they came; but they are obscure to you, both by reason of your voluntary blindness, who have shut your eyes and your mind against the saving doctrine of the gospel; and from the just judgment of the Messias, who justly preached in clouds and in covered expressions to them who would not see the sun and the open light.

II. How those words have wracked interpreters, " Is a candle put under a bushel," &c.; and, " There is nothing hidden," &c.: you may see also without a candle. A very easy sense of them is gathered from the context. When Christ speaks in parables, " A light is put under a bushel:" but " the light (saith he) is not come for this end," that it should be so hidden; nor, indeed, were it fit so to hide it, but that the divine justice would have it so, that they who will not see the light should not enjoy the light. But " there is nothing hid " which shall not be made manifest by the brightness of the doctrine of the gospel, so there be eyes that do not refuse the light, nor voluntarily become purblind. Therefore, take you heed how you hear, lest ye be like them, and divine justice mete to you by the same measure as is measured to them; namely, that they shall never hear, because they will not hear.

CHAP. V.[i]

VER. 1 : Εἰς τὴν χώραν τῶν Γαδαρηνῶν· *Into the country of the Gadarenes.*] So also Luke: but Matthew, εἰς τὴν χώραν Γεργεσηνῶν, *into the country of the Gergesenes.* And, which ought not to be passed over without observation, Mark and Luke, who call it *the country of the Gadarenes,* make mention only of *one* possessed person; but Matthew, who calls it *the country of the Gergesenes,* speaks of *two.* We know what is here said by commentators to reconcile the evangelists. We fetch their reconciliation from the very distinction of the words which the evangelists use, and that from those conclusions :

I. We say the region of the *Gergesenes* was of broader extent and signification than the region of the *Gadarenes*

<hr>

[i] *English folio edition,* vol. ii. p. 340.

was, and that the region of the *Gadarenes* was included
within it.   For whether it were called so from the old *Ger-
gashite* family of the Canaanites, or from the muddy and
clayey nature of the soil, which was called גרגשתא *Gergishta*
by the Jews, which we rather believe; it was of wider ex-
tension than the country of the *Gadarenes;* which denoted
only one city, and the smaller country about it, and that
belonged to *Gadara.*   But this country comprehended within
it the country of *Gadara,* of Hippo, and of Magdala, if not
others also.

II. We say *Gadara* was a city of heathens, (hence it is
less marvel if there were swine among them:) which we
prove also elsewhere, when we treat of the region of
Decapolis.

III. We say there were two possessed persons according
to Matthew, one a *Gadarene,* another coming from some
other place than the country of *Gadara,* namely, from some
place in the country of the *Gergesenes.*

IV. We believe that that *Gadarene* was a heathen; and
that Mark and Luke mentioned only him on set purpose,
that so they might make the story the more famous.   Any
one skilled in the chorography of the land of Israel might
understand that *the country of the Gadarenes* was of heathen
possession: they therefore mark him with that name, that it
might presently be perceived that Christ now had to do
with a heathen possessed person; which was somewhat rare,
and except the daughter of the Syrophœnician woman,
without any example.   Matthew would describe the great-
ness of the miracle; he therefore mentions *two* most miserably possessed persons: but Mark and Luke choose out only
one, and him more remarkable for this very thing, that he
was a *Gadarene,* and by consequence a heathen.   These
things, well weighed, do not only confirm the concord between the evangelists, but render the story far clearer.
For,

First, It is to be marked that the devil adjures Christ
not to "torment" him, ver. 7, which is not elsewhere done by
him: as though he were without Christ's jurisdiction, not
being among his people the Jews, but among the heathens.
And,

Secondly, Christ does not elsewhere ask any about their name, besides this alone, as being of more singular example and story.

Thirdly, The heathen name λεγεὼν, *legion*, argues him a heathen concerning whom the story is.

Fourthly, The devils besought him much that he would not send them out of the country; for being among heathens, they thought they were among their own.

Our Saviour, therefore, healed those two in Matthew together, the one, a *Gadarene* and heathen, and the other from some other place, a *Gergesene* and a Jew; and that not without a mystery; namely, that there should be comfort in Christ both to Jews and Gentiles, against the power and tyranny of Satan. Of those two, Mark and Luke mention the more remarkable.

Ver. 9 : Λεγεὼν ὄνομά μοι· *My name is Legion.*]   I. This name speaks a numerous company, the devil himself being the interpreter ; " *Legion* (saith he) *is my name*, for we are many."

And among the Jews, when a man would express a great number of any thing, it was not unusual to name *a legion*: " R. Eliezer[k] Ben Simeon saith, נוח לו לאדם לגדל לגיון אחד של זיתים בגליל *It*[1] *is easier for a man to nourish a legion of olives in Galilee*, than to bring up one child in the land of Israel."

II. Among the Talmudists, *a legion* bespeaks an unclean company ; at least, they reckoned all the legions for unclean : " The[m] Rabbins deliver: לגיון העובר *a legion that passeth* from place to place, if it enter into any house, the house is thereby become unclean. שאין לך כל לגיון ולגיון שאין לו כמה קרקפלין *for there is no legion which hath not some car-caphalia.* And wonder not at this, when the *carcaphalion* of R. Ismael was fastened to the heads of kings." קרקפל " ' *Carcaphal*' (saith the Gloss) is the skin of a head pulled off from a dead person, which they make use of in enchantments." It is a Greek word, saith the Aruch, καρακεφαλή.

III. What the Romans thought of their *legions*, take from

---

the words of Cæsar to the Spaniards : "Did[n] ye not consider, if I were overthrown, that the people of Rome have ten *legions*, which could not only resist you, but pull down even heaven itself?" What then is the power of "more than twelve *legions* of angels !"

Ver. 14: 'Ανήγγειλαν εἰς τοὺς ἀγρούς· *Told it in the country.*] *Told it* εἰς τοὺς ἀγροὺς, *in the fields.* But to whom? To them that laboured, or that travelled in the fields? So chap. vi. 36 : 'Απελθόντες εἰς τοὺς κύκλῳ ἀγροὺς, ἀγοράσωσιν ἑαυτοῖς ἄρτους· *That they may go away into the 'fields' round about, and buy themselves bread.* From whom, I pray, should they buy in the *fields*? And ver. 56 : Καὶ ὅπου ἂν εἰσεπορεύετο εἰς κώμας ἢ ἀγροὺς, ἐν ταῖς ἀγοραῖς ἐτίθουν τοὺς ἀσθενοῦντας· *And wheresoever they entered into towns or 'fields,' they laid the sick in the streets, or markets.* What *streets* or *markets* are there in the *fields*?

"Rabba[o] saith, That food made of meal, דחקלאי דמפישי ביה *of those that dwell in the fields, in which they mingle much meal, over it they give thanks.*" חקלאי, saith the Gloss, are בני כפר *inhabitants of the villages.* And the *Aruch* saith, "חקלייתא are private men who dwell in the fields:" that is, in houses scattered here and there, and not built together in one place, as it is in towns and cities.

Ver. 15: Σωφρονοῦντα· *In his right mind.*] נכונה דעתו : *firm*, or *sound of understanding*, in Talmudic speech.

Ver. 23: Τὸ θυγάτριόν μου· *My little daughter.*] Ἦν γὰρ ἐτῶν δώδεκα· *For she was twelve years old*, ver. 42 : "A[P] daughter from her birthday, until she is *twelve years old* complete, קטנה נקראת או תינוקת *is called 'little,' or 'a little maid.'* מבת יב' שנה ויום אחד *but when she is full twelve years old and one day over*, נקראת נערה *she is called 'a young woman.'*

Ver. 26: Καὶ πολλὰ παθοῦσα ὑπὸ πολλῶν ἰατρῶν· *And had suffered many things of many physicians.*] And it is no wonder: for see what various and manifold kinds of medicines are prescribed to a woman labouring under a flux:

[n] Comment. de Bell. Civil. lib. vi. [c. 42.] [An me deleto non animadvertebatis, decem legiones habere populum Romanum, quæ non solum vobis obsistere, sed etiam cœlum diruere possent.]

[o] Babyl. Beracoth, fol. 37. 2.

[P] Maimon. in אישות cap. 2.

" R. Jochanan saith[q], לייתי מתקל זוזא קימא אלכסנדריא
Bring (or *take*) *of gum of Alexandria the weight of a zuzee:*
ומתקל זוזא גביא גילא *and of alum, the weight of a zuzee:*
ומתקל זוזא כורכמא רישקא *and of crocus hortensis the*
weight of a zuzee: ולישחקינהו בהדי הדדי לזבה תלתא
בחמרא *let these be bruised together, and be given in wine to the*
woman that hath an issue of blood, &c.

" But if this 'does not benefit, לייתי תלתא קפיזי שמכי
פרסאי *take of Persian onions thrice three logs,* boil them in
wine, and then give it her to drink, and say קום מזבויך *Arise*
from thy flux.

" But if this does not prevail, לותבה אפרש דרכים *set her*
in a place where two ways meet, and let her hold a cup of wine
in her hand; and let somebody come behind her and affright
her, and say, קום מזבויך *Arise from thy flux.*

" But if that do no good, לייתי בונא דכמונא *take a*
handful of cummin, ובונא דמריקא *and a handful of crocus,*
ובונא דשבלילתא *and a handful of fœnum græcum.* Let
these be boiled in wine, and give them her to drink, and say,
Arise from thy flux."

But[r] if these do not benefit, other doses and others still are
prescribed, in number ten or more, which see, if you please, in
the place cited.   Among them I cannot omit this:

" וליקלי בהו ליכרי ז' בירי *Let them dig seven ditches:*
שבישתא ילדה דערלה *in which let them burn some cuttings*
of such vines as are not circumcised, [that is, that are not yet
four years old.] And ולנקטיה כסא דחמרא בידיה *let her*
take in her hand a cup of wine. And לוקמה מהא ולותבה
אהא *let them lead her away from this ditch, and make her*
sit down over that. And ולוקמה מהא ולותבה אהא *let*
them remove her from that, and make her sit down over another.
And ואכל חדא וחדא לימא לה קום מזבויך *in every re-*
moval you must say to her, Arise from thy flux," &c.

Ver. 29: Ἐξηράνθη ἡ πηγὴ τοῦ αἵματος αὐτῆς· *The fountain*
of her blood was dried up.]   Of the fountain of the blood, or
of the flux, called by the Hebrews מקור, see *Niddah,* cap. 2.
hal. 4; *Maimon. in Issure biah,* cap. 5, 6.   Where also it is
treated of זבה גדולה *the greater profluvious woman,* and

זבה קטנה *the lesser.* The former title you may well bestow upon this woman, who had laboured under a flux for twelve years.

Ver. 41 : Ταλιθὰ, κοῦμι· *Talitha kumi.*] "Rabbi Jochanan saith[s], We remember when מטיילן טלייא וטלייתא *boys and girls* of sixteen and seventeen years old *played* in the streets, and nobody was offended with them." Where the Gloss is, טלייא וטלייתא *Tali and Talitha is a boy and a girl.*

Τὸ κοράσιον, [σοὶ λέγω,] ἔγειραι· *Damsel, I say unto thee, arise.*] *Talitha kumi* signifies only Τὸ κοράσιον, ἔγειραι· *Maid, arise.* How comes that clause then, *I say unto thee,* to be inserted ?

I. You may recollect here, and perhaps not without profit, that which was alleged before ; namely, that it was customary among the Jews, that, when they applied physic to the pro-fluvious woman, they said, " Arise from thy flux ;" which very probably they used in other diseases also.

II. Christ[t] said nothing else than what sounded all one with, *Maid, arise:* but in the pronouncing and uttering those words that authority and commanding power shined forth, that they sounded no less than if he had said, " Maid, I say to thee, or I command thee, arise." They said, "Arise from thy disease ;" that is, " I wish thou wouldst arise :" but Christ saith, *Maid, arise;* that is, " I command thee, arise."

Ver. 43 : Εἶπε δοθῆναι αὐτῇ φαγεῖν· *He commanded that something should be given her to eat.*] Not as she was alive only, and now in good health, but as she was in a most perfect state of health, and hungry : " The son of Rabban Gamaliel was sick. He sent, therefore, two scholars of the wise men to R. Chaninah Ben Dusa into his city. He saith to them, ' Wait for me, until I go up into the upper chamber.' He went up into the upper chamber, and came down again, and said, ' I am sure that the son of Rabban Gamaliel is freed from his disease.' The same hour he asked for food."

[s] Bava Bathra, fol. 91. 2.　　　[t] *Leusden's edit.*, vol. ii. p. 444.

CHAP. VI.[u]

VER. 3 : Οὐχ οὖτός ἐστιν ὁ τέκτων; *Is not this the carpenter ?*
Among other things to be performed by the father for his
son this was one, to bring him up in some art or trade.
" It[x] is incumbent on the father to circumcise his son, to
redeem him, to teach him the law, and to teach him some
occupation. R. Judah saith, ' Whosoever teacheth not his
son to do some work, is as if he taught him robbery.'"
" R. Meir[y] saith, ' Let a man always endeavour to teach his
son אומנות נקייה *an honest art,*'" &c. Joseph instructs and
brings up Christ in his carpenter's trade.

Ver. 8 : Μὴ πήραν· *Nor scrip.*] Concerning the *scrip*
we said somewhat at Matt. x. 10 : let us add this story :
" The[z] Rabbins deliver : There is a story of a certain man,
whose sons behaved not themselves well. He stood forth
and assigned over his wealth to Jonathan Ben Uzziel. What
did Jonathan Ben Uzziel do? He sold a third part ; a third
part he dedicated to holy uses ; and a third part he gave
back to the sons of the deceased. Shammai came to him
במקלו ותרמילו *with his staff and with his scrip.*" The
Gloss saith, " He came to contend with Jonathan, because
he had violated the will of the dead." Behold the vice-president of the Sanhedrim carrying a *scrip,* in which he laid up
victuals for his journey.

Ver. 13 : Ἤλειφον ἐλαίῳ πολλοὺς ἀρρώστους· *Anointed with
oil many that were sick.*] " *The oil,* therefore, was (saith the
famous Beza) a symbol of that miraculous power, not a me-
dicament whereby they cured diseases." But the Jews say,
and that truly, such an *anointing* was physical, although it
did not always obtain its end. But this *anointing* of the apostles ever obtained its end : " R. Simeon[a] Ben Eliezer saith,
' R. Meir permitted the mingling of wine and oil, and to
anoint the sick on the sabbath. But when he once was sick,
and we would do the same to him, he permitted it not.'"
This story is recited elsewhere, *Schab.* f. 14. 3 ; where for
' *R. Simeon* Ben Eliezer,' is ' *R. Samuel* Ben Eliezer.' Per-

[u] *English folio edition*, vol. ii. p.
343.
[x] Tosapht. in Kiddush. cap. 1.

[y] Kiddush. cap. 4. hal. 11.
[z] Bava Bathra, fol. 133. 2.
[a] Hieros. Berac. fol. 3. 1.

haps in the manuscript copy it was written with an abbreviation רש׳, and thence came the ambiguity of the name.

Let it be granted such anointing was medicinal, which cannot possibly be denied; and then there is nothing obscure in the words of James, chap. v. 14; " Let the elders of the church be called, and let the sick man be anointed by them, or by others present, that their prayers may be joined with the ordinary means.

Ver. 27: Σπεκουλάτωρα· *An executioner.*] So the Targum of Jonathan upon Gen. xxxix. 1: רב סְפוּקְלְטוֹרִיא *Rab Speculatoraia.* See the Aruch, in the word סְפֶקְלָטוֹר *Speculator.*

Ver. 37: Διακοσίων δηναρίων· *Two hundred pence.*] I. דינר *Denarius* and זוז *zuz* are of the same value among the Rabbins. "The [b] fourth part of a shekel of silver in the Targum is זוּזָא חַד דִּכְסְפָּא *one zuz of silver.* For a shekel of the law was סלַע *selaa.* And so in the Targum, שְׁקַל *a shekel*, is סלָעָא *selaa*, and is worth four *denarii*," or *pence.*

But now a *penny* and *zuz* are the same: "They [c] call *pence*, in the language of the Gemara, *zuzim.*"

II. But [d] now two hundred *zuzees*, or *pence*, was a sum very famous, and of very frequent mention. "If [e] one of elder years lay with a woman of less years, or if one of less years lay with a woman of elder years, or one that is wounded, their portion is מאתים *two hundred zuzees.*" "If [f] one gives another a blow upon the cheek, נותן לו מאתי זוז *let him give him two hundred zuzees.*" "A [g] woman that is now become a widow, or [h] dismissed by a divorce, who was married a virgin, let her have for her portion *two hundred zuzees.*"

Hence, perhaps, is the same number of *two hundred pence* in the mouth of the disciples, because it was a most celebrated sum, and of very frequent mention in the mouths of all."

Ver. 40: Πρασιαὶ πρασιαί· *By ranks.*] שורות שורות *rank by rank*, in Talmudic language. The university of Jabneh is very frequently celebrated under the name of כרם ביבנה *the vineyard in Jabneh.* And R. Solomon gives

[b] Aruch in זוז.
[c] Gloss. in Bathra, fol. 166. 1.
[d] *English folio edition*, vol. ii. p. 344.

[e] Chetub. cap. 1. hal. 2.
[f] Bava Kama, cap. 8. hal. 6.
[g] Chetub. fol. 17. 1.
[h] *Leusden's edit.*, vol. ii. p. 445.

the reason[i]; שחיו יושבין שורות שורות *Because the scholars sat there ranks by ranks,* ככרם הנטוע שורות שורות *like a vineyard which is planted* πρασιαὶ πρασιαὶ, *rank by rank.*

CHAP. VII.

VER. 3 : Ἐὰν μὴ πυγμῇ νίψωνται· *Except they wash their hands oft.*] Πυγμῇ, *the fist.* When they washed their hands, they washed the fist עד הפרק *unto the joining of the arm.* ידים מטמאות ומיטהרות עד הפרק *the [k] hands are polluted, and made clean unto the joining of the arm.* " The[l] Rabbins deliver : The washing of hands לחולין עד הפרק *as to common things* (or *common food*) *was unto the joining of the arm.* And the cleansing of hands and feet in the Temple was to the joint." פרק, *saith the Aruch, is where the arm is distinguished from the hand.* So, also, where the foot is distinguished from the leg.

" The[m] second waters cleanse whatsoever parts of the hands the first waters had washed. But if the first waters had gone above the juncture of the arm, the second waters do not cleanse, לפי שאין מטהרין אלא עד הפרק *because they do not cleanse beyond the juncture.* If, therefore, the waters which went above the juncture return upon the hands again, they are unclean."

Ver. 4 : Καὶ ἀπὸ ἀγορᾶς, ἐὰν μὴ βαπτίσωνται· *And when they come from the market, except they wash.*] The Jews used נטילת ידים *the washing of the hands,* and טבילת ידים *the plunging of the hands.* And the word νίψωνται, *wash,* in our evangelist seems to answer to the former, and βαπτίζωνται, *baptize,* to the latter.

I. That the *plunging* of the whole body is not understood here, may be sufficiently proved hence ; that such *plunging* is not used but when pollution is contracted from the more principal causes of uncleanness. " A[n] man and vessels contract not uncleanness, אלא מאב הטומאה *but from the father of uncleanness :* such as uncleanness from a creeping thing, from the seed in the unclean act, from him that is polluted by the dead, from a leper, from the water of purification,

---

[i] In Jevamoth, cap. 8.
[k] Judaim, cap. 2. hal. 3.
[l] Cholin, fol. 106.

[m] Gloss. in Judaim, in the place above.
[n] R. Sol. in Kelim, cap. 1.

from him that lies with a menstruous woman, from the flux
of him that hath the gonorrhœa, from his spittle, from his
urine, from the blood of a menstruous woman, from a pro-
fluvious man," &c.   By these a man was so polluted, that it
was טיבול יום *a day's washing ;* and he must *plunge* his
whole body.   But for smaller uncleannesses it was enough to
cleanse the hands.

II. Much less is it to be understood of the things bought ;
as if they, when they were bought for the market, were to
be *washed* (in which sense some interpreters render the
words, " And what they buy out of the market, unless they
wash it, they eat it not "), when there were some things which
would not endure water, some things which, when bought,
were not presently[o] eaten ; and the traditional canons distinguish between those things which were lawful as soon as
they came from the market, and those which were not.

III. The phrase, therefore, seems to be meant of the *im-
mersion,* or *plunging of the hands only ;* and the word πυγμῇ,
fist, is here to be understood also in common.   Those that
remain at home eat not, ἐὰν μὴ πυγμῇ νίψωνται, *unless they
wash the fist.*   But those that come from the market eat not,
ἐὰν μὴ πυγμῇ βαπτίζωνται, *unless they plunge their fist into the
water,* being ignorant and uncertain what uncleanness they
came near unto in the market.

" The[p] *washing* of the hands, and *the plunging* of the
hands, were from the scribes.   The hands which had need of
טבילה *plunging,* they dipped not but in a fit place ; that is,
where there was a confluence of forty *seahs* of water.   For
in the place where any dipped vessels, it was lawful to dip
the hands.   But the hands which have need of נטילה *washing* only, if they dip them in the confluence of waters, they
are clean ; whether they dip them in waters that are drawn,
or in vessels, or in the pavement.   They do not cleanse the
hands [*as to washing*], until waters are poured upon the hands
out of a vessel : for they do not *wash* the hands but out of a
vessel."

Ξεστῶν· *Pots.*]   It is doubtful whether this word be derived
from ξέστης, *a sextary* (a certain measure), or from ξεστὰ,
vessels planed or *engraven.*   To take it as speaking of *sex-*

---

[o] *English folio edit.,* vol. ii. p. 345.   [p] Maimon. in Mikvaoth, cap. 11.

taries is, indeed, very agreeable to the word, and not much different from the matter.   And so also it is, if you derive it from ξεστὰ, by which word are denoted vessels *planed* or *turned*[q], that is, of wood.   And perhaps those vessels which are. called by the Rabbins פשוטים *flat*, and are opposed to מקבלים *such as may contain something within them*, are expressed by this word.   Of that sort were knives, tables, seats, &c.   Concerning which, as capable of pollution, see Maimonides[r], and the Talmudic tract *Kelim*[s]: where are reckoned up, 1. שלחן The very *table* at which they ate.   2. הדלופקי *The little table*, or the wooden side-table, where wine[t] and fruits were set, that were presently to be brought to table. 3. ספסל *A seat*.   4. שרפרף *The footstool* for the feet under the seat.

Χαλκίων· *Brazen vessels.*] כלי מתכת.

Κλινῶν· *Of beds.*] *Beds* contracted uncleanness; either that which they called טומאת מדרס, or that which they called טומאת מגע מדרס.   One can hardly put these into good English without a paraphrase.   מטה טמאה מדרס was a *bed*, on which a profluvious man or woman, or a menstruous woman, or a woman in childbirth, or a leper, had either sat or stood, or lain, or leaned, or hung.   מטה טמאה מגע מדרס was a *bed*, which any thing had touched, that had been touched before by any of these[u].

The word, therefore, βαπτισμοὺς, *washings*, applied to all these, properly and strictly is not to be taken of *dipping* or *plunging*, but, in respect of some things, of *washing* only, and, in respect of others, of sprinkling only.

Ver. 11 : Κορβᾶν (ὅ ἐστι, Δῶρον)· *Corban (that is, 'a gift').*] The word δῶρον, *a gift*, was. known and common among the Talmudists : אמר רבא עולה דורון היא *Rabba*[v] *saith, A burnt sacrifice is* δῶρον, '*a gift.*'   Where the Gloss writes thus; " A burnt sacrifice is not offered to expiate for any deed : but after repentance hath expiated the deed, the burnt sacrifice comes להקביל פנים, *that the man may be received with favour.*   As when any hath sinned against the king, וריצהו עי" פרקלטין *and hath appeased him by a paraclete* [*an*

q [rasilia, tornatilia.]
r In Kelim, cap. 4.   s Cap. 21.
t *Leusden's edit.*, vol. ii. p. 446.

u [See Buxtorf Lex T. & R. sub
v. מדרס col. 580.]
v Zevachin, fol. 7. 2.

advocate], and comes to implore his favour, he brings דורון
δῶρον, *a gift*."

מצרים שתביא דורון למשיח: *Egypt*[v] *shall bring* δῶρον,
' *a gift*,' *to the Messiah.*

Ver. 19[x] : Ἀφεδρῶνα· *The draught.*] בית הכסא *The house
of the secret seat.*

CHAP. VIII.

Ver. 12 : Τί ἡ γενεὰ αὕτη σημεῖον ἐπιζητεῖ; *Why doth this
generation seek after a sign?*] Instead of a comment, take a
story : " On y that day, R. Eliezer answered to all the questions in the whole world, but they hearkened not to him. He
said therefore to them, 'If the tradition be according to what
I say,'let this siliqua [*a kind of tree*] bear witness.' The siliqua was rooted up, and removed a hundred cubits from its
place : there are some who say four hundred. They say to
him, ' A proof is not to be fetched from a siliqua.' He saith
to them again, ' If the tradition be with me, let the rivers of
waters testify :' the rivers of waters are turned backward.
They say to him, ' A proof is not to be fetched from the
rivers of waters.' He said to them again, ' If the tradition
be with me, let the walls of the school testify :' the walls
bowed, as if they were falling. R. Josua chid them, saying, ' If there be a controversy between the disciples of the
wise men about tradition, what is that to you ?' Therefore the walls fell not in honour of R. Josua. Yet they
stood not upright again in honour of R. Eliezer. He said
to them, moreover, ' If the tradition be with me, let the
heavens bear witness.' The Bath Kol went forth and said,
' Why do ye contend with R. Eliezer, with whom the tradition always is ?' R. Jonah rose up upon his feet, and said,
' It is not in heaven' (Deut. xxx. 12). What do these words,
' It is not in heaven,' mean ? R. Jeremiah saith, When the
law is given from mount Sinai, we do not care for the Bath
Kol."

Shall we laugh at the fable, or shall we suspect some
truth in the story ? For my part, when I recollect with
myself, how addicted to and skilful that nation was in art-

---

v Pesachin, fol. 118. 2.   x *English folio edition*, vol. ii. p. 345.
y Bab. Mezia, fol. 59. 2.

magic; which is abundantly asserted not only by the Talmudists, but by the Holy Scriptures; I am ready to give some credit to this story, and many others of the same nature: namely, that the thing was really acted by the art and help of the devil by those ensign-bearers and captains of errors, the more to establish their honour and tradition.

Therefore, from the story, be it true or false, we observe these two things:—

I. How tenacious the Jews were of their traditions, and how unmovable in them even beyond the evidence of miracles. That Eliezer was of great fame among them, but he was a follower of Shammai. Hence he is called[z] once and again שמותי *the Shammean.* When, therefore, he taught something against the school of Hillel, although he did miracles (as they themselves relate), they gave no credit to him, nay, they derided him. The same was their practice, the same was their mind, against the miracles of Christ. And to this may these words of our Saviour tend, "Why does this generation seek a sign?" a generation, which is not only altogether unworthy of miracles, but also which is sworn to retain their traditions and doctrines, although infinite miracles be done to the contrary.

II. You see how the last testimony of the miracles of this conjuror is fetched from heaven: " For the Bath Kol went forth," &c. Which the followers of Hillel nevertheless received not: and therein not justly indeed; when they feign such a voice to have come to themselves from heaven, as a definitive oracle for the authority of the school of Hillel, not to be gainsaid: concerning which the Talmudists speak very frequently, and very boastingly.

After the same manner they require a sign from heaven of our Saviour; not content with those infinite miracles that he had done, the healing of diseases, the casting out devils, the multiplying of loaves[a], &c. They would also have somewhat from heaven, either after the example of Moses fetching manna from thence; or of Elias fetching down fire; or of Joshua staying the sun; or of Isaiah bringing it backwards.

---

[z] Hieros. Trumah, fol. 43. 3. Jom Tobh, fol. 60. 3, &c.
[a] *Leusden's edition,* vol. ii. p. 447.

CHAP. IX.[b]

Ver. i : Τὴν βασιλείαν τοῦ Θεοῦ ἐληλυθυῖαν ἐν δυνάμει· *The kingdom of God coming in power.*] In Matthew, it is τὸν υἱὸν τοῦ ἀνθρώπου ἐρχόμενον ἐν τῇ βασιλείᾳ αὐτοῦ, *the Son of man coming in his kingdom.* The coming of Christ in his vengeance and power to destroy the unbelieving and most wicked nation of the Jews is expressed under these forms of speech. Hence the day of judgment and vengeance :

I. It is called " the great and terrible day of the Lord," Acts ii. 20 ; 2 Thess. ii. 2, 3.

II. It is described as " the end of the world," Jer. iv. 27 ; Matt. xxiv. 29, &c.

III. In that phrase, " in the last times," Isa. ii. 2 ; Acts ii. 17; 1 Tim. iv. 1; 2 Pet. iii. 3; that is, in the last times of that city and dispensation.

IV. Thence, the beginning of the " new world," Isa. lxv. 17; 2 Pet. iii. 13.

V. The vengeance of Christ upon that nation is described as his " coming," John xxi. 22 ; Heb. x. 37 : his " coming in the clouds," Rev. i. 7 : " in glory with the angels," Matt. xxiv. 30, &c.

VI. It is described as the ' enthroning of Christ, and his twelve apostles judging the twelve tribes of Israel,' Matt. xix. 28 ; Luke xxii. 30.

Hence this is the sense of the present place : Our Saviour had said in the last verse of the former chapter, " Whosoever shall be ashamed of me and of my words in this adulterous and sinful generation ; of him also shall the Son of man be ashamed, when he cometh in the glory of his Father with the holy angels," to take punishment of that adulterous and sinful generation. And he suggests, with good reason, that that his coming in glory should be in the lifetime of some that stood there.

Ver. 2 : Εἰς ὄρος ὑψηλόν· *Into a high mountain.*] Now your pardon, reader ; I know it will be laughed at if I should doubt whether Christ were transfigured upon mount Tabor ; for who ever doubted of this thing ? But let me, before I give faith to the thing, reveal my doubts concerning it : and the reader, laying before his eyes some geographical map of Galilee, perhaps, when he shall have heard me, will judge more favourably of my doubting.

I. Let him consider that Christ, in the story next going before, was in the coast of Cæsarea Philippi, Matt. xvi. 13 ; Mark viii. 27 ; Luke ix. 18 ; and, for any thing that can be gathered out of the evangelists, changed not his place before this story. Who will deny that those words, " There are some that stand here who shall not taste of death," &c., were uttered in those coasts of Cæsarea Philippi ? And presently the story of the transfiguration followed.

II. Six days indeed came between : in which, you will say, Christ might travel from Cæsarea Philippi to Tabor. He might, indeed : but, 1. The evangelists intimate no change from place to place, saying only this, That he led up into the mountain three of his disciples. 2. It seems, indeed, a wonder that our Saviour would tire himself with so long a journey, to choose Tabor whereon to be transfigured, when, as far as we read, he had never before been in that mountain; and there were mountains elsewhere where he conversed frequently. 3. Follow the footsteps of the history, and of Christ in his travel, from his transfiguration onwards. When he came down from the mountain, he healed a child possessed with a devil : and when he betook himself into the house they said, " Why could not we cast out the devil? &c. And they departed thence, and passed through Galilee, and came to Capernaum," Mark ix. 28, 30, 33.

III. And now, reader, look upon the chorographical map, and how incongruous will this travelling seem ! 1. From Cæsarea Philippi to mount Tabor through the whole length almost of Galilee. 2. Then from mount Tabor by a course back again to Capernaum, a great part of Galilee (especially as the maps place Capernaum) being again passed over. Whereas Capernaum was in the way from Cæsarea Philippi to Tabor, and there was a mountain there well known to Christ, and very much frequented by him.

IV. So[c] that it seems far more consonant to the history of the gospel, that Christ was transfigured in some mountain near Cæsarea Philippi; perhaps that which, Josephus being witness, was the highest, and hung over the very fountains of Jordan, and at the foot whereof Cæsarea was placed.

In that place, formerly called *Dan*, was the first idolatry set up, and now in the same place the eternal Son of God is shewn, both in the confession of Peter, and in the unspeakably clear and illustrious demonstration of the Messias.

Ver. 38 : Εἴδομέν τινα ἐν τῷ ὀνόματί σου ἐκβάλλοντα δαιμόνια· *We saw one casting out devils in thy name.*] I. Without doubt he truly did this work, whosoever he were. He cast out devils truly and really, and that by the divine power; otherwise Christ had not said those things which he did, " Forbid him not: for there is no man which shall do a miracle in my name, that can lightly speak evil of me," &c.

II. Whence then could any one that followed not Christ cast out devils? Or whence could any one that cast out devils not follow Christ?

I answer[d] : We suppose,

I. That this man cast not out devils in the name of Jesus, but in the name of Christ, or Messias : and that it was not out of contempt that he followed not Jesus, but out of ignorance; namely, because he knew not yet that Jesus was the Messias.

II. We therefore conjecture that he had been heretofore some disciple of John, who had received his baptism in the name of the Messias now speedily to come, (which all the disciples of John had;) but he knew not as yet that Jesus of Nazareth was the Messias : which John himself knew not until it was revealed to him from heaven.

III. It is probable, therefore, that God granted the gifts of miracles to some lately baptized by John, to do them in the name of the Messias; and that, to lay a plainer way for the receiving of the Messias, when he should manifest himself under the name of ' Jesus of Nazareth.'

See ver. 41 : *In my name,* ὅτι Χριστοῦ ἐστε, *because ye belong to Christ;* and chap. xiii. 6, " Many shall come in my name;" not in the name of Jesus, but in the name of the Messias : for those false prophets assumed to themselves the name of the Messias, to bring to nought the name of Jesus.

---

[d] *Leusden's edition,* vol. ii. p. 448.

That, John xvi. 24, "Hitherto ye have asked nothing in my name," differs not much from this sense : ' The apostles poured out their prayers, and all the holy men theirs, in the name of the Messias ; but ye have as yet asked nothing in my name *Jesus*,' &c.

Ver. 43 : 'Απόκοψον αὐτήν· *Cut it off*.] " Rabh Mona[e], in the name of R. Judah, saith, A drop of cold water in the morning [*applied to the eye*], and the washing of the hands and feet in the evening, מכל קילורין שבעולם *is good beyond all the collyrium [eyesalve] in the whole world*. For he said, יד לעין תקצע *The hand applied to the eye [in the morning, before washing*], *let it be cut off*. The hand applied to the nostril, let it be cut off : the hand put to the ear, let it be cut off," &c.

Ver. 49 : Πᾶς γὰρ πυρὶ ἁλισθήσεται· *For every one shall be salted with fire*.] The great Scaliger is well chastised, and not without cause, by John Cloppenberg[f], because he changed the reading here into πᾶσα πυρία ἁλισθήσεται, *every sacrifice shall be salted*. See what he saith.

Πᾶς, *all*, is not to be understood of every man, but of every one of them " whose worm dieth not," &c.

The sense of the place is to be fetched from those words, and the sense of those words from Isa. lxvi. 24 : " And they shall go forth, and look upon the carcases of the men that have transgressed against me : for their worm shall not die, neither shall their fire be quenched ; and they shall be an abhorring unto all flesh." Upon which place thus the Jews write ; " ' They shall go forth and look,' &c. Is not the finger of a man, if it be put into the fire, immediately burnt ? But God gives power (*or being*) to wicked men to receive[g] torments." Kimchi upon the place thus : " They shall see the carcases of them full of worms, and fire burning in them :" and yet the worms die not.

The words therefore of our Saviour respect this : " Their worm dieth not, and the fire is not quenched ; for every one of them shall be seasoned with fire itself, so as to become unconsumable, and shall endure for ever to be tormented, as salt preserves from corruption.

---

e Bab. Schabb. fol. 108. 2.   f In Spicileg. Scholæ sacrific. Problem. 3.
g *English folio edit.*, vol. ii. p. 347.

That very learned man mentioned before called the common reading very improper. For what is it, saith he, ἀλίζειν πυρί, *to season with fire?* Let me retort, And what is it πυρίζειν ἀλί, *to fire with salt?* And yet that sense occurs very frequently in the Talmudists. For in them הקדית is *to burn,* (which it signifies properly indeed,) and very frequently it is, *to corrupt any thing with too much salting,* so that it cannot be eaten: *to be fired with salt.* So in this place, *to be salted with fire,* that it cannot be corrupted or consumed.

Καὶ πᾶσα θυσία ἀλὶ ἀλισθήσεται· *And every sacrifice shall be salted with salt.*] Here the discourse is of salting, which was done at the altar, see Levit. ii. 13: "In[h] the ascent of the altar, they salted the parts of the sacrifice: and on the top of the altar they salt the handful of meal, of frankincense, of incense, and the mincha of the priests, and the mincha of the anointed priest, and the mincha of the drink-offerings, and the sacrifice of birds." Yea[i], עצים קרבן מנחה הן וטעונין מלח *the very wood is a corban of the mincha, and is to be salted.*

But in the former clause, the allusion was not to the fire of the altar, but to the fire in the valley of Hinnom, where dead carcases, bones, and other filthy things were consumed. Carcases crawl with worms; and instead of salt which secures against worms, they shall be cast into the fire, and shall be seasoned with flames, and yet the worms shall not die. But he that is a true sacrifice to God shall be seasoned with the salt of grace to the incorruption of glory.

Our Saviour speaks in this place with Isaiah, chap. lxvi. 20: Ἄξουσι τοὺς ἀδελφοὺς ὑμῶν ἐκ πάντων τῶν ἐθνῶν δῶρον Κυρίῳ—ὡς ἀνενέγκαισαν οἱ υἱοὶ Ἰσραὴλ τὰς θυσίας αὐτῶν ἐμοὶ μετὰ ψαλμῶν εἰς τὸν οἶκον Κυρίου· *They shall bring your brethren out of all the nations for a gift to the Lord,——as the children of Israel offer their sacrifices to me with psalms in the house of the Lord.* And ver. 24: Καὶ ἐξελεύσονται, καὶ ὄψονται τὰ κῶλα τῶν ἀνθρώπων τῶν παραβεβηκότων ἐν ἐμοί· ὁ γὰρ σκώληξ αὐτῶν οὐ τελευτήσει, καὶ τὸ πῦρ αὐτῶν οὐ σβεσθήσεται, &c. *And they shall go forth, and look upon the limbs of men that transgressed against me: for their worm shall not die, and their fire shall not be quenched,* &c.

[h] Menacoth, fol. 21. 2.   [i] Fol. 20. 2.

Πᾶσα θυσία, *every sacrifice,* saith our Saviour, concerning holy men seasoned with grace: so the prophet, " They shall bring your brethren for a gift to the Lord, as the children of Israel do the sacrifices."

'Ἁλισθήσονται πυρὶ, *shall be seasoned with fire,* saith our Saviour of wicked men: in the same sense Isaiah, " They shall be in unquenchable[k] fire, and yet their worm shall not die."

Their fire and *their* worm: whose? Concerning the former, it is somewhat obscure in our Saviour's words, and so, indeed, that it is without all obscurity that he refers his words only to the words of Isaiah: but who they are in Isaiah is plain enough.

CHAP. X.

VER. 1 : Ἔρχεται εἰς τὰ ὅρια τῆς Ἰουδαίας, διὰ τοῦ πέραν τοῦ Ἰορδάνου· *Cometh into the coasts of Judea by the further side of Jordan.*] Here is need of a discerning eye to distinguish of the true time and method of this story, and of Christ's journey. If you make use of such an eye, you will find half a year, or thereabouts, to come between the uttering of the words immediately before-going, and this travel of our Saviour; however it seems to be intimated by our evangelist, and likewise by Matthew, that when he had finished those words, forthwith he entered upon his journey: when, in truth, he went before to Jerusalem, through the midst of Samaria, to the feast of Tabernacles, Luke ix. 51, &c. John vii. And again, from Galilee, after he had returned thither, through the cities and towns to Jerusalem, Luke xiii. 22; to the feast of Dedication, John x. 22: and again[l], " beyond Jordan" indeed, John x. 40; but first taking his way into Galilee, and thence beyond Jordan, according to that story which is before us. The studious reader, and that in good earnest employeth his labour upon this business, has no need of further proof; his own eyes will witness this sufficiently. Thus, the wisdom and Spirit of God directed the pens of these holy writers, that some omitted some things to be supplied by others; and others supplied those things which they had omitted: and so

k *Leusden's edit.,* vol. ii. p. 449.   l *English folio edit.,* vol. ii. p. 347.

a full and complete history was not composed but of all joined and compared together.

I wish the reverend Beza had sufficiently considered this, who rendereth πέραν 'Ιορδάνου, not *beyond*, but *by* Jordan, and corrects the Vulgar interpreter and Erasmus, who render it ' *beyond* Jordan,' properly and most truly: " As if, by Perea (saith he), or the country beyond Jordan, Christ, passing over Jordan or the lake of Tiberias, came into Judea out of Galilee; which is not true." But take heed you do not mistake, reverend old man. For he went over Jordan from Capernaum, as it is very probable, by the bridge built over Jordan between Chammath, near to Tiberias, at the Gadarene country: he betook himself to Bethabara, and stayed some time there, John x. 40: thence he went along Perea to the bank over against Jericho. While he tarrieth there, a messenger, sent from Mary, comes to him concerning the death of Lazarus, John xi; and thence, after two days, he passeth Jordan in Judea.

Ver. 17: Γονυπετήσας αὐτόν· *Kneeled to him.*] So chap. i. 40, Παρακαλῶν αὐτὸν, καὶ γονυπετῶν αὐτόν· *Beseeching him, and kneeling to him.* This is variously rendered, *procidit ad pedes, genu flexo, genu petens, ad genua procidens,* &c. *He fell at his feet, bowing the knee, beseeching upon his knee, falling down at his knees.* Which renderings are not improper, but I suspect something more is included. For, 1. It was customary for those that so adored to take hold of the knees or the legs, 2 Kings iv. 27; Matt. xxviii. 9. 2. To kiss the knees or the feet. See what we have said at Matt. xxviii. 9.

When R. Akiba[m] had been twelve years absent from his wife, and at last came back, his wife went out to meet him: " and when she came to him, falling upon her face, קא מנשקה ליה לכרעיה *she kissed his knees.*" And a little after, when he was entered into the city, his father-in-law not knowing who he was, but suspecting him to be some great Rabbin, went to him, and falling upon his face נשקיה ליה לכרעיה *kissed his knees.* Speaking[n] of Job, בא שטן נשקיה לכרעיה " *Satan came, and he kissed his knees:* but in all this Job sinned

---

[m] Bab. Chetub. fol. 63. 1.   [n] Id. Bava Bathr.

not with his lips," &c. When[o] a certain Rabbin had discoursed of divers things, קם בר חמא ונשקיה אכרעיה *Bar Chama rose up and kissed his knees.*

Ver. 21 : 'Ηγάπησεν αὐτόν· *Loved him.*] That is, he manifested by some outward gesture that this man pleased him, both in his question and in his answer : when he both seriously inquired concerning attaining eternal life; and seriously professed that he had addicted himself to God's commandments with all care and circumspection.

Let us compare the customs of the Masters among the Jews : Eliezer[p] Ben Erech obtained leave from Rabban Jochanan Ben Zaccai to discourse of some things before him. He discoursed of Ezekiel's *chariot* (מעשה מרכבה Ezek. chap. 1), or, *of mystical divinity*[q]. " When he had made an end, Rabban Jochanan arose up, ונשקיה בראשיה *and kissed his head.*" " R. Abba[r] Bar Cahna heard R. Levi disputing profoundly. When he had made an end, R. Abba rose up and kissed his head." There is a story[s] of a certain Nazarite young man that exceedingly pleased[t] Simeon the Just with a certain answer that he gave. Whereupon, said Simeon, " I bowed towards him with my head, and said, O son, let such as you be multiplied in Israel." The story is found elsewhere[u], where for הרכנתיו בראשי *I bowed towards him with my head,* it is חבקתיו ונשקתיו על ראשו *I embraced him and kissed his head.* " Miriam[x], before the birth of Moses, had prophesied, My mother shall bring forth a son who shall deliver Israel. When he was born the whole house was filled with light. His father stood forth, ונשקה על ראשה *and kissed her upon the head,* and said, Thy prophecy is fulfilled. And when they cast him into the river, טפחה על ראשה *he struck her upon the head.*"

What if our Saviour used this very gesture towards this young man? And that the more conveniently, when he was now upon his knees before him. Some gesture, at least, he

---

o Sanhedr. fol. 27. 2.
p Hieros. Chagigah, f. 77. 1.
q [Hebræi vocant principium Ezechielis מעשה מרכבה *opus quadrigæ.* Hoc *opus* mysterio plenum est, ideoque non quibuslibet explicandum. Buxtorf Lex. T. & R. sub

v. מרכבה col. 2258. q. v.]
r Hieros. Horaioth, fol. 48. 3.
s Id. Nedarim, fol. 36. 4.
t *Leusden's edition,* vol. ii. p. 450.
u Nazir. fol. 51. 3.
x Bab. Megill. fol. 14. 1.

used, whereby it appeared, both to the young man and to the
standers-by, thatʸ the young man did not a little please him,
both by his question and by his answer. So אָהַבְתִּי *I have
loved*, Psalm cxvi. 1, in the LXX, ἠγάπησα, *I have loved*, one
may render well, *complacet mihi, it pleaseth me well*. So Jo-
sephusᶻ of David's soldiers, (1 Sam. xxx. 22): " Those four
hundred who went to the battle would not impart the spoils
to the two hundred who were faint and weary ; Ἀγαπήσειν δὲ
σεσωσμένας γυναῖκας ἀπολαμβάνοντας ἔλεγον· *and said, That they
should ' love'* [that is, *be well pleased*] *that they had received
their wives safe again*."

In some parity of sense, John is called the disciple, ὃν ἠγάπα
ὁ Ἰησοῦς, *whom Jesus loved ;* not that Jesus loved him more
than the rest with his eternal, infinite, saving love, but he
favoured him more with some outward kindness and more
intimate friendship and familiarity. And why ? Because John
had promised that he would take care of Christ's mother after
his death.   For those words of our Saviour upon the cross to
John, ' Behold thy mother !' and to his mother, ' Behold thy
son !' and that from thence John took her home, do carry a
fair probability with them, that that was not the first time
that John heard of such a matter, but that long before he had
so promised.

Ἠγάπησά σε, *I have loved thee*, Isa. lx.10, is the rendering of
רִחַמְתִּיךְ *I have had pity upon thee :* which may here also
agree very well, " Jesus *had pity* upon him."

Ver. 46 : Υἱὸς Τιμαίου Βαρτίμαιος· *Bartimæus, the son of Timæus.*] Some suspect the evangelist here guilty of a solecism,
by making a tautology : for it was neither necessary, as they
think, so to render the Syriac word in Greek ; nor is it done
so elsewhere in proper names of that nature. For it is not
said by any evangelist, Bartholomeus, *the son of Tholomeus :*
Bar Abbas, *the son of Abbas :* Bar Jesus, *the son of Jesus :* nor
in the like names. True, indeed ; but,

I. When the denomination is made from a common name,
and not a proper, then it is not so ill sounding to interpret
the word : which is done once and again ; Mark iii.17, Βοανερ-
γὲς, ὅ ἐστιν, υἱοὶ βροντῆς· *Boanerges, which is, The sons of thunder :*

Acts iv. 36, Βαρνάβας, ὅ ἐστιν, υἱὸς παρακλήσεως· *Barnabas, which is, A son of consolation.*

II. *Bar Timai* may be rendered otherwise than *the son of Timæus*: namely, either בר תימה *a son of admiration;* or, which is more proper, בר טימי *a son of profit.* The Targum in Esther iii. 8; ולמלכא לית ליה טימי מנדהון *To the king ariseth no profit ('Timai') from them.* The evangelist therefore, deservedly, that he might shew that this *Bartimæus* was not named from this, or that, or some other etymology, but from his father's name, so interprets his name, Βαρτιμαῖος, υἱὸς Τιμαίου, *Bartimeus, the son of Timeus.*

III. Perhaps there was a *Timeus* of some more noted name in that age, either for some good report or some bad : so that it might not be absurd to the Jews that then conversed there to say, This blind *Bartimæus* is the son of the so much famed *Timæus.* So it is unknown to us who Alexander and Rufus were, chap. xv. 21 : but they were without doubt of most eminent fame, either among the disciples, or among the Jews.

IV. What if תימיא *Thima* be the same with סימיא *Simai, blind,* from the use of ת [Thau] for ס [Samech] among the Chaldeans? so that *Bartimæus the son of Timæus* might sound no more than *the blind son of a blind father.*

CHAP. XI.

VER. 11: Καὶ περιβλεψάμενος πάντα· *And when he had looked round about upon all things.*] Compare Mark with the other evangelists concerning the time of casting out the merchants of the Temple, and it will appear that the word περιβλεψάμενος, *he looked about,* denotes not a bare beholding or looking upon, but a beholding with reproof and correction ; אזהרה *admonition,* among the Jews.

Ver. 13 : Οὐ γὰρ ἦν καιρὸς σύκων· *For the time of figs was not yet.*] See what we have said at Matt. xxi. 19. The sum is this :

I. *The time of figs* was so far off, that the time of leaves was scarcely yet present.

II. The[a] other fig trees in the mount were of the common kind of fig trees : and on them were not leaves as yet to be

<hr>

a *English folio edition,* vol. ii. p. 348.

seen. But that which Christ saw with leaves on it, and therefore went to it, was a fig tree of an extraordinary kind.

III. For there was a certain fig tree called בנות שוח
Benoth Shuach, which never wanted leaves, and never wanted
figs. For every year it bare fruit, but that fruit came not to
full ripeness before the third year: and such, we suppose, was
this fig tree.

Ver. 16[b]: Καὶ οὐκ ἤφιεν ἵνα τὶς διενέγκῃ σκεῦος διὰ τοῦ ἱεροῦ·
*And would not suffer that any man should carry any vessel through
the Temple.*] "What[c] is the reverence of the Temple? That
none go into the Mountain of the Temple" [or the Court of
the Gentiles] "with his staff, and his shoes, with his purse,
and dust upon his feet: ולא יעשנו קפנדריא ורקיק *and that
none make it his common thoroughfare, nor make it a place of
spitting.*"

The same thing is ordered concerning a synagogue; yea,
concerning a synagogue that is now laid waste, much more
of one that flourisheth: "A[d] synagogue now laid waste,
לא עושין קפנדריא *let not men make it a common passage.*"
And[e] "his disciples asked R. Eleazar Ben Shammua, Whence
hast thou lived so long? He answered, I never made a synagogue a common thoroughfare."

It is therefore forbid by the masters, that the court of the
Temple be not made a passage for a shorter way. And was
not this bridle sufficient wherewith all might be kept back
from carrying vessels through the Temple? But the 'castle
of Antonia' joined to the court; and there were shops in the
Court of the Gentiles where many things were sold; and that
profane vessels were brought hither is scarcely to be denied.
And these vessels might be said to be carried διὰ τοῦ ἱεροῦ,
through the Temple; although those that carried them went
not through the whole Temple.

CHAP. XII.

Ver. i: Ἀμπελῶνα ἐφύτευσεν ἄνθρωπος, &c. *A certain man
planted a vineyard.*] The priests and Pharisees knew, saith
Matthew, that "these things were spoken of them," Matt.
xxi. 45. Nor is it any wonder; for the Jews boasted that

[b] *Leusden's edition*, vol. ii. p. 451.   [d] Megill. fol. 28. 1.
[c] Bab. Jevamoth, fol. 6. 2.   [e] Fol. 27. 2.

they were the Lord's vineyard : and they readily observed a
wrong done to that vineyard by any : but how far were they
from taking notice, how unfruitful they were, and unthankful
to the Lord of the vineyard !

"The[f] matter may be compared to a king that had a
vineyard ; and there were three who were enemies to it.
What were they? One cut down the branches. The second
cut off the bunches. And the third rooted up the vines.
That king is the King of kings, the Blessed Lord. The vineyard of the Lord is the house of Israel. The three enemies
are Pharaoh, Nebuchadnezzar, and Haman," &c.

'Αμπελῶνα· *A vineyard.*] "If[g] a man plants one row of
five vines, the school of Shammai saith, That it is a vineyard.
But the school of Hillel saith, It is not a vineyard, until there
be two rows of vines there."

Περιέθηκε φραγμόν· *Set a hedge about it.*] "What[h] is a
hedge? Let it be ten handbreadths high:" less than so is
not a hedge.

῎Ωρυξεν ὑπολήνιον· *Digged a place for the wine-fat.*] חריץ
שהוא עמוק י' ורחב ד' : Let[i] the fat be ten handbreadths
deep, and four broad.

'Ωικοδόμησε[k] πύργον· *Built a tower.*] שומרה שבכרם גבוהה י'
ורחבה ד' : Let[l] the watchhouse, which is in the vineyard, be
ten high, and four broad. Cubits are to be understood. For
Rambam saith, שומרה *is a high place where the vine-dresser
stands to overlook the vineyard.*

'Εξέδοτο αὐτὸν γεωργοῖς· *Let it out to husbandmen.*] המוסר
כרמו לשומר 'Ο ἀποδοὺς ἀμπελῶνα αὐτοῦ, &c. "He[m] that
lets out his vineyard to a keeper, בין באריסות בין בשמירו
חנם *either as a* γεωργὸς, *a husbandman, or as one to keep it
gratis,* and he enters into covenant with him, to dig it, prune
it, dress it, at his own cost ; but he neglects it, and doth not
so ; he is guilty, as if he should with his own hand lay the
vineyard waste."

Ver. 2 : 'Απέστειλε πρὸς τοὺς γεωργοὺς τῷ καιρῷ· *And at the
season he sent to the husbandmen.*] That is, in the fourth year
after the first planting it : when it now was כרם רבעי *a*

---

[f] Tanchum, fol. 54. 3.
[g] Kilaim, cap. 4. hal. 5.
[h] Ibid. hal. 3.   [i] Ibid.
[k] *English folio edit.*, vol. ii. p. 349.
[l] Ibid. cap. 5. hal. 3.
[m] Maimon. in שכירות c. 2.

vineyard of four years old; at least before that year there
was no profit of the fruits. כרם רבעי מציינין אותו בקוזות
אדמה *" They* [n] *paint* [or *note*] *a vineyard of four years old by
some turf* [or *clod*] *of earth,* coloured; של ערלה בחרסית
and that uncircumcised with clay; and sepulchres with chalk."

The Gloss is this : " On a vineyard of four years old they
paint some marks out of the turf of the earth, that men may
know that it is a vineyard of four years old, and eat not of it,
because it is holy, as the Lord saith, Lev. xix. 24 ; and the
owners ought to eat the fruit of it at Jerusalem, as the
second tithe.   And an uncircumcised vineyard," [that is,
which was not yet four years old ; see Lev. xix. 23,] "they
mark with *clay,* הוא טיט השרוף *that is, digested in fire.*
For the prohibition of (*a vineyard*) uncircumcised, is greater
than the prohibition concerning that of four years old : for
that of four years old is fit for eating; but that uncircumcised is not admitted to any use.   Therefore, they marked
not that by the turf, lest the mark might perhaps be de-
faced, and perish ; and men not seeing it might eat of
it," &c.

Ver. 4 [o] : Λιθοβολήσαντες ἐκεφαλαίωσαν· *At him they cast
stones, and wounded him in the head.*]   I. I see no need to
wrest the word ἐκεφαλαίωσαν from its true and genuine sense.
Κεφαλαιοῦν signifies *to reduce and gather into a certain sum,*
as the lexicons teach us : and why not in the same sense in
this place ? They cast stones at the servant, and deriding
him, made up the sum with him : saying, perhaps this, or
some such thing to him, " Do you come for fruit and rent ?
Behold this fruit," (casting a stone at him;) "behold another
fruit," (casting another stone ;) and so many times together :
and so they sen him away ἠτιμωμένον, *derided, and loaded
with disgrace.*

II. But be it that the word is to be translated as it is
commonly rendered, "they wounded him in the head :" then
this way of stoning is thus distinguished from that whereby
they were slain who were stoned by the Sanhedrim.   That
was called λιθοβολία, *stone-casting :* for it was the cast of a
stone, indeed, but of one only, and that a very great one;
and that upon the heart of the condemned person, when now

[n] Maasar Sheni, c. 5. hal. 1.   [o] *Leusden's edition,* vol. ii. p. 452.

he lay along upon his back.   But this stoning was of many
stones, thrown out of the hand through the air, striking him
here and there and everywhere.   The head of him that was
stoned by the Sanhedrim was unhurt, and without any
wound; but here, *They cast stones at him, and wounded him
in the head.*

Ver. 10: Λίθον, ὃν ἀπεδοκίμασαν· *The stone which the builders
rejected.*]   The Targum upon Psalm cxviii, thus, טליא
שביקו אדרכליא *the builders rejected the child.*   [Either for
אבן he read הבן, or rendered it according to the Arabic
idiom, *the son:* so also R. Solomon.]   And ver. 27, כפתו
טליא לנכסת חגא *"Bind the child to the sacrifice of the
solemnity* with chains, until ye shall have sacrificed him, and
poured out his blood upon the horns of the altar: said
Samuel the prophet."

Ver. 16 P: Τίνος ἡ εἰκών; Καίσαρος· *Whose is this image?
Cæsar's.*]   I. This was *a Cæsar's penny.*   דינרא קיסראנה
denarius Cæsareanus.   For *zuz,* among the Jews, was also a
penny, as we shewed elsewhere; but we scarce believe it was
of the same form and inscription: ההוא מינאה דשדר ליה
דינרא קיסראנה *"A q certain heathen sent to R. Judah the
prince a Cæsarean penny,* and that on a certain festival
day of the heathens.   Resh Lachish sat before him.   R.
Judah said, What shall I do?   If I receive it, I shall consent
(*to their festival*): if I receive it not, enmity will rise against
me.   Resh Lachish answered, Take the penny, and while
he looks upon you cast it into the well," &c.

II. It was a silver penny, not a gold one. דינרין סתם משם
של כסף *Pence, absolutely put, are to be understood silver pence.*
Where the Gloss is, " Pence, absolutely put, are silver, until
it is explained that they are gold."

But now a gold penny was worth five-and-twenty silver
pence.   "When r turtle-doves and young pigeons were sold
at Jerusalem sometime for a gold penny, Rabban Simeon
Ben Gamaliel said, By this Temple, I will not rest this night,
unless they are sold for a silver penny."   Where the Gloss,
" A gold penny is worth five-and-twenty silver pence."

III. It was צורי a *Roman penny,* not פשיטי a *Jerusalem:*

p *English folio edit.*, vol. ii. p. 349.   q Bab. Avod. Zar. fol. 6. 2.
r Cherithuth, cap. 1. hal. 7.

for this distinction they sometimes use. זוזי פשיטי, the Gloss
being witness, are זוזי מדינה *Jerusalem zuzees.* But more
frequently, מטבע של מדינה and מטבע צורי *money of
Tzur, and money of Jerusalem.* מטבע צורי one may well
render *Tyrian money.* But hear the *Aruch,* where he had
been treating of money צורי *of Tzur ;* at length he brings in
this passage : " R. Eliezer saith, Wheresoever in the Scripture צור *Tzur* is written full, the Scripture speaks of the
city *Tyre :* but where it is written defectively [צר without ו
(Vau)], it speaks of *Rome.*" Be it Tyrian or Roman money,
this held among the masters : " Wheresoever[s] any thing is
said of the silver money של מדינה *of Jerusalem,* it is the
eighth part of the Tyrian money."

Hence I should resolve that riddle at which the Glosser
himself sticks, if I may have leave to conjecture in a Jewish
affair, after a doubting Jew. In the tract now cited[t] there
is a discourse concerning מעות כוזביות ירושלמיות *Jerusalem Cozbian moneys.* A riddle truly. Ben Cozbi, indeed,
coined moneys when he made an insurrection against the
Romans[u]. But whence is this called *Jerusalem money,* when,
in the days of Ben Cozbi, Jerusalem lay buried in its own
rubbish ? If I may be the resolver, it was so called, because
it was of the same weight and value with the *Jerusalem money,*
and not with that of Tyre.

" The *Jerusalem money* (say they) is the eighth part of the
Tyrian." Here again some words of the masters entangle
me in a riddle. The Aruch[x] saith, " A penny and *zuz* are the
same." And elsewhere[y], " They call pence, in the Gemaristic
language, *Zuzim ;*" which we observed at chap. vi. ver. 37.
' *Zuz*' was Jerusalem money : how, then, was it the same with
a penny, which was Tyrian money, when it was the eighth
part only ? And these words spoken by Rambam[z] do add
a scruple over and above ; הדינר ר' זוזים *a penny contains
six zuzim.* If[a] he had said *eight zuzim,* it had been without
scruple. But what shall we say now ?

The former knot you may thus untie : that *zuz,* among the

[s] Bava Kama, fol. 36. 2, in Gloss.
[t] Bava Kama, fol. 97. 2.
[u] Hieros. Maasar Sheni, fol. 52. 4.
[x] In זוז.

[y] Gloss in Bava Bathra, fol. 166. 1.
[z] In Peah, cap. 8. hal. 7.
[a] *Leusden's edition,* vol. ii. 453.

Jews, is called also *a penny* ; a Jewish penny, indeed, but different from the Roman : as the Scots have their *shilling*, but much different from our English. But the second knot let him try to untie that is at leisure.

IV. This money was signed with the image of Cæsar; but of the Jerusalem money, thus the Jews write, whom you may believe when you please : " What[b] is the Jerusalem money? דוד ושלמה בצד אחד *David and Solomon were stamped on one side;* and on the reverse, ירושלם עיר הקודש *Jerusalem the holy city.*" But the Glosser inquires whether it were lawful to stamp the image of David and Solomon upon money, which he scarcely thinks. He concludes therefore that their names were only inscribed, not their effigies.

" Upon[c] Abraham's money were stamped, on one side, an old man and an old woman ; on the other, a young man and a young maid. On Joshua's money, on one side, an ox ; on the other, a monoceros. On David's money, on one side, a staff and a scrip ; on the other, a tower. On Mardochai's money, on one side, sackcloth and ashes ; on the other, a crown." Let the truth of this be upon the credit of the authors.

Ver. 28[d] : Ποία ἐστὶ πρώτη πασῶν ἐντολή ; *Which is the first commandment of all?*] It is not seldom that this distinction occurs in the Rabbins, between תורה *the law*, and מצוה *the precept :* by the latter they understand some special or greater rite (themselves being judges); such as circumcision, the repeating of the phylacteries, keeping the sabbath, &c. This question, propounded by the scribe, seems to respect the same : namely, whether those great precepts (as they were esteemed) and other ceremonial precepts of that nature, such as sacrifices, purifications, keeping festivals, were the greatest precepts of the law, or no : and if it were so, which among them was the first?

By his answer he seems to incline to the negative, and to prefer the moral law. Whence Christ saith, " That he was not far from the kingdom of heaven :" and while he suits an answer to him from that very passage, which was the first in the reciting of the phylacteries, שמע ישראל *Hear, O Israel,*—he directs the eyes and the minds of those that

---

b Bava Kama, fol. 97. 2.   c Bereshith Rab. fol. 24. 2.
d *English folio edition*, vol. ii. p. 350.

repeated them to the sense and the marrow of the thing repeated,—and that they rest not in the bare work of repeating
them.

Ver. 41: Ὄχλος βάλλει χαλκόν· *The people cast money.*]
היו מטילין שם המעות: *They*[e] *were casting in small money
there.* According[f] to his pleasure, any one might cast into
the chests how little soever he would; namely, in the chest
which was for gold, as little gold as a grain of barley would
weigh; and in the chest for frankincense, as much frankincense as weighed a grain of barley. But if he should say,
הרי עלי *Behold, I vow* wood; he shall not offer less than
two pieces of a cubit long, and breadth proportionable. Behold, I vow frankincense; he shall not offer less than a .pugil
of frankincense:" that is, not less money than that which
will buy so much.

Ver. 42: Λεπτὰ δύο, ὅ ἐστι κοδράντης· *Two mites, which
make a farthing.*] ב' פרוטות קדריונטס: *Two*[g] *prutahs are
a farthing.* "A[h] *prutah* is the eighth part of an Italian *assarius.* An *assarius* is the twenty-fourth part of a silver
penny." We rendered before, "The people cast money,
χαλκὸν, *brass,*" by היו מטילין מעות *they were casting in small
money:* one would think it should rather be rendered, היו
מטילין נחשת *They were casting in brass.* But consider well
this passage: הפורט סלע של מעשר שני *He*[i] *that changeth
the 'selaa' of the second tenth,* the school of Shammai saith,
מעות כל סלע *Let him change the whole 'selaa' into* מעות.
You would perhaps render it, *into moneys,* or *into meahs,* but
it is properly to be rendered *into brass,* as appears by what
follows: "The school of Hillel saith, שקל כסף ושקל מעות
into a shekel of silver, and a shekel of brass." So also the
Glossers; and the *Aruch* moreover[k], "He that changeth a
selaa, and receives for it מעות של נחושת שהן פרוטות
brass money, that is, prutahs."

None might, by the canon even now mentioned, enter into
the Temple, no, nor indeed into the Court of the Gentiles,
with his purse, therefore much less into the Court of the
Women; and yet scarce any entered who carried no money

[e] Gloss. in Shekal. fol. 8. 4.
[f] Ibid.
[g] Hieros. Kiddush. fol. 58. 4.
[h] Bava Mezia, fol. 44. 2.

[i] Maasar Sheni, cap. 2. hal. 8, 9.
Adajoth. cap. 1. 9, 10.
[k] In the word פורט.

with him to be offered to the Corban, whether in his hand, or in his bosom, or elsewhere, we do not define: so did this very poor woman, who for two mites purchased herself an eternal fame, our Saviour himself setting a value upon the thing above all the gifts of them that offered.

CHAP. XIII.[1]

VER. 3 : Εἰς τὸ ὄρος τῶν Ἐλαιῶν κατέναντι τοῦ ἱεροῦ· *Upon the mount of Olives, over against the Temple.*] "The east[m] gate of the Court of the Gentiles had the metropolis Sushan painted on it. And through this gate the high priest went out to burn the red cow." And, "All[n] the walls of that court were high, except the east wall; because of the priest, when he burnt the red cow, stood upon the top of mount *Olivet*[o], and took his aim, and looked upon the gate of the Temple, in that time when he sprinkled the blood." And, "The[p] priest stood with his face turned westward, kills the cow with his right hand, and receives the blood with the left, but sprinkleth it with his right, and that seven times, directly towards the Holy of Holies."

It is true, indeed, the Temple might be well seen from any tract of *Olivet*: but the word κατέναντι, *over against,* if it doth not direct to this very place, yet to some place certainly in the same line: and it cannot but recall to our mind that action of the high priest.

Ver. 7 : Μὴ θροεῖσθε· *Be not troubled.*] Think here, how the traditions of the scribes affrighted the nation with the report of Gog and Magog, immediately to go before the coming of the Messiah :—

"R. Eliezer Ben Abina saith[q], When you see the kingdoms disturbing one another, צפה לרגלי של משיח *then expect the footsteps of the Messiah.* And know that this is true from hence, that so it was in the days of Abraham; for kingdoms disturbed one another, and then came redemption to Abraham." And elsewhere; "So[r] they came against Abraham, and so they shall come with Gog and Magog." And again,

[1] *English folio edition,* vol. ii. p. 350.
[m] Middoth, cap. i. hal. 3.
[n] Cap. 2. hal. 4.
[o] *Leusden's edit.,* vol. ii. p. 454.
[p] Parah, cap. 3. hal. 9.
[q] Beresh. Rabb. sect. 41.
[r] Bab. Sanhedr. fol. 95. 2.

"The[s] Rabbins deliver.   In the first year of that week [*of
years*] that the Son of David is to come, shall that be fulfilled,
' I will rain upon one city, but I will not rain upon another,'
Amos iv. 7.   The second year, the arrows of famine shall be
sent forth.   The third, the famine shall be grievous, and men
and women and children, holy men, and men of good works,
shall die.   And there shall be a forgetfulness of the law
among those that learn it.   The fourth year, fulness, and not
fulness.   The fifth year, great fulness ; for they shall eat and
drink and rejoice, and the law shall return to its scholars.
The sixth year, voices.   (The Gloss is, ' A fame shall be
spread, that the Son of David comes,' or, ' they shall sound
with a trumpet.')   The seventh year, wars ; and in the going
out of that seventh year the Son of David shall come."

Ver. 8 : Ἀρχαὶ ὠδίνων ταῦτα·   *These are the beginnings of
sorrows.*]   Isa. lxvi. 7, 8 : Πρὶν τὴν ὠδίνουσαν τεκεῖν, πρὶν ἐλθεῖν
τὸν πόνον τῶν ὠδίνων, ἐξέφυγε καὶ ἔτεκεν ἄρσεν.   Τίς ἤκουσε
τοιοῦτο ; &c.   *Before she travailed she brought forth ; before the
labour of pains came she was delivered, and brought forth a male.
Who hath heard such a thing ?* &c.   Εἰ ὤδινε γῆ ἐν ἡμέρᾳ μιᾷ,
ἢ καὶ ἐτέχθη ἔθνος εἰς ἅπαξ, ὅτι ὤδινε καὶ ἔτεκε Σιὼν τὰ παιδία
αὐτῆς ;   *Does the earth bring forth in one day, or is a nation also
brought forth at once ?   For Sion was in travail and brought
forth her sons.*

The prophet here says two things :—

I. That Christ should be born before the destruction of
Jerusalem.   The Jews themselves collect and acknowledge
this out of this prophecy : "It[t] is in the *Great Genesis*,
[*Bereshith Rabba*] a very ancient book : thus R. Samuel Bar
Nachaman said, Whence prove you, that in the day when the
destruction of the Temple was, Messias was born ? He answered,
From this that is said in the last chapter of Isaiah, ' Before she
travailed she brought forth ; before her bringing forth shall
come, she brought forth a male child.' In the same hour that
the destruction of the Temple was, Israel cried out as though
she were bringing forth. And Jonathan in the Chaldee translation said, Before her trouble came she was saved; and
before pains of childbirth came upon her, Messiah was re-

[s] Ibid. fol. 97. 1.
[t] Hieron. a sancta fide, [Joshua
Lork.] lib. 1. contra Judæos, cap. 2.

[Max. Biblioth. Vet. Patrum, Tom.
xxvi. p. 533. De la Bigne.]

vealed." In the Chaldee it is, יתגלי מלכה *A king shall manifest himself.*

"In[u] like manner in the same book: R. Samuel Bar Nachaman said, It happened that Elias went by the way in the day wherein the destruction of the Temple was, and he heard a certain voice crying out and saying, 'The holy Temple is destroyed.' Which when he heard, he imagined how he could destroy the world: but travelling forward he saw men ploughing and sowing, to whom he said, 'God is angry with the world and will destroy his house, and lead his children captives to the Gentiles; and do you labour for temporal victuals?' And another voice was heard, saying, 'Let them work, for the Saviour of Israel is born.' And Elias said, 'Where is he?' And the voice said, 'In Bethlehem of Judah,'" &c. These words this author speaks, and these words they speak.

II. As it is not without good reason gathered, that Christ shall be born before the destruction of the city, from that clause, "Before she travailed she brought forth, before her bringing forth came [πόνος τῶν ὠδίνων, *the pangs of travail*], she brought forth a male child;" so also, from that clause, εἰ ἐτέχθη ἔθνος εἰς ἅπαξ, ὅτι ὤδινε καὶ ἔτεκε Σιών, &c. *Is a nation brought forth at once? for Sion travailed and brought forth her children,* is gathered as well, that the Gentiles were to be gathered and called to the faith before that destruction; which our Saviour most plainly teacheth, ver. 10, "But the gospel must first be preached among all nations." For how the Gentiles, which should believe, are called 'the children of Sion,' and 'the children of the church of Israel,' every where in the prophets, there is no need to show, for every one knows it.

In this sense is the word ὠδίνων, *pangs* or *sorrows,* in this place to be understood; and it agrees not only with the sense of the prophet alleged, but with a most common phrase and opinion in the nation concerning חבלי משיח *the sorrows of the Messiah,* that is, concerning the calamities which they expected would happen at the coming of the Messiah. אמר עולא ייתי ולא איחמיניה *"Ulla[x] saith, The*

---

u *English folio edition,* vol. ii. p. 351.   x Sanhedr. fol. 98. 2.

Messias shall come, but I shall not see him. So also saith
Rabba, Messias shall come, but I shall not see him; that is,
he shall not be to be seen. Abai saith to Rabba, Why?
משיח של חבלו משום *because of the sorrows of the Messias.*
It is a tradition. His disciples asked R. Eliezer, What may
a man do to be delivered from the sorrows of Messias? Let
him be conversant in the law and in the works of mercy."
The Glossy is, "חבלו that is, the terrors and the sorrows
which shall be in his days." "He[z] that feasts thrice on the
sabbath day shall be delivered from three miseries, של מחבלו
משיח *from the sorrows of Messiah,* from the judgment of
hell, and from the war of Gog and Magog." Where the Gloss
is this, "' From the sorrows of Messias :' for in that age,
wherein the Son of David shall come, there will be קטגוריא
an accusation of the scholars of the wise men. חבלי לשון
יולדת חבלי *The word* חבלי *denotes such pains as women in
childbirth endure.*"

Ver. 32 : Περὶ δὲ τῆς ἡμέρας ἐκείνης καὶ τῆς ὥρας, οὐδεὶς οἶδεν·
But of that day and hour knoweth no man.] Of what *day* and
hour? That the discourse is of the day of the destruction of
Jerusalem is so evident, both by the disciples' question, and
by the whole thread of Christ's discourse, that it is a wonder
any should understand these words of the *day and hour* of the
last judgment.

Two things are demanded of our Saviour, ver. 4 : the one
is, " When shall these things be, that one stone shall not be
left upon another?" And the second is, " What shall be the
sign of this consummation?" To the latter he answereth
throughout the whole chapter hitherto : to the former in the
present words. He had said, indeed, in the verse before,
" Heaven and earth shall pass away," &c.; not for resolution
to the question propounded (for there was no inquiry at all
concerning the dissolution of heaven and earth), but for confirmation of the truth of the thing which he had related. As
though he had said, " Ye ask *when* such an overthrow of the
Temple shall happen; when it shall be, and what shall be the
signs of it. I answer, These and those, and the other signs
shall go before it ; and these my words of the thing itself to

come to pass, and of the signs going before, are firmer than heaven and earth itself. But whereas ye inquire of the precise time, that is not to be inquired after; for *of that day and hour knoweth no man.*"

We cannot but remember here, that even among the beholders of the destruction of the Temple there is a difference concerning the day of the destruction; that that day and hour was so little known before the event, that even after the event, they who saw the flames disagreed among themselves concerning the *day.* Josephus, an eyewitness, saw the burning of the Temple, and he ascribed it to the tenth day of the month Ab or Lous. For thus he[a]; "The Temple perished the tenth day of the month Lous (or *August*), a[b] day fatal to the Temple, as having been on that day consumed in flames by the king of Babylon." Rabban Jochanan Ben Zaccai saw the same conflagration; and he, together with the whole Jewish nation, ascribes it to the ninth day of that month, not the tenth; yet so that he saith, "If I had not lived in that age I had not judged it but to have happened on the tenth day." For as the Gloss upon Maimonides[c] writes, "It was the evening when they set fire to it, and the Temple burnt until sunset the tenth day. In the Jerusalem Talmud, therefore, Rabbi and R. Joshua Ben Levi fasted the ninth and tenth days." See also the tract *Bab. Taanith*[d].

Οὐδὲ οἱ ἄγγελοι· *Neither the angels.*] "' For[e] the day of vengeance is in mine heart, and the year of my redeemed is come,' Isa. lxiii. 4. What means 'the day of vengeance is in mine heart?' R. Jochanan saith, I have revealed it to my heart, to my members I have not revealed it. R. Simeon Ben Lachish saith, I have revealed it to my heart, למלאכי השרת לא גליתי *but to the ministering angels I have not revealed it.*" And *Jalkut* on that place thus: לבא לפומא לא גלי פומא למאן גלי *My heart reveals it not to my mouth; to whom should my mouth reveal it?*

Οὐδὲ ὁ υἱός· *Nor the Son.*] Οὐδὲ ἄγγελοι οὐδὲ υἱός, that is, *Neither the angels, nor the Messias.* For in that sense the word Υἱός, *Son,* is to be taken in this place and elsewhere

---

a De Bell. lib. 6. cap. 26. [Hudson, p. 1278. l. 19.] [vi. 4, 5.]
b *English folio edit.*, vol. ii. p. 351.
c In Taanith, cap. 5.
d Fol. 29. 1.
e Bab. Sanhedr. fol. 99. 1.

very often: as in that passage, John v. 19, "The Son," that is, the Messias, "can do nothing of himself, but what he seeth the Father do:" ver. 20, "The Father loveth the Messias," &c.: ver. 26, "He hath given to the Messias to have life in himself," &c. And that the word *Son* is to be rendered in this sense, appears from ver. 27; "He hath given him authority to execute judgment also, because he is the Son of man." Observe that, "because he is the Son of man."

I. It is one thing to understand "the Son of God" barely and abstractly for the second person in the Holy Trinity; another to understand him for the Messias, or that second person incarnate. To say that the second person in the Trinity knows not something is blasphemous; to say so of the Messias, is not so, who, nevertheless, was the same with the second person in the Trinity: for although the second person, abstractly considered according to his mere Deity, was co-equal with the Father, co-omnipotent, co-omniscient, co-eternal with him, &c.; yet Messias, who was God-man, considered as Messias, was a servant and a messenger of the Father, and received commands and authority from the Father. And those expressions, "The Son can do nothing of himself," &c. will not in the least serve the Arian's turn; if you take them in this sense, which you must necessarily do; "Messias can do nothing of himself, because he is a servant and a deputy."

II. We must distinguish between the excellences and perfections of Christ, which flowed from the hypostatical union of the natures, and those which flowed from the donation and anointing of the Holy Spirit. From the hypostatical union of the natures flowed the infinite dignity of his person, his impeccability, his infinite[f] self-sufficiency to perform the law, and to satisfy the divine justice. From the anointing of the Spirit flowed his power of miracles, his foreknowledge of things to come, and all kind of knowledge of evangelic mysteries. *Those* rendered him a fit and perfect Redeemer; *these* a fit and perfect Minister of the gospel.

Now, therefore, the foreknowledge of things to come, of which the discourse here is, is to be numbered among those

---

[f] *Leusden's edition*, vol. ii. p. 456.

things which flowed from the anointing of the Holy Spirit, and from immediate revelation; not from the hypostatic union of the natures. So that those things which were revealed by Christ to his church, he had them from the revelation of the Spirit, not from that union. Nor is it any derogation or detraction from the dignity of his person, that he saith, ' He knew not that day and hour of the destruction of Jerusalem;' yea, it excellently agrees with his office and deputation, who, being the Father's servant, messenger, and minister, followed the orders of the Father, and obeyed him in all things. " The Son knoweth not," that is, it is not revealed to him from the Father to reveal to the church. Rev. i. 1, " The revelation of Jesus Christ, which God gave unto him."

We omit inquiring concerning the knowledge of Christ, being now raised from death: whether, and how far, it exceeded his knowledge, while yet he conversed on earth. It is without doubt, that, being now raised from the dead, he merited all kind of revelation (see Rev. v. 9, " And they sung a new song, saying, Thou art worthy to take the book, and to open the seals thereof: for thou wast slain," &c.); and that he, conversing on earth before his death, acted with the vigour of the Holy Spirit and of that unspeakable holiness which flowed from the union of the human nature with the divine, the divine⁵ nature, in the meantime, suspending its infinite activity of omnipotence. So that Christ might work miracles, and know things to come, in the same manner as the prophets also did, namely, by the Holy Ghost, but in a larger measure; and might overcome the devil not so much by the omnipotence of the divine nature, as by the infinite holiness of his person, and of his obedience. So that if you either look upon him as the minister and servant of God; or if you look upon the constitution, as I may so call it, and condition of his person, these words of his, " Of that day and hour knoweth not the Son also," carry nothing of incongruity along with them; yea, do excellently speak out his substitution as a servant, and the constitution of his person as Θεάν-θρωπος, *God-man.*

The reason why the divine wisdom would have the time of the destruction of Jerusalem so concealed, is well known to itself; but by men, since the time of it was unsearchable, the reason certainly is not easy to be searched. We may conjecture that the time was hid, partly, lest the godly might be terrified with the sound of it, as 2 Thess. ii. 2; partly, that the ungodly, and those that would be secure, might be taken in the snares of their own security, as Matt. xxiv. 38. But let secret things belong to God.

CHAP. XIV.

Ver. 3: Νάρδου πιστικῆς· *Of spikenard.*] What if I should render it, *nardinum balaninum, nardin of balanus?* "Nardin consists [h] of omphacium, balaninum, bulrush, nard, amomum, myrrh, balsam," &c. And again [i], "Myrobalanum is common to the Troglodytes, and to Thebais, and to that part of Arabia which divides Judea from Egypt; a growing ointment, as appears by the very name, whereby also is shown that it is the mast [*glans*] of a tree."

Βάλανος, as all know, among the Greeks, is *glans, mast,* or an *acorn:* so also is פסתקא *pistaca,* among the Talmudists. There are prescribed by the Talmudists various [k] remedies for various diseases: among others, this; לברסם ליתי כי פיסתקא דנישדור *For a pleurisy* (or, as others will have it, a certain disease of the head), *take to the quantity of the mast of ammoniac.* The Gloss is, פיסתקא *is the mast of cedar.* The *Aruch* saith, "פיסתקא is the grain of a fruit, which is called גלנדא *glans.*"

The word νάρδου, *nard,* is Hebrew from the word נרד *nerad;* and the word πιστική is Syriac, from the word פיסתקא *pistaca.* So that the ointment might be called *unguentum balaninum, balanine ointment,* in the composition of which, nard and פיסתקא *mast,* or *myrobalane,* were the chief ingredients.

Κατέχεεν αὐτοῦ κατὰ τῆς κεφαλῆς· *Poured it on his head.*] In Talmudic language, דרדיגה משחא ארישיה. "What [l] are the testimonies, that the woman married is a virgin? If she goes forth to be married בהינומא *with a veil* let down over

---

h Pliny, lib. xiii. cap. 1.   k Bab. Gittin, fol. 69. 1.
i Idem, lib. xii. cap. 21.   l Bab. Chetubh. fol. 17. 2.

her eyes, yet with her head not veiled. The scattering of
nuts is also a testimony. These are in Judea; but what are
in Babylon? Rabh saith, דמשחא ארישא דרבנין *If ointment
be upon the head of the Rabbins.*" (The Gloss is, "The women
poured ointment upon the heads תלמידין *of the scholars,* and
anointed them.") "Rabh Papa said to Abai, משחא
דחפיפותא קאמר מר *Does that doctor speak of the aromatic
ointment used in bridechambers?*" (The Gloss is, "Are the
Rabbins such, to be anointed with such ointments?") "He
answered, יתמא *O orphan*" (that is, O thou unacquainted with
the customs), לא עבדא לך אמך דרדוגי משחא ארישא
דרבנין "*did not thy mother pour out ointment for you* (at thy
wedding) *upon the heads of the Rabbins?* Thus, a certain
Rabbin got a wife for his son in the house of Rabbah Bar
Ulla; and they said to him, Rabbah Bar Ulla also got a wife
in the house of a certain Rabbin for his son, ודרדיג משחא
ארישא דרבנין *and he poured out ointment upon the head of the
Rabbins.*"

From the tradition produced it may be asked, whether it
were customary[m] in Judea to wet the heads of the Rabbins
with ointments, in the marriages of virgins, as it was in
Babylon? Or, whether it were so customary otherwise to
anoint their heads; as that such an anointing at weddings
were not so memorable a matter as it was in Babylon? Certainly, in both places, however they anointed men's heads for
health's sake[n], it was accounted unfitting for Rabbins to
smell of aromatical ointments: "It is indecent (say the
Jerusalem Talmudists[o]) for a scholar of the wise men to
smell of spices." And you have the judgment of the Babylonians in this very place, when it is inquired among them,
and that, as it were, with a certain kind of dissatisfaction,
Whether Rabbins be such as that they should be anointed
with aromatical ointments, as the more nice sort are wont to
be anointed? From this opinion, everywhere received among
them, you may more aptly understand, why the other disciples as well as Judas, did bear the lavish of the ointment
with some indignation: *he,* out of wicked covetousness; but
they, partly, as not willing that so precious a thing should be

lost, and partly as not liking so nice a custom should be used towards their master, from which the masters of the Jews themselves were so averse. And our Saviour, taking off the envy of what was done, applies this anointing to his burial, both in his intention and in the intention of the woman; that it might not seem to be done out of some delicate niceness.

Ver. 5: Ἐπάνω τριακοσίων δηναρίων· *More than three hundred pence.*] I. The prices of such precious ointments (as it seems in Pliny) were commonly known. For thus he, "The P price of *costus* is sixteen pounds. The price of *spike* (*nard*) is ninety pounds. The leaves have made a difference in the value. From the broadness of them it is called Hadrosphærum; with greater leaves it is worth X. xxx," that is, *thirty pence.* "That with a lesser leaf is called Mesosphærum, it is sold at X. lx," *sixty pence.* "The most esteemed is that called Microsphærum, having the least leaf, and the price of it is X. lxxv.," *seventy-five pence.* And elsewhere q : "To these the merchants have added that which they call Daphnois, surnamed Isocinnamon, and they make the price of it to be X. ccc" (τριακοσίους δηναρίους, *three hundred pence*). See more there.

II. It is not easy to reduce this sum of three hundred pence to its proper sense; partly because a penny was twofold, a silver penny, and a gold one: partly because there was a double value and estimation of money, namely, that of Jerusalem and that of Tyre, as we observed before. Let these be silver (which we believe), which are of much less value than gold : and let them be Jerusalem pence (which we also believe), which are cheaper than the Tyrian; yet they plainly speak the great wealth of Magdalene, who poured out an ointment of such a value, when before she had spent some such other.

Which brings to my mind those things which are spoken by the Masters concerning קופת הבשמים *the box of spices,* which the husband was bound to give the wife according to the proportion of her dowry: "But r this is not spoken, saith Rabh Ishai, but of Jerusalem people. There is an example

---

P Lib. xii. c. 12.   q Cap. 20.   r Bab. Chetub. fol. 66. 2.

of a daughter of נקדימון *Nicodemus* Ben Gorion, to whom
the wise men appointed four hundred crowns of gold for a
chest of spices for one day. She said to them, ' I wish you
may so appoint for their daughters ;' and they answered after
her, ' Amen.' " The Gloss is, " The husband was to give to
his wife ten *zuzees* for every *manah*, which she brought with
her to buy spices, with which she used to wash herself," &c.
Behold ! a most wealthy woman of Jerusalem, daughter of
Nicodemus, in the contract and instrument of whose marriage
was written, " A thousand thousand gold pence out of the
house of her father, besides those she had out of the house
of her father-in-law :" whom yet you have in the same story
reduced to that extreme poverty, that she picked up barleycorns for her food out of the cattle's dung.

Ver. 7 : Πάντοτε γὰρ τοὺς πτωχοὺς ἔχετε μεθ' ἑαυτῶν· *For ye
have the poor with you always.*] " Samuel saith [s], ' There is no
difference between this world and the days of the Messias,'
אלא שעבוד מלכיות *unless in regard of the affliction of the
heathen kingdoms;* as it is said, ' A poor man shall not be
wanting out of the midst of the earth,' " Deut. xv. 11.   Observe a Jew confessing, that there shall be poor men even in
the days of the Messias : which how it agrees with their received opinion of the pompous kingdom of the Messias, let
him look to it.   " R. Solomon and Aben Ezra write, ' If thou
shalt obey the words of the Lord, there shall not be a poor
man in thee : but thou wilt not obey ; therefore a poor man
shall never be wanting." Upon this received reason of the
thing, confess also, O Samuel, that there shall be disobedient
persons in the days of the Messias ; which, indeed, when the
true Messias came, proved too, too true, in thy nation.

Ver. 12 [t] : Καὶ τῇ πρώτῃ ἡμέρᾳ τῶν ἀζύμων· *And the first
day of unleavened bread.*] So Matt. xxvi. 17 ; Luke xxii. 7.
And now let them tell me, who think that Christ indeed
kept his Passover the fourteenth day, but the Jews not
before the fifteenth, because this year their Passover was
transferred unto the fifteenth day by reason of the following
sabbath : let them tell me, I say, whether the evangelists
speak according to the day prescribed by Moses, or according to the day prescribed by the masters of the tradi-

[s] Bab. Schabb. fol. 63. 1.   [t] *English folio edit.*, vol. ii. p. 353.

tions, and used by the nation. If according to Moses, then the fifteenth day was πρώτη ἀζύμων, *the first of unleavened bread,* Exod. xii. 15, 18 : but if according to the manner of the nation, then it was the fourteenth. And whether the evangelists speak according to this custom, let us inquire briefly.

Sometime, indeed, the whole seven days' feast was transferred [u] to another month ; and that not only from that law, Numb. ix, but from other causes also : concerning which see the places quoted in the margin [x]. But when the time appointed for the feast occurred, the lamb was always slain on the fourteenth day.

I. Let us begin with a story where an occasion occurs not very unlike that for which they of whom we speak think the Passover this year was transferred; namely, because of the following sabbath. The story is this : " After [y] the death of Shemaiah and Abtalion, the sons of Betira obtained the chief place. Hillel went up from Babylon to inquire concerning three doubts. When he was now at Jerusalem, and the fourteenth day of the first month fell out on the sabbath [*observe that*], it appeared not to the sons of Betira, whether the Passover drove off the sabbath or no. Which when Hillel had determined in many words, and had added, moreover, that he had learned this from Shemaiah and Abtalion, they laid down their authority, and made Hillel president. When they had chosen him president, he derided them, saying, ' What need have you of this Babylonian ? Did you not serve the two chief men of the world, Shemaiah and Abtalion, who sat among you ?' " These things which are already said make enough to our purpose, but, with the reader's leave, let us add the whole story : " While he thus scoffed at them, he forgot a tradition. For they said, ' What is to be done with the people if they bring not their knives ?' He answered, ' I have heard this tradition, but I have forgot. But let them alone ; for although they are not prophets, they are prophets' sons.' Presently every one whose passover was a lamb stuck his knife into the fleece of it ; and

[u] *Leusden's edition,* vol. ii. p. 458.
[x] Hieros. in Maasar Sheni, fol.
56. 3. Maimon. in Kiddush. Hodesh. cap. 4.
[y] Hieros. Pesachin, fol. 33. 1.

whose passover was a kid, hung his knife upon the horns of it."

And now let the impartial reader judge between the reason which is given for the transferring the Passover this year unto the fifteenth day, namely, because of the sabbath following, that they might not be forced to abstain from servile work for two days together; and the reason for which it might with good reason be transferred that year concerning which the story is. The fourteenth day fell on a sabbath; a scruple ariseth, whether the sabbath gives way to the Passover, or the Passover to the sabbath. The very chief men of the Sanhedrim, and the oracles of traditions, are not able to resolve the business. A great article of religion is transacting; and what is here to be done! O ye sons of Betira, transfer but the Passover unto the next day, and the knot is untied. Certainly if this had been either usual or lawful, they had provided that the affairs of religion, and their authority and fame, should not have stuck in this strait. But that was not to be suffered.

II. Let us add a tradition which you may justly wonder at: "Five[z] things, if they come in uncleanness, are not eaten in uncleanness: the sheaf of firstfruits, the two loaves, the shewbread, the peace offerings of the congregation, and the goats of the new moons. But הפסח שבא בטומאה נאכל בטומאה *the Passover which comes in uncleanness is eaten in uncleanness:* because it comes not originally unless to be eaten."

Upon which tradition thus Maimonides: "The Lord saith, 'And there were some that were unclean by the carcase of a man,' Numb. ix. 6, and he determines of them, that they be put off from the Passover of the first month to the Passover of the second. And the tradition is, that it was thus determined, because they were few. But if the whole congregation should have been unclean, or if the greatest part of it should have been unclean, yet they offer the Passover, though they are unclean. Therefore they say, 'Particular men are put off to the second Passover, but the whole congregation is not put off to the second Passover. In like manner all the

---

[z] Pesachin, cap. 7. hal. 4.

oblations of the congregation, they offer them in uncleanness if the most are unclean; which we learn also from the Passover. For the Lord saith of the Passover, [Numb. ix. 2.] בְּמוֹעֲדוֹ that it is to be offered *in its set time* [note that]; and saith also of the oblations of the congregation, Ye shall do this to the Lord in your set times, and to them all he prescribes a set time. Every thing, therefore, to which a time is set, is also offered in uncleanness, if so be very many of the congregation, or very many of the priests, be unclean."

"We [a] find [b] that the congregation makes their Passover in uncleanness, in that time when most of them are unclean. And if known uncleanness be thus dispensed with, much more doubted uncleanness." But what need is there of such dispensation? Could ye not put off the Passover, O ye fathers of the Sanhedrim, for one or two days, that the people might be purified? By no means: for the Passover is to be offered בְּמוֹעֲדוֹ *in its set time*, the fourteenth day, without any dispensation. For,

III. Thus the canons of that church concerning that day: אוֹר לִיד׳ בּוֹדְקִין אֶת הֶחָמֵץ לְאוֹר הַנֵּר *in* [c] *the light of the fourteenth day, they seek for leaven by candlelight.* The Gloss is; "In the night, to which the day following is the fourteenth day." And go to all the commentators, and they will teach, that this was done upon the going out of the thirteenth day. And Maimonides; "From [d] the words of the scribes, they look for and rid away leaven in the beginning of the night of the fourteenth day, and that by the light of the candle. For in the night time all are within their houses, and a candle is most proper for such a search. Therefore, they do not appoint employments in the end of the thirteenth day, nor doth a wise man begin to recite his phylacteries in that time, lest thereby, by reason of their length [e], he be hindered from seeking for leaven in its season." And the same author elsewhere [f]; "It is forbidden to eat leaven on the fourteenth day from noon and onwards, viz. from the beginning of the seventh hour. Our wise men also forbade eating it from the beginning of the sixth hour. Nay, the

[a] *English folio edit.*, vol. ii. p. 353.
[b] Hieros. Sotah, fol. 16. 3.
[c] Pesach. cap. 2. hal. 1.
[d] In חמץ ומצה cap. 2.
[e] *Leusden's edit.*, vol. ii. p. 459.
[f] Ibid. cap. 1.

fifth hour they eat not leaven, lest perhaps the day be cloudy, and so a mistake arise about the time. Behold, you learn that it is lawful to eat leaven on the fourteenth day, to the end of the fourth hour; but in the fifth hour it is not to be used." The same author elsewhere[g] writes thus; "The passover was not to be killed but in the court, where the other sacrifices were killed. And it was to be killed on the fourteenth day afternoon, after the daily sacrifice."

And now, reader, tell me what day the evangelists call πρώτην ἀζύμων, *the first day of unleavened bread*: and whether it be any thing probable that the Passover was ever transferred unto the fifteenth day? Much less is it probable that Christ this year kept his Passover one day before the Passovers of the Jews.

For the Passover was not to be slain but in the court, where the other sacrifices were slain, as we heard just now from Maimonides: and see the rubric[h] of bringing in the lambs into the court, and of slaying them. And then tell me seriously whether it be credible, that the priests in the Temple, against the set decree of the Sanhedrim that year (as the opinion we contradict imports), would kill Christ's one, only, single lamb; when by that decree it ought not to be killed before to-morrow? When Christ said to his disciples, " Ye know, that after two days is the Passover;" and when he commanded them, " Go ye, and prepare for us the Passover," it is a wonder they did not reply, " True, indeed, Sir, it ought to be after two days; but it is put off this year to a day later, so that now it is after three days; it is impossible therefore that we should obey you now, for the priests will not allow of killing before to-morrow."

We have said enough, I suppose, in this matter. But while I am speaking of the day of the Passover, let me add a few words, although not to the business concerning which we have been treating; and they perhaps not unworthy of our consideration :

" He[i] that mourns washes himself, and eats his Passover in the even. A proselyte, which is made a proselyte on the eve of the Passover, the school of Shammai saith, Let him be

---

g In Corban Pesach. cap. i.   h Pesach. cap. 3. hal. 5, 6.
i Pesach. cap. 8.

baptized, and eat his Passover in the even: the school of
Hillel saith, He that separates himself from uncircumcision
[*that is, from heathens and heathenism*] is as if he separated
himself from a sepulchre." The Gloss, " And hath need of
seven days' purification." אסרטוטות היו בירושלם " *There*[k]
were soldiers at Jerusalem, who baptized themselves, and ate
their Passovers in the even." A thing certainly to be noted,
proselytes the same day made proselytes, and eating the
Passover; and that as it seems without circumcision, but
admitted only by baptism.

The care of the school of Hillel in this case did not so
much repulse a proselyte from eating the Passover, who was
made a proselyte and baptized on the day of the Passover;
as provided for the future, that such a one in following years
should not obtrude himself to eat the Passover in uncleanness. For while he was in heathenism, he contracted not
uncleanness from the touch of a sepulchre; but being made
a proselyte, he contracted uncleanness by it. These are the
words of the Gloss.

Ἐτοιμάσωμεν ἵνα φάγῃς τὸ πάσχα· *That we prepare that
thou mayest eat the Passover.*] For the Passovers were prepared by the servants for their masters. "If[l] any say to his
servant, ' Go and kill me the passover,' and he kills a kid, let
him eat of it: if he kill a lamb, let him eat of it: if a kid and
a lamb, let him eat of the former," &c.

Ver. 26[m]: Καὶ ὑμνήσαντες· *And when they had sung an
hymn.*] I. "What[n] difference is there between the first
Passover and the second?" [that is, the Passover of the
first month and of the second, Num. ix.] " In the first, every
one is bound under that law, ' Leaven shall not be seen nor
found among you.' In the second, ' Leaven and unleavened
bread may be with a man in his house.' In the first, he is
bound to a *hymn* when he eats the Passover. In the second,
he is not bound to a *hymn* when he eats it. In both, he is
bound to a *hymn* while he makes *or* kills. Both are to be
eaten roast, and with unleavened bread, and bitter herbs,
and both drive away the sabbath." The Gemarists ask,
" Whence this is, that they are bound to *a hymn*, while they

k Hieros. Pesach. fol. 36. 2.
l Pesachin, cap. 8. hal. 2.

m *English folio edit.*, vol. ii. p. 354.
n Pesach. cap. 9. hal. 3.

eat the Passover? R. Jochanan in the name of R. Simeon
Ben Josedek saith, The Scripture saith, 'You shall have a
song, as in the night when a feast is kept,' Isa. xxx. 29. The
night which is set apart for a feast is bound to *a hymn :* the
night which is not set apart for a feast is not bound to *a
hymn.*" The Gloss writes thus ; " As ye are wont to sing in
the night when a feast is kept: but there is no night wherein
they are obliged to a song, besides the night when the Passover is eaten."

II. That hymn is called by the Rabbins the *Hallel ;* and
was from the beginning of Psalm cxiii, to the end of Psalm
cxviii, which they cut in two parts; and a part of it they
repeated in the very middle of the banquet, and they reserved
a part to the end.

How far the former portion extended, is disputed between
the schools of Shammai and Hillel. That of Shammai saith,
Unto the end of Psalm cxiii. That of Hillel saith, Unto the
end of Psalm cxiv. But these things must not stop us.
The hymn which Christ now sang with his disciples after
meat was the latter part. In which, as the Masters of the
Traditions observe, these five things are mentioned: "The[o]
going out[p] of Egypt. The cutting in two of the Red Sea.
The delivery of the law. The resurrection of the dead : and
the sorrows of the Messias. The going out of Egypt, as it
is written, ' When Israel went out of Egypt.' The cutting
in two of the Red Sea, as it is written, ' The sea saw it, and
fled.' The delivery of the law, as it is written, The mountains leaped like rams.' The resurrection of the dead, as it
is written, 'I will walk before the Lord in the land of the
living.' And the sorrows of the Messias, as it is written,
' Not unto us, Lord, not unto us.'

Ἐξῆλθον εἰς τὸ ὄρος τῶν ἐλαιῶν· *They went out into the mount
of Olives.*] They were bound by the traditional canons to
lodge within Jerusalem. " On[q] the first Passover, every one
is bound to lodge [*pernoctationem*] (טעון לינה) also on the
second Passover he is bound to lodge." The Gloss thus :
" He that keeps the Passover is bound to lodge in Jerusalem
the first night." But it is disputed, whether it be the same

---

[o] Pesachin, fol. 118. 1.   [p] *Leusden's edition,* vol. ii. p. 460.
          [q] Pesach. fol. 95. 2.

night wherein the lamb is eaten; or the night first following the feast day. See the place: and let not the lion of the tribe of Judah be restrained in those cobwebs.

Ver. 36: Ἀββᾶ, ὁ πατήρ· *Abba, Father.*] As it is necessary to distinguish between the Hebrew and Chaldee idiom in the words אבי *Abbi,* and אבא *Abba,* so you *may,* I had almost said, you *must,* distinguish of their sense. For the word אבי *Abi,* signifies indeed a natural father, but withal a civil father also, an elder, a master, a doctor, a magistrate: but the word אבא *Abba,* denotes only a natural father, with which we comprehend also an adopting father: yea, it denotes, *My father.*

שלא יאמר אדם לחבירו אבא גדול מאביך *Let[r] no man say to his neighbour,* אבא '*My father*' *is nobler than thy father.* "R. Chaija[s] asked Rabh the son of his brother, when he came into the land of Israel, אבא קיים *Doth my father live?* And he answereth, אמא קיימת *And doth your mother live?*" As if he should have said, You know your mother is dead, so you may know your father is dead. "Solomon[t] said, Observe ye מה פירש אבא *what my father saith?*" So in the Targum infinite times.

And we may observe in the Holy Scriptures, wheresoever mention is made of a natural father, the Targumists use the word אבא *Abba:* but when of a civil father, they use another word:—

I. Of[u] a natural father.

Gen xxii. 7, וַיֹּאמֶר אָבִי "*And he said,* '*Abi,*' *my father.*" The Targum reads, ואמר אבא "*And said,* '*Abba,*' *my father.*"

Gen. xxvii. 34: בָּרְכֵנִי גַם־אָנִי אָבִי "Bless me, even me also אָבִי '*Abi,*' O *my father.*" The Targum reads, ברכני אף אנא אבא *Bless me also,* '*Abba,*' *my father.*

Gen. xlviii. 18: לֹא כֵן אָבִי *Not so,* '*Abi,*' *my father.* Targum, לא כדין אבא *Not so,* '*Abba,*' *my father.*

Judg. xi. 36: אָבִי פָּצִיתָה אֶת־פִּיהָ '*Abi,*' *my father, if thou hast opened thy mouth.* Targum, אבא פתחת פומך '*Abba,*' *my father, if thou hast opened thy mouth.*

---

r Bab. Sanhedr. fol. 37. 1.
s Aruch in אבא.
t Bathr. fol. 10. 2.
u *English folio edit.*, vol. ii. p. 354.

Isa. viii. 4 : The Targum reads, עד לא ידע עולמא למקרי
אבא ואמא *before the child shall know to cry ' Abba,' my father,
and my mother.* See also the Targum upon Josh. ii. 13, and
Judg. xiv. 16, and elsewhere very frequently.

II. Of a civil father.

Gen. iv. 20, 21 : הוּא הָיָה אֲבִי *He was ' Abi,' the father of*
such as dwell in tents. "He was '*Abi*,' the father of such as
handle the harp," &c. The Targum reads, הוא הוה רבהון
He was ' Rabba,' the prince or *the master of them.*

1 Sam. x. 12 : וּמִי אֲבִיהֶם *But who is ' Abihem,' their father ?*
Targum, ומי רבהון *Who is their ' Rab,' master* or *prince ?*

2 Kings ii. 12 : אָבִי אָבִי *' Abi' ' Abi,' my father, my father.*
The Targum, רבי רבי *Rabbi, Rabbi.*

2 Kings v. 13 : וַיֹּאמְרוּ אָבִי *And they said, ' Abi,' my
father.* The Targum, ואמרו מרי *And they said, ' Mari,' my
Lord.*

2 Kings vi. 21 : הַאַכֶּה אָבִי *' Abi,' my father, shall I smite
them ?* Targum, אקטול רבי *' Rabbi,' shall I kill,* &c.

Hence appears the reason of those words of the apostle,
Rom. viii. 15 : Ἐλάβετε πνεῦμα υἱοθεσίας, ἐν ᾧ κράζομεν Ἀββᾶ
ὁ Πατήρ· *Ye have received the Spirit of adoption, whereby we
cry, Abba, Father.* And Gal. iv. 6 : "Because ye are sons,
God hath sent forth the Spirit of his Son into your hearts,
crying *Abba, Father.*" It was one thing to call God אבי
Abi, Father, that is, *Lord, King, Teacher, Governor, &c.*; and
another to call him אבא *Abba, My Father.* The doctrine of
adoption, in the proper sense, was altogether unknown to the
Jewish schools (though they boasted that the people of Israel
alone were adopted by God above all other nations); and yet
they called God אבי *Father,* and אבינו *our Father,* that is,
our God, Lord, and King, &c. But "since ye are sons (saith
the apostle), ye cry, אבא *Abba, O my Father,*" in the proper
and truly paternal sense.

Thus Christ in this place, however under an unspeakable
agony, and compassed about on all sides with anguishments,
and with a very cloudy and darksome providence ; yet he acknowledges, invokes, and finds God אבא *his Father,* in a
most sweet sense.

Κράζομεν, Ἀββᾶ, ὁ πατήρ· *We cry, ' Abba,' Father.* Did the

saints, invoking God, and calling him *Abba*, add also *Father?*
Did Christ also use the same addition of the Greek word
πατὴρ, *Father*, and did he repeat the word 'Αββᾶ *Abba* or
אבי *Abi? Father* seems rather here to be added by Mark,
and there also by St. Paul, for explication of the word ' *Abba :'*
and this is so much the more probable also, because it is expressed ὁ Πατὴρ, *Father*, and not ὦ Πάτερ, *O Father*, in the
vocative.

Ver. 51: Περιβεβλημένος σινδόνα ἐπὶ γυμνοῦ· *Having a linen
cloth cast about his naked body.*] It is well rendered by the
Vulgar *amictus sindone, clothed in sindon* or *fine linen :* for to
that the words have respect : not that he had some linen
loosely and by chance cast about him, but that the garment
wherewith he always went clothed, was of *sindon*, that is,
of *linen*. Let us hearken a little to the Talmudists.

" The Rabbins deliver[x] : סידון בציצית *Sindon* [*linen*] *with
fringes*, what of them ? The school of Shammai absolves, the
school of Hillel binds, and the wise men determine according
to the school[y] of Hillel. R. Eliezer Ben R. Zadok saith,
Whosoever wears hyacinth [*purple*] in Jerusalem, is among
those who make men admire." By *hyacinthinum* [תכלת
purple] they understand those fringes that were to put them
in mind of the law, Num. xv. And by סידון *sindon, linen*, is
understood טלית *a cloak,* or that garment, which, as it serves
for clothing the body, so it is doubly serviceable to religion.
For, 1. To this garment were ציצית *the fringes* fastened,
concerning which mention is made, Num. xv. 38. 2. With
this garment they commonly covered their heads when they
prayed. Hence that in the Gemarists in the place quoted :
טלית שמתכסה בו קטון ראשו ורובו *talith,* or *the cloak
whereby the boy covereth his head, and a great part of himself;*
if any one of elder years goes forth[z] clothed with it in a more
immodest manner, he is bound to wear fringes." And elsewhere, "The[a] priests who veil themselves when they go up
into the pulpit, בטלית שאינו להם *with a cloak which is not
their own,"* &c.

But now it was customary to wear this cloak, in the sum-

---

[x] Menacoth, fol. 40. 1.
[y] *Leusden's edition*, vol. ii. p. 149.
[z] *English folio edit.*, vol. ii. p. 355.
[a] Piske Tosaphoth in Menacoth numer. 150.

mer especially, and in Jerusalem for the most part, made of
sindon or of *linen.* And the question between the schools of
Shammai and Hillel arose hence, that when the fringes were
woollen, and the cloak linen, how would the suspicion of wearing things of different sorts be avoided? שרא ר׳ זירא לסדיניה
R. Zeira loosed his sindon. The Gloss is: " He loosed his
fringes from his sindon [that is, from his *talith*, which was
of ' *sindon,*' *linen*], because it was of *linen*," &c. " The[b] angel
found Rabh Ketina דמיכסי סדינא *clothed in sindon*; and
said to him, O Ketina, Ketina, סדינא בקייטא *sindon in the
summer*, וסרבלא בסיתוא *and a short cloak in the winter.*

You see that word which is spoke by the evangelist, ἐπὶ
γυμνοῦ, *about his naked body*, carries an emphasis: for it was
most usual to be clothed with sindon for an outer garment.
What therefore must we say of this young man? I suppose in
the first place, that he was not a disciple of Jesus; but that
he now followed, as some curious looker on, to see what this
multitude would at last produce. And to such a suspicion
they certainly do consent, who think him to have been roused
from his bed, and hastily followed the rout with nothing but
his shirt on, without any other clothes. I suppose, secondly,
St. Mark in the phrase περιβεβλημένος σινδόνα *having a sindon
cast about him*, spake according to the known and vulgar
dialect of the nation, מיכסי סדינא or מתכסה סדין *clothed
with a sindon.* For none shall ever persuade me that he would
use an idiom, any thing uncouth or strange to the nation;
and that when he used the very same phrase in Greek with
that Jewish one, he intended not to propound the very same
sense. But now you clearly see, they themselves being our
teachers, what is the meaning of *being clothed with a sindon*,
with them, namely, to have a *talith* or *cloak made of linen*;
that garment to which the fringes hung. I suppose, in the
last place, that this young man, out of religion, or superstition
rather, more than ordinary, had put on his *sindon*, and nothing
but that *upon his naked body*, neglecting his inner garment
(commonly called חלוק *chaluk*), and indeed neglecting his
body. For there were some amongst the Jews that did so
macerate their bodies, and afflict them with hunger and cold,
even above the severe rule of other sects.

Josephus in his own Life writes thus[c]: " I was sixteen years

b Ibid. fol. 41. 1.   c [Hudson, p. 905. l. 9.] [cap. 2.]

old, and I resolved to make trial of the institution of the three sects among us, the Pharisees, the Sadducees, and the Essenes; for I judged I should be able very well to choose the best of them, if I thoroughly learned them all. Afflicting, therefore, and much tormenting myself, I tried them all. Καὶ μηδὲ τὴν ἐντεῦθεν ἐμπειρίαν ἱκανὴν ἐμαυτῷ νομίσας εἶναι, &c. *But judging with myself that it was not enough to have tried these sects,* and hearing of one Banus, that lived in the wilderness, that he used a garment ἀπὸ δένδρων made *of leaves,* or *the bark of trees,* and no food but what grew of its own accord, and often by day and by night washing himself in cold water, I became a follower of him, and for three years abode with him."

And in that place in the Talmudists, which we but now produced, at that very story of Rabh Ketina, wearing a *sindon* in the winter for his *talith,* we have these words; " The religious in elder times, when they had wove three wings [*of the talith*], they joined תכלת *the purple,*" whereof the fringes were made: "but otherwise, חסידים דמחמרי לנפשייהו *they are religious who impose upon themselves things heavier than ordinary.*" And immediately follows the story of the angel and Ketina, who did so. There were some who heaped up upon themselves burdens and yokes of religion above the common rule, and that this is to be understood by מחמרי לנפשייהו *such as laid upon themselves heavier things than ordinary,* both the practice of some Jews persuade, and the word itself speaks it, being used by the Gemarists in the same sense elsewhere.

Such, we suppose, was this *young man* (as Josephus was, when a young man, of whom before), who, when others armed themselves against the cold with a double garment, namely, חלוק an *inner garment,* and טלית a *talith* or *cloak,* clothed himself with a single garment, and that of *sindon* or *linen,* and under the show of some more austere religion, neglecting the ordinary custom and care of himself.

The thing, taken in the sense which we propound, speaks the furious madness of this most wicked rout so much the more, inasmuch as they spared not a man, and him *a young man,* bearing most evident marks of a more severe religion.

Ver. 56[d]: Ἴσαι αἱ μαρτυρίαι οὐκ ἦσαν· *Their witness agreed*

[d] *English folio edition,* vol. ii. p. 355.

not together.] The traditional canons, in these things, divide testimonies into three parts :—

I. There was עדות במילה *a vain testimony :* which being heard, there is no more inquiry[e] made from that witness, there is no more use made of him, but he is set aside, as speaking nothing to the business.

II. There was עדות קיימת *a standing testimony,* for let me so turn it here, which, although it proved not the matter without doubt, yet it was not rejected by the judges, but admitted to examination by הזמה *citation,* that is, others being admitted to try to disprove it if they could.

III. There was the testimony כשדבריהם מכוונים *of the words of them that agreed* or *fitted together* (this also was עדות קיימת *a standing evidence*), when the words of two witnesses agreed, and were to the same purpose: μαρτυρία ἴση, *an even evidence.* Of these, see the tract *Sanhedrin*[f]; where also discourse is had concerning exact search and examination of the witnesses by בדוקות and חקירות and הזמה *inquisition,* and *scrutiny,* and *citation:* by which curious disquisition if they had examined the witnesses that babbled and barked against Christ, Oh! the unspeakable and infinite innocence of the most blessed Jesus, which envy and madness itself, never so much sworn together against his life, could not have fastened any crime upon!

It is said, ver. 55, Ἐζήτουν κατὰ τοῦ Ἰησοῦ μαρτυρίαν· *they sought for witness against Jesus.* This is neither equal, O fathers of the Sanhedrim! nor agreeable to your rule: דיני נפשות פותחין לזכות ואין פותחין לחובה *In[g] judgments about the life of any man, they begin first to transact about quitting the party who is tried; and they begin not with those things which make for his condemnation.* Whether the Sanhedrim now followed that canon in their scrutiny about Christ's case, let them look to it: by their whole process it sufficiently appears, whither their disquisition tended. And let it be granted, that they pretended some colour of justice and mercy, and permitted that any one who would, might come forth, ללמד עליו זכות *and testify something in his behalf,* where was any such now to be found? when all his

disciples turned their backs upon him, and the Fathers of the
Traditions had provided, that whosoever should confess him
to be Christ should be struck with the thunder of their excommunication, John ix. 22.

CHAP. XV.

VER. 1 : Ἐπὶ τὸ πρωὶ συμβούλιον ποιήσαντες,......καὶ ὅλον τὸ
συνέδριον· *In the morning they held a consultation,......and the
whole council.*] "At[h] what time do the judges sit in judgment? The lesser Sanhedrim and the bench of three sit,
after morning prayers are ended, until the end of the sixth
hour. But the great Sanhedrim sits after the morning daily
sacrifice to the afternoon daily sacrifice. And on sabbaths
and feast days" [as this day was that is here spoken of], "it
sat in *Beth-midrash*" (or *the chapel*), "in the Court of the
Gentiles."

"The Sanhedrim of one-and-seventy elders, it is not necessary that they all sit in their place, which is in the Temple.
But when it is necessary that all meet together, let all meet
together (ὅλον τὸ συνέδριον· *the whole council*).

"But in other times, he that hath business of his own, let
him attend his own business, and then return. With this
proviso, that nothing be wanting of the number of three-and-
twenty upon the bench continually during the whole time of
the session (συμβούλιον, *the consultation*). If any must go out,
let him look round, whether his colleagues be three-and-
twenty: if they be, let him go out: but if not, let him wait
till another enter in."

VER. 6[i] : Κατὰ δὲ ἑορτὴν ἀπέλυεν, &c. *At that feast he re-
leased, &c.*] The Syriac reads, עאדא בכל ; and so the Arab,
פי כל עיד *every feast*: Beza, *singulis festis, at each of the feasts,*
which pleases me not at all. For it is plainly said by Pilate
himself, "that I should release unto you one at the Passover," John xviii. 39: and the releasing of a prisoner suits
not so well to the other feasts as to the Passover; because
the Passover carries with it the memory of the release of the
people out of Egypt: but other feasts had other respects.
Κατὰ ἑορτὴν, I would render by way of paraphrase, *according*

---

[h] Maimon. Sanhedr. cap. 3.   [i] *English folio edition*, vol. ii. p. 356.

to the nature and quality of the feast, which was a monument of release.

The words עאדא and עיד, here and there used by the Syrian and the Arabic for *feast,* and especially עיד, remind me of that disputation of the Gemarists upon the second word in the tract *Avodah Zarah;* namely, whether it be to be writ אידידן or עידידין, whereby is denoted *a feast day* of the heathens.

Ver. 7 : Βαραββᾶς· *Barabbas.*] Let us mention also with him a very famous rogue in the Talmudists, בן דינאי *Ben Dinai,* whose name also was Eleazar. Of whom they have this passage worthy of chronological observation ; " From[k] the time that murderers were multiplied, the beheading the red cow ceased ; namely, from the time that Eleazar Ben Dinai came ; who was also called Techinnah Ben Perishah : but again they called him, בן הרצחן *The son of a murderer."* Of him mention is made elsewhere[l], where it is written בן דונא *Ben Donai.* See also בן נצר *Ben Nezer,* the king of the robbers[m].

Ver. 21 : Ἐρχόμενον ἀπ' ἀγροῦ· *Coming out of the country,* or *field.*] מביאים עצים מן השדה : " They[n] bring wood out of the field [on a feast-day], either bound together, or בן הקרפף *from some place fenced round or scattered."* The Gloss there is; " They bring wood on a feast day out of the field, which is within the limits of the sabbath, if it be bound together on the eve of the feast-day, &c. קרפף *is a place watched and fenced in every way."* And Rambam writes, " Rabbi Jose saith, If there be a door in קרפף *such a fenced place,* although it be distant from the city almost two thousand cubits, which are the limits of the sabbath, one may bring wood thence."

It may be conceived, that Simon the Cyrenean came out of the field thus loaded with wood; and you may conceive that he had given occasion[o] to the soldiers or executioners, why they would lay the cross upon him, namely, because they saw that he was a strong bearer; and instead of one burden, they laid this other upon him to bear.

Ver. 25 : Ἦν δ' ὥρα τρίτη, καὶ ἐσταύρωσαν αὐτόν· *And it was*

---

[k] Sotah, fol. 47. 1.
[l] Chetubh. fol. 27. 1. Kelim, fol. 12. 2.
[m] Chetubh. fol. 51. 2.
[n] Betsah, fol. 31. 1.
[o] *Leusden's edition,* vol. ii. p. 463.

the third hour, and they crucified him.] But John saith, chap. xix. 14, Ἦν δὲ παρασκευὴ τοῦ Πάσχα, ὥρα δὲ ὡσεὶ ἕκτη· *And it was the preparation of the Passover, and about the sixth hour ;* namely, when Pilate delivered him to be crucified. From the former clause, *it was the preparation of the Passover,* hath sprung that opinion, of which we have said something before concerning the transferring of the eating of the lamb this year to the fifteenth day. For they think by *the preparation of the Passover* is to be understood the preparation of the lamb, or for the eating of the lamb. For which interpretation they think that makes, which is said by the same John, chap. xviii. 28, " They would not go into the judgment-hall, lest they should be defiled, but that they might eat the Passover." And hence it is confidently concluded by them, that however Christ ate his lamb the day before, yet the Jews were to eat theirs this very day.

We will discourse first of the *day,* as it here occurs under the name of παρασκευὴ τοῦ πάσχα, *the preparation of the Pass-over ;* and then of the *hour :—*

I. Every[p] Israelite was bound, within that seven days' so-lemnity, after the lamb was eaten, to these two things : 1. To appear before the Lord in the court, and that with a sacrifice. 2. To solemn joy and mirth, and that also with sacrifices. The former was called by the Jews ראייה *Appearance.* The latter חגיגה *Chagigah, the festival.*

הכל חייבין בראייה "All[q] are bound to appear, except deaf-and-dumb, fools, young children," &c. And a little after; " The school of Shammai saith, *Let the Appearance be with two silver pieces of money* ראייה בשתי כסף, *and the Chagigah be with a 'meah' of silver* וחגיגה מעה כסף. The school of Hillel saith, Let the *Appearance* be with a *meah* of silver, and the *Chagigah* with two pieces of silver." The Gloss writes thus ; " All are bound to make their appearance from that precept, ' All thy males shall appear,' &c. Exod. xxiii. 17 : and it is necessary that they appear in the court in the feast. He that appears when he placeth himself in the court, let him bring a burnt offering, which is by no means to be of less price than two pieces of silver, that is, of two *meahs* of silver.

---

[p] *English folio edition,* vol. ii. p. 356.   [q] Chagigah, cap. 1. hal. 1.

They are bound also to the peace offerings of the *Chagigah* by
that law, וְחַגֹּתֶם אוֹתוֹ חַג לַיהוָה *Ye shall keep it a feast to
the LORD,*" Exod. xii. 14. Rambam upon the place thus;
" The Lord saith, ' Let them not appear before me empty,'
Deut. xvi. 16. That is, קרבן עולה Let him bring *an oblation
of a burnt sacrifice* in his hand when he goes up to the feast.
And those burnt sacrifices are called עולות ראייה *burnt-
sacrifices of appearance*, and also ראייה *appearance*, without
the addition of the word *burnt sacrifice.* And the *Chagigah* :
From thence, because the Lord saith, ' Ye shall keep it a
feast to the Lord,' it means this, שיביא קרבן שלמים *That a
man bring peace offerings*, and these peace offerings are called
Chagigah."

II. Of these two, namely, the *appearance* and the *Chagigah*,
the *Chagigah* was the greater and more famous.   For

First, certain persons were obliged to the *Chagigah*, who
were not obliged to the *appearance* : " He𝑟 that indeed is not
deaf, but yet is dumb, is not obliged to *appearance* ; but yet
he is obliged לשמחה *to rejoice.*"   It is true some of the
Gemarists distinguish between חגיגה *Chagigah* and שמחה
*rejoicing*ˢ.   But one Glosser upon the place alleged כי קאמר
דמחייב בשמחה הוא דין חגיגה *that which he saith of
' rejoicing,' obtains also of the ' Chagigah.'*   And another saith,
" He is bound לשמחה *to rejoicing,* namely, to rejoice in the
feast ; as it is written, ' And thou shalt rejoice in thy feast.'
And they say elsewhere, that that rejoicing is over the peace-
offerings, namely, in eating flesh."

Secondly, *appearance* was not tied so strictly to the first
day, but the *Chagigah* was tied to it. עולות נדרים ונדבות
במועד באות ביט" אינן באות *burnt sacrifices by vow, and
free will offerings are offered on the common days of the feast, they
are not offered on a feast day :* ועולה וראייה באה אפילו ביט"
*but the burnt sacrifices of appearance may be offered also on a
feast day :* and when they are offered, let them not be offered
but מן החולין *out of common cattle :* ושלמי שמחה *but the
peace offerings of rejoicing* also out of the tithes וחגיגת יום
טוב הראשון של פסח *the ' Chagigah' of the first feast day of
the Passover.*   The school of Shammai saith, Let it be of

(חולין) *common cattle:* the school of Hillel saith, Let it be of
the tithes.   What is it that it teaches of *the Chagigah of
the first feast day of the Passover?*   Rabh Ishai saith, חגיגת
טו׳ אין *the ' Chagigah' of the fifteenth day is so:* חגיגת יד׳ לא
the ' Chagigah' of the fourteenth, not."   The Gloss is; "The
burnt offerings of appearance were not offered the first day of
the feast, although they were due to the feast, because compensation might be made by them the day following."

"The *'Chagigah'* of the first feast day was without doubt
due; although it had flesh enough otherways."   For, as it is
said a little before, "They offered peace offerings on that
feast day לפי שיש בהם צורך למאכל הדיוט, *because they
had need of them for private food:*" and although there was
food enough, yet the *Chagigah* was to be offered as the due of
the day.

"The *Chagigah* of the fourteenth day was this, בשהיתה
הבורת פסח מרובה *when any* φρατρία, *company, was numerous,*
they joined the *Chagigah* also with the paschal lamb, that they
might eat the passover, even till they were filled.   But now
the *Chagigah* of that first day was not but of common cattle:
but the *Chagigah* of the fourteenth day might also be of the
tithes."

It was a greater[t] matter to offer of common cattle (or
cholin) than of the tithes of the first-born, for they were
owing to the Lord by right: but to offer the *cholin* [חולין]
was the part of further devotion and free will.

That therefore which John saith, that "the Jews would
not go into the judgment hall lest they should be polluted,
but that they might eat the passover," is to be understood
of that *Chagigah* of the fifteenth day, not of the paschal lamb:
for that also is called the passover, Deut. xvi. 2; "Thou shalt
sacrifice the *passover* to the Lord of thy flocks and of thy
herds."   *Of thy flocks;* this indeed, by virtue of that precept,
Exod. xii. 3: but what have we to do with *herds?* "'Of thy
herds,' saith R. Solomon, for the *Chagigah.*"   And Aben Ezra
saith, "'Of thy flocks,' according to the duty of the passover;
'of thy[u] herds,' for the peace offerings," and produceth that,
2 Chron. xxx. 24; xxxv. 8.   The Targum of Jonathan writes;

[t] *Leusden's edition,* vol. ii. p. 464.   [u] *English folio edition,* vol. ii. p. 357.

" Ye shall kill the passover before the Lord your God, between the eves, and your sheep and oxen on the morrow, in
that very day, in joy of the feast."

In one Glosser[x] mention is made of פסח קטון *the less
passover;* by which if he understands not the passover of the
second month, which is very usually called by them פסח שני
the second passover, or the passover of the second month, instruct me what he means by it. However this matter is clear
in Moses, that oxen, or the sacrifices offered after the lamb
eaten, are called the ' passover,' as well as the lamb itself.

And no wonder, when the lamb was the very least part of
the joy, and there were seven feast-days after he was eaten:
and when the lamb was a thing rubbing up the remembrance
of affliction, rather than denoting gladness and making merry.
For the unleavened bread was marked out by the holy Scripture under that very notion, and so also the bitter herbs,
which were things that belonged to the lamb. But how much
of the solemnity of the feast is attributed to the *Chagigah,*
and the other sacrifices after that, it would be too much to
mention, since it occurs everywhere.

Hear the author of the *Aruch* concerning the *Chagigah*
of Pentecost: " The word חג *chag* denotes dancing, and
clapping hands for joy. In the Syriac language it is חיגא
chigah: and so in the Scripture יָחוֹגּוּ וְיָנוּעוּ כַּשִּׁכּוֹר [Psalm
cvii. 27. The interlinear version reads, *They went in a round,
and moved themselves like a drunken man*]: and from this root
it is, because they eat, and drink, and dance [or make holiday.]
And the sacrifice of the *Chagigah,* which they were bound to
bring on a feastday, is that concerning which the Scripture
saith, וְעָשִׂיתָ חַג שָׁבוּעוֹת *and thou shalt make* חג *chag, a
solemnity of weeks* to the Lord thy God, a free will offering of
thy hand,' " &c. Deut. xvi. 10.

And now tell me whence received that feast its denomination, that it should be called חג *the feast* of weeks? Not
from the offering of the loaves of first fruits, but from the
Chagigah, and the feasting on the *Chagigah.* The same is
to be said of the feast of the Passover. So that John said
nothing strange to the ears of the Jews, when he said, " They

went not into the judgment hall lest they might be polluted, but that they might eat the passover;" pointing with his finger to the *Chagigah,* and not to the lamb, eaten indeed the day before.

The word *passover* might sound to the same sense in those words of his also, "It was the preparation of the passover, and about the sixth hour." It was the preparation to the *Chagigah,* and not to the lamb. But I suspect something more may be understood; namely, that on that day both food was prepared, and the mind too for the mirth of the whole feast. So that the passover denotes τὴν ἑορτὴν, *the feast,* not this or that particular appendage to the feast. The burnt sacrifices which were offered in the *appearance,* כּ־לה לגבוה *they all became God's,* as the masters say truly; and he who offered them carried not back the least part of them with him. But the sacrifices of the *Chagigah,* whether they were oxen or sheep, the greatest part of them returned to them that offered them; and with them they and their friends made solemn and joyful feastings while they tarried at Jerusalem. So that the oblation of these on the first day of the feast was παρασκευὴ τοῦ πάσχα, *the preparation of the passover,* and παρασκευὴ τῆς Πεντηκοστῆς, *the preparation of Pentecost,* and παρασκευὴ τῆς Σκηνοπηγίας, *the preparation of the feast of Tabernacles:* that is, the day and manner of preparing food for the following mirth of the feast. In the same sense was παρασκευὴ, *the preparation of the sabbath,* namely, *the preparation* of food and things necessary to the sabbath. Of which we shall speak at ver. 42.

Having thus despatched these things, let us now come to the *hour* itself. "It was the preparation of the passover (saith John), and about the *sixth* hour," when Pilate delivered Christ to be crucified. "And it was the *third* hour (saith Mark), and they crucified him."

It is disputed by the Gemarists[y], how far the evidences of two men may agree and consent, whereof one saith, "This I saw done in that hour;' and the other saith, ' I saw it done another hour.' "One saith, the second hour; another, the third: עדותן קיימה *their testimony consists together.* One saith the third hour, another the fifth; עדותן בטילה *their*

testimony is vain, as R. Meir saith. But saith R. Judah, their
testimony consists together. But if one saith, the fifth hour,
another, the seventh hour, their testimony is vain; because
in the fifth hour the sun is in the east part of heaven; in the
seventh, in the west part." They dispute largely concerning
this matter in the place alleged, and concerning evidences differing in words; nevertheless, as to the thing itself, they conclude that both may be true, because witnesses may be deceived in the computation of hours: which to conclude concerning the evangelists, were impious and blasphemous. But
there is one supposes the copiers were deceived in their trans-
scription, and would have the computation of John corrected
into ἦν δὲ ὥρα ὡσεὶ τρίτη, *and it was about the third hour*: too
boldly, and indeed without any reason, for it is neither credible nor[z] possible indeed, that those things which went before our Saviour's crucifixion should be done בתלת שעי
קמייתא (to use the words of the Talmudists[a]) *in the three
first hours of the day.* The harmony therefore of the evangelists is to be fetched elsewhere.

I. Let us repeat that out of Maimonides; "The great
Sanhedrim sat from the morning daily sacrifice, until the
afternoon daily sacrifice." But now when the morning daily
sacrifice was at the third hour, the Sanhedrim sat not before
that hour. Take heed, therefore, thou that wouldest have
the words of John, "and it was about the *sixth* hour," to be
changed into, "and it was about the *third* hour," lest thou
becomest guilty of a great solecism. For Pilate could not
deliver Christ to be crucified about the third hour, when the
Sanhedrim sat not before the third hour, and Christ was not
yet delivered to Pilate.

But you will say, the words of Mark do obscure these
things much more. For if the Sanhedrim that delivered up
Christ met not together before the third hour, one can no way
say that they crucified him the third hour.

We do here propound two things for the explanation of
this matter.

Let the first be taken from the *day* itself, and from the

z *English folio edit.*, vol. ii. p. 357. *Leusden's edit.*, vol. ii. p. 465.
a Sanhedr. fol. 105. 2.

hour itself. That day was "the preparation of the passover," a day of high solemnity, and when it behoved the priests and the other fathers of the Sanhedrim to be present at the third hour in the Temple, and to offer their Chagigahs that were preparative to the whole seven days' festivity: but they employed themselves in another thing, namely this. You may observe that he saith not, "it was the third hour *when*;" but "it was the third hour, *and* they crucified him." That is, when the third hour now was, and was passed, yet they omitted not to prosecute his crucifixion, when indeed, according to the manner of the feast and the obligation of religion, they ought to have been employed otherwise. I indeed should rather sit down satisfied with this interpretation, than accuse the holy text as depraved, or to deprave it more with my amendment. But,

Secondly, there is another sense also not to be despised, if our judgment is any thing, which we fetch from a custom usual in the Sanhedrim, but from which they now swerved. They are treating[b] concerning a guilty person condemned to hanging, with whom they deal in this process: משחין אותו עד סמוך לשקיעת החמה *they tarry until sunset approach,* וגומרין את דינו וממיתין אותו *and then they finish his judgment and put him to death.* Note that: ' They finish not his judgment until sunset draw near.' If you ask the reason, a more general one may be given which respected all persons condemned to die, and a more special one which respected him which was to be hanged.

1. There was that which is called by the Talmudists עינוי הדין *the affliction of judgment:* by which phrase they understand not judgment that is not just, but when he that is condemned, after judgment passed, is not presently put to death. לגמרית לדיניה בשבתא וליקטליה בחד בשבא "If[c] you *finish his judgment on the sabbath* [mark that], *and put him to death on the first day of the week,* נמצא אתה מענה את דינו *you afflict his judgment.* Where the Gloss is, " As long as his judgment is not finished, it is not the affliction of judgment, because he expects every hour to be absolved: but when judgment is ended, he expects death," &c. Therefore they

---

delayed but little between the finishing of judgment and
execution.

II. As to those that were to be hanged, את אותו משחין
גמר דינו *they delayed the finishing his judgment,* and they
hanged him not in the morning, lest they might grow slack
about his burial, and might fall into forgetfulness," and might
sin against the law, Deut. xxi. 23; "but near sunset, that
they might presently bury him." So the Gloss. They put
him to death not sooner, for this reason; they finished not his
judgment sooner for the reason above said.

And now let us resume the words of Mark, "And it was
the third hour, and they crucified him." The Sanhedrim used
not to finish the judgment of hanging until they were now
ready to rise up and depart from the council and bench after
the Mincha, the day now inclining towards sunset: but these
men finished the judgment of Jesus, and hastened him to the
cross, when they first came into the court at the third hour,
at the time of the daily sacrifice, which was very unusual, and
different from the custom.

Ver. 34[d]: Ἐλωΐ, Ἐλωΐ· *Eloi, Eloi.*] In Matthew it is אלי אלי
Eli, Eli, in the very same syllables of Psalm xxii. 1: Mark,
according to the present dialect (namely, the Chaldee), useth
the pronunciation of the word אלהא, or at least according to
the pronunciation of the word אלהים, Ἠλωΐ, *Eloi,* Judg. v. 5.
in the LXX.

Ver. 42: Παρασκευὴ, ὅ ἐστι προσάββατον· *The preparation,
that is, the day of the sabbath.*] You will ask, whether any day
going before the sabbath was called *parasceue, the preparation.*
Among the Hebrews, indeed, it is commonly said ערב השבת
the eve of the sabbath. But be it granted; whence is it called
the preparation? Either that *they prepared themselves* for the
sabbath; or rather, that *they prepared provisions* to be eaten
on the sabbath; and that by the law, "On the sixth day they
shall prepare, &c. Whatsoever ye will bake, bake to-day;
and whatsoever ye will seethe, seethe to-day," &c. Exod.
xvi. 5, 23. Hence הכנה that is, *preparation,* is a very usual
word with them in this sense חול מכין לשבת וחול מכין ליט"
a[e] common day prepares for the sabbath, and a common day

---

[d] *English folio edit.,* vol. ii. p. 358.   [e] Maimon. in Jom Tobh, c. 1.

prepares for a feast day. "But[f] those reasons do not hold good לְאַסוּר הַכְנָה *to forbid the preparation*[g], while as yet there remains much of the day:" הכנה, παρασκευή, *preparation.*"

But you will say, "If a feast day prepares not for the sabbath (which Maimonides saith), such an interpretation will not suit with the words which we are now handling, that it should be called *the preparation*, in respect of provisions prepared for the sabbath on that day. Let the masters themselves answer.

יום טוב שחל להיות ערב שבת: "*On*[h] *a feast day, which happens on the sabbath eve*, let not a man in the beginning seethe food after the feast day for the sabbath day, but let him seethe for the feast day, and if any remain, let it be reserved for the sabbath. But עושה תבשיל" (according to the letter, *Let him make a boiling*, but the sense is) "*Let him prepare food* on the eve of the feast day, and let him depend upon it for the sabbath. The school of Shammai saith, שני תבשילין, *a twofold food:* that of Hillel saith, One food."

Maimonides speaks[i] plainer: "On a feast day that falls in with a sabbath eve, they do not bake nor seethe on the feast day what they eat on the sabbath. And this prohibition is from the words of the scribes: namely, That none seethe on a feast day for a common day; for this is arguing *a majori ad minus, from the greater to the less:* if a man seethe not for the sabbath day, much less for a common day. But if he provides food on the eve of the feast day, *on which he may depend* (שסומך עליו), then if he bake or seethe on the feast day for the sabbath, it is permitted: and that on which he depends is called עירוב תבשילין *the mixing of food*. And why is it called עירוב *mixing* [συναναμιξις, *a mingling together*]? namely, as that *mixing* which they make concerning the courts or the vestries on the sabbath eve is for acknowledgment, that is, that they should not think that it is lawful to carry any thing from place to place on the sabbath; so this food is for acknowledgment and remembrance, that

---

[f] Gloss. ibid. in cap. 6.

[g] *Leusden's edit.*, vol. ii. p. 466.

[h] Bab. Jom Tobh, fol. 15. 1.

[i] Jom Tobh, cap. 6.

they should not think or imagine that it is lawful to bake any thing on a feast day which is not eaten that day : therefore this food is called עירובי תבשילין *the mixing of food.*

Of עירובי חצירות *the mixing of courts,* we speak 1 Cor. x. 16. The sum of the matter is this, many families dwelt by one common court. Now therefore when it was not lawful to carry out any thing on the sabbath מרשות לרשות *from a place which was of one right and condition, to a place which was of another ;* therefore it was not lawful for any one of those families to carry out any thing out of his house into the court joining to his door, and on the contrary ; all partook of the communion and *mixture* of the right, and that by eating together of that food which was brought together by them all ; and then it was lawful. So in this case whereof we are now treating. Since it was not lawful by the canons of the scribes to prepare any food on a feast day for the sabbath that followed on the morrow, and since of necessity something was to be prepared for the sabbath, they mollified the rigour of the canon thus ; that first some food should be prepared on the feast day, which was עירוב *a mixture* as it were of right, and depending upon this thus prepared, they might prepare any thing for the morrow sabbath.

Of[k] עירובי תבשילין *the mixture of foods,* mention occurs in the Talmudists infinite times ; and these things which have been spoken concerning them afford not a little light to the clause which we are now handling, and to others where the word *preparation* occurs ; and make those things plainer which we have said concerning *the preparation of the Passover ;* namely, that it denoteth not either *the preparation* of the Paschal lamb, nor *the preparation* of the people to eat the lamb ; but *the preparation of meats to be eaten in the Passover week.* Nor in this place, if it be applied to the sabbath, doth it denote any other thing than *the preparation of food* for the sabbath now approaching. So that that day wherein Christ was crucified was a double *preparation* in the double sense alleged : namely, the whole day, but especially from the third hour, was *the preparation of the Passover,* or of the whole week following ; and the evening of

---

[k] *English folio edition,* vol. ii. p. 358.

the day was *the preparation* of the sabbath following on the morrow.

Of that sabbath John saith, which we cannot let pass, that μεγάλη ἦν ἡ ἡμέρα ἐκείνου τοῦ σαββάτου· that *the day of that sabbath was a great day,* chap. xix. 31. For it was the day of the people's appearance in the Temple; it was the day of the offering of the sheaf of firstfruits: and I ask, whether before that day Christ's persecutors had offered their *Chagigahs?*

Ver. 43: Εὐσχήμων βουλευτής· *An honourable counsellor.*] The Vulgar reads, *nobilis decurio, a noble officer:* Erasmus, *honestus senator, an honourable senator:* Beza, *honoratus senator, an honourable senator.* The Talmud may serve here instead of a lexicon.

"Was it the[m] chamber פרהידרין προέδρων, *of the chief men?* Was it not the chamber בולוטי βουλευτῶν, *of the counsellors?* First it was called, לשכת בולוטי *the chamber of the counsellors:* but when the high priesthood was bought with money, and yearly changed, כפרהידרין הללו, *as the* πρόεδροι, *the chief counsellors* of the king are yearly changed, thence it was called לשכת פרהידרין *the chamber* προέδρων, *of proedri, chief men."* The Gloss is, בולוטי לשון שרים, βουλευταί, *counsellors, denotes princes.* True, indeed, and hence בולוטיא ופגניא *noble*[n] *men and common persons* are contradistinguished. But why should one not understand those princes and nobles in the proper sense of the word βουλευταί, that is, *counsellors?* For who sees not that the word is Greek? and so the *Aruch;* לשון יון חוא *it is a Greek word.*

Which fixeth our eyes faster upon the words of the Gloss at the Gemara in the place alleged; "From the beginning, in the days of Simeon the Just, who lived a greater while, they called it לשכת בולוטי *the chamber* βουλευτῶν, *of the counsellors."* What? did the Greek language so flourish at Jerusalem in the times of Simeon the Just, that a chamber in the Temple should be called by a Greek name? If that Simeon be he who met Alexander the Great, which the Talmudists[o] suppose, then some reason appears for it; but if not, inquire

---

[m] Bab. Joma, fol. 8. 2.　　　[n] Hieros. Schab. fol. 13. 3.
[o] Joma, fol. 69. 1.

further. However, that was the chamber of the high priest,
as appears often[p] in the Talmudists; not that he always
lived there, nor that once in the year he resorted thither;
but because it was that place where he sat with the council
of the priests, and consulted concerning the public service
and affairs of the Temple. Hence in the Jerusalem writers
mention is made of שמעון בולוטא *Simeon the counsellor.*
And in this sense is that to be taken, if I mistake not, which
occurs once and again in the Babylonian Talmudists, concerning בני כהנים הגדולים *the sons of the high priests,*
deciding several things; and בית דין של כהנים *the house of
judgment of the priests*[q].

Hence we think *Joseph of Arimathea* was called with good
reason βουλευτὴς, *a counsellor,* because he was a priest, and
one of that sacerdotal bench. לשכת בולוטי פירוש חכמי
עצה *it was called the chamber* βουλευτῶν, (saith the *Aruch,*)
that is, of counsellors.

CHAP. XVI.[r]

VER. 1 : ῞Ινα ἐλθοῦσαι ἀλείψωσιν αὐτόν· *That they might come
and anoint him.*] "What[s] is that, that is allowed as to the
living [on the sabbath day], but as to the dead it is not? It
is *anointing.*"

Ver. 2 : Καὶ λίαν πρωὶ, &c. *And very early in the morning,
&c.*] The distinction of the twilight among the Rabbins was
this :

I. איילתא דשחרא *the hind* [*cerva*] *of the morning :* the
first appearance of light. "R. Chaija[t] Rabba, and R. Simeon
Ben Chalaphta, travelling together in a certain morning, in
the valley of Arbel, saw *the hind of the morning,* that its light
spread the sky. R. Chaija said, Such shall be the redemption
of Israel. First, It goes forward by degrees, and by little
and little ; but by how much the more it shall go forward, by
so much the more it shall increase."

It was at that time that Christ arose ; namely, in the first
morning; as may be gathered from the words of Matthew.

[p] *Leusden's edition,* vol. ii. p. 467.   [s] Hieros. Schab. fol. 12. 1.
[q] Chetub. cap. 1.   [t] Hieros. Berac. fol. 2. 3.
[r] *English folio edit.,* vol. ii. p. 359.

And to this the title of the two-and-twentieth Psalm seems to have respect, עַל־אַיֶּלֶת הַשַּׁחַר[u]. See also Rev. xxii. 16; "I am the bright and morning star." And now you may imagine the women went out of their houses towards the sepulchre.

II. משיכיר בין תכלת ללבן *when one may distinguish between purple colour and white.* " From[x] what time do they recite their phylacterical prayers in the morning? From that time, that one may distinguish between purple colour and white. R. Eliezer saith, Between purple colour and green." Before this time was *obscurum adhuc cœptæ lucis, the obscurity of the begun light,* as Tacitus's expression is [y].

III. משיאור המזרח *when the east begins to lighten.*

IV. בנץ החמה *sunrise.* " From[z] *the hind of the morning* going forth, until the east begins to lighten; and from the time the east begins to lighten, until sunrise," &c.

According to these four parts of time, one might not improperly suit the four phrases of the evangelists. According to the first, Matthew's τῇ ἐπιφωσκούσῃ, *as it began to dawn.* According to the second, John's πρωὶ σκοτίας ἔτι οὔσης, *early in the morning, when it was yet dark.* To the third, Luke's ὄρθρου βαθέως, *very early in the morning.* To the fourth, Mark's λίαν πρωὶ, *very early in the morning,* and yet ἀνατείλαντος τοῦ ἡλίου, *at the rising of the sun.*

For the women came twice to the sepulchre, as John teacheth; by whom the other evangelists are to be explained: which being well considered, the reconciling them together is very easy.

Ver. 13: Οὐδὲ ἐκείνοις ἐπίστευσαν· *Neither believed they them.*] That in the verses immediately going before the discourse, the question is of the two disciples going to Emmaus, is without all controversy: and then how do these things consist with that relation in Luke, who saith, that "they...... returned to Jerusalem and found the eleven gathered together, and them that were with them, saying, The Lord is risen indeed, and hath appeared to Simon," Luke xxiv. 33, 34.

---

[u] [*Upon Aijeleth Shahar, The hind of the morning,* A. V. margin.]

[x] Berac. cap. 1. hal. 2.
[y] Hist. lib. iv. cap. 11.
[z] Hieros. in the place before.

The word λέγοντας, *saying*, evidently makes those to be the
words τῶν ἕνδεκα, *of the eleven*, and of those that were gathered
together with them : which, when you read the versions, you
would scarcely suspect.   For when that word is rendered by
the Syriac כד אמרין ; by the Arabic והם יקולון ; by the
Vulgar *dicentes ;* by the Italian *dicendo ;* by the French
disans ; by the English *saying ;* who, I pray, would take it
in another sense than that those two that returned from
Emmaus said, " The Lord is risen indeed," &c. ? But in the
original Greek, since it is the accusative case, it is plainly to
be referred to the eleven disciples, and those that were
together with them.   As if they had discourse among themselves of the appearance made to Peter, either before, or now
in the very access of those two coming from Emmaus.   And
yet saith this our evangelist, that when those two had related
the whole business[a], they gave credit no not to them.   So
that according to Luke they believed Christ was risen and
had appeared to Simon, before they told their story ; but
according to Mark, they believed it not, no not when they
had told it.

The reconciling, therefore, of the evangelists, is to be fetched
thence, that those words pronounced by the eleven, Ὅτι ἠγέρθη
ὁ Κύριος ὄντως, &c., *The Lord is risen indeed*, &c., doth not
manifest their absolute confession of the resurrection of Christ,
but a conjectural reason of the sudden and unexpected return
of Peter.

I believe that Peter was going with Cleophas into Galilee,
and that being moved with the words of Christ told him by
the women, " Say to his disciples and Peter, I go before you
into Galilee."   Think with yourself, how doubtful Peter was,
and how he fluctuated within himself after his threefold de-
nial ; and how he gasped to see the Lord again, if he were
risen, and to cast himself an humble supplicant at his feet.
When, therefore, he heard these things from the women (and
he had heard it indeed from Christ[b] himself, while he was yet
alive, that " when he arose he would go before them into
Galilee"), and when the rest were very little moved with the
report of his resurrection, nor as yet stirred from that place,

[a] *English folio edit.*, vol. ii. p. 359.   [b] *Leusden's edition*, vol. ii. p. 468.

he will try a journey into Galilee, and Alpheus with him.
Which when it was well known to the rest, and they saw him
return so soon, and so unexpectedly, " Certainly (say they)
the Lord is risen, and hath appeared to Peter; otherwise, he
had not so soon come back again." And yet when he and
Cleophas open the whole matter, they do not yet believe even
them.

Ver. 15 : Πάσῃ τῇ κτίσει· *To every creature*.] לכל הבריות
To every creature, a manner of speech most common among
the Jews: by which,

I. Are denoted *all men*. " The[c] Wise men say, Let the
mind of man always be מעורבת עם הבריות *mingled* [or com-
placent] *to the* ' *creatures*.' " The Gloss there is; " To do with
every man according to complacency." משרה רוח קדש על
הבריות He[d] *makes the Holy Spirit to dwell upon the* '*creatures* :'
that is, *upon men*. " In[e] every judge in the bench of three is
required prudence, mercy, religion, hatred of money, love of
truth, ואהבת הבריות *and love of the* ' *creatures* :' " that is,
φιλανθρωπία, *the love of mankind*.

II. But especially by that phrase the *Gentiles* are understood. " R. Jose saith[f], אוי להם לבריות *Woe to* ' *the creatures*,' which see, and know not what they see; which stand,
and know not upon what they stand ; namely, upon what the
earth stands," &c. He understands *the heathens* especially,
who were not instructed concerning the creation of things.
שיחתן של בריות The[g] *speech of all the* ' *creatures*' (that is, of
the heathens) " is only of earthly things, וכל תפלתן של בריות
And all the prayers of the ' *creatures*' are for earthly things ;
' Lord, let the earth be fruitful, let the earth prosper.' But
all the prayers of Israelites are only for the holy place ; ' Lord,
let the Temple be built,' " &c. Observe, how בריות *the creatures* are opposed to *Israelites*.

And the parallel words of Matthew, chap. xxviii, do sufficiently prove this to be the sense of the phrase, πάσῃ κτίσει,
every creature, in this place : that which in Mark is, κηρύξατε
πάσῃ τῇ κτίσει, *preach to every creature*, in that place in Mat-

---

c Bab. Chetub. fol. 17. 1.   f Bab. Chagig. fol. 12. 2.
d Midr. Till. in Psal. cxxxv.   g Beresh. Rabba, sect. 13.
e Maimon. in Sanhedr. cap. 2.

thew is, μαθητεύσατε πάντα τὰ ἔθνη, *disciple all nations;* as
those words also of St. Paul, Colos. i. 23, εὐαγγελίου τοῦ κη-
ρυχθέντος ἐν πάσῃ τῇ κτίσει, *the gospel that was preached in all
the creation.*

In the same sense you must, of necessity, understand the
same phrase, Rom. viii. 22. Where, if you take the whole
passage concerning the Gentiles breathing after the evangelical liberty of the sons of God, you render the sense very
easy, and very agreeable to the mind of the apostle, and to
the signification of the word κτίσις, *creature,* or *creation:* when
they who render it otherwise dash upon I know not what
rough and knotty sense. Let me, although it is out of my
road, thus paraphrase the whole place:—

Rom. viii. 19: Ἡ γὰρ ἀποκαραδοκία τῆς κτίσεως, &c. "' *For the
earnest expectation of the creature,* or of the heathen world,
waiteth for the revelation of the sons of God.' For God had
promised, and had very often pronounced by his prophets,
that he would gather together, and adopt to himself, innumerable sons among the Gentiles. Therefore, the whole
Gentile world doth now greedily expect the revelation and
production of those sons."

Ver. 20: Τῇ γὰρ ματαιότητι ἡ κτίσις ὑπετάγη, &c. "*For the
creature,* the whole heathen world, *was subjected to the vanity*
of their mind (as Rom. i. 21, ἐματαιώθησαν ἐν τοῖς διαλογισμοῖς
αὐτῶν, *became vain in their imaginations;* and Eph. iv. 17, ἔθνη
περιπατεῖ ἐν[h] ματαιότητι τοῦ νοὸς αὐτῶν, *the Gentiles walk in the
vanity of their mind*), not willingly, but because of him that
subjected it."

Ver. 21: " Under hope, because *the creature* also" (or that
heathen world) " shall be freed from the service of" (sinful)
" corruption" (which is in the world through lust, 2 Pet. i. 4),
" into the (gospel) liberty of the sons of God:" from the service of Satan, of idols, and of lusts, into the liberty which the
sons of God enjoy through the gospel.

Ver. 22: Οἴδαμεν γὰρ, ὅτι πᾶσα ἡ κτίσις, &c. " For we
know, that the whole *creature*" (or *heathen world*) " groaneth
together, and travaileth, and, as it were, with a convex weight,

boweth down unto this very time, to be born and brought forth."

Ver. 23 : Οὐ μόνον δὲ, ἀλλὰ καὶ αὐτοὶ, &c.   "Neither the Gentiles only, but we Jews also (however we belong to a nation envious of the heathen), to whom God hath granted the first-fruits of the Spirit, we sigh among ourselves for their sakes, waiting for the adoption, that is, the redemption of our mystical body, whereof the Gentiles make a very great part."